Now you can modify the data in using your own labor rates ... and generate a complete PDF version of your customized BNi Costbook in just minutes!

Dear valued customer:

Your paid purchase of this 2008 BNi Costbook entitles you to create a custom, PDF (Adobe Acrobat format) version of the entire book with all unit costs adjusted to reflect your labor rates. You can even create a customized title page of the book!

The wage rates used in this book reflect national averages and are applicable for a wide range of estimating needs. But as you know, actual rates can vary significantly from state to state, as well as in open-shop environments.

Now this problem is solved!

Starting right now, you can simply plug-in your own rates for 13 different labor classifications – and have every unit cost in the entire book completely recalculated! And then you can generate a PDF version to print and/or share with the other members of your staff.

TRY IT FREE!

This new service is available exclusively to paid buyers of this book. And you can generate a 32-page sample document for Free! An online demo/tutorial guides you every step of the way.

All you need to get started is a User id and a PIN number. To get your PIN number and temporary User Id, just go to www.bnibooks.com/costbooks and enter your BNI Invoice Number. If you don't have your invoice number (or if you purchased this book from one of our associates), just call us at 1.888.BNI.BOOK and we'll get you set up right away.

Then, for just $9.95, you can create a complete, customized version of this book that you can print, share, or save to your PC. We're providing this value-added service to help our customers extend the value of this book with faster and more accurate estimates.

Sincerely,

William D. Mahoney, P.E.
Editor-in-Chief

PS: If you received this book on a courtesy free preview basis, you can get your PIN number right away by calling us with your credit card payment information at 1.888.BNI.BOOK

BNi Building News

990 Park Center Drive, Suite E, Vista, CA 92081-8352

BNI Building News

PUBLIC WORKS

2008 COSTBOOK

FIFTEENTH EDITION

BNI Building News

• Los Angeles • Anaheim • Vista • New England

BNi Building News

EDITOR-IN-CHIEF
William D. Mahoney, P.E.

TECHNICAL SERVICES
Edward B. Wetherill, CSI
Anthony Jackson
Ana Varela
Heidi Hassan

GRAPHIC DESIGN
Robert O. Wright Jr.

BNI Publications, Inc.

LOS ANGELES
10801 NATIONAL BLVD. SUITE 100
LOS ANGELES, CA 90064

NEW ENGLAND
1800 MINERAL SPRING AVE. #101
NORTH PROVIDENCE, RI 02901-3927

ANAHEIM
1612 S. CLEMENTINE STREET
ANAHEIM, CA 92802

VISTA
990 PARK CENTER DRIVE, SUITE E
VISTA, CA 92081

1-888-BNI-BOOK (1-888-264-2665)
www.bnibooks.com

ISBN 978-1-55701-586-0

Cover Photography by: shutterstock.com and iStockphotos.com

PREFACE

For the past 60 years, Building News has been dedicated to providing construction professionals with timely and reliable information. Based on this experience, our staff has researched and compiled thousands of up-to-the-minute costs for the **Building News 2008 Costbooks**. This book is an essential reference for contractors, engineers, architects, facilities managers — any construction professional who must provide an estimate or any type of building project.

Whether working up a preliminary estimate or submitting a formal bid, the costs listed here can quickly and easily be tailored to your needs. All costs are based on national averages, while a table of modifiers is provided for regional adjustments. Overhead and profit are included in all costs.

Complete man-hour tables follow the unit costs to provide data on typical durations of specific tasks. This information can be used to schedule projects as well as to determine specific labor costs based on local labor rates.

All data is categorized according to the MASTERFORMAT of the Construction Specifications Institute (CSI). This industry standard provides an all-inclusive checklist to ensure that no element of a project is overlooked. In addition, to make specific items even easier to locate, there is a complete alphabetical index.

This costbook contains an appendix with reference charts and tables taken from an array of sources. Text explains the costs in certain categories and provides helpful pointers that should be taken into account with every estimate.

A section on square foot costs provides an overview of project costs for different building types — commercial, residential, etc. — with summaries of the actual projects. Square foot costs are invaluable for making budget estimates and checking prices when time is a factor.

The "Features in this Book" section presents a clear overview of the many features of this book. Included is an explanation of the data, sample page layout and discussion of how to best use the information in the book.

Of course, all buildings and construction projects are unique. The costs provided in this book are based on averages from well-managed projects with good labor productivity under normal working conditions (eight hours a day). Other circumstances affecting costs such as overtime, unusual working conditions, savings from buying bulk quantities for large projects, and unusual or hidden costs must be factored in as they arise.

The data provided in this book is for estimating purposes only. Check all applicable federal, state and local codes and regulations for specific requirements.

BNi. Building News

TABLE OF CONTENTS

CSI MASTERFORMAT

All data in the Costbook pages and Man-Hour tables is organized according to the CSI MASTERFORMAT — the industry standard numbering/classification system. The data is divided into the 16 divisions as shown below. The five digit numbers within each division correspond to the MASTERFORMAT Broadscope designations. Each section is further broken down into MASTERFORMAT Mediumscope designations. These numbers, in most cases, are the same as those used in architectural and engineering specifications.

The construction estimating information in this book is divided into two main sections:

Costbook Pages and Man-Hour Tables. Each is organized to the 16 divisions of the CSI MASTERFORMAT as shown below. In addition, there are extensive Construction Reference Tables, Geographic Cost Modifiers, Square Foot Tables and a detailed Index. Sample pages with graphic explanations are included before the Costbook pages, Man-Hour Tables and Square Foot Tables. These explanations, along with the discussions below, will provide a good understanding of what is included in this book and how it can best be used for construction estimating.

FEATURES IN THIS BOOK

The construction estimating information in this book is divided into two main sections: Costbook Pages and Man-Hour Tables. Each section is organized according to the 16 divisions of the MASTERFORMAT as shown on the previous pages. In addition, there are extensive Supporting Construction Reference tables, Geographic Costs Modifiers, Square Foot tables and a detailed Index.

Sample pages with graphic explanations are included before the Costbook pages and Man-Hour tables. These explanations, along with the discussions below, will provide a good understanding of what is included in this book and how it can best be used in construction estimating.

Material Costs

The material costs used in this book represent national averages for prices that a contractor would expect to pay plus an allowance for freight (if applicable), handling and storage. These costs reflect neither the lowest or highest prices, but rather a typical average cost over time. Periodic fluctuations in availability and in certain commodities (e.g. copper, lumber) can significantly affect local material pricing. In the final estimating and bidding stages of a project when the highest degree of accuracy is required, it is best to check local, current prices.

Labor Costs

Labor costs include the basic wage, plus commonly applicable taxes, insurance and markups for overhead and profit. The labor rates used here to develop the costs are typical average prevailing wage rates. Rates for different trades are used where appropriate for each type of work.

Taxes and insurance which are most often applied to labor rates include employer-paid Social Security/Medicare taxes (FICA), Worker's Compensation insurance, state and federal unemployment taxes, and business insurance. Fixed government rates as well as average allowances are included in the labor costs. However, most of these items vary significantly from state to state and within states. For more specific data, local agencies and sources should be consulted.

Equipment Costs

Costs for various types and pieces of equipment are included in Division 1 - General Requirements and can be included in an estimate when required either as a total "Equipment" category or with specific appropriate trades. Costs for equipment are included when appropriate in the installation costs in the Costbook pages.

Overhead And Profit

Included in the labor costs are allowances for overhead and profit for the contractor/employer whose workers are performing the specific tasks. No cost allowances or fees are included for management of subcontractors by the general contractor or construction manager. These costs, where appropriate, must be added to the costs as listed in the book.

The allowance for overhead is included to account for office overhead, the contractors' typical costs of doing business. These costs normally include in-house office staff salaries and benefits, office rent and operating expenses, professional fees, vehicle costs and other operating costs which are not directly applicable to specific jobs. It should be noted for this book that office overhead as included should be distinguished from project overhead, the General Requirements (CSI Division 1) which are specific to particular projects. Project overhead should be included on an item by item basis for each job.

Depending on the trade, an allowance of 10-15 percent is incorporated into the labor/installation costs to account for typical profit of the installing contractor. See Division 1, General Requirements, for a more detailed review of typical profit allowances.

Adjustments to Costs

The costs as presented in this book attempt to represent national averages. Costs, however, vary among regions, states and even between adjacent localities.

In order to more closely approximate the probable costs for specific locations throughout the U.S., a table of Geographic Cost Modifiers is provided. These adjustment factors are used to modify costs obtained from this book to help account for regional variations of construction costs. Whenever local current costs are known, whether material or equipment prices or labor rates, they should be used if more accuracy is required.

Man-Hour Tables

The man-hour data used to develop the labor costs are listed in the second main section of this book, the "Man-Hour Tables". These productivties represent typical installation labor for thousands of construction items. The data takes into account all activities involved in normal construction under commonly experienced working conditions such as site movement, material handling, start-up, etc. As with the Costbook pages, these items are listed according to the CSI MASTERFORMAT.

Square Foot Tables

Included as an additional reference are Square Foot Tables which list hundreds of actual projects for dozens of building types, each with associated building size and total square foot building cost. This data provides an overview of construction costs by building type. These costs are for actual projects. The variations within similar building types may be due, among other factors, to size, location, quality and specified components, material and processes. Depending upon all such factors, specific building costs can vary significantly and may not necessarily fall within the range of costs as presented.

Editor's Note: The **Building News 2008 Costbooks** are intended to provide accurate, reliable, average costs and typical productivities for thousands of common construction components. The data is developed and compiled from various industry sources, including government, manufacturers, suppliers and working professionals. The intent of the information is to provide assistance and guidelines to construction professionals in estimating. The user should be aware that local conditions, material and labor availability and cost variations, economic considerations, weather, local codes and regulations, etc., all affect the actual cost of construction. These and other such factors must be considered and incorporated into any and all construction estimates.

Sample Costbook Page

In order to best use the information in this book, please review this sample page and read the "Features In This Book" section.

CSI MASTERFORMAT Division

CSI Broadscope Category

CSI Mediumscope Category (First 5 Digits)

Detailed Descriptions
Complete descriptions of items may include information listed above a particular line. Review of the whole category is recommended for a complete description.

Material Cost
Material cost represent average contractor prices plus an allowance for freight, handling and storage.

Installation Cost
Installation cost includes basic wage rates, markups for taxes, insurance overhead and profit and also includes equipment costs where appropriate.

Total Cost
The total cost is the sum of material and installation costs. This total represents typical contractors' costs including overhead and profit, but does not include markups for the general contractor or construction management fees.

Unit of Measurement
Each item (and cost) is defined in terms of the common estimating unit. All costs are listed in dollars per unit.

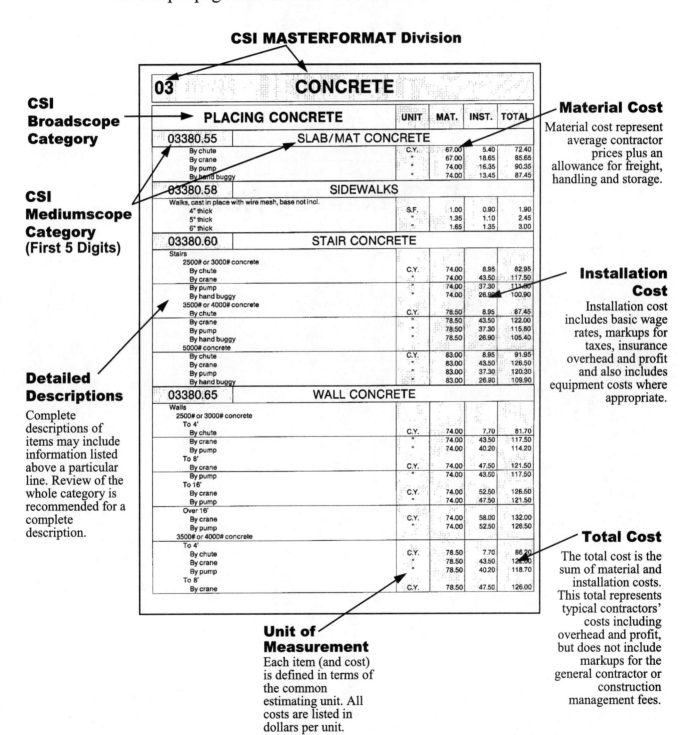

03	CONCRETE				
PLACING CONCRETE		UNIT	MAT.	INST.	TOTAL
03380.55	SLAB/MAT CONCRETE				
By chute		C.Y.	67.00	5.40	72.40
By crane		"	67.00	18.65	85.65
By pump		"	74.00	16.35	90.35
By hand buggy		"	74.00	13.45	87.45
03380.58	SIDEWALKS				
Walks, cast in place with wire mesh, base not incl.					
4" thick		S.F.	1.00	0.90	1.90
5" thick		"	1.35	1.10	2.45
6" thick		"	1.65	1.35	3.00
03380.60	STAIR CONCRETE				
Stairs					
2500# or 3000# concrete					
By chute		C.Y.	74.00	8.95	82.95
By crane		"	74.00	43.50	117.50
By pump		"	74.00	37.30	111.80
By hand buggy		"	74.00	26.90	100.90
3500# or 4000# concrete					
By chute		C.Y.	78.50	8.95	87.45
By crane		"	78.50	43.50	122.00
By pump		"	78.50	37.30	115.80
By hand buggy		"	78.50	26.90	105.40
5000# concrete					
By chute		C.Y.	83.00	8.95	91.95
By crane		"	83.00	43.50	126.50
By pump		"	83.00	37.30	120.30
By hand buggy		"	83.00	26.90	109.90
03380.65	WALL CONCRETE				
Walls					
2500# or 3000# concrete					
To 4'					
By chute		C.Y.	74.00	7.70	81.70
By crane		"	74.00	43.50	117.50
By pump		"	74.00	40.20	114.20
To 8'					
By crane		C.Y.	74.00	47.50	121.50
By pump		"	74.00	43.50	117.50
To 16'					
By crane		C.Y.	74.00	52.50	126.50
By pump		"	74.00	47.50	121.50
Over 16'					
By crane		C.Y.	74.00	58.00	132.00
By pump		"	74.00	52.50	126.50
3500# or 4000# concrete					
To 4'					
By chute		C.Y.	78.50	7.70	86.20
By crane		"	78.50	43.50	122.00
By pump		"	78.50	40.20	118.70
To 8'					
By crane		C.Y.	78.50	47.50	126.00

BNi . *Building News*

Requirements	UNIT	MAT.	INST.	TOTAL
01020.10 Allowances				
Overhead				
$20,000 project				
Minimum	PCT.			15.00
Average	"			20.00
Maximum	"			40.00
$100,000 project				
Minimum	PCT.			12.00
Average	"			15.00
Maximum	"			25.00
$500,000 project				
Minimum	PCT.			10.00
Average	"			12.00
Maximum	"			20.00
$1,000,000 project				
Minimum	PCT.			6.00
Average	"			10.00
Maximum	"			12.00
$10,000,000 project				
Minimum	PCT.			1.50
Average	"			5.00
Maximum	"			8.00
Profit				
$20,000 project				
Minimum	PCT.			10.00
Average	"			15.00
Maximum	"			25.00
$100,000 project				
Minimum	PCT.			10.00
Average	"			12.00
Maximum	"			20.00
$500,000 project				
Minimum	PCT.			5.00
Average	"			10.00
Maximum	"			15.00
$1,000,000 project				
Minimum	PCT.			3.00
Average	"			8.00
Maximum	"			15.00
Professional fees				
Architectural				
$100,000 project				
Minimum	PCT.			5.00
Average	"			10.00
Maximum	"			20.00
$500,000 project				
Minimum	PCT.			5.00
Average	"			8.00
Maximum	"			12.00
$1,000,000 project				
Minimum	PCT.			3.50
Average	"			7.00
Maximum	"			10.00

Requirements	UNIT	MAT.	INST.	TOTAL
01020.10 Allowances				
Structural engineering				
Minimum	PCT.			2.00
Average	"			3.00
Maximum	"			5.00
Mechanical engineering				
Minimum	PCT.			4.00
Average	"			5.00
Maximum	"			15.00
Electrical engineering				
Minimum	PCT.			3.00
Average	"			5.00
Maximum	"			12.00
Taxes				
Sales tax				
Minimum	PCT.			4.00
Average	"			5.00
Maximum	"			10.00
Unemployment				
Minimum	PCT.			3.00
Average	"			6.50
Maximum	"			8.00
Social security (FICA)	"			7.85
01050.10 Field Staff				
Superintendent				
Minimum	YEAR			71,885
Average	"			104,675
Maximum	"			151,337
Field engineer				
Minimum	YEAR			56,752
Average	"			84,497
Maximum	"			121,070
Foreman				
Minimum	YEAR			40,357
Average	"			64,318
Maximum	"			95,847
Bookkeeper/timekeeper				
Minimum	YEAR			23,962
Average	"			31,529
Maximum	"			49,185
Watchman				
Minimum	YEAR			16,143
Average	"			20,178
Maximum	"			32,790
01310.10 Scheduling				
Scheduling for				
$100,000 project				
Minimum	PCT.			1.00
Average	"			2.00
Maximum	"			4.00
$500,000 project				

Requirements	UNIT	MAT.	INST.	TOTAL
01310.10 — Scheduling				
Minimum	PCT.			0.50
Average	"			1.00
Maximum	"			2.00
$1,000,000 project				
Minimum	PCT.			0.30
Average	"			0.80
Maximum	"			1.50
Scheduling software, not including computer				
Minimum	EA.			385.00
Average	"			2,200
Maximum	"			44,000
01330.10 — Surveying				
Surveying				
Small crew	DAY		800.00	800.00
Average crew	"		1,210	1,210
Large crew	"		1,600	1,600
Lot lines and boundaries				
Minimum	ACRE		570.00	570.00
Average	"		1,210	1,210
Maximum	"		2,000	2,000
01380.10 — Job Requirements				
Job photographs, small jobs				
Minimum	EA.			110.00
Average	"			165.00
Maximum	"			385.00
Large projects				
Minimum	EA.			550.00
Average	"			825.00
Maximum	"			2,750
01410.10 — Testing				
Testing concrete, per test				
Minimum	EA.			18.19
Average	"			30.32
Maximum	"			60.64
Soil, per test				
Minimum	EA.			36.38
Average	"			90.96
Maximum	"			242.55
Welding, per test				
Minimum	EA.			18.19
Average	"			30.32
Maximum	"			121.28
01500.10 — Temporary Facilities				
Barricades, temporary				
Highway				
Concrete	L.F.	10.75	4.00	14.75
Wood	"	3.50	1.60	5.10
Steel	"	3.75	1.35	5.10
Pedestrian barricades				

Requirements	UNIT	MAT.	INST.	TOTAL
01500.10 — Temporary Facilities				
Plywood	S.F.	2.50	1.35	3.85
Chain link fence	"	2.80	1.35	4.15
Trailers, general office type, per month				
Minimum	EA.			187.39
Average	"			312.31
Maximum	"			624.62
Crew change trailers, per month				
Minimum	EA.			112.43
Average	"			124.93
Maximum	"			187.39
01505.10 — Mobilization				
Equipment mobilization				
Bulldozer				
Minimum	EA.			171.86
Average	"			359.64
Maximum	"			601.52
Backhoe/front-end loader				
Minimum	EA.			103.27
Average	"			179.82
Maximum	"			393.05
Crane, crawler type				
Minimum	EA.			1,892
Average	"			4,647
Maximum	"			9,981
Truck crane				
Minimum	EA.			445.57
Average	"			669.94
Maximum	"			1,152
Pile driving rig				
Minimum	EA.			8,604
Average	"			17,210
Maximum	"			30,978
01525.10 — Construction Aids				
Scaffolding/staging, rent per month				
Measured by lineal feet of base				
10' high	L.F.			10.95
20' high	"			19.78
30' high	"			27.68
40' high	"			31.94
50' high	"			38.02
Measured by square foot of surface				
Minimum	S.F.			0.49
Average	"			0.84
Maximum	"			1.50
Safety nets, heavy duty, per job				
Minimum	S.F.			0.32
Average	"			0.39
Maximum	"			0.85
Tarpaulins, fabric, per job				
Minimum	S.F.			0.22

Requirements	UNIT	MAT.	INST.	TOTAL
01525.10 Construction Aids				
Average	S.F.			0.39
Maximum	"			0.99
01570.10 Signs				
Construction signs, temporary				
Signs, 2' x 4'				
Minimum	EA.			31.58
Average	"			75.80
Maximum	"			266.51
Signs, 4' x 8'				
Minimum	EA.			66.33
Average	"			172.29
Maximum	"			740.28
Signs, 8' x 8'				
Minimum	EA.			85.28
Average	"			267.20
Maximum	"			2,763
01600.10 Equipment				
Air compressor				
60 cfm				
By day	EA.			83.69
By week	"			249.27
By month	"			755.91
300 cfm				
By day	EA.			175.16
By week	"			528.24
By month	"			1,591
600 cfm				
By day	EA.			482.12
By week	"			1,448
By month	"			4,345
Air tools, per compressor, per day				
Minimum	EA.			32.19
Average	"			40.25
Maximum	"			56.33
Generators, 5 kw				
By day	EA.			80.48
By week	"			239.57
By month	"			738.05
Heaters, salamander type, per week				
Minimum	EA.			96.56
Average	"			136.80
Maximum	"			288.67
Pumps, submersible				
50 gpm				
By day	EA.			64.37
By week	"			191.95
By month	"			577.35
100 gpm				
By day	EA.			80.48
By week	"			239.57

Requirements	UNIT	MAT.	INST.	TOTAL
01600.10	Equipment			
By month	EA.			723.17
500 gpm				
By day	EA.			128.74
By week	"			385.39
By month	"			1,158
Diaphragm pump, by week				
Minimum	EA.			112.66
Average	"			191.95
Maximum	"			400.28
Pickup truck				
By day	EA.			120.70
By week	"			352.66
By month	"			1,094
Dump truck				
6 cy truck				
By day	EA.			321.41
By week	"			964.23
By month	"			2,896
10 cy truck				
By day	EA.			400.28
By week	"			1,205
By month	"			3,619
16 cy truck				
By day	EA.			642.82
By week	"			1,930
By month	"			5,793
Backhoe, track mounted				
1/2 cy capacity				
By day	EA.			659.19
By week	"			2,010
By month	"			5,954
1 cy capacity				
By day	EA.			1,045
By week	"			3,137
By month	"			9,413
2 cy capacity				
By day	EA.			1,769
By week	"			5,309
By month	"			15,931
3 cy capacity				
By day	EA.			3,379
By week	"			10,138
By month	"			30,415
Backhoe/loader, rubber tired				
1/2 cy capacity				
By day	EA.			400.28
By week	"			1,205
By month	"			3,619
3/4 cy capacity				
By day	EA.			482.12
By week	"			1,448
By month	"			4,345

Requirements	UNIT	MAT.	INST.	TOTAL
01600.10 — Equipment				
Bulldozer				
75 hp				
By day	EA.			562.47
By week	"			1,689
By month	"			5,068
200 hp				
By day	EA.			1,609
By week	"			4,827
By month	"			14,483
400 hp				
By day	EA.			2,414
By week	"			7,241
By month	"			21,725
Cranes, crawler type				
15 ton capacity				
By day	EA.			723.17
By week	"			2,171
By month	"			6,516
25 ton capacity				
By day	EA.			883.88
By week	"			2,653
By month	"			7,964
50 ton capacity				
By day	EA.			1,609
By week	"			4,827
By month	"			14,483
100 ton capacity				
By day	EA.			2,412
By week	"			7,241
By month	"			21,725
Truck mounted, hydraulic				
15 ton capacity				
By day	EA.			681.51
By week	"			2,050
By month	"			5,917
Loader, rubber tired				
1 cy capacity				
By day	EA.			482.12
By week	"			1,448
By month	"			4,345
2 cy capacity				
By day	EA.			723.17
By week	"			2,815
By month	"			8,447
3 cy capacity				
By day	EA.			1,287
By week	"			3,861
By month	"			11,586

01   GENERAL

Requirements	UNIT	MAT.	INST.	TOTAL
01740.10 Bonds				
Performance bonds				
Minimum	PCT.			0.64
Average	"			2.01
Maximum	"			3.18

Soil Tests	UNIT	MAT.	INST.	TOTAL
02010.10 Soil Boring				
Borings, uncased, stable earth				
2-1/2" dia.				
Minimum	L.F.		17.80	17.80
Average	"		26.70	26.70
Maximum	"		42.80	42.80
4" dia.				
Minimum	L.F.		19.45	19.45
Average	"		30.50	30.50
Maximum	"		53.50	53.50
Cased, including samples				
2-1/2" dia.				
Minimum	L.F.		21.40	21.40
Average	"		35.60	35.60
Maximum	"		71.50	71.50
4" dia.				
Minumum	L.F.		42.80	42.80
Average	"		61.00	61.00
Maximum	"		85.50	85.50
Drilling in rock				
No sampling				
Minimum	L.F.		38.90	38.90
Average	"		56.50	56.50
Maximum	"		76.50	76.50
With casing and sampling				
Minimum	L.F.		53.50	53.50
Average	"		71.50	71.50
Maximum	"		110.00	110.00
Test pits				
Light soil				
Minimum	EA.		270.00	270.00
Average	"		360.00	360.00
Maximum	"		710.00	710.00
Heavy soil				
Minimum	EA.		430.00	430.00
Average	"		530.00	530.00
Maximum	"		1,070	1,070

Demolition	UNIT	MAT.	INST.	TOTAL
02060.10 Building Demolition				
Building, complete with disposal				
Wood frame	C.F.		0.31	0.31
Concrete	"		0.47	0.47
Steel frame	"		0.63	0.63
Partition removal				
Concrete block partitions				

Demolition	UNIT	MAT.	INST.	TOTAL
02060.10	**Building Demolition**			
4" thick	S.F.		2.00	2.00
8" thick	"		2.65	2.65
12" thick	"		3.65	3.65
Brick masonry partitions				
4" thick	S.F.		2.00	2.00
8" thick	"		2.50	2.50
12" thick	"		3.35	3.35
16" thick	"		5.00	5.00
Cast in place concrete partitions				
Unreinforced				
6" thick	S.F.		14.25	14.25
8" thick	"		15.25	15.25
10" thick	"		17.80	17.80
12" thick	"		21.40	21.40
Reinforced				
6" thick	S.F.		16.45	16.45
8" thick	"		21.40	21.40
10" thick	"		23.75	23.75
12" thick	"		28.50	28.50
Terra cotta				
To 6" thick	S.F.		2.00	2.00
Stud partitions				
Metal or wood, with drywall both sides	S.F.		2.00	2.00
Metal studs, both sides, lath and plaster	"		2.65	2.65
Door and frame removal				
Hollow metal in masonry wall				
Single				
2'6"x6'8"	EA.		50.00	50.00
3'x7'	"		66.50	66.50
Double				
3'x7'	EA.		80.00	80.00
4'x8'	"		80.00	80.00
Wood in framed wall				
Single				
2'6"x6'8"	EA.		28.60	28.60
3'x6'8"	"		33.30	33.30
Double				
2'6"x6'8"	EA.		40.00	40.00
3'x6'8"	"		44.40	44.40
Remove for re-use				
Hollow metal	EA.		100.00	100.00
Wood	"		66.50	66.50
Floor removal				
Brick flooring	S.F.		1.60	1.60
Ceramic or quarry tile	"		0.89	0.89
Terrazzo	"		1.80	1.80
Heavy wood	"		1.05	1.05
Residential wood	"		1.15	1.15
Resilient tile or linoleum	"		0.40	0.40
Ceiling removal				
Acoustical tile ceiling				
Adhesive fastened	S.F.		0.40	0.40

Demolition	UNIT	MAT.	INST.	TOTAL
02060.10	**Building Demolition**			
Furred and glued	S.F.		0.33	0.33
Suspended grid	"		0.25	0.25
Drywall ceiling				
Furred and nailed	S.F.		0.44	0.44
Nailed to framing	"		0.40	0.40
Plastered ceiling				
Furred on framing	S.F.		1.00	1.00
Suspended system	"		1.35	1.35
Roofing removal				
Steel frame				
Corrugated metal roofing	S.F.		0.80	0.80
Built-up roof on metal deck	"		1.35	1.35
Wood frame				
Built up roof on wood deck	S.F.		1.25	1.25
Roof shingles	"		0.67	0.67
Roof tiles	"		1.35	1.35
Concrete frame	C.F.		2.65	2.65
Concrete plank	S.F.		2.00	2.00
Built-up roof on concrete	"		1.15	1.15
Cut-outs				
Concrete, elevated slabs, mesh reinforcing				
Under 5 cf	C.F.		40.00	40.00
Over 5 cf	"		33.30	33.30
Bar reinforcing				
Under 5 cf	C.F.		66.50	66.50
Over 5 cf	"		50.00	50.00
Window removal				
Metal windows, trim included				
2'x3'	EA.		40.00	40.00
2'x4'	"		44.40	44.40
2'x6'	"		50.00	50.00
3'x4'	"		50.00	50.00
3'x6'	"		57.00	57.00
3'x8'	"		66.50	66.50
4'x4'	"		66.50	66.50
4'x6'	"		80.00	80.00
4'x8'	"		100.00	100.00
Wood windows, trim included				
2'x3'	EA.		22.20	22.20
2'x4'	"		23.55	23.55
2'x6'	"		25.00	25.00
3'x4'	"		26.70	26.70
3'x6'	"		28.60	28.60
3'x8'	"		30.80	30.80
6'x4'	"		33.30	33.30
6'x6'	"		36.40	36.40
6'x8'	"		40.00	40.00
Walls, concrete, bar reinforcing				
Small jobs	C.F.		26.70	26.70
Large jobs	"		22.20	22.20
Brick walls, not including toothing				
4" thick	S.F.		2.00	2.00

Demolition	UNIT	MAT.	INST.	TOTAL
02060.10 Building Demolition				
8" thick	S.F.		2.50	2.50
12" thick	"		3.35	3.35
16" thick	"		5.00	5.00
Concrete block walls, not including toothing				
4" thick	S.F.		2.20	2.20
6" thick	"		2.35	2.35
8" thick	"		2.50	2.50
10" thick	"		2.85	2.85
12" thick	"		3.35	3.35
Rubbish handling				
Load in dumpster or truck				
Minimum	C.F.		0.89	0.89
Maximum	"		1.35	1.35
For use of elevators, add				
Minimum	C.F.		0.20	0.20
Maximum	"		0.40	0.40
Rubbish hauling				
Hand loaded on trucks, 2 mile trip	C.Y.		32.80	32.80
Machine loaded on trucks, 2 mile trip	"		21.40	21.40

Highway Demolition	UNIT	MAT.	INST.	TOTAL
02065.10 Pavement Demolition				
Bituminous pavement, up to 3" thick				
On streets				
Minimum	S.Y.		6.10	6.10
Average	"		8.55	8.55
Maximum	"		14.25	14.25
On pipe trench				
Minimum	S.Y.		8.55	8.55
Average	"		10.70	10.70
Maximum	"		21.40	21.40
Concrete pavement, 6" thick				
No reinforcement				
Minimum	S.Y.		10.70	10.70
Average	"		14.25	14.25
Maximum	"		21.40	21.40
With wire mesh				
Minimum	S.Y.		16.45	16.45
Average	"		21.40	21.40
Maximum	"		26.70	26.70
With rebars				
Minimum	S.Y.		21.40	21.40
Average	"		26.70	26.70
Maximum	"		35.60	35.60
9" thick				

Highway Demolition	UNIT	MAT.	INST.	TOTAL
02065.10 — Pavement Demolition				
No reinforcement				
Minimum	S.Y.		14.25	14.25
Average	"		17.80	17.80
Maximum	"		21.40	21.40
With wire mesh				
Minimum	S.Y.		22.50	22.50
Average	"		26.70	26.70
Maximum	"		32.90	32.90
With rebars				
Minimum	S.Y.		28.50	28.50
Average	"		35.60	35.60
Maximum	"		47.50	47.50
12" thick				
No reinforcement				
Minimum	S.Y.		17.80	17.80
Average	"		21.40	21.40
Maximum	"		26.70	26.70
With wire mesh				
Minimum	S.Y.		25.20	25.20
Average	"		30.50	30.50
Maximum	"		38.90	38.90
With rebars				
Minimum	S.Y.		35.60	35.60
Average	"		42.80	42.80
Maximum	"		53.50	53.50
Sidewalk, 4" thick, with disposal				
Minimum	S.Y.		5.10	5.10
Average	"		7.15	7.15
Maximum	"		10.20	10.20
Removal of pavement markings by waterblasting				
Minimum	S.F.		0.17	0.17
Average	"		0.20	0.20
Maximum	"		0.40	0.40
02065.15 — Saw Cutting Pavement				
Pavement, bituminous				
2" thick	L.F.		1.65	1.65
3" thick	"		2.05	2.05
4" thick	"		2.55	2.55
5" thick	"		2.75	2.75
6" thick	"		2.95	2.95
Concrete pavement, with wire mesh				
4" thick	L.F.		3.15	3.15
5" thick	"		3.40	3.40
6" thick	"		3.75	3.75
8" thick	"		4.10	4.10
10" thick	"		4.55	4.55
Plain concrete, unreinforced				
4" thick	L.F.		2.75	2.75
5" thick	"		3.15	3.15
6" thick	"		3.40	3.40
8" thick	"		3.75	3.75

Highway Demolition	UNIT	MAT.	INST.	TOTAL
02065.15 Saw Cutting Pavement				
10" thick	L.F.		4.10	4.10
02065.80 Curb & Gutter				
Curb removal				
Concrete, unreinforced				
Minimum	L.F.		4.30	4.30
Average	"		5.35	5.35
Maximum	"		6.70	6.70
Reinforced				
Minimum	L.F.		6.90	6.90
Average	"		7.65	7.65
Maximum	"		8.55	8.55
Combination curb and 2' gutter				
Unreinforced				
Minimum	L.F.		5.65	5.65
Average	"		7.35	7.35
Maximum	"		10.70	10.70
Reinforced				
Minimum	L.F.		8.90	8.90
Average	"		11.90	11.90
Maximum	"		21.40	21.40
Granite curb				
Minimum	L.F.		6.10	6.10
Average	"		7.15	7.15
Maximum	"		8.20	8.20
Asphalt curb				
Minimum	L.F.		3.55	3.55
Average	"		4.30	4.30
Maximum	"		5.10	5.10
02065.85 Guardrails				
Remove standard guardrail				
Steel				
Minimum	L.F.		5.35	5.35
Average	"		7.15	7.15
Maximum	"		10.70	10.70
Wood				
Minimum	L.F.		4.65	4.65
Average	"		5.50	5.50
Maximum	"		8.90	8.90
02075.80 Core Drilling				
Concrete				
6" thick				
3" dia.	EA.		36.80	36.80
4" dia.	"		42.90	42.90
6" dia.	"		51.50	51.50
8" dia.	"		86.00	86.00
8" thick				
3" dia.	EA.		51.50	51.50
4" dia.	"		64.50	64.50
6" dia.	"		73.50	73.50

Highway Demolition	UNIT	MAT.	INST.	TOTAL
02075.80	\multicolumn{4}{c} Core Drilling

Highway Demolition	UNIT	MAT.	INST.	TOTAL
8" dia.	EA.		100.00	100.00
10" thick				
3" dia.	EA.		64.50	64.50
4" dia.	"		73.50	73.50
6" dia.	"		86.00	86.00
8" dia.	"		130.00	130.00
12" thick				
3" dia.	EA.		86.00	86.00
4" dia.	"		100.00	100.00
6" dia.	"		130.00	130.00
8" dia.	"		170.00	170.00

Hazardous Waste	UNIT	MAT.	INST.	TOTAL
02080.10	\multicolumn{4}{c} Asbestos Removal
Enclosure using wood studs & poly, install & remove	S.F.	1.20	1.00	2.20
Trailer (change room)	DAY			110.07
Disposal suits (4 suits per man day)	"			45.11
Type C respirator mask, includes hose & filters, per man	"			22.55
Respirator mask & filter, light contamination	"			8.82
Air monitoring test, 12 tests per day				
Off job testing	DAY			1,163
On the job testing	"			1,541
Asbestos vacuum with attachments	EA.			674.84
Hydraspray piston pump	"			862.65
Negative air pressure system	"			787.84
Grade D breathing air equipment	"			1,974
Glove bag, 44" x 60" x 6 mil plastic	"			6.01
40 CY asbestos dumpster				
Weekly rental	EA.			749.64
Pick up/delivery	"			354.93
Asbestos dump fee	"			186.22
02080.12	\multicolumn{4}{c} Duct Insulation Removal
Remove duct insulation, duct size				
6" x 12"	L.F.		2.20	2.20
x 18"	"		3.10	3.10
x 24"	"		4.45	4.45
8" x 12"	"		3.35	3.35
x 18"	"		3.65	3.65
x 24"	"		5.00	5.00
12" x 12"	"		3.35	3.35
x 18"	"		4.45	4.45
x 24"	"		5.70	5.70

Hazardous Waste	UNIT	MAT.	INST.	TOTAL
02080.15 — Pipe Insulation Removal				
Removal, asbestos insulation				
2" thick, pipe				
1" to 3" dia.	L.F.		3.35	3.35
4" to 6" dia.	"		3.80	3.80
3" thick				
7" to 8" dia.	L.F.		4.00	4.00
9" to 10" dia.	"		4.20	4.20
11" to 12" dia.	"		4.45	4.45
13" to 14" dia.	"		4.70	4.70
15" to 18" dia.	"		5.00	5.00

Site Demolition	UNIT	MAT.	INST.	TOTAL
02105.10 — Catch Basins/manholes				
Abandon catch basin or manhole (fill with sand)				
Minimum	EA.		270.00	270.00
Average	"		430.00	430.00
Maximum	"		710.00	710.00
Remove and reset frame and cover				
Minimum	EA.		140.00	140.00
Average	"		210.00	210.00
Maximum	"		360.00	360.00
Remove catch basin, to 10' deep				
Masonry				
Minumum	EA.		430.00	430.00
Average	"		530.00	530.00
Maximum	"		710.00	710.00
Concrete				
Minimum	EA.		530.00	530.00
Average	"		710.00	710.00
Maximum	"		860.00	860.00
02105.20 — Fences				
Remove fencing				
Chain link, 8' high				
For disposal	L.F.		2.00	2.00
For reuse	"		5.00	5.00
Wood				
4' high	S.F.		1.35	1.35
6' high	"		1.60	1.60
8' high	"		2.00	2.00
Masonry				
8" thick				
4' high	S.F.		4.00	4.00
6' high	"		5.00	5.00
8' high	"		5.70	5.70

Site Demolition	UNIT	MAT.	INST.	TOTAL
02105.20 Fences				
12" thick				
4' high	S.F.		6.65	6.65
6' high	"		8.00	8.00
8' high	"		10.00	10.00
12' high	"		13.35	13.35
02105.30 Hydrants				
Remove fire hydrant				
Minimum	EA.		270.00	270.00
Average	"		360.00	360.00
Maximum	"		530.00	530.00
Remove and reset fire hydrant				
Minimum	EA.		710.00	710.00
Average	"		1,070	1,070
Maximum	"		2,140	2,140
02105.42 Drainage Piping				
Remove drainage pipe, not including excavation				
12" dia.				
Minimum	L.F.		7.15	7.15
Average	"		8.90	8.90
Maximum	"		11.25	11.25
18" dia.				
Minimum	L.F.		9.70	9.70
Average	"		11.25	11.25
Maximum	"		14.25	14.25
24" dia.				
Minimum	L.F.		11.90	11.90
Average	"		14.25	14.25
Maximum	"		17.80	17.80
36" dia.				
Minimum	L.F.		14.25	14.25
Average	"		17.80	17.80
Maximum	"		22.50	22.50
02105.43 Gas Piping				
Remove welded steel pipe, not including excavation				
4" dia.				
Minimum	L.F.		10.70	10.70
Average	"		13.35	13.35
Maximum	"		17.80	17.80
5" dia.				
Minimum	L.F.		17.80	17.80
Average	"		21.40	21.40
Maximum	"		26.70	26.70
6" dia.				
Minimum	L.F.		22.50	22.50
Average	"		26.70	26.70
Maximum	"		35.60	35.60
8" dia.				
Minimum	L.F.		32.90	32.90
Average	"		42.80	42.80

Site Demolition	UNIT	MAT.	INST.	TOTAL
02105.43 — Gas Piping				
Maximum	L.F.		56.50	56.50
10" dia.				
Minimum	L.F.		42.80	42.80
Average	"		53.50	53.50
Maximum	"		71.50	71.50
02105.45 — Sanitary Piping				
Remove sewer pipe, not including excavation				
4" dia.				
Minimum	L.F.		5.95	5.95
Average	"		8.55	8.55
Maximum	"		14.25	14.25
6" dia.				
Minimum	L.F.		6.70	6.70
Average	"		9.70	9.70
Maximum	"		17.80	17.80
8" dia.				
Minimum	L.F.		7.15	7.15
Average	"		10.70	10.70
Maximum	"		21.40	21.40
10" dia.				
Minimum	L.F.		7.65	7.65
Average	"		11.25	11.25
Maximum	"		23.75	23.75
12" dia.				
Minimum	L.F.		8.20	8.20
Average	"		11.90	11.90
Maximum	"		26.70	26.70
15" dia.				
Minimum	L.F.		8.90	8.90
Average	"		12.60	12.60
Maximum	"		30.50	30.50
18" dia.				
Minimum	L.F.		9.70	9.70
Average	"		14.25	14.25
Maximum	"		35.60	35.60
24" dia.				
Minimum	L.F.		10.70	10.70
Average	"		17.80	17.80
Maximum	"		42.80	42.80
30" dia.				
Minimum	L.F.		11.90	11.90
Average	"		21.40	21.40
Maximum	"		53.50	53.50
36" dia.				
Minimum	L.F.		14.25	14.25
Average	"		26.70	26.70
Maximum	"		71.50	71.50

Site Demolition	UNIT	MAT.	INST.	TOTAL
02105.48		Water Piping		
Remove water pipe, not including excavation				
4" dia.				
Minimum	L.F.		8.55	8.55
Average	"		9.70	9.70
Maximum	"		11.25	11.25
6" dia.				
Minimum	L.F.		8.90	8.90
Average	"		10.20	10.20
Maximum	"		11.90	11.90
8" dia.				
Minimum	L.F.		9.70	9.70
Average	"		11.25	11.25
Maximum	"		13.35	13.35
10" dia.				
Minimum	L.F.		10.20	10.20
Average	"		11.90	11.90
Maximum	"		14.25	14.25
12" dia.				
Minimum	L.F.		10.70	10.70
Average	"		12.60	12.60
Maximum	"		15.25	15.25
14" dia.				
Minimum	L.F.		11.25	11.25
Average	"		13.35	13.35
Maximum	"		16.45	16.45
16" dia.				
Minimum	L.F.		11.90	11.90
Average	"		14.25	14.25
Maximum	"		17.80	17.80
18" dia.				
Minimum	L.F.		12.60	12.60
Average	"		15.25	15.25
Maximum	"		19.45	19.45
20" dia.				
Minimum	L.F.		13.35	13.35
Average	"		16.45	16.45
Maximum	"		21.40	21.40
Remove valves				
6"	EA.		110.00	110.00
10"	"		120.00	120.00
14"	"		130.00	130.00
18"	"		180.00	180.00
02105.60		Underground Tanks		
Remove underground storage tank, and backfill				
50 to 250 gals	EA.		710.00	710.00
600 gals	"		710.00	710.00
1000 gals	"		1,070	1,070
4000 gals	"		1,710	1,710
5000 gals	"		1,710	1,710
10,000 gals	"		2,850	2,850
12,000 gals	"		3,560	3,560

Site Demolition	UNIT	MAT.	INST.	TOTAL
02105.60 Underground Tanks				
15,000 gals	EA.		4,280	4,280
20,000 gals	"		5,350	5,350
02105.66 Septic Tanks				
Remove septic tank				
1000 gals	EA.		180.00	180.00
2000 gals	"		210.00	210.00
5000 gals	"		270.00	270.00
15,000 gals	"		2,140	2,140
25,000 gals	"		2,850	2,850
40,000 gals	"		4,280	4,280
02105.80 Walls, Exterior				
Concrete wall				
Light reinforcing				
6" thick	S.F.		10.70	10.70
8" thick	"		11.25	11.25
10" thick	"		11.90	11.90
12" thick	"		13.35	13.35
Medium reinforcing				
6" thick	S.F.		11.25	11.25
8" thick	"		11.90	11.90
10" thick	"		13.35	13.35
12" thick	"		15.25	15.25
Heavy reinforcing				
6" thick	S.F.		12.60	12.60
8" thick	"		13.35	13.35
10" thick	"		15.25	15.25
12" thick	"		17.80	17.80
Masonry				
No reinforcing				
8" thick	S.F.		4.75	4.75
12" thick	"		5.35	5.35
16" thick	"		6.10	6.10
Horizontal reinforcing				
8" thick	S.F.		5.35	5.35
12" thick	"		5.80	5.80
16" thick	"		6.90	6.90
Vertical reinforcing				
8" thick	S.F.		6.90	6.90
12" thick	"		7.90	7.90
16" thick	"		9.70	9.70
Remove concrete headwall				
15" pipe	EA.		150.00	150.00
18" pipe	"		180.00	180.00
24" pipe	"		190.00	190.00
30" pipe	"		210.00	210.00
36" pipe	"		240.00	240.00
48" pipe	"		310.00	310.00
60" pipe	"		430.00	430.00

Site Demolition	UNIT	MAT.	INST.	TOTAL
02110.10 — Clearing And Grubbing				
Clear wooded area				
Light density	ACRE		5,350	5,350
Medium density	"		7,130	7,130
Heavy density	"		8,550	8,550
02110.50 — Tree Cutting & Clearing				
Cut trees and clear out stumps				
9" to 12" dia.	EA.		430.00	430.00
To 24" dia.	"		530.00	530.00
24" dia. and up	"		710.00	710.00
Loading and trucking				
For machine load, per load, round trip				
1 mile	EA.		85.50	85.50
3 mile	"		97.00	97.00
5 mile	"		110.00	110.00
10 mile	"		140.00	140.00
20 mile	"		210.00	210.00
Hand loaded, round trip				
1 mile	EA.		210.00	210.00
3 mile	"		230.00	230.00
5 mile	"		270.00	270.00
10 mile	"		330.00	330.00
20 mile	"		410.00	410.00
Tree trimming for pole line construction				
Light cutting	L.F.		1.05	1.05
Medium cutting	"		1.45	1.45
Heavy cutting	"		2.15	2.15

Dewatering	UNIT	MAT.	INST.	TOTAL
02144.10 — Wellpoint Systems				
Pumping, gas driven, 50' hose				
3" header pipe	DAY		820.00	820.00
6" header pipe	"		1,030	1,030
Wellpoint system per job				
6" header pipe	L.F.	1.85	3.30	5.15
8" header pipe	"	2.35	4.10	6.45
10" header pipe	"	3.10	5.45	8.55
Jetting wellpoint system				
14' long	EA.	60.50	54.50	115.00
18' long	"	70.00	68.50	138.50
Sand filter for wellpoints	L.F.	2.90	1.35	4.25
Replacement of wellpoint components	EA.		16.40	16.40

Shoring And Underpinning	UNIT	MAT.	INST.	TOTAL
02162.10 Trench Sheeting				
Closed timber, including pull and salvage, excavation				
8' deep	S.F.	3.10	7.50	10.60
10' deep	"	3.10	7.90	11.00
12' deep	"	3.10	8.35	11.45
14' deep	"	3.10	8.80	11.90
16' deep	"	3.10	9.35	12.45
18' deep	"	3.10	10.70	13.80
20' deep	"	3.10	11.55	14.65
02170.10 Cofferdams				
Cofferdam, steel, driven from shore				
15' deep	S.F.	14.70	18.25	32.95
20' deep	"	14.70	17.05	31.75
25' deep	"	14.70	16.00	30.70
30' deep	"	14.70	15.05	29.75
40' deep	"	14.70	14.20	28.90
Driven from barge				
20' deep	S.F.	14.70	19.70	34.40
30' deep	"	14.70	18.25	32.95
40' deep	"	14.70	17.05	31.75
50' deep	"	14.70	16.00	30.70

Earthwork	UNIT	MAT.	INST.	TOTAL
02210.10 Hauling Material				
Haul material by 10 cy dump truck, round trip distance				
1 mile	C.Y.		4.55	4.55
2 mile	"		5.45	5.45
5 mile	"		7.45	7.45
10 mile	"		8.20	8.20
20 mile	"		9.10	9.10
30 mile	"		10.95	10.95
Site grading, cut & fill, sandy clay, 200' haul, 75 hp dozer	"		3.30	3.30
Spread topsoil by equipment on site	"		3.65	3.65
Site grading (cut and fill to 6") less than 1 acre				
75 hp dozer	C.Y.		5.45	5.45
1.5 cy backhoe/loader	"		8.20	8.20
02210.30 Bulk Excavation				
Excavation, by small dozer				
Large areas	C.Y.		1.65	1.65
Small areas	"		2.75	2.75
Trim banks	"		4.10	4.10
Drag line				
1-1/2 cy bucket				
Sand or gravel	C.Y.		3.55	3.55

Earthwork	UNIT	MAT.	INST.	TOTAL
02210.30 Bulk Excavation				
Light clay	C.Y.		4.75	4.75
Heavy clay	"		5.35	5.35
Unclassified	"		5.70	5.70
2 cy bucket				
Sand or gravel	C.Y.		3.30	3.30
Light clay	"		4.30	4.30
Heavy clay	"		4.75	4.75
Unclassified	"		5.05	5.05
2-1/2 cy bucket				
Sand or gravel	C.Y.		3.05	3.05
Light clay	"		3.90	3.90
Heavy clay	"		4.30	4.30
Unclassified	"		4.50	4.50
3 cy bucket				
Sand or gravel	C.Y.		2.65	2.65
Light clay	"		3.55	3.55
Heavy clay	"		3.90	3.90
Unclassified	"		4.05	4.05
Hydraulic excavator				
1 cy capacity				
Light material	C.Y.		3.55	3.55
Medium material	"		4.30	4.30
Wet material	"		5.35	5.35
Blasted rock	"		6.10	6.10
1-1/2 cy capacity				
Light material	C.Y.		1.45	1.45
Medium material	"		1.90	1.90
Wet material	"		2.30	2.30
Blasted rock	"		2.85	2.85
2 cy capacity				
Light material	C.Y.		1.25	1.25
Medium material	"		1.65	1.65
Wet material	"		1.90	1.90
Blasted rock	"		2.30	2.30
Wheel mounted front-end loader				
7/8 cy capacity				
Light material	C.Y.		2.85	2.85
Medium material	"		3.25	3.25
Wet material	"		3.80	3.80
Blasted rock	"		4.60	4.60
1-1/2 cy capacity				
Light material	C.Y.		1.65	1.65
Medium material	"		1.75	1.75
Wet material	"		1.90	1.90
Blasted rock	"		2.10	2.10
2-1/2 cy capacity				
Light material	C.Y.		1.35	1.35
Medium material	"		1.45	1.45
Wet material	"		1.55	1.55
Blasted rock	"		1.65	1.65
3-1/2 cy capacity				
Light material	C.Y.		1.25	1.25

Earthwork	UNIT	MAT.	INST.	TOTAL
02210.30 **Bulk Excavation**				
Medium material	C.Y.		1.35	1.35
Wet material	"		1.45	1.45
Blasted rock	"		1.55	1.55
6 cy capacity				
Light material	C.Y.		0.76	0.76
Medium material	"		0.82	0.82
Wet material	"		0.88	0.88
Blasted rock	"		0.95	0.95
Track mounted front-end loader				
1-1/2 cy capacity				
Light material	C.Y.		1.90	1.90
Medium material	"		2.10	2.10
Wet material	"		2.30	2.30
Blasted rock	"		2.55	2.55
2-3/4 cy capacity				
Light material	C.Y.		1.15	1.15
Medium material	"		1.25	1.25
Wet material	"		1.45	1.45
Blasted rock	"		1.65	1.65
02220.10 **Borrow**				
Borrow fill, F.O.B. at pit				
Sand, haul to site, round trip				
10 mile	C.Y.	13.25	11.45	24.70
20 mile	"	13.25	19.10	32.35
30 mile	"	13.25	28.60	41.85
Place borrow fill and compact				
Less than 1 in 4 slope	C.Y.	13.25	5.75	19.00
Greater than 1 in 4 slope	"	13.25	7.65	20.90
02220.20 **Gravel And Stone**				
F.O.B. PLANT				
No. 21 crusher run stone	C.Y.			28.53
No. 26 crusher run stone	"			27.74
No. 57 stone	"			29.34
No. 67 gravel	"			14.26
No. 68 stone	"			28.53
No. 78 stone	"			28.53
No. 78 gravel, (pea gravel)	"			16.64
No. 357 or B-3 stone	"			29.34
Structural & foundation backfill				
No. 21 crusher run stone	TON			25.35
No. 26 crusher run stone	"			26.16
No. 57 stone	"			28.53
No. 67 gravel	"			12.69
No. 68 stone	"			24.37
No. 78 stone	"			24.37
No. 78 gravel, (pea gravel)	"			19.82
No. 357 or B-3 stone	"			28.21

Earthwork	UNIT	MAT.	INST.	TOTAL
02220.40 — Building Excavation				
Structural excavation, unclassified earth				
3/8 cy backhoe	C.Y.		15.25	15.25
3/4 cy backhoe	"		11.45	11.45
1 cy backhoe	"		9.55	9.55
Foundation backfill and compaction by machine	"		22.90	22.90
02220.50 — Utility Excavation				
Trencher, sandy clay, 8" wide trench				
18" deep	L.F.		1.80	1.80
24" deep	"		2.05	2.05
36" deep	"		2.35	2.35
Trench backfill, 95% compaction				
Tamp by hand	C.Y.		25.00	25.00
Vibratory compaction	"		20.00	20.00
Trench backfilling, with borrow sand, place & compact	"	12.30	20.00	32.30
02220.60 — Trenching				
Trenching and continuous footing excavation				
By gradall				
1 cy capacity				
Light soil	C.Y.		3.25	3.25
Medium soil	"		3.50	3.50
Heavy/wet soil	"		3.80	3.80
Loose rock	"		4.15	4.15
Blasted rock	"		4.40	4.40
By hydraulic excavator				
1/2 cy capacity				
Light soil	C.Y.		3.80	3.80
Medium soil	"		4.15	4.15
Heavy/wet soil	"		4.60	4.60
Loose rock	"		5.10	5.10
Blasted rock	"		5.75	5.75
1 cy capacity				
Light soil	C.Y.		2.70	2.70
Medium soil	"		2.85	2.85
Heavy/wet soil	"		3.05	3.05
Loose rock	"		3.25	3.25
Blasted rock	"		3.50	3.50
1-1/2 cy capacity				
Light soil	C.Y.		2.40	2.40
Medium soil	"		2.55	2.55
Heavy/wet soil	"		2.70	2.70
Loose rock	"		2.85	2.85
Blasted rock	"		3.05	3.05
2 cy capacity				
Light soil	C.Y.		2.30	2.30
Medium soil	"		2.40	2.40
Heavy/wet soil	"		2.55	2.55
Loose rock	"		2.70	2.70
Blasted rock	"		2.85	2.85
2-1/2 cy capacity				
Light soil	C.Y.		2.10	2.10

Earthwork	UNIT	MAT.	INST.	TOTAL
02220.60	Trenching			
Medium soil	C.Y.		2.20	2.20
Heavy/wet soil	"		2.30	2.30
Loose rock	"		2.40	2.40
Blasted rock	"		2.55	2.55
Trencher, chain, 1' wide to 4' deep				
Light soil	C.Y.		2.05	2.05
Medium soil	"		2.35	2.35
Heavy soil	"		2.75	2.75
Hand excavation				
Bulk, wheeled 100'				
Normal soil	C.Y.		44.40	44.40
Sand or gravel	"		40.00	40.00
Medium clay	"		57.00	57.00
Heavy clay	"		80.00	80.00
Loose rock	"		100.00	100.00
Trenches, up to 2' deep				
Normal soil	C.Y.		50.00	50.00
Sand or gravel	"		44.40	44.40
Medium clay	"		66.50	66.50
Heavy clay	"		100.00	100.00
Loose rock	"		130.00	130.00
Trenches, to 6' deep				
Normal soil	C.Y.		57.00	57.00
Sand or gravel	"		50.00	50.00
Medium clay	"		80.00	80.00
Heavy clay	"		130.00	130.00
Loose rock	"		200.00	200.00
Backfill trenches				
With compaction				
By hand	C.Y.		33.30	33.30
By 60 hp tracked dozer	"		2.05	2.05
By 200 hp tracked dozer	"		1.25	1.25
By small front-end loader	"		2.35	2.35
Spread dumped fill or gravel, no compaction				
6" layers	S.Y.		1.35	1.35
12" layers	"		1.65	1.65
Compaction in 6" layers				
By hand with air tamper	S.Y.		1.05	1.05
Backfill trenches, sand bedding, no compaction				
By hand	C.Y.	12.30	33.30	45.60
By small front-end loader	"	12.30	3.25	15.55
02220.70	Roadway Excavation			
Roadway excavation				
1/4 mile haul	C.Y.		2.30	2.30
2 mile haul	"		3.80	3.80
5 mile haul	"		5.75	5.75
Excavation of open ditches	"		1.65	1.65
Trim banks, swales or ditches	S.Y.		1.90	1.90
Bulk swale excavation by dragline				
Small jobs	C.Y.		5.35	5.35
Large jobs	"		3.05	3.05

Earthwork	UNIT	MAT.	INST.	TOTAL
02220.70	**Roadway Excavation**			
Spread base course	C.Y.		2.85	2.85
Roll and compact	"		3.80	3.80
02220.71	**Base Course**			
Base course, crushed stone				
3" thick	S.Y.	2.90	0.57	3.47
4" thick	"	3.85	0.62	4.47
6" thick	"	5.85	0.67	6.52
8" thick	"	7.40	0.76	8.16
10" thick	"	9.10	0.82	9.92
12" thick	"	9.90	0.95	10.85
Base course, bank run gravel				
4" deep	S.Y.	2.10	0.60	2.70
6" deep	"	3.10	0.65	3.75
8" deep	"	4.00	0.72	4.72
10" deep	"	5.15	0.76	5.91
12" deep	"	6.00	0.88	6.88
Prepare and roll sub base				
Minimum	S.Y.		0.57	0.57
Average	"		0.72	0.72
Maximum	"		0.95	0.95
02220.90	**Hand Excavation**			
Excavation				
To 2' deep				
Normal soil	C.Y.		44.40	44.40
Sand and gravel	"		40.00	40.00
Medium clay	"		50.00	50.00
Heavy clay	"		57.00	57.00
Loose rock	"		66.50	66.50
To 6' deep				
Normal soil	C.Y.		57.00	57.00
Sand and gravel	"		50.00	50.00
Medium clay	"		66.50	66.50
Heavy clay	"		80.00	80.00
Loose rock	"		100.00	100.00
Backfilling foundation without compaction, 6" lifts	"		25.00	25.00
Compaction of backfill around structures or in trench				
By hand with air tamper	C.Y.		28.60	28.60
By hand with vibrating plate tamper	"		26.70	26.70
1 ton roller	"		41.10	41.10
Miscellaneous hand labor				
Trim slopes, sides of excavation	S.F.		0.07	0.07
Trim bottom of excavation	"		0.08	0.08
Excavation around obstructions and services	C.Y.		130.00	130.00
02240.05	**Soil Stabilization**			
Straw bale secured with rebar	L.F.	1.75	1.35	3.10
Filter barrier, 18" high filter fabric	"	1.75	4.00	5.75
Sediment fence, 36" fabric with 6" mesh	"	4.15	5.00	9.15
Soil stabilization with tar paper, burlap, straw and stakes	S.F.	0.35	0.06	0.41

Earthwork	UNIT	MAT.	INST.	TOTAL
02240.30	Geotextile			
Filter cloth, light reinforcement				
Woven				
12'-6" wide x 50' long	S.F.	0.33	0.06	0.39
Various lengths	"	0.50	0.06	0.55
Non-woven				
14'-8" wide x 430' long	S.F.	0.18	0.06	0.24
Various lengths	"	0.26	0.06	0.31
02270.10	Slope Protection			
Gabions, stone filled				
6" deep	S.Y.	25.90	20.50	46.40
9" deep	"	31.80	23.45	55.25
12" deep	"	42.00	27.40	69.40
18" deep	"	54.00	32.80	86.80
36" deep	"	95.50	54.50	150.00
02270.40	Riprap			
Riprap				
Crushed stone blanket, max size 2-1/2"	TON	28.90	62.50	91.40
Stone, quarry run, 300 lb. stones	"	36.10	57.50	93.60
400 lb. stones	"	36.10	53.50	89.60
500 lb. stones	"	36.10	50.00	86.10
750 lb. stones	"	36.10	46.90	83.00
Dry concrete riprap in bags 3" thick, 80 lb. per bag	BAG	5.80	3.10	8.90
02280.20	Soil Treatment			
Soil treatment, termite control pretreatment				
Under slabs	S.F.	0.17	0.22	0.39
By walls	"	0.17	0.27	0.43
02290.30	Weed Control			
Weed control, bromicil, 15 lb./acre, wettable powder	ACRE	280.00	200.00	480.00
Vegetation control, by application of plant killer	S.Y.	0.03	0.16	0.19
Weed killer, lawns and fields	"	0.23	0.08	0.31

Tunneling	UNIT	MAT.	INST.	TOTAL
02300.10	Pipe Jacking			
Pipe casing, horizontal jacking				
18" dia.	L.F.	87.00	83.50	170.50
21" dia.	"	100.00	89.50	189.50
24" dia.	"	110.00	94.00	204.00
27" dia.	"	120.00	94.00	214.00
30" dia.	"	130.00	98.50	228.50
36" dia.	"	150.00	110.00	260.00
42" dia.	"	210.00	120.00	330.00

Tunneling	UNIT	MAT.	INST.	TOTAL
02300.10		Pipe Jacking		
48" dia.	L.F.	260.00	130.00	390.00

Piles And Caissons	UNIT	MAT.	INST.	TOTAL
02360.50		Prestressed Piling		
Prestressed concrete piling, less than 60' long				
10" sq.	L.F.	10.95	5.35	16.30
12" sq.	"	15.30	5.55	20.85
14" sq.	"	15.95	5.70	21.65
16" sq.	"	19.60	5.80	25.40
18" sq.	"	27.10	6.25	33.35
20" sq.	"	36.70	6.40	43.10
24" sq.	"	46.90	6.55	53.45
More than 60' long				
12" sq.	L.F.	15.65	4.55	20.20
14" sq.	"	17.20	4.65	21.85
16" sq.	"	20.70	4.75	25.45
18" sq.	"	27.20	4.85	32.05
20" sq.	"	36.70	4.90	41.60
24" sq.	"	43.80	5.00	48.80
Straight cylinder, less than 60' long				
12" dia.	L.F.	14.25	5.80	20.05
14" dia.	"	19.25	5.95	25.20
16" dia.	"	23.45	6.10	29.55
18" dia.	"	29.70	6.25	35.95
20" dia.	"	35.10	6.40	41.50
24" dia.	"	43.50	6.55	50.05
More than 60' long				
12" dia.	L.F.	14.25	4.65	18.90
14" dia.	"	19.25	4.75	24.00
16" dia.	"	23.45	4.85	28.30
18" dia.	"	29.70	4.90	34.60
20" dia.	"	35.10	5.00	40.10
24" dia.	"	44.40	5.10	49.50
Concrete sheet piling				
12" thick x 20' long	S.F.	16.25	12.80	29.05
25' long	"	16.25	11.65	27.90
30' long	"	16.25	10.65	26.90
35' long	"	16.25	9.85	26.10
40' long	"	16.25	9.15	25.40
16" thick x 40' long	"	22.30	7.10	29.40
45' long	"	22.30	6.75	29.05
50' long	"	22.30	6.40	28.70
55' long	"	22.30	6.10	28.40
60' long	"	22.30	5.80	28.10

Piles And Caissons	UNIT	MAT.	INST.	TOTAL
02360.60 Steel Piles				
H-section piles				
8x8				
36 lb/ft				
30' long	L.F.	14.95	10.65	25.60
40' long	"	14.95	8.55	23.50
50' long	"	14.95	7.10	22.05
10x10				
42 lb/ft				
30' long	L.F.	17.00	10.65	27.65
40' long	"	17.00	8.55	25.55
50' long	"	17.00	7.10	24.10
57 lb/ft				
30' long	L.F.	21.75	10.65	32.40
40' long	"	21.75	8.55	30.30
50' long	"	21.75	7.10	28.85
12x12				
53 lb/ft				
30' long	L.F.	20.40	11.65	32.05
40' long	"	20.40	9.15	29.55
50' long	"	20.40	7.10	27.50
74 lb/ft				
30' long	L.F.	27.20	11.65	38.85
40' long	"	27.20	9.15	36.35
50' long	"	27.20	7.10	34.30
14x14				
73 lb/ft				
40' long	L.F.	27.20	11.65	38.85
50' long	"	27.20	9.15	36.35
60' long	"	27.20	7.10	34.30
89 lb/ft				
40' long	L.F.	34.00	11.65	45.65
50' long	"	34.00	9.15	43.15
60' long	"	34.00	7.10	41.10
102 lb/ft				
40' long	L.F.	39.50	11.65	51.15
50' long	"	39.50	9.15	48.65
60' long	"	39.50	7.10	46.60
117 lb/ft				
40' long	L.F.	44.90	12.20	57.10
50' long	"	44.90	9.50	54.40
60' long	"	44.90	7.30	52.20
Splice				
8"	EA.	75.00	66.50	141.50
10"	"	81.50	80.00	161.50
12"	"	110.00	80.00	190.00
14"	"	140.00	100.00	240.00
Driving cap				
8"	EA.	42.20	40.00	82.20
10"	"	42.20	50.00	92.20
12"	"	42.20	50.00	92.20
14"	"	42.20	57.00	99.20
Standard point				

Piles And Caissons	UNIT	MAT.	INST.	TOTAL
02360.60 Steel Piles				
8"	EA.	54.50	40.00	94.50
10"	"	67.50	50.00	117.50
12"	"	95.50	57.00	152.50
14"	"	130.00	66.50	196.50
Heavy duty point				
8"	EA.	62.50	44.40	106.90
10"	"	83.50	57.00	140.50
12"	"	110.00	66.50	176.50
14"	"	140.00	80.00	220.00
Tapered friction piles, with fluted steel casing, up to 50'				
With 4000 psi concrete no reinforcing				
12" dia.	L.F.	18.80	6.40	25.20
14" dia.	"	21.70	6.55	28.25
16" dia.	"	26.10	6.75	32.85
18" dia.	"	29.20	7.50	36.70
02360.65 Steel Pipe Piles				
Concrete filled, 3000# concrete, up to 40'				
8" dia.	L.F.	18.55	9.15	27.70
10" dia.	"	22.80	9.50	32.30
12" dia.	"	27.80	9.85	37.65
14" dia.	"	30.70	10.25	40.95
16" dia.	"	34.70	10.65	45.35
18" dia.	"	42.20	11.10	53.30
Pipe piles, non-filled				
8" dia.	L.F.	14.65	7.10	21.75
10" dia.	"	17.25	7.30	24.55
12" dia.	"	21.25	7.50	28.75
14" dia.	"	22.55	8.00	30.55
16" dia.	"	26.50	8.25	34.75
18" dia.	"	29.20	8.55	37.75
Splice				
8" dia.	EA.	50.00	80.00	130.00
10" dia.	"	53.00	80.00	133.00
12" dia.	"	59.50	100.00	159.50
14" dia.	"	66.50	100.00	166.50
16" dia.	"	88.50	130.00	218.50
18" dia.	"	120.00	130.00	250.00
Standard point				
8" dia.	EA.	64.50	80.00	144.50
10" dia.	"	72.50	80.00	152.50
12" dia.	"	110.00	100.00	210.00
14" dia.	"	160.00	100.00	260.00
16" dia.	"	180.00	130.00	310.00
18" dia.	"	220.00	130.00	350.00
Heavy duty point				
8" dia.	EA.	80.50	100.00	180.50
10" dia.	"	96.50	100.00	196.50
12" dia.	"	130.00	130.00	260.00
14" dia.	"	180.00	130.00	310.00
16" dia.	"	220.00	160.00	380.00
18" dia.	"	290.00	160.00	450.00

Piles And Caissons	UNIT	MAT.	INST.	TOTAL
02360.70 Steel Sheet Piling				
Steel sheet piling,12" wide				
20' long	S.F.	11.80	12.80	24.60
35' long	"	11.80	9.15	20.95
50' long	"	11.80	6.40	18.20
Over 50' long	"	11.80	5.80	17.60
02360.80 Wood And Timber Piles				
Treated wood piles, 12" butt, 8" tip				
25' long	L.F.	8.70	12.80	21.50
30' long	"	9.30	10.65	19.95
35' long	"	9.30	9.15	18.45
40' long	"	9.30	8.00	17.30
12" butt, 7" tip				
40' long	L.F.	10.50	8.00	18.50
45' long	"	10.50	7.10	17.60
50' long	"	12.70	6.40	19.10
55' long	"	12.70	5.80	18.50
60' long	"	12.70	5.35	18.05
02360.90 Pile Testing				
Pile test				
50 ton to 100 ton	EA.			18,169
To 200 ton	"			26,969
To 300 ton	"			29,808
To 400 ton	"			45,422
To 600 ton	"			52,519
02380.10 Caissons				
Caisson, including 3000# concrete, in stable ground				
18" dia.	L.F.	15.15	25.60	40.75
24" dia.	"	25.30	26.70	52.00
30" dia.	"	39.80	32.00	71.80
36" dia.	"	55.50	36.50	92.00
48" dia.	"	95.50	42.60	138.10
60" dia.	"	160.00	58.00	218.00
72" dia.	"	240.00	71.00	311.00
84" dia.	"	290.00	91.50	381.50
Wet ground, casing required but pulled				
18" dia.	L.F.	15.15	32.00	47.15
24" dia.	"	25.30	35.50	60.80
30" dia.	"	39.80	40.00	79.80
36" dia.	"	55.50	42.60	98.10
48" dia.	"	95.50	53.50	149.00
60" dia.	"	160.00	71.00	231.00
72" dia.	"	240.00	110.00	350.00
84" dia.	"	290.00	160.00	450.00
Soft rock				
18" dia.	L.F.	15.15	91.50	106.65
24" dia.	"	25.30	160.00	185.30
30" dia.	"	39.80	210.00	249.80
36" dia.	"	55.50	320.00	375.50
48" dia.	"	95.50	430.00	525.50

Piles And Caissons	UNIT	MAT.	INST.	TOTAL
02380.10 Caissons				
60" dia.	L.F.	160.00	640.00	800.00
72" dia.	"	240.00	710.00	950.00
84" dia.	"	290.00	800.00	1,090

Railroad Work	UNIT	MAT.	INST.	TOTAL
02450.10 Railroad Work				
Rail				
90 lb	L.F.	24.85	0.86	25.71
100 lb	"	28.40	0.86	29.26
115 lb	"	31.90	0.86	32.76
132 lb	"	35.50	0.86	36.36
Rail relay				
90 lb	L.F.	9.95	0.86	10.81
100 lb	"	11.00	0.86	11.86
115 lb	"	13.30	0.86	14.16
132 lb	"	16.15	0.86	17.01
New angle bars, per pair				
90 lb	EA.	92.00	1.05	93.05
100 lb	"	100.00	1.05	101.05
115 lb	"	130.00	1.05	131.05
132 lb	"	150.00	1.05	151.05
Angle bar relay				
90 lb	EA.	38.20	1.05	39.25
100 lb	"	38.90	1.05	39.95
115 lb	"	40.80	1.05	41.85
132 lb	"	43.50	1.05	44.55
New tie plates				
90 lb	EA.	12.40	0.76	13.16
100 lb	"	12.95	0.76	13.71
115 lb	"	14.20	0.76	14.96
132 lb	"	15.10	0.76	15.86
Tie plate relay				
90 lb	EA.	3.90	0.76	4.66
100 lb	"	5.50	0.76	6.26
115 lb	"	5.50	0.76	6.26
132 lb	"	6.75	0.76	7.51
Track accessories				
Wooden cross ties, 8'	EA.	46.00	5.35	51.35
Concrete cross ties, 8'	"	300.00	10.70	310.70
Tie plugs, 5"	"	18.90	0.54	19.44
Track bolts and nuts, 1"	"	4.80	0.54	5.34
Lockwashers, 1"	"	1.25	0.36	1.61
Track spikes, 6"	"	1.20	2.15	3.35
Wooden switch ties	B.F.	1.65	0.54	2.19
Rail anchors	EA.	4.85	1.95	6.80

Railroad Work	UNIT	MAT.	INST.	TOTAL
02450.10 Railroad Work				
Ballast	TON	14.20	10.70	24.90
Gauge rods	EA.	38.90	8.55	47.45
Compromise splice bars	"	490.00	14.25	504.25
Turnout				
90 lb	EA.	13,310	2,140	15,450
100 lb	"	14,010	2,140	16,150
110 lb	"	15,080	2,140	17,220
115 lb	"	15,430	2,140	17,570
132 lb	"	16,850	2,140	18,990
Turnout relay				
90 lb	EA.	8,510	2,140	10,650
100 lb	"	9,400	2,140	11,540
110 lb	"	9,760	2,140	11,900
115 lb	"	10,290	2,140	12,430
132 lb	"	11,180	2,140	13,320
Railroad track in place, complete				
New rail				
90 lb	L.F.	170.00	21.40	191.40
100 lb	"	170.00	21.40	191.40
110 lb	"	160.00	21.40	181.40
115 lb	"	170.00	21.40	191.40
132 lb	"	180.00	21.40	201.40
Rail relay				
90 lb	L.F.	93.00	21.40	114.40
100 lb	"	100.00	21.40	121.40
110 lb	"	100.00	21.40	121.40
115 lb	"	110.00	21.40	131.40
132 lb	"	120.00	21.40	141.40
No. 8 turnout				
90 lb	EA.	33,350	2,850	36,200
100 lb	"	37,080	2,850	39,930
110 lb	"	40,630	2,850	43,480
115 lb	"	41,510	2,850	44,360
132 lb	"	42,400	2,850	45,250
No. 8 turnout relay				
90 lb	EA.	27,680	2,850	30,530
100 lb	"	27,680	2,850	30,530
110 lb	"	27,680	2,850	30,530
115 lb	"	31,400	2,850	34,250
132 lb	"	31,400	2,850	34,250
Railroad crossings, asphalt, based on 8" thick x 20'				
Including track and approach				
12' roadway	EA.	830.00	530.00	1,360
15' roadway	"	970.00	610.00	1,580
18' roadway	"	1,140	710.00	1,850
21' roadway	"	1,270	860.00	2,130
24' roadway	"	1,430	1,070	2,500
Precast concrete inserts				
12' roadway	EA.	1,190	210.00	1,400
15' roadway	"	1,430	270.00	1,700
18' roadway	"	1,710	360.00	2,070
21' roadway	"	2,210	430.00	2,640

Railroad Work	UNIT	MAT.	INST.	TOTAL
02450.10 Railroad Work				
24' roadway	EA.	2,670	480.00	3,150
Molded rubber, with headers				
12' roadway	EA.	7,210	210.00	7,420
15' roadway	"	9,010	270.00	9,280
18' roadway	"	10,670	360.00	11,030
21' roadway	"	11,770	430.00	12,200
24' roadway	"	14,350	480.00	14,830

Paving And Surfacing	UNIT	MAT.	INST.	TOTAL
02510.20 Asphalt Surfaces				
Asphalt wearing surface, for flexible pavement				
1" thick	S.Y.	4.45	2.15	6.60
1-1/2" thick	"	6.85	2.55	9.40
2" thick	"	9.05	3.20	12.25
3" thick	"	13.35	4.25	17.60
Binder course				
1-1/2" thick	S.Y.	5.85	2.35	8.20
2" thick	"	7.80	2.90	10.70
3" thick	"	11.70	3.90	15.60
4" thick	"	15.60	4.25	19.85
5" thick	"	20.05	4.75	24.80
6" thick	"	23.95	5.35	29.30
Bituminous sidewalk, no base				
2" thick	S.Y.	9.75	2.50	12.25
3" thick	"	14.50	2.65	17.15
02520.10 Concrete Paving				
Concrete paving, reinforced, 5000 psi concrete				
6" thick	S.Y.	24.45	20.00	44.45
7" thick	"	26.90	21.30	48.20
8" thick	"	30.40	22.85	53.25
9" thick	"	31.30	24.60	55.90
10" thick	"	35.90	26.70	62.60
11" thick	"	39.90	29.10	69.00
12" thick	"	42.30	32.00	74.30
15" thick	"	53.00	40.00	93.00
Concrete paving, for pipe trench, reinforced				
7" thick	S.Y.	50.00	21.40	71.40
8" thick	"	57.50	23.75	81.25
9" thick	"	60.50	26.70	87.20
10" thick	"	68.00	30.50	98.50
Fibrous concrete				
5" thick	S.Y.	23.90	24.60	48.50
8" thick	"	30.50	26.70	57.20
Roller compacted concrete, (RCC), place and compact				

Paving And Surfacing	UNIT	MAT.	INST.	TOTAL
02520.10 — Concrete Paving				
8" thick	S.Y.	29.50	32.00	61.50
12" thick	"	44.80	40.00	84.80
Steel edge forms up to				
12" deep	L.F.	0.74	1.35	2.08
15" deep	"	0.94	1.60	2.54
Paving finishes				
Belt dragged	S.Y.		2.00	2.00
Curing	"	0.36	0.40	0.76
02545.10 — Asphalt Repair				
Coal tar emulsion seal coat, rubber additive, fuel resistant	S.Y.	2.10	0.57	2.67
Bituminous surface treatment, single	"	1.95	0.40	2.35
Double	"	2.60	0.04	2.64
Bituminous prime coat	"	1.30	0.05	1.35
Tack coat	"	0.64	0.04	0.68
Crack sealing, concrete paving	L.F.	1.10	0.27	1.37
Bituminous paving for pipe trench, 4" thick	S.Y.	12.45	14.25	26.70
Polypropylene, nonwoven paving fabric	"	1.65	0.20	1.85
Rubberized asphalt	"	2.60	3.65	6.25
Asphalt slurry seal	"	6.40	2.35	8.75
02580.10 — Pavement Markings				
Pavement line marking, paint				
4" wide	L.F.	0.09	0.10	0.19
6" wide	"	0.12	0.22	0.34
8" wide	"	0.13	0.33	0.47
Reflective paint, 4" wide	"	0.34	0.33	0.67
Airfield markings, retro-reflective				
White	L.F.	0.55	0.33	0.88
Yellow	"	0.59	0.33	0.92
Preformed tape, 4" wide				
Inlaid reflective	L.F.	1.55	0.06	1.61
Reflective paint	"	1.05	0.10	1.15
Thermoplastic				
White	L.F.	0.59	0.20	0.79
Yellow	"	0.59	0.20	0.79
12" wide, thermoplastic, white	"	1.25	0.57	1.82
Directional arrows, reflective preformed tape	EA.	110.00	40.00	150.00
Messages, reflective preformed tape (per letter)	"	55.00	20.00	75.00
Handicap symbol, preformed tape	"	92.00	40.00	132.00
Parking stall painting	"	1.45	8.00	9.45

Utilities	UNIT	MAT.	INST.	TOTAL
02605.30			Manholes	
Precast sections, 48" dia.				
Base section	EA.	180.00	180.00	360.00
1'0" riser	"	52.00	140.00	192.00
1'4" riser	"	63.00	150.00	213.00
2'8" riser	"	94.00	160.00	254.00
4'0" riser	"	180.00	180.00	360.00
2'8" cone top	"	110.00	210.00	320.00
Precast manholes, 48" dia.				
4' deep	EA.	430.00	430.00	860.00
6' deep	"	650.00	530.00	1,180
7' deep	"	740.00	610.00	1,350
8' deep	"	840.00	710.00	1,550
10' deep	"	940.00	860.00	1,800
Cast-in-place, 48" dia., with frame and cover				
5' deep	EA.	560.00	1,070	1,630
6' deep	"	730.00	1,220	1,950
8' deep	"	1,070	1,430	2,500
10' deep	"	1,250	1,710	2,960
Brick manholes, 48" dia. with cover, 8" thick				
4' deep	EA.	660.00	500.00	1,160
6' deep	"	830.00	550.00	1,380
8' deep	"	1,060	620.00	1,680
10' deep	"	1,320	710.00	2,030
12' deep	"	1,660	830.00	2,490
14' deep	"	2,010	1,000	3,010
Inverts for manholes				
Single channel	EA.	110.00	200.00	310.00
Triple channel	"	130.00	250.00	380.00
Frames and covers, 24" diameter				
300 lb	EA.	360.00	40.00	400.00
400 lb	"	380.00	44.40	424.40
500 lb	"	440.00	57.00	497.00
Watertight, 350 lb	"	460.00	130.00	590.00
For heavy equipment, 1200 lb	"	1,000	200.00	1,200
Steps for manholes				
7" x 9"	EA.	12.55	8.00	20.55
8" x 9"	"	15.90	8.90	24.80
Curb inlet, 4' throat, cast in place				
12"-30" pipe	EA.	360.00	1,070	1,430
36"-48" pipe	"	390.00	1,220	1,610
Raise exist frame and cover, when repaving	"		430.00	430.00
02610.10			Cast Iron Flanged Pipe	
Cast iron flanged sections				
4" pipe, with one bolt set				
3' section	EA.	190.00	19.45	209.45
4' section	"	200.00	21.40	221.40
5' section	"	220.00	23.75	243.75
6' section	"	240.00	26.70	266.70
8' section	"	280.00	30.50	310.50
10' section	"	310.00	42.80	352.80
12' section	"	340.00	71.50	411.50

Utilities	UNIT	MAT.	INST.	TOTAL
02610.10 Cast Iron Flanged Pipe				
15' section	EA.	400.00	110.00	510.00
18' section	"	440.00	140.00	580.00
6" pipe, with one bolt set				
3' section	EA.	240.00	21.40	261.40
4' section	"	260.00	25.20	285.20
5' section	"	280.00	28.50	308.50
6' section	"	310.00	32.90	342.90
8' section	"	340.00	47.50	387.50
10' section	"	390.00	53.50	443.50
12' section	"	430.00	71.50	501.50
15' section	"	500.00	110.00	610.00
18' section	"	640.00	150.00	790.00
8" pipe, with one bolt set				
3' section	EA.	320.00	26.70	346.70
4' section	"	360.00	30.50	390.50
5' section	"	390.00	35.60	425.60
6' section	"	410.00	42.80	452.80
8' section	"	460.00	61.00	521.00
10' section	"	520.00	71.50	591.50
12' section	"	550.00	110.00	660.00
15' section	"	660.00	140.00	800.00
18' section	"	810.00	180.00	990.00
10" pipe, with one bolt set				
3' section	EA.	420.00	27.40	447.40
4' section	"	470.00	31.40	501.40
5' section	"	510.00	36.90	546.90
6' section	"	550.00	44.50	594.50
8' section	"	610.00	65.00	675.00
10' section	"	670.00	76.50	746.50
12' section	"	760.00	120.00	880.00
15' section	"	830.00	150.00	980.00
18' section	"	1,020	210.00	1,230
12" pipe, with one bolt set				
3' section	EA.	550.00	29.70	579.70
4' section	"	590.00	34.50	624.50
5' section	"	650.00	41.10	691.10
6' section	"	690.00	48.60	738.60
8' section	"	780.00	71.50	851.50
10' section	"	870.00	82.00	952.00
12' section	"	960.00	130.00	1,090
15' section	"	1,100	180.00	1,280
18' section	"	1,160	240.00	1,400
02610.11 Cast Iron Fittings				
Mechanical joint, with 2 bolt kits				
90 deg bend				
4"	EA.	130.00	26.70	156.70
6"	"	170.00	30.80	200.80
8"	"	210.00	40.00	250.00
10"	"	320.00	57.00	377.00
12"	"	480.00	80.00	560.00
14"	"	670.00	100.00	770.00

Utilities	UNIT	MAT.	INST.	TOTAL
02610.11 Cast Iron Fittings				
16"	EA.	770.00	130.00	900.00
45 deg bend				
4"	EA.	120.00	26.70	146.70
6"	"	150.00	30.80	180.80
8"	"	210.00	40.00	250.00
10"	"	270.00	57.00	327.00
12"	"	370.00	80.00	450.00
14"	"	440.00	100.00	540.00
16"	"	570.00	130.00	700.00
Tee, with 3 bolt kits				
4" x 4"	EA.	200.00	40.00	240.00
6" x 6"	"	290.00	50.00	340.00
8" x 8"	"	380.00	66.50	446.50
10" x 10"	"	570.00	100.00	670.00
12" x 12"	"	770.00	130.00	900.00
Wye, with 3 bolt kits				
6" x 6"	EA.	380.00	50.00	430.00
8" x 8"	"	570.00	66.50	636.50
10" x 10"	"	770.00	100.00	870.00
12" x 12"	"	1,050	130.00	1,180
Reducer, with 2 bolt kits				
6" x 4"	EA.	140.00	50.00	190.00
8" x 6"	"	190.00	66.50	256.50
10" x 8"	"	340.00	100.00	440.00
12" x 10"	"	420.00	130.00	550.00
Flanged, 90 deg bend, 125 lb.				
4"	EA.	86.50	33.30	119.80
6"	"	120.00	40.00	160.00
8"	"	170.00	50.00	220.00
10"	"	300.00	66.50	366.50
12"	"	410.00	100.00	510.00
14"	"	820.00	130.00	950.00
16"	"	1,230	130.00	1,360
Tee				
4"	EA.	150.00	50.00	200.00
6"	"	210.00	57.00	267.00
8"	"	320.00	66.50	386.50
10"	"	590.00	80.00	670.00
12"	"	800.00	100.00	900.00
14"	"	1,780	130.00	1,910
16"	"	2,690	200.00	2,890
02610.13 Gate Valves				
Gate valve, (AWWA) mechanical joint, with adjustable box				
4" valve	EA.	730.00	71.50	801.50
6" valve	"	820.00	85.50	905.50
8" valve	"	1,090	110.00	1,200
10" valve	"	1,640	130.00	1,770
12" valve	"	2,190	150.00	2,340
14" valve	"	5,470	180.00	5,650
16" valve	"	7,290	190.00	7,480
18" valve	"	9,110	210.00	9,320

Utilities	UNIT	MAT.	INST.	TOTAL
02610.13 Gate Valves				
Flanged, with box, post indicator (AWWA)				
4" valve	EA.	650.00	85.50	735.50
6" valve	"	770.00	97.00	867.00
8" valve	"	1,090	120.00	1,210
10" valve	"	1,640	140.00	1,780
12" valve	"	2,370	180.00	2,550
14" valve	"	5,470	210.00	5,680
16" valve	"	7,290	270.00	7,560
02610.15 Water Meters				
Water meter, displacement type				
1"	EA.	270.00	57.00	327.00
1-1/2"	"	920.00	63.00	983.00
2"	"	1,380	71.00	1,451
02610.17 Corporation Stops				
Stop for flared copper service pipe				
3/4"	EA.	34.50	28.50	63.00
1"	"	46.70	31.60	78.30
1-1/4"	"	130.00	37.90	167.90
1-1/2"	"	150.00	47.40	197.40
2"	"	210.00	57.00	267.00
02610.40 Ductile Iron Pipe				
Ductile iron pipe, cement lined, slip-on joints				
4"	L.F.	13.75	5.95	19.70
6"	"	16.70	6.30	23.00
8"	"	21.80	6.70	28.50
10"	"	30.00	7.15	37.15
12"	"	37.00	8.55	45.55
14"	"	46.70	10.70	57.40
16"	"	57.50	11.90	69.40
18"	"	64.50	13.35	77.85
20"	"	73.50	15.25	88.75
Mechanical joint pipe				
4"	L.F.	16.40	8.20	24.60
6"	"	19.55	8.90	28.45
8"	"	25.80	9.70	35.50
10"	"	33.70	10.70	44.40
12"	"	42.80	14.25	57.05
14"	"	54.00	16.45	70.45
16"	"	59.00	19.45	78.45
18"	"	66.50	21.40	87.90
20"	"	76.50	23.75	100.25
Fittings, mechanical joint				
90 degree elbow				
4"	EA.	200.00	26.70	226.70
6"	"	260.00	30.80	290.80
8"	"	380.00	40.00	420.00
10"	"	550.00	57.00	607.00
12"	"	740.00	80.00	820.00
14"	"	1,140	100.00	1,240

Utilities	UNIT	MAT.	INST.	TOTAL
02610.40 Ductile Iron Pipe				
16"	EA.	1,430	130.00	1,560
18"	"	2,150	160.00	2,310
20"	"	2,380	200.00	2,580
45 degree elbow				
4"	EA.	210.00	26.70	236.70
6"	"	240.00	30.80	270.80
8"	"	330.00	40.00	370.00
10"	"	480.00	57.00	537.00
12"	"	690.00	80.00	770.00
14"	"	950.00	100.00	1,050
16"	"	1,140	130.00	1,270
18"	"	1,670	200.00	1,870
20"	"	1,980	200.00	2,180
Tee				
4"x3"	EA.	280.00	50.00	330.00
4"x4"	"	310.00	50.00	360.00
6"x3"	"	360.00	57.00	417.00
6"x4"	"	370.00	57.00	427.00
6"x6"	"	400.00	57.00	457.00
8"x4"	"	500.00	66.50	566.50
8"x6"	"	570.00	66.50	636.50
8"x8"	"	530.00	66.50	596.50
10"x4"	"	670.00	80.00	750.00
10"x6"	"	740.00	80.00	820.00
10"x8"	"	760.00	80.00	840.00
10"x10"	"	860.00	80.00	940.00
12"x4"	"	750.00	100.00	850.00
12"x6"	"	810.00	100.00	910.00
12"x8"	"	880.00	100.00	980.00
12"x10"	"	1,000	100.00	1,100
12"x12"	"	1,070	110.00	1,180
14"x4"	"	1,310	110.00	1,420
14"x6"	"	1,390	110.00	1,500
14"x8"	"	1,420	110.00	1,530
14"x10"	"	1,470	110.00	1,580
14"x12"	"	1,500	120.00	1,620
14"x14"	"	1,490	120.00	1,610
16"x4"	"	1,690	130.00	1,820
16"x6"	"	1,730	130.00	1,860
16"x8"	"	1,540	130.00	1,670
16"x10"	"	1,560	130.00	1,690
16"x12"	"	1,530	130.00	1,660
16"x14"	"	1,610	130.00	1,740
16"x16"	"	1,650	130.00	1,780
18"x6"	"	1,970	150.00	2,120
18"x8"	"	2,000	150.00	2,150
18"x10"	"	2,040	150.00	2,190
18"x12"	"	2,080	150.00	2,230
18"x14"	"	2,320	150.00	2,470
18"x16"	"	2,290	150.00	2,440
18"x18"	"	2,600	150.00	2,750
20"x6"	"	2,500	160.00	2,660

Utilities	UNIT	MAT.	INST.	TOTAL
02610.40 — Ductile Iron Pipe				
20"x8"	EA.	2,530	160.00	2,690
20"x10"	"	2,580	160.00	2,740
20"x12"	"	2,620	160.00	2,780
20"x14"	"	2,700	160.00	2,860
20"x16"	"	3,150	160.00	3,310
20"x18"	"	3,290	160.00	3,450
20"x20"	"	3,360	160.00	3,520
Cross				
4"x3"	EA.	360.00	66.50	426.50
4"x4"	"	390.00	66.50	456.50
6"x3"	"	400.00	80.00	480.00
6"x4"	"	430.00	80.00	510.00
6"x6"	"	480.00	80.00	560.00
8"x4"	"	550.00	89.00	639.00
8"x6"	"	600.00	89.00	689.00
8"x8"	"	650.00	89.00	739.00
10"x4"	"	760.00	100.00	860.00
10"x6"	"	810.00	100.00	910.00
10"x8"	"	880.00	100.00	980.00
10"x10"	"	1,050	100.00	1,150
12"x4"	"	980.00	110.00	1,090
12"x6"	"	1,100	110.00	1,210
12"x8"	"	1,070	110.00	1,180
12"x10"	"	1,240	120.00	1,360
12"x12"	"	1,340	120.00	1,460
14"x4"	"	1,260	130.00	1,390
14"x6"	"	1,430	130.00	1,560
14"x8"	"	1,490	130.00	1,620
14"x10"	"	1,600	130.00	1,730
14"x12"	"	1,720	150.00	1,870
14"x14"	"	1,880	150.00	2,030
16"x4"	"	1,650	160.00	1,810
16"x6"	"	1,690	160.00	1,850
16"x8"	"	1,790	160.00	1,950
16"x10"	"	1,910	160.00	2,070
16"x12"	"	1,990	160.00	2,150
16"x14"	"	2,160	160.00	2,320
16"x16"	"	2,290	160.00	2,450
18"x6"	"	2,120	180.00	2,300
18"x8"	"	2,200	180.00	2,380
18"x10"	"	2,290	180.00	2,470
18"x12"	"	2,410	180.00	2,590
18"x14"	"	2,860	180.00	3,040
18"x16"	"	3,060	180.00	3,240
18"x18"	"	3,220	180.00	3,400
20"x6"	"	2,550	190.00	2,740
20"x8"	"	2,620	190.00	2,810
20"x10"	"	2,740	190.00	2,930
20"x12"	"	2,860	190.00	3,050
20"x14"	"	3,010	190.00	3,200
20"x16"	"	3,480	190.00	3,670
20"x18"	"	3,720	200.00	3,920

SITEWORK

Utilities	UNIT	MAT.	INST.	TOTAL
02610.40 Ductile Iron Pipe				
20"x20"	EA.	3,940	200.00	4,140
02610.60 Plastic Pipe				
PVC, class 150 pipe				
4" dia.	L.F.	6.95	5.35	12.30
6" dia.	"	13.10	5.80	18.90
8" dia.	"	20.80	6.10	26.90
10" dia.	"	29.60	6.70	36.30
12" dia.	"	43.70	7.15	50.85
Schedule 40 pipe				
1-1/2" dia.	L.F.	3.85	2.35	6.20
2" dia.	"	4.50	2.50	7.00
2-1/2" dia.	"	5.00	2.65	7.65
3" dia.	"	7.20	2.85	10.05
4" dia.	"	10.30	3.35	13.65
6" dia.	"	17.35	4.00	21.35
90 degree elbows				
1"	EA.	2.60	6.65	9.25
1-1/2"	"	4.35	6.65	11.00
2"	"	4.90	7.25	12.15
2-1/2"	"	12.35	8.00	20.35
3"	"	14.90	8.90	23.80
4"	"	41.10	10.00	51.10
6"	"	92.50	13.35	105.85
45 degree elbows				
1"	EA.	2.80	6.65	9.45
1-1/2"	"	4.65	6.65	11.30
2"	"	6.15	7.25	13.40
2-1/2"	"	12.60	8.00	20.60
3"	"	15.30	8.90	24.20
4"	"	45.00	10.00	55.00
6"	"	97.50	13.35	110.85
Tees				
1"	EA.	3.35	8.00	11.35
1-1/2"	"	4.90	8.00	12.90
2"	"	6.65	8.90	15.55
2-1/2"	"	12.05	10.00	22.05
3"	"	16.45	11.45	27.90
4"	"	46.30	13.35	59.65
6"	"	92.50	16.00	108.50
Couplings				
1"	EA.	1.55	6.65	8.20
1-1/2"	"	1.80	6.65	8.45
2"	"	3.10	7.25	10.35
2-1/2"	"	6.15	8.00	14.15
3"	"	11.55	8.90	20.45
4"	"	25.70	10.00	35.70
6"	"	33.40	13.35	46.75
Drainage pipe				
PVC schedule 80				
1" dia.	L.F.	2.40	2.35	4.75
1-1/2" dia.	"	2.90	2.35	5.25

Utilities	UNIT	MAT.	INST.	TOTAL
02610.60 Plastic Pipe				
ABS, 2" dia.	L.F.	3.70	2.50	6.20
2-1/2" dia.	"	5.25	2.65	7.90
3" dia.	"	6.15	2.85	9.00
4" dia.	"	8.40	3.35	11.75
6" dia.	"	13.90	4.00	17.90
8" dia.	"	18.60	5.65	24.25
10" dia.	"	24.90	6.70	31.60
12" dia.	"	40.60	7.15	47.75
90 degree elbows				
1"	EA.	4.20	6.65	10.85
1-1/2"	"	5.25	6.65	11.90
2"	"	6.30	7.25	13.55
2-1/2"	"	15.10	8.00	23.10
3"	"	15.60	8.90	24.50
4"	"	27.50	10.00	37.50
6"	"	60.50	13.35	73.85
45 degree elbows				
1"	EA.	6.80	6.65	13.45
1-1/2"	"	8.65	6.65	15.30
2"	"	10.75	7.25	18.00
2-1/2"	"	20.20	8.00	28.20
3"	"	21.50	8.90	30.40
4"	"	40.60	10.00	50.60
6"	"	94.50	13.35	107.85
Tees				
1"	EA.	4.45	8.00	12.45
1-1/2"	"	14.15	8.00	22.15
2"	"	17.30	8.90	26.20
2-1/2"	"	20.20	10.00	30.20
3"	"	22.05	11.45	33.50
4"	"	41.90	13.35	55.25
6"	"	82.50	16.00	98.50
Couplings				
1"	EA.	3.70	6.65	10.35
1-1/2"	"	6.30	6.65	12.95
2"	"	9.30	7.25	16.55
2-1/2"	"	19.65	8.00	27.65
3"	"	20.20	8.90	29.10
4"	"	20.95	10.00	30.95
6"	"	35.40	13.35	48.75
Pressure pipe				
PVC, class 200 pipe				
3/4"	L.F.	2.30	2.00	4.30
1"	"	2.60	2.10	4.70
1-1/4"	"	2.90	2.20	5.10
1-1/2"	"	3.50	2.35	5.85
2"	"	3.75	2.50	6.25
2-1/2"	"	5.50	2.65	8.15
3"	"	6.95	2.85	9.80
4"	"	12.05	3.35	15.40
6"	"	22.80	4.00	26.80
8"	"	34.60	6.10	40.70

Utilities	UNIT	MAT.	INST.	TOTAL
02610.60 Plastic Pipe				
90 degree elbows				
3/4"	EA.	1.15	6.65	7.80
1"	"	1.45	6.65	8.10
1-1/4"	"	2.30	6.65	8.95
1-1/2"	"	2.75	6.65	9.40
2"	"	5.50	7.25	12.75
2-1/2"	"	7.90	8.00	15.90
3"	"	17.95	8.90	26.85
4"	"	46.10	10.00	56.10
6"	"	88.00	13.35	101.35
8"	"	170.00	20.00	190.00
45 degree elbows				
3/4"	EA.	1.70	6.65	8.35
1"	"	2.20	6.65	8.85
1-1/4"	"	3.10	6.65	9.75
1-1/2"	"	3.80	6.65	10.45
2"	"	5.35	7.25	12.60
2-1/2"	"	8.80	8.00	16.80
3"	"	20.20	8.90	29.10
4"	"	37.80	10.00	47.80
6"	"	93.00	13.35	106.35
8"	"	190.00	20.00	210.00
Tees				
3/4"	EA.	1.45	8.00	9.45
1"	"	1.85	8.00	9.85
1-1/4"	"	2.70	8.00	10.70
1-1/2"	"	3.75	8.00	11.75
2"	"	5.50	8.90	14.40
2-1/2"	"	8.65	10.00	18.65
3"	"	26.60	11.45	38.05
4"	"	38.00	13.35	51.35
6"	"	130.00	16.00	146.00
8"	"	270.00	22.20	292.20
Couplings				
3/4"	EA.	0.89	6.65	7.54
1"	"	1.30	6.65	7.95
1-1/4"	"	1.70	6.65	8.35
1-1/2"	"	1.85	6.65	8.50
2"	"	2.60	7.25	9.85
2-1/2"	"	5.50	8.00	13.50
3"	"	8.65	8.90	17.55
4"	"	12.15	8.90	21.05
6"	"	38.00	10.00	48.00
8"	"	68.00	13.35	81.35
02610.90 Vitrified Clay Pipe				
Vitrified clay pipe, extra strength				
6" dia.	L.F.	4.25	9.70	13.95
8" dia.	"	5.10	10.20	15.30
10" dia.	"	7.80	10.70	18.50
12" dia.	"	11.20	14.25	25.45
15" dia.	"	20.35	21.40	41.75

Utilities	UNIT	MAT.	INST.	TOTAL
02610.90 — Vitrified Clay Pipe				
18" dia.	L.F.	30.60	23.75	54.35
24" dia.	"	56.00	30.50	86.50
30" dia.	"	95.00	42.80	137.80
36" dia.	"	140.00	61.00	201.00
02630.10 — Tapping Saddles & Sleeves				
Tapping saddle, tap size to 2"				
4" saddle	EA.	64.00	20.00	84.00
6" saddle	"	75.00	25.00	100.00
8" saddle	"	87.50	33.30	120.80
10" saddle	"	100.00	40.00	140.00
12" saddle	"	120.00	57.00	177.00
14" saddle	"	140.00	80.00	220.00
Tapping sleeve				
4x4	EA.	680.00	26.70	706.70
6x4	"	870.00	30.80	900.80
6x6	"	890.00	30.80	920.80
8x4	"	910.00	40.00	950.00
8x6	"	930.00	40.00	970.00
10x4	"	1,480	85.50	1,566
10x6	"	2,140	85.50	2,226
10x8	"	2,230	85.50	2,316
10x10	"	2,280	89.00	2,369
12x4	"	2,300	89.00	2,389
12x6	"	2,320	97.00	2,417
12x8	"	2,370	110.00	2,480
12x10	"	2,500	120.00	2,620
12x12	"	2,580	130.00	2,710
Tapping valve, mechanical joint				
4" valve	EA.	640.00	270.00	910.00
6" valve	"	760.00	360.00	1,120
8" valve	"	1,140	530.00	1,670
10" valve	"	1,820	710.00	2,530
12" valve	"	3,210	1,070	4,280
Tap hole in pipe				
4" hole	EA.		50.00	50.00
6" hole	"		80.00	80.00
8" hole	"		130.00	130.00
10" hole	"		160.00	160.00
12" hole	"		200.00	200.00
02640.15 — Valve Boxes				
Valve box, adjustable, for valves up to 20"				
3' deep	EA.	160.00	13.35	173.35
4' deep	"	160.00	16.00	176.00
5' deep	"	160.00	20.00	180.00
02640.19 — Thrust Blocks				
Thrust block, 3000# concrete				
1/4 c.y.	EA.	110.00	86.00	196.00
1/2 c.y.	"	140.00	100.00	240.00
3/4 c.y.	"	160.00	170.00	330.00

Utilities	UNIT	MAT.	INST.	TOTAL
02640.19 Thrust Blocks				
1 c.y.	EA.	200.00	340.00	540.00
02645.10 Fire Hydrants				
Standard, 3 way post, 6" mechanical joint				
2' deep	EA.	1,610	710.00	2,320
4' deep	"	1,730	860.00	2,590
6' deep	"	1,930	1,070	3,000
8' deep	"	2,160	1,220	3,380
02665.10 Chilled Water Systems				
Chilled water pipe, 2" thick insulation, w/casing				
Align and tack weld on sleepers				
1-1/2" dia.	L.F.	18.40	1.95	20.35
3" dia.	"	29.50	3.05	32.55
4" dia.	"	33.90	4.30	38.20
6" dia.	"	38.80	5.35	44.15
8" dia.	"	54.50	6.10	60.60
10" dia.	"	69.50	7.15	76.65
12" dia.	"	83.00	8.55	91.55
14" dia.	"	110.00	9.30	119.30
16" dia.	"	140.00	10.70	150.70
Align and tack weld on trench bottom				
18" dia.	L.F.	150.00	11.90	161.90
20" dia.	"	190.00	13.35	203.35
Preinsulated fittings				
Align and tack weld on sleepers				
Elbows				
1-1/2"	EA.	380.00	35.60	415.60
3"	"	480.00	57.00	537.00
4"	"	630.00	71.00	701.00
6"	"	870.00	95.00	965.00
8"	"	1,230	110.00	1,340
Tees				
1-1/2"	EA.	590.00	37.90	627.90
3"	"	830.00	63.00	893.00
4"	"	630.00	81.50	711.50
6"	"	1,350	110.00	1,460
8"	"	1,800	140.00	1,940
Reducers				
3"	EA.	630.00	47.40	677.40
4"	"	990.00	57.00	1,047
6"	"	1,330	71.00	1,401
8"	"	1,440	95.00	1,535
Anchors, not including concrete				
4"	EA.	270.00	71.00	341.00
6"	"	390.00	71.00	461.00
Align and tack weld on trench bottom				
Elbows				
10"	EA.	1,620	130.00	1,750
12"	"	1,940	150.00	2,090
14"	"	2,440	160.00	2,600
16"	"	2,620	180.00	2,800

Utilities	UNIT	MAT.	INST.	TOTAL
02665.10 **Chilled Water Systems**				
18"	EA.	2,930	190.00	3,120
20"	"	3,530	210.00	3,740
Tees				
10"	EA.	2,620	130.00	2,750
12"	"	3,330	150.00	3,480
14"	"	3,530	160.00	3,690
16"	"	3,730	180.00	3,910
18"	"	4,240	190.00	4,430
20"	"	4,840	210.00	5,050
Reducers				
10"	EA.	2,000	89.00	2,089
12"	"	2,420	97.00	2,517
14"	"	2,620	110.00	2,730
16"	"	3,230	120.00	3,350
18"	"	3,530	130.00	3,660
20"	"	3,730	150.00	3,880
Anchors, not including concrete				
10"	EA.	530.00	89.00	619.00
12"	"	590.00	97.00	687.00
14"	"	680.00	110.00	790.00
16"	"	950.00	120.00	1,070
18"	"	1,330	130.00	1,460
20"	"	1,800	150.00	1,950
02670.10 **Wells**				
Domestic water, drilled and cased				
4" dia.	L.F.	16.60	64.00	80.60
6" dia.	"	18.25	71.00	89.25
8" dia.	"	21.60	80.00	101.60
02685.10 **Gas Distribution**				
Gas distribution lines				
Polyethylene, 60 psi coils				
1-1/4" dia.	L.F.	1.50	3.80	5.30
1-1/2" dia.	"	2.05	4.05	6.10
2" dia.	"	2.55	4.75	7.30
3" dia.	"	5.45	5.70	11.15
30' pipe lengths				
3" dia.	L.F.	5.35	6.30	11.65
4" dia.	"	8.35	7.10	15.45
6" dia.	"	13.20	9.50	22.70
8" dia.	"	24.50	11.40	35.90
Steel, schedule 40, plain end				
1" dia.	L.F.	5.25	4.75	10.00
2" dia.	"	7.25	5.15	12.40
3" dia.	"	12.50	5.70	18.20
4" dia.	"	15.35	14.25	29.60
5" dia.	"	28.80	15.25	44.05
6" dia.	"	38.40	17.80	56.20
8" dia.	"	48.00	19.45	67.45
Natural gas meters, direct digital reading, threaded				
250 cfh @ 5 lbs	EA.	180.00	110.00	290.00

02   SITEWORK

Utilities	UNIT	MAT.	INST.	TOTAL
02685.10 Gas Distribution				
425 cfh @ 10 lbs	EA.	460.00	110.00	570.00
800 cfh @ 20 lbs	"	640.00	140.00	780.00
1,000 cfh @ 25 lbs	"	1,890	140.00	2,030
1,400 cfh @ 100 lbs	"	4,370	190.00	4,560
2,300 cfh @ 100 lbs	"	6,090	280.00	6,370
5,000 cfh @ 100 lbs	"	8,940	570.00	9,510
Gas pressure regulators				
Threaded				
3/4"	EA.	79.00	71.00	150.00
1"	"	83.00	95.00	178.00
1-1/4"	"	86.50	95.00	181.50
1-1/2"	"	560.00	95.00	655.00
2"	"	580.00	110.00	690.00
Flanged				
3"	EA.	1,640	140.00	1,780
4"	"	2,450	190.00	2,640
02690.10 Storage Tanks				
Oil storage tank, underground				
Steel				
500 gals	EA.	810.00	270.00	1,080
1,000 gals	"	1,410	360.00	1,770
4,000 gals	"	3,870	710.00	4,580
5,000 gals	"	5,280	1,070	6,350
10,000 gals	"	7,560	2,140	9,700
Fiberglass, double wall				
550 gals	EA.	2,700	360.00	3,060
1,000 gals	"	3,490	360.00	3,850
2,000 gals	"	4,120	530.00	4,650
4,000 gals	"	5,550	1,070	6,620
6,000 gals	"	6,350	1,430	7,780
8,000 gals	"	8,570	2,140	10,710
10,000 gals	"	10,790	2,670	13,460
12,000 gals	"	12,850	3,560	16,410
15,000 gals	"	15,230	4,750	19,980
20,000 gals	"	19,350	5,350	24,700
Above ground				
Steel				
275 gals	EA.	330.00	210.00	540.00
500 gals	"	1,050	360.00	1,410
1,000 gals	"	1,580	430.00	2,010
1,500 gals	"	2,640	530.00	3,170
2,000 gals	"	3,320	710.00	4,030
5,000 gals	"	8,620	1,070	9,690
Fill cap	"	43.70	57.00	100.70
Vent cap	"	43.70	57.00	100.70
Level indicator	"	100.00	57.00	157.00
02695.40 Steel Pipe				
Steel pipe, extra heavy, A 53, grade B, seamless				
1/2" dia.	L.F.	2.35	5.70	8.05
3/4" dia.	"	3.75	6.00	9.75

Utilities	UNIT	MAT.	INST.	TOTAL
02695.40 Steel Pipe				
1" dia.	L.F.	4.90	6.30	11.20
1-1/4" dia.	"	5.90	7.10	13.00
1-1/2" dia.	"	6.70	8.15	14.85
2" dia.	"	7.70	9.50	17.20
3" dia.	"	14.80	10.70	25.50
4" dia.	"	25.70	11.90	37.60
6" dia.	"	63.00	13.35	76.35
8" dia.	"	82.50	15.25	97.75
10" dia.	"	120.00	17.80	137.80
12" dia.	"	150.00	21.40	171.40
02695.80 Steam Meters				
In-line turbine, direct reading, 300 lb, flanged				
2"	EA.	5,050	71.00	5,121
3"	"	5,410	95.00	5,505
4"	"	5,950	110.00	6,060
Threaded, 2"				
5" line	EA.	9,550	570.00	10,120
6" line	"	9,730	570.00	10,300
8" line	"	9,910	570.00	10,480
10" line	"	10,450	570.00	11,020
12" line	"	10,630	570.00	11,200
14" line	"	11,000	570.00	11,570
16" line	"	11,720	570.00	12,290

Sewerage And Drainage	UNIT	MAT.	INST.	TOTAL
02720.10 Catch Basins				
Standard concrete catch basin				
Cast in place, 3'8" x 3'8", 6" thick wall				
2' deep	EA.	290.00	530.00	820.00
3' deep	"	390.00	530.00	920.00
4' deep	"	510.00	710.00	1,220
5' deep	"	610.00	710.00	1,320
6' deep	"	680.00	860.00	1,540
4'x4', 8" thick wall, cast in place				
2' deep	EA.	310.00	530.00	840.00
3' deep	"	440.00	530.00	970.00
4' deep	"	580.00	710.00	1,290
5' deep	"	670.00	710.00	1,380
6' deep	"	740.00	860.00	1,600
Frames and covers, cast iron				
Round				
24" dia.	EA.	290.00	100.00	390.00
26" dia.	"	320.00	100.00	420.00
28" dia.	"	390.00	100.00	490.00

Sewerage And Drainage	UNIT	MAT.	INST.	TOTAL
02720.10 — Catch Basins				
Rectangular				
23"x23"	EA.	260.00	100.00	360.00
27"x20"	"	310.00	100.00	410.00
24"x24"	"	300.00	100.00	400.00
26"x26"	"	330.00	100.00	430.00
Curb inlet frames and covers				
27"x27"	EA.	630.00	100.00	730.00
24"x36"	"	380.00	100.00	480.00
24"x25"	"	350.00	100.00	450.00
24"x22"	"	300.00	100.00	400.00
20"x22"	"	400.00	100.00	500.00
Airfield catch basin frame and grating, galvanized				
2'x4'	EA.	730.00	100.00	830.00
2'x2'	"	510.00	100.00	610.00
02720.40 — Storm Drainage				
Headwalls, cast in place, 30 deg wingwall				
12" pipe	EA.	410.00	130.00	540.00
15" pipe	"	500.00	130.00	630.00
18" pipe	"	610.00	150.00	760.00
24" pipe	"	900.00	150.00	1,050
30" pipe	"	1,080	170.00	1,250
36" pipe	"	1,180	260.00	1,440
42" pipe	"	1,470	260.00	1,730
48" pipe	"	1,560	340.00	1,900
54" pipe	"	1,770	430.00	2,200
60" pipe	"	2,120	520.00	2,640
4" cleanout for storm drain				
4" pipe	EA.	590.00	50.00	640.00
6" pipe	"	720.00	50.00	770.00
8" pipe	"	1,000	50.00	1,050
Connect new drain line				
To existing manhole	EA.	140.00	130.00	270.00
To new manhole	"	120.00	80.00	200.00
02720.45 — Storm Drainage, Con. Pipe				
Concrete pipe				
Unreinforced, plain, bell and spigot, Class II				
Pipe diameter 6"	L.F.	5.65	9.70	15.35
8"	"	6.20	10.70	16.90
10"	"	6.40	11.25	17.65
12"	"	7.50	11.90	19.40
15"	"	9.10	12.60	21.70
18"	"	12.35	13.35	25.70
21"	"	15.45	14.25	29.70
24"	"	19.35	15.25	34.60
Reinforced, bell and spigot, Class III				
Pipe diameter 12"	L.F.	13.40	11.90	25.30
15"	"	15.05	12.60	27.65
18"	"	16.75	13.35	30.10
21"	"	21.75	14.25	36.00
24"	"	28.40	15.25	43.65

Sewerage And Drainage	UNIT	MAT.	INST.	TOTAL
02720.45 Storm Drainage, Con. Pipe				
27"	L.F.	33.50	16.45	49.95
30"	"	36.80	17.80	54.60
36"	"	55.00	19.45	74.45
42"	"	68.50	21.40	89.90
48"	"	95.50	23.75	119.25
54"	"	110.00	26.70	136.70
60"	"	120.00	30.50	150.50
66"	"	150.00	35.60	185.60
72"	"	180.00	42.80	222.80
78"	"	230.00	47.50	277.50
84"	"	270.00	53.50	323.50
90"	"	280.00	58.00	338.00
96"	"	330.00	61.00	391.00
Class IV				
Pipe diameter 12"	L.F.	12.20	11.90	24.10
15"	"	12.55	12.60	25.15
18"	"	15.90	13.35	29.25
21"	"	23.40	14.25	37.65
24"	"	29.30	15.25	44.55
27"	"	34.30	16.45	50.75
30"	"	36.80	17.80	54.60
36"	"	56.00	19.45	75.45
42"	"	72.00	21.40	93.40
48"	"	97.00	23.75	120.75
54"	"	130.00	26.70	156.70
60"	"	150.00	30.50	180.50
66"	"	170.00	35.60	205.60
72"	"	230.00	42.80	272.80
78"	"	270.00	47.50	317.50
84"	"	310.00	53.50	363.50
90"	"	330.00	58.00	388.00
96"	"	380.00	61.00	441.00
Class V				
Pipe diameter 12"	L.F.	15.05	11.90	26.95
15"	"	15.40	12.60	28.00
18"	"	20.90	13.35	34.25
21"	"	26.80	14.25	41.05
24"	"	33.50	15.25	48.75
27"	"	41.80	16.45	58.25
30"	"	48.50	17.80	66.30
36"	"	67.00	19.45	86.45
42"	"	87.00	21.40	108.40
48"	"	110.00	23.75	133.75
54"	"	140.00	26.70	166.70
60"	"	180.00	30.50	210.50
66"	"	200.00	35.60	235.60
72"	"	260.00	42.80	302.80
78"	"	320.00	47.50	367.50
84"	"	350.00	53.50	403.50
90"	"	370.00	58.00	428.00
96"	"	420.00	61.00	481.00
Eliptical pipe, reinforced				

Sewerage And Drainage	UNIT	MAT.	INST.	TOTAL
02720.45 Storm Drainage, Con. Pipe				
Class III				
20" x 30"	L.F.	41.80	15.25	57.05
22" x 34 "	"	46.80	16.45	63.25
24" x 38"	"	63.50	17.80	81.30
27" x 42"	"	80.50	19.45	99.95
29" x 45"	"	100.00	20.35	120.35
32" x 49"	"	110.00	21.40	131.40
34" x 54"	"	110.00	23.75	133.75
38" x 60"	"	130.00	26.70	156.70
43" x 68"	"	130.00	30.50	160.50
48" x 76"	"	160.00	32.90	192.90
53" x 83"	"	220.00	35.60	255.60
62" x 98"	"	300.00	42.80	342.80
82" x 128"	"	420.00	61.00	481.00
Flared end section pipe				
Pipe diameter 12"	L.F.	61.00	11.90	72.90
15"	"	71.50	12.60	84.10
18"	"	80.00	13.35	93.35
24"	"	99.00	15.25	114.25
30"	"	120.00	17.80	137.80
36"	"	170.00	19.45	189.45
42"	"	180.00	21.40	201.40
48"	"	200.00	23.75	223.75
54"	"	220.00	26.70	246.70
60"	"	240.00	30.50	270.50
Porous concrete pipe, standard strength				
Pipe diameter 4"	L.F.	3.85	8.20	12.05
6"	"	4.20	8.55	12.75
8"	"	4.80	8.90	13.70
10"	"	10.05	9.30	19.35
12"	"	13.40	9.30	22.70
02720.50 Storm Drainage, Steel Pipe				
Steel pipe				
Coated,corrugated metal pipe, paved invert				
16 gauge, pipe diameter 8"	L.F.	9.40	7.15	16.55
12"	"	14.15	7.65	21.80
15"	"	17.30	8.20	25.50
18"	"	20.40	8.90	29.30
21"	"	25.10	9.70	34.80
24"	"	29.80	10.70	40.50
30"	"	39.30	11.90	51.20
36"	"	53.50	13.35	66.85
42"	"	78.00	14.25	92.25
48"	"	110.00	15.25	125.25
14 gauge, pipe diameter 12"	"	17.45	7.65	25.10
15"	"	20.75	8.20	28.95
18"	"	24.20	8.90	33.10
21"	"	29.40	9.70	39.10
24"	"	37.70	10.70	48.40
30"	"	42.40	11.90	54.30
36"	"	60.50	13.35	73.85

Sewerage And Drainage	UNIT	MAT.	INST.	TOTAL
02720.50 Storm Drainage, Steel Pipe				
42"	L.F.	81.00	14.25	95.25
48"	"	110.00	15.25	125.25
54"	"	130.00	16.45	146.45
60"	"	150.00	17.80	167.80
66"	"	170.00	19.45	189.45
12 gauge, pipe diameter 18"	"	32.80	8.90	41.70
21"	"	39.70	9.70	49.40
24"	"	46.70	10.70	57.40
30"	"	64.00	11.90	75.90
36"	"	74.00	13.35	87.35
42"	"	98.50	14.25	112.75
48"	"	96.00	15.25	111.25
54"	"	150.00	16.45	166.45
60"	"	160.00	17.80	177.80
66"	"	190.00	19.45	209.45
72"	"	200.00	21.40	221.40
78"	"	220.00	22.50	242.50
10 gauge, pipe diameter 24"	"	60.50	10.70	71.20
30"	"	78.00	11.90	89.90
36"	"	95.00	13.35	108.35
42"	"	110.00	14.25	124.25
48"	"	140.00	15.25	155.25
54"	"	160.00	16.45	176.45
60"	"	160.00	17.80	177.80
66"	"	190.00	19.45	209.45
72"	"	160.00	21.40	181.40
78"	"	240.00	22.50	262.50
84"	"	260.00	23.75	283.75
90"	"	270.00	25.20	295.20
8 gauge, pipe diameter 48"	"	150.00	15.25	165.25
54"	"	170.00	16.45	186.45
60"	"	180.00	17.80	197.80
66"	"	190.00	19.45	209.45
72"	"	210.00	21.40	231.40
78"	"	250.00	22.50	272.50
84"	"	270.00	23.75	293.75
90"	"	290.00	25.20	315.20
96"	"	330.00	26.70	356.70
Plain,corrugated metal pipe				
16 gauge, pipe diameter 8"	L.F.	7.85	7.15	15.00
12"	"	11.00	7.65	18.65
15"	"	12.55	8.20	20.75
18"	"	18.85	8.90	27.75
21"	"	28.30	9.70	38.00
24"	"	28.30	10.70	39.00
30"	"	37.70	11.90	49.60
36"	"	47.10	13.35	60.45
42"	"	62.00	14.25	76.25
48"	"	86.50	15.25	101.75
14 gauge, pipe diameter 12"	"	16.05	7.65	23.70
15"	"	20.20	8.20	28.40
18"	"	23.15	8.90	32.05

Sewerage And Drainage	UNIT	MAT.	INST.	TOTAL
02720.50 Storm Drainage, Steel Pipe				
21"	L.F.	26.80	9.70	36.50
24"	"	31.10	10.70	41.80
30"	"	38.00	11.90	49.90
36"	"	52.00	13.35	65.35
42"	"	71.50	14.25	85.75
48"	"	100.00	15.25	115.25
54"	"	120.00	16.45	136.45
60"	"	130.00	17.80	147.80
66"	"	150.00	19.45	169.45
12 gauge, pipe diameter 18"	"	25.90	8.90	34.80
21"	"	29.40	9.70	39.10
24"	"	34.60	10.70	45.30
30"	"	41.50	11.90	53.40
36"	"	60.50	13.35	73.85
42"	"	82.50	14.25	96.75
48"	"	86.50	15.25	101.75
54"	"	130.00	16.45	146.45
60"	"	150.00	17.80	167.80
66"	"	170.00	19.45	189.45
72"	"	190.00	21.40	211.40
78"	"	200.00	22.50	222.50
10 gauge, pipe diameter 24"	"	41.50	10.70	52.20
30"	"	46.70	11.90	58.60
36"	"	69.00	13.35	82.35
42"	"	90.00	14.25	104.25
48"	"	120.00	15.25	135.25
54"	"	140.00	16.45	156.45
60"	"	120.00	17.80	137.80
66"	"	180.00	19.45	199.45
72"	"	190.00	21.40	211.40
78"	"	220.00	22.50	242.50
84"	"	240.00	23.75	263.75
90"	"	260.00	25.20	285.20
8 gauge, pipe diameter 48"	"	130.00	15.25	145.25
54"	"	140.00	16.45	156.45
60"	"	160.00	17.80	177.80
66"	"	190.00	19.45	209.45
72"	"	210.00	21.40	231.40
78"	"	230.00	22.50	252.50
84"	"	260.00	23.75	283.75
90"	"	290.00	25.20	315.20
96"	"	320.00	26.70	346.70
Steel arch				
Coated, corrugated				
16 gauge, 17" x 13"	L.F.	22.25	9.70	31.95
21" x 15"	"	29.80	10.70	40.50
14 gauge, 29" x 18"	"	44.00	11.90	55.90
36" x 22"	"	56.50	15.25	71.75
12 gauge, 43" x 28"	"	75.50	17.80	93.30
50" x 30"	"	86.50	19.45	105.95
58" x 36"	"	99.00	21.40	120.40
66" x 40"	"	120.00	22.50	142.50

Sewerage And Drainage	UNIT	MAT.	INST.	TOTAL
02720.50 Storm Drainage, Steel Pipe				
72" x 44"	L.F.	140.00	23.75	163.75
Plain, corrugated				
16 gauge, 17" x 13"	L.F.	13.05	9.70	22.75
21" x 15"	"	18.85	10.70	29.55
14 gauge, 29" x 18"	"	36.10	11.90	48.00
36" x 22"	"	44.00	15.25	59.25
12 gauge, 43" x 28"	"	50.50	17.80	68.30
50" x 30"	"	59.50	19.45	78.95
58" x 36"	"	66.00	21.40	87.40
66" x 40"	"	75.50	22.50	98.00
72" x 44"	"	120.00	23.75	143.75
Nestable corrugated metal pipe				
16 gauge, pipe diameter 10"	L.F.	12.55	7.35	19.90
12"	"	15.70	7.65	23.35
15"	"	20.40	8.20	28.60
18"	"	23.55	8.90	32.45
24"	"	33.00	10.70	43.70
30"	"	40.80	11.90	52.70
14 gauge, pipe diameter 12"	"	15.70	7.65	23.35
15"	"	20.40	8.20	28.60
18"	"	29.80	8.90	38.70
24"	"	37.70	10.70	48.40
30"	"	40.80	11.90	52.70
36"	"	47.10	13.35	60.45
02720.70 Underdrain				
Drain tile, clay				
6" pipe	L.F.	4.05	4.75	8.80
8" pipe	"	6.45	4.95	11.40
12" pipe	"	13.00	5.35	18.35
Porous concrete, standard strength				
6" pipe	L.F.	3.70	4.75	8.45
8" pipe	"	5.40	4.95	10.35
12" pipe	"	10.15	5.35	15.50
15" pipe	"	11.90	5.95	17.85
18" pipe	"	15.50	7.15	22.65
Corrugated metal pipe, perforated type				
6" pipe	L.F.	6.90	5.35	12.25
8" pipe	"	8.15	5.65	13.80
10" pipe	"	9.90	5.95	15.85
12" pipe	"	14.00	6.30	20.30
18" pipe	"	17.30	6.70	24.00
Perforated clay pipe				
6" pipe	L.F.	4.85	6.10	10.95
8" pipe	"	6.50	6.30	12.80
12" pipe	"	11.35	6.50	17.85
Drain tile, concrete				
6" pipe	L.F.	3.10	4.75	7.85
8" pipe	"	4.80	4.95	9.75
12" pipe	"	9.55	5.35	14.90
Perforated rigid PVC underdrain pipe				
4" pipe	L.F.	1.75	3.55	5.30

Sewerage And Drainage	UNIT	MAT.	INST.	TOTAL
02720.70 Underdrain				
6" pipe	L.F.	3.25	4.30	7.55
8" pipe	"	4.55	4.75	9.30
10" pipe	"	7.05	5.35	12.40
12" pipe	"	11.85	6.10	17.95
Underslab drainage, crushed stone				
3" thick	S.F.	0.29	0.71	1.00
4" thick	"	0.35	0.82	1.17
6" thick	"	0.37	0.89	1.26
8" thick	"	0.44	0.93	1.37
Plastic filter fabric for drain lines	"	0.14	0.40	0.54
Gravel fill in trench, crushed or bank run, 1/2" to 3/4"	C.Y.	29.70	53.50	83.20
02730.10 Sanitary Sewers				
Clay				
6" pipe	L.F.	4.85	7.15	12.00
8" pipe	"	6.45	7.65	14.10
10" pipe	"	8.10	8.20	16.30
12" pipe	"	12.95	8.90	21.85
PVC				
4" pipe	L.F.	2.45	5.35	7.80
6" pipe	"	4.90	5.65	10.55
8" pipe	"	7.35	5.95	13.30
10" pipe	"	9.80	6.30	16.10
12" pipe	"	14.70	6.70	21.40
Cleanout				
4" pipe	EA.	8.75	50.00	58.75
6" pipe	"	19.25	50.00	69.25
8" pipe	"	57.00	50.00	107.00
Connect new sewer line				
To existing manhole	EA.	93.00	130.00	223.00
To new manhole	"	66.50	80.00	146.50
02740.10 Drainage Fields				
Perforated PVC pipe, for drain field				
4" pipe	L.F.	1.85	4.75	6.60
6" pipe	"	3.45	5.10	8.55
02740.50 Septic Tanks				
Septic tank, precast concrete				
1000 gals	EA.	730.00	360.00	1,090
2000 gals	"	1,380	530.00	1,910
5000 gals	"	6,020	1,070	7,090
25,000 gals	"	24,400	4,280	28,680
40,000 gals	"	39,090	7,130	46,220
Leaching pit, precast concrete, 72" diameter				
3' deep	EA.	540.00	270.00	810.00
6' deep	"	680.00	310.00	990.00
8' deep	"	850.00	360.00	1,210
02760.10 Pipeline Restoration				
Relining existing water main				
6" dia.	L.F.	7.60	32.00	39.60
8" dia.	"	8.55	33.70	42.25

Sewerage And Drainage	UNIT	MAT.	INST.	TOTAL
02760.10 Pipeline Restoration				
10" dia.	L.F.	9.60	35.50	45.10
12" dia.	"	10.45	37.60	48.05
14" dia.	"	11.20	40.00	51.20
16" dia.	"	12.15	42.60	54.75
18" dia.	"	13.10	45.70	58.80
20" dia.	"	14.45	49.20	63.65
24" dia.	"	15.35	53.50	68.85
36" dia.	"	16.70	64.00	80.70
48" dia.	"	18.60	71.00	89.60
72" dia.	"	23.75	80.00	103.75
Replacing in line gate valves				
6" valve	EA.	820.00	430.00	1,250
8" valve	"	1,280	530.00	1,810
10" valve	"	1,920	640.00	2,560
12" valve	"	3,330	800.00	4,130
16" valve	"	7,570	910.00	8,480
18" valve	"	11,460	1,070	12,530
20" valve	"	15,760	1,280	17,040
24" valve	"	22,510	1,600	24,110
36" valve	"	61,390	2,130	63,520

Power & Communications	UNIT	MAT.	INST.	TOTAL
02780.20 High Voltage Cable				
High voltage XLP copper cable, shielded, 5000v				
#6 awg	L.F.	2.15	0.86	3.01
#4 awg	"	2.45	1.05	3.50
#2 awg	"	3.20	1.25	4.45
#1 awg	"	3.40	1.40	4.80
#1/0 awg	"	4.05	1.55	5.60
#2/0 awg	"	6.75	1.90	8.65
#3/0 awg	"	6.90	2.25	9.15
#4/0 awg	"	7.25	2.40	9.05
#250 awg	"	8.40	2.85	11.25
#300 awg	"	9.60	3.20	12.80
#350 awg	"	10.80	3.50	14.30
#500 awg	"	15.40	4.80	20.20
#750 awg	"	22.70	5.25	27.95
Ungrounded, 15,000v				
#1 awg	L.F.	5.15	2.05	7.20
#1/0 awg	"	6.05	2.25	8.30
#2/0 awg	"	6.95	2.40	9.35
#3/0 awg	"	8.05	2.65	10.70
#4/0 awg	"	8.85	3.00	11.85
#250 awg	"	9.95	3.20	13.15
#300 awg	"	11.25	3.50	14.75

Power & Communications	UNIT	MAT.	INST.	TOTAL
02780.20 High Voltage Cable				
#350 awg	L.F.	12.50	4.05	16.55
#500 awg	"	16.50	5.25	21.75
#750 awg	"	24.40	6.45	30.85
#1000 awg	"	35.90	8.10	44.00
Aluminum cable, shielded, 5000v				
#6 awg	L.F.	1.75	0.72	2.47
#4 awg	"	1.90	0.86	2.76
#2 awg	"	2.10	0.99	3.09
#1 awg	"	2.30	1.10	3.40
#1/0 awg	"	2.55	1.25	3.80
#2/0 awg	"	2.80	1.30	4.10
#3/0 awg	"	3.20	1.40	4.60
#4/0 awg	"	3.55	1.55	5.10
#250 awg	"	3.80	1.70	5.50
#300 awg	"	4.15	2.05	6.20
#350 awg	"	4.45	2.25	6.70
#500 awg	"	5.40	2.40	7.80
#750 awg	"	6.95	2.95	9.90
#1000 awg	"	7.85	3.30	11.15
Ungrounded, 15,000v				
#1 awg	L.F.	3.15	1.40	4.55
#1/0 awg	"	3.35	1.65	5.00
#2/0 awg	"	3.60	1.80	5.40
#3/0 awg	"	3.95	1.85	5.80
#4/0 awg	"	4.30	1.90	6.20
#250 awg	"	4.55	2.05	6.60
#300 awg	"	4.95	2.10	7.05
#350 awg	"	5.35	2.40	7.75
#500 awg	"	6.25	2.85	9.10
#750 awg	"	8.20	3.40	11.60
#1000 awg	"	10.80	4.20	15.00
Indoor terminations, 5000v				
#6 - #4	EA.	66.00	10.35	76.35
#2 - #2/0	"	77.00	10.35	87.35
#3/0 - #250	"	98.50	10.35	108.85
#300 - #750	"	110.00	180.00	290.00
#1000	"	130.00	250.00	380.00
In-line splice, 5000v				
#6 - #4/0	EA.	140.00	250.00	390.00
#250 - #500	"	150.00	660.00	810.00
#750 - #1000	"	210.00	860.00	1,070
T-splice, 5000v				
#2 - #4/0	EA.	140.00	790.00	930.00
#250 - #500	"	150.00	1,320	1,470
#750 - #1000	"	210.00	1,650	1,860
Indoor terminations, 15,000v				
#2 - #2/0	EA.	88.00	230.00	318.00
#3/0 - #500	"	110.00	350.00	460.00
#750 - #1000	"	130.00	410.00	540.00
In-line splice, 15,000v				
#2 - #4/0	EA.	150.00	590.00	740.00
#250 - #500	"	210.00	790.00	1,000

Power & Communications	UNIT	MAT.	INST.	TOTAL
02780.20 High Voltage Cable				
#750 - #1000	EA.	260.00	1,190	1,450
T-splice, 15,000v				
#4	EA.	150.00	1,190	1,340
#250 - #500	"	210.00	1,970	2,180
#750 - #1000	"	260.00	2,960	3,220
Compression lugs, 15,000v				
#4	EA.	10.35	26.40	36.75
#2	"	11.95	35.10	47.05
#1	"	13.05	35.10	48.15
#1/0	"	19.95	43.90	63.85
#2/0	"	20.95	43.90	64.85
#3/0	"	23.55	56.00	79.55
#4/0	"	25.90	56.00	81.90
#250	"	30.30	63.00	93.30
#300	"	35.10	63.00	98.10
#350	"	36.20	76.50	112.70
#500	"	55.00	82.50	137.50
#750	"	87.00	100.00	187.00
#1000	"	130.00	130.00	260.00
Compression splices, 15,000v				
#4	EA.	11.65	43.90	55.55
#2	"	12.80	47.90	60.70
#1	"	14.60	59.00	73.60
#1/0	"	15.45	66.00	81.45
#2/0	"	16.65	76.50	93.15
#3/0	"	18.10	82.50	100.60
#4/0	"	19.75	92.50	112.25
#250	"	21.65	100.00	121.65
#350	"	24.60	110.00	134.60
#500	"	36.40	130.00	166.40
#750	"	59.50	160.00	219.50
02780.40 Supports & Connectors				
Cable supports for conduit				
1-1/2"	EA.	66.50	22.90	89.40
2"	"	92.00	22.90	114.90
2-1/2"	"	100.00	26.40	126.40
3"	"	130.00	26.40	156.40
3-1/2"	"	170.00	33.00	203.00
4"	"	210.00	33.00	243.00
5"	"	380.00	43.90	423.90
6"	"	800.00	47.90	847.90
Split bolt connectors				
#10	EA.	2.05	13.20	15.25
#8	"	2.40	13.20	15.60
#6	"	2.65	13.20	15.85
#4	"	3.10	26.40	29.50
#3	"	4.45	26.40	30.85
#2	"	5.00	26.40	31.40
#1/0	"	6.50	43.90	50.40
#2/0	"	10.35	43.90	54.25
#3/0	"	15.75	43.90	59.65

Power & Communications	UNIT	MAT.	INST.	TOTAL
02780.40 Supports & Connectors				
#4/0	EA.	17.85	43.90	61.75
#250	"	18.40	66.00	84.40
#350	"	32.60	66.00	98.60
#500	"	42.70	66.00	108.70
#750	"	72.50	100.00	172.50
#1000	"	100.00	100.00	200.00
Single barrel lugs				
#6	EA.	0.72	16.45	17.17
#1/0	"	1.40	33.00	34.40
#250	"	3.40	43.90	47.30
#350	"	4.45	43.90	48.35
#500	"	8.55	43.90	52.45
#600	"	9.05	59.00	68.05
#800	"	10.35	59.00	69.35
#1000	"	12.40	59.00	71.40
Double barrel lugs				
#1/0	EA.	2.80	59.00	61.80
#250	"	8.15	85.00	93.15
#350	"	11.55	85.00	96.55
#600	"	17.55	130.00	147.55
#800	"	20.05	130.00	150.05
#1000	"	20.60	130.00	150.60
Three barrel lugs				
#2/0	EA.	22.40	85.00	107.40
#250	"	42.90	130.00	172.90
#350	"	70.00	130.00	200.00
#600	"	77.00	180.00	257.00
#800	"	120.00	180.00	300.00
#1000	"	170.00	180.00	350.00
Four barrel lugs				
#250	EA.	47.70	180.00	227.70
#350	"	79.50	180.00	259.50
#600	"	87.00	230.00	317.00
#800	"	140.00	230.00	370.00
Compression conductor adapters				
#6	EA.	6.20	19.55	25.75
#4	"	6.50	22.90	29.40
#2	"	6.80	29.30	36.10
#1	"	7.85	29.30	37.15
#1/0	"	8.15	35.10	43.25
#250	"	15.50	52.50	68.00
#350	"	18.40	56.00	74.40
#500	"	23.95	72.00	95.95
#750	"	32.80	75.50	108.30
Terminal blocks, 2 screw				
3 circuit	EA.	17.75	13.20	30.95
6 circuit	"	24.50	13.20	37.70
8 circuit	"	28.60	13.20	41.80
10 circuit	"	33.10	19.55	52.65
12 circuit	"	37.40	19.55	56.95
18 circuit	"	50.50	19.55	70.05
24 circuit	"	63.50	22.90	86.40

Power & Communications	UNIT	MAT.	INST.	TOTAL
02780.40 Supports & Connectors				
36 circuit	EA.	89.00	22.90	111.90
Compression splice				
#8 awg	EA.	3.00	25.10	28.10
#6 awg	"	3.60	18.20	21.80
#4 awg	"	3.80	18.20	22.00
#2 awg	"	5.90	35.10	41.00
#1 awg	"	8.25	35.10	43.35
#1/0 awg	"	10.10	35.10	45.20
#2/0 awg	"	10.75	56.00	66.75
#3/0 awg	"	12.60	56.00	68.60
#4/0 awg	"	13.30	56.00	69.30
#250 awg	"	14.15	89.50	103.65
#300 awg	"	15.40	89.50	104.90
#350 awg	"	15.70	92.50	108.20
#400 awg	"	21.30	92.50	113.80
#500 awg	"	24.90	100.00	124.90
#600 awg	"	37.70	100.00	137.70
#750 awg	"	40.00	110.00	150.00
#1000 awg	"	51.00	110.00	161.00

Site Improvements	UNIT	MAT.	INST.	TOTAL
02810.40 Lawn Irrigation				
Residential system, complete				
Minimum	ACRE			19,343
Maximum	"			36,819
Commercial system, complete				
Minimum	ACRE			28,015
Maximum	"			46,424
Components				
Pipe				
Schedule 40, PVC				
1/2"	L.F.	0.51	2.10	2.61
3/4"	"	0.73	2.20	2.93
1"	"	1.10	2.30	3.40
1-1/4"	"	1.45	2.30	3.75
1-1/2"	"	1.70	2.35	4.05
2"	"	2.55	2.50	5.05
2-1/2"	"	3.85	2.65	6.50
3"	"	5.20	2.85	8.05
4"	"	7.35	3.35	10.70
6"	"	12.95	4.00	16.95
Class 200				
3/4"	L.F.	0.37	2.20	2.57
1"	"	0.54	2.30	2.84
1-1/4"	"	0.91	2.30	3.21

Site Improvements	UNIT	MAT.	INST.	TOTAL
02810.40 Lawn Irrigation				
1-1/2"	L.F.	1.10	2.35	3.45
2"	"	1.80	2.50	4.30
2-1/2"	"	2.70	2.65	5.35
3"	"	4.15	2.85	7.00
4"	"	7.20	3.35	10.55
6"	"	14.35	4.00	18.35
Class 315				
1/2"	L.F.	0.33	2.10	2.43
2"	"	2.80	2.50	5.30
2-1/2"	"	3.80	2.65	6.45
3"	"	5.40	2.85	8.25
4"	"	9.90	3.35	13.25
Fittings				
Tee				
1/2"	EA.	0.87	6.65	7.52
3/4"	"	0.99	6.65	7.64
1"	"	1.80	6.65	8.45
1-1/4"	"	3.25	7.25	10.50
1-1/2"	"	3.70	8.00	11.70
2"	"	5.20	8.90	14.10
2-1/2"	"	19.55	10.00	29.55
3"	"	25.10	11.45	36.55
4"	"	44.90	13.35	58.25
6"	"	190.00	16.00	206.00
El				
1/2"	EA.	0.73	6.15	6.88
3/4"	"	0.82	6.65	7.47
1"	"	1.45	6.65	8.10
1-1/4"	"	2.55	6.65	9.20
1-1/2"	"	2.85	6.65	9.50
2"	"	4.30	7.25	11.55
2-1/2"	"	14.20	8.00	22.20
3"	"	17.95	8.90	26.85
4"	"	29.60	10.00	39.60
6"	"	130.00	13.35	143.35
Coupling				
1/2"	EA.	0.54	6.15	6.69
3/4"	"	0.73	6.65	7.38
1"	"	1.25	6.65	7.90
1-1/4"	"	1.60	6.65	8.25
1-1/2"	"	1.70	6.65	8.35
2"	"	2.70	7.25	9.95
2-1/2"	"	6.10	8.00	14.10
3"	"	10.75	8.90	19.65
4"	"	13.45	10.00	23.45
6"	"	57.50	13.35	70.85
45 El				
1/2"	EA.	1.10	6.15	7.25
3/4"	"	1.80	6.65	8.45
1"	"	2.55	6.65	9.20
1-1/4"	"	3.40	6.65	10.05
1-1/2"	"	4.15	6.65	10.80

Site Improvements	UNIT	MAT.	INST.	TOTAL
02810.40		Lawn Irrigation		
2"	EA.	5.40	7.25	12.65
2-1/2"	"	16.15	8.00	24.15
3"	"	23.35	8.90	32.25
4"	"	43.10	10.00	53.10
6"	"	140.00	13.35	153.35
Riser, 1/2" diameter				
2" (close)	EA.	0.63	10.00	10.63
3"	"	0.73	10.00	10.73
4"	"	0.91	11.45	12.36
5"	"	0.99	11.45	12.44
6"	"	1.25	11.45	12.70
10"	"	1.25	13.35	14.60
12"	"	1.45	13.35	14.80
3/4" diameter				
2" (close)	EA.	0.63	10.00	10.63
3"	"	0.73	10.00	10.73
4"	"	0.82	11.45	12.27
5"	"	1.10	11.45	12.55
6"	"	1.15	11.45	12.60
10"	"	1.60	13.35	14.95
12"	"	1.70	13.35	15.05
1" diameter				
2" (close)	EA.	0.91	10.00	10.91
3"	"	1.15	10.00	11.15
4"	"	1.35	11.45	12.80
5"	"	1.70	11.45	13.15
6"	"	1.75	11.45	13.20
10"	"	2.70	13.35	16.05
12"	"	2.85	13.35	16.20
Street El PVC				
1/2"	EA.	2.15	6.65	8.80
3/4"	"	2.85	7.25	10.10
1"	"	5.05	8.00	13.05
Valve Box				
Concrete, Square				
12" x 22"	EA.	77.00	50.00	127.00
18" x 20"	"	100.00	57.00	157.00
24" x 13"	"	86.00	66.50	152.50
Round				
12"	EA.	34.10	40.00	74.10
Plastic				
Square				
12"	EA.	35.90	50.00	85.90
18"	"			
Round				
6"	EA.	8.95	50.00	58.95
10"	"	19.75	50.00	69.75
12"	"	28.70	57.00	85.70
Sprinkler, Pop-Up				
Spray				
2" high	EA.	5.75	66.50	72.25
3" high	"	6.30	66.50	72.80

Site Improvements	UNIT	MAT.	INST.	TOTAL
02810.40 Lawn Irrigation				
4" high	EA.	6.85	80.00	86.85
6" high	"	14.35	80.00	94.35
12" high	"	18.30	80.00	98.30
Rotor				
4" high	EA.	26.90	66.50	93.40
6" high	"	35.90	80.00	115.90
Impact				
Brass	EA.	35.90	66.50	102.40
Plastic	"	17.95	80.00	97.95
Shrub Head				
Spray	EA.	10.75	66.50	77.25
Rotor	"	26.90	80.00	106.90
Time Clocks				
Minimum	EA.	180.00	100.00	280.00
Average	"	360.00	130.00	490.00
Maximum	"	3,230	200.00	3,430
Valves				
Anti-siphon				
Brass				
3/4"	EA.	77.00	66.50	143.50
1"	"	95.00	66.50	161.50
Plastic				
3/4"	EA.	44.90	66.50	111.40
1"	"	54.00	66.50	120.50
Ball Valve				
Plastic				
1/2"	EA.	9.90	66.50	76.40
3/4"	"	10.75	66.50	77.25
1"	"	14.35	66.50	80.85
1-1/2"	"	28.70	80.00	108.70
2"	"	37.70	80.00	117.70
Brass				
1/2"	EA.	9.90	66.50	76.40
3/4"	"	15.25	66.50	81.75
1"	"	24.25	66.50	90.75
1-1/2"	"	44.90	80.00	124.90
2"	"	63.00	80.00	143.00
Gate valves, Brass				
1/2"	EA.	21.55	66.50	88.05
3/4"	"	35.90	66.50	102.40
1"	"	50.00	66.50	116.50
1-1/2"	"	86.00	80.00	166.00
2"	"	110.00	80.00	190.00
In-line				
Brass				
1"	EA.	180.00	66.50	246.50
1-1/2"	"	270.00	80.00	350.00
2"	"	360.00	80.00	440.00
Plastic				
3/4"	EA.	35.90	66.50	102.40
1"	"	110.00	66.50	176.50
1-1/2"	"	140.00	80.00	220.00

Site Improvements	UNIT	MAT.	INST.	TOTAL
02810.40		Lawn Irrigation		
2"	EA.	210.00	80.00	290.00
Vacuum Breakers				
Brass				
3/4"	EA.	140.00	130.00	270.00
1"	"	200.00	130.00	330.00
1-1/2"	"	390.00	130.00	520.00
2"	"	560.00	130.00	690.00
Plastic				
3/4"	EA.	110.00	130.00	240.00
1"	"	130.00	130.00	260.00
1-1/2"	"	200.00	130.00	330.00
2"	"	230.00	130.00	360.00
Backflow Preventors, Brass				
3/4"	EA.	360.00	1,330	1,690
1"	"	390.00	1,330	1,720
1-1/2"	"	860.00	1,330	2,190
2"	"	1,080	1,600	2,680
Pressure Regulators, Brass				
3/4"	EA.	89.50	40.00	129.50
1"	"	130.00	40.00	170.00
1-1/2"	"	380.00	44.40	424.40
2"	"	450.00	50.00	500.00
Quick Coupler Valve				
3/4"	EA.	80.50	66.50	147.00
1"	"	120.00	66.50	186.50
02830.10		Chain Link Fence		
Chain link fence, 9 ga., galvanized, with posts 10' o.c.				
4' high	L.F.	6.40	2.85	9.25
5' high	"	8.55	3.65	12.20
6' high	"	9.65	5.00	14.65
7' high	"	11.00	6.15	17.15
8' high	"	12.70	8.00	20.70
For barbed wire with hangers, add				
3 strand	L.F.	2.35	2.00	4.35
6 strand	"	3.95	3.35	7.30
Corner or gate post, 3" post				
4' high	EA.	74.50	13.35	87.85
5' high	"	82.50	14.80	97.30
6' high	"	91.50	17.40	108.90
7' high	"	110.00	20.00	130.00
8' high	"	120.00	22.20	142.20
4" post				
4' high	EA.	130.00	14.80	144.80
5' high	"	150.00	17.40	167.40
6' high	"	170.00	20.00	190.00
7' high	"	180.00	22.20	202.20
8' high	"	200.00	25.00	225.00
Gate with gate posts, galvanized, 3' wide				
4' high	EA.	82.50	100.00	182.50
5' high	"	110.00	130.00	240.00
6' high	"	130.00	130.00	260.00

Site Improvements	UNIT	MAT.	INST.	TOTAL
02830.10 Chain Link Fence				
7' high	EA.	150.00	200.00	350.00
8' high	"	160.00	200.00	360.00
Fabric, galvanized chain link, 2" mesh, 9 ga.				
4' high	L.F.	2.90	1.35	4.25
5' high	"	3.55	1.60	5.15
6' high	"	3.70	2.00	5.70
8' high	"	5.70	2.65	8.35
Line post, no rail fitting, galvanized, 2-1/2" dia.				
4' high	EA.	22.00	11.45	33.45
5' high	"	23.95	12.50	36.45
6' high	"	26.20	13.35	39.55
7' high	"	29.80	16.00	45.80
8' high	"	33.20	20.00	53.20
1-7/8" H beam				
4' high	EA.	30.10	11.45	41.55
5' high	"	33.70	12.50	46.20
6' high	"	40.30	13.35	53.65
7' high	"	45.80	16.00	61.80
8' high	"	49.50	20.00	69.50
2-1/4" H beam				
4' high	EA.	22.00	11.45	33.45
5' high	"	27.40	12.50	39.90
6' high	"	31.50	13.35	44.85
7' high	"	36.50	16.00	52.50
8' high	"	42.40	20.00	62.40
Vinyl coated, 9 ga., with posts 10' o.c.				
4' high	L.F.	6.90	2.85	9.75
5' high	"	8.20	3.65	11.85
6' high	"	9.85	5.00	14.85
7' high	"	10.75	6.15	16.90
8' high	"	12.25	8.00	20.25
For barbed wire w/hangers, add				
3 strand	L.F.	2.50	2.00	4.50
6 Strand	"	4.05	3.35	7.40
Corner, or gate post, 4' high				
3" dia.	EA.	91.50	13.35	104.85
4" dia.	"	140.00	13.35	153.35
6" dia.	"	160.00	16.00	176.00
Gate, with posts, 3' wide				
4' high	EA.	100.00	100.00	200.00
5' high	"	120.00	130.00	250.00
6' high	"	140.00	130.00	270.00
7' high	"	160.00	200.00	360.00
8' high	"	180.00	200.00	380.00
Line post, no rail fitting, 2-1/2" dia.				
4' high	EA.	38.50	11.45	49.95
5' high	"	52.50	12.50	65.00
6' high	"	63.00	13.35	76.35
7' high	"	74.00	16.00	90.00
8' high	"	81.00	20.00	101.00
Corner post, no top rail fitting, 4" dia.				
4' high	EA.	150.00	13.35	163.35

Site Improvements	UNIT	MAT.	INST.	TOTAL
02830.10 Chain Link Fence				
5' high	EA.	170.00	14.80	184.80
6' high	"	200.00	17.40	217.40
7' high	"	220.00	20.00	240.00
8' high	"	230.00	22.20	252.20
Fabric, vinyl, chain link, 2" mesh, 9 ga.				
4' high	L.F.	5.30	1.35	6.65
5' high	"	6.40	1.60	8.00
6' high	"	7.50	2.00	9.50
8' high	"	10.00	2.65	12.65
Swing gates, galvanized, 4' high				
Single gate				
3' wide	EA.	190.00	100.00	290.00
4' wide	"	210.00	100.00	310.00
Double gate				
10' wide	EA.	490.00	160.00	650.00
12' wide	"	530.00	160.00	690.00
14' wide	"	540.00	160.00	700.00
16' wide	"	610.00	160.00	770.00
18' wide	"	650.00	230.00	880.00
20' wide	"	690.00	230.00	920.00
22' wide	"	770.00	230.00	1,000
24' wide	"	790.00	270.00	1,060
26' wide	"	820.00	270.00	1,090
28' wide	"	880.00	320.00	1,200
30' wide	"	930.00	320.00	1,250
5' high				
Single gate				
3' wide	EA.	200.00	130.00	330.00
4' wide	"	230.00	130.00	360.00
Double gate				
10' wide	EA.	530.00	200.00	730.00
12' wide	"	570.00	200.00	770.00
14' wide	"	970.00	200.00	1,170
16' wide	"	640.00	200.00	840.00
18' wide	"	650.00	230.00	880.00
20' wide	"	740.00	230.00	970.00
22' wide	"	780.00	230.00	1,010
24' wide	"	810.00	270.00	1,080
26' wide	"	850.00	270.00	1,120
28' wide	"	950.00	320.00	1,270
30' wide	"	980.00	320.00	1,300
6' high				
Single gate				
3' wide	EA.	230.00	130.00	360.00
4' wide	"	250.00	130.00	380.00
Double gate				
10' wide	EA.	550.00	200.00	750.00
12' wide	"	620.00	200.00	820.00
14' wide	"	660.00	200.00	860.00
16' wide	"	710.00	200.00	910.00
18' wide	"	760.00	230.00	990.00
20' wide	"	780.00	230.00	1,010

Site Improvements	UNIT	MAT.	INST.	TOTAL
02830.10 Chain Link Fence				
22' wide	EA.	840.00	230.00	1,070
24' wide	"	900.00	270.00	1,170
26' wide	"	930.00	270.00	1,200
28' wide	"	1,010	320.00	1,330
30' wide	"	1,060	320.00	1,380
7' high				
Single gate				
3' wide	EA.	250.00	200.00	450.00
4' wide	"	280.00	200.00	480.00
Double gate				
10' wide	EA.	650.00	270.00	920.00
12' wide	"	720.00	270.00	990.00
14' wide	"	770.00	270.00	1,040
16' wide	"	820.00	270.00	1,090
18' wide	"	880.00	320.00	1,200
20' wide	"	930.00	320.00	1,250
22' wide	"	980.00	320.00	1,300
24' wide	"	1,050	400.00	1,450
26' wide	"	1,120	400.00	1,520
28' wide	"	1,180	500.00	1,680
30' wide	"	1,350	500.00	1,850
8' high				
Single gate				
3' wide	EA.	270.00	200.00	470.00
4' wide	"	290.00	200.00	490.00
Double gate				
10' wide	EA.	720.00	270.00	990.00
12' wide	"	760.00	270.00	1,030
14' wide	"	820.00	270.00	1,090
16' wide	"	890.00	270.00	1,160
18' wide	"	930.00	320.00	1,250
20' wide	"	970.00	320.00	1,290
22' wide	"	1,020	320.00	1,340
24' wide	"	1,130	400.00	1,530
26' wide	"	1,170	400.00	1,570
28' wide	"	1,240	500.00	1,740
30' wide	"	1,370	500.00	1,870
Vinyl coated swing gates, 4' high				
Single gate				
3' wide	EA.	290.00	100.00	390.00
4' wide	"	310.00	100.00	410.00
Double gate				
10' wide	EA.	690.00	160.00	850.00
12' wide	"	880.00	160.00	1,040
14' wide	"	930.00	160.00	1,090
16' wide	"	1,030	160.00	1,190
18' wide	"	1,170	230.00	1,400
20' wide	"	1,380	230.00	1,610
22' wide	"	1,530	230.00	1,760
24' wide	"	1,650	270.00	1,920
26' wide	"	1,730	270.00	2,000
28' wide	"	2,010	320.00	2,330

Site Improvements	UNIT	MAT.	INST.	TOTAL
02830.10 Chain Link Fence				
30' wide	EA.	2,110	320.00	2,430
5' high				
Single gate				
3' wide	EA.	320.00	130.00	450.00
4' wide	"	360.00	130.00	490.00
Double gate				
10' wide	EA.	940.00	200.00	1,140
12' wide	"	1,000	200.00	1,200
14' wide	"	1,120	200.00	1,320
16' wide	"	1,170	200.00	1,370
18' wide	"	1,410	230.00	1,640
20' wide	"	1,530	230.00	1,760
22' wide	"	1,680	230.00	1,910
24' wide	"	1,910	270.00	2,180
26' wide	"	2,000	270.00	2,270
28' wide	"	2,230	320.00	2,550
30' wide	"	2,400	320.00	2,720
6' high				
Single gate				
3' wide	EA.	340.00	130.00	470.00
4' wide	"	350.00	130.00	480.00
Double gate				
10' wide	EA.	830.00	200.00	1,030
12' wide	"	960.00	200.00	1,160
14' wide	"	1,100	200.00	1,300
16' wide	"	1,280	200.00	1,480
18' wide	"	1,420	230.00	1,650
20' wide	"	1,530	230.00	1,760
22' wide	"	1,660	230.00	1,890
24' wide	"	1,860	270.00	2,130
26' wide	"	1,970	270.00	2,240
28' wide	"	2,330	320.00	2,650
30' wide	"	2,410	320.00	2,730
7' high				
Single gate				
3' wide	EA.	370.00	200.00	570.00
4' wide	"	480.00	200.00	680.00
Double gate				
10' wide	EA.	940.00	270.00	1,210
12' wide	"	1,110	270.00	1,380
14' wide	"	1,260	270.00	1,530
16' wide	"	1,410	270.00	1,680
18' wide	"	1,590	320.00	1,910
20' wide	"	1,820	320.00	2,140
22' wide	"	2,020	320.00	2,340
24' wide	"	2,220	400.00	2,620
26' wide	"	2,400	400.00	2,800
28' wide	"	2,590	500.00	3,090
30' wide	"	2,780	500.00	3,280
8' high				
Single gate				
3' wide	EA.	390.00	200.00	590.00

Site Improvements	UNIT	MAT.	INST.	TOTAL
02830.10 **Chain Link Fence**				
4' wide	EA.	480.00	200.00	680.00
Double gate				
10' wide	EA.	960.00	270.00	1,230
12' wide	"	1,110	270.00	1,380
14' wide	"	1,270	270.00	1,540
16' wide	"	900.00	270.00	1,170
18' wide	"	1,610	320.00	1,930
20' wide	"	1,870	320.00	2,190
22' wide	"	2,140	320.00	2,460
24' wide	"	2,280	400.00	2,680
28' wide	"	2,660	400.00	3,060
30' wide	"	2,850	500.00	3,350
Motor operator for gates, no wiring	"			5,493
Drilling fence post holes				
In soil				
By hand	EA.		20.00	20.00
By machine auger	"		12.85	12.85
In rock				
By jackhammer	EA.		170.00	170.00
By rock drill	"		51.50	51.50
Aluminum privacy slats, installed vertically	S.F.	0.96	1.00	1.96
Post hole, dig by hand	EA.		26.70	26.70
Set fence post in concrete	"	9.25	20.00	29.25
02830.70 **Recreational Courts**				
Walls, galvanized steel				
8' high	L.F.	13.10	8.00	21.10
10' high	"	15.60	8.90	24.50
12' high	"	17.90	10.55	28.45
Vinyl coated				
8' high	L.F.	12.60	8.00	20.60
10' high	"	15.40	8.90	24.30
12' high	"	17.10	10.55	27.65
Gates, galvanized steel				
Single, 3' transom				
3'x7'	EA.	310.00	200.00	510.00
4'x7'	"	330.00	230.00	560.00
5'x7'	"	440.00	270.00	710.00
6'x7'	"	480.00	320.00	800.00
Double, 3' transom				
10'x7'	EA.	750.00	800.00	1,550
12'x7'	"	960.00	890.00	1,850
14'x7'	"	1,150	1,000	2,150
Double, no transom				
10'x10'	EA.	810.00	670.00	1,480
12'x10'	"	960.00	800.00	1,760
14'x10'	"	1,110	890.00	2,000
Vinyl coated				
Single, 3' transom				
3'x7'	EA.	600.00	200.00	800.00
4'x7'	"	650.00	230.00	880.00
5'x7'	"	650.00	270.00	920.00

Site Improvements	UNIT	MAT.	INST.	TOTAL
02830.70		Recreational Courts		
6'x7'	EA.	670.00	320.00	990.00
Double, 3'				
10'x7'	EA.	1,780	800.00	2,580
12'x7'	"	1,820	890.00	2,710
14'x7'	"	1,970	1,000	2,970
Double, no transom				
10'x10'	EA.	1,770	670.00	2,440
12'x10'	"	1,790	800.00	2,590
14'x10'	"	1,970	890.00	2,860
Baseball backstop, regulation				
Galvanized	EA.			7,445
Vinyl coated	"			10,368
Softball backstop, regulation				
14' high				
Galvanized	EA.			6,913
Vinyl coated	"			10,280
18' high				
Galvanized	EA.			8,153
Vinyl coated	"			11,786
20' high				
Galvanized	EA.			9,659
Vinyl coated	"			13,913
22' high				
Galvanized	EA.			11,168
Vinyl coated	"			16,307
24' high				
Galvanized	EA.			13,577
Vinyl coated	"			22,334
Wire and miscellaneous metal fences				
Chicken wire, post 4' o.c.				
2" mesh				
4' high	L.F.	1.45	2.00	3.45
6' high	"	1.65	2.65	4.30
Galvanized steel				
12 gauge, 2" by 4" mesh, posts 5' o.c.				
3' high	L.F.	2.35	2.00	4.35
5' high	"	3.35	2.50	5.85
14 gauge, 1" by 2" mesh, posts 5' o.c.				
3' high	L.F.	1.95	2.00	3.95
5' high	"	3.20	2.50	5.70
02840.30		Guardrails		
Pipe bollard, steel pipe, concrete filled, painted				
6" dia.	EA.	200.00	33.30	233.30
8" dia.	"	250.00	50.00	300.00
12" dia.	"	400.00	130.00	530.00
Corrugated steel, guardrail, galvanized	L.F.	24.25	3.55	27.80
End section, wrap around or flared	EA.	64.50	40.00	104.50
Timber guardrail, 4" x 8"	L.F.	28.30	2.65	30.95
Guard rail, 3 cables, 3/4" dia.				
Steel posts	L.F.	12.55	10.70	23.25
Wood posts	"	14.30	8.55	22.85

Site Improvements	UNIT	MAT.	INST.	TOTAL
02840.30 Guardrails				
Steel box beam				
6" x 6"	L.F.	52.00	11.90	63.90
6" x 8"	"	55.00	13.35	68.35
Concrete posts	EA.	34.20	20.00	54.20
Barrel type impact barrier	"	430.00	40.00	470.00
Light shield, 6' high	L.F.	28.40	8.00	36.40
02840.40 Parking Barriers				
Timber, treated, 4' long				
4" x 4"	EA.	16.80	33.30	50.10
6" x 6"	"	31.20	40.00	71.20
Precast concrete, 6' long, with dowels				
12" x 6"	EA.	32.50	20.00	52.50
12" x 8"	"	35.60	22.20	57.80
02840.60 Signage				
Traffic signs				
Reflectorized signs per OSHA standards, including post				
Stop, 24"x24"	EA.	63.50	26.70	90.20
Yield, 30" triangle	"	37.10	26.70	63.80
Speed limit, 12"x18"	"	42.40	26.70	69.10
Directional, 12"x18"	"	58.00	26.70	84.70
Exit, 12"x18"	"	58.00	26.70	84.70
Entry, 12"x18"	"	58.00	26.70	84.70
Warning, 24"x24"	"	74.00	26.70	100.70
Informational, 12"x18"	"	26.50	26.70	53.20
Handicap parking, 12"x18"	"	28.20	26.70	54.90
02860.40 Recreational Facilities				
Bleachers, outdoor, portable, per seat				
10 tiers				
Minimum	EA.	33.50	13.35	46.85
Maximum	"	65.00	17.80	82.80
20 tiers				
Minimum	EA.	40.90	12.60	53.50
Maximum	"	78.00	16.45	94.45
Grandstands, fixed, wood seat, steel frame, per seat				
15 tiers				
Minimum	EA.	57.50	21.40	78.90
Maximum	"	98.50	35.60	134.10
30 tiers				
Minimum	EA.	59.50	19.45	78.95
Maximum	"	130.00	30.50	160.50
Seats				
Seat backs only				
Fiberglass	EA.	32.90	4.00	36.90
Steel and wood seat	"	47.60	4.00	51.60
Seat restoration, fiberglass on wood				
Seats	EA.	23.75	8.00	31.75
Plain bench, no backs	"	14.60	3.35	17.95
Benches				
Park, precast concrete with backs				

Site Improvements	UNIT	MAT.	INST.	TOTAL
02860.40			Recreational Facilities	
4' long	EA.	910.00	130.00	1,040
8' long	"	2,010	200.00	2,210
Fiberglass, with backs				
4' long	EA.	730.00	100.00	830.00
8' long	"	1,390	130.00	1,520
Wood, with backs and fiberglass supports				
4' long	EA.	410.00	100.00	510.00
8' long	"	420.00	130.00	550.00
Steel frame, 6' long				
All steel	EA.	340.00	100.00	440.00
Hardwood boards	"	240.00	100.00	340.00
Players bench (no back), steel frame, fir seat, 10' long	"	260.00	130.00	390.00
Backstops				
Handball or squash court, outdoor				
Wood	EA.			33,420
Masonry	"			30,207
Soccer goal posts	PAIR			2,699
Running track				
Gravel and cinders over stone base	S.Y.	8.30	5.35	13.65
Rubber-cork base resilient pavement	"	11.70	42.80	54.50
For colored surfaces, add	"	7.35	4.30	11.65
Colored rubberized asphalt	"	15.65	53.50	69.15
Artificial resilient mat over asphalt	"	36.90	110.00	146.90
Tennis courts				
Bituminous pavement, 2-1/2" thick	S.Y.	11.85	13.35	25.20
Colored sealer, acrylic emulsion				
3 coats	S.Y.	6.20	2.65	8.85
For 2 color seal coating, add	"	1.15	0.40	1.55
For preparing old courts, add	"	2.65	0.27	2.92
Net, nylon, 42' long	EA.	360.00	50.00	410.00
Paint markings on asphalt, 2 coats	"	93.00	400.00	493.00
Complete court with fence, etc., bituminous				
Minimum	EA.			14,558
Average	"			25,055
Maximum	"			35,552
Clay court				
Minimum	EA.			15,150
Average	"			20,651
Maximum	"			31,318
Playground equipment				
Basketball backboard				
Minimum	EA.	640.00	100.00	740.00
Maximum	"	1,220	110.00	1,330
Bike rack, 10' long	"	490.00	80.00	570.00
Golf shelter, fiberglass	"	2,450	100.00	2,550
Ground socket for movable posts				
Minimum	EA.	110.00	25.00	135.00
Maximum	"	230.00	25.00	255.00
Horizontal monkey ladder, 14' long	"	750.00	66.50	816.50
Posts, tether ball	"	360.00	20.00	380.00
Multiple purpose, 10' long	"	370.00	40.00	410.00
See-saw, steel				

Site Improvements	UNIT	MAT.	INST.	TOTAL
02860.40 Recreational Facilities				
Minimum	EA.	610.00	160.00	770.00
Average	"	1,140	200.00	1,340
Maximum	"	1,740	270.00	2,010
Slide				
Minimum	EA.	1,100	320.00	1,420
Maximum	"	1,910	360.00	2,270
Swings, plain seats				
8' high				
Minimum	EA.	820.00	270.00	1,090
Maximum	"	1,550	310.00	1,860
12' high				
Minimum	EA.	1,250	310.00	1,560
Maximum	"	2,260	440.00	2,700
02870.10 Prefabricated Planters				
Concrete precast, circular				
24" dia., 18" high	EA.	290.00	40.00	330.00
42" dia., 30" high	"	390.00	50.00	440.00
Fiberglass, circular				
36" dia., 27" high	EA.	540.00	20.00	560.00
60" dia., 39" high	"	1,250	22.20	1,272
Tapered, circular				
24" dia., 36" high	EA.	430.00	18.20	448.20
40" dia., 36" high	"	700.00	20.00	720.00
Square				
2' by 2', 17" high	EA.	360.00	18.20	378.20
4' by 4', 39" high	"	1,250	22.20	1,272
Rectangular				
4' by 1', 18" high	EA.	400.00	20.00	420.00

Landscaping	UNIT	MAT.	INST.	TOTAL
02910.10 Shrub & Tree Maintenance				
Moving shrubs on site				
12" ball	EA.		50.00	50.00
24" ball	"		66.50	66.50
3' high	"		40.00	40.00
4' high	"		44.40	44.40
5' high	"		50.00	50.00
18" spread	"		57.00	57.00
30" spread	"		66.50	66.50
Moving trees on site				
24" ball	EA.		110.00	110.00
48" ball	"		140.00	140.00
Trees				
3' high	EA.		42.80	42.80

Landscaping	UNIT	MAT.	INST.	TOTAL
02910.10 Shrub & Tree Maintenance				
6' high	EA.		47.50	47.50
8' high	"		53.50	53.50
10' high	"		71.50	71.50
Palm trees				
7' high	EA.		53.50	53.50
10' high	"		71.50	71.50
20' high	"		210.00	210.00
40' high	"		430.00	430.00
Guying trees				
4" dia.	EA.	7.25	20.00	27.25
8" dia.	"	7.25	25.00	32.25
02920.10 Topsoil				
Spread topsoil, with equipment				
Minimum	C.Y.		11.45	11.45
Maximum	"		14.30	14.30
By hand				
Minimum	C.Y.		40.00	40.00
Maximum	"		50.00	50.00
Area preparation for seeding (grade, rake and clean)				
Square yard	S.Y.		0.32	0.32
By acre	ACRE		1,600	1,600
Remove topsoil and stockpile on site				
4" deep	C.Y.		9.55	9.55
6" deep	"		8.80	8.80
Spreading topsoil from stock pile				
By loader	C.Y.		10.40	10.40
By hand	"		110.00	110.00
Top dress by hand	S.Y.		1.15	1.15
Place imported top soil				
By loader				
4" deep	S.Y.		1.15	1.15
6" deep	"		1.25	1.25
By hand				
4" deep	S.Y.		4.45	4.45
6" deep	"		5.00	5.00
Plant bed preparation, 18" deep				
With backhoe/loader	S.Y.		2.85	2.85
By hand	"		6.65	6.65
02930.30 Seeding				
Mechanical seeding, 175 lb/acre				
By square yard	S.Y.	0.65	0.10	0.76
By acre	ACRE	2,610	520.00	3,130
450 lb/acre				
By square yard	S.Y.	1.05	0.13	1.18
By acre	ACRE	3,990	640.00	4,630
Seeding by hand, 10 lb per 100 s.y.				
By square yard	S.Y.	0.70	0.13	0.83
By acre	ACRE	2,760	670.00	3,430
Reseed disturbed areas	S.F.	0.62	0.20	0.82

Landscaping	UNIT	MAT.	INST.	TOTAL
02950.10 Plants				
Euonymus coloratus, 18" (Purple Wintercreeper)	EA.	2.00	6.65	8.65
Hedera Helix, 2-1/4" pot (English ivy)	"	0.81	6.65	7.46
Liriope muscari, 2" clumps	"	3.50	4.00	7.50
Santolina, 12"	"	3.95	4.00	7.95
Vinca major or minor, 3" pot	"	0.64	4.00	4.64
Cortaderia argentia, 2 gallon (Pampas Grass)	"	12.65	4.00	16.65
Ophiopogan japonicus, 1 quart (4" pot)	"	3.50	4.00	7.50
Ajuga reptans, 2-3/4" pot (carpet bugle)	"	0.64	4.00	4.64
Pachysandra terminalis, 2-3/4" pot (Japanese Spurge)	"	0.88	4.00	4.88
02950.30 Shrubs				
Juniperus conferia litoralis, 18"-24" (Shore Juniper)	EA.	29.30	16.00	45.30
Horizontalis plumosa, 18"-24" (Andorra Juniper)	"	31.00	16.00	47.00
Sabina tamar-iscfolia-tamarix juniper, 18"-24"	"	31.00	16.00	47.00
Chin San Jose, 18"-24" (San Jose Juniper)	"	31.00	16.00	47.00
Sargenti, 18"-24" (Sargent's Juniper)	"	29.30	16.00	45.30
Nandina domestica, 18"-24" (Heavenly Bamboo)	"	19.60	16.00	35.60
Raphiolepis Indica Springtime, 18"-24" (Indian Hawthorn)	"	21.10	16.00	37.10
Osmanthus Heterophyllus Gulftide, 18"-24" (Osmanthus)	"	22.55	16.00	38.55
Ilex Cornuta Burfordi Nana, 18"-24" (Dwarf Burford Holly)	"	25.70	16.00	41.70
Glabra, 18"-24" (Inkberry Holly)	"	24.20	16.00	40.20
Azalea, Indica types, 18"-24"	"	27.30	16.00	43.30
Kurume types, 18"-24"	"	30.50	16.00	46.50
Berberis Julianae, 18"-24" (Wintergreen Barberry)	"	17.90	16.00	33.90
Pieris Japonica Japanese, 18"-24" (Japanese Pieris)	"	17.90	16.00	33.90
Ilex Cornuta Rotunda, 18"-24" (Dwarf Chinese Holly)	"	21.20	16.00	37.20
Juniperus Horiz. Plumosa, 24"-30" (Andorra Juniper)	"	19.55	20.00	39.55
Rhodopendrow Hybrids, 24"-30"	"	52.00	20.00	72.00
Aucuba Japonica Varigata, 24"-30" (Gold Dust Aucuba)	"	17.80	20.00	37.80
Ilex Crenata Willow Leaf, 24"-30" (Japanese Holly)	"	19.55	20.00	39.55
Cleyera Japonica, 30"-36" (Japanese Cleyera)	"	22.85	25.00	47.85
Pittosporum Tobira, 30"-36"	"	26.10	25.00	51.10
Prumus Laurocerasus, 30"-36"	"	49.00	25.00	74.00
Ilex Cornuta Burfordi, 30"-36" (Burford Holly)	"	26.10	25.00	51.10
Abelia Grandiflora, 24"-36" (Yew Podocarpus)	"	17.90	20.00	37.90
Podocarpos Macrophylla, 24"-36" (Yew Podocarpus)	"	29.30	20.00	49.30
Pyracantha Coccinea Lalandi, 3'-4' (Firethorn)	"	16.70	25.00	41.70
Photinia Frazieri, 3'-4' (Red Photinia)	"	26.50	25.00	51.50
Forsythia Suspensa, 3'-4' (Weeping Forsythia)	"	16.70	25.00	41.70
Camellia Japonica, 3'-4' (Common Camellia)	"	29.40	25.00	54.40
Juniperus Chin Torulosa, 3'-4' (Hollywood Juniper)	"	31.20	25.00	56.20
Cupressocyparis Leylandi, 3'-4'	"	26.30	25.00	51.30
Ilex Opaca Fosteri, 5'-6' (Foster's Holly)	"	110.00	33.30	143.30
Opaca, 5'-6' (American Holly)	"	150.00	33.30	183.30
Nyrica Cerifera, 4'-5' (Southern Wax Myrtles)	"	33.20	28.60	61.80
Ligustrum Japonicum, 4'-5' (Japanese Privet)	"	26.10	28.60	54.70
02950.60 Trees				
Cornus Florida, 5'-6' (White flowering Dogwood)	EA.	73.50	33.30	106.80
Prunus Serrulata Kwanzan, 6'-8' (Kwanzan Cherry)	"	81.50	40.00	121.50
Caroliniana, 6'-8' (Carolina Cherry Laurel)	"	96.50	40.00	136.50
Cercis Canadensis, 6'-8' (Eastern Redbud)	"	66.50	40.00	106.50

Landscaping	UNIT	MAT.	INST.	TOTAL
02950.60 Trees				
Koelreuteria Paniculata, 8'-10' (Goldenrain Tree)	EA.	110.00	50.00	160.00
Acer Platanoides, 1-3/4"-2" (11'-13') (Norway Maple)	"	150.00	66.50	216.50
Rubrum, 1-3/4"-2" (11'-13') (Red Maple)	"	110.00	66.50	176.50
Saccharum, 1-3/4"-2" (Sugar Maple)	"	200.00	66.50	266.50
Fraxinus Pennsylvanica, 1-3/4"-2" (Laneolata-Green Ash)	"	98.00	66.50	164.50
Celtis Occidentalis, 1-3/4"-2" (American Hackberry)	"	150.00	66.50	216.50
Glenditsia Triacantos Inermis, 2"	"	130.00	66.50	196.50
Prunus Cerasifera 'Thundercloud', 6'-8'	"	77.50	40.00	117.50
Yeodensis, 6'-8' (Yoshino Cherry)	"	82.00	40.00	122.00
Lagerstroemia Indica, 8'-10' (Crapemyrtle)	"	130.00	50.00	180.00
Crataegus Phaenopyrum, 8'-10' (Washington Hawthorn)	"	200.00	50.00	250.00
Quercus Borealis, 1-3/4"-2" (Northern Red Oak)	"	120.00	66.50	186.50
Quercus Acutissima, 1-3/4"-2" (8'-10') (Sawtooth Oak)	"	110.00	66.50	176.50
Saliz Babylonica, 1-3/4"-2" (Weeping Willow)	"	57.00	66.50	123.50
Tilia Cordata Greenspire, 1-3/4"-2" (10'-12')	"	250.00	66.50	316.50
Malus, 2"-2-1/2" (8'-10') (Flowering Crabapple)	"	120.00	66.50	186.50
Platanus Occidentalis, (12'-14')	"	190.00	80.00	270.00
Pyrus Calleryana Bradford, 2"-2-1/2" (Bradford Pear)	"	150.00	66.50	216.50
Quercus Palustris, 2"-2-1/2" (12'-14') (Pin Oak)	"	160.00	66.50	226.50
Phellos, 2-1/2"-3" (Willow Oak)	"	180.00	80.00	260.00
Nigra, 2"-2-1/2" (Water Oak)	"	150.00	66.50	216.50
Magnolia Soulangeana, 4'-5' (Saucer Magnolia)	"	88.50	33.30	121.80
Grandiflora, 6'-8' (Southern Magnolia)	"	120.00	40.00	160.00
Cedrus Deodara, 10'-12' (Deodare Cedar)	"	200.00	66.50	266.50
Gingko Biloba, 10'-12' (2"-2-1/2") (Maidenhair Tree)	"	190.00	66.50	256.50
Pinus Thunbergi, 5'-6' (Japanese Black Pine)	"	74.50	33.30	107.80
Strobus, 6'-8' (White Pine)	"	82.00	40.00	122.00
Taeda, 6'-8' (Loblolly Pine)	"	69.50	40.00	109.50
Quercus Virginiana, 2"-2-1/2" (Live Oak)	"	180.00	80.00	260.00
02970.10 Fertilizing				
Fertilizing (23#/1000 sf)				
By square yard	S.Y.	0.03	0.13	0.15
By acre	ACRE	130.00	640.00	770.00
Liming (70#/1000 sf)				
By square yard	S.Y.	0.03	0.17	0.20
By acre	ACRE	130.00	860.00	990.00
02980.10 Landscape Accessories				
Steel edging, 3/16" x 4"	L.F.	0.59	0.50	1.09
Landscaping stepping stones, 15"x15", white	EA.	5.30	2.00	7.30
Wood chip mulch	C.Y.	44.40	26.70	71.10
2" thick	S.Y.	2.75	0.80	3.55
4" thick	"	5.15	1.15	6.30
6" thick	"	7.70	1.45	9.15
Gravel mulch, 3/4" stone	C.Y.	34.10	40.00	74.10
White marble chips, 1" deep	S.F.	0.68	0.40	1.08
Peat moss				
2" thick	S.Y.	3.20	0.89	4.09
4" thick	"	6.15	1.35	7.50
6" thick	"	9.40	1.65	11.05
Landscaping timbers, treated lumber				

Landscaping		UNIT	MAT.	INST.	TOTAL
02980.10	Landscape Accessories				
4" x 4"		L.F.	1.25	1.35	2.60
6" x 6"		"	2.50	1.45	3.95
8" x 8"		"	4.05	1.65	5.70

CONCRETE

Formwork	UNIT	MAT.	INST.	TOTAL
03110.05		Beam Formwork		
Beam forms, job built				
Beam bottoms				
1 use	S.F.	4.30	8.60	12.90
2 uses	"	2.55	8.20	10.75
3 uses	"	1.95	7.95	9.90
4 uses	"	1.60	7.60	9.20
5 uses	"	1.45	7.35	8.80
Beam sides				
1 use	S.F.	3.10	5.75	8.85
2 uses	"	1.85	5.45	7.30
3 uses	"	1.60	5.15	6.75
4 uses	"	1.45	4.90	6.35
5 uses	"	1.30	4.70	6.00
03110.10		Box Culvert Formwork		
Box culverts, job built				
6' x 6'				
1 use	S.F.	2.95	5.15	8.10
2 uses	"	1.60	4.90	6.50
3 uses	"	1.35	4.70	6.05
4 uses	"	1.10	4.50	5.60
5 uses	"	1.00	4.30	5.30
8' x 12'				
1 use	S.F.	2.95	4.30	7.25
2 uses	"	1.60	4.15	5.75
3 uses	"	1.35	3.95	5.30
4 uses	"	1.10	3.80	4.90
5 uses	"	1.00	3.70	4.70
03110.15		Column Formwork		
Column, square forms, job built				
8" x 8" columns				
1 use	S.F.	3.40	10.30	13.70
2 uses	"	1.85	9.90	11.75
3 uses	"	1.55	9.55	11.10
4 uses	"	1.40	9.20	10.60
5 uses	"	1.20	8.90	10.10
12" x 12" columns				
1 use	S.F.	3.10	9.40	12.50
2 uses	"	1.70	9.05	10.75
3 uses	"	1.35	8.75	10.10
4 uses	"	1.20	8.45	9.65
5 uses	"	1.00	8.20	9.20
16" x 16" columns				
1 use	S.F.	2.95	8.60	11.55
2 uses	"	1.55	8.30	9.85
3 uses	"	1.25	8.05	9.30
4 uses	"	1.15	7.80	8.95
5 uses	"	0.93	7.60	8.53
24" x 24" columns				
1 use	S.F.	2.95	7.95	10.90
2 uses	"	1.35	7.70	9.05

Formwork	UNIT	MAT.	INST.	TOTAL
03110.15 Column Formwork				
3 uses	S.F.	1.10	7.50	8.60
4 uses	"	0.93	7.25	8.18
5 uses	"	0.86	7.05	7.91
36" x 36" columns				
1 use	S.F.	2.95	7.35	10.30
2 uses	"	1.40	7.15	8.55
3 uses	"	1.15	6.95	8.10
4 uses	"	1.00	6.80	7.80
5 uses	"	0.93	6.60	7.53
Round fiber forms, 1 use				
10" dia.	L.F.	3.95	10.30	14.25
12" dia.	"	4.90	10.55	15.45
14" dia.	"	6.40	11.00	17.40
16" dia.	"	8.40	11.45	19.85
18" dia.	"	13.75	12.30	26.05
24" dia.	"	16.80	13.25	30.05
30" dia.	"	25.20	14.35	39.55
36" dia.	"	31.30	15.65	46.95
42" dia.	"	57.50	17.20	74.70
03110.18 Curb Formwork				
Curb forms				
Straight, 6" high				
1 use	L.F.	2.00	5.15	7.15
2 uses	"	1.20	4.90	6.10
3 uses	"	0.89	4.70	5.59
4 uses	"	0.80	4.50	5.30
5 uses	"	0.72	4.30	5.02
Curved, 6" high				
1 use	L.F.	2.15	6.45	8.60
2 uses	"	1.35	6.05	7.40
3 uses	"	1.05	5.75	6.80
4 uses	"	0.94	5.50	6.44
5 uses	"	0.89	5.25	6.14
03110.20 Elevated Slab Formwork				
Elevated slab formwork				
Slab, with drop panels				
1 use	S.F.	3.55	4.15	7.70
2 uses	"	2.05	3.95	6.00
3 uses	"	1.60	3.80	5.40
4 uses	"	1.40	3.70	5.10
5 uses	"	1.25	3.55	4.80
Floor slab, hung from steel beams				
1 use	S.F.	2.85	3.95	6.80
2 uses	"	1.55	3.80	5.35
3 uses	"	1.45	3.70	5.15
4 uses	"	1.25	3.55	4.80
5 uses	"	1.05	3.45	4.50
Floor slab, with pans or domes				
1 use	S.F.	5.10	4.70	9.80
2 uses	"	3.40	4.50	7.90

Formwork	UNIT	MAT.	INST.	TOTAL
03110.20 Elevated Slab Formwork				
3 uses	S.F.	3.10	4.30	7.40
4 uses	"	2.90	4.15	7.05
5 uses	"	2.55	3.95	6.50
Equipment curbs, 12" high				
1 use	L.F.	2.65	5.15	7.80
2 uses	"	1.70	4.90	6.60
3 uses	"	1.45	4.70	6.15
4 uses	"	1.35	4.50	5.85
5 uses	"	1.10	4.30	5.40
03110.25 Equipment Pad Formwork				
Equipment pad, job built				
1 use	S.F.	3.45	6.45	9.90
2 uses	"	2.10	6.05	8.15
3 uses	"	1.65	5.75	7.40
4 uses	"	1.30	5.45	6.75
5 uses	"	1.05	5.15	6.20
03110.35 Footing Formwork				
Wall footings, job built, continuous				
1 use	S.F.	1.65	5.15	6.80
2 uses	"	1.15	4.90	6.05
3 uses	"	0.95	4.70	5.65
4 uses	"	0.83	4.50	5.33
5 uses	"	0.73	4.30	5.03
Column footings, spread				
1 use	S.F.	1.70	6.45	8.15
2 uses	"	1.30	6.05	7.35
3 uses	"	0.92	5.75	6.67
4 uses	"	0.77	5.45	6.22
5 uses	"	0.70	5.15	5.85
03110.50 Grade Beam Formwork				
Grade beams, job built				
1 use	S.F.	2.55	5.15	7.70
2 uses	"	1.45	4.90	6.35
3 uses	"	1.10	4.70	5.80
4 uses	"	0.93	4.50	5.43
5 uses	"	0.78	4.30	5.08
03110.53 Pile Cap Formwork				
Pile cap forms, job built				
Square				
1 use	S.F.	2.90	6.45	9.35
2 uses	"	1.70	6.05	7.75
3 uses	"	1.35	5.75	7.10
4 uses	"	1.20	5.45	6.65
5 uses	"	0.98	5.15	6.13
Triangular				
1 use	S.F.	3.10	7.35	10.45
2 uses	"	2.05	6.90	8.95
3 uses	"	1.65	6.45	8.10
4 uses	"	1.35	6.05	7.40

CONCRETE

Formwork	UNIT	MAT.	INST.	TOTAL
03110.53	**Pile Cap Formwork**			
5 uses	S.F.	1.05	5.75	6.80
03110.55	**Slab/mat Formwork**			
Mat foundations, job built				
1 use	S.F.	2.55	6.45	9.00
2 uses	"	1.45	6.05	7.50
3 uses	"	1.10	5.75	6.85
4 uses	"	0.92	5.45	6.37
5 uses	"	0.73	5.15	5.88
Edge forms				
6" high				
1 use	L.F.	2.55	4.70	7.25
2 uses	"	1.45	4.50	5.95
3 uses	"	1.10	4.30	5.40
4 uses	"	0.92	4.15	5.07
5 uses	"	0.73	3.95	4.68
12" high				
1 use	L.F.	2.40	5.15	7.55
2 uses	"	1.35	4.90	6.25
3 uses	"	1.00	4.70	5.70
4 uses	"	0.83	4.50	5.33
5 uses	"	0.68	4.30	4.98
Formwork for openings				
1 use	S.F.	3.50	10.30	13.80
2 uses	"	2.00	9.40	11.40
3 uses	"	1.65	8.60	10.25
4 uses	"	1.30	7.95	9.25
5 uses	"	1.05	7.35	8.40
03110.60	**Stair Formwork**			
Stairway forms, job built				
1 use	S.F.	4.35	10.30	14.65
2 uses	"	2.45	9.40	11.85
3 uses	"	1.90	8.60	10.50
4 uses	"	1.75	7.95	9.70
5 uses	"	1.45	7.35	8.80
Stairs, elevated				
1 use	S.F.	5.25	10.30	15.55
2 uses	"	2.80	8.60	11.40
3 uses	"	2.45	7.35	9.80
4 uses	"	2.10	6.90	9.00
5 uses	"	1.75	6.45	8.20
03110.65	**Wall Formwork**			
Wall forms, exterior, job built				
Up to 8' high wall				
1 use	S.F.	2.80	5.15	7.95
2 uses	"	1.55	4.90	6.45
3 uses	"	1.35	4.70	6.05
4 uses	"	1.20	4.50	5.70
5 uses	"	1.05	4.30	5.35
Over 8' high wall				

Formwork	UNIT	MAT.	INST.	TOTAL
03110.65 Wall Formwork				
1 use	S.F.	3.10	6.45	9.55
2 uses	"	1.75	6.05	7.80
3 uses	"	1.60	5.75	7.35
4 uses	"	1.45	5.45	6.90
5 uses	"	1.30	5.15	6.45
Over 16' high wall				
1 use	S.F.	3.25	7.35	10.60
2 uses	"	1.95	6.90	8.85
3 uses	"	1.75	6.45	8.20
4 uses	"	1.60	6.05	7.65
5 uses	"	1.45	5.75	7.20
Radial wall forms				
1 use	S.F.	3.05	7.95	11.00
2 uses	"	1.80	7.35	9.15
3 uses	"	1.70	6.90	8.60
4 uses	"	1.50	6.45	7.95
5 uses	"	1.35	6.05	7.40
Retaining wall forms				
1 use	S.F.	2.60	5.75	8.35
2 uses	"	1.40	5.45	6.85
3 uses	"	1.20	5.15	6.35
4 uses	"	1.05	4.90	5.95
5 uses	"	0.89	4.70	5.59
Radial retaining wall forms				
1 use	S.F.	2.75	8.60	11.35
2 uses	"	1.70	7.95	9.65
3 uses	"	1.45	7.35	8.80
4 uses	"	1.40	6.90	8.30
5 uses	"	1.20	6.45	7.65
Column pier and pilaster				
1 use	S.F.	3.10	10.30	13.40
2 uses	"	1.85	9.40	11.25
3 uses	"	1.70	8.60	10.30
4 uses	"	1.55	7.95	9.50
5 uses	"	1.40	7.35	8.75
Interior wall forms				
Up to 8' high				
1 use	S.F.	2.80	4.70	7.50
2 uses	"	1.55	4.50	6.05
3 uses	"	1.40	4.30	5.70
4 uses	"	1.20	4.15	5.35
5 uses	"	1.00	3.95	4.95
Over 8' high				
1 use	S.F.	3.10	5.75	8.85
2 uses	"	1.75	5.45	7.20
3 uses	"	1.60	5.15	6.75
4 uses	"	1.45	4.90	6.35
5 uses	"	1.30	4.70	6.00
Over 16' high				
1 use	S.F.	3.25	6.45	9.70
2 uses	"	1.95	6.05	8.00
3 uses	"	1.75	5.75	7.50

Formwork	UNIT	MAT.	INST.	TOTAL

03110.65 — Wall Formwork

	UNIT	MAT.	INST.	TOTAL
4 uses	S.F.	1.60	5.45	7.05
5 uses	"	1.45	5.15	6.60
Radial wall forms				
1 use	S.F.	3.05	6.90	9.95
2 uses	"	1.80	6.45	8.25
3 uses	"	1.70	6.05	7.75
4 uses	"	1.50	5.75	7.25
5 uses	"	1.35	5.45	6.80
Curved wall forms, 24" sections				
1 use	S.F.	2.90	10.30	13.20
2 uses	"	1.75	9.40	11.15
3 uses	"	1.60	8.60	10.20
4 uses	"	1.45	7.95	9.40
5 uses	"	1.30	7.35	8.65
PVC form liner, per side, smooth finish				
1 use	S.F.	6.35	4.30	10.65
2 uses	"	3.45	4.15	7.60
3 uses	"	2.90	3.95	6.85
4 uses	"	2.25	3.70	5.95
5 uses	"	1.80	3.45	5.25

03110.90 — Miscellaneous Formwork

	UNIT	MAT.	INST.	TOTAL
Keyway forms (5 uses)				
2 x 4	L.F.	0.19	2.60	2.78
2 x 6	"	0.28	2.85	3.13
Bulkheads				
Walls, with keyways				
2 piece	L.F.	3.15	4.70	7.85
3 piece	"	3.90	5.15	9.05
Elevated slab, with keyway				
2 piece	L.F.	3.60	4.30	7.90
3 piece	"	5.20	4.70	9.90
Ground slab, with keyway				
2 piece	L.F.	3.90	3.70	7.60
3 piece	"	5.20	3.95	9.15
Chamfer strips				
Wood				
1/2" wide	L.F.	0.24	1.15	1.39
3/4" wide	"	0.31	1.15	1.45
1" wide	"	0.40	1.15	1.55
PVC				
1/2" wide	L.F.	0.85	1.15	2.00
3/4" wide	"	0.94	1.15	2.09
1" wide	"	1.20	1.15	2.35
Radius				
1"	L.F.	1.05	1.25	2.30
1-1/2"	"	1.80	1.25	3.05
Reglets				
Galvanized steel, 24 ga.	L.F.	1.20	2.05	3.25
Metal formwork				
Straight edge forms				
4" high	L.F.	0.17	3.20	3.37

Formwork	UNIT	MAT.	INST.	TOTAL
03110.90 Miscellaneous Formwork				
6" high	L.F.	0.19	3.45	3.64
8" high	"	0.22	3.70	3.92
12" high	"	0.28	3.95	4.23
16" high	"	0.33	4.30	4.63
Curb form, S-shape				
12" x				
1'-6"	L.F.	0.33	7.35	7.68
2'	"	0.41	6.90	7.31
2'-6"	"	0.47	6.45	6.92
3'	"	0.52	5.75	6.27

Reinforcement	UNIT	MAT.	INST.	TOTAL
03210.05 Beam Reinforcing				
Beam-girders				
#3 - #4	TON	1,130	1,440	2,570
#5 - #6	"	990.00	1,150	2,140
#7 - #8	"	940.00	960.00	1,900
#9 - #10	"	940.00	820.00	1,760
#11 - #12	"	940.00	770.00	1,710
#13 - #14	"	940.00	720.00	1,660
Galvanized				
#3 - #4	TON	1,920	1,440	3,360
#5 - #6	"	1,820	1,150	2,970
#7 - #8	"	1,750	960.00	2,710
#9 - #10	"	1,750	820.00	2,570
#11 - #12	"	1,750	770.00	2,520
#13 - #14	"	1,750	720.00	2,470
Epoxy coated				
#3 - #4	TON	1,660	1,640	3,300
#5 - #6	"	1,560	1,280	2,840
#7 - #8	"	1,510	1,040	2,550
#9 - #10	"	1,510	880.00	2,390
#11 - #12	"	1,510	820.00	2,330
#13 - #14	"	1,510	770.00	2,280
Bond Beams				
#3 - #4	TON	1,130	1,910	3,040
#5 - #6	"	990.00	1,440	2,430
#7 - #8	"	940.00	1,280	2,220
Galvanized				
#3 - #4	TON	1,840	1,910	3,750
#5 - #6	"	1,820	1,440	3,260
#7 - #8	"	1,750	1,280	3,030
Epoxy coated				
#3 - #4	TON	1,660	2,300	3,960
#5 - #6	"	1,560	1,640	3,200

Reinforcement	UNIT	MAT.	INST.	TOTAL
03210.05 — Beam Reinforcing				
#7 - #8	TON	1,510	1,440	2,950
03210.10 — Box Culvert Reinforcing				
Box culverts				
#3 - #4	TON	1,130	720.00	1,850
#5 - #6	"	990.00	640.00	1,630
#7 - #8	"	940.00	570.00	1,510
#9 - #10	"	940.00	520.00	1,460
#11 - #12	"	940.00	480.00	1,420
Galvanized				
#3 - #4	TON	1,840	720.00	2,560
#5 - #6	"	1,820	640.00	2,460
#7 - #8	"	1,750	570.00	2,320
#9 - #10	"	1,750	520.00	2,270
#11 - #12	"	1,750	480.00	2,230
Epoxy coated				
#3 - #4	TON	1,660	770.00	2,430
#5 - #6	"	1,560	680.00	2,240
#7 - #8	"	1,510	600.00	2,110
#9 - #10	"	1,510	550.00	2,060
#11 - #12	"	1,510	500.00	2,010
03210.15 — Column Reinforcing				
Columns				
#3 - #4	TON	1,130	1,640	2,770
#5 - #6	"	990.00	1,280	2,270
#7 - #8	"	940.00	1,150	2,090
#9 - #10	"	940.00	1,040	1,980
#11 - #12	"	940.00	960.00	1,900
#13 - #14	"	940.00	880.00	1,820
#15 - #16	"	940.00	820.00	1,760
Galvanized				
#3 - #4	TON	1,920	1,640	3,560
#5 - #6	"	1,820	1,280	3,100
#7 - #8	"	1,750	1,150	2,900
#9 - #10	"	1,750	1,040	2,790
#11 - #12	"	1,750	960.00	2,710
#13 - #14	"	1,750	880.00	2,630
#15 - #16	"	1,750	820.00	2,570
Epoxy coated				
#3 - #4	TON	1,660	1,910	3,570
#5 - #6	"	1,560	1,440	3,000
#7 - #8	"	1,510	1,280	2,790
#9 - #10	"	1,510	1,150	2,660
#11 - #12	"	1,510	1,040	2,550
#13 - #14	"	1,510	960.00	2,470
#15 - #16	"	1,510	880.00	2,390
Spirals				
8" to 24" dia.	TON	1,750	1,440	3,190
24" to 48" dia.	"	1,750	1,280	3,030
48" to 84" dia.	"	1,920	1,150	3,070

Reinforcement	UNIT	MAT.	INST.	TOTAL
03210.20 Elevated Slab Reinforcing				
Elevated slab				
#3 - #4	TON	1,130	720.00	1,850
#5 - #6	"	990.00	640.00	1,630
#7 - #8	"	940.00	570.00	1,510
#9 - #10	"	940.00	520.00	1,460
#11 - #12	"	940.00	480.00	1,420
Galvanized				
#3 - #4	TON	1,840	720.00	2,560
#5 - #6	"	1,820	640.00	2,460
#7 - #8	"	1,750	570.00	2,320
#9 - #10	"	1,750	520.00	2,270
#11 - #12	"	1,750	480.00	2,230
Epoxy coated				
#3 - #4	TON	1,660	770.00	2,430
#5 - #6	"	1,560	680.00	2,240
#7 - #8	"	1,510	600.00	2,110
#9 - #10	"	1,510	550.00	2,060
#11 - #12	"	1,510	500.00	2,010
03210.25 Equip. Pad Reinforcing				
Equipment pad				
#3 - #4	TON	1,130	1,150	2,280
#5 - #6	"	990.00	1,040	2,030
#7 - #8	"	940.00	960.00	1,900
#9 - #10	"	940.00	880.00	1,820
#11 - #12	"	940.00	820.00	1,760
03210.35 Footing Reinforcing				
Footings				
Grade 50				
#3 - #4	TON	1,130	960.00	2,090
#5 - #6	"	990.00	820.00	1,810
#7 - #8	"	940.00	720.00	1,660
#9 - #10	"	940.00	640.00	1,580
Grade 60				
#3 - #4	TON	1,130	960.00	2,090
#5 - #6	"	990.00	820.00	1,810
#7 - #8	"	940.00	720.00	1,660
#9 - #10	"	940.00	640.00	1,580
Grade 70				
#3 - #4	TON	1,130	960.00	2,090
#5 - #6	"	990.00	820.00	1,810
#7 - #8	"	940.00	720.00	1,660
#9 - #10	"	940.00	640.00	1,580
#11- #12	"	940.00	570.00	1,510
Straight dowels, 24" long				
1" dia. (#8)	EA.	3.50	5.75	9.25
3/4" dia. (#6)	"	3.15	5.75	8.90
5/8" dia. (#5)	"	2.75	4.80	7.55
1/2" dia. (#4)	"	2.05	4.10	6.15

Reinforcement	UNIT	MAT.	INST.	TOTAL
03210.45 — Foundation Reinforcing				
Foundations				
#3 - #4	TON	1,130	960.00	2,090
#5 - #6	"	990.00	820.00	1,810
#7 - #8	"	940.00	720.00	1,660
#9 - #10	"	940.00	640.00	1,580
#11 - #12	"	940.00	570.00	1,510
Galvanized				
#3 - #4	TON	1,920	960.00	2,880
#5 - #6	"	1,820	820.00	2,640
#7 - #8	"	1,750	720.00	2,470
#9 - #10	"	1,750	640.00	2,390
#11 - #12	"	1,750	570.00	2,320
Epoxy Coated				
#3 - #4	TON	1,660	1,040	2,700
#5 - #6	"	1,560	880.00	2,440
#7 - #8	"	1,510	770.00	2,280
#9 - #10	"	1,510	680.00	2,190
#11 - #12	"	1,510	600.00	2,110
03210.50 — Grade Beam Reinforcing				
Grade beams				
#3 - #4	TON	1,130	880.00	2,010
#5 - #6	"	990.00	770.00	1,760
#7 - #8	"	940.00	680.00	1,620
#9 - #10	"	940.00	600.00	1,540
#11 - #12	"	940.00	550.00	1,490
Galvanized				
#3 - #4	TON	1,920	880.00	2,800
#5 - #6	"	1,820	770.00	2,590
#7 - #8	"	1,750	680.00	2,430
#9 - #10	"	1,750	600.00	2,350
#11 - #12	"	1,750	550.00	2,300
Epoxy coated				
#3 - #4	TON	1,660	960.00	2,620
#5 - #6	"	1,560	820.00	2,380
#7 - #8	"	1,510	720.00	2,230
#9 - #10	"	1,510	640.00	2,150
#11 - #12	"	1,510	570.00	2,080
03210.53 — Pile Cap Reinforcing				
Pile caps				
#3 - #4	TON	1,130	1,440	2,570
#5 - #6	"	990.00	1,280	2,270
#7 - #8	"	940.00	1,150	2,090
#9 - #10	"	940.00	1,040	1,980
#11 - #12	"	940.00	960.00	1,900
Galvanized				
#3 - #4	TON	1,920	1,440	3,360
#5 - #6	"	1,820	1,280	3,100
#7 - #8	"	1,750	1,150	2,900
#9 - #10	"	1,750	1,040	2,790
#11 - #12	"	1,750	960.00	2,710

Reinforcement	UNIT	MAT.	INST.	TOTAL
03210.53 Pile Cap Reinforcing				
Epoxy coated				
#3 - #4	TON	1,660	1,640	3,300
#5 - #6	"	1,560	1,440	3,000
#7 - #8	"	1,510	1,280	2,790
#9 - #10	"	1,510	1,150	2,660
#11 - #12	"	1,510	1,040	2,550
03210.55 Slab/mat Reinforcing				
Bars, slabs				
#3 - #4	TON	1,130	960.00	2,090
#5 - #6	"	990.00	820.00	1,810
#7 - #8	"	940.00	720.00	1,660
#9 - #10	"	940.00	640.00	1,580
#11 - #12	"	940.00	570.00	1,510
Galvanized				
#3 - #4	TON	1,920	960.00	2,880
#5 - #6	"	1,820	820.00	2,640
#7 - #8	"	1,750	720.00	2,470
#9 - #10	"	1,750	640.00	2,390
#11 - #12	"	1,750	570.00	2,320
Epoxy coated				
#3 - #4	TON	1,660	1,040	2,700
#5 - #6	"	1,560	880.00	2,440
#7 - #8	"	1,510	770.00	2,280
#9 - #10	"	1,510	680.00	2,190
#11 - #12	"	1,510	600.00	2,110
Wire mesh, slabs				
Galvanized				
4x4				
W1.4xW1.4	S.F.	0.28	0.38	0.66
W2.0xW2.0	"	0.36	0.41	0.77
W2.9xW2.9	"	0.51	0.44	0.95
W4.0xW4.0	"	0.76	0.48	1.24
6x6				
W1.4xW1.4	S.F.	0.26	0.29	0.55
W2.0xW2.0	"	0.36	0.32	0.68
W2.9xW2.9	"	0.50	0.34	0.83
W4.0xW4.0	"	0.53	0.38	0.91
Standard				
2x2				
W.9xW.9	S.F.	0.28	0.38	0.66
4x4				
W1.4xW1.4	S.F.	0.18	0.38	0.56
W2.0xW2.0	"	0.25	0.41	0.66
W2.9xW2.9	"	0.33	0.44	0.77
W4.0xW4.0	"	0.51	0.48	0.99
6x6				
W1.4xW1.4	S.F.	0.12	0.29	0.40
W2.0xW2.0	"	0.17	0.32	0.48
W2.9xW2.9	"	0.25	0.34	0.59
W4.0xW4.0	"	0.35	0.38	0.73

Reinforcement		UNIT	MAT.	INST.	TOTAL
03210.60	Stair Reinforcing				
Stairs					
#3 - #4		TON	1,130	1,150	2,280
#5 - #6		"	990.00	960.00	1,950
#7 - #8		"	940.00	820.00	1,760
#9 - #10		"	940.00	720.00	1,660
Galvanized					
#3 - #4		TON	1,920	1,150	3,070
#5 - #6		"	1,820	960.00	2,780
#7 - #8		"	1,750	820.00	2,570
#9 - #10		"	1,750	720.00	2,470
Epoxy coated					
#3 - #4		TON	1,660	1,280	2,940
#5 - #6		"	1,560	1,040	2,600
#7 - #8		"	1,510	880.00	2,390
#9 - #10		"	1,510	770.00	2,280
03210.65	Wall Reinforcing				
Walls					
#3 - #4		TON	1,130	820.00	1,950
#5 - #6		"	990.00	720.00	1,710
#7 - #8		"	940.00	640.00	1,580
#9 - #10		"	940.00	570.00	1,510
Galvanized					
#3 - #4		TON	1,920	820.00	2,740
#5 - #6		"	1,820	720.00	2,540
#7 - #8		"	1,750	640.00	2,390
#9 - #10		"	1,750	570.00	2,320
Epoxy coated					
#3 - #4		TON	1,660	880.00	2,540
#5 - #6		"	1,560	770.00	2,330
#7 - #8		"	1,510	680.00	2,190
#9 - #10		"	1,510	600.00	2,110
Masonry wall (horizontal)					
#3 - #4		TON	1,130	2,300	3,430
#5 - #6		"	990.00	1,910	2,900
Galvanized					
#3 - #4		TON	1,920	2,300	4,220
#5 - #6		"	1,820	1,910	3,730
Masonry wall (vertical)					
#3 - #4		TON	1,130	2,870	4,000
#5 - #6		"	990.00	2,300	3,290
Galvanized					
#3 - #4		TON	1,920	2,870	4,790
#5 - #6		"	1,820	2,300	4,120

Accessories	UNIT	MAT.	INST.	TOTAL
03250.40 Concrete Accessories				
Expansion joint, poured				
Asphalt				
1/2" x 1"	L.F.	0.69	0.80	1.49
1" x 2"	"	2.10	0.87	2.97
Liquid neoprene, cold applied				
1/2" x 1"	L.F.	2.50	0.82	3.32
1" x 2"	"	10.30	0.89	11.19
Polyurethane, 2 parts				
1/2" x 1"	L.F.	2.35	1.35	3.70
1" x 2"	"	9.65	1.45	11.10
Rubberized asphalt, cold				
1/2" x 1"	L.F.	0.58	0.80	1.38
1" x 2"	"	1.80	0.87	2.67
Hot, fuel resistant				
1/2" x 1"	L.F.	1.10	0.80	1.90
1" x 2"	"	5.35	0.87	6.22
Expansion joint, premolded, in slabs				
Asphalt				
1/2" x 6"	L.F.	0.77	1.00	1.77
1" x 12"	"	1.30	1.35	2.65
Cork				
1/2" x 6"	L.F.	1.55	1.00	2.55
1" x 12"	"	5.95	1.35	7.30
Neoprene sponge				
1/2" x 6"	L.F.	2.35	1.00	3.35
1" x 12"	"	8.50	1.35	9.85
Polyethylene foam				
1/2" x 6"	L.F.	0.89	1.00	1.89
1" x 12"	"	4.25	1.35	5.60
Polyurethane foam				
1/2" x 6"	L.F.	1.15	1.00	2.15
1" x 12"	"	2.60	1.35	3.95
Polyvinyl chloride foam				
1/2" x 6"	L.F.	2.50	1.00	3.50
1" x 12"	"	9.10	1.35	10.45
Rubber, gray sponge				
1/2" x 6"	L.F.	4.05	1.00	5.05
1" x 12"	"	17.15	1.35	18.50
Asphalt felt control joints or bond breaker, screed joints				
4" slab	L.F.	1.10	0.80	1.90
6" slab	"	1.40	0.89	2.29
8" slab	"	1.85	1.00	2.85
10" slab	"	2.60	1.15	3.75
Keyed cold expansion and control joints, 24 ga.				
4" slab	L.F.	0.96	2.50	3.46
5" slab	"	1.20	2.50	3.70
6" slab	"	1.40	2.65	4.05
8" slab	"	1.75	2.85	4.60
10" slab	"	1.95	3.10	5.05
Waterstops				
Polyvinyl chloride				
Ribbed				

Accessories	UNIT	MAT.	INST.	TOTAL
03250.40 — Concrete Accessories				
3/16" thick x				
4" wide	L.F.	1.60	2.00	3.60
6" wide	"	1.90	2.20	4.10
1/2" thick x				
9" wide	L.F.	5.30	2.50	7.80
Ribbed with center bulb				
3/16" thick x 9" wide	L.F.	4.50	2.50	7.00
3/8" thick x 9" wide	"	5.50	2.50	8.00
Dumbbell type, 3/8" thick x 6" wide	"	5.50	2.20	7.70
Plain, 3/8" thick x 9" wide	"	6.80	2.50	9.30
Center bulb, 3/8" thick x 9" wide	"	9.10	2.50	11.60
Rubber				
Flat dumbbell				
3/8" thick x				
6" wide	L.F.	8.85	2.20	11.05
9" wide	"	13.95	2.50	16.45
Center bulb				
3/8" thick x				
6" wide	L.F.	8.25	2.20	10.45
9" wide	"	16.70	2.50	19.20
Vapor barrier				
4 mil polyethylene	S.F.	0.04	0.13	0.17
6 mil polyethylene	"	0.06	0.13	0.19
Gravel porous fill, under floor slabs, 3/4" stone	C.Y.	21.60	66.50	88.10
Reinforcing accessories				
Beam bolsters				
1-1/2" high, plain	L.F.	0.47	0.57	1.05
Galvanized	"	0.59	0.57	1.16
3" high				
Plain	L.F.	1.10	0.72	1.82
Galvanized	"	1.20	0.72	1.92
Slab bolsters				
1" high				
Plain	L.F.	0.31	0.29	0.60
Galvanized	"	0.44	0.29	0.73
2" high				
Plain	L.F.	0.44	0.32	0.76
Galvanized	"	0.50	0.32	0.82
Chairs, high chairs				
3" high				
Plain	EA.	0.51	1.45	1.96
Galvanized	"	0.67	1.45	2.12
5" high				
Plain	EA.	0.67	1.50	2.17
Galvanized	"	0.83	1.50	2.33
8" high				
Plain	EA.	1.35	1.65	3.00
Galvanized	"	1.80	1.65	3.45
12" high				
Plain	EA.	2.90	1.90	4.80
Galvanized	"	3.45	1.90	5.35
Continuous, high chair				

Accessories	UNIT	MAT.	INST.	TOTAL
03250.40	**Concrete Accessories**			
3" high				
Plain	L.F.	0.60	0.38	0.98
Galvanized	"	0.73	0.38	1.11
5" high				
Plain	L.F.	0.90	0.41	1.31
Galvanized	"	1.20	0.41	1.61
8" high				
Plain	L.F.	1.20	0.44	1.64
Galvanized	"	1.60	0.44	2.04
12" high				
Plain	L.F.	2.60	0.48	3.08
Galvanized	"	3.10	0.48	3.58

Cast-in-place Concrete	UNIT	MAT.	INST.	TOTAL
03300.10	**Concrete Admixtures**			
Concrete admixtures				
Water reducing admixture	GAL			15.83
Set retarder	"			28.37
Air entraining agent	"			9.65
03350.10	**Concrete Finishes**			
Floor finishes				
Broom	S.F.		0.57	0.57
Screed	"		0.50	0.50
Darby	"		0.50	0.50
Steel float	"		0.67	0.67
Granolithic topping				
1/2" thick	S.F.	0.25	1.80	2.05
1" thick	"	0.47	2.00	2.47
2" thick	"	0.80	2.20	3.00
Wall finishes				
Burlap rub, with cement paste	S.F.	0.06	0.67	0.72
Float finish	"	0.08	1.00	1.08
Etch with acid	"	0.30	0.67	0.96
Sandblast				
Minimum	S.F.	0.06	1.05	1.11
Maximum	"	0.39	1.05	1.44
Bush hammer				
Green concrete	S.F.		2.00	2.00
Cured concrete	"		3.10	3.10
Break ties and patch holes	"		0.80	0.80
Carborundum				
Dry rub	S.F.		1.35	1.35
Wet rub	"		2.00	2.00
Floor hardeners				

Cast-in-place Concrete

	UNIT	MAT.	INST.	TOTAL
03350.10 Concrete Finishes				
Metallic				
Light service	S.F.	0.26	0.50	0.76
Heavy service	"	0.87	0.67	1.54
Non-metallic				
Light service	S.F.	0.14	0.50	0.64
Heavy service	"	0.63	0.67	1.29
Rusticated concrete finish				
Beveled edge	L.F.	0.31	2.20	2.51
Square edge	"	0.42	2.85	3.27
Solid board concrete finish				
Standard	S.F.	0.79	3.35	4.14
Rustic	"	0.70	4.00	4.70
03360.10 Pneumatic Concrete				
Pneumatic applied concrete (gunite)				
2" thick	S.F.	4.75	2.65	7.40
3" thick	"	5.90	3.55	9.45
4" thick	"	7.05	4.30	11.35
Finish surface				
Minimum	S.F.		2.60	2.60
Maximum	"		5.15	5.15
03370.10 Curing Concrete				
Sprayed membrane				
Slabs	S.F.	0.04	0.08	0.12
Walls	"	0.07	0.10	0.17
Curing paper				
Slabs	S.F.	0.07	0.11	0.17
Walls	"	0.07	0.12	0.18
Burlap				
7.5 oz.	S.F.	0.06	0.13	0.19
12 oz.	"	0.08	0.14	0.22

Placing Concrete

	UNIT	MAT.	INST.	TOTAL
03380.05 Beam Concrete				
Beams and girders				
2500# or 3000# concrete				
By crane	C.Y.	98.00	77.50	175.50
By pump	"	98.00	70.50	168.50
By hand buggy	"	98.00	40.00	138.00
3500# or 4000# concrete				
By crane	C.Y.	100.00	77.50	177.50
By pump	"	100.00	70.50	170.50
By hand buggy	"	100.00	40.00	140.00
5000# concrete				

03 CONCRETE

Placing Concrete	UNIT	MAT.	INST.	TOTAL
03380.05 Beam Concrete				
By crane	C.Y.	110.00	77.50	187.50
By pump	"	110.00	70.50	180.50
By hand buggy	"	110.00	40.00	150.00
Bond beam, 3000# concrete				
By pump				
8" high				
4" wide	L.F.	0.27	1.55	1.82
6" wide	"	0.65	1.75	2.40
8" wide	"	0.84	1.95	2.79
10" wide	"	1.10	2.15	3.25
12" wide	"	1.50	2.40	3.90
16" high				
8" wide	L.F.	2.05	2.40	4.45
10" wide	"	2.75	2.75	5.50
12" wide	"	3.65	3.25	6.90
By crane				
8" high				
4" wide	L.F.	0.32	1.70	2.02
6" wide	"	0.62	1.85	2.46
8" wide	"	0.79	1.95	2.74
10" wide	"	1.05	2.15	3.20
12" wide	"	1.40	2.40	3.80
16" high				
8" wide	L.F.	1.95	2.40	4.35
10" wide	"	2.60	2.60	5.20
12" wide	"	3.40	3.00	6.40
03380.15 Column Concrete				
Columns				
2500# or 3000# concrete				
By crane	C.Y.	98.00	70.50	168.50
By pump	"	98.00	64.50	162.50
3500# or 4000# concrete				
By crane	C.Y.	100.00	70.50	170.50
By pump	"	100.00	64.50	164.50
5000# concrete				
By crane	C.Y.	110.00	70.50	180.50
By pump	"	110.00	64.50	174.50
03380.20 Elevated Slab Concrete				
Elevated slab				
2500# or 3000# concrete				
By crane	C.Y.	98.00	38.80	136.80
By pump	"	98.00	29.80	127.80
By hand buggy	"	98.00	40.00	138.00
3500# or 4000# concrete				
By crane	C.Y.	100.00	38.80	138.80
By pump	"	100.00	29.80	129.80
By hand buggy	"	100.00	40.00	140.00
5000# concrete				
By crane	C.Y.	110.00	38.80	148.80
By pump	"	110.00	29.80	139.80

Placing Concrete	UNIT	MAT.	INST.	TOTAL
03380.20 Elevated Slab Concrete				
By hand buggy	C.Y.	110.00	40.00	150.00
Topping				
2500# or 3000# concrete				
By crane	C.Y.	98.00	38.80	136.80
By pump	"	98.00	29.80	127.80
By hand buggy	"	98.00	40.00	138.00
3500# or 4000# concrete				
By crane	C.Y.	100.00	38.80	138.80
By pump	"	100.00	29.80	129.80
By hand buggy	"	100.00	40.00	140.00
5000# concrete				
By crane	C.Y.	110.00	38.80	148.80
By pump	"	110.00	29.80	139.80
By hand buggy	"	110.00	40.00	150.00
03380.25 Equipment Pad Concrete				
Equipment pad				
2500# or 3000# concrete				
By chute	C.Y.	98.00	13.35	111.35
By pump	"	98.00	55.50	153.50
By crane	"	98.00	64.50	162.50
3500# or 4000# concrete				
By chute	C.Y.	100.00	13.35	113.35
By pump	"	100.00	55.50	155.50
By crane	"	100.00	64.50	164.50
5000# concrete				
By chute	C.Y.	110.00	13.35	123.35
By pump	"	110.00	55.50	165.50
By crane	"	110.00	64.50	174.50
03380.35 Footing Concrete				
Continuous footing				
2500# or 3000# concrete				
By chute	C.Y.	98.00	13.35	111.35
By pump	"	98.00	48.50	146.50
By crane	"	98.00	55.50	153.50
3500# or 4000# concrete				
By chute	C.Y.	100.00	13.35	113.35
By pump	"	100.00	48.50	148.50
By crane	"	100.00	55.50	155.50
5000# concrete				
By chute	C.Y.	110.00	13.35	123.35
By pump	"	110.00	48.50	158.50
By crane	"	110.00	55.50	165.50
Spread footing				
2500# or 3000# concrete				
Under 5 cy				
By chute	C.Y.	98.00	13.35	111.35
By pump	"	98.00	51.50	149.50
By crane	"	98.00	59.50	157.50
Over 5 cy				
By chute	C.Y.	98.00	10.00	108.00

Placing Concrete	UNIT	MAT.	INST.	TOTAL
03380.35 Footing Concrete				
By pump	C.Y.	98.00	45.60	143.60
By crane	"	98.00	51.50	149.50
3500# or 4000# concrete				
Under 5 c.y.				
By chute	C.Y.	100.00	13.35	113.35
By pump	"	100.00	51.50	151.50
By crane	"	100.00	59.50	159.50
Over 5 c.y.				
By chute	C.Y.	100.00	10.00	110.00
By pump	"	100.00	45.60	145.60
By crane	"	100.00	51.50	151.50
5000# concrete				
Under 5 c.y.				
By chute	C.Y.	110.00	13.35	123.35
By pump	"	110.00	51.50	161.50
By crane	"	110.00	59.50	169.50
Over 5 c.y.				
By chute	C.Y.	110.00	10.00	120.00
By pump	"	110.00	45.60	155.60
By crane	"	110.00	51.50	161.50
03380.50 Grade Beam Concrete				
Grade beam				
2500# or 3000# concrete				
By chute	C.Y.	98.00	13.35	111.35
By crane	"	98.00	55.50	153.50
By pump	"	98.00	48.50	146.50
By hand buggy	"	98.00	40.00	138.00
3500# or 4000# concrete				
By chute	C.Y.	100.00	13.35	113.35
By crane	"	100.00	55.50	155.50
By pump	"	100.00	48.50	148.50
By hand buggy	"	100.00	40.00	140.00
5000# concrete				
By chute	C.Y.	110.00	13.35	123.35
By crane	"	110.00	55.50	165.50
By pump	"	110.00	48.50	158.50
By hand buggy	"	110.00	40.00	150.00
03380.53 Pile Cap Concrete				
Pile cap				
2500# or 3000 concrete				
By chute	C.Y.	98.00	13.35	111.35
By crane	"	98.00	64.50	162.50
By pump	"	98.00	55.50	153.50
By hand buggy	"	98.00	40.00	138.00
3500# or 4000# concrete				
By chute	C.Y.	100.00	13.35	113.35
By crane	"	100.00	64.50	164.50
By pump	"	100.00	55.50	155.50
By hand buggy	"	100.00	40.00	140.00
5000# concrete				

Placing Concrete	UNIT	MAT.	INST.	TOTAL
03380.53 Pile Cap Concrete				
By chute	C.Y.	110.00	13.35	123.35
By crane	"	110.00	64.50	174.50
By pump	"	110.00	55.50	165.50
By hand buggy	"	110.00	40.00	150.00
03380.55 Slab/mat Concrete				
Slab on grade				
2500# or 3000# concrete				
By chute	C.Y.	98.00	10.00	108.00
By crane	"	98.00	32.30	130.30
By pump	"	98.00	27.70	125.70
By hand buggy	"	98.00	26.70	124.70
3500# or 4000# concrete				
By chute	C.Y.	100.00	10.00	110.00
By crane	"	100.00	32.30	132.30
By pump	"	100.00	27.70	127.70
By hand buggy	"	100.00	26.70	126.70
5000# concrete				
By chute	C.Y.	110.00	10.00	120.00
By crane	"	110.00	32.30	142.30
By pump	"	110.00	27.70	137.70
By hand buggy	"	110.00	26.70	136.70
Foundation mat				
2500# or 3000# concrete, over 20 cy				
By chute	C.Y.	98.00	8.00	106.00
By crane	"	98.00	27.70	125.70
By pump	"	98.00	24.25	122.25
By hand buggy	"	98.00	20.00	118.00
03380.58 Sidewalks				
Walks, cast in place with wire mesh, base not incl.				
4" thick	S.F.	1.35	1.35	2.70
5" thick	"	1.80	1.60	3.40
6" thick	"	2.25	2.00	4.25
03380.60 Stair Concrete				
Stairs				
2500# or 3000# concrete				
By chute	C.Y.	98.00	13.35	111.35
By crane	"	98.00	64.50	162.50
By pump	"	98.00	55.50	153.50
By hand buggy	"	98.00	40.00	138.00
3500# or 4000# concrete				
By chute	C.Y.	100.00	13.35	113.35
By crane	"	100.00	64.50	164.50
By pump	"	100.00	55.50	155.50
By hand buggy	"	100.00	40.00	140.00
5000# concrete				
By chute	C.Y.	110.00	13.35	123.35
By crane	"	110.00	64.50	174.50
By pump	"	110.00	55.50	165.50
By hand buggy	"	110.00	40.00	150.00

Placing Concrete	UNIT	MAT.	INST.	TOTAL
03380.65 Wall Concrete				
Walls				
2500# or 3000# concrete				
To 4'				
By chute	C.Y.	98.00	11.45	109.45
By crane	"	98.00	64.50	162.50
By pump	"	98.00	59.50	157.50
To 8'				
By crane	C.Y.	98.00	70.50	168.50
By pump	"	98.00	64.50	162.50
To 16'				
By crane	C.Y.	98.00	77.50	175.50
By pump	"	98.00	70.50	168.50
Over 16'				
By crane	C.Y.	98.00	86.00	184.00
By pump	"	98.00	77.50	175.50
3500# or 4000# concrete				
To 4'				
By chute	C.Y.	100.00	11.45	111.45
By crane	"	100.00	64.50	164.50
By pump	"	100.00	59.50	159.50
To 8'				
By crane	C.Y.	100.00	70.50	170.50
By pump	"	100.00	64.50	164.50
To 16'				
By crane	C.Y.	100.00	77.50	177.50
By pump	"	100.00	70.50	170.50
Over 16'				
By crane	C.Y.	100.00	86.00	186.00
By pump	"	100.00	77.50	177.50
5000# concrete				
To 4'				
By chute	C.Y.	110.00	11.45	121.45
By crane	"	110.00	64.50	174.50
By pump	"	110.00	59.50	169.50
To 8'				
By crane	C.Y.	110.00	70.50	180.50
By pump	"	110.00	64.50	174.50
To 16'				
By crane	C.Y.	110.00	77.50	187.50
By pump	"	110.00	70.50	180.50
Filled block (CMU)				
3000# concrete, by pump				
4" wide	S.F.	0.37	2.75	3.12
6" wide	"	0.85	3.25	4.10
8" wide	"	1.30	3.90	5.20
10" wide	"	1.75	4.55	6.30
12" wide	"	2.25	5.55	7.80
Pilasters, 3000# concrete	C.F.	5.15	77.50	82.65
Wall cavity, 2" thick, 3000# concrete	S.F.	0.95	2.60	3.55

Precast Concrete	UNIT	MAT.	INST.	TOTAL
03400.10 Precast Beams				
Prestressed, double tee, 24" deep, 8' wide				
35' span				
115 psf	S.F.	9.20	1.05	10.25
140 psf	"	9.75	1.05	10.80
40' span				
80 psf	S.F.	8.85	1.15	10.00
143 psf	"	9.40	1.15	10.55
45' span				
50 psf	S.F.	8.45	0.98	9.43
70 psf	"	9.05	0.98	10.03
100 psf	"	9.20	0.98	10.18
130 psf	"	10.15	0.98	11.13
50' span				
75 psf	S.F.	8.45	0.89	9.34
100 psf	"	9.20	0.89	10.09
Precast beams, girders and joists				
1000 lb/lf live load				
10' span	L.F.	78.00	21.30	99.30
20' span	"	82.50	12.80	95.30
30' span	"	100.00	10.65	110.65
3000 lb/lf live load				
10' span	L.F.	81.50	21.30	102.80
20' span	"	92.50	12.80	105.30
30' span	"	120.00	10.65	130.65
5000 lb/lf live load				
10' span	L.F.	83.50	21.30	104.80
20' span	"	110.00	12.80	122.80
30' span	"	140.00	10.65	150.65
03400.20 Precast Columns				
Prestressed concrete columns				
10" x 10"				
10' long	EA.	220.00	130.00	350.00
15' long	"	340.00	130.00	470.00
20' long	"	450.00	140.00	590.00
25' long	"	580.00	150.00	730.00
30' long	"	690.00	160.00	850.00
12" x 12"				
20' long	EA.	620.00	160.00	780.00
25' long	"	750.00	170.00	920.00
30' long	"	960.00	180.00	1,140
16" x 16"				
20' long	EA.	960.00	160.00	1,120
25' long	"	1,410	170.00	1,580
30' long	"	1,670	180.00	1,850
20" x 20"				
20' long	EA.	1,720	170.00	1,890
25' long	"	2,350	180.00	2,530
30' long	"	2,760	190.00	2,950
24" x 24"				
20' long	EA.	2,630	180.00	2,810
25' long	"	3,190	190.00	3,380

Precast Concrete	UNIT	MAT.	INST.	TOTAL
03400.20		Precast Columns		
30' long	EA.	3,940	200.00	4,140
28" x 28"				
20' long	EA.	3,570	200.00	3,770
25' long	"	4,320	210.00	4,530
30' long	"	5,350	230.00	5,580
32" x 32"				
20' long	EA.	4,510	210.00	4,720
25' long	"	5,820	230.00	6,050
30' long	"	6,670	250.00	6,920
36" x 36"				
20' long	EA.	5,630	230.00	5,860
25' long	"	7,040	250.00	7,290
30' long	"	8,450	270.00	8,720
03400.30		Precast Slabs		
Prestressed flat slab				
6" thick, 4' wide				
20' span				
80 psf	S.F.	13.45	2.65	16.10
110 psf	"	13.50	2.65	16.15
25' span				
80 psf	S.F.	14.10	2.55	16.65
Cored slab				
6" thick, 4' wide				
20' span				
80 psf	S.F.	7.05	2.65	9.70
100 psf	"	7.20	2.65	9.85
130 psf	"	7.35	2.65	10.00
8" thick, 4' wide				
25' span				
70 psf	S.F.	7.05	2.55	9.60
125 psf	"	7.50	2.55	10.05
170 psf	"	7.40	2.55	9.95
30' span				
70 psf	S.F.	7.05	2.15	9.20
90 psf	"	7.50	2.15	9.65
35' span				
70 psf	S.F.	7.40	2.00	9.40
10" thick, 4' wide				
30' span				
75 psf	S.F.	7.40	2.15	9.55
100 psf	"	7.60	2.15	9.75
130 psf	"	7.80	2.15	9.95
35' span				
60 psf	S.F.	7.60	2.00	9.60
80 psf	"	7.80	2.00	9.80
120 psf	"	8.15	2.00	10.15
40' span				
65 psf	S.F.	8.15	1.60	9.75
Slabs, roof and floor members, 4' wide				
6" thick, 25' span	S.F.	6.50	2.55	9.05
8" thick, 30' span	"	7.50	1.95	9.45

Precast Concrete	UNIT	MAT.	INST.	TOTAL
03400.30 — Precast Slabs				
10" thick, 40' span	S.F.	9.20	1.75	10.95
Tee members				
Multiple tee, roof and floor				
Minimum	S.F.	8.50	1.60	10.10
Maximum	"	10.70	3.20	13.90
Double tee wall member				
Minimum	S.F.	7.80	1.85	9.65
Maximum	"	9.90	3.55	13.45
Single tee				
Short span, roof members				
Minimum	S.F.	8.80	1.95	10.75
Maximum	"	10.90	4.00	14.90
Long span, roof members				
Minimum	S.F.	11.10	1.60	12.70
Maximum	"	13.25	3.20	16.45
03400.40 — Precast Walls				
Wall panel, 8' x 20'				
Gray cement				
Liner finish				
4" wall	S.F.	10.30	1.85	12.15
5" wall	"	11.05	1.90	12.95
6" wall	"	12.65	1.95	14.60
8" wall	"	13.10	2.00	15.10
Sandblast finish				
4" wall	S.F.	11.85	1.85	13.70
5" wall	"	12.95	1.90	14.85
6" wall	"	14.20	1.95	16.15
8" wall	"	14.85	2.00	16.85
White cement				
Liner finish				
4" wall	S.F.	12.50	1.85	14.35
5" wall	"	13.25	1.90	15.15
6" wall	"	14.55	1.95	16.50
8" wall	"	15.50	2.00	17.50
Sandblast finish				
4" wall	S.F.	13.45	1.85	15.30
5" wall	"	14.20	1.90	16.10
6" wall	"	14.55	1.95	16.50
8" wall	"	16.10	2.00	18.10
Double tee wall panel, 24" deep				
Gray cement				
Liner finish	S.F.	7.40	2.15	9.55
Sandblast finish	"	9.35	2.15	11.50
White cement				
Form liner finish	S.F.	10.40	2.15	12.55
Sandblast finish	"	13.40	2.15	15.55
Partition panels				
4" wall	S.F.	11.10	2.15	13.25
5" wall	"	12.05	2.15	14.20
6" wall	"	13.25	2.15	15.40
8" wall	"	14.30	2.15	16.45

4

Precast Concrete	UNIT	MAT.	INST.	TOTAL
03400.40 Precast Walls				
Cladding panels				
4" wall	S.F.	11.05	2.30	13.35
5" wall	"	12.05	2.30	14.35
6" wall	"	13.35	2.30	15.65
8" wall	"	14.15	2.30	16.45
Sandwich panel, 2.5" cladding panel, 2" insulation				
5" wall	S.F.	16.30	2.30	18.60
6" wall	"	17.10	2.30	19.40
8" wall	"	18.05	2.30	20.35
Adjustable tilt-up brace	EA.		10.00	10.00
03400.90 Precast Specialties				
Precast concrete, coping, 4' to 8' long				
12" wide	L.F.	7.45	5.35	12.80
10" wide	"	6.60	6.10	12.70
Splash block, 30"x12"x4"	EA.	11.05	35.60	46.65
Stair unit, per riser	"	72.50	35.60	108.10
Sun screen and trellis, 8' long, 12" high				
4" thick blades	EA.	79.50	26.70	106.20
5" thick blades	"	98.00	26.70	124.70
6" thick blades	"	120.00	28.50	148.50
8" thick blades	"	160.00	28.50	188.50
Bearing pads for precast members, 2" wide strips				
1/8" thick	L.F.	0.26	0.16	0.42
1/4" thick	"	0.36	0.16	0.52
1/2" thick	"	0.39	0.16	0.55
3/4" thick	"	0.78	0.18	0.96
1" thick	"	0.82	0.20	1.02
1-1/2" thick	"	1.00	0.20	1.20

Cementitous Toppings	UNIT	MAT.	INST.	TOTAL
03550.10 Concrete Toppings				
Gypsum fill				
2" thick	S.F.	1.60	0.40	2.00
2-1/2" thick	"	1.85	0.41	2.26
3" thick	"	2.25	0.42	2.67
3-1/2" thick	"	2.60	0.43	3.03
4" thick	"	3.00	0.49	3.49
Formboard				
Mineral fiber board				
1" thick	S.F.	1.45	1.00	2.45
1-1/2" thick	"	3.80	1.15	4.95
Cement fiber board				
1" thick	S.F.	1.10	1.35	2.45
1-1/2" thick	"	1.45	1.55	3.00

Cementitous Toppings	UNIT	MAT.	INST.	TOTAL
03550.10 Concrete Toppings				
Glass fiber board				
1" thick	S.F.	1.70	1.00	2.70
1-1/2" thick	"	2.30	1.15	3.45
Poured deck				
Vermiculite or perlite				
1 to 4 mix	C.Y.	150.00	64.50	214.50
1 to 6 mix	"	140.00	59.50	199.50
Vermiculite or perlite				
2" thick				
1 to 4 mix	S.F.	1.45	0.41	1.86
1 to 6 mix	"	1.05	0.37	1.42
3" thick				
1 to 4 mix	S.F.	1.95	0.60	2.55
1 to 6 mix	"	1.55	0.55	2.10
Concrete plank, lightweight				
2" thick	S.F.	7.45	3.20	10.65
2-1/2" thick	"	7.65	3.20	10.85
3-1/2" thick	"	7.95	3.55	11.50
4" thick	"	8.30	3.55	11.85
Channel slab, lightweight, straight				
2-3/4" thick	S.F.	6.00	3.20	9.20
3-1/2" thick	"	6.30	3.20	9.50
3-3/4" thick	"	6.65	3.20	9.85
4-3/4" thick	"	8.45	3.55	12.00
Gypsum plank				
2" thick	S.F.	2.90	3.20	6.10
3" thick	"	3.05	3.20	6.25
Cement fiber, T and G planks				
1" thick	S.F.	1.55	2.90	4.45
1-1/2" thick	"	1.65	2.90	4.55
2" thick	"	1.90	3.20	5.10
2-1/2" thick	"	2.00	3.20	5.20
3" thick	"	2.65	3.20	5.85
3-1/2" thick	"	3.00	3.55	6.55
4" thick	"	3.40	3.55	6.95

Grout	UNIT	MAT.	INST.	TOTAL
03600.10 Grouting				
Grouting for bases				
Nonshrink				
Metallic grout				
1" deep	S.F.	6.55	10.30	16.85
2" deep	"	12.35	11.45	23.80
Non-metallic grout				
1" deep	S.F.	4.85	10.30	15.15

Grout	UNIT	MAT.	INST.	TOTAL
03600.10 Grouting				
2" deep	S.F.	9.40	11.45	20.85
Fluid type				
Non-metallic				
1" deep	S.F.	4.85	10.30	15.15
2" deep	"	9.05	11.45	20.50
Grouting for joints				
Portland cement grout (1 cement to 3 sand, by volume)				
1/2" joint thickness				
6" wide joints	L.F.	0.12	1.70	1.82
8" wide joints	"	0.17	2.05	2.22
1" joint thickness				
4" wide joints	L.F.	0.17	1.60	1.77
6" wide joints	"	0.29	1.80	2.09
8" wide joints	"	0.35	2.15	2.50
Nonshrink, nonmetallic grout				
1/2" joint thickness				
4" wide joint	L.F.	0.81	1.45	2.26
6" wide joint	"	1.15	1.70	2.85
8" wide joint	"	1.55	2.05	3.60
1" joint thickness				
4" wide joint	L.F.	1.55	1.60	3.15
6" wide joint	"	2.35	1.80	4.15
8" wide joint	"	3.10	2.15	5.25

Concrete Restoration	UNIT	MAT.	INST.	TOTAL
03730.10 Concrete Repair				
Epoxy grout floor patch, 1/4" thick	S.F.	5.80	4.00	9.80
Grout, epoxy, 2 component system	C.F.			279.14
Epoxy sand	BAG			18.91
Epoxy modifier	GAL			121.27
Epoxy gel grout	S.F.	2.80	40.00	42.80
Injection valve, 1 way, threaded plastic	EA.	7.75	8.00	15.75
Grout crack seal, 2 component	C.F.	650.00	40.00	690.00
Grout, non shrink	"	66.50	40.00	106.50
Concrete, epoxy modified				
Sand mix	C.F.	110.00	16.00	126.00
Gravel mix	"	81.00	14.80	95.80
Concrete repair				
Soffit repair				
16" wide	L.F.	3.35	8.00	11.35
18" wide	"	3.50	8.35	11.85
24" wide	"	4.15	8.90	13.05
30" wide	"	4.75	9.50	14.25
32" wide	"	5.10	10.00	15.10
Edge repair				

Concrete Restoration	UNIT	MAT.	INST.	TOTAL
03730.10		Concrete Repair		
2" spall	L.F.	1.60	10.00	11.60
3" spall	"	1.60	10.55	12.15
4" spall	"	1.70	10.80	12.50
6" spall	"	1.75	11.10	12.85
8" spall	"	1.85	11.75	13.60
9" spall	"	1.90	13.35	15.25
Crack repair, 1/8" crack	"	3.10	4.00	7.10
Reinforcing steel repair				
1 bar, 4 ft				
#4 bar	L.F.	0.45	7.15	7.60
#5 bar	"	0.63	7.15	7.78
#6 bar	"	0.77	7.65	8.42
#8 bar	"	1.40	7.65	9.05
#9 bar	"	1.75	8.20	9.95
#11 bar	"	2.75	8.20	10.95
Form fabric, nylon				
18" diameter	L.F.			11.77
20" diameter	"			11.98
24" diameter	"			19.68
30" diameter	"			20.22
36" diameter	"			23.19
Pile repairs				
Polyethylene wrap				
30 mil thick				
60" wide	S.F.	12.65	13.35	26.00
72" wide	"	13.75	16.00	29.75
60 mil thick				
60" wide	S.F.	15.20	13.35	28.55
80" wide	"	17.55	18.20	35.75
Pile spall, average repair 3'				
18" x 18"	EA.	39.50	33.30	72.80
20" x 20"	"	52.50	40.00	92.50

Mortar And Grout	UNIT	MAT.	INST.	TOTAL
04100.10 — Masonry Grout				
Grout, non shrink, non-metallic, trowelable	C.F.	13.05	1.45	14.50
Grout door frame, hollow metal				
Single	EA.	19.00	53.50	72.50
Double	"	28.40	56.50	84.90
Grout-filled concrete block (CMU)				
4" wide	S.F.	0.55	1.80	2.35
6" wide	"	1.15	1.95	3.10
8" wide	"	2.00	2.15	4.15
12" wide	"	2.85	2.25	5.10
Grout-filled individual CMU cells				
4" wide	L.F.	0.29	1.05	1.34
6" wide	"	0.60	1.05	1.65
8" wide	"	0.79	1.05	1.84
10" wide	"	1.05	1.20	2.25
12" wide	"	1.20	1.20	2.40
Bond beams or lintels, 8" deep				
6" thick	L.F.	1.20	1.75	2.95
8" thick	"	1.55	1.95	3.50
10" thick	"	1.90	2.15	4.05
12" thick	"	2.20	2.40	4.60
Cavity walls				
2" thick	S.F.	1.30	2.60	3.90
3" thick	"	1.95	2.60	4.55
4" thick	"	2.60	2.75	5.35
6" thick	"	3.90	3.25	7.15
04150.10 — Masonry Accessories				
Foundation vents	EA.	27.10	19.95	47.05
Bar reinforcing				
Horizontal				
#3 - #4	Lb.	0.53	2.00	2.53
#5 - #6	"	0.50	1.65	2.15
Vertical				
#3 - #4	Lb.	0.53	2.50	3.03
#5 - #6	"	0.50	2.00	2.50
Horizontal joint reinforcing				
Truss type				
4" wide, 6" wall	L.F.	0.21	0.20	0.41
6" wide, 8" wall	"	0.21	0.21	0.41
8" wide, 10" wall	"	0.25	0.22	0.47
10" wide, 12" wall	"	0.25	0.23	0.48
12" wide, 14" wall	"	0.31	0.24	0.55
Ladder type				
4" wide, 6" wall	L.F.	0.15	0.20	0.35
6" wide, 8" wall	"	0.16	0.21	0.37
8" wide, 10" wall	"	0.18	0.22	0.39
10" wide, 12" wall	"	0.21	0.22	0.42
Rectangular wall ties				
3/16" dia., galvanized				
2" x 6"	EA.	0.22	0.83	1.05
2" x 8"	"	0.24	0.83	1.07
2" x 10"	"	0.27	0.83	1.10

Mortar And Grout	UNIT	MAT.	INST.	TOTAL
04150.10 Masonry Accessories				
2" x 12"	EA.	0.31	0.83	1.14
4" x 6"	"	0.25	1.00	1.25
4" x 8"	"	0.28	1.00	1.28
4" x 10"	"	0.37	1.00	1.37
4" x 12"	"	0.43	1.00	1.42
1/4" dia., galvanized				
2" x 6"	EA.	0.41	0.83	1.24
2" x 8"	"	0.46	0.83	1.29
2" x 10"	"	0.52	0.83	1.35
2" x 12"	"	0.59	0.83	1.42
4" x 6"	"	0.47	1.00	1.47
4" x 8"	"	0.52	1.00	1.51
4" x 10"	"	0.59	1.00	1.59
4" x 12"	"	0.62	1.00	1.62
"Z" type wall ties, galvanized				
6" long				
1/8" dia.	EA.	0.22	0.83	1.05
3/16" dia.	"	0.24	0.83	1.07
1/4" dia.	"	0.25	0.83	1.08
8" long				
1/8" dia.	EA.	0.24	0.83	1.07
3/16" dia.	"	0.25	0.83	1.08
1/4" dia.	"	0.27	0.83	1.10
10" long				
1/8" dia.	EA.	0.25	0.83	1.08
3/16" dia.	"	0.28	0.83	1.11
1/4" dia.	"	0.32	0.83	1.15
Dovetail anchor slots				
Galvanized steel, filled				
24 ga.	L.F.	0.59	1.25	1.84
20 ga.	"	0.74	1.25	1.99
16 oz. copper, foam filled	"	1.45	1.25	2.70
Dovetail anchors				
16 ga.				
3-1/2" long	EA.	0.18	0.83	1.01
5-1/2" long	"	0.21	0.83	1.04
12 ga.				
3-1/2" long	EA.	0.22	0.83	1.05
5-1/2" long	"	0.45	0.83	1.28
Dovetail, triangular galvanized ties, 12 ga.				
3" x 3"	EA.	0.40	0.83	1.24
5" x 5"	"	0.43	0.83	1.26
7" x 7"	"	0.49	0.83	1.32
7" x 9"	"	0.52	0.83	1.35
Brick anchors				
Corrugated, 3-1/2" long				
16 ga.	EA.	0.16	0.83	0.99
12 ga.	"	0.27	0.83	1.11
Non-corrugated, 3-1/2" long				
16 ga.	EA.	0.22	0.83	1.05
12 ga.	"	0.39	0.83	1.22

Mortar And Grout	UNIT	MAT.	INST.	TOTAL
04150.20 Masonry Control Joints				
Control joint, cross shaped PVC	L.F.	4.80	1.25	6.05
Closed cell joint filler				
1/2"	L.F.	0.73	1.25	1.98
3/4"	"	1.30	1.25	2.55
Rubber, for				
4" wall	L.F.	5.20	1.25	6.45
6" wall	"	8.15	1.30	9.45
8" wall	"	9.60	1.40	11.00
PVC, for				
4" wall	L.F.	4.00	1.25	5.25
6" wall	"	5.00	1.30	6.30
8" wall	"	5.65	1.40	7.05
04150.50 Masonry Flashing				
Through-wall flashing				
5 oz. coated copper	S.F.	6.25	4.15	10.40
0.030" elastomeric	"	1.10	3.35	4.45

Unit Masonry	UNIT	MAT.	INST.	TOTAL
04210.10 Brick Masonry				
Standard size brick, running bond				
Face brick, red (6.4/sf)				
Veneer	S.F.	3.30	8.30	11.60
Cavity wall	"	3.30	7.15	10.45
9" solid wall	"	6.35	14.25	20.60
Back-up				
4" thick	S.F.	3.40	6.25	9.65
8" thick	"	6.70	10.00	16.70
Firewall				
12" thick	S.F.	10.20	16.65	26.85
16" thick	"	13.50	22.65	36.15
Glazed brick (7.4/sf)				
Veneer	S.F.	10.85	9.05	19.90
Buff or gray face brick (6.4/sf)				
Veneer	S.F.	3.70	8.30	12.00
Cavity wall	"	3.70	7.15	10.85
Jumbo or oversize brick (3/sf)				
4" veneer	S.F.	4.25	5.00	9.25
4" back-up	"	4.25	4.15	8.40
8" back-up	"	9.95	7.15	17.10
12" firewall	"	14.20	12.45	26.65
16" firewall	"	21.00	16.65	37.65
Norman brick, red face, (4.5/sf)				
4" veneer	S.F.	4.95	6.25	11.20
Cavity wall	"	4.95	5.55	10.50

Unit Masonry	UNIT	MAT.	INST.	TOTAL
04210.10 Brick Masonry				
Chimney, standard brick, including flue				
16" x 16"	L.F.	19.85	49.90	69.75
16" x 20"	"	23.45	49.90	73.35
16" x 24"	"	27.80	49.90	77.70
20" x 20"	"	30.40	62.50	92.90
20" x 24"	"	39.10	62.50	101.60
20" x 32"	"	49.20	71.50	120.70
Window sill, face brick on edge	"	2.95	12.45	15.40
04210.20 Structural Tile				
Structural glazed tile				
6T series, 5-1/2" x 12"				
Glazed on one side				
2" thick	S.F.	7.85	5.00	12.85
4" thick	"	9.80	5.00	14.80
6" thick	"	14.30	5.55	19.85
8" thick	"	18.85	6.25	25.10
Glazed on two sides				
4" thick	S.F.	15.05	6.25	21.30
6" thick	"	22.60	7.15	29.75
04210.60 Pavers, Masonry				
Brick walk laid on sand, sand joints				
Laid flat, (4.5 per sf)	S.F.	3.50	5.55	9.05
Laid on edge, (7.2 per sf)	"	5.50	8.30	13.80
Precast concrete patio blocks				
2" thick				
Natural	S.F.	2.70	1.65	4.35
Colors	"	3.75	1.65	5.40
Exposed aggregates, local aggregate				
Natural	S.F.	3.15	1.65	4.80
Colors	"	4.20	1.65	5.85
Granite or limestone aggregate	"	5.75	1.65	7.40
White tumblestone aggregate	"	4.50	1.65	6.15
Stone pavers, set in mortar				
Bluestone				
1" thick				
Irregular	S.F.	2.90	12.45	15.35
Snapped rectangular	"	4.40	10.00	14.40
1-1/2" thick, random rectangular	"	5.05	12.45	17.50
2" thick, random rectangular	"	6.00	14.25	20.25
Slate				
Natural cleft				
Irregular, 3/4" thick	S.F.	2.90	14.25	17.15
Random rectangular				
1-1/4" thick	S.F.	6.30	12.45	18.75
1-1/2" thick	"	7.10	13.85	20.95
Granite blocks				
3" thick, 3" to 6" wide				
4" to 12" long	S.F.	6.75	16.65	23.40
6" to 15" long	"	3.95	14.25	18.20
Crushed stone, white marble, 3" thick	"	1.60	0.80	2.40

Unit Masonry	UNIT	MAT.	INST.	TOTAL
04220.10		Concrete Masonry Units		
Hollow, load bearing				
4"	S.F.	1.60	3.70	5.30
6"	"	2.00	3.85	5.85
8"	"	2.60	4.15	6.75
10"	"	3.50	4.55	8.05
12"	"	3.65	5.00	8.65
Solid, load bearing				
4"	S.F.	2.15	3.70	5.85
6"	"	2.55	3.85	6.40
8"	"	3.00	4.15	7.15
10"	"	4.05	4.55	8.60
12"	"	4.50	5.00	9.50
Back-up block, 8" x 16"				
2"	S.F.	1.05	2.85	3.90
4"	"	1.50	2.95	4.45
6"	"	1.95	3.10	5.05
8"	"	2.25	3.35	5.60
10"	"	3.00	3.55	6.55
12"	"	3.15	3.85	7.00
Foundation wall, 8" x 16"				
6"	S.F.	2.05	3.55	5.60
8"	"	2.30	3.85	6.15
10"	"	3.50	4.15	7.65
12"	"	3.85	4.55	8.40
Solid				
6"	S.F.	2.85	3.85	6.70
8"	"	3.55	4.15	7.70
10"	"	4.30	4.55	8.85
12"	"	5.25	5.00	10.25
Exterior, styrofoam inserts, standard weight, 8" x 16"				
6"	S.F.	3.90	3.85	7.75
8"	"	3.40	4.15	7.55
10"	"	4.85	4.55	9.40
12"	"	5.05	5.00	10.05
Acoustical slotted block				
4"	S.F.	3.40	4.55	7.95
6"	"	4.15	4.55	8.70
8"	"	6.20	5.00	11.20
Filled cavities				
4"	S.F.	4.30	5.55	9.85
6"	"	5.30	5.85	11.15
8"	"	7.10	6.25	13.35
Hollow, split face				
4"	S.F.	3.25	3.70	6.95
6"	"	3.75	3.85	7.60
8"	"	3.40	4.15	7.55
10"	"	4.45	4.55	9.00
12"	"	4.75	5.00	9.75
Split rib profile				
4"	S.F.	2.35	4.55	6.90
6"	"	2.75	4.55	7.30
8"	"	2.95	5.00	7.95

Unit Masonry	UNIT	MAT.	INST.	TOTAL
04220.10 Concrete Masonry Units				
10"	S.F.	3.25	5.00	8.25
12"	"	3.55	5.00	8.55
High strength block, 3500 psi				
2"	S.F.	1.55	3.70	5.25
4"	"	1.95	3.85	5.80
6"	"	2.30	3.85	6.15
8"	"	2.60	4.15	6.75
10"	"	3.00	4.55	7.55
12"	"	3.60	5.00	8.60
Solar screen concrete block				
4" thick				
6" x 6"	S.F.	4.60	11.10	15.70
8" x 8"	"	5.50	10.00	15.50
12" x 12"	"	3.20	7.65	10.85
8" thick				
8" x 16"	S.F.	3.40	7.15	10.55
Glazed block				
Cove base, glazed 1 side, 2"	L.F.	10.45	5.55	16.00
4"	"	10.45	5.55	16.00
6"	"	11.05	6.25	17.30
8"	"	11.80	6.25	18.05
Single face				
2"	S.F.	7.75	4.15	11.90
4"	"	8.40	4.15	12.55
6"	"	8.50	4.55	13.05
8"	"	8.80	5.00	13.80
10"	"	9.10	5.55	14.65
12"	"	9.40	5.85	15.25
Double face				
4"	S.F.	12.40	5.25	17.65
6"	"	13.40	5.55	18.95
8"	"	13.80	6.25	20.05
Corner or bullnose				
2"	EA.	10.45	6.25	16.70
4"	"	13.40	7.15	20.55
6"	"	16.40	7.15	23.55
8"	"	17.90	8.30	26.20
10"	"	19.40	9.05	28.45
12"	"	20.90	10.00	30.90
04220.90 Bond Beams & Lintels				
Bond beam, no grout or reinforcement				
8" x 16" x				
4" thick	L.F.	2.05	3.85	5.90
6" thick	"	2.50	4.00	6.50
8" thick	"	3.05	4.15	7.20
10" thick	"	3.20	4.35	7.55
12" thick	"	3.20	4.55	7.75
Beam lintel, no grout or reinforcement				
8" x 16" x				
10" thick	L.F.	5.60	5.00	10.60
12" thick	"	7.10	5.55	12.65

Unit Masonry	UNIT	MAT.	INST.	TOTAL
04220.90 — Bond Beams & Lintels				
Precast masonry lintel				
6 lf, 8" high x				
4" thick	L.F.	5.35	8.30	13.65
6" thick	"	6.85	8.30	15.15
8" thick	"	7.75	9.05	16.80
10" thick	"	9.25	9.05	18.30
10 lf, 8" high x				
4" thick	L.F.	6.75	5.00	11.75
6" thick	"	8.30	5.00	13.30
8" thick	"	9.25	5.55	14.80
10" thick	"	12.55	5.55	18.10
Steel angles and plates				
Minimum	Lb.	0.49	0.71	1.21
Maximum	"	0.68	1.25	1.93
Various size angle lintels				
1/4" stock				
3" x 3"	L.F.	3.40	3.10	6.50
3" x 3-1/2"	"	3.55	3.10	6.65
3/8" stock				
3" x 4"	L.F.	5.50	3.10	8.60
3-1/2" x 4"	"	5.75	3.10	8.85
4" x 4"	"	6.20	3.10	9.30
5" x 3-1/2"	"	6.50	3.10	9.60
6" x 3-1/2"	"	6.65	3.10	9.75
1/2" stock				
6" x 4"	L.F.	8.25	3.10	11.35
04270.10 — Glass Block				
Glass block, 4" thick				
6" x 6"	S.F.	33.40	16.65	50.05
8" x 8"	"	28.90	12.45	41.35
12" x 12"	"	28.90	10.00	38.90
Replacement glass blocks, 4" x 8" x 8"				
Minimum	S.F.	35.10	49.90	85.00
Maximum	"	41.50	100.00	141.50
04295.10 — Parging/masonry Plaster				
Parging				
1/2" thick	S.F.	0.66	3.35	4.01
3/4" thick	"	0.84	4.15	4.99
1" thick	"	1.15	5.00	6.15

Stone	UNIT	MAT.	INST.	TOTAL
04400.10	Stone			
Rubble stone				
Walls set in mortar				
8" thick	S.F.	14.60	12.45	27.05
12" thick	"	17.65	19.95	37.60
18" thick	"	23.40	24.95	48.35
24" thick	"	29.30	33.30	62.60
Dry set wall				
8" thick	S.F.	16.45	8.30	24.75
12" thick	"	18.55	12.45	31.00
18" thick	"	25.60	16.65	42.25
24" thick	"	31.30	19.95	51.25
Cut stone				
Facing panels				
3/4" thick	S.F.	39.00	19.95	58.95
1-1/2" thick	"	58.50	22.65	81.15

Masonry Restoration	UNIT	MAT.	INST.	TOTAL
04520.10	Restoration And Cleaning			
Masonry cleaning				
Washing brick				
Smooth surface	S.F.	0.43	0.83	1.26
Rough surface	"	0.60	1.10	1.69
Steam clean masonry				
Smooth face				
Minimum	S.F.		0.64	0.64
Maximum	"		0.94	0.94
Rough face				
Minimum	S.F.		0.86	0.86
Maximum	"		1.30	1.30
Sandblast masonry				
Minimum	S.F.	0.52	1.05	1.57
Maximum	"	0.77	1.70	2.47
Pointing masonry				
Brick	S.F.	1.35	2.00	3.35
Concrete block	"	0.61	1.45	2.06
Cut and repoint				
Brick				
Minimum	S.F.	0.37	2.50	2.87
Maximum	"	0.64	5.00	5.64
Stone work	L.F.	1.70	3.85	5.55
Cut and recaulk				
Oil base caulks	L.F.	1.30	3.35	4.65
Butyl caulks	"	1.15	3.35	4.50
Polysulfides and acrylics	"	2.25	3.35	5.60
Silicones	"	2.60	3.35	5.95

Masonry Restoration	UNIT	MAT.	INST.	TOTAL
04520.10 Restoration And Cleaning				
Cement and sand grout on walls, to 1/8" thick				
Minimum	S.F.	0.65	2.00	2.65
Maximum	"	1.65	2.50	4.15
Brick removal and replacement				
Minimum	EA.	0.68	6.25	6.93
Average	"	0.90	8.30	9.20
Maximum	"	1.80	24.95	26.75

Metal Fastening	UNIT	MAT.	INST.	TOTAL
05050.10	Structural Welding			
Welding				
Single pass				
1/8"	L.F.	0.58	2.85	3.43
3/16"	"	1.10	3.85	4.95
1/4"	"	1.50	4.80	6.30
Miscellaneous steel shapes				
Plain	Lb.	1.10	0.12	1.22
Galvanized	"	1.65	0.19	1.84
Plates				
Plain	Lb.	1.00	0.14	1.14
Galvanized	"	1.55	0.23	1.78
05050.90	Metal Anchors			
Anchor bolts				
1/2" x				
8" long	EA.			4.87
10" long	"			5.19
12" long	"			5.69
18" long	"			6.18
3/4" x				
8" long	EA.			6.49
12" long	"			7.31
18" long	"			10.06
24" long	"			13.31
1" x				
12" long	EA.			12.99
18" long	"			16.24
24" long	"			19.48
36" long	"			29.22
Expansion shield				
1/4"	EA.			0.97
3/8"	"			1.63
1/2"	"			3.25
5/8"	"			4.72
3/4"	"			5.69
1"	"			7.81
Non-drilling anchor				
1/4"	EA.			0.62
3/8"	"			0.77
1/2"	"			1.18
5/8"	"			1.93
3/4"	"			3.30
Self-drilling anchor				
1/4"	EA.			1.63
5/16"	"			2.03
3/8"	"			2.44
1/2"	"			3.25
5/8"	"			6.18
3/4"	"			8.12
7/8"	"			11.37
Add 25% for galvanized anchor bolts				
Channel door frame, with anchors	Lb.	1.60	0.64	2.24

Metal Fastening	UNIT	MAT.	INST.	TOTAL
05050.90	Metal Anchors			
Corner guard angle, with anchors	Lb.	1.45	0.96	2.41
05050.95	Metal Lintels			
Lintels, steel				
Plain	Lb.	1.20	1.45	2.65
Galvanized	"	1.80	1.45	3.25
05120.10	Structural Steel			
Beams and girders, A-36				
Welded	TON	2,030	640.00	2,670
Bolted	"	1,990	580.00	2,570
Columns				
Pipe				
6" dia.	Lb.	1.35	0.64	1.99
12" dia.	"	1.15	0.53	1.68
Purlins and girts				
Welded	TON	2,530	1,070	3,600
Bolted	"	2,490	910.00	3,400
Column base plates				
Up to 150 lb each	Lb.	1.45	0.38	1.83
Over 150 lb each	"	1.20	0.48	1.68
Structural pipe				
3" to 5" o.d.	TON	2,730	1,280	4,010
6" to 12" o.d.	"	2,530	910.00	3,440
Structural tube				
6" square				
Light sections	TON	3,170	1,280	4,450
Heavy sections	"	2,970	910.00	3,880
6" wide rectangular				
Light sections	TON	3,170	1,070	4,240
Heavy sections	"	2,970	800.00	3,770
Greater than 6" wide rectangular				
Light sections	TON	3,480	1,070	4,550
Heavy sections	"	3,270	800.00	4,070
Miscellaneous structural shapes				
Steel angle	TON	2,250	1,600	3,850
Steel plate	"	2,560	1,070	3,630
Trusses, field welded				
60 lb/lf	TON	3,270	800.00	4,070
100 lb/lf	"	2,860	640.00	3,500
150 lb/lf	"	2,700	530.00	3,230
Bolted				
60 lb/lf	TON	3,230	710.00	3,940
100 lb/lf	"	2,820	580.00	3,400
150 lb/lf	"	2,680	490.00	3,170
Add for galvanizing	"			642.85

Cold Formed Framing

Cold Formed Framing	UNIT	MAT.	INST.	TOTAL
05410.10		Metal Framing		
Furring channel, galvanized				
Beams and columns, 3/4"				
12" o.c.	S.F.	0.53	5.75	6.28
16" o.c.	"	0.44	5.20	5.64
Walls, 3/4"				
12" o.c.	S.F.	0.52	2.85	3.37
16" o.c.	"	0.41	2.40	2.81
24" o.c.	"	0.30	1.90	2.20
1-1/2"				
12" o.c.	S.F.	0.66	2.85	3.51
16" o.c.	"	0.53	2.40	2.93
24" o.c.	"	0.41	1.90	2.31
Stud, load bearing				
16" o.c.				
16 ga.				
2-1/2"	S.F.	1.35	2.55	3.90
3-5/8"	"	1.75	2.55	4.30
4"	"	1.90	2.55	4.45
6"	"	2.75	2.85	5.60
24" o.c.				
16 ga.				
2-1/2"	S.F.	1.10	2.20	3.30
3-5/8"	"	1.45	2.20	3.65
4"	"	1.65	2.20	3.85
6"	"	2.40	2.40	4.80
8"	"	2.55	2.40	4.95

Metal Fabrications

Metal Fabrications	UNIT	MAT.	INST.	TOTAL
05510.10		Stairs		
Stock unit, steel, complete, per riser				
Tread				
3'-6" wide	EA.	120.00	72.00	192.00
4' wide	"	140.00	82.00	222.00
5' wide	"	170.00	95.50	265.50
Metal pan stair, cement filled, per riser				
3'-6" wide	EA.	130.00	57.50	187.50
4' wide	"	150.00	64.00	214.00
5' wide	"	170.00	72.00	242.00
Landing, steel pan	S.F.	53.00	14.35	67.35
Cast iron tread, steel stringers, stock units, per riser				
Tread				
3'-6" wide	EA.	240.00	72.00	312.00
4' wide	"	270.00	82.00	352.00
5' wide	"	320.00	95.50	415.50
Stair treads, abrasive, 12" x 3'-6"				

Metal Fabrications	UNIT	MAT.	INST.	TOTAL
05510.10 Stairs				
Cast iron				
3/8"	EA.	130.00	28.70	158.70
1/2"	"	160.00	28.70	188.70
Cast aluminum				
5/16"	EA.	150.00	28.70	178.70
3/8"	"	160.00	28.70	188.70
1/2"	"	190.00	28.70	218.70
05515.10 Ladders				
Ladder, 18" wide				
With cage	L.F.	93.50	38.30	131.80
Without cage	"	59.50	28.70	88.20
05520.10 Railings				
Railing, pipe				
1-1/4" diameter, welded steel				
2-rail				
Primed	L.F.	19.05	11.50	30.55
Galvanized	"	24.25	11.50	35.75
3-rail				
Primed	L.F.	24.25	14.35	38.60
Galvanized	"	31.20	14.35	45.55
Wall mounted, single rail, welded steel				
Primed	L.F.	8.10	8.85	16.95
Galvanized	"	12.10	8.85	20.95
1-1/2" diameter, welded steel				
2-rail				
Primed	L.F.	20.80	11.50	32.30
Galvanized	"	26.00	11.50	37.50
3-rail				
Primed	L.F.	26.00	14.35	40.35
Galvanized	"	32.80	14.35	47.15
Wall mounted, single rail, welded steel				
Primed	L.F.	9.50	8.85	18.35
Galvanized	"	13.00	8.85	21.85
2" diameter, welded steel				
2-rail				
Primed	L.F.	26.00	12.75	38.75
Galvanized	"	32.90	12.75	45.65
3-rail				
Primed	L.F.	32.90	16.40	49.30
Galvanized	"	39.80	16.40	56.20
Wall mounted, single rail, welded steel				
Primed	L.F.	10.40	9.55	19.95
Galvanized	"	13.00	9.55	22.55
05530.10 Metal Grating				
Floor plate, checkered, steel				
1/4"				
Primed	S.F.	7.75	0.82	8.57
Galvanized	"	10.30	0.82	11.12
3/8"				

Metal Fabrications	UNIT	MAT.	INST.	TOTAL
05530.10				**Metal Grating**
Primed	S.F.	10.30	0.88	11.18
Galvanized	"	13.75	0.88	14.63
Aluminum grating, pressure-locked bearing bars				
3/4" x 1/8"	S.F.	16.55	1.45	18.00
1" x 1/8"	"	18.20	1.45	19.65
1-1/4" x 1/8"	"	23.15	1.45	24.60
1-1/4" x 3/16"	"	24.80	1.45	26.25
1-1/2" x 1/8"	"	26.40	1.45	27.85
1-3/4" x 3/16"	"	29.70	1.45	31.15
Miscellaneous expenses				
Cutting				
Minimum	L.F.		3.85	3.85
Maximum	"		5.75	5.75
Banding				
Minimum	L.F.		9.55	9.55
Maximum	"		11.50	11.50
Toe plates				
Minimum	L.F.		11.50	11.50
Maximum	"		14.35	14.35
Steel grating, primed				
3/4" x 1/8"	S.F.	7.35	1.90	9.25
1" x 1/8"	"	7.55	1.90	9.45
1-1/4" x 1/8"	"	8.10	1.90	10.00
1-1/4" x 3/16"	"	9.90	1.90	11.80
1-1/2" x 1/8"	"	9.05	1.90	10.95
1-3/4" x 3/16"	"	12.90	1.90	14.80
Galvanized				
3/4" x 1/8"	S.F.	9.05	1.90	10.95
1" x 1/8"	"	9.65	1.90	11.55
1-1/4" x 1/8"	"	10.50	1.90	12.40
1-1/4" x 3/16"	"	12.50	1.90	14.40
1-1/2" x 1/8"	"	11.20	1.90	13.10
1-3/4" x 3/16"	"	16.35	1.90	18.25
Miscellaneous expenses				
Cutting				
Minimum	L.F.		4.10	4.10
Maximum	"		6.40	6.40
Banding				
Minimum	L.F.		10.45	10.45
Maximum	"		12.75	12.75
Toe plates				
Minimum	L.F.		12.75	12.75
Maximum	"		16.40	16.40
05540.10				**Castings**
Miscellaneous castings				
Light sections	Lb.	1.65	1.15	2.80
Heavy sections	"	1.40	0.82	2.22
Manhole covers and frames				
Regular, city type				
18" dia.				
100 lb	EA.	340.00	110.00	450.00

Metal Fabrications	UNIT	MAT.	INST.	TOTAL
05540.10 Castings				
24" dia.				
200 lb	EA.	350.00	110.00	460.00
300 lb	"	360.00	130.00	490.00
400 lb	"	380.00	130.00	510.00
26" dia., 475 lb	"	460.00	140.00	600.00
30" dia., 600 lb	"	530.00	160.00	690.00
8" square, 75 lb	"	150.00	22.95	172.95
24" square				
126 lb	EA.	330.00	110.00	440.00
500 lb	"	530.00	140.00	670.00
Watertight type				
20" dia., 200 lb	EA.	300.00	140.00	440.00
24" dia., 350 lb	"	510.00	190.00	700.00
Steps, cast iron				
7" x 9"	EA.	14.55	11.50	26.05
8" x 9"	"	17.40	12.75	30.15
Manhole covers and frames, aluminum				
12" x 12"	EA.	69.50	22.95	92.45
18" x 18"	"	72.00	22.95	94.95
24" x 24"	"	79.00	28.70	107.70
Corner protection				
Steel angle guard with anchors				
2" x 2" x 3/16"	L.F.	15.10	8.20	23.30
2" x 3" x 1/4"	"	17.10	8.20	25.30
3" x 3" x 5/16"	"	19.90	8.20	28.10
3" x 4" x 5/16"	"	23.90	8.85	32.75
4" x 4" x 5/16"	"	24.85	8.85	33.70

Misc. Fabrications	UNIT	MAT.	INST.	TOTAL
05580.10 Metal Specialties				
Kick plate				
4" high x 1/4" thick				
Primed	L.F.	7.25	11.50	18.75
Galvanized	"	8.25	11.50	19.75
6" high x 1/4" thick				
Primed	L.F.	7.90	12.75	20.65
Galvanized	"	9.40	12.75	22.15
05700.10 Ornamental Metal				
Railings, vertical square bars, 6" o.c., with shaped top rails				
Steel	L.F.	79.00	28.70	107.70
Aluminum	"	110.00	28.70	138.70
Bronze	"	170.00	38.30	208.30
Stainless steel	"	160.00	38.30	198.30
Laminated metal or wood handrails with metal supports				

Misc. Fabrications	UNIT	MAT.	INST.	TOTAL
05700.10 — Ornamental Metal				
2-1/2" round or oval shape	L.F.	150.00	28.70	178.70
05800.10 — Expansion Control				
Expansion joints with covers, floor assembly type				
With 1" space				
Aluminum	L.F.	27.30	9.55	36.85
Bronze	"	57.00	9.55	66.55
Stainless steel	"	44.20	9.55	53.75
With 2" space				
Aluminum	L.F.	33.80	9.55	43.35
Bronze	"	60.00	9.55	69.55
Stainless steel	"	52.50	9.55	62.05
Ceiling and wall assembly type				
With 1" space				
Aluminum	L.F.	17.50	11.50	29.00
Bronze	"	60.00	11.50	71.50
Stainless steel	"	54.00	11.50	65.50
With 2" space				
Aluminum	L.F.	19.30	11.50	30.80
Bronze	"	65.00	11.50	76.50
Stainless steel	"	57.00	11.50	68.50
Exterior roof and wall, aluminum				
Roof to roof				
With 1" space	L.F.	51.00	9.55	60.55
With 2" space	"	55.00	9.55	64.55
Roof to wall				
With 1" space	L.F.	39.70	10.45	50.15
With 2" space	"	47.10	10.45	57.55

Fasteners And Adhesives	UNIT	MAT.	INST.	TOTAL
06050.10 Accessories				
Column/post base, cast aluminum				
4" x 4"	EA.	3.10	12.90	16.00
6" x 6"	"	6.75	12.90	19.65
Bridging, metal, per pair				
12" o.c.	EA.	1.15	5.15	6.30
16" o.c.	"	1.15	4.70	5.85
Anchors				
Bolts, threaded two ends, with nuts and washers				
1/2" dia.				
4" long	EA.	1.55	3.20	4.75
7-1/2" long	"	1.85	3.20	5.05
15" long	"	3.80	3.20	7.00
Bolts, carriage				
1/4 x 4	EA.	1.55	5.15	6.70
5/16 x 6	"	1.65	5.45	7.10
Joist and beam hangers				
18 ga.				
2 x 4	EA.	0.74	5.15	5.89
2 x 6	"	0.98	5.15	6.13
2 x 8	"	1.15	5.15	6.30
2 x 10	"	1.30	5.75	7.05
2 x 12	"	1.55	6.45	8.00
16 ga.				
3 x 6	EA.	2.70	5.75	8.45
3 x 8	"	2.80	5.75	8.55
3 x 10	"	3.20	6.05	9.25
3 x 12	"	3.50	6.90	10.40
3 x 14	"	3.75	7.35	11.10
4 x 6	"	3.05	5.75	8.80
4 x 8	"	3.50	5.75	9.25
4 x 10	"	4.40	6.05	10.45
4 x 12	"	4.90	6.90	11.80
4 x 14	"	5.35	7.35	12.70
Rafter anchors, 18 ga., 1-1/2" wide				
5-1/4" long	EA.	0.82	4.30	5.12
10-3/4" long	"	1.25	4.30	5.55
Sill anchors				
Embedded in concrete	EA.	2.05	5.15	7.20
Strap ties, 14 ga., 1-3/8" wide				
12" long	EA.	1.70	4.30	6.00

Rough Carpentry	UNIT	MAT.	INST.	TOTAL
06110.10 Blocking				
Steel construction				
Walls				
2x4	L.F.	0.63	3.45	4.08
2x6	"	0.89	3.95	4.84
2x8	"	1.25	4.30	5.55
2x10	"	1.75	4.70	6.45
2x12	"	2.30	5.15	7.45
Ceilings				
2x4	L.F.	0.63	3.95	4.58
2x6	"	0.89	4.70	5.59
2x8	"	1.25	5.15	6.40
2x10	"	1.75	5.75	7.50
2x12	"	2.30	6.45	8.75
Wood construction				
Walls				
2x4	L.F.	0.63	2.85	3.48
2x6	"	0.89	3.20	4.09
2x8	"	1.25	3.45	4.70
2x10	"	1.75	3.70	5.45
2x12	"	2.30	3.95	6.25
Ceilings				
2x4	L.F.	0.63	3.20	3.83
2x6	"	0.89	3.70	4.59
2x8	"	1.25	3.95	5.20
2x10	"	1.75	4.30	6.05
2x12	"	2.30	4.70	7.00
06110.20 Ceiling Framing				
Ceiling joists				
16" o.c.				
2x4	S.F.	0.63	0.99	1.62
2x6	"	0.95	1.05	2.00
2x8	"	1.30	1.05	2.35
2x10	"	1.95	1.10	3.05
2x12	"	2.55	1.15	3.70
Headers and nailers				
2x4	L.F.	0.63	1.65	2.28
2x6	"	0.89	1.70	2.59
2x8	"	1.25	1.85	3.10
2x10	"	1.75	2.00	3.75
2x12	"	2.30	2.15	4.45
Sister joists for ceilings				
2x4	L.F.	0.63	3.70	4.33
2x6	"	0.89	4.30	5.19
2x8	"	1.25	5.15	6.40
2x10	"	1.75	6.45	8.20
2x12	"	2.30	8.60	10.90
06110.30 Floor Framing				
Floor joists				
16" o.c.				
2x6	S.F.	0.95	0.86	1.81

Rough Carpentry	UNIT	MAT.	INST.	TOTAL
06110.30 Floor Framing				
2x8	S.F.	1.30	0.88	2.18
2x10	"	1.95	0.89	2.84
2x12	"	2.55	0.92	3.47
2x14	"	3.15	0.96	4.11
3x6	"	2.10	0.89	2.99
3x8	"	2.75	0.92	3.67
3x10	"	3.45	0.96	4.41
3x12	"	4.10	0.99	5.09
3x14	"	4.85	1.05	5.90
4x6	"	2.75	0.89	3.64
4x8	"	3.70	0.92	4.62
4x10	"	4.60	0.96	5.56
4x12	"	5.45	0.99	6.44
4x14	"	6.45	1.05	7.50
Sister joists for floors				
2x4	L.F.	0.63	3.20	3.83
2x6	"	0.89	3.70	4.59
2x8	"	1.25	4.30	5.55
2x10	"	1.75	5.15	6.90
2x12	"	2.30	6.45	8.75
06110.40 Furring				
Furring, wood strips				
Walls				
On masonry or concrete walls				
1x2 furring				
12" o.c.	S.F.	0.29	1.60	1.89
16" o.c.	"	0.25	1.45	1.70
24" o.c.	"	0.20	1.35	1.55
1x3 furring				
12" o.c.	S.F.	0.42	1.60	2.02
16" o.c.	"	0.36	1.45	1.81
24" o.c.	"	0.29	1.35	1.64
On wood walls				
1x2 furring				
12" o.c.	S.F.	0.29	1.15	1.44
16" o.c.	"	0.25	1.05	1.30
24" o.c.	"	0.20	0.94	1.14
1x3 furring				
12" o.c.	S.F.	0.42	1.15	1.57
16" o.c.	"	0.36	1.05	1.41
24" o.c.	"	0.29	0.94	1.23
Ceilings				
On masonry or concrete ceilings				
1x2 furring				
12" o.c.	S.F.	0.29	2.85	3.14
16" o.c.	"	0.25	2.60	2.85
24" o.c.	"	0.20	2.35	2.55
1x3 furring				
12" o.c.	S.F.	0.42	2.85	3.27
16" o.c.	"	0.36	2.60	2.96
24" o.c.	"	0.29	2.35	2.64

Rough Carpentry	UNIT	MAT.	INST.	TOTAL
06110.40 Furring				
On wood ceilings				
1x2 furring				
12" o.c.	S.F.	0.29	1.90	2.19
16" o.c.	"	0.25	1.70	1.95
24" o.c.	"	0.20	1.55	1.75
1x3				
12" o.c.	S.F.	0.42	1.90	2.32
16" o.c.	"	0.36	1.70	2.06
24" o.c.	"	0.29	1.55	1.84
06110.50 Roof Framing				
Roof framing				
Rafters, gable end				
4-6 pitch (4-in-12 to 6-in-12)				
16" o.c.				
2x6	S.F.	0.99	0.96	1.95
2x8	"	1.45	0.99	2.44
2x10	"	2.10	1.05	3.15
2x12	"	2.80	1.05	3.85
24" o.c.				
2x6	S.F.	0.80	0.81	1.61
2x8	"	1.10	0.83	1.93
2x10	"	1.65	0.89	2.54
2x12	"	2.25	0.99	3.24
Ridge boards				
2x6	L.F.	0.89	2.60	3.49
2x8	"	1.25	2.85	4.10
2x10	"	1.75	3.20	4.95
2x12	"	2.30	3.70	6.00
Hip rafters				
2x6	L.F.	0.89	1.85	2.74
2x8	"	1.25	1.90	3.15
2x10	"	1.75	2.00	3.75
2x12	"	2.30	2.05	4.35
Jack rafters				
4-6 pitch (4-in-12 to 6-in-12)				
16" o.c.				
2x6	S.F.	1.00	1.50	2.50
2x8	"	1.45	1.55	3.00
2x10	"	2.10	1.65	3.75
2x12	"	2.80	1.70	4.50
24" o.c.				
2x6	S.F.	0.80	1.15	1.95
2x8	"	1.10	1.20	2.30
2x10	"	1.65	1.25	2.90
2x12	"	2.25	1.30	3.55
Sister rafters				
2x4	L.F.	0.63	3.70	4.33
2x6	"	0.89	4.30	5.19
2x8	"	1.25	5.15	6.40
2x10	"	1.75	6.45	8.20
2x12	"	2.30	8.60	10.90

Rough Carpentry	UNIT	MAT.	INST.	TOTAL
06110.50 — Roof Framing				
Fascia boards				
2x4	L.F.	0.63	2.60	3.23
2x6	"	0.89	2.60	3.49
2x8	"	1.25	2.85	4.10
2x10	"	1.75	2.85	4.60
2x12	"	2.30	3.20	5.50
Cant strips				
Fiber				
3x3	L.F.	0.31	1.45	1.76
4x4	"	0.41	1.55	1.96
Wood				
3x3	L.F.	1.70	1.55	3.25
06110.60 — Sleepers				
Sleepers, over concrete				
12" o.c.				
1x2	S.F.	0.26	1.15	1.41
1x3	"	0.36	1.25	1.61
2x4	"	0.76	1.45	2.21
2x6	"	1.10	1.50	2.60
16" o.c.				
1x2	S.F.	0.22	1.05	1.27
1x3	"	0.31	1.05	1.36
2x4	"	0.63	1.25	1.88
2x6	"	0.95	1.30	2.25
06110.65 — Soffits				
Soffit framing				
2x3	L.F.	0.50	3.70	4.19
2x4	"	0.63	3.95	4.58
2x6	"	0.89	4.30	5.19
2x8	"	1.25	4.70	5.95
06110.70 — Wall Framing				
Framing wall, studs				
12" o.c.				
2x3	S.F.	0.54	0.96	1.49
2x4	"	0.76	0.96	1.71
2x6	"	1.10	1.05	2.15
2x8	"	1.55	1.05	2.60
16" o.c.				
2x3	S.F.	0.47	0.81	1.27
2x4	"	0.63	0.81	1.43
2x6	"	0.89	0.86	1.75
2x8	"	1.30	0.89	2.19
24" o.c.				
2x3	S.F.	0.35	0.70	1.05
2x4	"	0.51	0.70	1.21
2x6	"	0.76	0.74	1.49
2x8	"	1.00	0.76	1.76
Plates, top or bottom				
2x3	L.F.	0.50	1.50	1.99

Rough Carpentry	UNIT	MAT.	INST.	TOTAL
06110.70 — Wall Framing				
2x4	L.F.	0.63	1.60	2.23
2x6	"	0.89	1.70	2.59
2x8	"	1.25	1.85	3.10
Headers, door or window				
2x8				
Single				
4' long	EA.	5.25	32.30	37.55
8' long	"	10.55	39.70	50.25
Double				
4' long	EA.	10.55	36.90	47.45
8' long	"	21.10	46.90	68.00
2x12				
Single				
6' long	EA.	15.20	39.70	54.90
12' long	"	30.40	51.50	81.90
Double				
6' long	EA.	30.40	46.90	77.30
12' long	"	61.00	57.50	118.50
06115.10 — Floor Sheathing				
Sub-flooring, plywood, CDX				
1/2" thick	S.F.	0.69	0.65	1.34
5/8" thick	"	0.83	0.74	1.57
3/4" thick	"	0.99	0.86	1.85
Structural plywood				
1/2" thick	S.F.	0.77	0.65	1.42
5/8" thick	"	0.91	0.74	1.65
3/4" thick	"	1.10	0.79	1.89
Underlayment				
Hardboard, 1/4" tempered	S.F.	0.50	0.65	1.14
Plywood, CDX				
3/8" thick	S.F.	0.62	0.65	1.26
1/2" thick	"	0.71	0.69	1.40
5/8" thick	"	0.85	0.74	1.58
3/4" thick	"	1.00	0.79	1.79
06115.20 — Roof Sheathing				
Sheathing				
Plywood, CDX				
3/8" thick	S.F.	0.62	0.67	1.28
1/2" thick	"	0.71	0.69	1.40
5/8" thick	"	0.85	0.74	1.58
3/4" thick	"	1.00	0.79	1.79
06115.30 — Wall Sheathing				
Sheathing				
Plywood, CDX				
3/8" thick	S.F.	0.62	0.76	1.38
1/2" thick	"	0.71	0.79	1.50
5/8" thick	"	0.85	0.86	1.71
3/4" thick	"	1.00	0.94	1.94

Rough Carpentry	UNIT	MAT.	INST.	TOTAL
06125.10 Wood Decking				
Decking, T&G solid				
Fir				
3" thick	S.F.	3.30	1.30	4.60
4" thick	"	4.05	1.40	5.45
Southern yellow pine				
3" thick	S.F.	3.25	1.45	4.70
4" thick	"	3.50	1.60	5.10
White pine				
3" thick	S.F.	4.10	1.30	5.40
4" thick	"	5.40	1.40	6.80
06130.10 Heavy Timber				
Mill framed structures				
Beams to 20' long				
Douglas fir				
6x8	L.F.	5.85	6.45	12.30
6x10	"	6.90	6.70	13.60
Southern yellow pine				
6x8	L.F.	4.65	6.45	11.10
6x10	"	5.60	6.70	12.30
Columns to 12' high				
6x6	L.F.	4.20	9.70	13.90
10x10	"	12.55	10.80	23.35
06190.20 Wood Trusses				
Truss, fink, 2x4 members				
3-in-12 slope				
24' span	EA.	74.50	55.50	130.00
30' span	"	95.50	59.00	154.50

Finish Carpentry	UNIT	MAT.	INST.	TOTAL
06200.10 Finish Carpentry				
Casing				
11/16 x 2-1/2	L.F.	1.55	2.35	3.90
11/16 x 3-1/2	"	2.00	2.45	4.45
Half round				
1/2	L.F.	0.62	2.05	2.67
5/8	"	0.82	2.05	2.87
Railings, balusters				
1-1/8 x 1-1/8	L.F.	2.70	5.15	7.85
1-1/2 x 1-1/2	"	3.15	4.70	7.85
Stop				
5/8 x 1-5/8				
Colonial	L.F.	0.63	3.20	3.83
Ranch	"	0.62	3.20	3.82

Finish Carpentry	UNIT	MAT.	INST.	TOTAL
06200.10 Finish Carpentry				
Exterior trim, casing, select pine, 1x3	L.F.	2.10	2.60	4.70
Douglas fir				
1x3	L.F.	1.15	2.60	3.75
1x4	"	1.55	2.60	4.15
1x6	"	1.85	2.85	4.70
Cornices, white pine, #2 or better				
1x2	L.F.	0.69	2.60	3.29
1x4	"	1.05	2.60	3.65
1x8	"	1.85	3.05	4.90
Shelving, pine				
1x8	L.F.	2.20	3.95	6.15
1x10	"	2.70	4.15	6.85
1x12	"	3.50	4.30	7.80
06220.10 Millwork				
Countertop, laminated plastic				
25" x 7/8" thick				
Minimum	L.F.	17.35	12.90	30.25
Average	"	31.30	17.20	48.50
Maximum	"	52.00	20.65	72.65
Base cabinets, 34-1/2" high, 24" deep, hardwood, no tops				
Minimum	L.F.	66.50	20.65	87.15
Average	"	110.00	25.80	135.80
Maximum	"	180.00	34.40	214.40
Wall cabinets				
Minimum	L.F.	53.00	17.20	70.20
Average	"	85.00	20.65	105.65
Maximum	"	170.00	25.80	195.80

Wood Treatment	UNIT	MAT.	INST.	TOTAL
06300.10 Wood Treatment				
Creosote preservative treatment				
8 lb/cf	B.F.			0.47
10 lb/cf	"			0.61
Salt preservative treatment				
Oil borne				
Minimum	B.F.			0.35
Maximum	"			0.57
Water borne				
Minimum	B.F.			0.27
Maximum	"			0.44
Fire retardant treatment				
Minimum	B.F.			0.59
Maximum	"			0.71

Architectural Woodwork	UNIT	MAT.	INST.	TOTAL
06420.10 Panel Work				
Plywood unfinished, 1/4" thick				
Birch				
Natural	S.F.	1.55	1.70	3.25
Select	"	2.00	1.70	3.70
Knotty pine	"	2.00	1.70	3.70
Plywood, prefinished, 1/4" thick, premium grade				
Birch veneer	S.F.	2.70	2.05	4.75
Cherry veneer	"	3.05	2.05	5.10
06430.10 Stairwork				
Risers, 1x8, 42" wide				
White oak	EA.	22.10	25.80	47.90
Pine	"	15.65	25.80	41.45
Treads, 1-1/16" x 9-1/2" x 42"				
White oak	EA.	31.60	32.30	63.90
06440.10 Columns				
Column, hollow, round wood				
12" diameter				
10' high	EA.	640.00	71.50	711.50
12' high	"	780.00	76.50	856.50
24" diameter				
16' high	EA.	2,650	110.00	2,760
18' high	"	3,010	110.00	3,120

Moisture Protection	UNIT	MAT.	INST.	TOTAL
07100.10			Waterproofing	
Membrane waterproofing, elastomeric				
Butyl				
1/32" thick	S.F.	1.05	1.60	2.65
1/16" thick	"	1.40	1.65	3.05
Butyl with nylon				
1/32" thick	S.F.	1.25	1.60	2.85
1/16" thick	"	1.45	1.65	3.10
Neoprene				
1/32" thick	S.F.	1.70	1.60	3.30
1/16" thick	"	2.80	1.65	4.45
Neoprene with nylon				
1/32" thick	S.F.	1.90	1.60	3.50
1/16" thick	"	3.00	1.65	4.65
Plastic vapor barrier (polyethylene)				
4 mil	S.F.	0.02	0.16	0.18
6 mil	"	0.04	0.16	0.20
10 mil	"	0.09	0.20	0.29
Bituminous membrane waterproofing, asphalt felt, 15 lb.				
One ply	S.F.	0.63	1.00	1.63
Two ply	"	0.73	1.20	1.93
Three ply	"	0.91	1.45	2.36
Four ply	"	1.05	1.65	2.70
Five ply	"	1.15	2.10	3.25
Modified asphalt membrane waterproofing, fibrous asphalt				
One ply	S.F.	1.45	1.65	3.10
Two ply	"	2.15	2.00	4.15
Three ply	"	2.40	2.20	4.60
Four ply	"	2.90	2.65	5.55
Five ply	"	3.40	3.20	6.60
Asphalt coated protective board				
1/8" thick	S.F.	0.81	1.00	1.80
1/4" thick	"	1.15	1.00	2.15
3/8" thick	"	1.25	1.00	2.25
1/2" thick	"	1.50	1.05	2.55
Cement protective board				
3/8" thick	S.F.	2.75	1.35	4.10
1/2" thick	"	3.85	1.35	5.20
Fluid applied, neoprene				
50 mil	S.F.	3.35	1.35	4.70
90 mil	"	4.55	1.35	5.90
Tab extended polyurethane				
.050" thick	S.F.	1.80	1.00	2.80
Fluid applied rubber based polyurethane				
6 mil	S.F.	0.95	1.25	2.20
15 mil	"	1.80	1.00	2.80
Bentonite waterproofing, panels				
3/16" thick	S.F.	1.60	1.00	2.60
1/4" thick	"	1.80	1.00	2.80
5/8" thick	"	2.70	1.05	3.75
Granular admixtures, trowel on, 3/8" thick	"	2.25	1.00	3.25
Metallic oxide waterproofing, iron compound, troweled				
5/8" thick	S.F.	1.65	1.00	2.65

Moisture Protection	UNIT	MAT.	INST.	TOTAL
07100.10 Waterproofing				
3/4" thick	S.F.	2.00	1.15	3.15
07150.10 Dampproofing				
Silicone dampproofing, sprayed on				
Concrete surface				
1 coat	S.F.	0.65	0.22	0.87
2 coats	"	1.05	0.31	1.36
Concrete block				
1 coat	S.F.	0.65	0.27	0.91
2 coats	"	1.05	0.36	1.41
Brick				
1 coat	S.F.	0.75	0.31	1.06
2 coats	"	1.15	0.40	1.55
07160.10 Bituminous Dampproofing				
Building paper, asphalt felt				
15 lb	S.F.	0.15	1.60	1.75
30 lb	"	0.28	1.65	1.93
Asphalt dampproofing, troweled, cold, primer plus				
1 coat	S.F.	0.96	1.35	2.31
2 coats	"	1.45	2.00	3.45
3 coats	"	2.15	2.50	4.65
Fibrous asphalt dampproofing, hot troweled, primer plus				
1 coat	S.F.	1.50	1.60	3.10
2 coats	"	1.90	2.20	4.10
3 coats	"	2.05	2.85	4.90
Asphaltic paint dampproofing, per coat				
Brush on	S.F.	0.28	0.57	0.85
Spray on	"	0.49	0.44	0.94
07190.10 Vapor Barriers				
Vapor barrier, polyethylene				
2 mil	S.F.	0.02	0.20	0.22
6 mil	"	0.03	0.20	0.23
8 mil	"	0.05	0.22	0.27
10 mil	"	0.08	0.22	0.30

Insulation	UNIT	MAT.	INST.	TOTAL
07210.10 Batt Insulation				
Ceiling, fiberglass, unfaced				
3-1/2" thick, R11	S.F.	0.39	0.47	0.86
6" thick, R19	"	0.51	0.53	1.04
9" thick, R30	"	1.00	0.62	1.62
Suspended ceiling, unfaced				
3-1/2" thick, R11	S.F.	0.39	0.44	0.83

Insulation	UNIT	MAT.	INST.	TOTAL
07210.10 Batt Insulation				
6" thick, R19	S.F.	0.51	0.50	1.01
9" thick, R30	"	1.00	0.57	1.57
Wall, fiberglass				
Paper backed				
2" thick, R7	S.F.	0.26	0.42	0.68
3" thick, R8	"	0.27	0.44	0.71
4" thick, R11	"	0.45	0.47	0.92
6" thick, R19	"	0.68	0.50	1.18
Foil backed, 1 side				
2" thick, R7	S.F.	0.59	0.42	1.01
3" thick, R11	"	0.62	0.44	1.06
4" thick, R14	"	0.65	0.47	1.12
Foil backed, 2 sides				
Unfaced				
2" thick, R7	S.F.	0.38	0.42	0.80
3" thick, R9	"	0.42	0.44	0.86
4" thick, R11	"	0.45	0.47	0.92
6" thick, R19	"	0.59	0.50	1.09
07210.20 Board Insulation				
Insulation, rigid				
0.75" thick, R2.78	S.F.	0.36	0.36	0.72
1.06" thick, R4.17	"	0.56	0.38	0.94
1.31" thick, R5.26	"	0.74	0.40	1.14
1.63" thick, R6.67	"	0.92	0.42	1.34
2.25" thick, R8.33	"	1.00	0.44	1.44
Perlite board, roof				
1.00" thick, R2.78	S.F.	0.77	0.33	1.10
1.50" thick, R4.17	"	1.20	0.35	1.55
2.00" thick, R5.92	"	1.45	0.36	1.81
2.50" thick, R6.67	"	1.80	0.38	2.18
Rigid urethane				
Roof				
1" thick, R6.67	S.F.	1.05	0.33	1.38
1.20" thick, R8.33	"	1.20	0.34	1.54
1.50" thick, R11.11	"	1.40	0.35	1.75
2" thick, R14.29	"	1.85	0.36	2.21
2.25" thick, R16.67	"	2.40	0.38	2.78
Polystyrene				
Roof				
1.0" thick, R4.17	S.F.	0.98	0.33	1.31
1.5" thick, R6.26	"	1.65	0.35	2.00
2.0" thick, R8.33	"	1.80	0.36	2.16
Wall				
1.0" thick, R4.17	S.F.	0.98	0.42	1.40
1.5" thick, R6.26	"	1.65	0.44	2.09
2.0" thick, R8.33	"	1.80	0.47	2.27
07210.60 Loose Fill Insulation				
Blown-in type				
Fiberglass				
5" thick, R11	S.F.	0.36	0.33	0.69

Insulation	UNIT	MAT.	INST.	TOTAL
07210.60 Loose Fill Insulation				
6" thick, R13	S.F.	0.42	0.40	0.82
9" thick, R19	"	0.51	0.57	1.08
Poured type				
Fiberglass				
1" thick, R4	S.F.	0.33	0.25	0.58
2" thick, R8	"	0.62	0.29	0.90
3" thick, R12	"	0.90	0.33	1.23
4" thick, R16	"	1.20	0.40	1.60
Vermiculite or perlite				
2" thick, R4.8	S.F.	0.77	0.29	1.05
3" thick, R7.2	"	1.10	0.33	1.43
4" thick, R9.6	"	1.45	0.40	1.85
Masonry, poured vermiculite or perlite				
4" block	S.F.	0.59	0.20	0.79
6" block	"	0.74	0.25	0.99
8" block	"	1.10	0.29	1.39
10" block	"	1.30	0.31	1.61
12" block	"	1.50	0.33	1.83
07210.70 Sprayed Insulation				
Foam, sprayed on				
Polystyrene				
1" thick, R4	S.F.	0.74	0.40	1.14
2" thick, R8	"	1.50	0.53	2.03
Urethane				
1" thick, R4	S.F.	0.67	0.40	1.07
2" thick, R8	"	1.40	0.53	1.93
07250.10 Fireproofing				
Sprayed on				
1" thick				
On beams	S.F.	0.71	0.89	1.60
On columns	"	0.73	0.80	1.53
On decks				
Flat surface	S.F.	0.73	0.40	1.13
Fluted surface	"	0.92	0.50	1.42
1-1/2" thick				
On beams	S.F.	1.30	1.15	2.45
On columns	"	1.45	1.00	2.45
On decks				
Flat surface	S.F.	1.10	0.50	1.60
Fluted surface	"	1.30	0.67	1.97

Shingles And Tiles	UNIT	MAT.	INST.	TOTAL
07310.10 Asphalt Shingles				
Standard asphalt shingles, strip shingles				
210 lb/square	SQ.	68.00	49.50	117.50
240 lb/square	"	74.50	62.00	136.50
Roll roofing, mineral surface				
90 lb	SQ.	38.00	35.40	73.40
140 lb	"	65.50	49.50	115.00
07310.30 Metal Shingles				
Aluminum, .020" thick				
Plain	SQ.	260.00	100.00	360.00
Steel, galvanized				
Plain	SQ.	260.00	100.00	360.00
07310.60 Slate Shingles				
Slate shingles				
Ribbon	SQ.	620.00	250.00	870.00
Clear	"	810.00	250.00	1,060
Replacement shingles				
Small jobs	EA.	12.05	16.50	28.55
Large jobs	S.F.	9.50	8.25	17.75
07310.70 Wood Shingles				
Wood shingles, on roofs				
White cedar, #1 shingles				
4" exposure	SQ.	230.00	170.00	400.00
5" exposure	"	210.00	120.00	330.00
#2 shingles				
4" exposure	SQ.	160.00	170.00	330.00
5" exposure	"	140.00	120.00	260.00
Resquared and rebutted				
4" exposure	SQ.	210.00	170.00	380.00
5" exposure	"	170.00	120.00	290.00
Add for fire retarding	"			107.74
07310.80 Wood Shakes				
Shakes, hand split, 24" red cedar, on roofs				
5" exposure	SQ.	240.00	250.00	490.00
7" exposure	"	220.00	200.00	420.00
9" exposure	"	210.00	170.00	380.00
Add for fire retarding	"			74.00

Roofing And Siding

Roofing And Siding	UNIT	MAT.	INST.	TOTAL
07410.10 Manufactured Roofs				
Aluminum roof panels, for structural steel framing				
Corrugated				
Unpainted finish				
.024"	S.F.	1.80	1.25	3.05
.030"	"	2.10	1.25	3.35
Painted finish				
.024"	S.F.	2.25	1.25	3.50
.030"	"	2.75	1.25	4.00
Steel roof panels, for structural steel framing				
Corrugated, painted				
18 ga.	S.F.	5.60	1.25	6.85
20 ga.	"	5.25	1.25	6.50
07460.10 Metal Siding Panels				
Aluminum siding panels				
Corrugated				
Plain finish				
.024"	S.F.	1.55	2.30	3.85
.032"	"	1.85	2.30	4.15
Painted finish				
.024"	S.F.	1.90	2.30	4.20
.032"	"	2.25	2.30	4.55
Steel siding panels				
Corrugated				
22 ga.	S.F.	1.85	3.85	5.70
24 ga.	"	1.70	3.85	5.55
07460.70 Steel Siding				
Ribbed, sheets, galvanized				
22 ga.	S.F.	1.90	2.30	4.20
24 ga.	"	1.70	2.30	4.00
Primed				
24 ga.	S.F.	2.25	2.30	4.55
26 ga.	"	1.55	2.30	3.85

Membrane Roofing

Membrane Roofing	UNIT	MAT.	INST.	TOTAL
07510.10 Built-up Asphalt Roofing				
Built-up roofing, asphalt felt, including gravel				
2 ply	SQ.	55.00	120.00	175.00
3 ply	"	75.00	170.00	245.00
4 ply	"	110.00	200.00	310.00
Walkway, for built-up roofs				
3' x 3' x				
1/2" thick	S.F.	5.20	1.65	6.85
3/4" thick	"	6.90	1.65	8.55

Membrane Roofing	UNIT	MAT.	INST.	TOTAL
07510.10	Built-up Asphalt Roofing			
1" thick	S.F.	7.60	1.65	9.25
Roof bonds				
Asphalt felt				
10 yrs	SQ.			33.88
20 yrs	"			38.72
Cant strip, 4" x 4"				
Treated wood	L.F.	2.20	1.40	3.60
Foamglass	"	1.05	1.25	2.30
Mineral fiber	"	0.44	1.25	1.69
New gravel for built-up roofing, 400 lb/sq	SQ.	31.90	100.00	131.90
Roof gravel (ballast)	C.Y.	21.45	250.00	271.45
Aluminum coating, top surfacing, for built-up roofing	SQ.	33.80	82.50	116.30
Remove 4-ply built-up roof (includes gravel)	"		250.00	250.00
Remove & replace gravel, includes flood coat	"	48.40	170.00	218.40
07530.10	Single-ply Roofing			
Elastic sheet roofing				
Neoprene, 1/16" thick	S.F.	2.70	0.62	3.32
EPDM rubber				
45 mil	S.F.	1.45	0.62	2.07
PVC				
45 mil	S.F.	2.05	0.62	2.67
Flashing				
Pipe flashing, 90 mil thick				
1" pipe	EA.	28.60	12.40	41.00
Neoprene flashing, 60 mil thick strip				
6" wide	L.F.	1.75	4.15	5.90
12" wide	"	3.40	6.20	9.60
18" wide	"	5.05	8.25	13.30
24" wide	"	6.60	12.40	19.00
Adhesives				
Mastic sealer, applied at joints only				
1/4" bead	L.F.	0.11	0.25	0.35
Fluid applied roofing				
Urethane, 2 components, elastomeric top membrane				
1" thick	S.F.	2.95	0.83	3.78
Vinyl liquid roofing, 2 coats, 2 mils per coat	"	4.65	0.71	5.36
Silicone roofing, 2 coats sprayed, 16 mil per coat	"	3.45	0.83	4.28
Inverted roof system				
Insulated membrane with coarse gravel ballast				
3 ply with 2" polystyrene	S.F.	6.70	0.83	7.53
Ballast, 3/4" through 1-1/2" dia. river gravel, 100lb/sf	"	0.38	49.50	49.88
Walkway for membrane roofs, 1/2" thick	"	2.15	1.65	3.80

Flashing And Sheet Metal	UNIT	MAT.	INST.	TOTAL
07610.10 Metal Roofing				
Sheet metal roofing, copper, 16 oz, batten seam	SQ.	760.00	330.00	1,090
Standing seam	"	750.00	310.00	1,060
Aluminum roofing, natural finish				
Corrugated, on steel frame				
.0175" thick	SQ.	120.00	140.00	260.00
.0215" thick	"	160.00	140.00	300.00
.024" thick	"	190.00	140.00	330.00
.032" thick	"	240.00	140.00	380.00
Ridge cap				
.019" thick	L.F.	3.65	1.65	5.30
Corrugated galvanized steel roofing, on steel frame				
28 ga.	SQ.	120.00	140.00	260.00
26 ga.	"	140.00	140.00	280.00
24 ga.	"	160.00	140.00	300.00
22 ga.	"	170.00	140.00	310.00
07620.10 Flashing And Trim				
Counter flashing				
Aluminum, .032"	S.F.	1.45	4.95	6.40
Stainless steel, .015"	"	4.60	4.95	9.55
Copper				
16 oz.	S.F.	6.80	4.95	11.75
20 oz.	"	8.50	4.95	13.45
24 oz.	"	10.20	4.95	15.15
32 oz.	"	12.55	4.95	17.50
Valley flashing				
Aluminum, .032"	S.F.	1.55	3.10	4.65
Stainless steel, .015	"	4.80	3.10	7.90
Copper				
16 oz.	S.F.	6.80	3.10	9.90
20 oz.	"	8.50	4.15	12.65
24 oz.	"	10.20	3.10	13.30
32 oz.	"	12.55	3.10	15.65
Base flashing				
Aluminum, .040"	S.F.	2.60	4.15	6.75
Stainless steel, .018"	"	5.80	4.15	9.95
Copper				
16 oz.	S.F.	6.80	4.15	10.95
20 oz.	"	8.50	3.10	11.60
24 oz.	"	10.20	4.15	14.35
32 oz.	"	12.55	4.15	16.70
Flashing and trim, aluminum				
.019" thick	S.F.	1.30	3.55	4.85
.032" thick	"	1.55	3.55	5.10
.040" thick	"	2.70	3.80	6.50
Reglets, copper 10 oz.	L.F.	4.65	3.30	7.95
Stainless steel, .020"	"	2.75	3.30	6.05
Gravel stop				
Aluminum, .032"				
4"	L.F.	4.95	1.65	6.60
10"	"	10.35	1.90	12.25
Copper, 16 oz.				

Flashing And Sheet Metal	UNIT	MAT.	INST.	TOTAL
07620.10 Flashing And Trim				
4"	L.F.	10.55	1.65	12.20
10"	"	19.00	1.90	20.90
07700.10 Manufactured Specialties				
Smoke vent, 48" x 48"				
Aluminum	EA.	900.00	120.00	1,020
Galvanized steel	"	900.00	120.00	1,020
Heat/smoke vent, 48" x 96"				
Aluminum	EA.	2,750	170.00	2,920
Galvanized steel	"	2,750	170.00	2,920
Ridge vent strips				
Mill finish	L.F.	3.90	3.30	7.20
Soffit vents				
Mill finish				
2-1/2" wide	L.F.	0.48	2.00	2.48
Roof hatches				
Steel, plain, primed				
2'6" x 3'0"	EA.	630.00	120.00	750.00
Galvanized steel				
2'6" x 3'0"	EA.	650.00	120.00	770.00
Aluminum				
2'6" x 3'0"	EA.	680.00	120.00	800.00
Gravity ventilators, with curb, base, damper and screen				
Wind driven spinner				
6" dia.	EA.	56.00	33.00	89.00
12" dia.	"	75.50	33.00	108.50

Skylights	UNIT	MAT.	INST.	TOTAL
07810.10 Plastic Skylights				
Single thickness, not including mounting curb				
2' x 4'	EA.	360.00	62.00	422.00
4' x 4'	"	490.00	82.50	572.50
Double thickness, not including mounting curb				
2' x 4'	EA.	470.00	62.00	532.00
4' x 4'	"	600.00	82.50	682.50

Metal	UNIT	MAT.	INST.	TOTAL
08110.10 — Metal Doors				
Flush hollow metal, standard duty, 20 ga., 1-3/8" thick				
2-6 x 6-8	EA.	210.00	57.50	267.50
2-8 x 6-8	"	250.00	57.50	307.50
3-0 x 6-8	"	260.00	57.50	317.50
1-3/4" thick				
2-6 x 6-8	EA.	250.00	57.50	307.50
2-8 x 6-8	"	260.00	57.50	317.50
3-0 x 6-8	"	280.00	57.50	337.50
Heavy duty, 20 ga., unrated, 1-3/4"				
2-8 x 6-8	EA.	270.00	57.50	327.50
3-0 x 6-8	"	280.00	57.50	337.50
08110.40 — Metal Door Frames				
Hollow metal, stock, 18 ga., 4-3/4" x 1-3/4"				
2-0 x 7-0	EA.	130.00	64.50	194.50
2-4 x 7-0	"	130.00	64.50	194.50
2-6 x 7-0	"	140.00	64.50	204.50
3-0 x 7-0	"	150.00	64.50	214.50
08120.10 — Aluminum Doors				
Aluminum doors, commercial				
Narrow stile				
2-6 x 7-0	EA.	610.00	290.00	900.00
3-0 x 7-0	"	650.00	290.00	940.00
3-6 x 7-0	"	660.00	290.00	950.00
Wide stile				
2-6 x 7-0	EA.	950.00	290.00	1,240
3-0 x 7-0	"	980.00	290.00	1,270
3-6 x 7-0	"	1,010	290.00	1,300
08300.10 — Special Doors				
Overhead door, coiling insulated				
Chain gear, no frame, 12' x 12'	EA.	2,730	650.00	3,380
Sliding metal fire doors, motorized, fusible link, 3 hr.				
3-0 x 6-8	EA.	3,490	1,030	4,520
3-8 x 6-8	"	3,490	1,030	4,520
4-0 x 8-0	"	3,760	1,030	4,790
5-0 x 8-0	"	3,850	1,030	4,880
Counter doors, (roll-up shutters), standard, manual				
Opening, 4' high				
4' wide	EA.	1,240	430.00	1,670
6' wide	"	1,700	430.00	2,130
8' wide	"	1,970	470.00	2,440
10' wide	"	2,150	650.00	2,800
14' wide	"	2,680	650.00	3,330
6' high				
4' wide	EA.	1,530	430.00	1,960
6' wide	"	1,970	470.00	2,440
8' wide	"	2,130	520.00	2,650
10' wide	"	2,380	650.00	3,030
14' wide	"	2,560	740.00	3,300
For stainless steel, add to material, 40%				

Metal	UNIT	MAT.	INST.	TOTAL
08300.10		Special Doors		
For motor operator, add	EA.			1,362
Service doors, (roll up shutters), standard, manual				
Opening				
8' high x 8' wide	EA.	1,590	290.00	1,880
10' high x 10' wide	"	1,870	430.00	2,300
12' high x 12' wide	"	2,210	650.00	2,860
14' high x 14' wide	"	2,900	860.00	3,760
16' high x 14' wide	"	3,920	860.00	4,780
20' high x 14' wide	"	5,550	1,290	6,840
24' high x 16' wide	"	7,520	1,150	8,670
For motor operator				
Up to 12-0 x 12-0, add	EA.			1,537
Over 12-0 x 12-0, add	"			1,967
Roll-up doors				
13-0 high x 14-0 wide	EA.	1,360	740.00	2,100
12-0 high x 14-0 wide	"	1,700	740.00	2,440
Top coiling grilles, manually operated, steel or aluminum				
Opening, 4' high x				
4' wide	EA.	1,610	210.00	1,820
6' wide	"	1,640	210.00	1,850
8' wide	"	1,900	290.00	2,190
12' wide	"	2,210	290.00	2,500
16' wide	"	2,560	430.00	2,990
6' high x				
4' wide	EA.	1,700	430.00	2,130
6' wide	"	1,870	470.00	2,340
8' wide	"	1,960	520.00	2,480
12' wide	"	2,380	570.00	2,950
16' wide	"	3,070	740.00	3,810
Side coiling grilles, manually operated, aluminum				
Opening, 8' high x				
18' wide	EA.	11,930	4,850	16,780
24' wide	"	15,330	5,540	20,870
12' high x				
12' wide	EA.	11,930	4,850	16,780
18' wide	"	15,330	5,540	20,870
24' wide	"	20,440	6,470	26,910

Storefronts	UNIT	MAT.	INST.	TOTAL
08410.10		Storefronts		
Storefront, aluminum and glass				
Minimum	S.F.	17.35	7.15	24.50
Average	"	27.40	8.20	35.60
Maximum	"	47.70	9.55	57.25

Metal Windows	UNIT	MAT.	INST.	TOTAL
08510.10 Steel Windows				
Steel windows, primed				
Casements				
Operable				
Minimum	S.F.	34.80	3.40	38.20
Maximum	"	52.00	3.85	55.85
Fixed sash	"	27.80	2.85	30.65
Double hung	"	52.00	3.20	55.20
Industrial windows				
Horizontally pivoted sash	S.F.	48.70	3.85	52.55
Fixed sash	"	38.20	3.20	41.40
Security sash				
Operable	S.F.	61.00	3.85	64.85
Fixed	"	54.00	3.20	57.20
Picture window	"	26.10	3.20	29.30
Projecting sash				
Minimum	S.F.	45.20	3.60	48.80
Maximum	"	55.50	3.60	59.10
Mullions	L.F.	11.90	2.85	14.75
08520.10 Aluminum Windows				
Fixed window				
6 sf to 8 sf	S.F.	14.95	8.20	23.15
12 sf to 16 sf	"	13.25	6.40	19.65
Projecting window				
6 sf to 8 sf	S.F.	33.20	14.35	47.55
12 sf to 16 sf	"	29.80	9.55	39.35
Horizontal sliding				
6 sf to 8 sf	S.F.	21.55	7.15	28.70
12 sf to 16 sf	"	19.90	5.75	25.65
Double hung				
6 sf to 8 sf	S.F.	29.80	11.50	41.30
10 sf to 12 sf	"	26.50	9.55	36.05

Hardware	UNIT	MAT.	INST.	TOTAL
08710.10 Hinges				
Hinges				
3 x 3 butts, steel, interior, plain bearing	PAIR			17.90
4 x 4 butts, steel, standard	"			26.87
5 x 4-1/2 butts, bronze/s. steel, heavy duty	"			71.59
08710.20 Locksets				
Latchset, heavy duty				
Cylindrical	EA.	150.00	32.30	182.30
Mortise	"	150.00	51.50	201.50
Lockset, heavy duty				

Hardware	UNIT	MAT.	INST.	TOTAL
08710.20 Locksets				
Cylindrical	EA.	180.00	32.30	212.30
Mortise	"	210.00	51.50	261.50
08710.30 Closers				
Door closers				
Surface mounted, traditional type, parallel arm				
Standard	EA.	160.00	64.50	224.50
Heavy duty	"	180.00	64.50	244.50
08710.40 Door Trim				
Panic device				
Mortise	EA.	770.00	130.00	900.00
Vertical rod	"	890.00	130.00	1,020
Labelled, rim type	"	800.00	130.00	930.00
Mortise	"	960.00	130.00	1,090
Vertical rod	"	1,080	130.00	1,210
Door plates				
Kick plate, aluminum, 3 beveled edges				
10" x 28"	EA.	17.10	25.80	42.90
10" x 38"	"	23.65	25.80	49.45
Push plate, 4" x 16"				
Aluminum	EA.	16.90	10.30	27.20
Bronze	"	84.50	10.30	94.80
Stainless steel	"	67.50	10.30	77.80
08710.60 Weatherstripping				
Weatherstrip, head and jamb, metal strip, neoprene bulb				
Standard duty	L.F.	4.05	2.85	6.90
Heavy duty	"	5.10	3.20	8.30
Thresholds				
Bronze	L.F.	50.50	12.90	63.40
Aluminum				
Plain	L.F.	18.95	12.90	31.85
Vinyl insert	"	28.90	12.90	41.80
Aluminum with grit	"	27.10	12.90	40.00
Steel				
Plain	L.F.	18.95	12.90	31.85
Interlocking	"	28.90	43.00	71.90

Glazing	UNIT	MAT.	INST.	TOTAL
08810.10 Glazing				
Sheet glass, 1/8" thick	S.F.	7.20	3.20	10.40
Plate glass, bronze or grey, 1/4" thick	"	10.75	5.20	15.95
Clear	"	8.25	5.20	13.45
Polished	"	9.10	5.20	14.30

Glazing	UNIT	MAT.	INST.	TOTAL
08810.10	Glazing			
Plexiglass				
1/8" thick	S.F.	3.10	5.20	8.30
1/4" thick	"	5.75	3.20	8.95
Float glass, clear				
1/4" thick	S.F.	6.15	5.20	11.35
1/2" thick	"	20.70	9.55	30.25
3/4" thick	"	25.90	14.35	40.25
1" thick	"	45.60	19.15	64.75
Tinted glass, polished plate, twin ground				
1/4" thick	S.F.	8.20	5.20	13.40
1/2" thick	"	21.45	9.55	31.00
Total, full vision, all glass window system				
To 10' high				
Minimum	S.F.	33.30	14.35	47.65
Average	"	43.80	14.35	58.15
Maximum	"	52.50	14.35	66.85
10' to 20' high				
Minimum	S.F.	40.30	14.35	54.65
Average	"	49.10	14.35	63.45
Maximum	"	61.50	14.35	75.85
Insulated glass, bronze or gray				
1/2" thick	S.F.	15.30	9.55	24.85
1" thick	"	18.20	14.35	32.55
Spandrel glass, polished bronze/grey, 1 side, 1/4" thick	"	12.30	5.20	17.50
Tempered glass (safety)				
Clear sheet glass				
1/8" thick	S.F.	8.40	3.20	11.60
3/16" thick	"	10.20	4.40	14.60
Clear float glass				
1/4" thick	S.F.	8.75	4.80	13.55
1/2" thick	"	26.30	9.55	35.85
3/4" thick	"	36.80	19.15	55.95
Tinted float glass				
3/16" thick	S.F.	10.50	4.40	14.90
1/4" thick	"	11.60	4.80	16.40
3/8" thick	"	21.05	7.15	28.20
1/2" thick	"	28.10	9.55	37.65
Laminated glass				
Float safety glass with polyvinyl plastic interlayer				
1/4", sheet or float				
Two lites, 1/8" thick, clear glass	S.F.	12.25	4.80	17.05
1/2" thick, float glass				
Two lites, 1/4" thick, clear glass	S.F.	18.25	9.55	27.80
Tinted glass	"	21.85	9.55	31.40
Insulating glass, two lites, clear float glass				
1/2" thick	S.F.	11.95	9.55	21.50
3/4" thick	"	15.15	14.35	29.50
1" thick	"	17.05	19.15	36.20
Glass seal edge				
3/8" thick	S.F.	10.05	9.55	19.60
Tinted glass				
1/2" thick	S.F.	20.50	9.55	30.05

Glazing	UNIT	MAT.	INST.	TOTAL
08810.10	Glazing			
1" thick	S.F.	22.05	19.15	41.20
Tempered, clear				
1" thick	S.F.	40.10	19.15	59.25
Wire reinforced	"	51.00	19.15	70.15
Plate mirror glass				
1/4" thick				
15 sf	S.F.	10.50	5.75	16.25
Over 15 sf	"	9.65	5.20	14.85
Door type, 1/4" thick	"	11.00	5.75	16.75
Transparent, one way vision, 1/4" thick	"	23.35	5.75	29.10
Sheet mirror glass				
3/16" thick	S.F.	10.20	5.75	15.95
1/4" thick	"	10.70	4.80	15.50
Wall tiles, 12" x 12"				
Clear glass	S.F.	3.45	3.20	6.65
Veined glass	"	4.05	3.20	7.25
Wire glass, 1/4" thick				
Clear	S.F.	14.25	19.15	33.40
Hammered	"	14.40	19.15	33.55
Obscure	"	17.25	19.15	36.40
Glazing accessories				
Neoprene glazing gaskets				
1/4" glass	L.F.	1.40	2.30	3.70
1/2" glass	"	2.15	2.50	4.65
3/4" glass	"	2.95	2.60	5.55
1" glass	"	3.35	2.85	6.20
Mullion section				
1/4" glass	L.F.	0.58	1.15	1.72
3/8" glass	"	0.74	1.45	2.19
1/2" glass	"	1.10	1.65	2.75
3/4" glass	"	1.65	1.90	3.55
1" glass	"	2.20	2.30	4.50
Molded corners	EA.	2.35	38.30	40.65

Glazed Curtain Walls	UNIT	MAT.	INST.	TOTAL
08910.10	Glazed Curtain Walls			
Curtain wall, aluminum system, framing sections				
2" x 3"				
Jamb	L.F.	10.50	4.80	15.30
Horizontal	"	10.65	4.80	15.45
Mullion	"	14.25	4.80	19.05
2" x 4"				
Jamb	L.F.	14.25	7.15	21.40
Horizontal	"	14.65	7.15	21.80
Mullion	"	14.25	7.15	21.40

Glazed Curtain Walls	UNIT	MAT.	INST.	TOTAL
08910.10 Glazed Curtain Walls				
3" x 5-1/2"				
Jamb	L.F.	18.80	7.15	25.95
Horizontal	"	20.90	7.15	28.05
Mullion	"	18.95	7.15	26.10
4" corner mullion	"	25.10	9.55	34.65
Coping sections				
1/8" x 8"	L.F.	26.30	9.55	35.85
1/8" x 9"	"	26.50	9.55	36.05
1/8" x 12-1/2"	"	27.10	11.50	38.60
Sill section				
1/8" x 6"	L.F.	25.90	5.75	31.65
1/8" x 7"	"	26.20	5.75	31.95
1/8" x 8-1/2"	"	26.70	5.75	32.45
Column covers, aluminum				
1/8" x 26"	L.F.	25.90	14.35	40.25
1/8" x 34"	"	26.20	15.10	41.30
1/8" x 38"	"	26.50	15.10	41.60
Doors				
Aluminum framed, standard hardware				
Narrow stile				
2-6 x 7-0	EA.	580.00	290.00	870.00
3-0 x 7-0	"	590.00	290.00	880.00
3-6 x 7-0	"	610.00	290.00	900.00
Wide stile				
2-6 x 7-0	EA.	1,010	290.00	1,300
3-0 x 7-0	"	1,080	290.00	1,370
3-6 x 7-0	"	1,160	290.00	1,450
Window wall system, complete				
Minimum	S.F.	18.80	5.75	24.55
Average	"	30.10	6.40	36.50
Maximum	"	69.50	8.20	77.70
Added costs				
For bronze, add 20% to material				
For stainless steel, add 50% to material				

Support Systems	UNIT	MAT.	INST.	TOTAL
09110.10 Metal Studs				
Studs, non load bearing, galvanized				
2-1/2", 20 ga.				
12" o.c.	S.F.	0.94	1.05	1.99
16" o.c.	"	0.77	0.86	1.62
25 ga.				
12" o.c.	S.F.	0.65	1.05	1.70
16" o.c.	"	0.46	0.86	1.32
24" o.c.	"	0.41	0.72	1.13
3-5/8", 20 ga.				
12" o.c.	S.F.	1.10	1.30	2.40
16" o.c.	"	0.94	1.05	1.99
24" o.c.	"	0.75	0.86	1.61
25 ga.				
12" o.c.	S.F.	0.63	1.30	1.93
16" o.c.	"	0.54	1.05	1.59
24" o.c.	"	0.44	0.86	1.30
4", 20 ga.				
12" o.c.	S.F.	1.30	1.30	2.60
16" o.c.	"	1.05	1.05	2.10
24" o.c.	"	0.85	0.86	1.71
25 ga.				
12" o.c.	S.F.	0.75	1.30	2.05
16" o.c.	"	0.63	1.05	1.68
24" o.c.	"	0.53	0.86	1.39
6", 20 ga.				
12" o.c.	S.F.	1.55	1.60	3.15
16" o.c.	"	1.30	1.30	2.60
24" o.c.	"	1.00	1.05	2.05
25 ga.				
12" o.c.	S.F.	0.96	1.60	2.56
16" o.c.	"	0.77	1.30	2.06
24" o.c.	"	0.65	1.05	1.70
Load bearing studs, galvanized				
3-5/8", 16 ga.				
12" o.c.	S.F.	1.85	1.30	3.15
16" o.c.	"	1.50	1.05	2.55
18 ga.				
12" o.c.	S.F.	1.65	0.86	2.51
16" o.c.	"	1.30	1.05	2.35
4", 16 ga.				
12" o.c.	S.F.	2.00	1.30	3.30
16" o.c.	"	1.65	1.05	2.70
6", 16 ga.				
12" o.c.	S.F.	2.45	1.60	4.05
16" o.c.	"	2.00	1.30	3.30
Furring				
On beams and columns				
7/8" channel	L.F.	0.49	3.45	3.94
1-1/2" channel	"	0.57	3.95	4.52
On ceilings				
3/4" furring channels				
12" o.c.	S.F.	0.46	2.15	2.61

Support Systems	UNIT	MAT.	INST.	TOTAL
09110.10 Metal Studs				
16" o.c.	S.F.	0.40	2.05	2.45
24" o.c.	"	0.29	1.85	2.14
1-1/2" furring channels				
12" o.c.	S.F.	0.66	2.35	3.01
16" o.c.	"	0.57	2.15	2.72
24" o.c.	"	0.49	2.00	2.49
On walls				
3/4" furring channels				
12" o.c.	S.F.	0.47	1.70	2.17
16" o.c.	"	0.38	1.60	1.98
24" o.c.	"	0.29	1.50	1.79
1-1/2" furring channels				
12" o.c.	S.F.	0.66	1.85	2.51
16" o.c.	"	0.57	1.70	2.27

Lath And Plaster	UNIT	MAT.	INST.	TOTAL
09205.10 Gypsum Lath				
Gypsum lath, 1/2" thick				
Clipped	S.Y.	7.40	2.85	10.25
Nailed	"	7.20	3.20	10.40
09205.20 Metal Lath				
Stucco lath				
1.8 lb.	S.Y.	4.95	6.45	11.40
3.6 lb.	"	5.55	6.45	12.00
Paper backed				
Minimum	S.Y.	3.85	5.15	9.00
Maximum	"	6.20	7.35	13.55
09210.10 Plaster				
Gypsum plaster, trowel finish, 2 coats				
Ceilings	S.Y.	6.20	15.85	22.05
Walls	"	6.20	14.95	21.15
3 coats				
Ceilings	S.Y.	8.60	22.10	30.70
Walls	"	8.60	19.55	28.15
Patch holes, average size holes				
1 sf to 5 sf				
Minimum	S.F.	2.55	8.45	11.00
Average	"	3.45	10.15	13.60
Maximum	"	4.65	12.70	17.35
Over 5 sf				
Minimum	S.F.	2.25	5.10	7.35
Average	"	3.05	7.25	10.30
Maximum	"	3.80	8.45	12.25

Lath And Plaster	UNIT	MAT.	INST.	TOTAL
09210.10 **Plaster**				
Patch cracks				
Minimum	S.F.	1.35	1.70	3.05
average	"	1.55	2.55	4.10
Maximum	"	1.90	5.10	7.00
09220.10 **Portland Cement Plaster**				
Stucco, portland, gray, 3 coat, 1" thick				
Sand finish	S.Y.	7.75	22.10	29.85
Trowel finish	"	7.75	23.10	30.85
White cement				
Sand finish	S.Y.	8.85	23.10	31.95
Trowel finish	"	8.85	25.40	34.25
Scratch coat				
For ceramic tile	S.Y.	2.80	5.10	7.90
For quarry tile	"	2.80	5.10	7.90
Portland cement plaster				
2 coats, 1/2"	S.Y.	5.60	10.15	15.75
3 coats, 7/8"	"	6.65	12.70	19.35
09250.10 **Gypsum Board**				
Drywall, plasterboard, 3/8" clipped to				
Metal furred ceiling	S.F.	0.34	0.57	0.92
Columns and beams	"	0.34	1.30	1.64
Walls	"	0.34	0.52	0.86
Nailed or screwed to				
Wood framed ceiling	S.F.	0.34	0.52	0.86
Columns and beams	"	0.34	1.15	1.49
Walls	"	0.34	0.47	0.81
1/2", clipped to				
Metal furred ceiling	S.F.	0.36	0.57	0.93
Columns and beams	"	0.36	1.30	1.66
Walls	"	0.36	0.52	0.88
Nailed or screwed to				
Wood framed ceiling	S.F.	0.36	0.52	0.88
Columns and beams	"	0.36	1.15	1.51
Walls	"	0.36	0.47	0.83
5/8", clipped to				
Metal furred ceiling	S.F.	0.39	0.65	1.04
Columns and beams	"	0.39	1.45	1.84
Walls	"	0.39	0.57	0.96
Nailed or screwed to				
Wood framed ceiling	S.F.	0.39	0.65	1.04
Columns and beams	"	0.39	1.45	1.84
Walls	"	0.39	0.57	0.96
Taping and finishing joints				
Minimum	S.F.	0.05	0.34	0.39
Average	"	0.06	0.43	0.49
Maximum	"	0.09	0.52	0.61
Casing bead				
Minimum	L.F.	0.15	1.45	1.60
Average	"	0.17	1.70	1.86
Maximum	"	0.21	2.60	2.81

Lath And Plaster	UNIT	MAT.	INST.	TOTAL
09250.10 Gypsum Board				
Corner bead				
Minimum	L.F.	0.17	1.45	1.61
Average	"	0.21	1.70	1.91
Maximum	"	0.25	2.60	2.85

Tile	UNIT	MAT.	INST.	TOTAL
09310.10 Ceramic Tile				
Glazed wall tile, 4-1/4" x 4-1/4"				
Minimum	S.F.	2.30	3.55	5.85
Average	"	3.65	4.15	7.80
Maximum	"	9.95	5.00	14.95
Unglazed floor tile				
Portland cement bed, cushion edge, face mounted				
1" x 1"	S.F.	6.95	4.55	11.50
1" x 2"	"	11.15	4.35	15.50
2" x 2"	"	7.30	4.15	11.45
Adhesive bed, with white grout				
1" x 1"	S.F.	6.15	4.55	10.70
1" x 2"	"	6.40	4.35	10.75
2" x 2"	"	6.50	4.15	10.65
09330.10 Quarry Tile				
Floor				
4 x 4 x 1/2"	S.F.	5.40	6.65	12.05
6 x 6 x 1/2"	"	5.50	6.25	11.75
6 x 6 x 3/4"	"	6.45	6.25	12.70
Wall, applied to 3/4" portland cement bed				
4 x 4 x 1/2"	S.F.	4.95	10.00	14.95
6 x 6 x 3/4"	"	6.20	8.30	14.50
Cove base				
5 x 6 x 1/2" straight top	L.F.	4.80	8.30	13.10
6 x 6 x 3/4" round top	"	5.10	8.30	13.40
Stair treads 6 x 6 x 3/4"	"	8.55	12.45	21.00
Window sill 6 x 8 x 3/4"	"	6.90	10.00	16.90
For abrasive surface, add to material, 25%				
09410.10 Terrazzo				
Floors on concrete, 1-3/4" thick, 5/8" topping				
Gray cement	S.F.	4.70	7.25	11.95
White cement	"	5.10	7.25	12.35
Sand cushion, 3" thick, 5/8" top, 1/4"				
Gray cement	S.F.	5.55	8.45	14.00
White cement	"	6.15	8.45	14.60
Monolithic terrazzo, 3-1/2" base slab, 5/8" topping	"	3.95	6.35	10.30
Terrazzo wainscot, cast-in-place, 1/2" thick	"	8.30	12.70	21.00

Tile	UNIT	MAT.	INST.	TOTAL
09410.10 Terrazzo				
Base, cast in place, terrazzo cove type, 6" high	L.F.	8.85	7.25	16.10
Curb, cast in place, 6" wide x 6" high, polished top	"	9.85	25.40	35.25
For venetian type terrazzo, add to material, 10%				
For abrasive heavy duty terrazzo, add to material, 15%				
Divider strips				
Zinc	L.F.			1.50
Brass	"			2.80
Stairs, cast-in-place, topping on concrete or metal				
1-1/2" thick treads, 12" wide	L.F.	5.90	25.40	31.30
Combined tread and riser	"	8.85	63.50	72.35
Precast terrazzo, thin set				
Terrazzo tiles, non-slip surface				
9" x 9" x 1" thick	S.F.	18.75	7.25	26.00
12" x 12"				
1" thick	S.F.	20.20	6.75	26.95
1-1/2" thick	"	21.10	7.25	28.35
18" x 18" x 1-1/2" thick	"	27.60	7.25	34.85
24" x 24" x 1-1/2" thick	"	35.50	6.00	41.50
For white cement, add to material, 10%				
For venetian type terrazzo, add to material, 25%				
Terrazzo wainscot				
12" x 12" x 1" thick	S.F.	20.70	12.70	33.40
18" x 18" x 1-1/2" thick	"	32.50	14.50	47.00
Base				
6" high				
Straight	L.F.	13.35	3.90	17.25
Coved	"	15.80	3.90	19.70
8" high				
Straight	L.F.	14.95	4.25	19.20
Coved	"	17.55	4.25	21.80
Terrazzo curbs				
8" wide x 8" high	L.F.	31.50	20.30	51.80
6" wide x 6" high	"	28.60	16.95	45.55
Precast terrazzo stair treads, 12" wide				
1-1/2" thick				
Diamond pattern	L.F.	33.50	9.25	42.75
Non-slip surface	"	37.50	9.25	46.75
2" thick				
Diamond pattern	L.F.	37.50	9.25	46.75
Non-slip surface	"	41.40	10.15	51.55
Stair risers, 1" thick to 6" high				
Straight sections	L.F.	14.10	5.10	19.20
Cove sections	"	16.55	5.10	21.65
Combined tread and riser				
Straight sections				
1-1/2" tread, 3/4" riser	L.F.	68.50	14.50	83.00
3" tread, 1" riser	"	72.50	14.50	87.00
Curved sections				
2" tread, 1" riser	L.F.	77.50	16.95	94.45
3" tread, 1" riser	"	80.00	16.95	96.95
Stair stringers, notched for treads and risers				
1" thick	L.F.	36.40	12.70	49.10

Tile

	UNIT	MAT.	INST.	TOTAL
09410.10 Terrazzo				
2" thick	L.F.	37.80	16.95	54.75
Landings, structural, nonslip				
1-1/2" thick	S.F.	31.30	8.45	39.75
3" thick	"	30.50	10.15	40.65
Conductive terrazzo, spark proof industrial floor				
Epoxy terrazzo				
Floor	S.F.	13.20	3.15	16.35
Base	"	13.20	4.25	17.45
Polyacrylate				
Floor	S.F.	10.65	3.15	13.80
Base	"	10.65	4.25	14.90
Polyester				
Floor	S.F.	3.75	2.05	5.80
Base	"	3.75	2.55	6.30
Synthetic latex mastic				
Floor	S.F.	6.10	3.15	9.25
Base	"	6.10	4.25	10.35

Acoustical Treatment

	UNIT	MAT.	INST.	TOTAL
09510.10 Ceilings And Walls				
Acoustical panels, suspension system not included				
Fiberglass panels				
5/8" thick				
2' x 2'	S.F.	0.93	0.74	1.67
2' x 4'	"	0.93	0.57	1.50
3/4" thick				
2' x 2'	S.F.	1.15	0.74	1.89
2' x 4'	"	1.15	0.57	1.72
Mineral fiber panels				
5/8" thick				
2' x 2'	S.F.	1.15	0.74	1.89
2' x 4'	"	1.15	0.57	1.72
3/4" thick				
2' x 2'	S.F.	1.50	0.74	2.24
2' x 4'	"	1.50	0.57	2.07
Ceiling suspension systems				
T bar system				
2' x 4'	S.F.	1.15	0.52	1.67
2' x 2'	"	1.25	0.57	1.82

Flooring	UNIT	MAT.	INST.	TOTAL
09550.10 Wood Flooring				
Wood block industrial flooring				
Creosoted				
2" thick	S.F.	4.15	1.35	5.50
2-1/2" thick	"	4.30	1.60	5.90
3" thick	"	4.50	1.70	6.20
Gym floor, 2 ply felt, 25/32" maple, finished, in mastic	"	7.75	2.85	10.60
Over wood sleepers	"	8.65	3.20	11.85
Finishing, sand, fill, finish, and wax	"	0.67	1.30	1.97
Refinish sand, seal, and 2 coats of polyurethane	"	1.15	1.70	2.85
Clean and wax floors	"	0.20	0.26	0.45
09630.10 Unit Masonry Flooring				
Clay brick				
9 x 4-1/2 x 3" thick				
Glazed	S.F.	8.05	4.30	12.35
Unglazed	"	7.70	4.30	12.00
8 x 4 x 3/4" thick				
Glazed	S.F.	7.25	4.50	11.75
Unglazed	"	7.15	4.50	11.65
For herringbone pattern, add to labor, 15%				
09660.10 Resilient Tile Flooring				
Solid vinyl tile, 1/8" thick, 12" x 12"				
Marble patterns	S.F.	2.95	1.30	4.25
Solid colors	"	3.85	1.30	5.15
Travertine patterns	"	4.30	1.30	5.60
09665.10 Resilient Sheet Flooring				
Vinyl sheet flooring				
Minimum	S.F.	2.60	0.52	3.12
Average	"	3.75	0.62	4.37
Maximum	"	7.85	0.86	8.71
Cove, to 6"	L.F.	1.60	1.05	2.65
Fluid applied resilient flooring				
Polyurethane, poured in place, 3/8" thick	S.F.	10.60	4.30	14.90
09678.10 Resilient Base And Accessories				
Wall base, vinyl				
4" high	L.F.	1.05	1.70	2.75
6" high	"	1.45	1.70	3.15
Stair accessories				
Treads, 1/4" x 12", rubber diamond surface				
Marbled	L.F.	8.30	4.30	12.60
Plain	"	8.10	4.30	12.40
Grit strip safety tread, 12" wide, colors				
3/16" thick	L.F.	11.40	4.30	15.70
5/16" thick	"	15.95	4.30	20.25
Risers, 7" high, 1/8" thick, colors				
Flat	L.F.	2.40	2.60	5.00
Coved	"	4.00	2.60	6.60

Carpet	UNIT	MAT.	INST.	TOTAL
09680.10 Floor Leveling				
Repair and level floors to receive new flooring				
Minimum	S.Y.	0.89	1.70	2.59
Average	"	3.45	4.30	7.75
Maximum	"	5.10	5.15	10.25
09682.10 Carpet Padding				
Carpet padding				
Jute padding				
Minimum	S.Y.	4.20	2.35	6.55
Average	"	5.45	2.60	8.05
Maximum	"	8.20	2.85	11.05
Sponge rubber cushion				
Minimum	S.Y.	4.95	2.35	7.30
Average	"	6.60	2.60	9.20
Maximum	"	8.20	2.85	11.05
Urethane cushion, 3/8" thick				
Minimum	S.Y.	4.95	2.35	7.30
Average	"	5.75	2.60	8.35
Maximum	"	6.60	2.85	9.45
09685.10 Carpet				
Carpet, acrylic				
24 oz., light traffic	S.Y.	28.00	5.75	33.75
28 oz., medium traffic	"	35.40	5.75	41.15
Commercial				
Nylon				
28 oz., medium traffic	S.Y.	25.70	5.75	31.45
35 oz., heavy traffic	"	30.80	5.75	36.55
Wool				
30 oz., medium traffic	S.Y.	42.00	5.75	47.75
36 oz., medium traffic	"	44.30	5.75	50.05
42 oz., heavy traffic	"	58.50	5.75	64.25
Carpet tile				
Foam backed				
Clean and vacuum carpet				
Minimum	S.Y.	0.29	0.20	0.49
Average	"	0.47	0.34	0.81
Maximum	"	0.64	0.52	1.16
09700.10 Special Flooring				
Epoxy flooring, marble chips				
Epoxy with colored quartz chips in 1/4" base	S.F.	12.10	2.85	14.95
Heavy duty epoxy topping, 3/16" thick	"	10.65	2.85	13.50
Epoxy terrazzo				
1/4" thick chemical resistant	S.F.	12.40	3.20	15.60

Painting	UNIT	MAT.	INST.	TOTAL
09905.10 Painting Preparation				
Dropcloths				
Minimum	S.F.	0.02	0.03	0.06
Average	"	0.02	0.04	0.07
Maximum	"	0.02	0.06	0.08
Masking				
Paper and tape				
Minimum	L.F.	0.02	0.52	0.54
Average	"	0.02	0.65	0.67
Maximum	"	0.02	0.86	0.88
Doors				
Minimum	EA.	0.05	6.45	6.50
Average	"	0.05	8.60	8.65
Maximum	"	0.05	11.45	11.50
Windows				
Minimum	EA.	0.05	6.45	6.50
Average	"	0.05	8.60	8.65
Maximum	"	0.05	11.45	11.50
Sanding				
Walls and flat surfaces				
Minimum	S.F.		0.34	0.34
Average	"		0.43	0.43
Maximum	"		0.52	0.52
Doors and windows				
Minimum	EA.		8.60	8.60
Average	"		12.90	12.90
Maximum	"		17.20	17.20
Trim				
Minimum	L.F.		0.65	0.65
Average	"		0.86	0.86
Maximum	"		1.15	1.15
Puttying				
Minimum	S.F.	0.01	0.79	0.81
Average	"	0.01	1.05	1.06
Maximum	"	0.01	1.30	1.31
09910.05 Ext. Painting, Sitework				
Benches				
Brush				
First Coat				
Minimum	S.F.	0.17	0.52	0.69
Average	"	0.17	0.65	0.82
Maximum	"	0.17	0.86	1.03
Second Coat				
Minimum	S.F.	0.17	0.32	0.49
Average	"	0.17	0.37	0.54
Maximum	"	0.17	0.43	0.60
Roller				
First Coat				
Minimum	S.F.	0.17	0.26	0.43
Average	"	0.17	0.29	0.46
Maximum	"	0.17	0.32	0.49
Second Coat				

Painting	UNIT	MAT.	INST.	TOTAL
09910.05 Ext. Painting, Sitework				
Minimum	S.F.	0.17	0.18	0.36
Average	"	0.17	0.22	0.39
Maximum	"	0.17	0.24	0.41
Brickwork				
Brush				
First Coat				
Minimum	S.F.	0.17	0.32	0.49
Average	"	0.17	0.43	0.60
Maximum	"	0.17	0.65	0.82
Second Coat				
Minimum	S.F.	0.17	0.29	0.46
Average	"	0.17	0.34	0.52
Maximum	"	0.17	0.43	0.60
Roller				
First Coat				
Minimum	S.F.	0.17	0.26	0.43
Average	"	0.17	0.32	0.49
Maximum	"	0.17	0.43	0.60
Second Coat				
Minimum	S.F.	0.17	0.22	0.39
Average	"	0.17	0.26	0.43
Maximum	"	0.17	0.32	0.49
Spray				
First Coat				
Minimum	S.F.	0.14	0.14	0.29
Average	"	0.14	0.18	0.33
Maximum	"	0.14	0.24	0.38
Second Coat				
Minimum	S.F.	0.14	0.14	0.28
Average	"	0.14	0.17	0.31
Maximum	"	0.14	0.22	0.36
Concrete Block				
Roller				
First Coat				
Minimum	S.F.	0.17	0.26	0.43
Average	"	0.17	0.34	0.52
Maximum	"	0.17	0.52	0.69
Second Coat				
Minimum	S.F.	0.17	0.22	0.39
Average	"	0.17	0.29	0.46
Maximum	"	0.17	0.43	0.60
Spray				
First Coat				
Minimum	S.F.	0.14	0.14	0.29
Average	"	0.14	0.17	0.32
Maximum	"	0.14	0.20	0.34
Second Coat				
Minimum	S.F.	0.14	0.09	0.24
Average	"	0.14	0.12	0.26
Maximum	"	0.14	0.16	0.30
Fences, Chain Link				
Brush				

Painting	UNIT	MAT.	INST.	TOTAL
09910.05 Ext. Painting, Sitework				
First Coat				
Minimum	S.F.	0.11	0.52	0.63
Average	"	0.11	0.57	0.69
Maximum	"	0.11	0.65	0.76
Second Coat				
Minimum	S.F.	0.11	0.34	0.46
Average	"	0.11	0.40	0.51
Maximum	"	0.11	0.47	0.58
Roller				
First Coat				
Minimum	S.F.	0.11	0.37	0.48
Average	"	0.11	0.43	0.54
Maximum	"	0.11	0.49	0.61
Second Coat				
Minimum	S.F.	0.11	0.22	0.33
Average	"	0.11	0.26	0.37
Maximum	"	0.11	0.32	0.44
Spray				
First Coat				
Minimum	S.F.	0.09	0.16	0.25
Average	"	0.09	0.18	0.27
Maximum	"	0.09	0.22	0.30
Second Coat				
Minimum	S.F.	0.09	0.12	0.21
Average	"	0.09	0.14	0.23
Maximum	"	0.09	0.16	0.25
Fences, Wood or Masonry				
Brush				
First Coat				
Minimum	S.F.	0.17	0.54	0.71
Average	"	0.17	0.65	0.82
Maximum	"	0.17	0.86	1.03
Second Coat				
Minimum	S.F.	0.17	0.32	0.49
Average	"	0.17	0.40	0.57
Maximum	"	0.17	0.52	0.69
Roller				
First Coat				
Minimum	S.F.	0.17	0.29	0.46
Average	"	0.17	0.34	0.52
Maximum	"	0.17	0.40	0.57
Second Coat				
Minimum	S.F.	0.17	0.20	0.37
Average	"	0.17	0.25	0.42
Maximum	"	0.17	0.32	0.49
Spray				
First Coat				
Minimum	S.F.	0.14	0.18	0.33
Average	"	0.14	0.24	0.38
Maximum	"	0.14	0.32	0.47
Second Coat				
Minimum	S.F.	0.14	0.13	0.27

Painting	UNIT	MAT.	INST.	TOTAL
09910.05 Ext. Painting, Sitework				
Average	S.F.	0.14	0.16	0.30
Maximum	"	0.14	0.22	0.36
Storage Tanks				
Roller				
First Coat				
Minimum	S.F.	0.14	0.22	0.36
Average	"	0.14	0.26	0.40
Maximum	"	0.14	0.32	0.47
Second Coat				
Minimum	S.F.	0.14	0.17	0.32
Average	"	0.14	0.21	0.35
Maximum	"	0.14	0.26	0.40
Spray				
First Coat				
Minimum	S.F.	0.11	0.13	0.24
Average	"	0.11	0.15	0.27
Maximum	"	0.11	0.18	0.30
Second Coat				
Minimum	S.F.	0.11	0.10	0.22
Average	"	0.11	0.12	0.23
Maximum	"	0.11	0.13	0.24
09910.15 Ext. Painting, Buildings				
Decks, Wood, Stained				
Brush				
First Coat				
Minimum	S.F.	0.14	0.26	0.40
Average	"	0.14	0.29	0.43
Maximum	"	0.14	0.32	0.47
Second Coat				
Minimum	S.F.	0.14	0.18	0.33
Average	"	0.14	0.20	0.34
Maximum	"	0.14	0.22	0.36
Roller				
First Coat				
Minimum	S.F.	0.14	0.18	0.33
Average	"	0.14	0.20	0.34
Maximum	"	0.14	0.22	0.36
Second Coat				
Minimum	S.F.	0.14	0.16	0.30
Average	"	0.14	0.17	0.32
Maximum	"	0.14	0.20	0.34
Spray				
First Coat				
Minimum	S.F.	0.11	0.16	0.28
Average	"	0.11	0.17	0.29
Maximum	"	0.11	0.20	0.31
Second Coat				
Minimum	S.F.	0.11	0.14	0.26
Average	"	0.11	0.16	0.27
Maximum	"	0.11	0.17	0.29
Doors, Metal				

Painting	UNIT	MAT.	INST.	TOTAL
09910.15 — Ext. Painting, Buildings				
Roller				
First Coat				
Minimum	S.F.	0.14	0.37	0.51
Average	"	0.14	0.43	0.57
Maximum	"	0.14	0.52	0.66
Second Coat				
Minimum	S.F.	0.14	0.26	0.40
Average	"	0.14	0.29	0.43
Maximum	"	0.14	0.32	0.47
Spray				
First Coat				
Minimum	S.F.	0.11	0.32	0.44
Average	"	0.11	0.37	0.48
Maximum	"	0.11	0.43	0.54
Second Coat				
Minimum	S.F.	0.11	0.24	0.35
Average	"	0.11	0.26	0.37
Maximum	"	0.11	0.29	0.40
Door Frames, Metal				
Brush				
First Coat				
Minimum	L.F.	0.17	0.65	0.82
Average	"	0.17	0.81	0.98
Maximum	"	0.17	0.94	1.11
Second Coat				
Minimum	L.F.	0.17	0.37	0.54
Average	"	0.17	0.43	0.60
Maximum	"	0.17	0.52	0.69
Spray				
First Coat				
Minimum	L.F.	0.11	0.29	0.40
Average	"	0.11	0.37	0.48
Maximum	"	0.11	0.52	0.63
Second Coat				
Minimum	L.F.	0.11	0.24	0.35
Average	"	0.11	0.26	0.37
Maximum	"	0.11	0.29	0.40
Siding, Metal				
Roller				
First Coat				
Minimum	S.F.	0.14	0.22	0.36
Average	"	0.14	0.24	0.38
Maximum	"	0.14	0.26	0.40
Second Coat				
Minimum	S.F.	0.14	0.20	0.34
Average	"	0.14	0.22	0.36
Maximum	"	0.14	0.24	0.38
Spray				
First Coat				
Minimum	S.F.	0.11	0.16	0.28
Average	"	0.11	0.18	0.30
Maximum	"	0.11	0.22	0.33

Painting		UNIT	MAT.	INST.	TOTAL
09910.15	Ext. Painting, Buildings				
Minimum		S.F.	0.11	0.10	0.22
Average		"	0.11	0.13	0.24
Maximum		"	0.11	0.17	0.29
Stucco					
Roller					
First Coat					
Minimum		S.F.	0.17	0.24	0.41
Average		"	0.17	0.27	0.44
Maximum		"	0.17	0.32	0.49
Second Coat					
Minimum		S.F.	0.17	0.19	0.36
Average		"	0.17	0.22	0.39
Maximum		"	0.17	0.26	0.43
Spray					
First Coat					
Minimum		S.F.	0.13	0.16	0.29
Average		"	0.13	0.18	0.31
Maximum		"	0.13	0.22	0.34
Second Coat					
Minimum		S.F.	0.13	0.13	0.26
Average		"	0.13	0.15	0.28
Maximum		"	0.13	0.17	0.30
Trim					
Brush					
First Coat					
Minimum		L.F.	0.17	0.22	0.39
Average		"	0.17	0.26	0.43
Maximum		"	0.17	0.32	0.49
Second Coat					
Minimum		L.F.	0.17	0.16	0.33
Average		"	0.17	0.22	0.39
Maximum		"	0.17	0.32	0.49
Walls					
Roller					
First Coat					
Minimum		S.F.	0.14	0.18	0.33
Average		"	0.14	0.19	0.33
Maximum		"	0.14	0.21	0.35
Second Coat					
Minimum		S.F.	0.14	0.16	0.30
Average		"	0.14	0.17	0.32
Maximum		"	0.14	0.20	0.34
Spray					
First Coat					
Minimum		S.F.	0.11	0.08	0.20
Average		"	0.11	0.10	0.22
Maximum		"	0.11	0.13	0.24
Second Coat					
Minimum		S.F.	0.11	0.07	0.18
Average		"	0.11	0.09	0.20
Maximum		"	0.11	0.12	0.23
Windows					

Painting	UNIT	MAT.	INST.	TOTAL
09910.15 Ext. Painting, Buildings				
Brush				
First Coat				
Minimum	S.F.	0.11	0.86	0.97
Average	"	0.11	1.05	1.16
Maximum	"	0.11	1.30	1.41
Second Coat				
Minimum	S.F.	0.11	0.74	0.85
Average	"	0.11	0.86	0.97
Maximum	"	0.11	1.05	1.16
09910.25 Ext. Painting, Misc.				
Gratings, Metal				
Roller				
First Coat				
Minimum	S.F.	0.14	1.45	1.59
Average	"	0.14	1.70	1.84
Maximum	"	0.14	2.05	2.19
Second Coat				
Minimum	S.F.	0.14	1.05	1.19
Average	"	0.14	1.30	1.44
Maximum	"	0.14	1.70	1.84
Spray				
First Coat				
Minimum	S.F.	0.11	0.74	0.85
Average	"	0.11	0.86	0.97
Maximum	"	0.11	1.05	1.16
Second Coat				
Minimum	S.F.	0.11	0.57	0.69
Average	"	0.11	0.65	0.76
Maximum	"	0.11	0.74	0.85
Ladders				
Brush				
First Coat				
Minimum	L.F.	0.17	1.30	1.47
Average	"	0.17	1.45	1.62
Maximum	"	0.17	1.70	1.87
Second Coat				
Minimum	L.F.	0.17	1.05	1.22
Average	"	0.17	1.15	1.32
Maximum	"	0.17	1.30	1.47
Spray				
First Coat				
Minimum	L.F.	0.11	0.86	0.97
Average	"	0.11	0.94	1.05
Maximum	"	0.11	1.05	1.16
Second Coat				
Minimum	L.F.	0.11	0.74	0.85
Average	"	0.11	0.79	0.91
Maximum	"	0.11	0.86	0.97
Shutters and Louvres				
Brush				
First Coat				

Painting	UNIT	MAT.	INST.	TOTAL
09910.25 Ext. Painting, Misc.				
Minimum	EA.	0.17	10.30	10.47
Average	"	0.17	12.90	13.07
Maximum	"	0.17	17.20	17.37
Second Coat				
Minimum	EA.	0.17	6.45	6.62
Average	"	0.17	7.95	8.12
Maximum	"	0.17	10.30	10.47
Spray				
First Coat				
Minimum	EA.	0.11	3.45	3.56
Average	"	0.11	4.15	4.26
Maximum	"	0.11	5.15	5.26
Second Coat				
Minimum	EA.	0.11	2.60	2.71
Average	"	0.11	3.45	3.56
Maximum	"	0.11	4.15	4.26
Stairs, metal				
Brush				
First Coat				
Minimum	S.F.	0.17	0.57	0.74
Average	"	0.17	0.65	0.82
Maximum	"	0.17	0.74	0.91
Second Coat				
Minimum	S.F.	0.17	0.32	0.49
Average	"	0.17	0.37	0.54
Maximum	"	0.17	0.43	0.60
Spray				
First Coat				
Minimum	S.F.	0.11	0.29	0.40
Average	"		0.37	0.37
Maximum	"	0.11	0.40	0.51
Second Coat				
Minimum	S.F.	0.11	0.22	0.33
Average	"	0.11	0.26	0.37
Maximum	"	0.11	0.32	0.44
09910.35 Int. Painting, Buildings				
Ceilings				
Roller				
First Coat				
Minimum	S.F.	0.14	0.22	0.36
Average	"	0.14	0.24	0.38
Maximum	"	0.14	0.26	0.40
Second Coat				
Minimum	S.F.	0.14	0.17	0.32
Average	"	0.14	0.20	0.34
Maximum	"	0.14	0.22	0.36
Spray				
First Coat				
Minimum	S.F.	0.11	0.13	0.24
Average	"	0.11	0.14	0.26
Maximum	"	0.11	0.16	0.28

Painting	UNIT	MAT.	INST.	TOTAL
09910.35 Int. Painting, Buildings				
Second Coat				
Minimum	S.F.	0.11	0.10	0.21
Average	"	0.11	0.11	0.23
Maximum	"	0.11	0.13	0.24
Doors, Metal				
Roller				
First Coat				
Minimum	L.F.	0.17	0.34	0.52
Average	"	0.17	0.40	0.57
Maximum	"	0.17	0.47	0.64
Second Coat				
Minimum	L.F.	0.17	0.25	0.42
Average	"	0.17	0.27	0.44
Maximum	"	0.17	0.30	0.48
Spray				
First Coat				
Minimum	L.F.	0.11	0.29	0.40
Average	"	0.11	0.32	0.44
Maximum	"	0.11	0.37	0.48
Second Coat				
Minimum	L.F.	0.11	0.22	0.33
Average	"	0.11	0.24	0.35
Maximum	"	0.11	0.26	0.37
Floors				
Roller				
First Coat				
Minimum	S.F.	0.14	0.16	0.30
Average	"	0.14	0.19	0.33
Maximum	"	0.14	0.22	0.36
Second Coat				
Minimum	S.F.	0.14	0.13	0.27
Average	"	0.14	0.14	0.29
Maximum	"	0.14	0.15	0.30
Spray				
First Coat				
Minimum	S.F.	0.11	0.12	0.23
Average	"	0.11	0.12	0.24
Maximum	"	0.11	0.14	0.25
Second Coat				
Minimum	S.F.	0.11	0.10	0.21
Average	"	0.11	0.11	0.22
Maximum	"	0.11	0.12	0.23
Pipes to 6" diameter				
Brush				
Minimum	L.F.	0.17	0.65	0.82
Average	"	0.17	0.74	0.91
Maximum	"	0.17	0.86	1.03
Spray				
Minimum	L.F.	0.14	0.22	0.36
Average	"	0.14	0.26	0.40
Maximum	"	0.14	0.34	0.49
Pipes to 12" diameter				

Painting	UNIT	MAT.	INST.	TOTAL
09910.35 — Int. Painting, Buildings				
Brush				
Minimum	L.F.	0.29	1.30	1.59
Average	"	0.29	1.45	1.74
Maximum	"	0.29	1.70	1.99
Spray				
Minimum	L.F.	0.26	0.43	0.69
Average	"	0.26	0.52	0.77
Maximum	"	0.26	0.65	0.90
Trim				
Brush				
First Coat				
Minimum	L.F.	0.17	0.21	0.38
Average	"	0.17	0.24	0.41
Maximum	"	0.17	0.29	0.46
Second Coat				
Minimum	L.F.	0.17	0.15	0.32
Average	"	0.17	0.20	0.37
Maximum	"	0.17	0.29	0.46
Walls				
Roller				
First Coat				
Minimum	S.F.	0.14	0.18	0.33
Average	"	0.14	0.19	0.33
Maximum	"	0.14	0.22	0.36
Second Coat				
Minimum	S.F.	0.14	0.16	0.30
Average	"	0.14	0.17	0.32
Maximum	"	0.14	0.20	0.34
Spray				
First Coat				
Minimum	S.F.	0.11	0.08	0.20
Average	"	0.11	0.10	0.21
Maximum	"	0.11	0.13	0.24
Second Coat				
Minimum	S.F.	0.11	0.07	0.19
Average	"	0.11	0.09	0.20
Maximum	"	0.11	0.12	0.23
09955.10 — Wall Covering				
Vinyl wall covering				
Medium duty	S.F.	1.45	0.74	2.19
Heavy duty	"	2.15	0.86	3.01
Over pipes and irregular shapes				
Flexible gypsum coated wall fabric, fire resistant	S.F.	1.60	0.52	2.12
Vinyl corner guards				
3/4" x 3/4" x 8'	EA.	7.50	6.45	13.95
2-3/4" x 2-3/4" x 4'	"	4.45	6.45	10.90
09980.15 — Paint				
Paint, enamel				
600 sf per gal.	GAL			40.45
550 sf per gal.	"			36.47

Painting	UNIT	MAT.	INST.	TOTAL
09980.15 Paint				
500 sf per gal.	GAL			26.53
450 sf per gal.	"			24.86
350 sf per gal.	"			23.21
Filler, 60 sf per gal.	"			28.19
Latex, 400 sf per gal.	"			23.21
Aluminum				
400 sf per gal.	GAL			33.16
500 sf per gal.	"			59.67
Red lead, 350 sf per gal.	"			49.74
Primer				
400 sf per gal.	GAL			30.65
300 sf per gal.	"			30.77
Latex base, interior, white	"			25.75
Sealer and varnish				
400 sf per gal.	GAL			23.77
425 sf per gal.	"			34.78
600 sf per gal.	"			46.60

Specialties	UNIT	MAT.	INST.	TOTAL
10110.10 Chalkboards				
Chalkboard, metal frame, 1/4" thick				
48"x60"	EA.	270.00	51.50	321.50
48"x96"	"	440.00	57.50	497.50
48"x144"	"	570.00	64.50	634.50
48"x192"	"	800.00	73.50	873.50
Liquid chalkboard				
48"x60"	EA.	290.00	51.50	341.50
48"x96"	"	450.00	57.50	507.50
48"x144"	"	690.00	64.50	754.50
48"x192"	"	800.00	73.50	873.50
Map rail, deluxe	L.F.	8.15	2.60	10.75
Average	PCT.			4.16
10165.10 Toilet Partitions				
Toilet partition, plastic laminate				
Ceiling mounted	EA.	780.00	170.00	950.00
Floor mounted	"	700.00	130.00	830.00
Metal				
Ceiling mounted	EA.	610.00	170.00	780.00
Floor mounted	"	580.00	130.00	710.00
Wheel chair partition, plastic laminate				
Ceiling mounted	EA.	1,110	170.00	1,280
Floor mounted	"	1,040	130.00	1,170
Painted metal				
Ceiling mounted	EA.	880.00	170.00	1,050
Floor mounted	"	790.00	130.00	920.00
Urinal screen, plastic laminate				
Wall hung	EA.	390.00	64.50	454.50
Floor mounted	"	330.00	64.50	394.50
Porcelain enameled steel, floor mounted	"	460.00	64.50	524.50
Painted metal, floor mounted	"	290.00	64.50	354.50
Stainless steel, floor mounted	"	610.00	64.50	674.50
Metal toilet partitions				
Front door and side divider, floor mounted				
Porcelain enameled steel	EA.	1,030	130.00	1,160
Painted steel	"	580.00	130.00	710.00
Stainless steel	"	1,370	130.00	1,500
10185.10 Shower Stalls				
Shower receptors				
Precast, terrazzo				
32" x 32"	EA.	460.00	47.40	507.40
32" x 48"	"	580.00	57.00	637.00
Concrete				
32" x 32"	EA.	230.00	47.40	277.40
48" x 48"	"	280.00	63.00	343.00
Shower door, trim and hardware				
Porcelain enameled steel, flush	EA.	440.00	57.00	497.00
Baked enameled steel, flush	"	260.00	57.00	317.00
Aluminum frame, tempered glass, 48" wide, sliding	"	570.00	71.00	641.00
Folding	"	540.00	71.00	611.00
Shower compartment, precast concrete receptor				

Specialties	UNIT	MAT.	INST.	TOTAL
10185.10 Shower Stalls				
Single entry type				
Porcelain enameled steel	EA.	2,090	570.00	2,660
Baked enameled steel	"	1,210	570.00	1,780
Stainless steel	"	2,420	570.00	2,990
Double entry type				
Porcelain enameled steel	EA.	5,960	710.00	6,670
Baked enameled steel	"	3,860	710.00	4,570
Stainless steel	"	6,040	710.00	6,750
10210.10 Vents And Wall Louvres				
Vents w/screen, 4" deep, 8" wide, 5" high				
Modular	EA.	82.00	17.95	99.95
Aluminum gable louvers	S.F.	14.65	9.55	24.20
Vent screen aluminum, 4" wide, continuous	L.F.	4.10	1.90	6.00
Wall louvre, aluminum mill finish				
Under, 2 sf	S.F.	30.90	7.15	38.05
2 to 4 sf	"	26.00	6.40	32.40
5 to 10 sf	"	25.20	6.40	31.60
Galvanized steel				
Under 2 sf	S.F.	29.30	7.15	36.45
2 to 4 sf	"	21.20	6.40	27.60
5 to 10 sf	"	19.55	6.40	25.95
10225.10 Door Louvres				
Fixed, 1" thick, enameled steel				
8"x8"	EA.	48.10	6.45	54.55
12"x12"	"	61.50	7.35	68.85
20"x20"	"	120.00	20.65	140.65
24"x24"	"	130.00	23.45	153.45
10290.10 Pest Control				
Termite control				
Under slab spraying				
Minimum	S.F.	0.18	0.10	0.28
Average	"	0.24	0.20	0.44
Maximum	"	0.34	0.40	0.74
10350.10 Flagpoles				
Installed in concrete base				
Fiberglass				
25' high	EA.	1,230	340.00	1,570
50' high	"	5,520	860.00	6,380
Aluminum				
25' high	EA.	1,530	340.00	1,870
50' high	"	5,060	860.00	5,920
Bonderized steel				
25' high	EA.	2,410	400.00	2,810
50' high	"	5,620	1,030	6,650
Freestanding tapered, fiberglass				
30' high	EA.	1,380	370.00	1,750
40' high	"	2,420	470.00	2,890
50' high	"	4,910	520.00	5,430
60' high	"	6,440	610.00	7,050

Specialties	UNIT	MAT.	INST.	TOTAL
10350.10			Flagpoles	
Wall mounted, with collar, brushed aluminum finish				
15' long	EA.	1,070	260.00	1,330
18' long	"	1,380	260.00	1,640
20' long	"	1,530	270.00	1,800
24' long	"	1,690	300.00	1,990
Outrigger, wall, including base				
10' long	EA.	920.00	340.00	1,260
20' long	"	1,380	430.00	1,810
10400.10		Identifying Devices		
Directory and bulletin boards				
Open face boards				
Chrome plated steel frame	S.F.	28.20	25.80	54.00
Aluminum framed	"	24.75	25.80	50.55
Bronze framed	"	26.70	25.80	52.50
Stainless steel framed	"	53.00	25.80	78.80
Tack board, aluminum framed	"	15.90	25.80	41.70
Visual aid board, aluminum framed	"	15.90	25.80	41.70
Glass encased boards, hinged and keyed				
Aluminum framed	S.F.	61.50	64.50	126.00
Bronze framed	"	66.50	64.50	131.00
Stainless steel framed	"	150.00	64.50	214.50
Chrome plated steel framed	"	150.00	64.50	214.50
Metal plaque				
Cast bronze	S.F.	400.00	43.00	443.00
Aluminum	"	370.00	43.00	413.00
Metal engraved plaque				
Porcelain steel	S.F.	500.00	43.00	543.00
Stainless steel	"	460.00	43.00	503.00
Brass	"	500.00	43.00	543.00
Aluminum	"	230.00	43.00	273.00
Metal built-up plaque				
Bronze	S.F.	390.00	51.50	441.50
Copper and bronze	"	400.00	51.50	451.50
Copper and aluminum	"	440.00	51.50	491.50
Metal nameplate plaques				
Cast bronze	S.F.	390.00	32.30	422.30
Cast aluminum	"	350.00	32.30	382.30
Engraved, 1-1/2" x 6"				
Bronze	EA.	120.00	32.30	152.30
Aluminum	"	120.00	32.30	152.30
Letters, on masonry or concrete, aluminum, satin finish				
1/2" thick				
2" high	EA.	14.50	20.65	35.15
4" high	"	16.25	25.80	42.05
6" high	"	21.35	28.70	50.05
3/4" thick				
8" high	EA.	28.20	32.30	60.50
10" high	"	35.90	36.90	72.80
1" thick				
12" high	EA.	47.00	43.00	90.00
14" high	"	53.00	51.50	104.50

Specialties	UNIT	MAT.	INST.	TOTAL
10400.10 — Identifying Devices				
16" high	EA.	73.50	64.50	138.00
For polished aluminum add, 15%				
For clear anodized aluminum add, 15%				
For colored anodic aluminum add, 30%				
For profiled and color enameled letters add, 50%				
Cast bronze, satin finish letters				
3/8" thick				
2" high	EA.	26.50	20.65	47.15
4" high	"	28.70	25.80	54.50
1/2" thick, 6" high	"	37.30	28.70	66.00
5/8" thick, 8" high	"	48.10	32.30	80.40
1" thick				
10" high	EA.	73.00	36.90	109.90
12" high	"	93.00	43.00	136.00
14" high	"	100.00	51.50	151.50
16" high	"	130.00	64.50	194.50
Interior door signs, adhesive, flexible				
2" x 8"	EA.	17.40	10.00	27.40
4" x 4"	"	17.90	10.00	27.90
6" x 7"	"	23.40	10.00	33.40
6" x 9"	"	30.80	10.00	40.80
10" x 9"	"	41.00	10.00	51.00
10" x 12"	"	53.00	10.00	63.00
Hard plastic type, no frame				
3" x 8"	EA.	37.60	10.00	47.60
4" x 4"	"	35.90	10.00	45.90
4" x 12"	"	44.40	10.00	54.40
Hard plastic type, with frame				
3" x 8"	EA.	130.00	10.00	140.00
4" x 4"	"	97.50	10.00	107.50
4" x 12"	"	160.00	10.00	170.00
10450.10 — Control				
Access control, 7' high, indoor or outdoor impenetrability				
Remote or card control, type B	EA.	4,100	700.00	4,800
Free passage, type B	"	3,790	700.00	4,490
Remote or card control, type AA	"	5,370	700.00	6,070
Free passage, type AA	"	4,890	700.00	5,590
10500.10 — Lockers				
Locker bench, floor mounted, laminated maple				
4'	EA.	140.00	43.00	183.00
6'	"	210.00	43.00	253.00
Wardrobe locker, 12" x 60" x 15", baked on enamel				
1-tier	EA.	170.00	25.80	195.80
2-tier	"	190.00	25.80	215.80
3-tier	"	190.00	27.20	217.20
4-tier	"	230.00	27.20	257.20
12" x 72" x 15", baked on enamel				
1-tier	EA.	170.00	25.80	195.80
2-tier	"	210.00	25.80	235.80
4-tier	"	260.00	27.20	287.20

Specialties	UNIT	MAT.	INST.	TOTAL
10500.10 Lockers				
5-tier	EA.	260.00	27.20	287.20
15" x 60" x 15", baked on enamel				
1-tier	EA.	230.00	25.80	255.80
4-tier	"	250.00	27.20	277.20
Wardrobe locker, single tier type				
12" x 15" x 72"	EA.	170.00	51.50	221.50
18" x 15" x 72"	"	210.00	54.50	264.50
12" x 18" x 72"	"	200.00	57.50	257.50
18" x 18" x 72"	"	230.00	60.50	290.50
Double tier type				
12" x 15" x 36"	EA.	120.00	25.80	145.80
18" x 15" x 36"	"	130.00	25.80	155.80
12" x 18" x 36"	"	110.00	25.80	135.80
18" x 18" x 36"	"	130.00	25.80	155.80
Two person unit				
18" x 15" x 72"	EA.	340.00	86.00	426.00
18" x 18" x 72"	"	200.00	100.00	300.00
Duplex unit				
15" x 15" x 72"	EA.	330.00	51.50	381.50
15" x 21" x 72"	"	350.00	51.50	401.50
Basket lockers, basket sets with baskets				
24 basket set	SET	710.00	260.00	970.00
30 basket set	"	850.00	320.00	1,170
36 basket set	"	950.00	430.00	1,380
42 basket set	"	1,050	520.00	1,570
10520.10 Fire Protection				
Portable fire extinguishers				
Water pump tank type				
2.5 gal.				
Red enameled galvanized	EA.	110.00	26.70	136.70
Red enameled copper	"	130.00	26.70	156.70
Polished copper	"	190.00	26.70	216.70
Carbon dioxide type, red enamel steel				
Squeeze grip with hose and horn				
2.5 lb	EA.	65.00	26.70	91.70
5 lb	"	150.00	30.80	180.80
10 lb	"	230.00	40.00	270.00
15 lb	"	260.00	50.00	310.00
20 lb	"	310.00	50.00	360.00
Wheeled type				
125 lb	EA.	1,640	80.00	1,720
250 lb	"	1,690	80.00	1,770
500 lb	"	3,160	80.00	3,240
Dry chemical, pressurized type				
Red enameled steel				
2.5 lb	EA.	39.00	26.70	65.70
5 lb	"	65.00	30.80	95.80
10 lb	"	81.50	40.00	121.50
20 lb	"	130.00	50.00	180.00
30 lb	"	340.00	50.00	390.00
Chrome plated steel, 2.5 lb	"	81.50	26.70	108.20

Specialties	UNIT	MAT.	INST.	TOTAL
10520.10 Fire Protection				
Other type extinguishers				
2.5 gal, stainless steel, pressurized water tanks	EA.	81.50	26.70	108.20
Soda and acid type	"	150.00	26.70	176.70
Cartridge operated, water type	"	240.00	26.70	266.70
Loaded stream, water type	"	110.00	26.70	136.70
Foam type	"	94.50	26.70	121.20
40 gal, wheeled foam type	"	4,940	80.00	5,020
Fire extinguisher cabinets				
Enameled steel				
8" x 12" x 27"	EA.	180.00	80.00	260.00
8" x 16" x 38"	"	240.00	80.00	320.00
Aluminum				
8" x 12" x 27"	EA.	240.00	80.00	320.00
8" x 16" x 38"	"	280.00	80.00	360.00
8" x 12" x 27"	"	400.00	80.00	480.00
Stainless steel				
8" x 16" x 38"	EA.	510.00	80.00	590.00
10550.10 Postal Specialties				
Mail chutes				
Single mail chute				
Finished aluminum	L.F.	640.00	130.00	770.00
Bronze	"	940.00	130.00	1,070
Single mail chute receiving box				
Finished aluminum	EA.	1,010	260.00	1,270
Bronze	"	1,880	260.00	2,140
Twin mail chute, double parallel				
Finished aluminum	FLR	1,200	260.00	1,460
Bronze	"	1,880	260.00	2,140
Receiving box, 36" x 20" x 12"				
Finished aluminum	EA.	2,090	430.00	2,520
Bronze	"	2,990	430.00	3,420
Locked receiving mail box				
Finished aluminum	EA.	1,010	260.00	1,270
Bronze	"	1,710	260.00	1,970
Commercial postal accessories for mail chutes				
Letter slot, brass	EA.	330.00	86.00	416.00
Bulk mail slot, brass	"	950.00	86.00	1,036
Mail boxes				
Residential postal accessories				
Letter slot	EA.	100.00	25.80	125.80
Rural letter box	"	70.00	64.50	134.50
10670.10 Shelving				
Shelving, enamel, closed side and back, 12" x 36"				
5 shelves	EA.	170.00	86.00	256.00
8 shelves	"	210.00	110.00	320.00
Open				
5 shelves	EA.	110.00	86.00	196.00
8 shelves	"	110.00	110.00	220.00
Metal storage shelving, baked enamel				
7 shelf unit, 72" or 84" high				

Specialties	UNIT	MAT.	INST.	TOTAL
10670.10 Shelving				
12" shelf	L.F.	48.80	54.50	103.30
24" shelf	"	64.50	64.50	129.00
36" shelf	"	83.50	73.50	157.00
4 shelf unit, 40" high				
12" shelf	L.F.	41.80	46.90	88.70
24" shelf	"	59.00	57.50	116.50
3 shelf unit, 32" high				
12" shelf	L.F.	33.10	27.20	60.30
24" shelf	"	43.50	32.30	75.80
Single shelf unit, attached to masonry				
12" shelf	L.F.	13.05	9.40	22.45
24" shelf	"	18.30	11.20	29.50
For stainless steel, add to material, 120%				
For attachment to gypsum board, add to labor, 50%				
10800.10 Bath Accessories				
Ash receiver, wall mounted, aluminum	EA.	180.00	25.80	205.80
Grab bar, 1-1/2" dia., stainless steel, wall mounted				
24" long	EA.	50.00	25.80	75.80
36" long	"	72.50	27.20	99.70
48" long	"	100.00	30.40	130.40
1" dia., stainless steel				
12" long	EA.	39.60	22.45	62.05
24" long	"	46.60	25.80	72.40
36" long	"	58.50	28.70	87.20
48" long	"	60.50	30.40	90.90
Hand dryer, surface mounted, 110 volt	"	560.00	64.50	624.50
Medicine cabinet, 16 x 22, baked enamel, steel, lighted	"	89.50	20.65	110.15
With mirror, lighted	"	160.00	34.40	194.40
Mirror, 1/4" plate glass, up to 10 sf	S.F.	8.95	5.15	14.10
Mirror, stainless steel frame				
18"x24"	EA.	140.00	17.20	157.20
24"x30"	"	180.00	25.80	205.80
24"x48"	"	350.00	43.00	393.00
30"x30"	"	200.00	51.50	251.50
48"x72"	"	590.00	86.00	676.00
With shelf, 18"x24"	"	200.00	20.65	220.65
Sanitary napkin dispenser, stainless steel, wall mounted	"	480.00	34.40	514.40
Shower rod, 1" diameter				
Chrome finish over brass	EA.	81.00	25.80	106.80
Stainless steel	"	77.50	25.80	103.30
Soap dish, stainless steel, wall mounted	"	98.50	34.40	132.90
Toilet tissue dispenser, stainless, wall mounted				
Single roll	EA.	48.30	12.90	61.20
Double roll	"	76.00	14.75	90.75
Towel dispenser, stainless steel				
Flush mounted	EA.	140.00	28.70	168.70
Surface mounted	"	130.00	25.80	155.80
Combination towel dispenser and waste receptacle	"	430.00	34.40	464.40
Towel bar, stainless steel				
18" long	EA.	41.40	20.65	62.05
24" long	"	48.30	23.45	71.75

Specialties	UNIT	MAT.	INST.	TOTAL
10800.10		Bath Accessories		
30" long	EA.	51.50	25.80	77.30
36" long	"	57.00	28.70	85.70
Waste receptacle, stainless steel, wall mounted	"	290.00	43.00	333.00

Architectural Equipment	UNIT	MAT.	INST.	TOTAL
11020.10 Security Equipment				
Office safes, 30" x 20" x 20", 1 hr rating	EA.	2,520	130.00	2,650
30" x 16" x 15", 2 hr rating	"	2,370	100.00	2,470
30" x 28" x 20", H&G rating	"	11,050	64.50	11,115
Surveillance system				
Minimum	EA.	5,880	1,030	6,910
Maximum	"	45,600	5,160	50,760
Insulated file room door				
1 hr rating				
32" wide	EA.	3,980	520.00	4,500
40" wide	"	4,230	570.00	4,800
11161.10 Loading Dock Equipment				
Dock leveler, 10 ton capacity				
6' x 8'	EA.	4,740	520.00	5,260
7' x 8'	"	4,900	520.00	5,420
Bumpers, laminated rubber				
4-1/2" thick				
6" x 14"	EA.	80.50	10.30	90.80
10" x 14"	"	86.50	12.90	99.40
10" x 36"	"	110.00	17.20	127.20
12" x 14"	"	94.50	13.60	108.10
12" x 36"	"	130.00	19.10	149.10
6" thick				
10" x 14"	EA.	100.00	14.75	114.75
10" x 24"	"	130.00	17.80	147.80
10" x 36"	"	140.00	25.80	165.80
Extruded rubber bumpers				
T-section, 22" x 22" x 3"	EA.	130.00	10.30	140.30
Molded rubber bumpers				
24" x 12" x 3" thick	EA.	78.00	25.80	103.80
Door seal, 12" x 12", vinyl covered	L.F.	44.80	12.90	57.70
Dock boards, heavy duty, 5' x 5'				
5000 lb				
Minimum	EA.	1,260	430.00	1,690
Maximum	"	2,160	430.00	2,590
9000 lb				
Minimum	EA.	1,440	430.00	1,870
Maximum	"	2,400	470.00	2,870
15,000 lb	"	1,900	470.00	2,370
Truck shelters				
Minimum	EA.	1,510	400.00	1,910
Maximum	"	2,490	740.00	3,230
11170.10 Waste Handling				
Incinerator, electric				
100 lb/hr				
Minimum	EA.	22,240	530.00	22,770
Maximum	"	38,350	530.00	38,880
400 lb/hr				
Minimum	EA.	39,480	1,050	40,530
Maximum	"	76,680	1,050	77,730
1000 lb/hr				

Architectural Equipment	UNIT	MAT.	INST.	TOTAL
11170.10	\multicolumn{4}{Waste Handling}			
Minimum	EA.	76,690	1,600	78,290
Maximum	"	122,700	1,600	124,300
11480.10	\multicolumn{4}{Athletic Equipment}			
Basketball backboard				
Fixed	EA.	870.00	650.00	1,520
Swing-up	"	2,010	1,030	3,040
Portable, hydraulic	"	11,130	260.00	11,390
Suspended type, standard	"	3,930	1,030	4,960
For glass backboard, add	"			1,203
For electrically operated, add	"			1,588
Bleacher, telescoping, manual				
15 tier, minimum	SEAT	110.00	10.30	120.30
Maximum	"	130.00	10.30	140.30
20 tier, minimum	"	110.00	11.45	121.45
Maximum	"	130.00	11.45	141.45
30 tier, minimum	"	110.00	17.20	127.20
Maximum	"	130.00	17.20	147.20
Boxing ring elevated, complete, 22' x 22'	EA.	9,240	7,370	16,610
Gym divider curtain				
Minimum	S.F.	5.75	0.69	6.44
Maximum	"	9.00	0.69	9.69
Scoreboards, single face				
Minimum	EA.	4,100	520.00	4,620
Maximum	"	26,440	2,580	29,020
Parallel bars				
Minimum	EA.	1,370	520.00	1,890
Maximum	"	3,850	860.00	4,710
11500.10	\multicolumn{4}{Industrial Equipment}			
Vehicular paint spray booth, solid back, 14'4" x 9'6"				
24' deep	EA.	13,880	520.00	14,400
26'6" deep	"	14,040	520.00	14,560
28'6" deep	"	14,300	520.00	14,820
Drive through, 14'9" x 9'6"				
24' deep	EA.	14,300	520.00	14,820
26'6" deep	"	14,640	520.00	15,160
28'6" deep	"	14,800	520.00	15,320
Water wash, paint spray booth				
5' x 11'2" x 10'8"	EA.	7,190	520.00	7,710
6' x 11'2" x 10'8"	"	7,360	520.00	7,880
8' x 11'2" x 10'8"	"	9,300	520.00	9,820
10' x 11'2" x 11'2"	"	10,320	520.00	10,840
12' x 12'2" x 11'2"	"	12,610	520.00	13,130
14' x 12'2" x 11'2"	"	14,800	520.00	15,320
16' x 12'2" x 11'2"	"	16,670	520.00	17,190
20' x 12'2" x 11'2"	"	19,970	520.00	20,490
Dry type spray booth, with paint arrestors				
5'4" x 7'2" x 6'8"	EA.	3,130	520.00	3,650
6'4" x 7'2" x 6'8"	"	3,810	520.00	4,330
8'4" x 7'2" x 9'2"	"	4,310	520.00	4,830
10'4" x 7'2" x 9'2"	"	4,990	520.00	5,510

Architectural Equipment	UNIT	MAT.	INST.	TOTAL
11500.10 Industrial Equipment				
12'4" x 7'6" x 9'2"	EA.	4,900	520.00	5,420
14'4" x 7'6" x 9'8"	"	6,680	520.00	7,200
16'4" x 7'7" x 9'8"	"	7,530	520.00	8,050
20'4" x 7'7" x 10'8"	"	8,460	520.00	8,980
Air compressor, electric				
1 hp				
115 volt	EA.	1,040	340.00	1,380
7.5 hp				
115 volt	EA.	3,470	520.00	3,990
230 volt	"	4,040	520.00	4,560
Hydraulic lifts				
8,000 lb capacity	EA.	5,840	1,290	7,130
11,000 lb capacity	"	8,200	2,060	10,260
24,000 lb capacity	"	11,590	3,440	15,030
Power tools				
Band saws				
10"	EA.	790.00	43.00	833.00
14"	"	1,390	51.50	1,442
Motorized shaper	"	740.00	39.70	779.70
Motorized lathe	"	880.00	43.00	923.00
Bench saws				
9" saw	EA.	1,590	34.40	1,624
10" saw	"	2,450	36.90	2,487
12" saw	"	3,130	43.00	3,173
Electric grinders				
1/3 hp	EA.	300.00	20.65	320.65
1/2 hp	"	440.00	22.45	462.45
3/4 hp	"	520.00	22.45	542.45

12	FURNISHINGS				

Interior	UNIT	MAT.	INST.	TOTAL
12690.40	Floor Mats			
Recessed entrance mat, 3/8" thick, aluminum link	S.F.	24.90	25.80	50.70
Steel, flexible	"	11.00	25.80	36.80

Construction	UNIT	MAT.	INST.	TOTAL
13121.10 — Pre-engineered Buildings				
Pre-engineered metal building, 40'x100'				
14' eave height	S.F.	12.15	4.25	16.40
16' eave height	"	12.85	4.90	17.75
20' eave height	"	14.65	6.40	21.05
60'x100'				
14' eave height	S.F.	10.50	4.25	14.75
16' eave height	"	11.00	4.90	15.90
20' eave height	"	12.30	6.40	18.70
80'x100'				
14' eave height	S.F.	10.50	4.25	14.75
16' eave height	"	10.85	4.90	15.75
20' eave height	"	12.45	6.40	18.85
100'x100'				
14' eave height	S.F.	15.45	4.25	19.70
16' eave height	"	11.00	4.90	15.90
20' eave height	"	12.10	6.40	18.50
100'x150'				
14' eave height	S.F.	9.60	4.25	13.85
16' eave height	"	10.30	4.90	15.20
20' eave height	"	11.40	6.40	17.80
120'x150'				
14' eave height	S.F.	9.60	4.25	13.85
16' eave height	"	10.10	4.90	15.00
20' eave height	"	11.00	6.40	17.40
140'x150'				
14' eave height	S.F.	9.05	4.25	13.30
16' eave height	"	9.75	4.90	14.65
20' eave height	"	10.85	6.40	17.25
160'x200'				
14' eave height	S.F.	8.85	4.25	13.10
16' eave height	"	8.95	4.90	13.85
20' eave height	"	10.10	6.40	16.50
200'x200'				
14' eave height	S.F.	8.85	4.25	13.10
16' eave height	"	9.25	4.90	14.15
20' eave height	"	9.95	6.40	16.35
Hollow metal door and frame, 6' x 7'	EA.			937.06
Sectional steel overhead door, manually operated				
8' x 8'	EA.			1,013
12' x 12'	"			1,521
Roll-up steel door, manually operated				
10' x 10'	EA.			1,877
12' x 12'	"			2,255
For gravity ridge ventilator with birdscreen	"			692.95
9" throat x 10'	"			749.65
12" throat x 10'	"			787.44
For 20" rotary vent with damper	"			318.13
For 4' x 3' fixed louver	"			337.03
For 4' x 3' aluminum sliding window	"			346.48
For 3' x 9' fiberglass panels	"			139.06
Liner panel, 26 ga, painted steel	S.F.	2.15	1.45	3.60
Wall panel insulated, 26 ga. steel, foam core	"	6.95	1.45	8.40

Construction	UNIT	MAT.	INST.	TOTAL
13121.10 Pre-engineered Buildings				
Roof panel, 26 ga. painted steel	S.F.	1.80	0.82	2.62
Plastic (sky light)	"	5.10	0.82	5.92
Insulation, 3-1/2" thick blanket, R11	"	1.60	0.38	1.98

Elevators	UNIT	MAT.	INST.	TOTAL
14210.10		**Elevators**		
Passenger elevators, electric, geared				
Based on a shaft of 6 stops and 6 openings				
50 fpm, 2000 lb	EA.	100,430	2,140	102,570
100 fpm, 2000 lb	"	104,150	2,380	106,530
150 fpm				
2000 lb	EA.	115,300	2,670	117,970
3000 lb	"	145,060	3,050	148,110
4000 lb	"	150,640	3,560	154,200

Lifts	UNIT	MAT.	INST.	TOTAL
14410.10		**Personnel Lifts**		
Electrically operated, 1 or 2 person lift				
With attached foot platforms				
3 stops	EA.			21,133
5 stops	"			27,051
7 stops	"			32,121
For each additional stop, add $1250				
Residential stair climber, per story	EA.	6,250	440.00	6,690
14450.10		**Vehicle Lifts**		
Automotive hoist, one post, semi-hydraulic, 8,000 lb	EA.	5,100	2,140	7,240
Full hydraulic, 8,000 lb	"	4,830	2,140	6,970
2 post, semi-hydraulic, 10,000 lb	"	5,270	3,050	8,320
Full hydraulic				
10,000 lb	EA.	5,630	3,050	8,680
13,000 lb	"	6,940	5,350	12,290
18,500 lb	"	9,050	5,350	14,400
24,000 lb	"	12,220	5,350	17,570
26,000 lb	"	14,150	5,350	19,500
Pneumatic hoist, fully hydraulic				
11,000 lb	EA.	6,770	7,130	13,900
24,000 lb	"	11,870	7,130	19,000

Hoists And Cranes	UNIT	MAT.	INST.	TOTAL
14600.10		**Industrial Hoists**		
Industrial hoists, electric, light to medium duty				
500 lb	EA.	6,930	260.00	7,190
1000 lb	"	7,270	280.00	7,550

Hoists And Cranes	UNIT	MAT.	INST.	TOTAL
14600.10	Industrial Hoists			
2000 lb	EA.	7,460	290.00	7,750
5000 lb	"	12,140	350.00	12,490
10,000 lb	"	22,650	390.00	23,040
20,000 lb	"	39,730	440.00	40,170
30,000 lb	"	42,710	530.00	43,240
Heavy duty				
500 lb	EA.	10,230	260.00	10,490
1000 lb	"	10,540	280.00	10,820
2000 lb	"	11,720	290.00	12,010
5000 lb	"	13,590	350.00	13,940
10,000 lb	"	20,040	390.00	20,430
20,000 lb	"	27,350	440.00	27,790
30,000 lb	"	41,470	530.00	42,000
Air powered hoists				
500 lb	EA.	3,830	260.00	4,090
1000 lb	"	4,270	260.00	4,530
2000 lb	"	4,660	280.00	4,940
4000 lb	"	5,440	310.00	5,750
6000 lb	"	6,490	410.00	6,900
Overhead traveling bridge crane				
Single girder, 20' span				
3 ton	EA.	21,780	1,070	22,850
5 ton	"	23,960	1,070	25,030
7.5 ton	"	30,320	1,070	31,390
10 ton	"	32,440	1,340	33,780
15 ton	"	37,460	1,340	38,800
30' span				
3 ton	EA.	23,170	1,070	24,240
5 ton	"	25,610	1,070	26,680
10 ton	"	32,760	1,340	34,100
15 ton	"	39,200	1,340	40,540
Double girder, 40' span				
3 ton	EA.	44,950	2,380	47,330
5 ton	"	46,170	2,380	48,550
7.5 ton	"	47,740	2,380	50,120
10 ton	"	50,180	3,050	53,230
15 ton	"	56,450	3,050	59,500
25 ton	"	83,640	3,050	86,690
50' span				
3 ton	EA.	49,050	2,380	51,430
5 ton	"	50,790	2,380	53,170
7.5 ton	"	52,620	2,380	55,000
10 ton	"	57,150	3,050	60,200
15 ton	"	66,210	3,050	69,260
25 ton	"	91,360	3,050	94,410
14650.10	Jib Cranes			
Self supporting, swinging 8' boom, 200 deg rotation				
2000 lb	EA.	2,090	480.00	2,570
4000 lb	"	2,600	960.00	3,560
10,000 lb	"	4,130	960.00	5,090
Wall mounted, 180 deg rotation				

14	CONVEYING				

Hoists And Cranes		UNIT	MAT.	INST.	TOTAL
14650.10			Jib Cranes		
2000 lb		EA.	1,110	480.00	1,590
4000 lb		"	1,480	960.00	2,440
10,000 lb		"	3,310	960.00	4,270

Basic Materials	UNIT	MAT.	INST.	TOTAL
15100.10 Specialties				
Wall penetration				
Concrete wall, 6" thick				
2" dia.	EA.		13.35	13.35
4" dia.	"		20.00	20.00
12" thick				
2" dia.	EA.		18.20	18.20
4" dia.	"		28.60	28.60
15120.10 Backflow Preventers				
Backflow preventer, flanged, cast iron, with valves				
3" pipe	EA.	2,040	280.00	2,320
4" pipe	"	3,020	320.00	3,340
Threaded				
3/4" pipe	EA.	520.00	35.60	555.60
2" pipe	"	940.00	57.00	997.00
15140.11 Pipe Hangers, Light				
A band, black iron				
1/2"	EA.	0.80	4.05	4.85
1"	"	0.86	4.20	5.06
1-1/4"	"	0.89	4.40	5.29
1-1/2"	"	0.91	4.75	5.66
2"	"	0.97	5.15	6.12
2-1/2"	"	1.85	5.70	7.55
3"	"	1.95	6.30	8.25
4"	"	2.90	7.10	10.00
Copper				
1/2"	EA.	1.30	4.05	5.35
3/4"	"	1.30	4.20	5.50
1"	"	1.35	4.20	5.55
1-1/4"	"	1.40	4.40	5.80
1-1/2"	"	1.45	4.75	6.20
2"	"	1.55	5.15	6.70
2-1/2"	"	2.95	5.70	8.65
3"	"	3.15	6.30	9.45
4"	"	4.65	7.10	11.75
2 hole clips, galvanized				
3/4"	EA.	0.26	3.80	4.06
1"	"	0.30	3.95	4.25
1-1/4"	"	0.39	4.05	4.44
1-1/2"	"	0.47	4.20	4.67
2"	"	0.62	4.40	5.02
2-1/2"	"	1.10	4.55	5.65
3"	"	1.60	4.75	6.35
4"	"	3.45	5.15	8.60
Perforated strap				
3/4"				
Galvanized, 20 ga.	L.F.	0.41	2.85	3.26
Copper, 22 ga.	"	0.64	2.85	3.49
J-Hooks				
1/2"	EA.	0.42	2.60	3.02
3/4"	"	0.45	2.60	3.05

Basic Materials	UNIT	MAT.	INST.	TOTAL
15140.11 — Pipe Hangers, Light				
1"	EA.	0.46	2.70	3.16
1-1/4"	"	0.48	2.80	3.28
1-1/2"	"	0.50	2.85	3.35
2"	"	0.52	2.85	3.37
3"	"	0.59	3.00	3.59
4"	"	0.64	3.00	3.64
PVC coated hangers, galvanized, 28 ga.				
1-1/2" x 12"	EA.	1.25	3.80	5.05
2" x 12"	"	1.35	4.05	5.40
3" x 12"	"	1.55	4.40	5.95
4" x 12"	"	1.70	4.75	6.45
Copper, 30 ga.				
1-1/2" x 12"	EA.	1.75	3.80	5.55
2" x 12"	"	2.10	4.05	6.15
3" x 12"	"	2.30	4.40	6.70
4" x 12"	"	2.55	4.75	7.30
Wire hook hangers				
Black wire, 1/2" x				
4"	EA.	0.43	2.85	3.28
6"	"	0.50	3.00	3.50
Copper wire hooks				
1/2" x				
4"	EA.	0.59	2.85	3.44
6"	"	0.67	3.00	3.67
8"	"	0.76	3.15	3.91
10"	"	0.96	3.35	4.31
12"	"	1.10	3.55	4.65
15240.10 — Vibration Control				
Vibration isolator, in-line, stainless connector, screwed				
3/4"	EA.	100.00	33.50	133.50
1"	"	110.00	35.60	145.60
2"	"	180.00	43.80	223.80
3"	"	470.00	51.50	521.50
4"	"	630.00	57.00	687.00

Insulation	UNIT	MAT.	INST.	TOTAL
15260.10 — Fiberglass Pipe Insulation				
Fiberglass insulation on 1/2" pipe				
1" thick	L.F.	0.99	1.90	2.89
1-1/2" thick	"	2.10	2.35	4.45
3/4" pipe				
1" thick	L.F.	1.20	1.90	3.10
1-1/2" thick	"	2.20	2.35	4.55
1" pipe				

Insulation	UNIT	MAT.	INST.	TOTAL
15260.10 — Fiberglass Pipe Insulation				
1" thick	L.F.	1.20	1.90	3.10
1-1/2" thick	"	2.30	2.35	4.65
2" thick	"	3.55	2.85	6.40
1-1/4" pipe				
1" thick	L.F.	1.35	2.35	3.70
1-1/2" thick	"	2.55	2.60	5.15
1-1/2" pipe				
1" thick	L.F.	1.50	2.35	3.85
1-1/2" thick	"	2.60	2.60	5.20
2" pipe				
1" thick	L.F.	1.65	2.35	4.00
1-1/2" thick	"	2.85	2.60	5.45
2-1/2" pipe				
1" thick	L.F.	1.75	2.35	4.10
1-1/2" thick	"	3.10	2.60	5.70
3" pipe				
1" thick	L.F.	2.00	2.70	4.70
1-1/2" thick	"	3.20	2.85	6.05
4" pipe				
1" thick	L.F.	2.55	2.70	5.25
1-1/2" thick	"	3.65	2.85	6.50
6" pipe				
1" thick	L.F.	3.30	3.00	6.30
2" thick	"	6.80	3.15	9.95
10" pipe				
2" thick	L.F.	10.55	3.00	13.55
3" thick	"	15.60	3.15	18.75
15260.20 — Calcium Silicate				
Calcium silicate insulation, 6" pipe				
2" thick	L.F.	8.25	4.05	12.30
3" thick	"	15.50	4.75	20.25
6" thick	"	28.30	5.70	34.00
12" pipe				
2" thick	L.F.	13.75	4.40	18.15
3" thick	"	25.90	5.15	31.05
6" thick	"	47.90	6.30	54.20
15260.60 — Exterior Pipe Insulation				
Fiberglass insulation, aluminum jacket				
1/2" pipe				
1" thick	L.F.	1.50	4.40	5.90
1-1/2" thick	"	2.80	4.75	7.55
1" pipe				
1" thick	L.F.	1.80	4.40	6.20
1-1/2" thick	"	3.15	4.75	7.90
2" pipe				
1" thick	L.F.	2.45	5.15	7.60
1-1/2" thick	"	3.70	5.40	9.10
3" pipe				
1" thick	L.F.	2.95	5.70	8.65
1-1/2" thick	"	4.40	6.00	10.40

Insulation	UNIT	MAT.	INST.	TOTAL
15260.60 Exterior Pipe Insulation				
4" pipe				
1" thick	L.F.	3.75	5.70	9.45
1-1/2" thick	"	5.05	6.00	11.05
6" pipe				
1" thick	L.F.	4.95	6.30	11.25
2" thick	"	8.80	6.70	15.50
10" pipe				
2" thick	L.F.	12.55	6.30	18.85
3" thick	"	18.00	6.70	24.70
15260.90 Pipe Insulation Fittings				
Insulation protection saddle				
1" thick covering				
1/2" pipe	EA.	3.30	22.75	26.05
3/4" pipe	"	3.30	22.75	26.05
1" pipe	"	3.30	22.75	26.05
2" pipe	"	4.75	22.75	27.50
3" pipe	"	5.40	25.90	31.30
6" pipe	"	6.65	35.60	42.25
1-1/2" thick covering				
3/4" pipe	EA.	5.40	22.75	28.15
1" pipe	"	5.40	22.75	28.15
2" pipe	"	6.05	22.75	28.80
3" pipe	"	6.80	22.75	29.55
6" pipe	"	10.05	35.60	45.65
10" pipe	"	12.65	47.40	60.05
15280.10 Equipment Insulation				
Equipment insulation, 2" thick, cellular glass	S.F.	3.25	3.55	6.80
Urethane, rigid, field applied jacket, plastered finish	"	3.45	7.10	10.55
Fiberglass, rigid, with vapor barrier	"	3.25	3.15	6.40
15290.10 Ductwork Insulation				
Fiberglass duct insulation, plain blanket				
1-1/2" thick	S.F.	1.10	0.71	1.81
2" thick	"	1.30	0.95	2.25
With vapor barrier				
1-1/2" thick	S.F.	0.66	0.71	1.37
2" thick	"	0.74	0.95	1.69
Rigid with vapor barrier				
2" thick	S.F.	2.15	1.90	4.05

Fire Protection	UNIT	MAT.	INST.	TOTAL

15330.10   Wet Sprinkler System

	UNIT	MAT.	INST.	TOTAL
Sprinkler head, 212 deg, brass, exposed piping	EA.	9.60	22.75	32.35
Chrome, concealed piping	"	11.25	31.60	42.85
Water motor alarm	"	270.00	95.00	365.00
Fire department inlet connection	"	200.00	110.00	310.00
Wall plate for fire dept connection	"	94.50	47.40	141.90
Swing check valve flanged iron body, 4"	"	280.00	190.00	470.00
Check valve, 6"	"	900.00	280.00	1,180
Wet pipe valve, flange to groove, 4"	"	780.00	63.00	843.00
Flange to flange				
6"	EA.	1,160	95.00	1,255
8"	"	2,040	190.00	2,230
Alarm valve, flange to flange, (wet valve)				
4"	EA.	950.00	63.00	1,013
8"	"	2,090	470.00	2,560
Inspector's test connection	"	60.50	47.40	107.90
Wall hydrant, polished brass, 2-1/2" x 2-1/2", single	"	480.00	40.70	520.70
2-way	"	1,080	40.70	1,121
3-way	"	2,210	40.70	2,251
Wet valve trim, includes retard chamber & gauges, 4"-6"	"	760.00	47.40	807.40
Retard pressure switch for wet systems	"	1,320	110.00	1,430
Air maintenance device	"	400.00	47.40	447.40
Wall hydrant non-freeze, 8" thick wall, vacuum breaker	"	44.20	28.50	72.70
12" thick wall	"	48.20	28.50	76.70

Plumbing	UNIT	MAT.	INST.	TOTAL

15410.05   C.i. Pipe, Above Ground

	UNIT	MAT.	INST.	TOTAL
No hub pipe				
1-1/2" pipe	L.F.	5.95	4.05	10.00
2" pipe	"	6.05	4.75	10.80
3" pipe	"	8.35	5.70	14.05
4" pipe	"	10.90	9.50	20.40
No hub fittings, 1-1/2" pipe				
1/4 bend	EA.	10.55	18.95	29.50
1/8 bend	"	7.55	18.95	26.50
Sanitary tee	"	12.85	28.50	41.35
Sanitary cross	"	15.95	28.50	44.45
Plug	"			2.37
Coupling	"			14.08
Wye	"	14.00	28.50	42.50
2" pipe				
1/4 bend	EA.	10.80	22.75	33.55
1/8 bend	"	7.75	22.75	30.50
Sanitary tee	"	13.40	37.90	51.30
Coupling	"			14.08
Wye	"	15.00	47.40	62.40

Plumbing	UNIT	MAT.	INST.	TOTAL
15410.05	C.i. Pipe, Above Ground			
3" pipe				
1/4 bend	EA.	13.65	28.50	42.15
1/8 bend	"	12.25	28.50	40.75
Sanitary tee	"	15.95	35.60	51.55
Coupling	"			16.45
Wye	"	16.40	47.40	63.80
4" pipe				
1/4 bend	EA.	18.80	28.50	47.30
1/8 bend	"	15.95	28.50	44.45
Sanitary tee	"	23.45	47.40	70.85
Coupling	"			18.37
Wye	"	23.45	47.40	70.85
15410.06	C.i. Pipe, Below Ground			
No hub pipe				
1-1/2" pipe	L.F.	5.95	2.85	8.80
2" pipe	"	6.05	3.15	9.20
3" pipe	"	8.35	3.55	11.90
4" pipe	"	10.90	4.75	15.65
Fittings, 1-1/2"				
1/4 bend	EA.	10.55	16.25	26.80
1/8 bend	"	7.55	16.25	23.80
Plug	"			2.37
Wye	"	14.00	22.75	36.75
Wye & 1/8 bend	"	14.00	16.25	30.25
P-trap	"	20.45	16.25	36.70
2"				
1/4 bend	EA.	10.80	18.95	29.75
1/8 bend	"	7.75	18.95	26.70
Plug	"			2.86
Double wye	"	19.25	35.60	54.85
Wye & 1/8 bend	"	18.95	28.50	47.45
Double wye & 1/8 bend	"	28.20	35.60	63.80
P-trap	"	20.45	18.95	39.40
3"				
1/4 bend	EA.	13.65	22.75	36.40
1/8 bend	"	12.25	22.75	35.00
Plug	"			4.24
Wye	"	16.40	35.60	52.00
3x2" wye	"	16.90	35.60	52.50
Wye & 1/8 bend	"	21.10	35.60	56.70
Double wye & 1/8 bend	"	38.70	35.60	74.30
3x2" double wye & 1/8 bend	"	29.40	35.60	65.00
3x2" reducer	"	8.95	22.75	31.70
P-trap	"	24.65	22.75	47.40
4"				
1/4 bend	EA.	18.80	22.75	41.55
1/8 bend	"	15.95	22.75	38.70
Wye	"	23.45	35.60	59.05

Plumbing	UNIT	MAT.	INST.	TOTAL
15410.09 **Service Weight Pipe**				
Service weight pipe, single hub				
3" x 5'	EA.	50.50	12.10	62.60
4" x 5'	"	61.00	12.65	73.65
6" x 5'	"	97.00	14.25	111.25
1/8 bend				
3"	EA.	11.65	22.75	34.40
4"	"	16.10	25.90	42.00
6"	"	25.70	28.50	54.20
1/4 bend				
3"	EA.	14.55	22.75	37.30
4"	"	20.40	25.90	46.30
6"	"	34.80	28.50	63.30
Sweep				
3"	EA.	22.40	22.75	45.15
4"	"	31.30	25.90	57.20
6"	"	56.00	28.50	84.50
Sanitary T				
3"	EA.	23.55	40.70	64.25
4"	"	29.10	47.40	76.50
6"	"	58.50	51.50	110.00
Wye				
3"	EA.	25.70	31.60	57.30
4"	"	32.50	33.50	66.00
6"	"	67.00	40.70	107.70
15410.10 **Copper Pipe**				
Type "K" copper				
1/2"	L.F.	5.00	1.80	6.80
3/4"	"	9.25	1.90	11.15
1"	"	11.60	2.05	13.65
DWV, copper				
1-1/4"	L.F.	9.25	2.35	11.60
1-1/2"	"	11.90	2.60	14.50
2"	"	13.40	2.85	16.25
3"	"	25.20	3.15	28.35
4"	"	41.60	3.55	45.15
6"	"	160.00	4.05	164.05
Type "L" copper				
1/4"	L.F.	3.00	1.65	4.65
3/8"	"	3.30	1.65	4.95
1/2"	"	5.00	1.80	6.80
3/4"	"	5.65	1.90	7.55
1"	"	7.70	2.05	9.75
Type "M" copper				
1/2"	L.F.	3.55	1.80	5.35
3/4"	"	5.00	1.90	6.90
1"	"	6.15	2.05	8.20
Type "K" tube, coil				
1/4" x 60'	EA.			136.68
1/2" x 60'	"			255.48
3/4" x 60'	"			412.50
1" x 60'	"			621.50

15 MECHANICAL

Plumbing	UNIT	MAT.	INST.	TOTAL

15410.10 — Copper Pipe

	UNIT	MAT.	INST.	TOTAL
Type "L" tube, coil				
1/4" x 60'	EA.			130.74
3/8" x 60'	"			196.08
1/2" x 60'	"			261.47
3/4" x 60'	"			387.37
1" x 60'	"			666.05

15410.11 — Copper Fittings

	UNIT	MAT.	INST.	TOTAL
DWV fittings, coupling with stop				
1-1/4"	EA.	8.25	33.50	41.75
1-1/2"	"	9.40	35.60	45.00
1-1/2" x 1-1/4"	"	10.85	35.60	46.45
2"	"	10.60	37.90	48.50
2" x 1-1/4"	"	14.15	37.90	52.05
2" x 1-1/2"	"	14.15	37.90	52.05
3"	"	17.85	47.40	65.25
3" x 1-1/2"	"	35.30	47.40	82.70
3" x 2"	"	35.30	47.40	82.70
4"	"	37.60	57.00	94.60
Slip coupling				
1-1/2"	EA.	10.60	35.60	46.20
2"	"	11.55	37.90	49.45
3"	"	16.45	47.40	63.85
90 ells				
1-1/2"	EA.	19.75	35.60	55.35
1-1/2" x 1-1/4"	"	24.95	35.60	60.55
2"	"	21.15	37.90	59.05
2" x 1-1/2"	"	30.60	37.90	68.50
3"	"	61.00	47.40	108.40
4"	"	230.00	57.00	287.00
Street, 90 elbows				
1-1/2"	EA.	16.45	35.60	52.05
2"	"	27.70	37.90	65.60
3"	"	59.00	47.40	106.40
4"	"	250.00	57.00	307.00
45 ells				
1-1/4"	EA.	11.80	33.50	45.30
1-1/2"	"	10.85	35.60	46.45
2"	"	20.25	37.90	58.15
3"	"	37.60	47.40	85.00
4"	"	110.00	57.00	167.00
Street, 45 ell				
1-1/2"	EA.	13.15	35.60	48.75
2"	"	23.55	37.90	61.45
3"	"	56.50	47.40	103.90
Wye				
1-1/4"	EA.	37.60	33.50	71.10
1-1/2"	"	33.00	35.60	68.60
2"	"	54.00	37.90	91.90
3"	"	130.00	47.40	177.40
4"	"	280.00	57.00	337.00
Sanitary tee				

Plumbing	UNIT	MAT.	INST.	TOTAL
15410.11	**Copper Fittings**			
1-1/4"	EA.	27.10	33.50	60.60
1-1/2"	"	25.90	35.60	61.50
2"	"	37.60	37.90	75.50
3"	"	89.50	47.40	136.90
4"	"	230.00	57.00	287.00
No-hub adapters				
1-1/2" x 2"	EA.	26.00	35.60	61.60
2"	"	26.00	37.90	63.90
2" x 3"	"	70.50	37.90	108.40
3"	"	43.60	47.40	91.00
3" x 4"	"	73.00	47.40	120.40
4"	"	77.50	57.00	134.50
Fitting reducers				
1-1/2" x 1-1/4"	EA.	10.85	35.60	46.45
2" x 1-1/2"	"	10.60	37.90	48.50
3" x 1-1/2"	"	34.10	47.40	81.50
3" x 2"	"	34.90	47.40	82.30
Copper caps				
1-1/2"	EA.	18.35	35.60	53.95
2"	"	29.40	37.90	67.30
Copper pipe fittings				
1/2"				
90 deg ell	EA.	1.50	12.65	14.15
45 deg ell	"	1.95	12.65	14.60
Tee	"	2.55	16.25	18.80
Cap	"	1.05	6.30	7.35
Coupling	"	1.10	12.65	13.75
Union	"	7.70	14.25	21.95
3/4"				
90 deg ell	EA.	3.30	14.25	17.55
45 deg ell	"	3.90	14.25	18.15
Tee	"	5.55	18.95	24.50
Cap	"	2.05	6.70	8.75
Coupling	"	2.25	14.25	16.50
Union	"	11.35	16.25	27.60
1"				
90 deg ell	EA.	7.70	18.95	26.65
45 deg ell	"	10.05	18.95	29.00
Tee	"	12.65	22.75	35.40
Cap	"	3.75	9.50	13.25
Coupling	"	5.55	18.95	24.50
Union	"	14.90	18.95	33.85
1-1/4"				
90 deg ell	EA.	10.50	16.25	26.75
45 deg ell	"	13.05	16.25	29.30
Tee	"	17.15	28.50	45.65
Cap	"	3.00	9.50	12.50
Union	"	24.60	20.35	44.95
1-1/2"				
90 deg ell	EA.	13.70	20.35	34.05
45 deg ell	"	16.25	20.35	36.60
Tee	"	22.45	31.60	54.05

Plumbing	UNIT	MAT.	INST.	TOTAL
15410.11	Copper Fittings			
Cap	EA.	3.00	9.50	12.50
Coupling	"	10.05	18.95	29.00
Union	"	37.50	25.90	63.40
2"				
90 deg ell	EA.	26.70	22.75	49.45
45 deg ell	"	24.60	35.60	60.20
Tee	"	38.50	35.60	74.10
Cap	"	6.20	11.40	17.60
Coupling	"	16.25	22.75	39.00
Union	"	40.60	28.50	69.10
2-1/2"				
90 deg ell	EA.	51.50	28.50	80.00
45 deg ell	"	44.90	28.50	73.40
Tee	"	51.50	40.70	92.20
Cap	"	12.65	14.25	26.90
Coupling	"	24.60	28.50	53.10
Union	"	75.00	31.60	106.60
15410.15	Brass Fittings			
Compression fittings, union				
3/8"	EA.	6.80	9.50	16.30
1/2"	"	10.10	9.50	19.60
5/8"	"	12.45	9.50	21.95
Union elbow				
3/8"	EA.	11.25	9.50	20.75
1/2"	"	17.75	9.50	27.25
5/8"	"	22.20	9.50	31.70
Union tee				
3/8"	EA.	14.80	9.50	24.30
1/2"	"	23.70	9.50	33.20
5/8"	"	34.10	9.50	43.60
Male connector				
3/8"	EA.	4.75	9.50	14.25
1/2"	"	3.25	9.50	12.75
5/8"	"	7.40	9.50	16.90
Female connector				
3/8"	EA.	8.85	9.50	18.35
1/2"	"	11.25	9.50	20.75
5/8"	"	11.25	9.50	20.75
15410.30	Pvc/cpvc Pipe			
PVC schedule 40				
1/2" pipe	L.F.	0.44	2.35	2.79
3/4" pipe	"	0.61	2.60	3.21
1" pipe	"	0.88	2.85	3.73
1-1/4" pipe	"	1.20	3.15	4.35
1-1/2" pipe	"	1.35	3.55	4.90
2" pipe	"	1.85	4.05	5.90
2-1/2" pipe	"	3.00	4.75	7.75
3" pipe	"	3.85	5.70	9.55
4" pipe	"	5.50	7.10	12.60
6" pipe	"	9.60	14.25	23.85

Plumbing	UNIT	MAT.	INST.	TOTAL
15410.30		Pvc/cpvc Pipe		
8" pipe	L.F.	14.45	18.95	33.40
Fittings, 1/2"				
90 deg ell	EA.	0.48	7.10	7.58
45 deg ell	"	0.76	7.10	7.86
Tee	"	0.65	8.15	8.80
Polypropylene, acid resistant, DWV pipe				
Schedule 40				
1-1/2" pipe	L.F.	5.15	4.05	9.20
2" pipe	"	6.95	4.75	11.70
3" pipe	"	12.75	5.70	18.45
4" pipe	"	18.05	7.10	25.15
6" pipe	"	32.30	14.25	46.55
Polyethylene pipe and fittings				
SDR-21				
3" pipe	L.F.	3.40	7.10	10.50
4" pipe	"	5.10	9.50	14.60
6" pipe	"	8.50	14.25	22.75
8" pipe	"	13.60	16.25	29.85
10" pipe	"	15.30	18.95	34.25
12" pipe	"	23.80	22.75	46.55
14" pipe	"	30.60	28.50	59.10
16" pipe	"	37.30	35.60	72.90
18" pipe	"	40.90	43.80	84.70
20" pipe	"	51.00	57.00	108.00
22" pipe	"	59.50	63.00	122.50
24" pipe	"	72.50	71.00	143.50
Fittings, 3"				
90 deg elbow	EA.	92.50	28.50	121.00
45 deg elbow	"	57.50	28.50	86.00
Tee	"	52.50	47.40	99.90
45 deg wye	"	130.00	47.40	177.40
Reducer	"	26.10	35.60	61.70
Flange assembly	"	20.80	28.50	49.30
4"				
90 deg elbow	EA.	130.00	35.60	165.60
45 deg elbow	"	79.00	35.60	114.60
Tee	"	110.00	57.00	167.00
45 deg wye	"	210.00	57.00	267.00
Reducer	"	72.50	47.40	119.90
Flange assembly	"	72.50	35.60	108.10
8"				
90 deg elbow	EA.	360.00	71.00	431.00
45 deg elbow	"	200.00	71.00	271.00
Tee	"	340.00	110.00	450.00
45 deg wye	"	520.00	110.00	630.00
Reducer	"	180.00	95.00	275.00
Flange assembly	"	190.00	71.00	261.00
10"				
90 deg elbow	EA.	500.00	95.00	595.00
45 deg elbow	"	270.00	95.00	365.00
Tee	"	450.00	140.00	590.00
45 deg wye	"	710.00	140.00	850.00

Plumbing	UNIT	MAT.	INST.	TOTAL
15410.30			**Pvc/cpvc Pipe**	
Reducer	EA.	240.00	110.00	350.00
Flange assembly	"	230.00	95.00	325.00
12"				
90 deg elbow	EA.	810.00	110.00	920.00
45 deg elbow	"	500.00	110.00	610.00
Tee	"	630.00	190.00	820.00
45 deg wye	"	990.00	190.00	1,180
Reducer	"	380.00	140.00	520.00
Flange assembly	"	300.00	110.00	410.00
14"				
90 deg elbow	EA.	1,100	140.00	1,240
45 deg elbow	"	630.00	140.00	770.00
Tee	"	810.00	230.00	1,040
45 deg wye	"	1,490	230.00	1,720
Reducer	"	320.00	190.00	510.00
Flange assembly	"	370.00	140.00	510.00
16"				
90 deg elbow	EA.	1,380	140.00	1,520
45 deg elbow	"	820.00	140.00	960.00
Tee	"	1,000	230.00	1,230
45 deg wye	"	1,660	230.00	1,890
Reducer	"	640.00	190.00	830.00
Flange assembly	"	460.00	140.00	600.00
18"				
90 deg elbow	EA.	2,110	190.00	2,300
45 deg elbow	"	1,360	190.00	1,550
Tee	"	1,620	280.00	1,900
45 deg wye	"	2,810	280.00	3,090
Reducer	"	600.00	190.00	790.00
Flange assembly	"	820.00	190.00	1,010
20"				
90 deg elbow	EA.	1,700	190.00	1,890
45 deg elbow	"	1,010	190.00	1,200
15410.33			**Abs Dwv Pipe**	
Schedule 40 ABS				
1-1/2" pipe	L.F.	0.83	2.85	3.68
2" pipe	"	1.05	3.15	4.20
3" pipe	"	2.10	4.05	6.15
4" pipe	"	2.95	5.70	8.65
6" pipe	"	6.05	7.10	13.15
15410.35			**Plastic Pipe**	
Fiberglass reinforced pipe				
2" pipe	L.F.	4.55	4.40	8.95
3" pipe	"	6.15	4.75	10.90
4" pipe	"	7.80	5.15	12.95
6" pipe	"	12.20	5.70	17.90
8" pipe	"	17.80	9.50	27.30
10" pipe	"	22.00	11.40	33.40
12" pipe	"	28.60	14.25	42.85
Fittings				

Plumbing	UNIT	MAT.	INST.	TOTAL
15410.35		**Plastic Pipe**		
90 deg elbow, flanged				
2"	EA.	140.00	57.00	197.00
3"	"	180.00	63.00	243.00
4"	"	220.00	71.00	291.00
6"	"	410.00	95.00	505.00
8"	"	740.00	110.00	850.00
10"	"	980.00	140.00	1,120
12"	"	1,310	190.00	1,500
45 deg elbow, flanged				
2"	EA.	140.00	47.40	187.40
3"	"	180.00	57.00	237.00
4"	"	220.00	71.00	291.00
6"	"	410.00	95.00	505.00
8"	"	620.00	110.00	730.00
10"	"	830.00	140.00	970.00
12"	"	1,050	190.00	1,240
Tee, flanged				
2"	EA.	180.00	71.00	251.00
3"	"	260.00	81.50	341.50
4"	"	290.00	95.00	385.00
6"	"	500.00	110.00	610.00
8"	"	870.00	140.00	1,010
10"	"	1,420	190.00	1,610
12"	"	1,960	280.00	2,240
Wye, flanged				
2"	EA.	360.00	71.00	431.00
3"	"	500.00	81.50	581.50
4"	"	650.00	95.00	745.00
6"	"	830.00	110.00	940.00
8"	"	1,400	140.00	1,540
10"	"	2,390	190.00	2,580
12"	"	3,060	280.00	3,340
Concentric reducer, flanged				
2"	EA.	140.00	47.40	187.40
4"	"	210.00	57.00	267.00
6"	"	280.00	81.50	361.50
8"	"	450.00	110.00	560.00
10"	"	700.00	140.00	840.00
12"	"	1,010	190.00	1,200
Adapter, bell x male or female				
2"	EA.	18.05	47.40	65.45
3"	"	36.00	51.50	87.50
4"	"	38.10	57.00	95.10
6"	"	81.50	81.50	163.00
8"	"	110.00	110.00	220.00
10"	"	170.00	140.00	310.00
12"	"	300.00	190.00	490.00
Nipples				
2" x 6"	EA.	7.60	5.70	13.30
2" x 12"	"	11.45	7.10	18.55
3" x 8"	"	11.45	8.75	20.20
3" x 12"	"	11.45	9.50	20.95

Plumbing	UNIT	MAT.	INST.	TOTAL
15410.35 — Plastic Pipe				
4" x 8"	EA.	11.45	9.50	20.95
4" x 12"	"	12.85	11.40	24.25
6" x 12"	"	29.40	14.25	43.65
8" x 18"	"	84.00	14.25	98.25
8" x 24"	"	99.00	16.25	115.25
10" x 18"	"	99.00	18.95	117.95
10" x 24"	"	130.00	22.75	152.75
12" x 18"	"	130.00	25.90	155.90
12" x 24"	"	160.00	28.50	188.50
Sleeve coupling				
2"	EA.	16.60	47.40	64.00
3"	"	18.25	57.00	75.25
4"	"	25.20	81.50	106.70
6"	"	60.50	110.00	170.50
8"	"	97.00	140.00	237.00
10"	"	150.00	190.00	340.00
Flanges				
2"	EA.	24.75	47.40	72.15
3"	"	33.40	57.00	90.40
4"	"	44.40	81.50	125.90
6"	"	76.00	110.00	186.00
8"	"	130.00	140.00	270.00
10"	"	180.00	190.00	370.00
12"	"	230.00	190.00	420.00
15410.70 — Stainless Steel Pipe				
Stainless steel, schedule 40, threaded				
1/2" pipe	L.F.	9.35	8.15	17.50
1" pipe	"	14.50	8.75	23.25
1-1/2" pipe	"	19.70	9.50	29.20
2" pipe	"	29.60	10.35	39.95
2-1/2" pipe	"	41.50	11.40	52.90
3" pipe	"	58.50	12.65	71.15
4" pipe	"	75.00	14.25	89.25
15410.80 — Steel Pipe				
Black steel, extra heavy pipe, threaded				
1/2" pipe	L.F.	2.25	2.30	4.55
3/4" pipe	"	2.70	2.30	5.00
1" pipe	"	3.75	2.85	6.60
1-1/2" pipe	"	5.60	3.15	8.75
2-1/2" pipe	"	11.20	7.10	18.30
3" pipe	"	14.90	9.50	24.40
4" pipe	"	22.65	11.40	34.05
5" pipe	"	30.50	14.25	44.75
6" pipe	"	38.10	14.25	52.35
8" pipe	"	56.00	18.95	74.95
10" pipe	"	88.00	22.75	110.75
12" pipe	"	120.00	28.50	148.50
Fittings, malleable iron, threaded, 1/2" pipe				
90 deg ell	EA.	2.30	18.95	21.25
45 deg ell	"	3.65	18.95	22.60

Plumbing	UNIT	MAT.	INST.	TOTAL
15410.80 Steel Pipe				
Tee	EA.	3.00	28.50	31.50
3/4" pipe				
90 deg ell	EA.	3.00	18.95	21.95
45 deg ell	"	4.95	28.50	33.45
Tee	"	5.05	28.50	33.55
1-1/2" pipe				
90 deg ell	EA.	9.45	28.50	37.95
45 deg ell	"	11.00	28.50	39.50
Tee	"	13.60	40.70	54.30
2-1/2" pipe				
90 deg ell	EA.	38.10	71.00	109.10
45 deg ell	"	47.50	71.00	118.50
Tee	"	51.50	95.00	146.50
3" pipe				
90 deg ell	EA.	55.00	95.00	150.00
45 deg ell	"	62.50	95.00	157.50
Tee	"	70.50	140.00	210.50
4" pipe				
90 deg ell	EA.	110.00	110.00	220.00
45 deg ell	"	110.00	110.00	220.00
Tee	"	170.00	190.00	360.00
6" pipe				
90 deg ell	EA.	310.00	110.00	420.00
45 deg ell	"	390.00	110.00	500.00
Tee	"	440.00	190.00	630.00
8" pipe				
90 deg ell	EA.	330.00	230.00	560.00
45 deg ell	"	400.00	230.00	630.00
Tee	"	470.00	360.00	830.00
10" pipe				
90 deg ell	EA.	360.00	280.00	640.00
45 deg ell	"	430.00	280.00	710.00
Tee	"	540.00	360.00	900.00
12" pipe				
90 deg ell	EA.	430.00	360.00	790.00
45 deg ell	"	500.00	360.00	860.00
Tee	"	630.00	470.00	1,100
Butt welded, 1/2" pipe				
90 deg ell	EA.	15.00	18.95	33.95
45 deg ell	"	21.55	18.95	40.50
Tee	"	49.50	28.50	78.00
3/4" pipe				
90 deg ell	EA.	15.00	18.95	33.95
45 deg. ell	"	21.90	18.95	40.85
Tee	"	49.50	28.50	78.00
1" pipe				
90 deg ell	EA.	19.80	22.75	42.55
45 deg ell	"	21.90	22.75	44.65
Tee	"	49.50	31.60	81.10
1-1/2" pipe				
90 deg ell	EA.	21.30	28.50	49.80
45 deg. ell	"	22.65	28.50	51.15

Plumbing	UNIT	MAT.	INST.	TOTAL
15410.80 Steel Pipe				
Tee	EA.	55.00	40.70	95.70
Reducing tee	"	37.50	40.70	78.20
Cap	"	20.00	22.75	42.75
2-1/2" pipe				
90 deg. ell	EA.	32.80	57.00	89.80
45 deg. ell	"	43.80	57.00	100.80
Tee	"	61.00	81.50	142.50
Reducing tee	"	37.50	81.50	119.00
Cap	"	22.00	28.50	50.50
3" pipe				
90 deg ell	EA.	38.50	71.00	109.50
45 deg. ell	"	43.80	71.00	114.80
Tee	"	61.00	95.00	156.00
Reducing tee	"	43.80	95.00	138.80
Cap	"	22.80	47.40	70.20
4" pipe				
90 deg ell	EA.	60.50	95.00	155.50
45 deg. ell	"	49.50	95.00	144.50
Tee	"	82.50	140.00	222.50
Reducing tee	"	55.00	140.00	195.00
Cap	"	24.75	47.40	72.15
6" pipe				
90 deg. ell	EA.	150.00	110.00	260.00
45 deg. ell	"	120.00	110.00	230.00
Tee	"	220.00	190.00	410.00
Reducing tee	"	210.00	190.00	400.00
Cap	"	43.80	57.00	100.80
8" pipe				
90 deg. ell	EA.	280.00	190.00	470.00
45 deg. ell	"	220.00	190.00	410.00
Tee	"	390.00	280.00	670.00
Reducing tee	"	240.00	280.00	520.00
Cap	"	66.50	110.00	176.50
10" pipe				
90 deg ell	EA.	500.00	190.00	690.00
45 deg. ell	"	440.00	190.00	630.00
Tee	"	500.00	280.00	780.00
Reducing tee	"	320.00	280.00	600.00
Cap	"	120.00	140.00	260.00
12" pipe				
90 deg. ell	EA.	720.00	230.00	950.00
45 deg. ell	"	490.00	230.00	720.00
Tee	"	720.00	410.00	1,130
Reducing tee	"	370.00	410.00	780.00
Cap	"	180.00	140.00	320.00
Cast iron fittings				
1/2" pipe				
90 deg. ell	EA.	3.80	18.95	22.75
45 deg. ell	"	7.65	18.95	26.60
Tee	"	4.95	28.50	33.45
Reducing tee	"	9.35	28.50	37.85
3/4" pipe				

Plumbing	UNIT	MAT.	INST.	TOTAL
15410.80 Steel Pipe				
90 deg. ell	EA.	4.00	18.95	22.95
45 deg. ell	"	4.95	18.95	23.90
Tee	"	6.20	28.50	34.70
Reducing tee	"	8.10	28.50	36.60
1" pipe				
90 deg. ell	EA.	4.85	22.75	27.60
45 deg. ell	"	6.65	22.75	29.40
Tee	"	6.10	31.60	37.70
Reducing tee	"	7.95	31.60	39.55
1-1/2" pipe				
90 deg. ell	EA.	9.45	28.50	37.95
45 deg. ell	"	13.45	28.50	41.95
Tee	"	13.45	40.70	54.15
Reducing tee	"	18.65	40.70	59.35
2-1/2" pipe				
90 deg. ell	EA.	30.10	57.00	87.10
45 deg. ell	"	35.80	57.00	92.80
Tee	"	42.90	81.50	124.40
Reducing tee	"	49.80	81.50	131.30
3" pipe				
90 deg. ell	EA.	48.70	71.00	119.70
45 deg. ell	"	56.00	71.00	127.00
Tee	"	65.00	110.00	175.00
Reducing tee	"	75.00	110.00	185.00
4" pipe				
90 deg. ell	EA.	87.50	95.00	182.50
45 deg. ell	"	110.00	95.00	205.00
Tee	"	120.00	140.00	260.00
Reducing tee	"	150.00	140.00	290.00
6" pipe				
90 deg. ell	EA.	210.00	95.00	305.00
45 deg. ell	"	230.00	95.00	325.00
Tee	"	290.00	140.00	430.00
Reducing tee	"	330.00	140.00	470.00
8" pipe				
90 deg. ell	EA.	420.00	190.00	610.00
45 deg. ell	"	460.00	190.00	650.00
Tee	"	590.00	280.00	870.00
Reducing tee	"	650.00	280.00	930.00
15410.82 Galvanized Steel Pipe				
Galvanized pipe				
1/2" pipe	L.F.	2.55	5.70	8.25
3/4" pipe	"	3.30	7.10	10.40
1" pipe	"	5.05	8.15	13.20
1-1/4" pipe	"	5.90	9.50	15.40
1-1/2" pipe	"	6.25	11.40	17.65
2" pipe	"	9.00	14.25	23.25
2-1/2" pipe	"	12.90	18.95	31.85
3" pipe	"	18.00	20.35	38.35
4" pipe	"	24.45	23.70	48.15
6" pipe	"	49.00	47.40	96.40

Plumbing	UNIT	MAT.	INST.	TOTAL
15430.23 Cleanouts				
Cleanout, wall				
2"	EA.	130.00	37.90	167.90
3"	"	150.00	37.90	187.90
4"	"	190.00	47.40	237.40
6"	"	320.00	57.00	377.00
8"	"	390.00	71.00	461.00
Floor				
2"	EA.	150.00	47.40	197.40
3"	"	180.00	47.40	227.40
4"	"	200.00	57.00	257.00
6"	"	280.00	71.00	351.00
8"	"	530.00	81.50	611.50
15430.24 Grease Traps				
Grease traps, cast iron, 3" pipe				
35 gpm, 70 lb capacity	EA.	3,200	570.00	3,770
50 gpm, 100 lb capacity	"	4,080	710.00	4,790
15430.25 Hose Bibbs				
Hose bibb				
1/2"	EA.	9.05	18.95	28.00
3/4"	"	9.60	18.95	28.55
15430.60 Valves				
Gate valve, 125 lb, bronze, soldered				
1/2"	EA.	26.20	14.25	40.45
3/4"	"	30.90	14.25	45.15
1"	"	38.10	18.95	57.05
1-1/2"	"	66.50	22.75	89.25
2"	"	93.00	28.50	121.50
2-1/2"	"	210.00	35.60	245.60
Threaded				
1/4", 125 lb	EA.	25.60	22.75	48.35
1/2"				
125 lb	EA.	28.50	22.75	51.25
150 lb	"	38.10	22.75	60.85
300 lb	"	71.50	22.75	94.25
3/4"				
125 lb	EA.	33.30	22.75	56.05
150 lb	"	45.20	22.75	67.95
300 lb	"	86.00	22.75	108.75
1"				
125 lb	EA.	42.80	22.75	65.55
150 lb	"	59.50	22.75	82.25
300 lb	"	120.00	28.50	148.50
1-1/2"				
125 lb	EA.	75.00	28.50	103.50
150 lb	"	100.00	28.50	128.50
300 lb	"	220.00	31.60	251.60
2"				
125 lb	EA.	93.50	40.70	134.20
150 lb	"	140.00	40.70	180.70

Plumbing	UNIT	MAT.	INST.	TOTAL
15430.60 Valves				
300 lb	EA.	330.00	47.40	377.40
Cast iron, flanged				
2", 150 lb	EA.	350.00	47.40	397.40
2-1/2"				
125 lb	EA.	340.00	47.40	387.40
150 lb	"	530.00	47.40	577.40
250 lb	"	680.00	47.40	727.40
3"				
125 lb	EA.	410.00	57.00	467.00
150 lb	"	550.00	57.00	607.00
250 lb	"	860.00	57.00	917.00
4"				
125 lb	EA.	660.00	81.50	741.50
150 lb	"	890.00	81.50	971.50
250 lb	"	1,160	81.50	1,242
6"				
125 lb	EA.	990.00	110.00	1,100
250 lb	"	2,010	110.00	2,120
8"				
125 lb	EA.	1,500	140.00	1,640
250 lb	"	4,490	140.00	4,630
OS&Y, flanged				
2"				
125 lb	EA.	300.00	47.40	347.40
250 lb	"	700.00	47.40	747.40
2-1/2"				
125 lb	EA.	320.00	47.40	367.40
250 lb	"	790.00	57.00	847.00
3"				
125 lb	EA.	320.00	57.00	377.00
250 lb	"	860.00	57.00	917.00
4"				
125 lb	EA.	460.00	95.00	555.00
250 lb	"	1,330	95.00	1,425
6"				
125 lb	EA.	730.00	110.00	840.00
250 lb	"	2,140	110.00	2,250
Check valve, bronze, soldered, 125 lb				
1/2"	EA.	31.10	14.25	45.35
3/4"	"	35.50	14.25	49.75
1"	"	46.80	18.95	65.75
1-1/4"	"	65.50	22.75	88.25
1-1/2"	"	76.50	22.75	99.25
2"	"	110.00	28.50	138.50
Threaded				
1/2"				
125 lb	EA.	25.70	18.95	44.65
150 lb	"	42.00	18.95	60.95
200 lb	"	43.00	18.95	61.95
3/4"				
125 lb	EA.	32.70	22.75	55.45
150 lb	"	51.50	22.75	74.25

Plumbing	UNIT	MAT.	INST.	TOTAL
15430.60 Valves				
200 lb	EA.	51.50	22.75	74.25
1"				
125 lb	EA.	41.60	28.50	70.10
150 lb	"	67.50	28.50	96.00
200 lb	"	67.50	28.50	96.00
Flow check valve, cast iron, threaded				
1"	EA.	60.00	22.75	82.75
1-1/4"	"	60.00	28.50	88.50
1-1/2"				
125 lb	EA.	58.50	28.50	87.00
150 lb	"	97.00	28.50	125.50
200 lb	"	97.00	31.60	128.60
2"				
125 lb	EA.	86.00	31.60	117.60
150 lb	"	140.00	31.60	171.60
200 lb	"	140.00	35.60	175.60
2-1/2"				
125 lb	EA.	200.00	47.40	247.40
250 lb	"	630.00	57.00	687.00
3"				
125 lb	EA.	220.00	57.00	277.00
250 lb	"	780.00	71.00	851.00
4"				
125 lb	EA.	340.00	81.50	421.50
250 lb	"	1,000	95.00	1,095
6"				
125 lb	EA.	460.00	110.00	570.00
250 lb	"	1,690	110.00	1,800
Vertical check valve, bronze, 125 lb, threaded				
1/2"	EA.	50.50	22.75	73.25
3/4"	"	67.50	25.90	93.40
1"	"	82.00	28.50	110.50
1-1/4"	"	100.00	31.60	131.60
1-1/2"	"	110.00	35.60	145.60
2"	"	190.00	40.70	230.70
Cast iron, flanged				
2-1/2"	EA.	280.00	57.00	337.00
3"	"	310.00	71.00	381.00
4"	"	480.00	95.00	575.00
6	"	820.00	110.00	930.00
8"	"	1,540	140.00	1,680
10"	"	2,630	190.00	2,820
12"	"	4,090	230.00	4,320
Globe valve, bronze, soldered, 125 lb				
1/2"	EA.	28.10	16.25	44.35
3/4"	"	32.70	17.80	50.50
1"	"	58.50	18.95	77.45
1-1/4"	"	91.50	20.35	111.85
1-1/2"	"	120.00	23.70	143.70
2"	"	210.00	28.50	238.50
Threaded				
1/2"				

Plumbing	UNIT	MAT.	INST.	TOTAL
15430.60		Valves		
125 lb	EA.	25.50	18.95	44.45
150 lb	"	72.00	18.95	90.95
300 lb	"	93.50	18.95	112.45
3/4"				
125 lb	EA.	29.70	22.75	52.45
150 lb	"	76.50	22.75	99.25
300 lb	"	93.50	22.75	116.25
1"				
125 lb	EA.	53.00	28.50	81.50
150 lb	"	170.00	28.50	198.50
300 lb	"	190.00	28.50	218.50
1-1/4"				
125 lb	EA.	95.50	28.50	124.00
150 lb	"	220.00	28.50	248.50
300 lb	"	260.00	28.50	288.50
1-1/2"				
125 lb	EA.	110.00	31.60	141.60
150 lb	"	240.00	31.60	271.60
300 lb	"	300.00	31.60	331.60
2"				
125 lb	EA.	190.00	37.90	227.90
150 lb	"	390.00	37.90	427.90
300 lb	"	480.00	37.90	517.90
Cast iron flanged				
2-1/2"				
125 lb	EA.	680.00	57.00	737.00
250 lb	"	1,180	57.00	1,237
3"				
125 lb	EA.	820.00	71.00	891.00
250 lb	"	1,210	71.00	1,281
4"				
125 lb	EA.	1,180	95.00	1,275
250 lb	"	1,790	95.00	1,885
6"				
125 lb	EA.	2,160	110.00	2,270
250 lb	"	3,180	110.00	3,290
8"				
125 lb	EA.	4,250	140.00	4,390
250 lb	"	4,960	140.00	5,100
Butterfly valve, cast iron, wafer type				
2"				
150 lb	EA.	120.00	40.70	160.70
200 lb	"	170.00	47.40	217.40
2-1/2"				
150 lb	EA.	170.00	47.40	217.40
200 lb	"	170.00	51.50	221.50
3"				
150 lb	EA.	170.00	57.00	227.00
200 lb	"	170.00	63.00	233.00
4"				
150 lb	EA.	180.00	81.50	261.50
200 lb	"	200.00	95.00	295.00

Plumbing	UNIT	MAT.	INST.	TOTAL
15430.60 Valves				
6"				
150 lb	EA.	220.00	110.00	330.00
200 lb	"	270.00	110.00	380.00
8"				
150 lb	EA.	270.00	130.00	400.00
200 lb	"	300.00	140.00	440.00
10"				
150 lb	EA.	330.00	140.00	470.00
200 lb	"	440.00	190.00	630.00
Ball valve, bronze, 250 lb, threaded				
1/2"	EA.	14.20	22.75	36.95
3/4"	"	21.25	22.75	44.00
1"	"	24.25	28.50	52.75
1-1/4"	"	39.40	31.60	71.00
1-1/2"	"	62.50	35.60	98.10
2"	"	71.00	40.70	111.70
Angle valve, bronze, 150 lb, threaded				
1/2"	EA.	84.50	20.35	104.85
3/4"	"	110.00	22.75	132.75
1"	"	170.00	22.75	192.75
1-1/4"	"	190.00	28.50	218.50
1-1/2"	"	240.00	31.60	271.60
Balancing valve, with meter connections, circuit setter				
1/2"	EA.	82.00	22.75	104.75
3/4"	"	86.50	25.90	112.40
1"	"	110.00	28.50	138.50
1-1/4"	"	150.00	31.60	181.60
1-1/2"	"	190.00	37.90	227.90
2"	"	260.00	47.40	307.40
2-1/2"	"	520.00	57.00	577.00
3"	"	760.00	71.00	831.00
4"	"	1,070	95.00	1,165
Balancing valve, straight type				
1/2"	EA.	22.15	22.75	44.90
3/4"	"	27.00	22.75	49.75
Angle type				
1/2"	EA.	29.90	22.75	52.65
3/4"	"	41.60	22.75	64.35
Square head cock, 125 lb, bronze body				
1/2"	EA.	17.50	18.95	36.45
3/4"	"	21.00	22.75	43.75
1"	"	29.30	25.90	55.20
1-1/4"	"	39.70	28.50	68.20
Pressure regulating valve, bronze, class 300				
1"	EA.	620.00	35.60	655.60
1-1/2"	"	830.00	43.80	873.80
2"	"	940.00	57.00	997.00
3"	"	1,060	81.50	1,142
4"	"	1,320	110.00	1,430
5"	"	2,000	140.00	2,140
6"	"	2,040	190.00	2,230

Plumbing	UNIT	MAT.	INST.	TOTAL
15430.68 Strainers				
Strainer, Y pattern, 125 psi, cast iron body, threaded				
3/4"	EA.	10.85	20.35	31.20
1"	"	13.00	22.75	35.75
1-1/4"	"	17.25	28.50	45.75
1-1/2"	"	21.55	28.50	50.05
2"	"	26.50	35.60	62.10
250 psi, brass body, threaded				
3/4"	EA.	29.80	22.75	52.55
1"	"	41.60	22.75	64.35
1-1/4"	"	52.00	28.50	80.50
1-1/2"	"	72.50	28.50	101.00
2"	"	130.00	35.60	165.60
Cast iron body, threaded				
3/4"	EA.	17.40	22.75	40.15
1"	"	22.10	22.75	44.85
1-1/4"	"	29.40	28.50	57.90
1-1/2"	"	38.90	28.50	67.40
2"	"	49.50	35.60	85.10
15430.70 Drains, Roof & Floor				
Floor drain, cast iron, with cast iron top				
2"	EA.	83.00	47.40	130.40
3"	"	120.00	47.40	167.40
4"	"	170.00	47.40	217.40
6"	"	310.00	57.00	367.00
Roof drain, cast iron				
2"	EA.	200.00	47.40	247.40
3"	"	220.00	47.40	267.40
4"	"	240.00	47.40	287.40
5"	"	310.00	57.00	367.00
6"	"	320.00	57.00	377.00

Plumbing Fixtures	UNIT	MAT.	INST.	TOTAL
15440.15 Faucets				
Washroom				
Minimum	EA.	200.00	95.00	295.00
Average	"	340.00	110.00	450.00
Maximum	"	510.00	140.00	650.00
Handicapped				
Minimum	EA.	250.00	110.00	360.00
Average	"	360.00	140.00	500.00
Maximum	"	560.00	190.00	750.00
For trim and rough-in				
Minimum	EA.	78.50	110.00	188.50
Average	"	120.00	140.00	260.00

Plumbing Fixtures	UNIT	MAT.	INST.	TOTAL
15440.15 — Faucets				
Maximum	EA.	200.00	280.00	480.00
15440.18 — Hydrants				
Wall hydrant				
8" thick	EA.	280.00	95.00	375.00
12" thick	"	330.00	110.00	440.00
18" thick	"	380.00	130.00	510.00
24" thick	"	430.00	140.00	570.00
Ground hydrant				
2' deep	EA.	560.00	71.00	631.00
4' deep	"	590.00	81.50	671.50
6' deep	"	640.00	95.00	735.00
8' deep	"	810.00	140.00	950.00
15440.20 — Lavatories				
Lavatory, counter top, porcelain enamel on cast iron				
Minimum	EA.	190.00	110.00	300.00
Average	"	290.00	140.00	430.00
Maximum	"	520.00	190.00	710.00
Wall hung, china				
Minimum	EA.	260.00	110.00	370.00
Average	"	310.00	140.00	450.00
Maximum	"	770.00	190.00	960.00
Handicapped				
Minimum	EA.	430.00	140.00	570.00
Average	"	500.00	190.00	690.00
Maximum	"	830.00	280.00	1,110
For trim and rough-in				
Minimum	EA.	220.00	140.00	360.00
Average	"	370.00	190.00	560.00
Maximum	"	460.00	280.00	740.00
15440.30 — Showers				
Shower, fiberglass, 36"x34"x84"				
Minimum	EA.	570.00	410.00	980.00
Average	"	800.00	570.00	1,370
Maximum	"	1,160	570.00	1,730
Steel, 1 piece, 36"x36"				
Minimum	EA.	530.00	410.00	940.00
Average	"	800.00	570.00	1,370
Maximum	"	950.00	570.00	1,520
Receptor, molded stone, 36"x36"				
Minimum	EA.	220.00	190.00	410.00
Average	"	370.00	280.00	650.00
Maximum	"	570.00	470.00	1,040
For trim and rough-in				
Minimum	EA.	220.00	260.00	480.00
Average	"	370.00	320.00	690.00
Maximum	"	460.00	570.00	1,030

Plumbing Fixtures	UNIT	MAT.	INST.	TOTAL
15440.40 Sinks				
Service sink, 24"x29"				
Minimum	EA.	640.00	140.00	780.00
Average	"	790.00	190.00	980.00
Maximum	"	1,170	280.00	1,450
Mop sink, 24"x36"x10"				
Minimum	EA.	480.00	110.00	590.00
Average	"	580.00	140.00	720.00
Maximum	"	780.00	190.00	970.00
For trim and rough-in				
Minimum	EA.	290.00	190.00	480.00
Average	"	440.00	280.00	720.00
Maximum	"	560.00	380.00	940.00
15440.50 Urinals				
Urinal, flush valve, floor mounted				
Minimum	EA.	500.00	140.00	640.00
Average	"	580.00	190.00	770.00
Maximum	"	680.00	280.00	960.00
Wall mounted				
Minimum	EA.	410.00	140.00	550.00
Average	"	560.00	190.00	750.00
Maximum	"	730.00	280.00	1,010
For trim and rough-in				
Minimum	EA.	180.00	140.00	320.00
Average	"	260.00	280.00	540.00
Maximum	"	360.00	380.00	740.00
15440.60 Water Closets				
Water closet flush tank, floor mounted				
Minimum	EA.	330.00	140.00	470.00
Average	"	650.00	190.00	840.00
Maximum	"	1,020	280.00	1,300
Handicapped				
Minimum	EA.	370.00	190.00	560.00
Average	"	670.00	280.00	950.00
Maximum	"	1,280	570.00	1,850
Bowl, with flush valve, floor mounted				
Minimum	EA.	460.00	140.00	600.00
Average	"	510.00	190.00	700.00
Maximum	"	990.00	280.00	1,270
Wall mounted				
Minimum	EA.	460.00	140.00	600.00
Average	"	540.00	190.00	730.00
Maximum	"	1,030	280.00	1,310
For trim and rough-in				
Minimum	EA.	210.00	140.00	350.00
Average	"	250.00	190.00	440.00
Maximum	"	330.00	280.00	610.00

Plumbing Fixtures	UNIT	MAT.	INST.	TOTAL
15440.70 Water Heaters				
Water heater, electric				
6 gal	EA.	330.00	95.00	425.00
10 gal	"	350.00	95.00	445.00
20 gal	"	410.00	110.00	520.00
40 gal	"	460.00	110.00	570.00
80 gal	"	830.00	140.00	970.00
100 gal	"	1,030	190.00	1,220
120 gal	"	1,320	190.00	1,510
15440.90 Miscellaneous Fixtures				
Electric water cooler				
Floor mounted	EA.	1,010	190.00	1,200
Wall mounted	"	950.00	190.00	1,140
Wash fountain				
Wall mounted	EA.	2,420	280.00	2,700
Circular, floor supported	"	4,240	570.00	4,810
Deluge shower and eye wash	"	1,010	280.00	1,290
15440.95 Fixture Carriers				
Water fountain, wall carrier				
Minimum	EA.	64.00	57.00	121.00
Average	"	86.00	71.00	157.00
Maximum	"	110.00	95.00	205.00
Lavatory, wall carrier				
Minimum	EA.	140.00	57.00	197.00
Average	"	210.00	71.00	281.00
Maximum	"	260.00	95.00	355.00
Sink, industrial, wall carrier				
Minimum	EA.	190.00	57.00	247.00
Average	"	220.00	71.00	291.00
Maximum	"	280.00	95.00	375.00
Toilets, water closets, wall carrier				
Minimum	EA.	280.00	57.00	337.00
Average	"	330.00	71.00	401.00
Maximum	"	430.00	95.00	525.00
Floor support				
Minimum	EA.	140.00	47.40	187.40
Average	"	170.00	57.00	227.00
Maximum	"	180.00	71.00	251.00
Urinals, wall carrier				
Minimum	EA.	150.00	57.00	207.00
Average	"	190.00	71.00	261.00
Maximum	"	230.00	95.00	325.00
Floor support				
Minimum	EA.	120.00	47.40	167.40
Average	"	180.00	57.00	237.00
Maximum	"	200.00	71.00	271.00
15450.30 Pumps				
In-line pump, bronze, centrifugal				
5 gpm, 20' head	EA.	470.00	35.60	505.60
20 gpm, 40' head	"	870.00	35.60	905.60

Plumbing Fixtures	UNIT	MAT.	INST.	TOTAL
15450.30 Pumps				
50 gpm				
50' head	EA.	1,150	71.00	1,221
100' head	"	1,320	71.00	1,391
70 gpm, 100' head	"	1,640	95.00	1,735
100 gpm, 80' head	"	1,750	95.00	1,845
250 gpm, 150' head	"	5,490	140.00	5,630
Cast iron, centrifugal				
50 gpm, 200' head	EA.	770.00	71.00	841.00
100 gpm				
100' head	EA.	1,860	95.00	1,955
200' head	"	2,170	95.00	2,265
200 gpm				
100' head	EA.	3,240	140.00	3,380
200' head	"	4,370	140.00	4,510
Centrifugal, close coupled, c.i., single stage				
50 gpm, 100' head	EA.	1,300	71.00	1,371
100 gpm, 100' head	"	1,580	95.00	1,675
Base mounted				
50 gpm, 100' head	EA.	2,660	71.00	2,731
100 gpm, 50' head	"	3,030	95.00	3,125
200 gpm, 100' head	"	3,870	140.00	4,010
300 gpm, 175' head	"	5,030	140.00	5,170
Suction diffuser, flanged, strainer				
3" inlet, 2-1/2" outlet	EA.	430.00	71.00	501.00
3" outlet	"	440.00	71.00	511.00
4" inlet				
3" outlet	EA.	520.00	95.00	615.00
4" outlet	"	610.00	95.00	705.00
6" inlet				
4" outlet	EA.	700.00	110.00	810.00
5" outlet	"	850.00	110.00	960.00
6" Outlet	"	880.00	110.00	990.00
8" inlet				
6" outlet	EA.	960.00	140.00	1,100
8" outlet	"	1,660	140.00	1,800
10" inlet				
8" outlet	EA.	2,230	190.00	2,420
Vertical turbine				
Single stage, C.I., 3550 rpm, 200 gpm, 50'head	EA.	5,690	190.00	5,880
Multi stage, 3550 rpm				
50 gpm, 100' head	EA.	5,690	140.00	5,830
100 gpm				
100' head	EA.	5,410	140.00	5,550
200 gpm				
50' head	EA.	6,360	190.00	6,550
100' head	"	6,470	190.00	6,660
Bronze				
Single stage, 3550 rpm, 100 gpm, 50' head	EA.	5,890	140.00	6,030
Multi stage, 3550 rpm, 50 gpm, 100' head	"	5,550	140.00	5,690
100 gpm				
100' head	EA.	6,110	140.00	6,250
200 gpm				

Plumbing Fixtures

	UNIT	MAT.	INST.	TOTAL
15450.30 — Pumps				
50' head	EA.	6,110	190.00	6,300
100' head	"	6,520	190.00	6,710
Sump pump, bronze, 1750 rpm, 25 gpm				
20' head	EA.	5,360	710.00	6,070
150' head	"	7,460	950.00	8,410
50 gpm				
100' head	EA.	6,370	710.00	7,080
100 gpm				
50' head	EA.	5,540	710.00	6,250
15480.10 — Special Systems				
Air compressor, air cooled, two stage				
5.0 cfm, 175 psi	EA.	2,350	1,140	3,490
10 cfm, 175 psi	"	2,870	1,260	4,130
20 cfm, 175 psi	"	3,960	1,360	5,320
50 cfm, 125 psi	"	5,780	1,500	7,280
80 cfm, 125 psi	"	8,260	1,630	9,890
Single stage, 125 psi				
1.0 cfm	EA.	2,270	810.00	3,080
1.5 cfm	"	2,310	810.00	3,120
2.0 cfm	"	2,370	810.00	3,180
Automotive, hose reel, air and water, 50' hose	"	1,060	470.00	1,530
Lube equipment, 3 reel, with pumps	"	5,530	2,280	7,810
Tire changer				
Truck	EA.	14,430	810.00	15,240
Passenger car	"	3,410	440.00	3,850
Air hose reel, includes, 50' hose	"	900.00	440.00	1,340
Hose reel, 5 reel, motor oil, gear oil, lube, air & water	"	8,420	2,280	10,700
Water hose reel, 50' hose	"	900.00	440.00	1,340
Pump, air operated, for motor or gear oil, fits 55 gal drum	"	1,180	57.00	1,237
For chassis lube	"	1,930	57.00	1,987
Fuel dispensing pump, lighted dial, one product				
One hose	EA.	4,200	470.00	4,670
Two hose	"	7,410	470.00	7,880
Two products, two hose	"	7,810	470.00	8,280

Heating & Ventilating

	UNIT	MAT.	INST.	TOTAL
15610.10 — Furnaces				
Electric, hot air				
40 mbh	EA.	810.00	280.00	1,090
80 mbh	"	960.00	320.00	1,280
100 mbh	"	1,080	330.00	1,410
160 mbh	"	1,820	360.00	2,180
200 mbh	"	2,640	370.00	3,010
400 mbh	"	4,680	380.00	5,060

Heating & Ventilating	UNIT	MAT.	INST.	TOTAL
15610.10 Furnaces				
Gas fired hot air				
40 mbh	EA.	810.00	280.00	1,090
80 mbh	"	1,000	320.00	1,320
100 mbh	"	1,050	330.00	1,380
160 mbh	"	1,360	360.00	1,720
200 mbh	"	2,430	370.00	2,800
400 mbh	"	4,680	380.00	5,060
Oil fired hot air				
40 mbh	EA.	1,090	280.00	1,370
80 mbh	"	1,430	320.00	1,750
100 mbh	"	1,670	330.00	2,000
160 mbh	"	2,010	360.00	2,370
200 mbh	"	2,590	370.00	2,960
400 mbh	"	5,470	380.00	5,850
15780.20 Rooftop Units				
Packaged, single zone rooftop unit, with roof curb				
2 ton	EA.	4,860	570.00	5,430
3 ton	"	5,080	570.00	5,650
4 ton	"	5,570	710.00	6,280
5 ton	"	6,050	950.00	7,000
7.5 ton	"	8,830	1,140	9,970
15830.70 Unit Heaters				
Steam unit heater, horizontal				
12,500 btuh, 200 cfm	EA.	630.00	95.00	725.00
17,000 btuh, 300 cfm	"	720.00	95.00	815.00
40,000 btuh, 500 cfm	"	890.00	95.00	985.00
60,000 btuh, 700 cfm	"	1,000	95.00	1,095
70,000 btuh, 1000 cfm	"	1,240	140.00	1,380
Vertical				
12,500 btuh, 200 cfm	EA.	540.00	95.00	635.00
17,000 btuh, 300 cfm	"	890.00	95.00	985.00
40,000 btuh, 500 cfm	"	1,070	95.00	1,165
60,000 btuh, 700 cfm	"	1,240	95.00	1,335
70,000 btuh, 1000 cfm	"	1,430	95.00	1,525
Gas unit heater, horizontal				
27,400 btuh	EA.	890.00	230.00	1,120
38,000 btuh	"	980.00	230.00	1,210
56,000 btuh	"	1,070	230.00	1,300
82,200 btuh	"	1,180	230.00	1,410
103,900 btuh	"	1,230	360.00	1,590
125,700 btuh	"	1,270	360.00	1,630
133,200 btuh	"	1,330	360.00	1,690
149,000 btuh	"	1,560	360.00	1,920
172,000 btuh	"	1,690	360.00	2,050
190,000 btuh	"	1,780	360.00	2,140
225,000 btuh	"	1,960	360.00	2,320
Hot water unit heater, horizontal				
12,500 btuh, 200 cfm	EA.	540.00	95.00	635.00
17,000 btuh, 300 cfm	"	630.00	95.00	725.00
25,000 btuh, 500 cfm	"	670.00	95.00	765.00

Heating & Ventilating	UNIT	MAT.	INST.	TOTAL
15830.70 Unit Heaters				
30,000 btuh, 700 cfm	EA.	800.00	95.00	895.00
50,000 btuh, 1000 cfm	"	890.00	140.00	1,030
60,000 btuh, 1300 cfm	"	1,240	140.00	1,380
Vertical				
12,500 btuh, 200 cfm	EA.	660.00	95.00	755.00
17,000 btuh, 300 cfm	"	720.00	95.00	815.00
25,000 btuh, 500 cfm	"	760.00	95.00	855.00
30,000 btuh, 700 cfm	"	810.00	95.00	905.00
50,000 btuh, 1000 cfm	"	890.00	95.00	985.00
60,000 btuh, 1300 cfm	"	980.00	95.00	1,075
Cabinet unit heaters, ceiling, exposed, hot water				
200 cfm	EA.	1,240	190.00	1,430
300 cfm	"	1,330	230.00	1,560
400 cfm	"	1,390	270.00	1,660
600 cfm	"	1,430	300.00	1,730
800 cfm	"	1,780	360.00	2,140
1000 cfm	"	2,320	410.00	2,730
1200 cfm	"	2,500	470.00	2,970
2000 cfm	"	4,280	630.00	4,910

Air Handling	UNIT	MAT.	INST.	TOTAL
15855.10 Air Handling Units				
Air handling unit, medium pressure, single zone				
1500 cfm	EA.	4,000	360.00	4,360
3000 cfm	"	5,010	630.00	5,640
4000 cfm	"	6,410	710.00	7,120
5000 cfm	"	8,090	760.00	8,850
6000 cfm	"	9,630	810.00	10,440
7000 cfm	"	11,190	880.00	12,070
8500 cfm	"	12,320	950.00	13,270
Rooftop air handling units				
4950 cfm	EA.	10,950	630.00	11,580
7370 cfm	"	11,860	810.00	12,670
15870.20 Exhaust Fans				
Belt drive roof exhaust fans				
640 cfm, 2618 fpm	EA.	1,030	71.00	1,101
940 cfm, 2604 fpm	"	1,340	71.00	1,411
1050 cfm, 3325 fpm	"	1,200	71.00	1,271
1170 cfm, 2373 fpm	"	1,740	71.00	1,811
2440 cfm, 4501 fpm	"	1,360	71.00	1,431

Air Distribution	UNIT	MAT.	INST.	TOTAL
15890.10	**Metal Ductwork**			
Rectangular duct				
Galvanized steel				
Minimum	Lb.	0.88	5.15	6.03
Average	"	1.10	6.30	7.40
Maximum	"	1.70	9.50	11.20
Aluminum				
Minimum	Lb.	2.10	11.40	13.50
Average	"	2.80	14.25	17.05
Maximum	"	3.45	18.95	22.40
Fittings				
Minimum	EA.	7.25	18.95	26.20
Average	"	10.90	28.50	39.40
Maximum	"	16.00	57.00	73.00
For work				
10-20' high, add per pound, $.30				
30-50', add per pound, $.50				
15890.30	**Flexible Ductwork**			
Flexible duct, 1.25" fiberglass				
6" dia.	L.F.	3.15	3.15	6.30
8" dia.	"	3.95	3.55	7.50
12" dia.	"	5.50	4.40	9.90
16" dia.	"	8.25	5.15	13.40
Flexible duct connector, 3" wide fabric	"	2.30	9.50	11.80
15910.10	**Dampers**			
Horizontal parallel aluminum backdraft damper				
12" x 12"	EA.	69.00	14.25	83.25
24" x 24"	"	110.00	28.50	138.50
36" x 36"	"	250.00	40.70	290.70
15940.10	**Diffusers**			
Ceiling diffusers, round, baked enamel finish				
6" dia.	EA.	51.50	18.95	70.45
8" dia.	"	62.00	23.70	85.70
12" dia.	"	92.50	23.70	116.20
16" dia.	"	140.00	25.90	165.90
20" dia.	"	190.00	28.50	218.50
Rectangular				
6x6"	EA.	57.50	18.95	76.45
12x12"	"	100.00	28.50	128.50
18x18"	"	160.00	28.50	188.50
24x24"	"	290.00	35.60	325.60
15940.40	**Registers And Grilles**			
Lay in flush mounted, perforated face, return				
6x6/24x24	EA.	46.30	22.75	69.05
8x8/24x24	"	46.30	22.75	69.05
9x9/24x24	"	50.00	22.75	72.75
10x10/24x24	"	54.00	22.75	76.75
12x12/24x24	"	54.00	22.75	76.75
Rectangular, ceiling return, single deflection				
10x10	EA.	27.80	28.50	56.30

15   MECHANICAL

Air Distribution	UNIT	MAT.	INST.	TOTAL
15940.40 Registers And Grilles				
12x12	EA.	32.50	28.50	61.00
16x16	"	32.50	28.50	61.00
20x20	"	60.00	28.50	88.50
24x18	"	110.00	28.50	138.50
36x24	"	220.00	31.60	251.60
36x30	"	320.00	31.60	351.60
Wall, return air register				
12x12	EA.	46.20	14.25	60.45
16x16	"	68.00	14.25	82.25
18x18	"	80.50	14.25	94.75
20x20	"	95.50	14.25	109.75
24x24	"	130.00	14.25	144.25

Basic Materials	UNIT	MAT.	INST.	TOTAL
16050.30 — Bus Duct				
Bus duct, 100a, plug-in				
10', 600v	EA.	230.00	180.00	410.00
With ground	"	310.00	280.00	590.00
Circuit breakers, with enclosure				
1 pole				
15a-60a	EA.	230.00	66.00	296.00
70a-100a	"	260.00	82.50	342.50
2 pole				
15a-60a	EA.	340.00	72.50	412.50
70a-100a	"	410.00	85.50	495.50
Circuit breaker, adapter cubicle				
225a	EA.	3,710	100.00	3,810
400a	"	4,380	110.00	4,490
Fusible switches, 240v, 3 phase				
30a	EA.	590.00	66.00	656.00
60a	"	730.00	82.50	812.50
100a	"	970.00	100.00	1,070
200a	"	1,690	140.00	1,830
16110.12 — Cable Tray				
Cable tray, 6"	L.F.	19.05	3.90	22.95
Ventilated cover	"	7.70	2.00	9.70
Solid cover	"	6.00	2.00	8.00
16110.20 — Conduit Specialties				
Rod beam clamp, 1/2"	EA.	5.70	3.30	9.00
Hanger rod				
3/8"	L.F.	1.20	2.65	3.85
1/2"	"	2.00	3.30	5.30
Hanger channel, 1-1/2"				
No holes	EA.	4.65	2.00	6.65
Holes	"	5.20	2.00	7.20
Channel strap				
1/2"	EA.	1.20	3.30	4.50
1"	"	1.60	3.30	4.90
2"	"	2.30	5.25	7.55
3"	"	2.70	8.10	10.80
4"	"	3.80	9.60	13.40
5"	"	5.35	9.60	14.95
6"	"	6.30	9.60	15.90
Conduit penetrations, roof and wall, 8" thick				
1/2"	EA.		40.60	40.60
1"	"		52.50	52.50
2"	"		110.00	110.00
3"	"		110.00	110.00
4"	"		130.00	130.00
Fireproofing, for conduit penetrations				
1/2"	EA.	2.80	33.00	35.80
1"	"	2.95	33.00	35.95
2"	"	4.25	47.90	52.15
3"	"	8.35	64.00	72.35
4"	"	11.80	100.00	111.80

Basic Materials	UNIT	MAT.	INST.	TOTAL
16110.21 Aluminum Conduit				
Aluminum conduit				
1/2"	L.F.	1.30	2.00	3.30
3/4"	"	1.65	2.65	4.30
1"	"	1.70	3.30	5.00
1-1/4"	"	3.20	3.90	7.10
1-1/2"	"	3.95	5.25	9.20
2"	"	5.30	5.85	11.15
2-1/2"	"	8.35	6.60	14.95
3"	"	10.95	7.05	18.00
3-1/2"	"	13.15	8.10	21.25
4"	"	15.55	9.60	25.15
5"	"	22.25	12.00	34.25
6"	"	29.40	13.20	42.60
16110.22 Emt Conduit				
EMT conduit				
1/2"	L.F.	0.33	2.00	2.33
3/4"	"	0.62	2.65	3.27
1"	"	0.98	3.30	4.28
1-1/4"	"	1.50	3.90	5.40
1-1/2"	"	1.85	5.25	7.10
2"	"	2.20	5.85	8.05
2-1/2"	"	4.75	6.60	11.35
3"	"	6.70	8.10	14.80
3-1/2"	"	8.85	9.60	18.45
4"	"	9.90	12.00	21.90
16110.23 Flexible Conduit				
Flexible conduit, steel				
3/8"	L.F.	0.35	2.00	2.35
1/2	"	0.40	2.00	2.40
3/4"	"	0.53	2.65	3.18
1"	"	1.05	2.65	3.70
1-1/4"	"	1.30	3.30	4.60
1-1/2"	"	2.10	3.90	6.00
2"	"	2.65	5.25	7.90
2-1/2"	"	3.05	5.85	8.90
3"	"	3.75	7.05	10.80
16110.24 Galvanized Conduit				
Galvanized rigid steel conduit				
1/2"	L.F.	1.30	2.65	3.95
3/4"	"	1.45	3.30	4.75
1"	"	2.30	3.90	6.20
1-1/4"	"	3.30	5.25	8.55
1-1/2"	"	3.90	5.85	9.75
2"	"	4.65	6.60	11.25
2-1/2"	"	7.70	9.60	17.30
3"	"	10.05	12.00	22.05
3-1/2"	"	10.35	12.55	22.90
4"	"	15.00	13.85	28.85
5"	"	30.60	18.85	49.45

16 ELECTRICAL

Basic Materials	UNIT	MAT.	INST.	TOTAL
16110.24 — Galvanized Conduit				
6"	L.F.	44.20	25.10	69.30
16110.25 — Plastic Conduit				
PVC conduit, schedule 40				
1/2"	L.F.	0.57	2.00	2.57
3/4"	"	0.77	2.00	2.77
1"	"	1.15	2.65	3.80
1-1/4"	"	1.55	2.65	4.20
1-1/2"	"	1.85	3.30	5.15
2"	"	2.45	3.30	5.75
2-1/2"	"	3.80	3.90	7.70
3"	"	4.35	3.90	8.25
3-1/2"	"	5.75	5.25	11.00
4"	"	6.30	5.25	11.55
5"	"	8.90	5.85	14.75
6"	"	11.80	6.60	18.40
16110.27 — Plastic Coated Conduit				
Rigid steel conduit, plastic coated				
1/2"	L.F.	4.30	3.30	7.60
3/4"	"	5.05	3.90	8.95
1"	"	6.55	5.25	11.80
1-1/4"	"	8.20	6.60	14.80
1-1/2"	"	9.95	8.10	18.05
2"	"	13.15	9.60	22.75
2-1/2"	"	19.95	12.55	32.50
3"	"	25.10	14.65	39.75
3-1/2"	"	30.60	16.45	47.05
4"	"	37.40	20.30	57.70
5"	"	64.00	25.10	89.10
90 degree elbows				
1/2"	EA.	16.55	20.30	36.85
3/4"	"	16.90	25.10	42.00
1"	"	19.65	29.30	48.95
1-1/4"	"	24.55	33.00	57.55
1-1/2"	"	29.70	40.60	70.30
2"	"	41.30	52.50	93.80
2-1/2"	"	80.00	75.50	155.50
3"	"	81.00	88.00	169.00
3-1/2"	"	180.00	110.00	290.00
4"	"	190.00	130.00	320.00
5"	"	420.00	160.00	580.00
Couplings				
1/2"	EA.	4.85	3.90	8.75
3/4"	"	5.10	5.25	10.35
1"	"	6.80	5.85	12.65
1-1/4"	"	7.95	7.05	15.00
1-1/2"	"	11.10	8.10	19.20
2"	"	13.90	9.60	23.50
2-1/2"	"	34.90	12.00	46.90
3"	"	40.60	12.55	53.15
3-1/2"	"	56.00	13.20	69.20

Basic Materials	UNIT	MAT.	INST.	TOTAL
16110.27 Plastic Coated Conduit				
4"	EA.	69.00	14.65	83.65
5"	"	200.00	16.45	216.45
1 hole conduit straps				
3/4"	EA.	8.00	3.30	11.30
1"	"	8.25	3.30	11.55
1-1/4"	"	12.00	3.90	15.90
1-1/2"	"	12.70	3.90	16.60
2"	"	18.45	3.90	22.35
3"	"	21.80	5.25	27.05
3-1/2"	"	24.35	5.25	29.60
4"	"	33.20	6.60	39.80
16110.28 Steel Conduit				
Intermediate metal conduit (IMC)				
1/2"	L.F.	1.45	2.00	3.45
3/4"	"	1.70	2.65	4.35
1"	"	2.25	3.30	5.55
1-1/4"	"	2.90	3.90	6.80
1-1/2"	"	3.45	5.25	8.70
2"	"	4.65	5.85	10.50
2-1/2"	"	7.10	7.85	14.95
3"	"	10.10	9.60	19.70
3-1/2"	"	13.10	12.00	25.10
4"	"	15.35	12.55	27.90
90 degree ell				
1/2"	EA.	9.20	16.45	25.65
3/4"	"	11.20	20.30	31.50
1"	"	16.15	25.10	41.25
1-1/4"	"	26.20	29.30	55.50
1-1/2"	"	29.40	33.00	62.40
2"	"	42.40	37.70	80.10
2-1/2"	"	73.50	43.90	117.40
3"	"	110.00	58.50	168.50
3-1/2"	"	200.00	75.50	275.50
4"	"	230.00	88.00	318.00
Couplings				
1/2"	EA.	1.85	3.30	5.15
3/4"	"	2.30	3.90	6.20
1"	"	3.40	5.25	8.65
1-1/4"	"	4.20	5.85	10.05
1-1/2"	"	5.30	6.60	11.90
2"	"	7.05	7.05	14.10
2-1/2"	"	15.65	8.10	23.75
3"	"	21.45	9.60	31.05
3-1/2"	"	28.60	9.60	38.20
4"	"	30.10	10.55	40.65
16110.35 Surface Mounted Raceway				
Single Raceway				
3/4" x 17/32" Conduit	L.F.	1.65	2.65	4.30
Mounting Strap	EA.	0.45	3.50	3.95
Connector	"	0.61	3.50	4.11

Basic Materials	UNIT	MAT.	INST.	TOTAL
16110.35 Surface Mounted Raceway				
Elbow				
45 degree	EA.	7.60	3.30	10.90
90 degree	"	2.45	3.30	5.75
internal	"	3.05	3.30	6.35
external	"	2.85	3.30	6.15
Switch	"	19.80	26.40	46.20
Utility Box	"	13.30	26.40	39.70
Receptacle	"	23.45	26.40	49.85
3/4" x 21/32" Conduit	L.F.	1.90	2.65	4.55
Mounting Strap	EA.	0.70	3.50	4.20
Connector	"	0.73	3.50	4.23
Elbow				
45 degree	EA.	9.40	3.30	12.70
90 degree	"	2.60	3.30	5.90
internal	"	3.50	3.30	6.80
external	"	3.50	3.30	6.80
Switch	"	19.80	26.40	46.20
Utility Box	"	13.30	26.40	39.70
Receptacle	"	23.45	26.40	49.85
16110.60 Trench Duct				
Trench duct, with cover				
9"	L.F.	110.00	11.20	121.20
12"	"	130.00	13.20	143.20
18"	"	180.00	17.55	197.55
Tees				
9"	EA.	420.00	110.00	530.00
12"	"	460.00	130.00	590.00
18"	"	590.00	150.00	740.00
Vertical elbows				
9"	EA.	140.00	52.50	192.50
12"	"	150.00	72.00	222.00
18"	"	190.00	89.50	279.50
Cabinet connectors				
9"	EA.	190.00	130.00	320.00
12"	"	210.00	140.00	350.00
18"	"	240.00	160.00	400.00
End closers				
9"	EA.	44.40	40.60	85.00
12"	"	46.00	43.90	89.90
18"	"	69.00	52.50	121.50
Horizontal elbows				
9"	EA.	420.00	100.00	520.00
12"	"	460.00	110.00	570.00
18"	"	590.00	140.00	730.00
Crosses				
9"	EA.	660.00	130.00	790.00
12"	"	690.00	150.00	840.00
18"	"	830.00	160.00	990.00

Basic Materials	UNIT	MAT.	INST.	TOTAL
16110.80 Wireways				
Wireway, hinge cover type				
2-1/2" x 2-1/2"				
1' section	EA.	14.25	10.15	24.40
2'	"	20.20	12.55	32.75
3'	"	27.40	16.45	43.85
16120.41 Aluminum Conductors				
Type XHHW, stranded aluminum, 600v				
#8	L.F.	0.22	0.33	0.55
#6	"	0.30	0.40	0.70
#4	"	0.39	0.53	0.91
#2	"	0.46	0.59	1.05
1/0	"	0.75	0.73	1.48
2/0	"	0.90	0.79	1.70
3/0	"	1.10	0.93	2.03
4/0	"	1.35	0.99	2.34
THW, stranded				
#8	L.F.	0.20	0.33	0.53
#6	"	0.21	0.40	0.61
#4	"	0.25	0.53	0.78
#3	"	0.33	0.59	0.92
#1	"	0.48	0.66	1.14
1/0	"	0.59	0.73	1.32
2/0	"	0.67	0.78	1.45
3/0	"	0.84	0.78	1.62
4/0	"	1.00	0.99	1.99
16120.43 Copper Conductors				
Copper conductors, type THW, solid				
#14	L.F.	0.12	0.26	0.39
#12	"	0.19	0.33	0.52
#10	"	0.29	0.40	0.68
Stranded				
#14	L.F.	0.13	0.26	0.40
#12	"	0.20	0.33	0.53
#10	"	0.30	0.40	0.70
#8	"	0.51	0.53	1.03
#6	"	0.86	0.59	1.45
#4	"	1.35	0.66	2.01
#3	"	1.70	0.66	2.36
#2	"	2.10	0.79	2.89
#1	"	2.70	0.93	3.63
1/0	"	3.20	1.05	4.25
2/0	"	4.00	1.30	5.30
3/0	"	5.05	1.65	6.70
4/0	"	6.35	1.85	8.20
THHN-THWN, solid				
#14	L.F.	0.12	0.26	0.39
#12	"	0.19	0.33	0.52
#10	"	0.29	0.40	0.68
Stranded				
#14	L.F.	0.13	0.26	0.40

Basic Materials	UNIT	MAT.	INST.	TOTAL
16120.43 Copper Conductors				
#12	L.F.	0.20	0.33	0.53
#10	"	0.30	0.40	0.70
#8	"	0.51	0.53	1.03
#6	"	0.86	0.59	1.45
#4	"	1.35	0.66	2.01
#2	"	2.10	0.79	2.89
#1	"	2.70	0.93	3.63
1/0	"	3.20	1.05	4.25
2/0	"	4.00	1.30	5.30
3/0	"	5.05	1.65	6.70
4/0	"	6.35	1.85	8.20
XLP, 600v				
#12	L.F.	0.40	0.33	0.73
#10	"	0.57	0.40	0.97
#8	"	0.70	0.53	1.23
#6	"	1.15	0.59	1.74
#4	"	1.75	0.66	2.41
#3	"	2.15	0.73	2.88
#2	"	2.70	0.79	3.49
#1	"	3.50	0.93	4.43
1/0	"	4.10	1.05	5.15
2/0	"	5.05	1.30	6.35
3/0	"	6.35	1.70	8.05
4/0	"	7.95	1.85	9.80
Bare solid wire				
#14	L.F.	0.11	0.26	0.37
#12	"	0.17	0.33	0.50
#10	"	0.26	0.40	0.66
#8	"	0.42	0.53	0.95
#6	"	0.75	0.59	1.34
#4	"	1.25	0.66	1.91
#2	"	1.95	0.79	2.74
Bare stranded wire				
#8	L.F.	0.45	0.53	0.98
#6	"	0.79	0.66	1.45
#4	"	1.25	0.66	1.91
#2	"	2.00	0.73	2.73
#1	"	2.50	0.93	3.43
1/0	"	2.95	1.20	4.15
2/0	"	3.70	1.30	5.00
3/0	"	4.70	1.65	6.35
4/0	"	5.90	1.85	7.75
Type "BX" solid armored cable				
#14/2	L.F.	0.61	1.65	2.26
#14/3	"	0.96	1.85	2.81
#14/4	"	1.40	2.05	3.45
#12/2	"	0.62	1.85	2.47
#12/3	"	0.98	2.05	3.03
#12/4	"	1.40	2.30	3.70
#10/2	"	1.10	2.05	3.15
#10/3	"	1.55	2.30	3.85
#10/4	"	2.40	2.65	5.05

Basic Materials	UNIT	MAT.	INST.	TOTAL
16120.43 Copper Conductors				
#8/2	L.F.	1.95	2.30	4.25
#8/3	"	2.45	2.65	5.10
Steel type, metal clad cable, solid, with ground				
#14/2	L.F.	0.68	1.20	1.88
#14/3	"	1.05	1.30	2.35
#14/4	"	1.40	1.50	2.90
#12/2	"	0.69	1.30	1.99
#12/3	"	1.10	1.65	2.75
#12/4	"	1.45	2.00	3.45
#10/2	"	1.25	1.50	2.75
#10/3	"	1.95	1.85	3.80
#10/4	"	3.05	2.20	5.25
Metal clad cable, stranded, with ground				
#8/2	L.F.	2.55	1.85	4.40
#8/3	"	3.65	2.30	5.95
#8/4	"	4.75	2.75	7.50
#6/2	"	3.80	2.00	5.80
#6/3	"	4.55	2.50	7.05
#6/4	"	5.45	2.95	8.40
#4/2	"	4.95	2.65	7.60
#4/3	"	6.45	2.95	9.40
#4/4	"	7.60	3.65	11.25
#3/3	"	7.90	3.30	11.20
#3/4	"	9.35	3.90	13.25
#2/3	"	9.40	3.75	13.15
#2/4	"	11.50	4.40	15.90
#1/3	"	11.35	5.00	16.35
#1/4	"	13.40	5.55	18.95
16120.47 Sheathed Cable				
Non-metallic sheathed cable				
Type NM cable with ground				
#14/2	L.F.	0.35	0.99	1.34
#12/2	"	0.54	1.05	1.59
#10/2	"	0.86	1.15	2.01
#8/2	"	1.40	1.30	2.70
#6/2	"	2.20	1.65	3.85
#14/3	"	0.50	1.70	2.20
#12/3	"	0.77	1.75	2.52
#10/3	"	1.20	1.80	3.00
#8/3	"	2.05	1.80	3.85
#6/3	"	3.30	1.85	5.15
#4/3	"	5.85	2.10	7.95
#2/3	"	8.75	2.30	11.05
Type U.F. cable with ground				
#14/2	L.F.	0.41	1.05	1.46
#12/2	"	0.62	1.25	1.87
#10/2	"	0.98	1.30	2.28
#8/2	"	1.70	1.50	3.20
#6/2	"	2.65	1.80	4.45
#14/3	"	0.57	1.30	1.87
#12/3	"	0.87	1.45	2.32

Basic Materials	UNIT	MAT.	INST.	TOTAL
16120.47	Sheathed Cable			
#10/3	L.F.	1.35	1.65	3.00
#8/3	"	2.55	1.85	4.40
#6/3	"	4.10	2.10	6.20
Type S.F.U. cable, 3 conductor				
#8	L.F.	1.75	1.85	3.60
#6	"	3.05	2.05	5.10
Type SER cable, 4 conductor				
#6	L.F.	4.40	2.40	6.80
#4	"	6.15	2.55	8.70
Flexible cord, type STO cord				
#18/2	L.F.	0.75	0.26	1.01
#18/3	"	0.87	0.33	1.20
#18/4	"	1.20	0.40	1.60
#16/2	"	0.86	0.26	1.12
#16/3	"	0.73	0.29	1.02
#16/4	"	1.00	0.33	1.33
#14/2	"	1.35	0.33	1.68
#14/3	"	1.20	0.41	1.61
#14/4	"	1.50	0.46	1.96
#12/2	"	1.70	0.40	2.10
#12/3	"	1.30	0.44	1.74
#12/4	"	1.85	0.53	2.38
#10/2	"	2.10	0.46	2.56
#10/3	"	2.00	0.53	2.53
#10/4	"	3.15	0.59	3.74
#8/2	"	3.50	0.53	4.03
#8/3	"	3.90	0.59	4.49
#8/4	"	5.50	0.66	6.16
16130.40	Boxes			
Round cast box, type SEH				
1/2"	EA.	24.35	22.90	47.25
3/4"	"	26.60	27.70	54.30
SEHC				
1/2"	EA.	30.60	22.90	53.50
3/4"	"	32.00	27.70	59.70
SEHL				
1/2"	EA.	37.70	22.90	60.60
3/4"	"	39.80	29.30	69.10
SEHT				
1/2"	EA.	42.90	27.70	70.60
3/4"	"	44.20	33.00	77.20
SEHX				
1/2"	EA.	46.40	33.00	79.40
3/4"	"	48.20	40.60	88.80
Blank cover	"	6.05	9.60	15.65
1/2", hub cover	"	4.60	9.60	14.20
Cover with gasket	"	5.05	11.70	16.75
Rectangle, type FS boxes				
1/2"	EA.	12.25	22.90	35.15
3/4"	"	12.95	26.40	39.35
1"	"	14.05	33.00	47.05

Basic Materials	UNIT	MAT.	INST.	TOTAL
16130.40 Boxes				
FSA				
1/2"	EA.	20.35	22.90	43.25
3/4"	"	21.85	26.40	48.25
FSC				
1/2"	EA.	13.55	22.90	36.45
3/4"	"	14.85	27.70	42.55
1"	"	18.50	33.00	51.50
FSL				
1/2"	EA.	15.65	22.90	38.55
3/4"	"	16.15	26.40	42.55
FSR				
1/2"	EA.	15.65	22.90	38.55
3/4"	"	19.50	26.40	45.90
FSS				
1/2"	EA.	13.55	22.90	36.45
3/4"	"	14.85	26.40	41.25
FSLA				
1/2"	EA.	15.65	22.90	38.55
3/4"	"	17.75	26.40	44.15
FSCA				
1/2"	EA.	20.80	22.90	43.70
3/4"	"	23.85	26.40	50.25
FSCC				
1/2"	EA.	16.60	26.40	43.00
3/4"	"	21.95	33.00	54.95
FSCT				
1/2"	EA.	16.60	26.40	43.00
3/4"	"	20.70	33.00	53.70
1"	"	27.90	37.70	65.60
FST				
1/2"	EA.	22.45	33.00	55.45
3/4"	"	24.25	37.70	61.95
FSX				
1/2"	EA.	22.85	40.60	63.45
3/4"	"	26.50	47.90	74.40
FSCD boxes				
1/2"	EA.	25.20	40.60	65.80
3/4"	"	26.70	47.90	74.60
Rectangle, type FS, 2 gang boxes				
1/2"	EA.	21.95	22.90	44.85
3/4"	"	22.60	26.40	49.00
1"	"	23.80	33.00	56.80
Weatherproof cast aluminum boxes, 1 gang, 3 outlets				
1/2"	EA.	6.55	26.40	32.95
3/4"	"	7.10	33.00	40.10
2 gang, 3 outlets				
1/2"	EA.	12.50	33.00	45.50
3/4"	"	13.35	35.10	48.45
1 gang, 4 outlets				
1/2"	EA.	8.05	40.60	48.65
3/4"	"	8.60	47.90	56.50
2 gang, 4 outlets				

Basic Materials	UNIT	MAT.	INST.	TOTAL
16130.40 Boxes				
1/2"	EA.	13.75	40.60	54.35
3/4"	"	14.50	47.90	62.40
Weatherproof and type FS box covers, blank, 1 gang	"	2.85	9.60	12.45
Tumbler switch, 1 gang	"	3.85	9.60	13.45
1 gang, single recept	"	3.85	9.60	13.45
Duplex recept	"	4.90	9.60	14.50
Despard	"	3.50	9.60	13.10
Red pilot light	"	23.20	9.60	32.80
SW and				
Single recept	EA.	10.35	13.20	23.55
Duplex recept	"	8.45	13.20	21.65
2 gang				
Blank	EA.	3.10	12.00	15.10
Tumbler switch	"	4.05	12.00	16.05
Single recept	"	4.05	12.00	16.05
Duplex recept	"	4.05	12.00	16.05
Box covers				
Surface	EA.	15.60	13.20	28.80
Sealing	"	17.00	13.20	30.20
Dome	"	23.55	13.20	36.75
1/2" nipple	"	30.00	13.20	43.20
3/4" nipple	"	30.90	13.20	44.10
16130.60 Pull And Junction Boxes				
4"				
Octagon box	EA.	2.55	7.55	10.10
Box extension	"	4.20	3.90	8.10
Plaster ring	"	2.80	3.90	6.70
Cover blank	"	1.05	3.90	4.95
Square box	"	3.10	7.55	10.65
Box extension	"	4.25	3.90	8.15
Plaster ring	"	2.35	3.90	6.25
Cover blank	"	1.20	3.90	5.10
4-11/16"				
Square box	EA.	9.70	7.55	17.25
Box extension	"	9.60	3.90	13.50
Plaster ring	"	6.40	3.90	10.30
Cover blank	"	2.15	3.90	6.05
Switch and device boxes				
2 gang	EA.	13.25	7.55	20.80
3 gang	"	16.35	7.55	23.90
4 gang	"	23.10	10.55	33.65
Device covers				
2 gang	EA.	11.55	3.90	15.45
3 gang	"	11.95	3.90	15.85
4 gang	"	16.20	3.90	20.10
Handy box	"	2.80	7.55	10.35
Extension	"	3.35	3.90	7.25
Switch cover	"	1.00	3.90	4.90
Switch box with knockout	"	2.85	9.60	12.45
Weatherproof cover, spring type	"	9.95	5.25	15.20
Cover plate, dryer receptacle 1 gang plastic	"	5.95	6.60	12.55

Basic Materials	UNIT	MAT.	INST.	TOTAL
16130.60 Pull And Junction Boxes				
For 4" receptacle, 2 gang	EA.	6.10	6.60	12.70
Duplex receptacle cover plate, plastic	"	0.90	3.90	4.80
4", vertical bracket box, 1-1/2" with				
RMX clamps	EA.	6.90	9.60	16.50
BX clamps	"	7.40	9.60	17.00
4", octagon device cover				
1 switch	EA.	3.15	3.90	7.05
1 duplex recept	"	2.90	3.90	6.80
4" octagon adjustable bar hangers				
18-1/2"	EA.	5.05	3.30	8.35
26-1/2"	"	5.50	3.30	8.80
With clip				
18-1/2"	EA.	3.75	3.30	7.05
26-1/2"	"	4.20	3.30	7.50
4" square to round plaster rings	"	2.35	3.90	6.25
2 gang device plaster rings	"	2.85	3.90	6.75
Surface covers				
1 gang switch	EA.	2.45	3.90	6.35
2 gang switch	"	2.55	3.90	6.45
1 single recept	"	3.75	3.90	7.65
1 20a twist lock recept	"	4.65	3.90	8.55
1 30a twist lock recept	"	5.95	3.90	9.85
1 duplex recept	"	2.30	3.90	6.20
2 duplex recept	"	2.30	3.90	6.20
Switch and duplex recept	"	3.85	3.90	7.75
4" plastic round boxes, ground straps				
Box only	EA.	1.60	9.60	11.20
Box w/clamps	"	1.90	13.20	15.10
Box w/16" bar	"	3.95	15.05	19.00
Box w/24" bar	"	3.95	16.45	20.40
4" plastic round box covers				
Blank cover	EA.	1.05	3.90	4.95
Plaster ring	"	1.70	3.90	5.60
4" plastic square boxes				
Box only	EA.	1.25	9.60	10.85
Box w/clamps	"	1.55	13.20	14.75
Box w/hanger	"	1.90	16.45	18.35
Box w/nails and clamp	"	2.70	16.45	19.15
4" plastic square box covers				
Blank cover	EA.	1.00	3.90	4.90
1 gang ring	"	1.25	3.90	5.15
2 gang ring	"	1.75	3.90	5.65
Round ring	"	1.35	3.90	5.25
16130.65 Pull Boxes And Cabinets				
Galvanized pull boxes, screw cover				
4x4x4	EA.	7.70	12.55	20.25
4x6x4	"	9.60	12.55	22.15

16 ELECTRICAL

Basic Materials	UNIT	MAT.	INST.	TOTAL

16130.80   Receptacles

	UNIT	MAT.	INST.	TOTAL
Contractor grade duplex receptacles, 15a 120v				
Duplex	EA.	0.84	13.20	14.04
125 volt, 20a, duplex, grounding type, standard grade	"	7.35	13.20	20.55
Ground fault interrupter type	"	9.80	19.55	29.35
250 volt, 20a, 2 pole, single receptacle, ground type	"	5.30	13.20	18.50
120/208v, 4 pole, single receptacle, twist lock				
20a	EA.	21.55	22.90	44.45
50a	"	41.00	22.90	63.90
125/250v, 3 pole, flush receptacle				
30a	EA.	6.80	19.55	26.35
50a	"	7.90	19.55	27.45
60a	"	31.90	22.90	54.80
Clock receptacle, 2 pole, grounding type	"	5.70	13.20	18.90
125/250v, 3 pole, 3 wire surface recepts				
30a	EA.	18.50	19.55	38.05
50a	"	20.55	19.55	40.10
60a	"	45.00	22.90	67.90
Cord set, 3 wire, 6' cord				
30a	EA.	16.50	19.55	36.05
50a	"	23.20	19.55	42.75
125/250v, 3 pole, 3 wire cap				
30a	EA.	16.30	26.40	42.70
50a	"	29.70	26.40	56.10
60a	"	38.20	29.30	67.50

16198.10   Electric Manholes

	UNIT	MAT.	INST.	TOTAL
Precast, handhole, 4' deep				
2'x2'	EA.	350.00	230.00	580.00
3'x3'	"	460.00	370.00	830.00
4'x4'	"	1,000	680.00	1,680
Power manhole, complete, precast, 8' deep				
4'x4'	EA.	1,420	920.00	2,340
6'x6'	"	1,900	1,320	3,220
8'x8'	"	2,260	1,390	3,650
6' deep, 9' x 12'	"	2,490	1,650	4,140
Cast in place, power manhole, 8' deep				
4'x4'	EA.	1,690	920.00	2,610
6'x6'	"	2,180	1,320	3,500
8'x8'	"	2,420	1,390	3,810

16199.10   Utility Poles & Fittings

	UNIT	MAT.	INST.	TOTAL
Wood pole, creosoted				
25'	EA.	450.00	160.00	610.00
30'	"	540.00	200.00	740.00
35'	"	720.00	230.00	950.00
40'	"	860.00	250.00	1,110
45'	"	990.00	460.00	1,450
50'	"	1,170	470.00	1,640
55'	"	1,340	500.00	1,840
Treated, wood preservative, 6"x6"				
8'	EA.	91.00	33.00	124.00
10'	"	130.00	52.50	182.50

Basic Materials	UNIT	MAT.	INST.	TOTAL
16199.10 Utility Poles & Fittings				
12'	EA.	140.00	58.50	198.50
14'	"	180.00	88.00	268.00
16'	"	210.00	110.00	320.00
18'	"	240.00	130.00	370.00
20'	"	310.00	130.00	440.00
Aluminum, brushed, no base				
8'	EA.	540.00	130.00	670.00
10'	"	620.00	180.00	800.00
15'	"	690.00	180.00	870.00
20'	"	920.00	210.00	1,130
25'	"	1,230	250.00	1,480
30'	"	1,850	290.00	2,140
35'	"	2,170	330.00	2,500
40'	"	2,780	410.00	3,190
Steel, no base				
10'	EA.	690.00	160.00	850.00
15'	"	760.00	200.00	960.00
20'	"	840.00	250.00	1,090
25'	"	1,090	300.00	1,390
30'	"	1,460	340.00	1,800
35'	"	2,020	410.00	2,430
Concrete, no base				
13'	EA.	850.00	360.00	1,210
16'	"	1,180	480.00	1,660
18'	"	1,420	580.00	2,000
25'	"	1,740	660.00	2,400
30'	"	2,310	800.00	3,110
35'	"	2,980	920.00	3,900
40'	"	3,480	1,050	4,530
45'	"	4,140	1,120	5,260
50'	"	5,130	1,200	6,330
55'	"	5,710	1,260	6,970
60'	"	6,530	1,320	7,850
Pole line hardware				
Wood crossarm				
4'	EA.	48.20	88.00	136.20
8'	"	96.50	110.00	206.50
10'	"	190.00	140.00	330.00
Angle steel brace				
1 piece	EA.	10.45	16.45	26.90
2 piece	"	22.35	22.90	45.25
Eye nut, 5/8"	"	5.15	3.30	8.45
Bolt (14-16"), 5/8"	"	13.65	13.20	26.85
Transformer, ground connection	"	6.10	16.45	22.55
Stirrup	"	18.65	20.30	38.95
Secondary lead support	"	20.80	26.40	47.20
Spool insulator	"	15.30	13.20	28.50
Guy grip, preformed				
7/16"	EA.	3.30	9.60	12.90
1/2"	"	4.95	9.60	14.55
Hook	"	3.30	16.45	19.75
Strain insulator	"	26.70	23.95	50.65

Basic Materials	UNIT	MAT.	INST.	TOTAL
16199.10 Utility Poles & Fittings				
Wire				
5/16"	L.F.	0.54	0.33	0.87
7/16"	"	1.10	0.40	1.50
1/2"	"	1.80	0.53	2.33
Soft drawn ground, copper, #8	"	0.45	0.53	0.98
Ground clamp	EA.	7.10	20.30	27.40
Perforated strapping for conduit, 1-1/2"	L.F.	2.75	9.60	12.35
Hot line clamp	EA.	20.80	52.50	73.30
Lightning arrester				
3kv	EA.	240.00	66.00	306.00
10kv	"	370.00	110.00	480.00
30kv	"	680.00	130.00	810.00
36kv	"	1,390	160.00	1,550
Fittings				
Plastic molding	L.F.	3.25	9.60	12.85
Molding staples	EA.	0.77	3.30	4.07
Ground wires staples	"	0.33	2.00	2.33
Copper butt plate	"	0.92	19.55	20.47
Anchor bond clamp	"	4.05	9.60	13.65
Guy wire				
1/4"	L.F.	0.45	2.00	2.45
3/8"	"	0.72	3.30	4.02
Guy grip				
1/4"	EA.	2.25	3.30	5.55
3/8"	"	3.95	3.30	7.25

Power Generation	UNIT	MAT.	INST.	TOTAL
16210.10 Generators				
Diesel generator, with auto transfer switch				
50kw	EA.	34,420	2,030	36,450
125kw	"	51,830	3,300	55,130
300kw	"	84,900	6,590	91,490
750kw	"	247,530	13,180	260,710
16320.10 Transformers				
Floor mounted, single phase, int. dry, 480v-120/240v				
3 kva	EA.	390.00	120.00	510.00
5 kva	"	530.00	200.00	730.00
7.5 kva	"	790.00	230.00	1,020
10 kva	"	910.00	250.00	1,160
15 kva	"	1,230	280.00	1,510
100 kva	"	4,280	760.00	5,040
Three phase, 480v-120/208v				
15 kva	EA.	1,470	400.00	1,870
30 kva	"	1,890	620.00	2,510

Power Generation	UNIT	MAT.	INST.	TOTAL
16320.10 Transformers				
45 kva	EA.	2,530	710.00	3,240
225 kva	"	8,330	1,010	9,340
16350.10 Circuit Breakers				
Molded case, 240v, 15-60a, bolt-on				
1 pole	EA.	16.55	16.45	33.00
2 pole	"	35.20	22.90	58.10
70-100a, 2 pole	"	100.00	35.10	135.10
15-60a, 3 pole	"	120.00	26.40	146.40
70-100a, 3 pole	"	200.00	40.60	240.60
480v, 2 pole				
15-60a	EA.	250.00	19.55	269.55
70-100a	"	330.00	26.40	356.40
3 pole				
15-60a	EA.	330.00	26.40	356.40
70-100a	"	390.00	29.30	419.30
70-225a	"	800.00	40.60	840.60
Load center circuit breakers, 240v				
1 pole, 10-60a	EA.	16.55	16.45	33.00
2 pole				
10-60a	EA.	35.20	26.40	61.60
70-100a	"	100.00	43.90	143.90
110-150a	"	200.00	47.90	247.90
3 pole				
10-60a	EA.	110.00	33.00	143.00
70-100a	"	170.00	47.90	217.90
Load center, G.F.I. breakers, 240v				
1 pole, 15-30a	EA.	110.00	19.55	129.55
2 pole, 15-30a	"	200.00	26.40	226.40
Key operated breakers, 240v, 1 pole, 10-30a	"	19.50	19.55	39.05
Tandem breakers, 240v				
1 pole, 15-30a	EA.	31.20	26.40	57.60
2 pole, 15-30a	"	57.00	35.10	92.10
Bolt-on, G.F.I. breakers, 240v, 1 pole, 15-30a	"	130.00	22.90	152.90
16360.10 Safety Switches				
Fused, 3 phase, 30 amp, 600v, heavy duty				
NEMA 1	EA.	200.00	75.50	275.50
NEMA 3r	"	340.00	75.50	415.50
NEMA 4	"	910.00	110.00	1,020
NEMA 12	"	330.00	110.00	440.00
60a				
NEMA 1	EA.	280.00	75.50	355.50
NEMA 3r	"	420.00	75.50	495.50
NEMA 4	"	1,090	110.00	1,200
NEMA 12	"	340.00	110.00	450.00
100a				
NEMA 1	EA.	510.00	110.00	620.00
NEMA 3r	"	700.00	110.00	810.00
NEMA 4	"	2,180	130.00	2,310
NEMA 12	"	610.00	160.00	770.00
200a				

	UNIT	MAT.	INST.	TOTAL
NEMA 4	"	3,090	180.00	3,270
NEMA 12	"	920.00	230.00	1,150
Non-fused, 240-600v, heavy duty, 3 phase, 30 amp				
NEMA 1	EA.	140.00	75.50	215.50
NEMA 3r	"	230.00	75.50	305.50
NEMA 4	"	910.00	110.00	1,020
NEMA 12	"	280.00	110.00	390.00
60a				
NEMA1	EA.	230.00	75.50	305.50
NEMA 3r	"	390.00	75.50	465.50
NEMA 4	"	1,090	110.00	1,200
NEMA 12	"	340.00	110.00	450.00
100a				
NEMA 1	EA.	360.00	110.00	470.00
NEMA 3r	"	550.00	110.00	660.00
NEMA 4	"	2,180	160.00	2,340
NEMA 12	"	470.00	160.00	630.00
200a, NEMA 1	"	560.00	160.00	720.00
600a, NEMA 12	"	2,450	810.00	3,260

16365.10 Fuses

	UNIT	MAT.	INST.	TOTAL
Fuse, one-time, 250v				
30a	EA.	1.90	3.30	5.20
60a	"	3.20	3.30	6.50
100a	"	13.40	3.30	16.70
200a	"	32.50	3.30	35.80
400a	"	72.50	3.30	75.80
600a	"	120.00	3.30	123.30
600v				
30a	EA.	9.55	3.30	12.85
60a	"	15.25	3.30	18.55
100a	"	29.00	3.30	32.30
200a	"	77.00	3.30	80.30
400a	"	160.00	3.30	163.30

16395.10 Grounding

	UNIT	MAT.	INST.	TOTAL
Ground rods, copper clad, 1/2" x				
6'	EA.	10.70	43.90	54.60
8'	"	14.75	47.90	62.65
10'	"	18.40	66.00	84.40
5/8" x				
5'	EA.	13.30	40.60	53.90
6'	"	14.25	47.90	62.15
8'	"	18.45	66.00	84.45
10'	"	22.80	82.50	105.30
3/4" x				
8'	EA.	32.70	47.90	80.60
10'	"	35.80	52.50	88.30
Ground rod clamp				
5/8"	EA.	5.45	8.10	13.55

ELECTRICAL

Power Generation	UNIT	MAT.	INST.	TOTAL
6395.10	Grounding			
3/4"	EA.	7.75	8.10	15.85
Ground rod couplings				
1/2"	EA.	10.00	6.60	16.60
5/8"	"	14.00	6.60	20.60
Ground rod, driving stud				
1/2"	EA.	8.05	6.60	14.65
5/8"	"	9.00	6.60	15.60
3/4"	"	10.00	6.60	16.60
Ground rod clamps, #8-2 to				
1" pipe	EA.	8.70	13.20	21.90
2" pipe	"	10.90	16.45	27.35
3" pipe	"	43.60	19.55	63.15
5" pipe	"	70.00	22.90	92.90
6" pipe	"	95.50	29.30	124.80

Service And Distribution	UNIT	MAT.	INST.	TOTAL
16425.10	Switchboards			
Switchboard, 90" high, no main disconnect, 208/120v				
400a	EA.	2,630	520.00	3,150
600a	"	4,080	530.00	4,610
1000a	"	5,140	530.00	5,670
1200a	"	5,430	660.00	6,090
1600a	"	5,970	790.00	6,760
2000a	"	6,410	920.00	7,330
2500a	"	5,260	1,050	6,310
277/480v				
600a	EA.	4,690	540.00	5,230
800a	"	5,140	540.00	5,680
1600a	"	6,470	790.00	7,260
2000a	"	6,920	920.00	7,840
2500a	"	7,370	1,050	8,420
3000a	"	8,480	1,820	10,300
4000a	"	10,270	1,950	12,220
16430.20	Metering			
Outdoor wp meter sockets, 1 gang, 240v, 1 phase				
Includes sealing ring, 100a	EA.	43.00	100.00	143.00
150a	"	57.00	120.00	177.00
200a	"	71.50	130.00	201.50
Die cast hubs, 1-1/4"	"	6.65	21.10	27.75
1-1/2"	"	7.65	21.10	28.75
2"	"	9.25	21.10	30.35

Service And Distribution

16470.10	Panelboards				
Indoor load center, 1 phase 240v main lug only					
30a - 2 spaces	EA.				
100a - 8 spaces	"		64.50	100.00	
150a - 16 spaces	"		150.00	200.00	
200a - 24 spaces	"		200.00	230.00	
200a - 42 spaces	"		370.00	260.00	630.00
Main circuit breaker					
100a - 8 spaces	EA.		150.00	160.00	310.00
100a - 16 spaces	"		200.00	180.00	380.00
150a - 16 spaces	"		320.00	200.00	520.00
150a - 24 spaces	"		370.00	210.00	580.00
200a - 24 spaces	"		390.00	230.00	620.00
200a - 42 spaces	"		530.00	240.00	770.00
3 phase, 480/277v, main lugs only, 120a, 30 circuits	"		1,050	230.00	1,280
277/480v, 4 wire, flush surface					
225a, 30 circuits	EA.		1,110	260.00	1,370
400a, 30 circuits	"		1,280	330.00	1,610
600a, 42 circuits	"		1,580	400.00	1,980
208/120v, main circuit breaker, 3 phase, 4 wire					
100a					
12 circuits	EA.		900.00	340.00	1,240
20 circuits	"		1,120	420.00	1,540
30 circuits	"		1,650	460.00	2,110
400a					
30 circuits	EA.		3,480	980.00	4,460
42 circuits	"		4,170	1,050	5,220
600a, 42 circuits	"		8,110	1,200	9,310
120/208v, flush, 3 ph., 4 wire, main only					
100a					
12 circuits	EA.		640.00	340.00	980.00
20 circuits	"		880.00	420.00	1,300
30 circuits	"		1,310	460.00	1,770
225a					
30 circuits	EA.		1,330	510.00	1,840
42 circuits	"		1,680	630.00	2,310
400a					
30 circuits	EA.		2,550	980.00	3,530
42 circuits	"		3,720	1,050	4,770
600a, 42 circuits	"		5,800	1,200	7,000

16480.10	Motor Controls				
Motor generator set, 3 phase, 480/277v, w/controls					
10kw	EA.		11,680	1,820	13,500
15kw	"		15,240	2,030	17,270
20kw	"		16,910	2,110	19,020
40kw	"		23,800	2,510	26,310
100kw	"		39,010	4,060	43,070
200kw	"		89,170	4,790	93,960
300kw	"		111,450	5,270	116,720
2 pole, 230 volt starter, w/NEMA-1					
1 hp, 9 amp, size 00	EA.		180.00	66.00	246.00
2 hp, 18amp, size 0	"		230.00	66.00	296.00

Service And Distribution	UNIT	MAT.	INST.	TOTAL
480.10 Motor Controls				
3 hp, 27amp, size 1	EA.	250.00	66.00	316.00
5 hp, 45amp, size 1p	"	320.00	66.00	386.00
7-1/2 hp, 45a, size 2	"	560.00	66.00	626.00
15 hp, 90a, size 3	"	840.00	66.00	906.00
16490.10 Switches				
Fused interrupter load, 35kv				
20A				
1 pole	EA.	23,640	1,050	24,690
2 pole	"	25,610	1,120	26,730
3 way	"	27,580	1,120	28,700
4 way	"	29,550	1,200	30,750
30a, 1 pole	"	23,640	1,050	24,690
3 way	"	27,580	1,120	28,700
4 way	"	29,550	1,200	30,750
Weatherproof switch, including box & cover, 20a				
1 pole	EA.	25,600	1,050	26,650
2 pole	"	27,580	1,120	28,700
3 way	"	29,550	1,200	30,750
4 way	"	31,530	1,200	32,730
Photo electric switches				
1000 watt				
105-135v	EA.	33.60	47.90	81.50
Dimmer switch and switch plate				
600w	EA.	30.90	20.30	51.20
Contractor grade wall switch 15a, 120v				
Single pole	EA.	1.65	10.55	12.20
Three way	"	2.95	13.20	16.15
Four way	"	9.60	17.55	27.15
Specification grade toggle switches, 20a, 120-277v				
Single pole	EA.	3.40	13.20	16.60
Double pole	"	9.85	19.55	29.40
3 way	"	4.80	16.45	21.25
4 way	"	18.15	19.55	37.70
Switch plates, plastic ivory				
1 gang	EA.	0.34	5.25	5.59
2 gang	"	0.69	6.60	7.29
3 gang	"	1.00	7.85	8.85
4 gang	"	1.65	9.60	11.25
5 gang	"	3.70	10.55	14.25
6 gang	"	4.35	12.00	16.35
Stainless steel				
1 gang	EA.	2.45	5.25	7.70
2 gang	"	3.40	6.60	10.00
3 gang	"	5.20	8.10	13.30
4 gang	"	9.90	9.60	19.50
5 gang	"	13.60	10.55	24.15
6 gang	"	16.90	12.00	28.90
Brass				
1 gang	EA.	4.55	5.25	9.80
2 gang	"	9.80	6.60	16.40
3 gang	"	15.10	8.10	23.20

Service And Distribution	UNIT	MAT.	INST.	TOTAL
16490.10 — Switches				
4 gang	EA.	22.55	9.60	32.15
5 gang	"	27.90	10.55	38.45
6 gang	"	33.70	12.00	45.70
16490.20 — Transfer Switches				
Automatic transfer switch 600v, 3 pole				
30a	EA.	2,410	230.00	2,640
100a	"	5,020	310.00	5,330
400a	"	11,040	660.00	11,700
800a	"	18,480	1,200	19,680
1200a	"	30,130	1,510	31,640
2600a	"	70,300	2,770	73,070
16490.80 — Safety Switches				
Safety switch, 600v, 3 pole, heavy duty, NEMA-1				
30a	EA.	200.00	66.00	266.00
60a	"	260.00	75.50	335.50
100a	"	510.00	110.00	620.00
200a	"	720.00	160.00	880.00
400a	"	1,800	360.00	2,160
600a	"	3,250	530.00	3,780
800a	"	4,990	690.00	5,680
1200a	"	6,180	940.00	7,120

Lighting	UNIT	MAT.	INST.	TOTAL
16510.05 — Interior Lighting				
Recessed fluorescent fixtures, 2'x2'				
2 lamp	EA.	63.00	47.90	110.90
4 lamp	"	85.00	47.90	132.90
2 lamp w/flange	"	79.00	66.00	145.00
4 lamp w/flange	"	97.00	66.00	163.00
1'x4'				
2 lamp	EA.	64.00	43.90	107.90
3 lamp	"	88.00	43.90	131.90
2 lamp w/flange	"	79.00	47.90	126.90
3 lamp w/flange	"	110.00	47.90	157.90
2'x4'				
2 lamp	EA.	79.00	47.90	126.90
3 lamp	"	97.00	47.90	144.90
4 lamp	"	88.00	47.90	135.90
2 lamp w/flange	"	97.00	66.00	163.00
3 lamp w/flange	"	110.00	66.00	176.00
4 lamp w/flange	"	110.00	66.00	176.00
4'x4'				
4 lamp	EA.	300.00	66.00	366.00

Lighting	UNIT	MAT.	INST.	TOTAL
16510.05 Interior Lighting				
6 lamp	EA.	360.00	66.00	426.00
8 lamp	"	390.00	66.00	456.00
4 lamp w/flange	"	370.00	100.00	470.00
6 lamp w/flange	"	460.00	100.00	560.00
8 lamp, w/flange	"	520.00	100.00	620.00
Surface mounted incandescent fixtures				
40w	EA.	71.50	43.90	115.40
75w	"	78.00	43.90	121.90
100w	"	92.50	43.90	136.40
150w	"	110.00	43.90	153.90
Pendant				
40w	EA.	78.00	52.50	130.50
75w	"	86.50	52.50	139.00
100w	"	98.50	52.50	151.00
150w	"	110.00	52.50	162.50
Recessed incandescent fixtures				
40w	EA.	130.00	100.00	230.00
75w	"	140.00	100.00	240.00
100w	"	150.00	100.00	250.00
150w	"	170.00	100.00	270.00
Exit lights, 120v				
Recessed	EA.	33.00	82.50	115.50
Back mount	"	55.00	47.90	102.90
Universal mount	"	33.00	47.90	80.90
Emergency battery units, 6v-120v, 50 unit	"	150.00	100.00	250.00
With 1 head	"	180.00	100.00	280.00
With 2 heads	"	200.00	100.00	300.00
Mounting bucket	"	30.70	47.90	78.60
Light track single circuit				
2'	EA.	37.50	33.00	70.50
4'	"	68.00	33.00	101.00
8'	"	120.00	66.00	186.00
12'	"	190.00	100.00	290.00
Fixtures, square				
R-20	EA.	58.50	9.60	68.10
R-30	"	60.50	9.60	70.10
Mini spot	"	75.00	9.60	84.60
16510.10 Lighting Industrial				
Surface mounted fluorescent, wrap around lens				
1 lamp	EA.	73.50	52.50	126.00
2 lamps	"	80.50	58.50	139.00
4 lamps	"	130.00	66.00	196.00
Wall mounted fluorescent				
2-20w lamps	EA.	59.50	33.00	92.50
2-30w lamps	"	63.50	33.00	96.50
2-40w lamps	"	73.50	43.90	117.40
Indirect, with wood shielding, 2049w lamps				
4'	EA.	130.00	66.00	196.00
8'	"	180.00	110.00	290.00
Industrial fluorescent, 2 lamp				
4'	EA.	130.00	47.90	177.90

Lighting	UNIT	MAT.	INST.	TOTAL
16510.10		Lighting Industrial		
8'	EA.	200.00	88.00	288.00
Strip fluorescent				
4'				
1 lamp	EA.	42.20	43.90	86.10
2 lamps	"	52.50	43.90	96.40
8'				
1 lamp	EA.	84.50	47.90	132.40
2 lamps	"	94.50	58.50	153.00
Wire guard for strip fixture, 4' long	"	21.10	22.90	44.00
Strip fluorescent, 8' long, two 4' lamps	"	130.00	88.00	218.00
With four 4' lamps	"	170.00	110.00	280.00
Wet location fluorescent, plastic housing				
4' long				
1 lamp	EA.	140.00	66.00	206.00
2 lamps	"	150.00	88.00	238.00
8' long				
2 lamps	EA.	260.00	110.00	370.00
4 lamps	"	350.00	110.00	460.00
Parabolic troffer, 2'x2'				
With 2 "U" lamps	EA.	180.00	66.00	246.00
With 3 "U" lamps	"	210.00	75.50	285.50
2'x4'				
With 2 40w lamps	EA.	240.00	75.50	315.50
With 3 40w lamps	"	260.00	88.00	348.00
With 4 40w lamps	"	300.00	88.00	388.00
1'x4'				
With 1 T-12 lamp, 9 cell	EA.	180.00	47.90	227.90
With 2 T-12 lamps	"	200.00	58.50	258.50
With 1 T-12 lamp, 20 cell	"	200.00	47.90	247.90
With 2 T-12 lamps	"	220.00	58.50	278.50
Steel sided surface fluorescent, 2'x4'				
3 lamps	EA.	150.00	88.00	238.00
4 lamps	"	170.00	88.00	258.00
Outdoor sign fluor., 1 lamp, remote ballast				
4' long	EA.	3,010	400.00	3,410
6' long	"	3,620	530.00	4,150
Recess mounted, commercial, 2'x2', 13" high				
100w	EA.	1,000	260.00	1,260
250w	"	1,100	300.00	1,400
High pressure sodium, hi-bay open				
400w	EA.	540.00	110.00	650.00
1000w	"	920.00	160.00	1,080
Enclosed				
400w	EA.	840.00	160.00	1,000
1000w	"	1,220	200.00	1,420
Metal halide hi-bay, open				
400w	EA.	480.00	110.00	590.00
1000w	"	830.00	160.00	990.00
Enclosed				
400w	EA.	780.00	160.00	940.00
1000w	"	1,170	200.00	1,370
High pressure sodium, low bay, surface mounted				

Lighting	UNIT	MAT.	INST.	TOTAL
16510.10	**Lighting Industrial**			
100w	EA.	340.00	66.00	406.00
150w	"	370.00	75.50	445.50
250w	"	420.00	88.00	508.00
400w	"	530.00	110.00	640.00
Metal halide, low bay, pendant mounted				
175w	EA.	370.00	88.00	458.00
250w	"	480.00	110.00	590.00
400w	"	610.00	150.00	760.00
Indirect luminare, square, metal halide, freestanding				
175w	EA.	980.00	66.00	1,046
250w	"	990.00	66.00	1,056
400w	"	1,070	66.00	1,136
High pressure sodium				
150w	EA.	990.00	66.00	1,056
250w	"	1,050	66.00	1,116
400w	"	1,130	66.00	1,196
Round, metal halide				
175w	EA.	920.00	66.00	986.00
250w	"	980.00	66.00	1,046
400w	"	1,010	66.00	1,076
High pressure sodium				
150w	EA.	940.00	66.00	1,006
250w	"	1,010	66.00	1,076
400w	"	1,060	66.00	1,126
Wall mounted, metal halide				
175w	EA.	760.00	160.00	920.00
250w	"	810.00	160.00	970.00
400w	"	1,340	210.00	1,550
High pressure sodium				
150w	EA.	870.00	160.00	1,030
250w	"	1,070	160.00	1,230
400w	"	1,390	210.00	1,600
Wall pack lithonia, high pressure sodium				
35w	EA.	230.00	58.50	288.50
55w	"	260.00	66.00	326.00
150w	"	290.00	110.00	400.00
250w	"	370.00	110.00	480.00
Low pressure sodium				
35w	EA.	330.00	110.00	440.00
55w	"	510.00	130.00	640.00
Wall pack hubbell, high pressure sodium				
35w	EA.	250.00	58.50	308.50
150w	"	320.00	110.00	430.00
250w	"	410.00	110.00	520.00
Compact fluorescent				
2-7w	EA.	150.00	66.00	216.00
2-13w	"	180.00	88.00	268.00
1-18w	"	210.00	88.00	298.00
Handball & racquet ball court, 2'x2', metal halide				
250w	EA.	550.00	160.00	710.00
400w	"	680.00	180.00	860.00
High pressure sodium				

Lighting	UNIT	MAT.	INST.	TOTAL
16510.10 Lighting Industrial				
250w	EA.	610.00	160.00	770.00
400w	"	660.00	180.00	840.00
Bollard light, 42" w/found., high pressure sodium				
70w	EA.	920.00	170.00	1,090
100w	"	950.00	170.00	1,120
150w	"	960.00	170.00	1,130
Light fixture lamps				
Lamp				
20w med. bipin base, cool white, 24"	EA.	6.85	9.60	16.45
30w cool white, rapid start, 36"	"	8.85	9.60	18.45
40w cool white "U", 3"	"	17.00	9.60	26.60
40w cool white, rapid start, 48"	"	4.05	9.60	13.65
70w high pressure sodium, mogul base	"	88.00	13.20	101.20
75w slimline, 96"	"	11.35	13.20	24.55
100w				
Incandescent, 100a, inside frost	EA.	3.50	6.60	10.10
Mercury vapor, clear, mogul base	"	43.00	13.20	56.20
High pressure sodium, mogul base	"	93.50	13.20	106.70
150w				
Par 38 flood or spot, incandescent	EA.	10.50	6.60	17.10
High pressure sodium, 1/2 mogul base	"	98.00	13.20	111.20
175w				
Mercury vapor, clear, mogul base	EA.	74.50	13.20	87.70
Metal halide, clear, mogul base	"	33.20	13.20	46.40
High pressure sodium, mogul base	"	45.00	13.20	58.20
250w				
Mercury vapor, clear, mogul base	EA.	59.00	13.20	72.20
Metal halide, clear, mogul base	"	93.50	13.20	106.70
High pressure sodium, mogul base	"	100.00	13.20	113.20
400w				
Mercury vapor, clear, mogul base	EA.	46.80	13.20	60.00
Metal halide, clear, mogul base	"	88.00	13.20	101.20
High pressure sodium, mogul base	"	110.00	13.20	123.20
1000w				
Mercury vapor, clear, mogul base	EA.	100.00	16.45	116.45
High pressure sodium, mogul base	"	260.00	16.45	276.45
16510.30 Exterior Lighting				
Exterior light fixtures				
Rectangle, high pressure sodium				
70w	EA.	300.00	160.00	460.00
100w	"	310.00	170.00	480.00
150w	"	330.00	170.00	500.00
250w	"	450.00	180.00	630.00
400w	"	500.00	230.00	730.00
Flood, rectangular, high pressure sodium				
70w	EA.	310.00	160.00	470.00
100w	"	320.00	170.00	490.00
150w	"	360.00	170.00	530.00
400w	"	530.00	230.00	760.00
1000w	"	800.00	300.00	1,100
Round				

Lighting	UNIT	MAT.	INST.	TOTAL
16510.30 Exterior Lighting				
400w	EA.	550.00	230.00	780.00
1000w	"	860.00	300.00	1,160
Round, metal halide				
400w	EA.	610.00	230.00	840.00
1000w	"	900.00	300.00	1,200
Light fixture arms, cobra head, 6', high press. sodium				
100w	EA.	330.00	130.00	460.00
150w	"	520.00	160.00	680.00
250w	"	540.00	160.00	700.00
400w	"	560.00	200.00	760.00
Flood, metal halide				
400w	EA.	580.00	230.00	810.00
1000w	"	870.00	300.00	1,170
1500w	"	1,180	400.00	1,580
Mercury vapor				
250w	EA.	340.00	180.00	520.00
400w	"	590.00	230.00	820.00
Incandescent				
300w	EA.	60.50	110.00	170.50
500w	"	100.00	130.00	230.00
1000w	"	120.00	210.00	330.00
16510.90 Power Line Filters				
Heavy duty power line filter, 240v				
100a	EA.	4,510	660.00	5,170
300a	"	14,970	1,050	16,020
600a	"	20,750	1,600	22,350
16610.30 Uninterruptible Power				
Uninterruptible power systems, (U.P.S.), 3kva	EA.	7,810	530.00	8,340
5 kva	"	8,760	730.00	9,490
7.5 kva	"	10,510	1,050	11,560
10 kva	"	13,140	1,450	14,590
15 kva	"	15,770	1,510	17,280
20 kva	"	21,900	1,580	23,480
25 kva	"	28,030	1,650	29,680
30 kva	"	28,910	1,710	30,620
35 kva	"	30,660	1,780	32,440
40 kva	"	33,290	1,840	35,130
45 kva	"	35,040	1,910	36,950
50 kva	"	37,670	1,970	39,640
62.5 kva	"	44,680	2,110	46,790
75 kva	"	51,680	2,300	53,980
100 kva	"	69,210	2,370	71,580
150 kva	"	105,130	3,300	108,430
200 kva	"	140,170	3,640	143,810
300 kva	"	210,250	4,930	215,180
400 kva	"	314,530	5,920	320,450
500 kva	"	393,170	7,220	400,390

Lighting	UNIT	MAT.	INST.	TOTAL
16670.10		Lightning Protection		
Lightning protection				
Copper point, nickel plated, 12'				
1/2" dia.	EA.	44.00	66.00	110.00
5/8" dia.	"	49.50	66.00	115.50

Communications	UNIT	MAT.	INST.	TOTAL
16720.10		Fire Alarm Systems		
Master fire alarm box, pedestal mounted	EA.	7,110	1,050	8,160
Master fire alarm box	"	3,650	400.00	4,050
Box light	"	200.00	33.00	233.00
Ground assembly for box	"	100.00	43.90	143.90
Bracket for pole type box	"	130.00	47.90	177.90
Pull station				
Waterproof	EA.	100.00	33.00	133.00
Manual	"	61.00	26.40	87.40
Horn, waterproof	"	91.50	66.00	157.50
Interior alarm	"	61.00	47.90	108.90
Coded transmitter, automatic	"	1,070	130.00	1,200
Control panel, 8 zone	"	2,150	530.00	2,680
Battery charger and cabinet	"	720.00	130.00	850.00
Batteries, nickel cadmium or lead calcium	"	540.00	330.00	870.00
CO2 pressure switch connection	"	100.00	47.90	147.90
Annunciator panels				
Fire detection annunciator, remote type, 8 zone	EA.	360.00	120.00	480.00
12 zone	"	460.00	130.00	590.00
16 zone	"	580.00	160.00	740.00
Fire alarm systems				
Bell	EA.	110.00	40.60	150.60
Weatherproof bell	"	140.00	43.90	183.90
Horn	"	65.00	47.90	112.90
Siren	"	660.00	130.00	790.00
Chime	"	81.50	40.60	122.10
Audio/visual	"	120.00	47.90	167.90
Strobe light	"	110.00	47.90	157.90
Smoke detector	"	180.00	43.90	223.90
Heat detection	"	30.50	33.00	63.50
Thermal detector	"	28.40	33.00	61.40
Ionization detector	"	140.00	35.10	175.10
Duct detector	"	470.00	180.00	650.00
Test switch	"	81.50	33.00	114.50
Remote indicator	"	41.00	37.70	78.70
Door holder	"	180.00	47.90	227.90
Telephone jack	"	30.50	19.55	50.05
Fireman phone	"	430.00	66.00	496.00
Speaker	"	87.00	52.50	139.50

Communications	UNIT	MAT.	INST.	TOTAL
16720.10	Fire Alarm Systems			
Remote fire alarm annunciator panel				
24 zone	EA.	2,230	440.00	2,670
48 zone	"	4,470	860.00	5,330
Control panel				
12 zone	EA.	1,520	200.00	1,720
16 zone	"	1,990	290.00	2,280
24 zone	"	3,050	440.00	3,490
48 zone	"	5,690	1,050	6,740
Power supply	"	350.00	100.00	450.00
Status command	"	9,640	330.00	9,970
Printer	"	3,750	100.00	3,850
Transponder	"	310.00	59.00	369.00
Transformer	"	220.00	43.90	263.90
Transceiver	"	310.00	47.90	357.90
Relays	"	120.00	33.00	153.00
Flow switch	"	400.00	130.00	530.00
Tamper switch	"	240.00	200.00	440.00
End of line resistor	"	17.20	22.90	40.10
Printed ckt. card	"	150.00	33.00	183.00
Central processing unit	"	19,890	410.00	20,300
UPS backup to c.p.u.	"	19,290	590.00	19,880
Smoke detector, fixed temp. & rate of rise comb.	"	310.00	110.00	420.00
16720.50	Security Systems			
Sensors				
Balanced magnetic door switch, surface mounted	EA.	150.00	33.00	183.00
With remote test	"	200.00	66.00	266.00
Flush mounted	"	140.00	120.00	260.00
Mounted bracket	"	10.95	22.90	33.85
Mounted bracket spacer	"	9.85	22.90	32.75
Photoelectric sensor, for fence				
6 beam	EA.	16,060	180.00	16,240
9 beam	"	19,640	280.00	19,920
Photoelectric sensor, 12 volt dc				
500' range	EA.	470.00	110.00	580.00
800' range	"	530.00	130.00	660.00
Monitor cabinet, wall mounted				
1 zone	EA.	760.00	66.00	826.00
5 zone	"	2,740	110.00	2,850
10 zone	"	1,250	110.00	1,360
20 zone	"	3,820	130.00	3,950
16730.20	Clock Systems			
Clock systems				
Single face	EA.	130.00	52.50	182.50
Double face	"	360.00	52.50	412.50
Skeleton	"	280.00	180.00	460.00
Master	"	2,860	330.00	3,190
Signal generator	"	2,480	260.00	2,740
Elapsed time indicator	"	490.00	52.50	542.50
Controller	"	110.00	35.10	145.10
Clock and speaker	"	210.00	72.00	282.00

Communications	UNIT	MAT.	INST.	TOTAL
16730.20 Clock Systems				
Bell				
Standard	EA.	77.00	35.10	112.10
Weatherproof	"	93.50	52.50	146.00
Horn				
Standard	EA.	49.50	47.90	97.40
Weatherproof	"	60.50	63.00	123.50
Chime	"	55.00	35.10	90.10
Buzzer	"	19.80	35.10	54.90
Flasher	"	77.00	40.60	117.60
Control Board	"	320.00	230.00	550.00
Program unit	"	350.00	330.00	680.00
Block back box	"	19.80	33.00	52.80
Double clock back box	"	44.00	43.90	87.90
Wire guard	"	13.20	13.20	26.40
16740.10 Telephone Systems				
Communication cable				
25 pair	L.F.	0.94	1.70	2.64
100 pair	"	4.45	1.90	6.35
150 pair	"	6.75	2.20	8.95
200 pair	"	9.15	2.65	11.80
300 pair	"	11.60	2.75	14.35
400 pair	"	15.80	2.95	18.75
Cable tap in manhole or junction box				
25 pair cable	EA.	6.50	250.00	256.50
50 pair cable	"	13.15	500.00	513.15
75 pair cable	"	19.65	740.00	759.65
100 pair cable	"	26.20	990.00	1,016
150 pair cable	"	39.30	1,460	1,499
200 pair cable	"	52.50	1,950	2,003
300 pair cable	"	78.50	2,930	3,009
400 pair cable	"	110.00	4,060	4,170
Cable terminations, manhole or junction box				
25 pair cable	EA.	6.50	250.00	256.50
50 pair cable	"	13.15	490.00	503.15
100 pair cable	"	26.20	990.00	1,016
150 pair cable	"	39.30	1,460	1,499
200 pair cable	"	52.50	1,950	2,003
300 pair cable	"	78.50	2,930	3,009
400 pair cable	"	81.50	4,060	4,142
Telephones, standard				
1 button	EA.	120.00	200.00	320.00
2 button	"	180.00	230.00	410.00
6 button	"	260.00	350.00	610.00
12 button	"	670.00	500.00	1,170
18 button	"	700.00	590.00	1,290
Hazardous area				
Desk	EA.	2,010	480.00	2,490
Wall	"	940.00	330.00	1,270
Accessories				
Standard ground	EA.	33.20	110.00	143.20
Push button	"	33.90	110.00	143.90

Communications	UNIT	MAT.	INST.	TOTAL
16740.10 Telephone Systems				
Buzzer	EA.	35.40	110.00	145.40
Interface device	"	18.80	52.50	71.30
Long cord	"	19.90	52.50	72.40
Interior jack	"	12.15	26.40	38.55
Exterior jack	"	24.30	40.60	64.90
Hazardous area				
Selector switch	EA.	200.00	210.00	410.00
Bell	"	300.00	210.00	510.00
Horn	"	450.00	280.00	730.00
Horn relay	"	370.00	200.00	570.00
16770.30 Sound Systems				
Power amplifiers	EA.	1,060	230.00	1,290
Pre-amplifiers	"	840.00	180.00	1,020
Tuner	"	540.00	96.00	636.00
Horn				
Equalizer	EA.	1,360	110.00	1,470
Mixer	"	560.00	150.00	710.00
Tape recorder	"	1,780	120.00	1,900
Microphone	"	150.00	66.00	216.00
Cassette Player	"	900.00	140.00	1,040
Record player	"	79.00	130.00	209.00
Equipment rack	"	100.00	85.00	185.00
Speaker				
Wall	EA.	560.00	260.00	820.00
Paging	"	200.00	52.50	252.50
Column	"	300.00	35.10	335.10
Single	"	67.50	40.60	108.10
Double	"	210.00	290.00	500.00
Volume control	"	67.50	35.10	102.60
Plug-in	"	210.00	52.50	262.50
Desk	"	170.00	26.40	196.40
Outlet	"	33.80	26.40	60.20
Stand	"	67.50	19.55	87.05
Console	"	15,920	530.00	16,450
Power supply	"	300.00	85.00	385.00
16780.10 Antennas And Towers				
Guy cable, alumaweld				
1x3, 7/32"	L.F.	0.45	3.30	3.75
1x3, 1/4"	"	0.53	3.30	3.83
1x3, 25/64"	"	0.75	3.90	4.65
1x19, 1/2"	"	1.85	4.60	6.45
1x7, 35/64"	"	2.15	5.25	7.40
1x19, 13/16"	"	2.30	6.60	8.90
Preformed alumaweld end grip				
1/4" cable	EA.	3.40	6.60	10.00
3/8" cable	"	4.50	6.60	11.10
1/2" cable	"	5.65	9.60	15.25
9/16" cable	"	7.05	13.20	20.25
5/8" cable	"	8.65	16.45	25.10
Fiberglass guy rod, white epoxy coated				

Communications	UNIT	MAT.	INST.	TOTAL
16780.10 Antennas And Towers				
1/4" dia.	L.F.	2.30	9.60	11.90
3/8" dia	"	3.45	9.60	13.05
1/2" dia	"	4.60	13.20	17.80
5/8" dia	"	5.75	16.45	22.20
Preformed glass grip end grip, guy rod				
1/4" dia.	EA.	12.75	9.60	22.35
3/8" dia.	"	14.80	13.20	28.00
1/2" dia.	"	18.10	16.45	34.55
5/8" dia.	"	20.30	16.45	36.75
Spelter socket end grip, 1/4" dia. guy rod				
Standard strength	EA.	37.70	33.00	70.70
High performance	"	46.50	33.00	79.50
3/8" dia. guy rod				
Standard strength	EA.	36.70	22.90	59.60
High performance	"	46.50	33.00	79.50
Timber pole, Douglas Fir				
80-85 ft	EA.	3,530	1,290	4,820
90-95 ft	"	4,420	1,460	5,880
Southern yellow pine				
35-45 ft	EA.	2,110	720.00	2,830
50-55 ft	"	2,950	920.00	3,870
16780.50 Television Systems				
TV outlet, self terminating, w/cover plate	EA.	5.95	20.30	26.25
Thru splitter	"	13.00	110.00	123.00
End of line	"	10.85	88.00	98.85
In line splitter multitap				
4 way	EA.	21.70	120.00	141.70
2 way	"	16.30	110.00	126.30
Equipment cabinet	"	54.00	110.00	164.00
Antenna				
Broad band uhf	EA.	110.00	230.00	340.00
Lightning arrester	"	33.00	47.90	80.90
TV cable	L.F.	0.50	0.33	0.83
Coaxial cable rg	"	0.33	0.33	0.66
Cable drill, with replacement tip	EA.	5.45	33.00	38.45
Cable blocks for in-line taps	"	10.85	47.90	58.75
In-line taps ptu-series 36 tv system	"	13.05	75.50	88.55
Control receptacles	"	8.50	29.60	38.10
Coupler	"	16.30	160.00	176.30
Head end equipment	"	2,050	440.00	2,490
TV camera	"	1,110	110.00	1,220
TV power bracket	"	99.00	52.50	151.50
TV monitor	"	850.00	96.00	946.00
Video recorder	"	1,650	140.00	1,790
Console	"	3,420	560.00	3,980
Selector switch	"	530.00	91.00	621.00
TV controller	"	250.00	92.50	342.50

Resistance Heating	UNIT	MAT.	INST.	TOTAL
16850.10		Electric Heating		
Baseboard heater				
2', 375w	EA.	48.40	66.00	114.40
3', 500w	"	57.00	66.00	123.00
4', 750w	"	61.50	75.50	137.00
5', 935w	"	84.50	88.00	172.50
6', 1125w	"	92.50	110.00	202.50
7', 1310w	"	110.00	120.00	230.00
8', 1500w	"	120.00	130.00	250.00
9', 1680w	"	170.00	150.00	320.00
10', 1875w	"	180.00	150.00	330.00
Unit heater, wall mounted				
750w	EA.	140.00	110.00	250.00
1500w	"	220.00	110.00	330.00
2000w	"	230.00	110.00	340.00
2500w	"	240.00	120.00	360.00
3000w	"	280.00	130.00	410.00
4000w	"	320.00	150.00	470.00
Thermostat				
Integral	EA.	37.40	33.00	70.40
Line voltage	"	38.50	33.00	71.50
Electric heater connection	"	1.65	16.45	18.10
Fittings				
Inside corner	EA.	24.20	26.40	50.60
Outside corner	"	26.40	26.40	52.80
Receptacle section	"	27.50	26.40	53.90
Blank section	"	34.10	26.40	60.50
Infrared heaters				
600w	EA.	150.00	66.00	216.00
2000w	"	160.00	78.50	238.50
3000w	"	240.00	130.00	370.00
4000w	"	340.00	160.00	500.00
Controller	"	65.00	43.90	108.90
Wall bracket	"	130.00	47.90	177.90
Radiant ceiling heater panels				
500w	EA.	180.00	66.00	246.00
750w	"	220.00	66.00	286.00
Unit heaters, suspended, single phase				
3.0 kw	EA.	390.00	180.00	570.00
5.0 kw	"	400.00	180.00	580.00
7.5 kw	"	620.00	210.00	830.00
10.0 kw	"	680.00	250.00	930.00
Three phase				
5 kw	EA.	480.00	180.00	660.00
7.5 kw	"	630.00	210.00	840.00
10 kw	"	680.00	250.00	930.00
15 kw	"	1,150	280.00	1,430
20 kw	"	1,540	350.00	1,890
25 kw	"	1,850	420.00	2,270
30 kw	"	2,160	530.00	2,690
35 kw	"	2,620	530.00	3,150
Unit heater thermostat	"	49.70	35.10	84.80
Mounting bracket	"	51.00	47.90	98.90

Resistance Heating	UNIT	MAT.	INST.	TOTAL
16850.10	Electric Heating			
Relay	EA.	65.00	40.60	105.60
Duct heaters, three phase				
10 kw	EA.	580.00	250.00	830.00
15 kw	"	700.00	250.00	950.00
17.5 kw	"	730.00	260.00	990.00
20 kw	"	780.00	410.00	1,190

Controls	UNIT	MAT.	INST.	TOTAL
16910.40	Control Cable			
Control cable, 600v, #14 THWN, PVC jacket				
2 wire	L.F.	0.32	0.53	0.85
4 wire	"	0.51	0.66	1.17
6 wire	"	0.88	8.65	9.53
8 wire	"	1.00	9.60	10.60
10 wire	"	1.20	10.55	11.75
12 wire	"	1.80	12.00	13.80
14 wire	"	2.00	13.85	15.85
16 wire	"	2.15	14.65	16.80
18 wire	"	2.55	16.00	18.55
20 wire	"	2.75	16.45	19.20
22 wire	"	2.90	18.85	21.75
Audio cables, shielded, #24 gauge				
3 conductor	L.F.	0.26	0.26	0.53
4 conductor	"	0.32	0.40	0.71
5 conductor	"	0.37	0.46	0.83
6 conductor	"	0.42	0.59	1.01
7 conductor	"	0.47	0.72	1.20
8 conductor	"	0.53	0.79	1.32
9 conductor	"	0.55	0.93	1.48
10 conductor	"	0.62	0.99	1.60
15 conductor	"	1.05	1.20	2.25
20 conductor	"	1.40	1.50	2.90
25 conductor	"	1.70	1.80	3.50
30 conductor	"	2.10	2.00	4.10
40 conductor	"	2.75	2.40	5.15
50 conductor	"	3.45	2.75	6.20
#22 gauge				
3 conductor	L.F.	0.23	0.26	0.50
4 conductor	"	0.55	0.40	0.95
#20 gauge				
3 conductor	L.F.	0.29	0.26	0.55
10 conductor	"	0.92	0.99	1.91
15 conductor	"	1.20	1.20	2.40
#18 gauge				
3 conductor	L.F.	0.37	0.26	0.64

Controls	UNIT	MAT.	INST.	TOTAL
16910.40	**Control Cable**			
4 conductor	L.F.	0.47	0.40	0.87
Microphone cables, #24 gauge				
2 conductor	L.F.	0.37	0.26	0.64
3 conductor	"	0.42	0.33	0.75
#20 gauge				
1 conductor	L.F.	0.41	0.26	0.67
2 conductor	"	0.64	0.26	0.90
2 conductor	"	0.73	0.26	0.99
3 conductor	"	0.88	0.40	1.28
4 conductor	"	1.25	0.46	1.71
5 conductor	"	1.50	0.59	2.09
7 conductor	"	1.65	0.72	2.37
8 conductor	"	1.85	0.79	2.64
Computer cables shielded, #24 gauge				
1 pair	L.F.	0.24	0.26	0.51
2 pair	"	0.33	0.26	0.59
3 pair	"	0.41	0.40	0.80
4 pair	"	0.47	0.46	0.93
5 pair	"	0.62	0.59	1.21
6 pair	"	0.73	0.73	1.45
7 pair	"	0.76	0.79	1.55
8 pair	"	0.88	0.93	1.81
50 pair	"	5.05	2.55	7.60
Fire alarm cables, #22 gauge				
6 conductor	L.F.	0.46	0.66	1.12
9 conductor	"	0.59	0.99	1.58
12 conductor	"	0.68	1.05	1.73
#18 gauge				
2 conductor	L.F.	0.46	0.33	0.79
4 conductor	"	0.59	0.46	1.05
#16 gauge				
2 conductor	L.F.	0.46	0.46	0.92
4 conductor	"	0.64	0.53	1.17
#14 gauge				
2 conductor	L.F.	0.68	0.53	1.21
#12 gauge				
2 conductor	L.F.	0.84	0.66	1.50
Plastic jacketed thermostat cable				
2 conductor	L.F.	0.12	0.26	0.39
3 conductor	"	0.17	0.33	0.50
4 conductor	"	0.22	0.40	0.62
5 conductor	"	0.28	0.53	0.80
6 conductor	"	0.33	0.59	0.92
7 conductor	"	0.36	0.79	1.16
8 conductor	"	0.53	0.86	1.39

Man-Hour Tables

The man-hour productivities used to develop the labor costs are listed in the following section of this book. These productivities represent typical installation labor for thousands of construction items. The data takes into account all activities involved in normal construction under commonly experienced working conditions. As with the Costbook pages, these items are listed according to the CSI MASTERFORMAT. In order to best use the information in this book, please review this sample page and read the "Features in this Book" section.

CSI MASTERFORMAT Division

CSI Broadscope Category

CSI Mediumscope Category (First 5 Digits)

Detailed Descriptions
Complete descriptions of items may include information listed above a particular line. Review of the whole category is recommended for a complete description.

Unit of Measurement
Each item is defined in terms of the common estimating unit. Quantities listed are defined as man-hour per unit.

Man-Hours
Man-hour quantities represent typical installation times and take into account all activities involved in normal construction under commonly experienced working conditions.

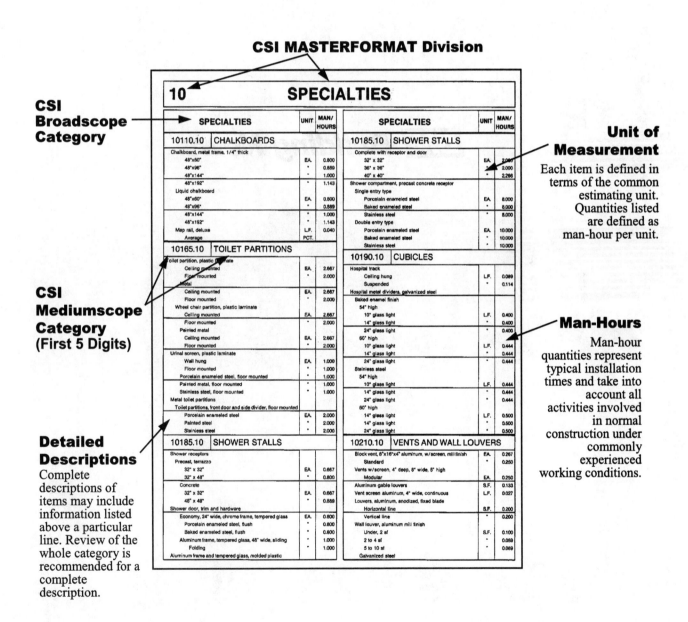

10 SPECIALTIES

SPECIALTIES	UNIT	MAN/HOURS
10110.10 CHALKBOARDS		
Chalkboard, metal frame, 1/4" thick		
48"x60"	EA.	0.800
48"x96"	"	0.889
48"x144"	"	1.000
48"x192"	"	1.143
Liquid chalkboard		
48"x60"	EA.	0.800
49"x96"	"	0.889
48"x144"	"	1.000
48"x192"	"	1.143
Map rail, deluxe	L.F.	0.040
Average	PCT.	
10165.10 TOILET PARTITIONS		
Toilet partition, plastic laminate		
Ceiling mounted	EA.	2.667
Floor mounted	"	2.000
Metal		
Ceiling mounted	EA.	2.667
Floor mounted	"	2.000
Wheel chair partition, plastic laminate		
Ceiling mounted	EA.	2.667
Floor mounted	"	2.000
Painted metal		
Ceiling mounted	EA.	2.667
Floor mounted	"	2.000
Urinal screen, plastic laminate		
Wall hung	EA.	1.000
Floor mounted	"	1.000
Porcelain enameled steel, floor mounted	"	1.000
Painted metal, floor mounted	"	1.000
Stainless steel, floor mounted	"	1.000
Metal toilet partitions		
Toilet partitions, front door and side divider, floor mounted		
Porcelain enameled steel	EA.	2.000
Painted steel	"	2.000
Stainless steel	"	2.000
10185.10 SHOWER STALLS		
Shower receptors		
Precast, terrazzo		
32" x 32"	EA.	0.667
32" x 48"	"	0.800
Concrete		
32" x 32"	EA.	0.667
48" x 48"	"	0.889
Shower door, trim and hardware		
Economy, 24" wide, chrome frame, tempered glass	EA.	0.800
Porcelain enameled steel, flush	"	0.800
Baked enameled steel, flush	"	0.800
Aluminum frame, tempered glass, 48" wide, sliding	"	1.000
Folding	"	1.000
Aluminum frame and tempered glass, molded plastic		

SPECIALTIES	UNIT	MAN/HOURS
10185.10 SHOWER STALLS		
Complete with receptor and door		
32" x 32"	EA.	2.000
36" x 36"	"	2.000
40" x 40"	"	2.286
Shower compartment, precast concrete receptor		
Single entry type		
Porcelain enameled steel	EA.	8.000
Baked enameled steel	"	8.000
Stainless steel	"	8.000
Double entry type		
Porcelain enameled steel	EA.	10.000
Baked enameled steel	"	10.000
Stainless steel	"	10.000
10190.10 CUBICLES		
Hospital track		
Ceiling hung	L.F.	0.089
Suspended	"	0.114
Hospital metal dividers, galvanized steel		
Baked enamel finish		
54" high		
10" glass light	L.F.	0.400
14" glass light	"	0.400
24" glass light	"	0.400
60" high		
10" glass light	L.F.	0.444
14" glass light	"	0.444
24" glass light	"	0.444
Stainless steel		
54" high		
10" glass light	L.F.	0.444
14" glass light	"	0.444
24" glass light	"	0.444
60" high		
14" glass light	L.F.	0.500
14" glass light	"	0.500
24" glass light	"	0.500
10210.10 VENTS AND WALL LOUVERS		
Block vent, 8"x16"x4" aluminum, w/screen, mill finish	EA.	0.267
Standard	"	0.250
Vents w/screen, 4" deep, 8" wide, 5" high		
Modular	EA.	0.250
Aluminum gable louvers	S.F.	0.133
Vent screen aluminum, 4" wide, continuous	L.F.	0.027
Louvers, aluminum, anodized, fixed blade		
Horizontal line	S.F.	0.200
Vertical line	"	0.200
Wall louver, aluminum mill finish		
Under, 2 sf	S.F.	0.100
2 to 4 sf	"	0.089
5 to 10 sf	"	0.089
Galvanized steel		

Soil Tests	UNIT	MAN/ HOURS
02010.10 Soil Boring		
Borings, uncased, stable earth		
2-1/2" dia.		
Minimum	L.F.	0.200
Average	L.F.	0.300
Maximum	L.F.	0.480
4" dia.		
Minimum	L.F.	0.218
Average	L.F.	0.343
Maximum	L.F.	0.600
Cased, including samples		
2-1/2" dia.		
Minimum	L.F.	0.240
Average	L.F.	0.400
Maximum	L.F.	0.800
4" dia.		
Minumum	L.F.	0.480
Average	L.F.	0.686
Maximum	L.F.	0.960
Drilling in rock		
No sampling		
Minimum	L.F.	0.436
Average	L.F.	0.632
Maximum	L.F.	0.857
With casing and sampling		
Minimum	L.F.	0.600
Average	L.F.	0.800
Maximum	L.F.	1.200
Test pits		
Light soil		
Minimum	EA.	3.000
Average	EA.	4.000
Maximum	EA.	8.000
Heavy soil		
Minimum	EA.	4.800
Average	EA.	6.000
Maximum	EA.	12.000

Demolition	UNIT	MAN/ HOURS
02060.10 Building Demolition		
Building, complete with disposal		
Wood frame	C.F.	0.003
Concrete	C.F.	0.004
Steel frame	C.F.	0.005
Partition removal		
Concrete block partitions		
4" thick	S.F.	0.040

Demolition	UNIT	MAN/ HOURS
02060.10 Building Demolition		
8" thick	S.F.	0.053
12" thick	S.F.	0.073
Brick masonry partitions		
4" thick	S.F.	0.040
8" thick	S.F.	0.050
12" thick	S.F.	0.067
16" thick	S.F.	0.100
Cast in place concrete partitions		
Unreinforced		
6" thick	S.F.	0.160
8" thick	S.F.	0.171
10" thick	S.F.	0.200
12" thick	S.F.	0.240
Reinforced		
6" thick	S.F.	0.185
8" thick	S.F.	0.240
10" thick	S.F.	0.267
12" thick	S.F.	0.320
Terra cotta		
To 6" thick	S.F.	0.040
Stud partitions		
Metal or wood, with drywall both sides	S.F.	0.040
Metal studs, both sides, lath and plaster	S.F.	0.053
Door and frame removal		
Hollow metal in masonry wall		
Single		
2'6"x6'8"	EA.	1.000
3'x7'	EA.	1.333
Double		
3'x7'	EA.	1.600
4'x8'	EA.	1.600
Wood in framed wall		
Single		
2'6"x6'8"	EA.	0.571
3'x6'8"	EA.	0.667
Double		
2'6"x6'8"	EA.	0.800
3'x6'8"	EA.	0.889
Remove for re-use		
Hollow metal	EA.	2.000
Wood	EA.	1.333
Floor removal		
Brick flooring	S.F.	0.032
Ceramic or quarry tile	S.F.	0.018
Terrazzo	S.F.	0.036
Heavy wood	S.F.	0.021
Residential wood	S.F.	0.023
Resilient tile or linoleum	S.F.	0.008
Ceiling removal		
Acoustical tile ceiling		
Adhesive fastened	S.F.	0.008
Furred and glued	S.F.	0.007
Suspended grid	S.F.	0.005
Drywall ceiling		

Demolition

	UNIT	MAN/HOURS
02060.10 Building Demolition		
Furred and nailed	S.F.	0.009
Nailed to framing	S.F.	0.008
Plastered ceiling		
Furred on framing	S.F.	0.020
Suspended system	S.F.	0.027
Roofing removal		
Steel frame		
Corrugated metal roofing	S.F.	0.016
Built-up roof on metal deck	S.F.	0.027
Wood frame		
Built up roof on wood deck	S.F.	0.025
Roof shingles	S.F.	0.013
Roof tiles	S.F.	0.027
Concrete frame	C.F.	0.053
Concrete plank	S.F.	0.040
Built-up roof on concrete	S.F.	0.023
Cut-outs		
Concrete, elevated slabs, mesh reinforcing		
Under 5 cf	C.F.	0.800
Over 5 cf	C.F.	0.667
Bar reinforcing		
Under 5 cf	C.F.	1.333
Over 5 cf	C.F.	1.000
Window removal		
Metal windows, trim included		
2'x3'	EA.	0.800
2'x4'	EA.	0.889
2'x6'	EA.	1.000
3'x4'	EA.	1.000
3'x6'	EA.	1.143
3'x8'	EA.	1.333
4'x4'	EA.	1.333
4'x6'	EA.	1.600
4'x8'	EA.	2.000
Wood windows, trim included		
2'x3'	EA.	0.444
2'x4'	EA.	0.471
2'x6'	EA.	0.500
3'x4'	EA.	0.533
3'x6'	EA.	0.571
3'x8'	EA.	0.615
6'x4'	EA.	0.667
6'x6'	EA.	0.727
6'x8'	EA.	0.800
Walls, concrete, bar reinforcing		
Small jobs	C.F.	0.533
Large jobs	C.F.	0.444
Brick walls, not including toothing		
4" thick	S.F.	0.040
8" thick	S.F.	0.050
12" thick	S.F.	0.067
16" thick	S.F.	0.100
Concrete block walls, not including toothing		
4" thick	S.F.	0.044

Demolition

	UNIT	MAN/HOURS
02060.10 Building Demolition		
6" thick	S.F.	0.047
8" thick	S.F.	0.050
10" thick	S.F.	0.057
12" thick	S.F.	0.067
Rubbish handling		
Load in dumpster or truck		
Minimum	C.F.	0.018
Maximum	C.F.	0.027
For use of elevators, add		
Minimum	C.F.	0.004
Maximum	C.F.	0.008
Rubbish hauling		
Hand loaded on trucks, 2 mile trip	C.Y.	0.320
Machine loaded on trucks, 2 mile trip	C.Y.	0.240

Highway Demolition

	UNIT	MAN/HOURS
02065.10 Pavement Demolition		
Bituminous pavement, up to 3" thick		
On streets		
Minimum	S.Y.	0.069
Average	S.Y.	0.096
Maximum	S.Y.	0.160
On pipe trench		
Minimum	S.Y.	0.096
Average	S.Y.	0.120
Maximum	S.Y.	0.240
Concrete pavement, 6" thick		
No reinforcement		
Minimum	S.Y.	0.120
Average	S.Y.	0.160
Maximum	S.Y.	0.240
With wire mesh		
Minimum	S.Y.	0.185
Average	S.Y.	0.240
Maximum	S.Y.	0.300
With rebars		
Minimum	S.Y.	0.240
Average	S.Y.	0.300
Maximum	S.Y.	0.400
9" thick		
No reinforcement		
Minimum	S.Y.	0.160
Average	S.Y.	0.200
Maximum	S.Y.	0.240
With wire mesh		
Minimum	S.Y.	0.253

Highway Demolition	UNIT	MAN/HOURS
02065.10 Pavement Demolition		
Average	S.Y.	0.300
Maximum	S.Y.	0.369
With rebars		
Minimum	S.Y.	0.320
Average	S.Y.	0.400
Maximum	S.Y.	0.533
12" thick		
No reinforcement		
Minimum	S.Y.	0.200
Average	S.Y.	0.240
Maximum	S.Y.	0.300
With wire mesh		
Minimum	S.Y.	0.282
Average	S.Y.	0.343
Maximum	S.Y.	0.436
With rebars		
Minimum	S.Y.	0.400
Average	S.Y.	0.480
Maximum	S.Y.	0.600
Sidewalk, 4" thick, with disposal		
Minimum	S.Y.	0.057
Average	S.Y.	0.080
Maximum	S.Y.	0.114
Removal of pavement markings by waterblasting		
Minimum	S.F.	0.003
Average	S.F.	0.004
Maximum	S.F.	0.008
02065.15 Saw Cutting Pavement		
Pavement, bituminous		
2" thick	L.F.	0.016
3" thick	L.F.	0.020
4" thick	L.F.	0.025
5" thick	L.F.	0.027
6" thick	L.F.	0.029
Concrete pavement, with wire mesh		
4" thick	L.F.	0.031
5" thick	L.F.	0.033
6" thick	L.F.	0.036
8" thick	L.F.	0.040
10" thick	L.F.	0.044
Plain concrete, unreinforced		
4" thick	L.F.	0.027
5" thick	L.F.	0.031
6" thick	L.F.	0.033
8" thick	L.F.	0.036
10" thick	L.F.	0.040
02065.80 Curb & Gutter		
Curb removal		
Concrete, unreinforced		
Minimum	L.F.	0.048
Average	L.F.	0.060
Maximum	L.F.	0.075

Highway Demolition	UNIT	MAN/HOURS
02065.80 Curb & Gutter		
Reinforced		
Minimum	L.F.	0.077
Average	L.F.	0.086
Maximum	L.F.	0.096
Combination curb and 2' gutter		
Unreinforced		
Minimum	L.F.	0.063
Average	L.F.	0.083
Maximum	L.F.	0.120
Reinforced		
Minimum	L.F.	0.100
Average	L.F.	0.133
Maximum	L.F.	0.240
Granite curb		
Minimum	L.F.	0.069
Average	L.F.	0.080
Maximum	L.F.	0.092
Asphalt curb		
Minimum	L.F.	0.040
Average	L.F.	0.048
Maximum	L.F.	0.057
02065.85 Guardrails		
Remove standard guardrail		
Steel		
Minimum	L.F.	0.060
Average	L.F.	0.080
Maximum	L.F.	0.120
Wood		
Minimum	L.F.	0.052
Average	L.F.	0.062
Maximum	L.F.	0.100
02075.80 Core Drilling		
Concrete		
6" thick		
3" dia.	EA.	0.571
4" dia.	EA.	0.667
6" dia.	EA.	0.800
8" dia.	EA.	1.333
8" thick		
3" dia.	EA.	0.800
4" dia.	EA.	1.000
6" dia.	EA.	1.143
8" dia.	EA.	1.600
10" thick		
3" dia.	EA.	1.000
4" dia.	EA.	1.143
6" dia.	EA.	1.333
8" dia.	EA.	2.000
12" thick		
3" dia.	EA.	1.333
4" dia.	EA.	1.600
6" dia.	EA.	2.000

Highway Demolition

02075.80 — Core Drilling

	UNIT	MAN/HOURS
8" dia.	EA.	2.667

Hazardous Waste

02080.10 — Asbestos Removal

	UNIT	MAN/HOURS
Enclosure using wood studs & poly, install & remove	S.F.	0.020

02080.12 — Duct Insulation Removal

	UNIT	MAN/HOURS
Remove duct insulation, duct size		
6" x 12"	L.F.	0.044
x 18"	L.F.	0.062
x 24"	L.F.	0.089
8" x 12"	L.F.	0.067
x 18"	L.F.	0.073
x 24"	L.F.	0.100
12" x 12"	L.F.	0.067
x 18"	L.F.	0.089
x 24"	L.F.	0.114

02080.15 — Pipe Insulation Removal

	UNIT	MAN/HOURS
Removal, asbestos insulation		
2" thick, pipe		
1" to 3" dia.	L.F.	0.067
4" to 6" dia.	L.F.	0.076
3" thick		
7" to 8" dia.	L.F.	0.080
9" to 10" dia.	L.F.	0.084
11" to 12" dia.	L.F.	0.089
13" to 14" dia.	L.F.	0.094
15" to 18" dia.	L.F.	0.100

Site Demolition

02105.10 — Catch Basins/manholes

	UNIT	MAN/HOURS
Abandon catch basin or manhole (fill with sand)		
Minimum	EA.	3.000
Average	EA.	4.800
Maximum	EA.	8.000
Remove and reset frame and cover		
Minimum	EA.	1.600
Average	EA.	2.400

Site Demolition

02105.10 — Catch Basins/manholes

	UNIT	MAN/HOURS
Maximum	EA.	4.000
Remove catch basin, to 10' deep		
Masonry		
Minumum	EA.	4.800
Average	EA.	6.000
Maximum	EA.	8.000
Concrete		
Minimum	EA.	6.000
Average	EA.	8.000
Maximum	EA.	9.600

02105.20 — Fences

	UNIT	MAN/HOURS
Remove fencing		
Chain link, 8' high		
For disposal	L.F.	0.040
For reuse	L.F.	0.100
Wood		
4' high	S.F.	0.027
6' high	S.F.	0.032
8' high	S.F.	0.040
Masonry		
8" thick		
4' high	S.F.	0.080
6' high	S.F.	0.100
8' high	S.F.	0.114
12" thick		
4' high	S.F.	0.133
6' high	S.F.	0.160
8' high	S.F.	0.200
12' high	S.F.	0.267

02105.30 — Hydrants

	UNIT	MAN/HOURS
Remove fire hydrant		
Minimum	EA.	3.000
Average	EA.	4.000
Maximum	EA.	6.000
Remove and reset fire hydrant		
Minimum	EA.	8.000
Average	EA.	12.000
Maximum	EA.	24.000

02105.42 — Drainage Piping

	UNIT	MAN/HOURS
Remove drainage pipe, not including excavation		
12" dia.		
Minimum	L.F.	0.080
Average	L.F.	0.100
Maximum	L.F.	0.126
18" dia.		
Minimum	L.F.	0.109
Average	L.F.	0.126
Maximum	L.F.	0.160
24" dia.		
Minimum	L.F.	0.133
Average	L.F.	0.160

Site Demolition

Site Demolition	UNIT	MAN/HOURS
02105.42 Drainage Piping		
Maximum	L.F.	0.200
36" dia.		
Minimum	L.F.	0.160
Average	L.F.	0.200
Maximum	L.F.	0.253
02105.43 Gas Piping		
Remove welded steel pipe, not including excavation		
4" dia.		
Minimum	L.F.	0.120
Average	L.F.	0.150
Maximum	L.F.	0.200
5" dia.		
Minimum	L.F.	0.200
Average	L.F.	0.240
Maximum	L.F.	0.300
6" dia.		
Minimum	L.F.	0.253
Average	L.F.	0.300
Maximum	L.F.	0.400
8" dia.		
Minimum	L.F.	0.369
Average	L.F.	0.480
Maximum	L.F.	0.632
10" dia.		
Minimum	L.F.	0.480
Average	L.F.	0.600
Maximum	L.F.	0.800
02105.45 Sanitary Piping		
Remove sewer pipe, not including excavation		
4" dia.		
Minimum	L.F.	0.067
Average	L.F.	0.096
Maximum	L.F.	0.160
6" dia.		
Minimum	L.F.	0.075
Average	L.F.	0.109
Maximum	L.F.	0.200
8" dia.		
Minimum	L.F.	0.080
Average	L.F.	0.120
Maximum	L.F.	0.240
10" dia.		
Minimum	L.F.	0.086
Average	L.F.	0.126
Maximum	L.F.	0.267
12" dia.		
Minimum	L.F.	0.092
Average	L.F.	0.133
Maximum	L.F.	0.300
15" dia.		
Minimum	L.F.	0.100
Average	L.F.	0.141

Site Demolition	UNIT	MAN/HOURS
02105.45 Sanitary Piping		
Maximum	L.F.	0.343
18" dia.		
Minimum	L.F.	0.109
Average	L.F.	0.160
Maximum	L.F.	0.400
24" dia.		
Minimum	L.F.	0.120
Average	L.F.	0.200
Maximum	L.F.	0.480
30" dia.		
Minimum	L.F.	0.133
Average	L.F.	0.240
Maximum	L.F.	0.600
36" dia.		
Minimum	L.F.	0.160
Average	L.F.	0.300
Maximum	L.F.	0.800
02105.48 Water Piping		
Remove water pipe, not including excavation		
4" dia.		
Minimum	L.F.	0.096
Average	L.F.	0.109
Maximum	L.F.	0.126
6" dia.		
Minimum	L.F.	0.100
Average	L.F.	0.114
Maximum	L.F.	0.133
8" dia.		
Minimum	L.F.	0.109
Average	L.F.	0.126
Maximum	L.F.	0.150
10" dia.		
Minimum	L.F.	0.114
Average	L.F.	0.133
Maximum	L.F.	0.160
12" dia.		
Minimum	L.F.	0.120
Average	L.F.	0.141
Maximum	L.F.	0.171
14" dia.		
Minimum	L.F.	0.126
Average	L.F.	0.150
Maximum	L.F.	0.185
16" dia.		
Minimum	L.F.	0.133
Average	L.F.	0.160
Maximum	L.F.	0.200
18" dia.		
Minimum	L.F.	0.141
Average	L.F.	0.171
Maximum	L.F.	0.218
20" dia.		
Minimum	L.F.	0.150

Site Demolition	UNIT	MAN/HOURS
02105.48 Water Piping		
Average	L.F.	0.185
Maximum	L.F.	0.240
Remove valves		
6"	EA.	1.200
10"	EA.	1.333
14"	EA.	1.500
18"	EA.	2.000
02105.60 Underground Tanks		
Remove underground storage tank, and backfill		
50 to 250 gals	EA.	8.000
600 gals	EA.	8.000
1000 gals	EA.	12.000
4000 gals	EA.	19.200
5000 gals	EA.	19.200
10,000 gals	EA.	32.000
12,000 gals	EA.	40.000
15,000 gals	EA.	48.000
20,000 gals	EA.	60.000
02105.66 Septic Tanks		
Remove septic tank		
1000 gals	EA.	2.000
2000 gals	EA.	2.400
5000 gals	EA.	3.000
15,000 gals	EA.	24.000
25,000 gals	EA.	32.000
40,000 gals	EA.	48.000
02105.80 Walls, Exterior		
Concrete wall		
Light reinforcing		
6" thick	S.F.	0.120
8" thick	S.F.	0.126
10" thick	S.F.	0.133
12" thick	S.F.	0.150
Medium reinforcing		
6" thick	S.F.	0.126
8" thick	S.F.	0.133
10" thick	S.F.	0.150
12" thick	S.F.	0.171
Heavy reinforcing		
6" thick	S.F.	0.141
8" thick	S.F.	0.150
10" thick	S.F.	0.171
12" thick	S.F.	0.200
Masonry		
No reinforcing		
8" thick	S.F.	0.053
12" thick	S.F.	0.060
16" thick	S.F.	0.069
Horizontal reinforcing		
8" thick	S.F.	0.060
12" thick	S.F.	0.065

Site Demolition	UNIT	MAN/HOURS
02105.80 Walls, Exterior		
16" thick	S.F.	0.077
Vertical reinforcing		
8" thick	S.F.	0.077
12" thick	S.F.	0.089
16" thick	S.F.	0.109
Remove concrete headwall		
15" pipe	EA.	1.714
18" pipe	EA.	2.000
24" pipe	EA.	2.182
30" pipe	EA.	2.400
36" pipe	EA.	2.667
48" pipe	EA.	3.429
60" pipe	EA.	4.800
02110.10 Clearing And Grubbing		
Clear wooded area		
Light density	ACRE	60.000
Medium density	ACRE	80.000
Heavy density	ACRE	96.000
02110.50 Tree Cutting & Clearing		
Cut trees and clear out stumps		
9" to 12" dia.	EA.	4.800
To 24" dia.	EA.	6.000
24" dia. and up	EA.	8.000
Loading and trucking		
For machine load, per load, round trip		
1 mile	EA.	0.960
3 mile	EA.	1.091
5 mile	EA.	1.200
10 mile	EA.	1.600
20 mile	EA.	2.400
Hand loaded, round trip		
1 mile	EA.	2.000
3 mile	EA.	2.286
5 mile	EA.	2.667
10 mile	EA.	3.200
20 mile	EA.	4.000
Tree trimming for pole line construction		
Light cutting	L.F.	0.012
Medium cutting	L.F.	0.016
Heavy cutting	L.F.	0.024

Dewatering

	UNIT	MAN/HOURS
02144.10 — Wellpoint Systems		
Pumping, gas driven, 50' hose		
3" header pipe	DAY	8.000
6" header pipe	DAY	10.000
Wellpoint system per job		
6" header pipe	L.F.	0.032
8" header pipe	L.F.	0.040
10" header pipe	L.F.	0.053
Jetting wellpoint system		
14' long	EA.	0.533
18' long	EA.	0.667
Sand filter for wellpoints	L.F.	0.013
Replacement of wellpoint components	EA.	0.160

Shoring And Underpinning

	UNIT	MAN/HOURS
02162.10 — Trench Sheeting		
Closed timber, including pull and salvage, excavation		
8' deep	S.F.	0.064
10' deep	S.F.	0.067
12' deep	S.F.	0.071
14' deep	S.F.	0.075
16' deep	S.F.	0.080
18' deep	S.F.	0.091
20' deep	S.F.	0.098
02170.10 — Cofferdams		
Cofferdam, steel, driven from shore		
15' deep	S.F.	0.137
20' deep	S.F.	0.128
25' deep	S.F.	0.120
30' deep	S.F.	0.113
40' deep	S.F.	0.107
Driven from barge		
20' deep	S.F.	0.148
30' deep	S.F.	0.137
40' deep	S.F.	0.128
50' deep	S.F.	0.120

Earthwork

	UNIT	MAN/HOURS
02210.10 — Hauling Material		
Haul material by 10 cy dump truck, round trip distance		
1 mile	C.Y.	0.044
2 mile	C.Y.	0.053
5 mile	C.Y.	0.073
10 mile	C.Y.	0.080
20 mile	C.Y.	0.089
30 mile	C.Y.	0.107
Site grading, cut & fill, sandy clay, 200' haul, 75 hp dozer	C.Y.	0.032
Spread topsoil by equipment on site	C.Y.	0.036
Site grading (cut and fill to 6") less than 1 acre		
75 hp dozer	C.Y.	0.053
1.5 cy backhoe/loader	C.Y.	0.080
02210.30 — Bulk Excavation		
Excavation, by small dozer		
Large areas	C.Y.	0.016
Small areas	C.Y.	0.027
Trim banks	C.Y.	0.040
Drag line		
1-1/2 cy bucket		
Sand or gravel	C.Y.	0.040
Light clay	C.Y.	0.053
Heavy clay	C.Y.	0.060
Unclassified	C.Y.	0.064
2 cy bucket		
Sand or gravel	C.Y.	0.037
Light clay	C.Y.	0.048
Heavy clay	C.Y.	0.053
Unclassified	C.Y.	0.056
2-1/2 cy bucket		
Sand or gravel	C.Y.	0.034
Light clay	C.Y.	0.044
Heavy clay	C.Y.	0.048
Unclassified	C.Y.	0.051
3 cy bucket		
Sand or gravel	C.Y.	0.030
Light clay	C.Y.	0.040
Heavy clay	C.Y.	0.044
Unclassified	C.Y.	0.046
Hydraulic excavator		
1 cy capacity		
Light material	C.Y.	0.040
Medium material	C.Y.	0.048
Wet material	C.Y.	0.060
Blasted rock	C.Y.	0.069
1-1/2 cy capacity		
Light material	C.Y.	0.010
Medium material	C.Y.	0.013
Wet material	C.Y.	0.016
Blasted rock	C.Y.	0.020
2 cy capacity		
Light material	C.Y.	0.009
Medium material	C.Y.	0.011
Wet material	C.Y.	0.013

4

Earthwork

02210.30 — Bulk Excavation

	UNIT	MAN/HOURS
Blasted rock	C.Y.	0.016
Wheel mounted front-end loader		
7/8 cy capacity		
Light material	C.Y.	0.020
Medium material	C.Y.	0.023
Wet material	C.Y.	0.027
Blasted rock	C.Y.	0.032
1-1/2 cy capacity		
Light material	C.Y.	0.011
Medium material	C.Y.	0.012
Wet material	C.Y.	0.013
Blasted rock	C.Y.	0.015
2-1/2 cy capacity		
Light material	C.Y.	0.009
Medium material	C.Y.	0.010
Wet material	C.Y.	0.011
Blasted rock	C.Y.	0.011
3-1/2 cy capacity		
Light material	C.Y.	0.009
Medium material	C.Y.	0.009
Wet material	C.Y.	0.010
Blasted rock	C.Y.	0.011
6 cy capacity		
Light material	C.Y.	0.005
Medium material	C.Y.	0.006
Wet material	C.Y.	0.006
Blasted rock	C.Y.	0.007
Track mounted front-end loader		
1-1/2 cy capacity		
Light material	C.Y.	0.013
Medium material	C.Y.	0.015
Wet material	C.Y.	0.016
Blasted rock	C.Y.	0.018
2-3/4 cy capacity		
Light material	C.Y.	0.008
Medium material	C.Y.	0.009
Wet material	C.Y.	0.010
Blasted rock	C.Y.	0.011

02220.10 — Borrow

	UNIT	MAN/HOURS
Borrow fill, F.O.B. at pit		
Sand, haul to site, round trip		
10 mile	C.Y.	0.080
20 mile	C.Y.	0.133
30 mile	C.Y.	0.200
Place borrow fill and compact		
Less than 1 in 4 slope	C.Y.	0.040
Greater than 1 in 4 slope	C.Y.	0.053

02220.40 — Building Excavation

	UNIT	MAN/HOURS
Structural excavation, unclassified earth		
3/8 cy backhoe	C.Y.	0.107
3/4 cy backhoe	C.Y.	0.080
1 cy backhoe	C.Y.	0.067

Earthwork

02220.40 — Building Excavation

	UNIT	MAN/HOURS
Foundation backfill and compaction by machine	C.Y.	0.160

02220.50 — Utility Excavation

	UNIT	MAN/HOURS
Trencher, sandy clay, 8" wide trench		
18" deep	L.F.	0.018
24" deep	L.F.	0.020
36" deep	L.F.	0.023
Trench backfill, 95% compaction		
Tamp by hand	C.Y.	0.500
Vibratory compaction	C.Y.	0.400
Trench backfilling, with borrow sand, place & compact	C.Y.	0.400

02220.60 — Trenching

	UNIT	MAN/HOURS
Trenching and continuous footing excavation		
By gradall		
1 cy capacity		
Light soil	C.Y.	0.023
Medium soil	C.Y.	0.025
Heavy/wet soil	C.Y.	0.027
Loose rock	C.Y.	0.029
Blasted rock	C.Y.	0.031
By hydraulic excavator		
1/2 cy capacity		
Light soil	C.Y.	0.027
Medium soil	C.Y.	0.029
Heavy/wet soil	C.Y.	0.032
Loose rock	C.Y.	0.036
Blasted rock	C.Y.	0.040
1 cy capacity		
Light soil	C.Y.	0.019
Medium soil	C.Y.	0.020
Heavy/wet soil	C.Y.	0.021
Loose rock	C.Y.	0.023
Blasted rock	C.Y.	0.025
1-1/2 cy capacity		
Light soil	C.Y.	0.017
Medium soil	C.Y.	0.018
Heavy/wet soil	C.Y.	0.019
Loose rock	C.Y.	0.020
Blasted rock	C.Y.	0.021
2 cy capacity		
Light soil	C.Y.	0.016
Medium soil	C.Y.	0.017
Heavy/wet soil	C.Y.	0.018
Loose rock	C.Y.	0.019
Blasted rock	C.Y.	0.020
2-1/2 cy capacity		
Light soil	C.Y.	0.015
Medium soil	C.Y.	0.015
Heavy/wet soil	C.Y.	0.016
Loose rock	C.Y.	0.017
Blasted rock	C.Y.	0.018
Trencher, chain, 1' wide to 4' deep		
Light soil	C.Y.	0.020

Earthwork

02220.60 — Trenching

	UNIT	MAN/HOURS
Medium soil	C.Y.	0.023
Heavy soil	C.Y.	0.027
Hand excavation		
Bulk, wheeled 100'		
Normal soil	C.Y.	0.889
Sand or gravel	C.Y.	0.800
Medium clay	C.Y.	1.143
Heavy clay	C.Y.	1.600
Loose rock	C.Y.	2.000
Trenches, up to 2' deep		
Normal soil	C.Y.	1.000
Sand or gravel	C.Y.	0.889
Medium clay	C.Y.	1.333
Heavy clay	C.Y.	2.000
Loose rock	C.Y.	2.667
Trenches, to 6' deep		
Normal soil	C.Y.	1.143
Sand or gravel	C.Y.	1.000
Medium clay	C.Y.	1.600
Heavy clay	C.Y.	2.667
Loose rock	C.Y.	4.000
Backfill trenches		
With compaction		
By hand	C.Y.	0.667
By 60 hp tracked dozer	C.Y.	0.020
By 200 hp tracked dozer	C.Y.	0.009
By small front-end loader	C.Y.	0.023
Spread dumped fill or gravel, no compaction		
6" layers	S.Y.	0.013
12" layers	S.Y.	0.016
Compaction in 6" layers		
By hand with air tamper	S.Y.	0.016
Backfill trenches, sand bedding, no compaction		
By hand	C.Y.	0.667
By small front-end loader	C.Y.	0.023

02220.70 — Roadway Excavation

	UNIT	MAN/HOURS
Roadway excavation		
1/4 mile haul	C.Y.	0.016
2 mile haul	C.Y.	0.027
5 mile haul	C.Y.	0.040
Excavation of open ditches	C.Y.	0.011
Trim banks, swales or ditches	S.Y.	0.013
Bulk swale excavation by dragline		
Small jobs	C.Y.	0.060
Large jobs	C.Y.	0.034
Spread base course	C.Y.	0.020
Roll and compact	C.Y.	0.027

02220.71 — Base Course

	UNIT	MAN/HOURS
Base course, crushed stone		
3" thick	S.Y.	0.004
4" thick	S.Y.	0.004
6" thick	S.Y.	0.005

Earthwork

02220.71 — Base Course

	UNIT	MAN/HOURS
8" thick	S.Y.	0.005
10" thick	S.Y.	0.006
12" thick	S.Y.	0.007
Base course, bank run gravel		
4" deep	S.Y.	0.004
6" deep	S.Y.	0.005
8" deep	S.Y.	0.005
10" deep	S.Y.	0.005
12" deep	S.Y.	0.006
Prepare and roll sub base		
Minimum	S.Y.	0.004
Average	S.Y.	0.005
Maximum	S.Y.	0.007

02220.90 — Hand Excavation

	UNIT	MAN/HOURS
Excavation		
To 2' deep		
Normal soil	C.Y.	0.889
Sand and gravel	C.Y.	0.800
Medium clay	C.Y.	1.000
Heavy clay	C.Y.	1.143
Loose rock	C.Y.	1.333
To 6' deep		
Normal soil	C.Y.	1.143
Sand and gravel	C.Y.	1.000
Medium clay	C.Y.	1.333
Heavy clay	C.Y.	1.600
Loose rock	C.Y.	2.000
Backfilling foundation without compaction, 6" lifts	C.Y.	0.500
Compaction of backfill around structures or in trench		
By hand with air tamper	C.Y.	0.571
By hand with vibrating plate tamper	C.Y.	0.533
1 ton roller	C.Y.	0.400
Miscellaneous hand labor		
Trim slopes, sides of excavation	S.F.	0.001
Trim bottom of excavation	S.F.	0.002
Excavation around obstructions and services	C.Y.	2.667

02240.05 — Soil Stabilization

	UNIT	MAN/HOURS
Straw bale secured with rebar	L.F.	0.027
Filter barrier, 18" high filter fabric	L.F.	0.080
Sediment fence, 36" fabric with 6" mesh	L.F.	0.100
Soil stabilization with tar paper, burlap, straw and stakes	S.F.	0.001

02240.30 — Geotextile

	UNIT	MAN/HOURS
Filter cloth, light reinforcement		
Woven		
12'-6" wide x 50' long	S.F.	0.001
Various lengths	S.F.	0.001
Non-woven		
14'-8" wide x 430' long	S.F.	0.001
Various lengths	S.F.	0.001

SITEWORK

Earthwork		UNIT	MAN/HOURS
02270.10	Slope Protection		
Gabions, stone filled			
6" deep		S.Y.	0.200
9" deep		S.Y.	0.229
12" deep		S.Y.	0.267
18" deep		S.Y.	0.320
36" deep		S.Y.	0.533
02270.40	Riprap		
Riprap			
Crushed stone blanket, max size 2-1/2"		TON	0.533
Stone, quarry run, 300 lb. stones		TON	0.492
400 lb. stones		TON	0.457
500 lb. stones		TON	0.427
750 lb. stones		TON	0.400
Dry concrete riprap in bags 3" thick, 80 lb. per bag		BAG	0.027
02280.20	Soil Treatment		
Soil treatment, termite control pretreatment			
Under slabs		S.F.	0.004
By walls		S.F.	0.005
02290.30	Weed Control		
Weed control, bromicil, 15 lb./acre, wettable powder		ACRE	4.000
Vegetation control, by application of plant killer		S.Y.	0.003
Weed killer, lawns and fields		S.Y.	0.002

Tunneling		UNIT	MAN/HOURS
02300.10	Pipe Jacking		
Pipe casing, horizontal jacking			
18" dia.		L.F.	0.711
21" dia.		L.F.	0.762
24" dia.		L.F.	0.800
27" dia.		L.F.	0.800
30" dia.		L.F.	0.842
36" dia.		L.F.	0.914
42" dia.		L.F.	1.000
48" dia.		L.F.	1.067

Piles And Caissons		UNIT	MAN/HOURS
02360.50	Prestressed Piling		
Prestressed concrete piling, less than 60' long			
10" sq.		L.F.	0.040
12" sq.		L.F.	0.042
14" sq.		L.F.	0.043
16" sq.		L.F.	0.044
18" sq.		L.F.	0.047
20" sq.		L.F.	0.048
24" sq.		L.F.	0.049
More than 60' long			
12" sq.		L.F.	0.034
14" sq.		L.F.	0.035
16" sq.		L.F.	0.036
18" sq.		L.F.	0.036
20" sq.		L.F.	0.037
24" sq.		L.F.	0.038
Straight cylinder, less than 60' long			
12" dia.		L.F.	0.044
14" dia.		L.F.	0.045
16" dia.		L.F.	0.046
18" dia.		L.F.	0.047
20" dia.		L.F.	0.048
24" dia.		L.F.	0.049
More than 60' long			
12" dia.		L.F.	0.035
14" dia.		L.F.	0.036
16" dia.		L.F.	0.036
18" dia.		L.F.	0.037
20" dia.		L.F.	0.038
24" dia.		L.F.	0.038
Concrete sheet piling			
12" thick x 20' long		S.F.	0.096
25' long		S.F.	0.087
30' long		S.F.	0.080
35' long		S.F.	0.074
40' long		S.F.	0.069
16" thick x 40' long		S.F.	0.053
45' long		S.F.	0.051
50' long		S.F.	0.048
55' long		S.F.	0.046
60' long		S.F.	0.044
02360.60	Steel Piles		
H-section piles			
8x8			
36 lb/ft			
30' long		L.F.	0.080
40' long		L.F.	0.064
50' long		L.F.	0.053
10x10			
42 lb/ft			
30' long		L.F.	0.080
40' long		L.F.	0.064
50' long		L.F.	0.053
57 lb/ft			

Piles And Caissons

Piles And Caissons	UNIT	MAN/HOURS
02360.60 Steel Piles		
30' long	L.F.	0.080
40' long	L.F.	0.064
50' long	L.F.	0.053
12x12		
53 lb/ft		
30' long	L.F.	0.087
40' long	L.F.	0.069
50' long	L.F.	0.053
74 lb/ft		
30' long	L.F.	0.087
40' long	L.F.	0.069
50' long	L.F.	0.053
14x14		
73 lb/ft		
40' long	L.F.	0.087
50' long	L.F.	0.069
60' long	L.F.	0.053
89 lb/ft		
40' long	L.F.	0.087
50' long	L.F.	0.069
60' long	L.F.	0.053
102 lb/ft		
40' long	L.F.	0.087
50' long	L.F.	0.069
60' long	L.F.	0.053
117 lb/ft		
40' long	L.F.	0.091
50' long	L.F.	0.071
60' long	L.F.	0.055
Splice		
8"	EA.	1.333
10"	EA.	1.600
12"	EA.	1.600
14"	EA.	2.000
Driving cap		
8"	EA.	0.800
10"	EA.	1.000
12"	EA.	1.000
14"	EA.	1.143
Standard point		
8"	EA.	0.800
10"	EA.	1.000
12"	EA.	1.143
14"	EA.	1.333
Heavy duty point		
8"	EA.	0.889
10"	EA.	1.143
12"	EA.	1.333
14"	EA.	1.600
Tapered friction piles, with fluted steel casing, up to 50'		
With 4000 psi concrete no reinforcing		
12" dia.	L.F.	0.048
14" dia.	L.F.	0.049
16" dia.	L.F.	0.051

Piles And Caissons	UNIT	MAN/HOURS
02360.60 Steel Piles		
18" dia.	L.F.	0.056
02360.65 Steel Pipe Piles		
Concrete filled, 3000# concrete, up to 40'		
8" dia.	L.F.	0.069
10" dia.	L.F.	0.071
12" dia.	L.F.	0.074
14" dia.	L.F.	0.077
16" dia.	L.F.	0.080
18" dia.	L.F.	0.083
Pipe piles, non-filled		
8" dia.	L.F.	0.053
10" dia.	L.F.	0.055
12" dia.	L.F.	0.056
14" dia.	L.F.	0.060
16" dia.	L.F.	0.062
18" dia.	L.F.	0.064
Splice		
8" dia.	EA.	1.600
10" dia.	EA.	1.600
12" dia.	EA.	2.000
14" dia.	EA.	2.000
16" dia.	EA.	2.667
18" dia.	EA.	2.667
Standard point		
8" dia.	EA.	1.600
10" dia.	EA.	1.600
12" dia.	EA.	2.000
14" dia.	EA.	2.000
16" dia.	EA.	2.667
18" dia.	EA.	2.667
Heavy duty point		
8" dia.	EA.	2.000
10" dia.	EA.	2.000
12" dia.	EA.	2.667
14" dia.	EA.	2.667
16" dia.	EA.	3.200
18" dia.	EA.	3.200
02360.70 Steel Sheet Piling		
Steel sheet piling,12" wide		
20' long	S.F.	0.096
35' long	S.F.	0.069
50' long	S.F.	0.048
Over 50' long	S.F.	0.044
02360.80 Wood And Timber Piles		
Treated wood piles, 12" butt, 8" tip		
25' long	L.F.	0.096
30' long	L.F.	0.080
35' long	L.F.	0.069
40' long	L.F.	0.060
12" butt, 7" tip		
40' long	L.F.	0.060

Piles And Caissons

Piles And Caissons	UNIT	MAN/HOURS

02360.80 — Wood And Timber Piles

	UNIT	MAN/HOURS
45' long	L.F.	0.053
50' long	L.F.	0.048
55' long	L.F.	0.044
60' long	L.F.	0.040

02380.10 — Caissons

	UNIT	MAN/HOURS
Caisson, including 3000# concrete, in stable ground		
18" dia.	L.F.	0.192
24" dia.	L.F.	0.200
30" dia.	L.F.	0.240
36" dia.	L.F.	0.274
48" dia.	L.F.	0.320
60" dia.	L.F.	0.436
72" dia.	L.F.	0.533
84" dia.	L.F.	0.686
Wet ground, casing required but pulled		
18" dia.	L.F.	0.240
24" dia.	L.F.	0.267
30" dia.	L.F.	0.300
36" dia.	L.F.	0.320
48" dia.	L.F.	0.400
60" dia.	L.F.	0.533
72" dia.	L.F.	0.800
84" dia.	L.F.	1.200
Soft rock		
18" dia.	L.F.	0.686
24" dia.	L.F.	1.200
30" dia.	L.F.	1.600
36" dia.	L.F.	2.400
48" dia.	L.F.	3.200
60" dia.	L.F.	4.800
72" dia.	L.F.	5.333
84" dia.	L.F.	6.000

Railroad Work

Railroad Work	UNIT	MAN/HOURS

02450.10 — Railroad Work

Rail	UNIT	MAN/HOURS
90 lb	L.F.	0.010
100 lb	L.F.	0.010
115 lb	L.F.	0.010
132 lb	L.F.	0.010
Rail relay		
90 lb	L.F.	0.010
100 lb	L.F.	0.010
115 lb	L.F.	0.010
132 lb	L.F.	0.010

Railroad Work

Railroad Work	UNIT	MAN/HOURS

02450.10 — Railroad Work

	UNIT	MAN/HOURS
New angle bars, per pair		
90 lb	EA.	0.012
100 lb	EA.	0.012
115 lb	EA.	0.012
132 lb	EA.	0.012
Angle bar relay		
90 lb	EA.	0.012
100 lb	EA.	0.012
115 lb	EA.	0.012
132 lb	EA.	0.012
New tie plates		
90 lb	EA.	0.009
100 lb	EA.	0.009
115 lb	EA.	0.009
132 lb	EA.	0.009
Tie plate relay		
90 lb	EA.	0.009
100 lb	EA.	0.009
115 lb	EA.	0.009
132 lb	EA.	0.009
Track accessories		
Wooden cross ties, 8'	EA.	0.060
Concrete cross ties, 8'	EA.	0.120
Tie plugs, 5"	EA.	0.006
Track bolts and nuts, 1"	EA.	0.006
Lockwashers, 1"	EA.	0.004
Track spikes, 6"	EA.	0.024
Wooden switch ties	B.F.	0.006
Rail anchors	EA.	0.022
Ballast	TON	0.120
Gauge rods	EA.	0.096
Compromise splice bars	EA.	0.160
Turnout		
90 lb	EA.	24.000
100 lb	EA.	24.000
110 lb	EA.	24.000
115 lb	EA.	24.000
132 lb	EA.	24.000
Turnout relay		
90 lb	EA.	24.000
100 lb	EA.	24.000
110 lb	EA.	24.000
115 lb	EA.	24.000
132 lb	EA.	24.000
Railroad track in place, complete		
New rail		
90 lb	L.F.	0.240
100 lb	L.F.	0.240
110 lb	L.F.	0.240
115 lb	L.F.	0.240
132 lb	L.F.	0.240
Rail relay		
90 lb	L.F.	0.240
100 lb	L.F.	0.240

Railroad Work

	UNIT	MAN/HOURS
02450.10 Railroad Work		
110 lb	L.F.	0.240
115 lb	L.F.	0.240
132 lb	L.F.	0.240
No. 8 turnout		
90 lb	EA.	32.000
100 lb	EA.	32.000
110 lb	EA.	32.000
115 lb	EA.	32.000
132 lb	EA.	32.000
No. 8 turnout relay		
90 lb	EA.	32.000
100 lb	EA.	32.000
110 lb	EA.	32.000
115 lb	EA.	32.000
132 lb	EA.	32.000
Railroad crossings, asphalt, based on 8" thick x 20'		
Including track and approach		
12' roadway	EA.	6.000
15' roadway	EA.	6.857
18' roadway	EA.	8.000
21' roadway	EA.	9.600
24' roadway	EA.	12.000
Precast concrete inserts		
12' roadway	EA.	2.400
15' roadway	EA.	3.000
18' roadway	EA.	4.000
21' roadway	EA.	4.800
24' roadway	EA.	5.333
Molded rubber, with headers		
12' roadway	EA.	2.400
15' roadway	EA.	3.000
18' roadway	EA.	4.000
21' roadway	EA.	4.800
24' roadway	EA.	5.333

Paving And Surfacing

	UNIT	MAN/HOURS
02510.20 Asphalt Surfaces		
Asphalt wearing surface, for flexible pavement		
1" thick	S.Y.	0.016
1-1/2" thick	S.Y.	0.019
2" thick	S.Y.	0.024
3" thick	S.Y.	0.032
Binder course		
1-1/2" thick	S.Y.	0.018
2" thick	S.Y.	0.022
3" thick	S.Y.	0.029

Paving And Surfacing

	UNIT	MAN/HOURS
02510.20 Asphalt Surfaces		
4" thick	S.Y.	0.032
5" thick	S.Y.	0.036
6" thick	S.Y.	0.040
Bituminous sidewalk, no base		
2" thick	S.Y.	0.028
3" thick	S.Y.	0.030
02520.10 Concrete Paving		
Concrete paving, reinforced, 5000 psi concrete		
6" thick	S.Y.	0.150
7" thick	S.Y.	0.160
8" thick	S.Y.	0.171
9" thick	S.Y.	0.185
10" thick	S.Y.	0.200
11" thick	S.Y.	0.218
12" thick	S.Y.	0.240
15" thick	S.Y.	0.300
Concrete paving, for pipe trench, reinforced		
7" thick	S.Y.	0.240
8" thick	S.Y.	0.267
9" thick	S.Y.	0.300
10" thick	S.Y.	0.343
Fibrous concrete		
5" thick	S.Y.	0.185
8" thick	S.Y.	0.200
Roller compacted concrete, (RCC), place and compact		
8" thick	S.Y.	0.240
12" thick	S.Y.	0.300
Steel edge forms up to		
12" deep	L.F.	0.027
15" deep	L.F.	0.032
Paving finishes		
Belt dragged	S.Y.	0.040
Curing	S.Y.	0.008
02545.10 Asphalt Repair		
Coal tar emulsion seal coat, rubber additive, fuel resistant	S.Y.	0.011
Bituminous surface treatment, single	S.Y.	0.008
Double	S.Y.	0.001
Bituminous prime coat	S.Y.	0.001
Tack coat	S.Y.	0.001
Crack sealing, concrete paving	L.F.	0.005
Bituminous paving for pipe trench, 4" thick	S.Y.	0.160
Polypropylene, nonwoven paving fabric	S.Y.	0.004
Rubberized asphalt	S.Y.	0.073
Asphalt slurry seal	S.Y.	0.047
02580.10 Pavement Markings		
Pavement line marking, paint		
4" wide	L.F.	0.002
6" wide	L.F.	0.004
8" wide	L.F.	0.007
Reflective paint, 4" wide	L.F.	0.007
Airfield markings, retro-reflective		

Paving And Surfacing	UNIT	MAN/HOURS
02580.10 Pavement Markings		
White	L.F.	0.007
Yellow	L.F.	0.007
Preformed tape, 4" wide		
Inlaid reflective	L.F.	0.001
Reflective paint	L.F.	0.002
Thermoplastic		
White	L.F.	0.004
Yellow	L.F.	0.004
12" wide, thermoplastic, white	L.F.	0.011
Directional arrows, reflective preformed tape	EA.	0.800
Messages, reflective preformed tape (per letter)	EA.	0.400
Handicap symbol, preformed tape	EA.	0.800
Parking stall painting	EA.	0.160

Utilities	UNIT	MAN/HOURS
02605.30 Manholes		
Precast sections, 48" dia.		
Base section	EA.	2.000
1'0" riser	EA.	1.600
1'4" riser	EA.	1.714
2'8" riser	EA.	1.846
4'0" riser	EA.	2.000
2'8" cone top	EA.	2.400
Precast manholes, 48" dia.		
4' deep	EA.	4.800
6' deep	EA.	6.000
7' deep	EA.	6.857
8' deep	EA.	8.000
10' deep	EA.	9.600
Cast-in-place, 48" dia., with frame and cover		
5' deep	EA.	12.000
6' deep	EA.	13.714
8' deep	EA.	16.000
10' deep	EA.	19.200
Brick manholes, 48" dia. with cover, 8" thick		
4' deep	EA.	8.000
6' deep	EA.	8.889
8' deep	EA.	10.000
10' deep	EA.	11.429
12' deep	EA.	13.333
14' deep	EA.	16.000
Inverts for manholes		
Single channel	EA.	3.200
Triple channel	EA.	4.000
Frames and covers, 24" diameter		
300 lb	EA.	0.800

Utilities	UNIT	MAN/HOURS
02605.30 Manholes		
400 lb	EA.	0.889
500 lb	EA.	1.143
Watertight, 350 lb	EA.	2.667
For heavy equipment, 1200 lb	EA.	4.000
Steps for manholes		
7" x 9"	EA.	0.160
8" x 9"	EA.	0.178
Curb inlet, 4' throat, cast in place		
12"-30" pipe	EA.	12.000
36"-48" pipe	EA.	13.714
Raise exist frame and cover, when repaving	EA.	4.800
02610.10 Cast Iron Flanged Pipe		
Cast iron flanged sections		
4" pipe, with one bolt set		
3' section	EA.	0.218
4' section	EA.	0.240
5' section	EA.	0.267
6' section	EA.	0.300
8' section	EA.	0.343
10' section	EA.	0.480
12' section	EA.	0.800
15' section	EA.	1.200
18' section	EA.	1.600
6" pipe, with one bolt set		
3' section	EA.	0.240
4' section	EA.	0.282
5' section	EA.	0.320
6' section	EA.	0.369
8' section	EA.	0.533
10' section	EA.	0.600
12' section	EA.	0.800
15' section	EA.	1.200
18' section	EA.	1.714
8" pipe, with one bolt set		
3' section	EA.	0.300
4' section	EA.	0.343
5' section	EA.	0.400
6' section	EA.	0.480
8' section	EA.	0.686
10' section	EA.	0.800
12' section	EA.	1.200
15' section	EA.	1.600
18' section	EA.	2.000
10" pipe, with one bolt set		
3' section	EA.	0.308
4' section	EA.	0.353
5' section	EA.	0.414
6' section	EA.	0.500
8' section	EA.	0.727
10' section	EA.	0.857
12' section	EA.	1.333
15' section	EA.	1.714
18' section	EA.	2.400

Utilities	UNIT	MAN/HOURS
02610.10 **Cast Iron Flanged Pipe**		
12" pipe, with one bolt set		
3' section	EA.	0.333
4' section	EA.	0.387
5' section	EA.	0.462
6' section	EA.	0.545
8' section	EA.	0.800
10' section	EA.	0.923
12' section	EA.	1.500
15' section	EA.	2.000
18' section	EA.	2.667
02610.11 **Cast Iron Fittings**		
Mechanical joint, with 2 bolt kits		
90 deg bend		
4"	EA.	0.533
6"	EA.	0.615
8"	EA.	0.800
10"	EA.	1.143
12"	EA.	1.600
14"	EA.	2.000
16"	EA.	2.667
45 deg bend		
4"	EA.	0.533
6"	EA.	0.615
8"	EA.	0.800
10"	EA.	1.143
12"	EA.	1.600
14"	EA.	2.000
16"	EA.	2.667
Tee, with 3 bolt kits		
4" x 4"	EA.	0.800
6" x 6"	EA.	1.000
8" x 8"	EA.	1.333
10" x 10"	EA.	2.000
12" x 12"	EA.	2.667
Wye, with 3 bolt kits		
6" x 6"	EA.	1.000
8" x 8"	EA.	1.333
10" x 10"	EA.	2.000
12" x 12"	EA.	2.667
Reducer, with 2 bolt kits		
6" x 4"	EA.	1.000
8" x 6"	EA.	1.333
10" x 8"	EA.	2.000
12" x 10"	EA.	2.667
Flanged, 90 deg bend, 125 lb.		
4"	EA.	0.667
6"	EA.	0.800
8"	EA.	1.000
10"	EA.	1.333
12"	EA.	2.000
14"	EA.	2.667
16"	EA.	2.667
Tee		

Utilities	UNIT	MAN/HOURS
02610.11 **Cast Iron Fittings**		
4"	EA.	1.000
6"	EA.	1.143
8"	EA.	1.333
10"	EA.	1.600
12"	EA.	2.000
14"	EA.	2.667
16"	EA.	4.000
02610.13 **Gate Valves**		
Gate valve, (AWWA) mechanical joint, with adjustable box		
4" valve	EA.	0.800
6" valve	EA.	0.960
8" valve	EA.	1.200
10" valve	EA.	1.412
12" valve	EA.	1.714
14" valve	EA.	2.000
16" valve	EA.	2.182
18" valve	EA.	2.400
Flanged, with box, post indicator (AWWA)		
4" valve	EA.	0.960
6" valve	EA.	1.091
8" valve	EA.	1.333
10" valve	EA.	1.600
12" valve	EA.	2.000
14" valve	EA.	2.400
16" valve	EA.	3.000
02610.15 **Water Meters**		
Water meter, displacement type		
1"	EA.	0.800
1-1/2"	EA.	0.889
2"	EA.	1.000
02610.17 **Corporation Stops**		
Stop for flared copper service pipe		
3/4"	EA.	0.400
1"	EA.	0.444
1-1/4"	EA.	0.533
1-1/2"	EA.	0.667
2"	EA.	0.800
02610.40 **Ductile Iron Pipe**		
Ductile iron pipe, cement lined, slip-on joints		
4"	L.F.	0.067
6"	L.F.	0.071
8"	L.F.	0.075
10"	L.F.	0.080
12"	L.F.	0.096
14"	L.F.	0.120
16"	L.F.	0.133
18"	L.F.	0.150
20"	L.F.	0.171
Mechanical joint pipe		
4"	L.F.	0.092

Utilities	UNIT	MAN/HOURS
02610.40 Ductile Iron Pipe		
6"	L.F.	0.100
8"	L.F.	0.109
10"	L.F.	0.120
12"	L.F.	0.160
14"	L.F.	0.185
16"	L.F.	0.218
18"	L.F.	0.240
20"	L.F.	0.267
Fittings, mechanical joint		
90 degree elbow		
4"	EA.	0.533
6"	EA.	0.615
8"	EA.	0.800
10"	EA.	1.143
12"	EA.	1.600
14"	EA.	2.000
16"	EA.	2.667
18"	EA.	3.200
20"	EA.	4.000
45 degree elbow		
4"	EA.	0.533
6"	EA.	0.615
8"	EA.	0.800
10"	EA.	1.143
12"	EA.	1.600
14"	EA.	2.000
16"	EA.	2.667
18"	EA.	4.000
20"	EA.	4.000
Tee		
4"x3"	EA.	1.000
4"x4"	EA.	1.000
6"x3"	EA.	1.143
6"x4"	EA.	1.143
6"x6"	EA.	1.143
8"x4"	EA.	1.333
8"x6"	EA.	1.333
8"x8"	EA.	1.333
10"x4"	EA.	1.600
10"x6"	EA.	1.600
10"x8"	EA.	1.600
10"x10"	EA.	1.600
12"x4"	EA.	2.000
12"x6"	EA.	2.000
12"x8"	EA.	2.000
12"x10"	EA.	2.000
12"x12"	EA.	2.133
14"x4"	EA.	2.286
14"x6"	EA.	2.286
14"x8"	EA.	2.286
14"x10"	EA.	2.286
14"x12"	EA.	2.462
14"x14"	EA.	2.462
16"x4"	EA.	2.667

Utilities	UNIT	MAN/HOURS
02610.40 Ductile Iron Pipe		
16"x6"	EA.	2.667
16"x8"	EA.	2.667
16"x10"	EA.	2.667
16"x12"	EA.	2.667
16"x14"	EA.	2.667
16"x16"	EA.	2.667
18"x6"	EA.	2.909
18"x8"	EA.	2.909
18"x10"	EA.	2.909
18"x12"	EA.	2.909
18"x14"	EA.	2.909
18"x16"	EA.	2.909
18"x18"	EA.	2.909
20"x6"	EA.	3.200
20"x8"	EA.	3.200
20"x10"	EA.	3.200
20"x12"	EA.	3.200
20"x14"	EA.	3.200
20"x16"	EA.	3.200
20"x18"	EA.	3.200
20"x20"	EA.	3.200
Cross		
4"x3"	EA.	1.333
4"x4"	EA.	1.333
6"x3"	EA.	1.600
6"x4"	EA.	1.600
6"x6"	EA.	1.600
8"x4"	EA.	1.778
8"x6"	EA.	1.778
8"x8"	EA.	1.778
10"x4"	EA.	2.000
10"x6"	EA.	2.000
10"x8"	EA.	2.000
10"x10"	EA.	2.000
12"x4"	EA.	2.286
12"x6"	EA.	2.286
12"x8"	EA.	2.286
12"x10"	EA.	2.462
12"x12"	EA.	2.462
14"x4"	EA.	2.667
14"x6"	EA.	2.667
14"x8"	EA.	2.667
14"x10"	EA.	2.667
14"x12"	EA.	2.909
14"x14"	EA.	2.909
16"x4"	EA.	3.200
16"x6"	EA.	3.200
16"x8"	EA.	3.200
16"x10"	EA.	3.200
16"x12"	EA.	3.200
16"x14"	EA.	3.200
16"x16"	EA.	3.200
18"x6"	EA.	3.556
18"x8"	EA.	3.556

Utilities		UNIT	MAN/HOURS
02610.40	**Ductile Iron Pipe**		
18"x10"		EA.	3.556
18"x12"		EA.	3.556
18"x14"		EA.	3.556
18"x16"		EA.	3.556
18"x18"		EA.	3.556
20"x6"		EA.	3.810
20"x8"		EA.	3.810
20"x10"		EA.	3.810
20"x12"		EA.	3.810
20"x14"		EA.	3.810
20"x16"		EA.	3.810
20"x18"		EA.	4.000
20"x20"		EA.	4.000
02610.60	**Plastic Pipe**		
PVC, class 150 pipe			
4" dia.		L.F.	0.060
6" dia.		L.F.	0.065
8" dia.		L.F.	0.069
10" dia.		L.F.	0.075
12" dia.		L.F.	0.080
Schedule 40 pipe			
1-1/2" dia.		L.F.	0.047
2" dia.		L.F.	0.050
2-1/2" dia.		L.F.	0.053
3" dia.		L.F.	0.057
4" dia.		L.F.	0.067
6" dia.		L.F.	0.080
90 degree elbows			
1"		EA.	0.133
1-1/2"		EA.	0.133
2"		EA.	0.145
2-1/2"		EA.	0.160
3"		EA.	0.178
4"		EA.	0.200
6"		EA.	0.267
45 degree elbows			
1"		EA.	0.133
1-1/2"		EA.	0.133
2"		EA.	0.145
2-1/2"		EA.	0.160
3"		EA.	0.178
4"		EA.	0.200
6"		EA.	0.267
Tees			
1"		EA.	0.160
1-1/2"		EA.	0.160
2"		EA.	0.178
2-1/2"		EA.	0.200
3"		EA.	0.229
4"		EA.	0.267
6"		EA.	0.320
Couplings			
1"		EA.	0.133

Utilities		UNIT	MAN/HOURS
02610.60	**Plastic Pipe**		
1-1/2"		EA.	0.133
2"		EA.	0.145
2-1/2"		EA.	0.160
3"		EA.	0.178
4"		EA.	0.200
6"		EA.	0.267
Drainage pipe			
PVC schedule 80			
1" dia.		L.F.	0.047
1-1/2" dia.		L.F.	0.047
ABS, 2" dia.		L.F.	0.050
2-1/2" dia.		L.F.	0.053
3" dia.		L.F.	0.057
4" dia.		L.F.	0.067
6" dia.		L.F.	0.080
8" dia.		L.F.	0.063
10" dia.		L.F.	0.075
12" dia.		L.F.	0.080
90 degree elbows			
1"		EA.	0.133
1-1/2"		EA.	0.133
2"		EA.	0.145
2-1/2"		EA.	0.160
3"		EA.	0.178
4"		EA.	0.200
6"		EA.	0.267
45 degree elbows			
1"		EA.	0.133
1-1/2"		EA.	0.133
2"		EA.	0.145
2-1/2"		EA.	0.160
3"		EA.	0.178
4"		EA.	0.200
6"		EA.	0.267
Tees			
1"		EA.	0.160
1-1/2"		EA.	0.160
2"		EA.	0.178
2-1/2"		EA.	0.200
3"		EA.	0.229
4"		EA.	0.267
6"		EA.	0.320
Couplings			
1"		EA.	0.133
1-1/2"		EA.	0.133
2"		EA.	0.145
2-1/2"		EA.	0.160
3"		EA.	0.178
4"		EA.	0.200
6"		EA.	0.267
Pressure pipe			
PVC, class 200 pipe			
3/4"		L.F.	0.040
1"		L.F.	0.042

Utilities	UNIT	MAN/HOURS
02610.60 — Plastic Pipe		
1-1/4"	L.F.	0.044
1-1/2"	L.F.	0.047
2"	L.F.	0.050
2-1/2"	L.F.	0.053
3"	L.F.	0.057
4"	L.F.	0.067
6"	L.F.	0.080
8"	L.F.	0.069
90 degree elbows		
3/4"	EA.	0.133
1"	EA.	0.133
1-1/4"	EA.	0.133
1-1/2"	EA.	0.133
2"	EA.	0.145
2-1/2"	EA.	0.160
3"	EA.	0.178
4"	EA.	0.200
6"	EA.	0.267
8"	EA.	0.400
45 degree elbows		
3/4"	EA.	0.133
1"	EA.	0.133
1-1/4"	EA.	0.133
1-1/2"	EA.	0.133
2"	EA.	0.145
2-1/2"	EA.	0.160
3"	EA.	0.178
4"	EA.	0.200
6"	EA.	0.267
8"	EA.	0.400
Tees		
3/4"	EA.	0.160
1"	EA.	0.160
1-1/4"	EA.	0.160
1-1/2"	EA.	0.160
2"	EA.	0.178
2-1/2"	EA.	0.200
3"	EA.	0.229
4"	EA.	0.267
6"	EA.	0.320
8"	EA.	0.444
Couplings		
3/4"	EA.	0.133
1"	EA.	0.133
1-1/4"	EA.	0.133
1-1/2"	EA.	0.133
2"	EA.	0.145
2-1/2"	EA.	0.160
3"	EA.	0.178
4"	EA.	0.178
6"	EA.	0.200
8"	EA.	0.267

Utilities	UNIT	MAN/HOURS
02610.90 — Vitrified Clay Pipe		
Vitrified clay pipe, extra strength		
6" dia.	L.F.	0.109
8" dia.	L.F.	0.114
10" dia.	L.F.	0.120
12" dia.	L.F.	0.160
15" dia.	L.F.	0.240
18" dia.	L.F.	0.267
24" dia.	L.F.	0.343
30" dia.	L.F.	0.480
36" dia.	L.F.	0.686
02630.10 — Tapping Saddles & Sleeves		
Tapping saddle, tap size to 2"		
4" saddle	EA.	0.400
6" saddle	EA.	0.500
8" saddle	EA.	0.667
10" saddle	EA.	0.800
12" saddle	EA.	1.143
14" saddle	EA.	1.600
Tapping sleeve		
4x4	EA.	0.533
6x4	EA.	0.615
6x6	EA.	0.615
8x4	EA.	0.800
8x6	EA.	0.800
10x4	EA.	0.960
10x6	EA.	0.960
10x8	EA.	0.960
10x10	EA.	1.000
12x4	EA.	1.000
12x6	EA.	1.091
12x8	EA.	1.200
12x10	EA.	1.333
12x12	EA.	1.500
Tapping valve, mechanical joint		
4" valve	EA.	3.000
6" valve	EA.	4.000
8" valve	EA.	6.000
10" valve	EA.	8.000
12" valve	EA.	12.000
Tap hole in pipe		
4" hole	EA.	1.000
6" hole	EA.	1.600
8" hole	EA.	2.667
10" hole	EA.	3.200
12" hole	EA.	4.000
02640.15 — Valve Boxes		
Valve box, adjustable, for valves up to 20"		
3' deep	EA.	0.267
4' deep	EA.	0.320
5' deep	EA.	0.400

Utilities	UNIT	MAN/ HOURS
02640.19 **Thrust Blocks**		
Thrust block, 3000# concrete		
1/4 c.y.	EA.	1.333
1/2 c.y.	EA.	1.600
3/4 c.y.	EA.	2.667
1 c.y.	EA.	5.333
02645.10 **Fire Hydrants**		
Standard, 3 way post, 6" mechanical joint		
2' deep	EA.	8.000
4' deep	EA.	9.600
6' deep	EA.	12.000
8' deep	EA.	13.714
02665.10 **Chilled Water Systems**		
Chilled water pipe, 2" thick insulation, w/casing		
Align and tack weld on sleepers		
1-1/2" dia.	L.F.	0.022
3" dia.	L.F.	0.034
4" dia.	L.F.	0.048
6" dia.	L.F.	0.060
8" dia.	L.F.	0.069
10" dia.	L.F.	0.080
12" dia.	L.F.	0.096
14" dia.	L.F.	0.104
16" dia.	L.F.	0.120
Align and tack weld on trench bottom		
18" dia.	L.F.	0.133
20" dia.	L.F.	0.150
Preinsulated fittings		
Align and tack weld on sleepers		
Elbows		
1-1/2"	EA.	0.500
3"	EA.	0.800
4"	EA.	1.000
6"	EA.	1.333
8"	EA.	1.600
Tees		
1-1/2"	EA.	0.533
3"	EA.	0.889
4"	EA.	1.143
6"	EA.	1.600
8"	EA.	2.000
Reducers		
3"	EA.	0.667
4"	EA.	0.800
6"	EA.	1.000
8"	EA.	1.333
Anchors, not including concrete		
4"	EA.	1.000
6"	EA.	1.000
Align and tack weld on trench bottom		
Elbows		
10"	EA.	1.500
12"	EA.	1.714

Utilities	UNIT	MAN/ HOURS
02665.10 **Chilled Water Systems**		
14"	EA.	1.846
16"	EA.	2.000
18"	EA.	2.182
20"	EA.	2.400
Tees		
10"	EA.	1.500
12"	EA.	1.714
14"	EA.	1.846
16"	EA.	2.000
18"	EA.	2.182
20"	EA.	2.400
Reducers		
10"	EA.	1.000
12"	EA.	1.091
14"	EA.	1.200
16"	EA.	1.333
18"	EA.	1.500
20"	EA.	1.714
Anchors, not including concrete		
10"	EA.	1.000
12"	EA.	1.091
14"	EA.	1.200
16"	EA.	1.333
18"	EA.	1.500
20"	EA.	1.714
02670.10 **Wells**		
Domestic water, drilled and cased		
4" dia.	L.F.	0.480
6" dia.	L.F.	0.533
8" dia.	L.F.	0.600
02685.10 **Gas Distribution**		
Gas distribution lines		
Polyethylene, 60 psi coils		
1-1/4" dia.	L.F.	0.053
1-1/2" dia.	L.F.	0.057
2" dia.	L.F.	0.067
3" dia.	L.F.	0.080
30' pipe lengths		
3" dia.	L.F.	0.089
4" dia.	L.F.	0.100
6" dia.	L.F.	0.133
8" dia.	L.F.	0.160
Steel, schedule 40, plain end		
1" dia.	L.F.	0.067
2" dia.	L.F.	0.073
3" dia.	L.F.	0.080
4" dia.	L.F.	0.160
5" dia.	L.F.	0.171
6" dia.	L.F.	0.200
8" dia.	L.F.	0.218
Natural gas meters, direct digital reading, threaded		
250 cfh @ 5 lbs	EA.	1.600

Utilities

	UNIT	MAN/HOURS
02685.10 Gas Distribution		
425 cfh @ 10 lbs	EA.	1.600
800 cfh @ 20 lbs	EA.	2.000
1,000 cfh @ 25 lbs	EA.	2.000
1,400 cfh @ 100 lbs	EA.	2.667
2,300 cfh @ 100 lbs	EA.	4.000
5,000 cfh @ 100 lbs	EA.	8.000
Gas pressure regulators		
Threaded		
3/4"	EA.	1.000
1"	EA.	1.333
1-1/4"	EA.	1.333
1-1/2"	EA.	1.333
2"	EA.	1.600
Flanged		
3"	EA.	2.000
4"	EA.	2.667
02690.10 Storage Tanks		
Oil storage tank, underground		
Steel		
500 gals	EA.	3.000
1,000 gals	EA.	4.000
4,000 gals	EA.	8.000
5,000 gals	EA.	12.000
10,000 gals	EA.	24.000
Fiberglass, double wall		
550 gals	EA.	4.000
1,000 gals	EA.	4.000
2,000 gals	EA.	6.000
4,000 gals	EA.	12.000
6,000 gals	EA.	16.000
8,000 gals	EA.	24.000
10,000 gals	EA.	30.000
12,000 gals	EA.	40.000
15,000 gals	EA.	53.333
20,000 gals	EA.	60.000
Above ground		
Steel		
275 gals	EA.	2.400
500 gals	EA.	4.000
1,000 gals	EA.	4.800
1,500 gals	EA.	6.000
2,000 gals	EA.	8.000
5,000 gals	EA.	12.000
Fill cap	EA.	0.800
Vent cap	EA.	0.800
Level indicator	EA.	0.800
02695.40 Steel Pipe		
Steel pipe, extra heavy, A 53, grade B, seamless		
1/2" dia.	L.F.	0.080
3/4" dia.	L.F.	0.084
1" dia.	L.F.	0.089
1-1/4" dia.	L.F.	0.100

Utilities

	UNIT	MAN/HOURS
02695.40 Steel Pipe		
1-1/2" dia.	L.F.	0.114
2" dia.	L.F.	0.133
3" dia.	L.F.	0.120
4" dia.	L.F.	0.133
6" dia.	L.F.	0.150
8" dia.	L.F.	0.171
10" dia.	L.F.	0.200
12" dia.	L.F.	0.240
02695.80 Steam Meters		
In-line turbine, direct reading, 300 lb, flanged		
2"	EA.	1.000
3"	EA.	1.333
4"	EA.	1.600
Threaded, 2"		
5" line	EA.	8.000
6" line	EA.	8.000
8" line	EA.	8.000
10" line	EA.	8.000
12" line	EA.	8.000
14" line	EA.	8.000
16" line	EA.	8.000

Sewerage And Drainage

	UNIT	MAN/HOURS
02720.10 Catch Basins		
Standard concrete catch basin		
Cast in place, 3'8" x 3'8", 6" thick wall		
2' deep	EA.	6.000
3' deep	EA.	6.000
4' deep	EA.	8.000
5' deep	EA.	8.000
6' deep	EA.	9.600
4'x4', 8" thick wall, cast in place		
2' deep	EA.	6.000
3' deep	EA.	6.000
4' deep	EA.	8.000
5' deep	EA.	8.000
6' deep	EA.	9.600
Frames and covers, cast iron		
Round		
24" dia.	EA.	2.000
26" dia.	EA.	2.000
28" dia.	EA.	2.000
Rectangular		
23"x23"	EA.	2.000
27"x20"	EA.	2.000

Sewerage And Drainage	UNIT	MAN/HOURS
02720.10 — Catch Basins		
24"x24"	EA.	2.000
26"x26"	EA.	2.000
Curb inlet frames and covers		
27"x27"	EA.	2.000
24"x36"	EA.	2.000
24"x25"	EA.	2.000
24"x22"	EA.	2.000
20"x22"	EA.	2.000
Airfield catch basin frame and grating, galvanized		
2'x4'	EA.	2.000
2'x2'	EA.	2.000
02720.40 — Storm Drainage		
Headwalls, cast in place, 30 deg wingwall		
12" pipe	EA.	2.000
15" pipe	EA.	2.000
18" pipe	EA.	2.286
24" pipe	EA.	2.286
30" pipe	EA.	2.667
36" pipe	EA.	4.000
42" pipe	EA.	4.000
48" pipe	EA.	5.333
54" pipe	EA.	6.667
60" pipe	EA.	8.000
4" cleanout for storm drain		
4" pipe	EA.	1.000
6" pipe	EA.	1.000
8" pipe	EA.	1.000
Connect new drain line		
To existing manhole	EA.	2.667
To new manhole	EA.	1.600
02720.45 — Storm Drainage, Con. Pipe		
Concrete pipe		
Unreinforced, plain, bell and spigot, Class II		
Pipe diameter 6"	L.F.	0.109
8"	L.F.	0.120
10"	L.F.	0.126
12"	L.F.	0.133
15"	L.F.	0.141
18"	L.F.	0.150
21"	L.F.	0.160
24"	L.F.	0.171
Reinforced, bell and spigot, Class III		
Pipe diameter 12"	L.F.	0.133
15"	L.F.	0.141
18"	L.F.	0.150
21"	L.F.	0.160
24"	L.F.	0.171
27"	L.F.	0.185
30"	L.F.	0.200
36"	L.F.	0.218
42"	L.F.	0.240
48"	L.F.	0.267

Sewerage And Drainage	UNIT	MAN/HOURS
02720.45 — Storm Drainage, Con. Pipe		
54"	L.F.	0.300
60"	L.F.	0.343
66"	L.F.	0.400
72"	L.F.	0.480
78"	L.F.	0.533
84"	L.F.	0.600
90"	L.F.	0.649
96"	L.F.	0.686
Class IV		
Pipe diameter 12"	L.F.	0.133
15"	L.F.	0.141
18"	L.F.	0.150
21"	L.F.	0.160
24"	L.F.	0.171
27"	L.F.	0.185
30"	L.F.	0.200
36"	L.F.	0.218
42"	L.F.	0.240
48"	L.F.	0.267
54"	L.F.	0.300
60"	L.F.	0.343
66"	L.F.	0.400
72"	L.F.	0.480
78"	L.F.	0.533
84"	L.F.	0.600
90"	L.F.	0.649
96"	L.F.	0.686
Class V		
Pipe diameter 12"	L.F.	0.133
15"	L.F.	0.141
18"	L.F.	0.150
21"	L.F.	0.160
24"	L.F.	0.171
27"	L.F.	0.185
30"	L.F.	0.200
36"	L.F.	0.218
42"	L.F.	0.240
48"	L.F.	0.267
54"	L.F.	0.300
60"	L.F.	0.343
66"	L.F.	0.400
72"	L.F.	0.480
78"	L.F.	0.533
84"	L.F.	0.600
90"	L.F.	0.649
96"	L.F.	0.686
Eliptical pipe, reinforced		
Class III		
20" x 30"	L.F.	0.171
22" x 34 "	L.F.	0.185
24" x 38"	L.F.	0.200
27" x 42"	L.F.	0.218
29" x 45"	L.F.	0.229
32" x 49"	L.F.	0.240

Sewerage And Drainage

02720.45 — Storm Drainage, Con. Pipe

	UNIT	MAN/HOURS
34" x 54"	L.F.	0.267
38" x 60"	L.F.	0.300
43" x 68"	L.F.	0.343
48" x 76"	L.F.	0.369
53" x 83"	L.F.	0.400
62" x 98"	L.F.	0.480
82" x 128"	L.F.	0.686
Flared end section pipe		
Pipe diameter 12"	L.F.	0.133
15"	L.F.	0.141
18"	L.F.	0.150
24"	L.F.	0.171
30"	L.F.	0.200
36"	L.F.	0.218
42"	L.F.	0.240
48"	L.F.	0.267
54"	L.F.	0.300
60"	L.F.	0.343
Porous concrete pipe, standard strength		
Pipe diameter 4"	L.F.	0.092
6"	L.F.	0.096
8"	L.F.	0.100
10"	L.F.	0.104
12"	L.F.	0.104

02720.50 — Storm Drainage, Steel Pipe

	UNIT	MAN/HOURS
Steel pipe		
Coated,corrugated metal pipe, paved invert		
16 gauge, pipe diameter 8"	L.F.	0.080
12"	L.F.	0.086
15"	L.F.	0.092
18"	L.F.	0.100
21"	L.F.	0.109
24"	L.F.	0.120
30"	L.F.	0.133
36"	L.F.	0.150
42"	L.F.	0.160
48"	L.F.	0.171
14 gauge, pipe diameter 12"	L.F.	0.086
15"	L.F.	0.092
18"	L.F.	0.100
21"	L.F.	0.109
24"	L.F.	0.120
30"	L.F.	0.133
36"	L.F.	0.150
42"	L.F.	0.160
48"	L.F.	0.171
54"	L.F.	0.185
60"	L.F.	0.200
66"	L.F.	0.218
12 gauge, pipe diameter 18"	L.F.	0.100
21"	L.F.	0.109
24"	L.F.	0.120
30"	L.F.	0.133

Sewerage And Drainage

02720.50 — Storm Drainage, Steel Pipe

	UNIT	MAN/HOURS
36"	L.F.	0.150
42"	L.F.	0.160
48"	L.F.	0.171
54"	L.F.	0.185
60"	L.F.	0.200
66"	L.F.	0.218
72"	L.F.	0.240
78"	L.F.	0.253
10 gauge, pipe diameter 24"	L.F.	0.120
30"	L.F.	0.133
36"	L.F.	0.150
42"	L.F.	0.160
48"	L.F.	0.171
54"	L.F.	0.185
60"	L.F.	0.200
66"	L.F.	0.218
72"	L.F.	0.240
78"	L.F.	0.253
84"	L.F.	0.267
90"	L.F.	0.282
8 gauge, pipe diameter 48"	L.F.	0.171
54"	L.F.	0.185
60"	L.F.	0.200
66"	L.F.	0.218
72"	L.F.	0.240
78"	L.F.	0.253
84"	L.F.	0.267
90"	L.F.	0.282
96"	L.F.	0.300
Plain,corrugated metal pipe		
16 gauge, pipe diameter 8"	L.F.	0.080
12"	L.F.	0.086
15"	L.F.	0.092
18"	L.F.	0.100
21"	L.F.	0.109
24"	L.F.	0.120
30"	L.F.	0.133
36"	L.F.	0.150
42"	L.F.	0.160
48"	L.F.	0.171
14 gauge, pipe diameter 12"	L.F.	0.086
15"	L.F.	0.092
18"	L.F.	0.100
21"	L.F.	0.109
24"	L.F.	0.120
30"	L.F.	0.133
36"	L.F.	0.150
42"	L.F.	0.160
48"	L.F.	0.171
54"	L.F.	0.185
60"	L.F.	0.200
66"	L.F.	0.218
12 gauge, pipe diameter 18"	L.F.	0.100
21"	L.F.	0.109

Sewerage And Drainage	UNIT	MAN/HOURS
02720.50 Storm Drainage, Steel Pipe		
24"	L.F.	0.120
30"	L.F.	0.133
36"	L.F.	0.150
42"	L.F.	0.160
48"	L.F.	0.171
54"	L.F.	0.185
60"	L.F.	0.200
66"	L.F.	0.218
72"	L.F.	0.240
78"	L.F.	0.253
10 gauge, pipe diameter 24"	L.F.	0.120
30"	L.F.	0.133
36"	L.F.	0.150
42"	L.F.	0.160
48"	L.F.	0.171
54"	L.F.	0.185
60"	L.F.	0.200
66"	L.F.	0.218
72"	L.F.	0.240
78"	L.F.	0.253
84"	L.F.	0.267
90"	L.F.	0.282
8 gauge, pipe diameter 48"	L.F.	0.171
54"	L.F.	0.185
60"	L.F.	0.200
66"	L.F.	0.218
72"	L.F.	0.240
78"	L.F.	0.253
84"	L.F.	0.267
90"	L.F.	0.282
96"	L.F.	0.300
Steel arch		
Coated, corrugated		
16 gauge, 17" x 13"	L.F.	0.109
21" x 15"	L.F.	0.120
14 gauge, 29" x 18"	L.F.	0.133
36" x 22"	L.F.	0.171
12 gauge, 43" x 28"	L.F.	0.200
50" x 30"	L.F.	0.218
58" x 36"	L.F.	0.240
66" x 40"	L.F.	0.253
72" x 44"	L.F.	0.267
Plain, corrugated		
16 gauge, 17" x 13"	L.F.	0.109
21" x 15"	L.F.	0.120
14 gauge, 29" x 18"	L.F.	0.133
36" x 22"	L.F.	0.171
12 gauge, 43" x 28"	L.F.	0.200
50" x 30"	L.F.	0.218
58" x 36"	L.F.	0.240
66" x 40"	L.F.	0.253
72" x 44"	L.F.	0.267
Nestable corrugated metal pipe		
16 gauge, pipe diameter 10"	L.F.	0.083

Sewerage And Drainage	UNIT	MAN/HOURS
02720.50 Storm Drainage, Steel Pipe		
12"	L.F.	0.086
15"	L.F.	0.092
18"	L.F.	0.100
24"	L.F.	0.120
30"	L.F.	0.133
14 gauge, pipe diameter 12"	L.F.	0.086
15"	L.F.	0.092
18"	L.F.	0.100
24"	L.F.	0.120
30"	L.F.	0.133
36"	L.F.	0.150
02720.70 Underdrain		
Drain tile, clay		
6" pipe	L.F.	0.053
8" pipe	L.F.	0.056
12" pipe	L.F.	0.060
Porous concrete, standard strength		
6" pipe	L.F.	0.053
8" pipe	L.F.	0.056
12" pipe	L.F.	0.060
15" pipe	L.F.	0.067
18" pipe	L.F.	0.080
Corrugated metal pipe, perforated type		
6" pipe	L.F.	0.060
8" pipe	L.F.	0.063
10" pipe	L.F.	0.067
12" pipe	L.F.	0.071
18" pipe	L.F.	0.075
Perforated clay pipe		
6" pipe	L.F.	0.069
8" pipe	L.F.	0.071
12" pipe	L.F.	0.073
Drain tile, concrete		
6" pipe	L.F.	0.053
8" pipe	L.F.	0.056
12" pipe	L.F.	0.060
Perforated rigid PVC underdrain pipe		
4" pipe	L.F.	0.040
6" pipe	L.F.	0.048
8" pipe	L.F.	0.053
10" pipe	L.F.	0.060
12" pipe	L.F.	0.069
Underslab drainage, crushed stone		
3" thick	S.F.	0.008
4" thick	S.F.	0.009
6" thick	S.F.	0.010
8" thick	S.F.	0.010
Plastic filter fabric for drain lines	S.F.	0.008
Gravel fill in trench, crushed or bank run, 1/2" to 3/4"	C.Y.	0.600

Sewerage And Drainage	UNIT	MAN/HOURS
02730.10 Sanitary Sewers		
Clay		
6" pipe	L.F.	0.080
8" pipe	L.F.	0.086
10" pipe	L.F.	0.092
12" pipe	L.F.	0.100
PVC		
4" pipe	L.F.	0.060
6" pipe	L.F.	0.063
8" pipe	L.F.	0.067
10" pipe	L.F.	0.071
12" pipe	L.F.	0.075
Cleanout		
4" pipe	EA.	1.000
6" pipe	EA.	1.000
8" pipe	EA.	1.000
Connect new sewer line		
To existing manhole	EA.	2.667
To new manhole	EA.	1.600
02740.10 Drainage Fields		
Perforated PVC pipe, for drain field		
4" pipe	L.F.	0.053
6" pipe	L.F.	0.057
02740.50 Septic Tanks		
Septic tank, precast concrete		
1000 gals	EA.	4.000
2000 gals	EA.	6.000
5000 gals	EA.	12.000
25,000 gals	EA.	48.000
40,000 gals	EA.	80.000
Leaching pit, precast concrete, 72" diameter		
3' deep	EA.	3.000
6' deep	EA.	3.429
8' deep	EA.	4.000
02760.10 Pipeline Restoration		
Relining existing water main		
6" dia.	L.F.	0.240
8" dia.	L.F.	0.253
10" dia.	L.F.	0.267
12" dia.	L.F.	0.282
14" dia.	L.F.	0.300
16" dia.	L.F.	0.320
18" dia.	L.F.	0.343
20" dia.	L.F.	0.369
24" dia.	L.F.	0.400
36" dia.	L.F.	0.480
48" dia.	L.F.	0.533
72" dia.	L.F.	0.600
Replacing in line gate valves		
6" valve	EA.	3.200
8" valve	EA.	4.000
10" valve	EA.	4.800

Sewerage And Drainage	UNIT	MAN/HOURS
02760.10 Pipeline Restoration		
12" valve	EA.	6.000
16" valve	EA.	6.857
18" valve	EA.	8.000
20" valve	EA.	9.600
24" valve	EA.	12.000
36" valve	EA.	16.000

Power & Communications	UNIT	MAN/HOURS
02780.20 High Voltage Cable		
High voltage XLP copper cable, shielded, 5000v		
#6 awg	L.F.	0.013
#4 awg	L.F.	0.016
#2 awg	L.F.	0.019
#1 awg	L.F.	0.021
#1/0 awg	L.F.	0.024
#2/0 awg	L.F.	0.029
#3/0 awg	L.F.	0.034
#4/0 awg	L.F.	0.036
#250 awg	L.F.	0.043
#300 awg	L.F.	0.048
#350 awg	L.F.	0.053
#500 awg	L.F.	0.073
#750 awg	L.F.	0.080
Ungrounded, 15,000v		
#1 awg	L.F.	0.031
#1/0 awg	L.F.	0.034
#2/0 awg	L.F.	0.036
#3/0 awg	L.F.	0.040
#4/0 awg	L.F.	0.046
#250 awg	L.F.	0.048
#300 awg	L.F.	0.053
#350 awg	L.F.	0.062
#500 awg	L.F.	0.080
#750 awg	L.F.	0.098
#1000 awg	L.F.	0.123
Aluminum cable, shielded, 5000v		
#6 awg	L.F.	0.011
#4 awg	L.F.	0.013
#2 awg	L.F.	0.015
#1 awg	L.F.	0.017
#1/0 awg	L.F.	0.019
#2/0 awg	L.F.	0.020
#3/0 awg	L.F.	0.021
#4/0 awg	L.F.	0.024
#250 awg	L.F.	0.026
#300 awg	L.F.	0.031

Power & Communications	UNIT	MAN/HOURS
02780.20 High Voltage Cable		
#350 awg	L.F.	0.034
#500 awg	L.F.	0.036
#750 awg	L.F.	0.044
#1000 awg	L.F.	0.050
Ungrounded, 15,000v		
#1 awg	L.F.	0.021
#1/0 awg	L.F.	0.025
#2/0 awg	L.F.	0.027
#3/0 awg	L.F.	0.028
#4/0 awg	L.F.	0.029
#250 awg	L.F.	0.031
#300 awg	L.F.	0.032
#350 awg	L.F.	0.036
#500 awg	L.F.	0.043
#750 awg	L.F.	0.052
#1000 awg	L.F.	0.064
Indoor terminations, 5000v		
#6 - #4	EA.	0.157
#2 - #2/0	EA.	0.157
#3/0 - #250	EA.	0.157
#300 - #750	EA.	2.759
#1000	EA.	3.810
In-line splice, 5000v		
#6 - #4/0	EA.	3.810
#250 - #500	EA.	10.000
#750 - #1000	EA.	13.008
T-splice, 5000v		
#2 - #4/0	EA.	11.994
#250 - #500	EA.	20.000
#750 - #1000	EA.	25.000
Indoor terminations, 15,000v		
#2 - #2/0	EA.	3.478
#3/0 - #500	EA.	5.333
#750 - #1000	EA.	6.154
In-line splice, 15,000v		
#2 - #4/0	EA.	8.999
#250 - #500	EA.	11.994
#750 - #1000	EA.	18.018
T-splice, 15,000v		
#4	EA.	18.018
#250 - #500	EA.	29.963
#750 - #1000	EA.	44.944
Compression lugs, 15,000v		
#4	EA.	0.400
#2	EA.	0.533
#1	EA.	0.533
#1/0	EA.	0.667
#2/0	EA.	0.667
#3/0	EA.	0.851
#4/0	EA.	0.851
#250	EA.	0.952
#300	EA.	0.952
#350	EA.	1.159
#500	EA.	1.250

Power & Communications	UNIT	MAN/HOURS
02780.20 High Voltage Cable		
#750	EA.	1.509
#1000	EA.	1.905
Compression splices, 15,000v		
#4	EA.	0.667
#2	EA.	0.727
#1	EA.	0.899
#1/0	EA.	1.000
#2/0	EA.	1.159
#3/0	EA.	1.250
#4/0	EA.	1.404
#250	EA.	1.509
#350	EA.	1.739
#500	EA.	2.000
#750	EA.	2.500
02780.40 Supports & Connectors		
Cable supports for conduit		
1-1/2"	EA.	0.348
2"	EA.	0.348
2-1/2"	EA.	0.400
3"	EA.	0.400
3-1/2"	EA.	0.500
4"	EA.	0.500
5"	EA.	0.667
6"	EA.	0.727
Split bolt connectors		
#10	EA.	0.200
#8	EA.	0.200
#6	EA.	0.200
#4	EA.	0.400
#3	EA.	0.400
#2	EA.	0.400
#1/0	EA.	0.667
#2/0	EA.	0.667
#3/0	EA.	0.667
#4/0	EA.	0.667
#250	EA.	1.000
#350	EA.	1.000
#500	EA.	1.000
#750	EA.	1.509
#1000	EA.	1.509
Single barrel lugs		
#6	EA.	0.250
#1/0	EA.	0.500
#250	EA.	0.667
#350	EA.	0.667
#500	EA.	0.667
#600	EA.	0.899
#800	EA.	0.899
#1000	EA.	0.899
Double barrel lugs		
#1/0	EA.	0.899
#250	EA.	1.290
#350	EA.	1.290

Power & Communications	UNIT	MAN/HOURS
02780.40 Supports & Connectors		
#600	EA.	1.905
#800	EA.	1.905
#1000	EA.	1.905
Three barrel lugs		
#2/0	EA.	1.290
#250	EA.	1.905
#350	EA.	1.905
#600	EA.	2.667
#800	EA.	2.667
#1000	EA.	2.667
Four barrel lugs		
#250	EA.	2.759
#350	EA.	2.759
#600	EA.	3.478
#800	EA.	3.478
Compression conductor adapters		
#6	EA.	0.296
#4	EA.	0.348
#2	EA.	0.444
#1	EA.	0.444
#1/0	EA.	0.533
#250	EA.	0.800
#350	EA.	0.851
#500	EA.	1.096
#750	EA.	1.143
Terminal blocks, 2 screw		
3 circuit	EA.	0.200
6 circuit	EA.	0.200
8 circuit	EA.	0.200
10 circuit	EA.	0.296
12 circuit	EA.	0.296
18 circuit	EA.	0.296
24 circuit	EA.	0.348
36 circuit	EA.	0.348
Compression splice		
#8 awg	EA.	0.381
#6 awg	EA.	0.276
#4 awg	EA.	0.276
#2 awg	EA.	0.533
#1 awg	EA.	0.533
#1/0 awg	EA.	0.533
#2/0 awg	EA.	0.851
#3/0 awg	EA.	0.851
#4/0 awg	EA.	0.851
#250 awg	EA.	1.356
#300 awg	EA.	1.356
#350 awg	EA.	1.404
#400 awg	EA.	1.404
#500 awg	EA.	1.509
#600 awg	EA.	1.509
#750 awg	EA.	1.739
#1000 awg	EA.	1.739

Site Improvements	UNIT	MAN/HOURS
02810.40 Lawn Irrigation		
Pipe		
Schedule 40, PVC		
1/2"	L.F.	0.042
3/4"	L.F.	0.044
1"	L.F.	0.046
1-1/4"	L.F.	0.046
1-1/2"	L.F.	0.047
2"	L.F.	0.050
2-1/2"	L.F.	0.053
3"	L.F.	0.057
4"	L.F.	0.067
6"	L.F.	0.080
Class 200		
3/4"	L.F.	0.044
1"	L.F.	0.046
1-1/4"	L.F.	0.046
1-1/2"	L.F.	0.047
2"	L.F.	0.050
2-1/2"	L.F.	0.053
3"	L.F.	0.057
4"	L.F.	0.067
6"	L.F.	0.080
Class 315		
1/2"	L.F.	0.042
2"	L.F.	0.050
2-1/2"	L.F.	0.053
3"	L.F.	0.057
4"	L.F.	0.067
Fittings		
Tee		
1/2"	EA.	0.133
3/4"	EA.	0.133
1"	EA.	0.133
1-1/4"	EA.	0.145
1-1/2"	EA.	0.160
2"	EA.	0.178
2-1/2"	EA.	0.200
3"	EA.	0.229
4"	EA.	0.267
6"	EA.	0.320
El		
1/2"	EA.	0.123
3/4"	EA.	0.133
1"	EA.	0.133
1-1/4"	EA.	0.133
1-1/2"	EA.	0.133
2"	EA.	0.145
2-1/2"	EA.	0.160
3"	EA.	0.178
4"	EA.	0.200
6"	EA.	0.267
Coupling		
1/2"	EA.	0.123
3/4"	EA.	0.133

Site Improvements	UNIT	MAN/ HOURS
02810.40 Lawn Irrigation		
1"	EA.	0.133
1-1/4"	EA.	0.133
1-1/2"	EA.	0.133
2"	EA.	0.145
2-1/2"	EA.	0.160
3"	EA.	0.178
4"	EA.	0.200
6"	EA.	0.267
45 El		
1/2"	EA.	0.123
3/4"	EA.	0.133
1"	EA.	0.133
1-1/4"	EA.	0.133
1-1/2"	EA.	0.133
2"	EA.	0.145
2-1/2"	EA.	0.160
3"	EA.	0.178
4"	EA.	0.200
6"	EA.	0.267
Riser, 1/2" diameter		
2" (close)	EA.	0.200
3"	EA.	0.200
4"	EA.	0.229
5"	EA.	0.229
6"	EA.	0.229
10"	EA.	0.267
12"	EA.	0.267
3/4" diameter		
2" (close)	EA.	0.200
3"	EA.	0.200
4"	EA.	0.229
5"	EA.	0.229
6"	EA.	0.229
10"	EA.	0.267
12"	EA.	0.267
1" diameter		
2" (close)	EA.	0.200
3"	EA.	0.200
4"	EA.	0.229
5"	EA.	0.229
6"	EA.	0.229
10"	EA.	0.267
12"	EA.	0.267
Street El PVC		
1/2"	EA.	0.133
3/4"	EA.	0.145
1"	EA.	0.160
Valve Box		
Concrete, Square		
12" x 22"	EA.	1.000
18" x 20"	EA.	1.143
24" x 13"	EA.	1.333
Round		
12"	EA.	0.800

Site Improvements	UNIT	MAN/ HOURS
02810.40 Lawn Irrigation		
Plastic		
Square		
12"	EA.	1.000
18"	EA.	
Round		
6"	EA.	1.000
10"	EA.	1.000
12"	EA.	1.143
Sprinkler, Pop-Up		
Spray		
2" high	EA.	1.333
3" high	EA.	1.333
4" high	EA.	1.600
6" high	EA.	1.600
12" high	EA.	1.600
Rotor		
4" high	EA.	1.333
6" high	EA.	1.600
Impact		
Brass	EA.	1.333
Plastic	EA.	1.600
Shrub Head		
Spray	EA.	1.333
Rotor	EA.	1.600
Time Clocks		
Minimum	EA.	2.000
Average	EA.	2.667
Maximum	EA.	4.000
Valves		
Anti-siphon		
Brass		
3/4"	EA.	1.333
1"	EA.	1.333
Plastic		
3/4"	EA.	1.333
1"	EA.	1.333
Ball Valve		
Plastic		
1/2"	EA.	1.333
3/4"	EA.	1.333
1"	EA.	1.333
1-1/2"	EA.	1.600
2"	EA.	1.600
Brass		
1/2"	EA.	1.333
3/4"	EA.	1.333
1"	EA.	1.333
1-1/2"	EA.	1.600
2"	EA.	1.600
Gate valves, Brass		
1/2"	EA.	1.333
3/4"	EA.	1.333
1"	EA.	1.333
1-1/2"	EA.	1.600

Site Improvements	UNIT	MAN/ HOURS
02810.40 Lawn Irrigation		
2"	EA.	1.600
In-line		
Brass		
1"	EA.	1.333
1-1/2"	EA.	1.600
2"	EA.	1.600
Plastic		
3/4"	EA.	1.333
1"	EA.	1.333
1-1/2"	EA.	1.600
2"	EA.	1.600
Vacuum Breakers		
Brass		
3/4"	EA.	2.667
1"	EA.	2.667
1-1/2"	EA.	2.667
2"	EA.	2.667
Plastic		
3/4"	EA.	2.667
1"	EA.	2.667
1-1/2"	EA.	2.667
2"	EA.	2.667
Backflow Preventors, Brass		
3/4"	EA.	26.667
1"	EA.	26.667
1-1/2"	EA.	26.667
2"	EA.	32.000
Pressure Regulators, Brass		
3/4"	EA.	0.800
1"	EA.	0.800
1-1/2"	EA.	0.889
2"	EA.	1.000
Quick Coupler Valve		
3/4"	EA.	1.333
1"	EA.	1.333
02830.10 Chain Link Fence		
Chain link fence, 9 ga., galvanized, with posts 10' o.c.		
4' high	L.F.	0.057
5' high	L.F.	0.073
6' high	L.F.	0.100
7' high	L.F.	0.123
8' high	L.F.	0.160
For barbed wire with hangers, add		
3 strand	L.F.	0.040
6 strand	L.F.	0.067
Corner or gate post, 3" post		
4' high	EA.	0.267
5' high	EA.	0.296
6' high	EA.	0.348
7' high	EA.	0.400
8' high	EA.	0.444
4" post		
4' high	EA.	0.296

Site Improvements	UNIT	MAN/ HOURS
02830.10 Chain Link Fence		
5' high	EA.	0.348
6' high	EA.	0.400
7' high	EA.	0.444
8' high	EA.	0.500
Gate with gate posts, galvanized, 3' wide		
4' high	EA.	2.000
5' high	EA.	2.667
6' high	EA.	2.667
7' high	EA.	4.000
8' high	EA.	4.000
Fabric, galvanized chain link, 2" mesh, 9 ga.		
4' high	L.F.	0.027
5' high	L.F.	0.032
6' high	L.F.	0.040
8' high	L.F.	0.053
Line post, no rail fitting, galvanized, 2-1/2" dia.		
4' high	EA.	0.229
5' high	EA.	0.250
6' high	EA.	0.267
7' high	EA.	0.320
8' high	EA.	0.400
1-7/8" H beam		
4' high	EA.	0.229
5' high	EA.	0.250
6' high	EA.	0.267
7' high	EA.	0.320
8' high	EA.	0.400
2-1/4" H beam		
4' high	EA.	0.229
5' high	EA.	0.250
6' high	EA.	0.267
7' high	EA.	0.320
8' high	EA.	0.400
Vinyl coated, 9 ga., with posts 10' o.c.		
4' high	L.F.	0.057
5' high	L.F.	0.073
6' high	L.F.	0.100
7' high	L.F.	0.123
8' high	L.F.	0.160
For barbed wire w/hangers, add		
3 strand	L.F.	0.040
6 Strand	L.F.	0.067
Corner, or gate post, 4' high		
3" dia.	EA.	0.267
4" dia.	EA.	0.267
6" dia.	EA.	0.320
Gate, with posts, 3' wide		
4' high	EA.	2.000
5' high	EA.	2.667
6' high	EA.	2.667
7' high	EA.	4.000
8' high	EA.	4.000
Line post, no rail fitting, 2-1/2" dia.		
4' high	EA.	0.229

Site Improvements	UNIT	MAN/HOURS
02830.10 Chain Link Fence		
5' high	EA.	0.250
6' high	EA.	0.267
7' high	EA.	0.320
8' high	EA.	0.400
Corner post, no top rail fitting, 4" dia.		
4' high	EA.	0.267
5' high	EA.	0.296
6' high	EA.	0.348
7' high	EA.	0.400
8' high	EA.	0.444
Fabric, vinyl, chain link, 2" mesh, 9 ga.		
4' high	L.F.	0.027
5' high	L.F.	0.032
6' high	L.F.	0.040
8' high	L.F.	0.053
Swing gates, galvanized, 4' high		
Single gate		
3' wide	EA.	2.000
4' wide	EA.	2.000
Double gate		
10' wide	EA.	3.200
12' wide	EA.	3.200
14' wide	EA.	3.200
16' wide	EA.	3.200
18' wide	EA.	4.571
20' wide	EA.	4.571
22' wide	EA.	4.571
24' wide	EA.	5.333
26' wide	EA.	5.333
28' wide	EA.	6.400
30' wide	EA.	6.400
5' high		
Single gate		
3' wide	EA.	2.667
4' wide	EA.	2.667
Double gate		
10' wide	EA.	4.000
12' wide	EA.	4.000
14' wide	EA.	4.000
16' wide	EA.	4.000
18' wide	EA.	4.571
20' wide	EA.	4.571
22' wide	EA.	4.571
24' wide	EA.	5.333
26' wide	EA.	5.333
28' wide	EA.	6.400
30' wide	EA.	6.400
6' high		
Single gate		
3' wide	EA.	2.667
4' wide	EA.	2.667
Double gate		
10' wide	EA.	4.000
12' wide	EA.	4.000

Site Improvements	UNIT	MAN/HOURS
02830.10 Chain Link Fence		
14' wide	EA.	4.000
16' wide	EA.	4.000
18' wide	EA.	4.571
20' wide	EA.	4.571
22' wide	EA.	4.571
24' wide	EA.	5.333
26' wide	EA.	5.333
28' wide	EA.	6.400
30' wide	EA.	6.400
7' high		
Single gate		
3' wide	EA.	4.000
4' wide	EA.	4.000
Double gate		
10' wide	EA.	5.333
12' wide	EA.	5.333
14' wide	EA.	5.333
16' wide	EA.	5.333
18' wide	EA.	6.400
20' wide	EA.	6.400
22' wide	EA.	6.400
24' wide	EA.	8.000
26' wide	EA.	8.000
28' wide	EA.	10.000
30' wide	EA.	10.000
8' high		
Single gate		
3' wide	EA.	4.000
4' wide	EA.	4.000
Double gate		
10' wide	EA.	5.333
12' wide	EA.	5.333
14' wide	EA.	5.333
16' wide	EA.	5.333
18' wide	EA.	6.400
20' wide	EA.	6.400
22' wide	EA.	6.400
24' wide	EA.	8.000
26' wide	EA.	8.000
28' wide	EA.	10.000
30' wide	EA.	10.000
Vinyl coated swing gates, 4' high		
Single gate		
3' wide	EA.	2.000
4' wide	EA.	2.000
Double gate		
10' wide	EA.	3.200
12' wide	EA.	3.200
14' wide	EA.	3.200
16' wide	EA.	3.200
18' wide	EA.	4.571
20' wide	EA.	4.571
22' wide	EA.	4.571
24' wide	EA.	5.333

Site Improvements	UNIT	MAN/HOURS
02830.10 Chain Link Fence		
26' wide	EA.	5.333
28' wide	EA.	6.400
30' wide	EA.	6.400
5' high		
Single gate		
3' wide	EA.	2.667
4' wide	EA.	2.667
Double gate		
10' wide	EA.	4.000
12' wide	EA.	4.000
14' wide	EA.	4.000
16' wide	EA.	4.000
18' wide	EA.	4.571
20' wide	EA.	4.571
22' wide	EA.	4.571
24' wide	EA.	5.333
26' wide	EA.	5.333
28' wide	EA.	6.400
30' wide	EA.	6.400
6' high		
Single gate		
3' wide	EA.	2.667
4' wide	EA.	2.667
Double gate		
10' wide	EA.	4.000
12' wide	EA.	4.000
14' wide	EA.	4.000
16' wide	EA.	4.000
18' wide	EA.	4.571
20' wide	EA.	4.571
22' wide	EA.	4.571
24' wide	EA.	5.333
26' wide	EA.	5.333
28' wide	EA.	6.400
30' wide	EA.	6.400
7' high		
Single gate		
3' wide	EA.	4.000
4' wide	EA.	4.000
Double gate		
10' wide	EA.	5.333
12' wide	EA.	5.333
14' wide	EA.	5.333
16' wide	EA.	5.333
18' wide	EA.	6.400
20' wide	EA.	6.400
22' wide	EA.	6.400
24' wide	EA.	8.000
26' wide	EA.	8.000
28' wide	EA.	10.000
30' wide	EA.	10.000
8' high		
Single gate		
3' wide	EA.	4.000

Site Improvements	UNIT	MAN/HOURS
02830.10 Chain Link Fence		
4' wide	EA.	4.000
Double gate		
10' wide	EA.	5.333
12' wide	EA.	5.333
14' wide	EA.	5.333
16' wide	EA.	5.333
18' wide	EA.	6.400
20' wide	EA.	6.400
22' wide	EA.	6.400
24' wide	EA.	8.000
28' wide	EA.	8.000
30' wide	EA.	10.000
Drilling fence post holes		
In soil		
By hand	EA.	0.400
By machine auger	EA.	0.200
In rock		
By jackhammer	EA.	2.667
By rock drill	EA.	0.800
Aluminum privacy slats, installed vertically	S.F.	0.020
Post hole, dig by hand	EA.	0.533
Set fence post in concrete	EA.	0.400
02830.70 Recreational Courts		
Walls, galvanized steel		
8' high	L.F.	0.160
10' high	L.F.	0.178
12' high	L.F.	0.211
Vinyl coated		
8' high	L.F.	0.160
10' high	L.F.	0.178
12' high	L.F.	0.211
Gates, galvanized steel		
Single, 3' transom		
3'x7'	EA.	4.000
4'x7'	EA.	4.571
5'x7'	EA.	5.333
6'x7'	EA.	6.400
Double, 3' transom		
10'x7'	EA.	16.000
12'x7'	EA.	17.778
14'x7'	EA.	20.000
Double, no transom		
10'x10'	EA.	13.333
12'x10'	EA.	16.000
14'x10'	EA.	17.778
Vinyl coated		
Single, 3' transom		
3'x7'	EA.	4.000
4'x7'	EA.	4.571
5'x7'	EA.	5.333
6'x7'	EA.	6.400
Double, 3'		
10'x7'	EA.	16.000

Site Improvements		UNIT	MAN/HOURS
02830.70	**Recreational Courts**		
12'x7'		EA.	17.778
14'x7'		EA.	20.000
Double, no transom			
10'x10'		EA.	13.333
12'x10'		EA.	16.000
14'x10'		EA.	17.778
Wire and miscellaneous metal fences			
Chicken wire, post 4' o.c.			
2" mesh			
4' high		L.F.	0.040
6' high		L.F.	0.053
Galvanized steel			
12 gauge, 2" by 4" mesh, posts 5' o.c.			
3' high		L.F.	0.040
5' high		L.F.	0.050
14 gauge, 1" by 2" mesh, posts 5' o.c.			
3' high		L.F.	0.040
5' high		L.F.	0.050
02840.30	**Guardrails**		
Pipe bollard, steel pipe, concrete filled, painted			
6" dia.		EA.	0.667
8" dia.		EA.	1.000
12" dia.		EA.	2.667
Corrugated steel, guardrail, galvanized		L.F.	0.040
End section, wrap around or flared		EA.	0.800
Timber guardrail, 4" x 8"		L.F.	0.030
Guard rail, 3 cables, 3/4" dia.			
Steel posts		L.F.	0.120
Wood posts		L.F.	0.096
Steel box beam			
6" x 6"		L.F.	0.133
6" x 8"		L.F.	0.150
Concrete posts		EA.	0.400
Barrel type impact barrier		EA.	0.800
Light shield, 6' high		L.F.	0.160
02840.40	**Parking Barriers**		
Timber, treated, 4' long			
4" x 4"		EA.	0.667
6" x 6"		EA.	0.800
Precast concrete, 6' long, with dowels			
12" x 6"		EA.	0.400
12" x 8"		EA.	0.444
02840.60	**Signage**		
Traffic signs			
Reflectorized signs per OSHA standards, including post			
Stop, 24"x24"		EA.	0.533
Yield, 30" triangle		EA.	0.533
Speed limit, 12"x18"		EA.	0.533
Directional, 12"x18"		EA.	0.533
Exit, 12"x18"		EA.	0.533
Entry, 12"x18"		EA.	0.533

Site Improvements		UNIT	MAN/HOURS
02840.60	**Signage**		
Warning, 24"x24"		EA.	0.533
Informational, 12"x18"		EA.	0.533
Handicap parking, 12"x18"		EA.	0.533
02860.40	**Recreational Facilities**		
Bleachers, outdoor, portable, per seat			
10 tiers			
Minimum		EA.	0.150
Maximum		EA.	0.200
20 tiers			
Minimum		EA.	0.141
Maximum		EA.	0.185
Grandstands, fixed, wood seat, steel frame, per seat			
15 tiers			
Minimum		EA.	0.240
Maximum		EA.	0.400
30 tiers			
Minimum		EA.	0.218
Maximum		EA.	0.343
Seats			
Seat backs only			
Fiberglass		EA.	0.080
Steel and wood seat		EA.	0.080
Seat restoration, fiberglass on wood			
Seats		EA.	0.160
Plain bench, no backs		EA.	0.067
Benches			
Park, precast concrete with backs			
4' long		EA.	2.667
8' long		EA.	4.000
Fiberglass, with backs			
4' long		EA.	2.000
8' long		EA.	2.667
Wood, with backs and fiberglass supports			
4' long		EA.	2.000
8' long		EA.	2.667
Steel frame, 6' long			
All steel		EA.	2.000
Hardwood boards		EA.	2.000
Players bench (no back), steel frame, fir seat, 10' long		EA.	2.667
Soccer goal posts		PAIR	
Running track			
Gravel and cinders over stone base		S.Y.	0.060
Rubber-cork base resilient pavement		S.Y.	0.480
For colored surfaces, add		S.Y.	0.048
Colored rubberized asphalt		S.Y.	0.600
Artificial resilient mat over asphalt		S.Y.	1.200
Tennis courts			
Bituminous pavement, 2-1/2" thick		S.Y.	0.150
Colored sealer, acrylic emulsion			
3 coats		S.Y.	0.053
For 2 color seal coating, add		S.Y.	0.008
For preparing old courts, add		S.Y.	0.005
Net, nylon, 42' long		EA.	1.000

Site Improvements

02860.40 — Recreational Facilities

	UNIT	MAN/HOURS
Paint markings on asphalt, 2 coats	EA.	8.000
Playground equipment		
Basketball backboard		
Minimum	EA.	2.000
Maximum	EA.	2.286
Bike rack, 10' long	EA.	1.600
Golf shelter, fiberglass	EA.	2.000
Ground socket for movable posts		
Minimum	EA.	0.500
Maximum	EA.	0.500
Horizontal monkey ladder, 14' long	EA.	1.333
Posts, tether ball	EA.	0.400
Multiple purpose, 10' long	EA.	0.800
See-saw, steel		
Minimum	EA.	3.200
Average	EA.	4.000
Maximum	EA.	5.333
Slide		
Minimum	EA.	6.400
Maximum	EA.	7.273
Swings, plain seats		
8' high		
Minimum	EA.	5.333
Maximum	EA.	6.154
12' high		
Minimum	EA.	6.154
Maximum	EA.	8.889

02870.10 — Prefabricated Planters

	UNIT	MAN/HOURS
Concrete precast, circular		
24" dia., 18" high	EA.	0.800
42" dia., 30" high	EA.	1.000
Fiberglass, circular		
36" dia., 27" high	EA.	0.400
60" dia., 39" high	EA.	0.444
Tapered, circular		
24" dia., 36" high	EA.	0.364
40" dia., 36" high	EA.	0.400
Square		
2' by 2', 17" high	EA.	0.364
4' by 4', 39" high	EA.	0.444
Rectangular		
4' by 1', 18" high	EA.	0.400

Landscaping

02910.10 — Shrub & Tree Maintenance

	UNIT	MAN/HOURS
Moving shrubs on site		
12" ball	EA.	1.000
24" ball	EA.	1.333
3' high	EA.	0.800
4' high	EA.	0.889
5' high	EA.	1.000
18" spread	EA.	1.143
30" spread	EA.	1.333
Moving trees on site		
24" ball	EA.	1.200
48" ball	EA.	1.600
Trees		
3' high	EA.	0.480
6' high	EA.	0.533
8' high	EA.	0.600
10' high	EA.	0.800
Palm trees		
7' high	EA.	0.600
10' high	EA.	0.800
20' high	EA.	2.400
40' high	EA.	4.800
Guying trees		
4" dia.	EA.	0.400
8" dia.	EA.	0.500

02920.10 — Topsoil

	UNIT	MAN/HOURS
Spread topsoil, with equipment		
Minimum	C.Y.	0.080
Maximum	C.Y.	0.100
By hand		
Minimum	C.Y.	0.800
Maximum	C.Y.	1.000
Area preparation for seeding (grade, rake and clean)		
Square yard	S.Y.	0.006
By acre	ACRE	32.000
Remove topsoil and stockpile on site		
4" deep	C.Y.	0.067
6" deep	C.Y.	0.062
Spreading topsoil from stock pile		
By loader	C.Y.	0.073
By hand	C.Y.	0.800
Top dress by hand	S.Y.	0.008
Place imported top soil		
By loader		
4" deep	S.Y.	0.008
6" deep	S.Y.	0.009
By hand		
4" deep	S.Y.	0.089
6" deep	S.Y.	0.100
Plant bed preparation, 18" deep		
With backhoe/loader	S.Y.	0.020
By hand	S.Y.	0.133

Landscaping	UNIT	MAN/HOURS
02930.30 — Seeding		
Mechanical seeding, 175 lb/acre		
By square yard	S.Y.	0.002
By acre	ACRE	8.000
450 lb/acre		
By square yard	S.Y.	0.002
By acre	ACRE	10.000
Seeding by hand, 10 lb per 100 s.y.		
By square yard	S.Y.	0.003
By acre	ACRE	13.333
Reseed disturbed areas	S.F.	0.004
02950.10 — Plants		
Euonymus coloratus, 18" (Purple Wintercreeper)	EA.	0.133
Hedera Helix, 2-1/4" pot (English ivy)	EA.	0.133
Liriope muscari, 2" clumps	EA.	0.080
Santolina, 12"	EA.	0.080
Vinca major or minor, 3" pot	EA.	0.080
Cortaderia argentia, 2 gallon (Pampas Grass)	EA.	0.080
Ophiopogan japonicus, 1 quart (4" pot)	EA.	0.080
Ajuga reptans, 2-3/4" pot (carpet bugle)	EA.	0.080
Pachysandra terminalis, 2-3/4" pot (Japanese Spurge)	EA.	0.080
02950.30 — Shrubs		
Juniperus conferia litoralis, 18"-24" (Shore Juniper)	EA.	0.320
Horizontalis plumosa, 18"-24" (Andorra Juniper)	EA.	0.320
Sabina tamar-iscfolia-tamarix juniper, 18"-24"	EA.	0.320
Chin San Jose, 18"-24" (San Jose Juniper)	EA.	0.320
Sargenti, 18"-24" (Sargent's Juniper)	EA.	0.320
Nandina domestica, 18"-24" (Heavenly Bamboo)	EA.	0.320
Raphiolepis Indica Springtime, 18"-24" (Indian Hawthorn)	EA.	0.320
Osmanthus Heterophyllus Gulftide, 18"-24" (Osmanthus)	EA.	0.320
Ilex Cornuta Burfordi Nana, 18"-24" (Dwarf Burford Holly)	EA.	0.320
Glabra, 18"-24" (Inkberry Holly)	EA.	0.320
Azalea, Indica types, 18"-24"	EA.	0.320
Kurume types, 18"-24"	EA.	0.320
Berberis Julianae, 18"-24" (Wintergreen Barberry)	EA.	0.320
Pieris Japonica Japanese, 18"-24" (Japanese Pieris)	EA.	0.320
Ilex Cornuta Rotunda, 18"-24" (Dwarf Chinese Holly)	EA.	0.320
Juniperus Horiz. Plumosa, 24"-30" (Andorra Juniper)	EA.	0.400
Rhodopendrow Hybrids, 24"-30"	EA.	0.400
Aucuba Japonica Varigata, 24"-30" (Gold Dust Aucuba)	EA.	0.400
Ilex Crenata Willow Leaf, 24"-30" (Japanese Holly)	EA.	0.400
Cleyera Japonica, 30"-36" (Japanese Cleyera)	EA.	0.500
Pittosporum Tobira, 30"-36"	EA.	0.500
Prumus Laurocerasus, 30"-36"	EA.	0.500
Ilex Cornuta Burfordi, 30"-36" (Burford Holly)	EA.	0.500
Abelia Grandiflora, 24"-36" (Yew Podocarpus)	EA.	0.400
Podocarpos Macrophylla, 24"-36" (Yew Podocarpus)	EA.	0.400
Pyracantha Coccinea Lalandi, 3'-4' (Firethorn)	EA.	0.500
Photinia Frazieri, 3'-4' (Red Photinia)	EA.	0.500
Forsythia Suspensa, 3'-4' (Weeping Forsythia)	EA.	0.500
Camellia Japonica, 3'-4' (Common Camellia)	EA.	0.500
Juniperus Chin Torulosa, 3'-4' (Hollywood Juniper)	EA.	0.500
Cupressocyparis Leylandi, 3'-4'	EA.	0.500

Landscaping	UNIT	MAN/HOURS
02950.30 — Shrubs		
Ilex Opaca Fosteri, 5'-6' (Foster's Holly)	EA.	0.667
Opaca, 5'-6' (American Holly)	EA.	0.667
Nyrica Cerifera, 4'-5' (Southern Wax Myrtles)	EA.	0.571
Ligustrum Japonicum, 4'-5' (Japanese Privet)	EA.	0.571
02950.60 — Trees		
Cornus Florida, 5'-6' (White flowering Dogwood)	EA.	0.667
Prunus Serrulata Kwanzan, 6'-8' (Kwanzan Cherry)	EA.	0.800
Caroliniana, 6'-8' (Carolina Cherry Laurel)	EA.	0.800
Cercis Canadensis, 6'-8' (Eastern Redbud)	EA.	0.800
Koelreuteria Paniculata, 8'-10' (Goldenrain Tree)	EA.	1.000
Acer Platanoides, 1-3/4"-2" (11'-13') (Norway Maple)	EA.	1.333
Rubrum, 1-3/4"-2" (11'-13') (Red Maple)	EA.	1.333
Saccharum, 1-3/4"-2" (Sugar Maple)	EA.	1.333
Fraxinus Pennsylvanica, 1-3/4"-2" (Laneolata-Green Ash)	EA.	1.333
Celtis Occidentalis, 1-3/4"-2" (American Hackberry)	EA.	1.333
Glenditsia Triacantos Inermis, 2"	EA.	1.333
Prunus Cerasifera 'Thundercloud', 6'-8'	EA.	0.800
Yeodensis, 6'-8' (Yoshino Cherry)	EA.	0.800
Lagerstroemia Indica, 8'-10' (Crapemyrtle)	EA.	1.000
Crataegus Phaenopyrum, 8'-10' (Washington Hawthorn)	EA.	1.000
Quercus Borealis, 1-3/4"-2" (Northern Red Oak)	EA.	1.333
Quercus Acutissima, 1-3/4"-2" (8'-10') (Sawtooth Oak)	EA.	1.333
Saliz Babylonica, 1-3/4"-2" (Weeping Willow)	EA.	1.333
Tilia Cordata Greenspire, 1-3/4"-2" (10'-12')	EA.	1.333
Malus, 2"-2-1/2" (8'-10') (Flowering Crabapple)	EA.	1.333
Platanus Occidentalis, (12'-14')	EA.	1.600
Pyrus Calleryana Bradford, 2"-2-1/2" (Bradford Pear)	EA.	1.333
Quercus Palustris, 2"-2-1/2" (12'-14') (Pin Oak)	EA.	1.333
Phellos, 2-1/2"-3" (Willow Oak)	EA.	1.600
Nigra, 2"-2-1/2" (Water Oak)	EA.	1.333
Magnolia Soulangeana, 4'-5' (Saucer Magnolia)	EA.	0.667
Grandiflora, 6'-8' (Southern Magnolia)	EA.	0.800
Cedrus Deodara, 10'-12' (Deodare Cedar)	EA.	1.333
Gingko Biloba, 10'-12' (2"-2-1/2") (Maidenhair Tree)	EA.	1.333
Pinus Thunbergi, 5'-6' (Japanese Black Pine)	EA.	0.667
Strobus, 6'-8' (White Pine)	EA.	0.800
Taeda, 6'-8' (Loblolly Pine)	EA.	0.800
Quercus Virginiana, 2"-2-1/2" (Live Oak)	EA.	1.600
02970.10 — Fertilizing		
Fertilizing (23#/1000 sf)		
By square yard	S.Y.	0.002
By acre	ACRE	10.000
Liming (70#/1000 sf)		
By square yard	S.Y.	0.003
By acre	ACRE	13.333
02980.10 — Landscape Accessories		
Steel edging, 3/16" x 4"	L.F.	0.010
Landscaping stepping stones, 15"x15", white	EA.	0.040
Wood chip mulch	C.Y.	0.533
2" thick	S.Y.	0.016
4" thick	S.Y.	0.023

285

Landscaping	UNIT	MAN/ HOURS
02980.10 Landscape Accessories		
6" thick	S.Y.	0.029
Gravel mulch, 3/4" stone	C.Y.	0.800
White marble chips, 1" deep	S.F.	0.008
Peat moss		
2" thick	S.Y.	0.018
4" thick	S.Y.	0.027
6" thick	S.Y.	0.033
Landscaping timbers, treated lumber		
4" x 4"	L.F.	0.027
6" x 6"	L.F.	0.029
8" x 8"	L.F.	0.033

Formwork

03110.05 — Beam Formwork

	UNIT	MAN/HOURS
Beam forms, job built		
Beam bottoms		
1 use	S.F.	0.133
2 uses	S.F.	0.127
3 uses	S.F.	0.123
4 uses	S.F.	0.118
5 uses	S.F.	0.114
Beam sides		
1 use	S.F.	0.089
2 uses	S.F.	0.084
3 uses	S.F.	0.080
4 uses	S.F.	0.076
5 uses	S.F.	0.073

03110.10 — Box Culvert Formwork

	UNIT	MAN/HOURS
Box culverts, job built		
6' x 6'		
1 use	S.F.	0.080
2 uses	S.F.	0.076
3 uses	S.F.	0.073
4 uses	S.F.	0.070
5 uses	S.F.	0.067
8' x 12'		
1 use	S.F.	0.067
2 uses	S.F.	0.064
3 uses	S.F.	0.062
4 uses	S.F.	0.059
5 uses	S.F.	0.057

03110.15 — Column Formwork

	UNIT	MAN/HOURS
Column, square forms, job built		
8" x 8" columns		
1 use	S.F.	0.160
2 uses	S.F.	0.154
3 uses	S.F.	0.148
4 uses	S.F.	0.143
5 uses	S.F.	0.138
12" x 12" columns		
1 use	S.F.	0.145
2 uses	S.F.	0.140
3 uses	S.F.	0.136
4 uses	S.F.	0.131
5 uses	S.F.	0.127
16" x 16" columns		
1 use	S.F.	0.133
2 uses	S.F.	0.129
3 uses	S.F.	0.125
4 uses	S.F.	0.121
5 uses	S.F.	0.118
24" x 24" columns		
1 use	S.F.	0.123
2 uses	S.F.	0.119
3 uses	S.F.	0.116
4 uses	S.F.	0.113

Formwork

03110.15 — Column Formwork

	UNIT	MAN/HOURS
5 uses	S.F.	0.110
36" x 36" columns		
1 use	S.F.	0.114
2 uses	S.F.	0.111
3 uses	S.F.	0.108
4 uses	S.F.	0.105
5 uses	S.F.	0.103
Round fiber forms, 1 use		
10" dia.	L.F.	0.160
12" dia.	L.F.	0.163
14" dia.	L.F.	0.170
16" dia.	L.F.	0.178
18" dia.	L.F.	0.190
24" dia.	L.F.	0.205
30" dia.	L.F.	0.222
36" dia.	L.F.	0.242
42" dia.	L.F.	0.267

03110.18 — Curb Formwork

	UNIT	MAN/HOURS
Curb forms		
Straight, 6" high		
1 use	L.F.	0.080
2 uses	L.F.	0.076
3 uses	L.F.	0.073
4 uses	L.F.	0.070
5 uses	L.F.	0.067
Curved, 6" high		
1 use	L.F.	0.100
2 uses	L.F.	0.094
3 uses	L.F.	0.089
4 uses	L.F.	0.085
5 uses	L.F.	0.082

03110.20 — Elevated Slab Formwork

	UNIT	MAN/HOURS
Elevated slab formwork		
Slab, with drop panels		
1 use	S.F.	0.064
2 uses	S.F.	0.062
3 uses	S.F.	0.059
4 uses	S.F.	0.057
5 uses	S.F.	0.055
Floor slab, hung from steel beams		
1 use	S.F.	0.062
2 uses	S.F.	0.059
3 uses	S.F.	0.057
4 uses	S.F.	0.055
5 uses	S.F.	0.053
Floor slab, with pans or domes		
1 use	S.F.	0.073
2 uses	S.F.	0.070
3 uses	S.F.	0.067
4 uses	S.F.	0.064
5 uses	S.F.	0.062
Equipment curbs, 12" high		

Formwork		UNIT	MAN/HOURS
03110.20	**Elevated Slab Formwork**		
1 use		L.F.	0.080
2 uses		L.F.	0.076
3 uses		L.F.	0.073
4 uses		L.F.	0.070
5 uses		L.F.	0.067
03110.25	**Equipment Pad Formwork**		
Equipment pad, job built			
1 use		S.F.	0.100
2 uses		S.F.	0.094
3 uses		S.F.	0.089
4 uses		S.F.	0.084
5 uses		S.F.	0.080
03110.35	**Footing Formwork**		
Wall footings, job built, continuous			
1 use		S.F.	0.080
2 uses		S.F.	0.076
3 uses		S.F.	0.073
4 uses		S.F.	0.070
5 uses		S.F.	0.067
Column footings, spread			
1 use		S.F.	0.100
2 uses		S.F.	0.094
3 uses		S.F.	0.089
4 uses		S.F.	0.084
5 uses		S.F.	0.080
03110.50	**Grade Beam Formwork**		
Grade beams, job built			
1 use		S.F.	0.080
2 uses		S.F.	0.076
3 uses		S.F.	0.073
4 uses		S.F.	0.070
5 uses		S.F.	0.067
03110.53	**Pile Cap Formwork**		
Pile cap forms, job built			
Square			
1 use		S.F.	0.100
2 uses		S.F.	0.094
3 uses		S.F.	0.089
4 uses		S.F.	0.084
5 uses		S.F.	0.080
Triangular			
1 use		S.F.	0.114
2 uses		S.F.	0.107
3 uses		S.F.	0.100
4 uses		S.F.	0.094
5 uses		S.F.	0.089

Formwork		UNIT	MAN/HOURS
03110.55	**Slab/mat Formwork**		
Mat foundations, job built			
1 use		S.F.	0.100
2 uses		S.F.	0.094
3 uses		S.F.	0.089
4 uses		S.F.	0.084
5 uses		S.F.	0.080
Edge forms			
6" high			
1 use		L.F.	0.073
2 uses		L.F.	0.070
3 uses		L.F.	0.067
4 uses		L.F.	0.064
5 uses		L.F.	0.062
12" high			
1 use		L.F.	0.080
2 uses		L.F.	0.076
3 uses		L.F.	0.073
4 uses		L.F.	0.070
5 uses		L.F.	0.067
Formwork for openings			
1 use		S.F.	0.160
2 uses		S.F.	0.145
3 uses		S.F.	0.133
4 uses		S.F.	0.123
5 uses		S.F.	0.114
03110.60	**Stair Formwork**		
Stairway forms, job built			
1 use		S.F.	0.160
2 uses		S.F.	0.145
3 uses		S.F.	0.133
4 uses		S.F.	0.123
5 uses		S.F.	0.114
Stairs, elevated			
1 use		S.F.	0.160
2 uses		S.F.	0.133
3 uses		S.F.	0.114
4 uses		S.F.	0.107
5 uses		S.F.	0.100
03110.65	**Wall Formwork**		
Wall forms, exterior, job built			
Up to 8' high wall			
1 use		S.F.	0.080
2 uses		S.F.	0.076
3 uses		S.F.	0.073
4 uses		S.F.	0.070
5 uses		S.F.	0.067
Over 8' high wall			
1 use		S.F.	0.100
2 uses		S.F.	0.094
3 uses		S.F.	0.089
4 uses		S.F.	0.084
5 uses		S.F.	0.080

Formwork	UNIT	MAN/HOURS
03110.65 Wall Formwork		
Over 16' high wall		
1 use	S.F.	0.114
2 uses	S.F.	0.107
3 uses	S.F.	0.100
4 uses	S.F.	0.094
5 uses	S.F.	0.089
Radial wall forms		
1 use	S.F.	0.123
2 uses	S.F.	0.114
3 uses	S.F.	0.107
4 uses	S.F.	0.100
5 uses	S.F.	0.094
Retaining wall forms		
1 use	S.F.	0.089
2 uses	S.F.	0.084
3 uses	S.F.	0.080
4 uses	S.F.	0.076
5 uses	S.F.	0.073
Radial retaining wall forms		
1 use	S.F.	0.133
2 uses	S.F.	0.123
3 uses	S.F.	0.114
4 uses	S.F.	0.107
5 uses	S.F.	0.100
Column pier and pilaster		
1 use	S.F.	0.160
2 uses	S.F.	0.145
3 uses	S.F.	0.133
4 uses	S.F.	0.123
5 uses	S.F.	0.114
Interior wall forms		
Up to 8' high		
1 use	S.F.	0.073
2 uses	S.F.	0.070
3 uses	S.F.	0.067
4 uses	S.F.	0.064
5 uses	S.F.	0.062
Over 8' high		
1 use	S.F.	0.089
2 uses	S.F.	0.084
3 uses	S.F.	0.080
4 uses	S.F.	0.076
5 uses	S.F.	0.073
Over 16' high		
1 use	S.F.	0.100
2 uses	S.F.	0.094
3 uses	S.F.	0.089
4 uses	S.F.	0.084
5 uses	S.F.	0.080
Radial wall forms		
1 use	S.F.	0.107
2 uses	S.F.	0.100
3 uses	S.F.	0.094
4 uses	S.F.	0.089

Formwork	UNIT	MAN/HOURS
03110.65 Wall Formwork		
5 uses	S.F.	0.084
Curved wall forms, 24" sections		
1 use	S.F.	0.160
2 uses	S.F.	0.145
3 uses	S.F.	0.133
4 uses	S.F.	0.123
5 uses	S.F.	0.114
PVC form liner, per side, smooth finish		
1 use	S.F.	0.067
2 uses	S.F.	0.064
3 uses	S.F.	0.062
4 uses	S.F.	0.057
5 uses	S.F.	0.053
03110.90 Miscellaneous Formwork		
Keyway forms (5 uses)		
2 x 4	L.F.	0.040
2 x 6	L.F.	0.044
Bulkheads		
Walls, with keyways		
2 piece	L.F.	0.073
3 piece	L.F.	0.080
Elevated slab, with keyway		
2 piece	L.F.	0.067
3 piece	L.F.	0.073
Ground slab, with keyway		
2 piece	L.F.	0.057
3 piece	L.F.	0.062
Chamfer strips		
Wood		
1/2" wide	L.F.	0.018
3/4" wide	L.F.	0.018
1" wide	L.F.	0.018
PVC		
1/2" wide	L.F.	0.018
3/4" wide	L.F.	0.018
1" wide	L.F.	0.018
Radius		
1"	L.F.	0.019
1-1/2"	L.F.	0.019
Reglets		
Galvanized steel, 24 ga.	L.F.	0.032
Metal formwork		
Straight edge forms		
4" high	L.F.	0.050
6" high	L.F.	0.053
8" high	L.F.	0.057
12" high	L.F.	0.062
16" high	L.F.	0.067
Curb form, S-shape		
12" x		
1'-6"	L.F.	0.114
2'	L.F.	0.107
2'-6"	L.F.	0.100

Formwork		UNIT	MAN/HOURS
03110.90 Miscellaneous Formwork			
3'		L.F.	0.089

Reinforcement		UNIT	MAN/HOURS
03210.05 Beam Reinforcing			
Beam-girders			
#3 - #4		TON	20.000
#5 - #6		TON	16.000
#7 - #8		TON	13.333
#9 - #10		TON	11.429
#11 - #12		TON	10.667
#13 - #14		TON	10.000
Galvanized			
#3 - #4		TON	20.000
#5 - #6		TON	16.000
#7 - #8		TON	13.333
#9 - #10		TON	11.429
#11 - #12		TON	10.667
#13 - #14		TON	10.000
Epoxy coated			
#3 - #4		TON	22.857
#5 - #6		TON	17.778
#7 - #8		TON	14.545
#9 - #10		TON	12.308
#11 - #12		TON	11.429
#13 - #14		TON	10.667
Bond Beams			
#3 - #4		TON	26.667
#5 - #6		TON	20.000
#7 - #8		TON	17.778
Galvanized			
#3 - #4		TON	26.667
#5 - #6		TON	20.000
#7 - #8		TON	17.778
Epoxy coated			
#3 - #4		TON	32.000
#5 - #6		TON	22.857
#7 - #8		TON	20.000
03210.10 Box Culvert Reinforcing			
Box culverts			
#3 - #4		TON	10.000
#5 - #6		TON	8.889
#7 - #8		TON	8.000
#9 - #10		TON	7.273
#11 - #12		TON	6.667
Galvanized			

Reinforcement		UNIT	MAN/HOURS
03210.10 Box Culvert Reinforcing			
#3 - #4		TON	10.000
#5 - #6		TON	8.889
#7 - #8		TON	8.000
#9 - #10		TON	7.273
#11 - #12		TON	6.667
Epoxy coated			
#3 - #4		TON	10.667
#5 - #6		TON	9.412
#7 - #8		TON	8.421
#9 - #10		TON	7.619
#11 - #12		TON	6.957
03210.15 Column Reinforcing			
Columns			
#3 - #4		TON	22.857
#5 - #6		TON	17.778
#7 - #8		TON	16.000
#9 - #10		TON	14.545
#11 - #12		TON	13.333
#13 - #14		TON	12.308
#15 - #16		TON	11.429
Galvanized			
#3 - #4		TON	22.857
#5 - #6		TON	17.778
#7 - #8		TON	16.000
#9 - #10		TON	14.545
#11 - #12		TON	13.333
#13 - #14		TON	12.308
#15 - #16		TON	11.429
Epoxy coated			
#3 - #4		TON	26.667
#5 - #6		TON	20.000
#7 - #8		TON	17.778
#9 - #10		TON	16.000
#11 - #12		TON	14.545
#13 - #14		TON	13.333
#15 - #16		TON	12.308
Spirals			
8" to 24" dia.		TON	20.000
24" to 48" dia.		TON	17.778
48" to 84" dia.		TON	16.000
03210.20 Elevated Slab Reinforcing			
Elevated slab			
#3 - #4		TON	10.000
#5 - #6		TON	8.889
#7 - #8		TON	8.000
#9 - #10		TON	7.273
#11 - #12		TON	6.667
Galvanized			
#3 - #4		TON	10.000
#5 - #6		TON	8.889
#7 - #8		TON	8.000
#9 - #10		TON	7.273

Reinforcement

03210.20 — Elevated Slab Reinforcing

	UNIT	MAN/HOURS
#11 - #12	TON	6.667
Epoxy coated		
#3 - #4	TON	10.667
#5 - #6	TON	9.412
#7 - #8	TON	8.421
#9 - #10	TON	7.619
#11 - #12	TON	6.957

03210.25 — Equip. Pad Reinforcing

	UNIT	MAN/HOURS
Equipment pad		
#3 - #4	TON	16.000
#5 - #6	TON	14.545
#7 - #8	TON	13.333
#9 - #10	TON	12.308
#11 - #12	TON	11.429

03210.35 — Footing Reinforcing

	UNIT	MAN/HOURS
Footings		
Grade 50		
#3 - #4	TON	13.333
#5 - #6	TON	11.429
#7 - #8	TON	10.000
#9 - #10	TON	8.889
Grade 60		
#3 - #4	TON	13.333
#5 - #6	TON	11.429
#7 - #8	TON	10.000
#9 - #10	TON	8.889
Grade 70		
#3 - #4	TON	13.333
#5 - #6	TON	11.429
#7 - #8	TON	10.000
#9 - #10	TON	8.889
#11- #12	TON	8.000
Straight dowels, 24" long		
1" dia. (#8)	EA.	0.080
3/4" dia. (#6)	EA.	0.080
5/8" dia. (#5)	EA.	0.067
1/2" dia. (#4)	EA.	0.057

03210.45 — Foundation Reinforcing

	UNIT	MAN/HOURS
Foundations		
#3 - #4	TON	13.333
#5 - #6	TON	11.429
#7 - #8	TON	10.000
#9 - #10	TON	8.889
#11 - #12	TON	8.000
Galvanized		
#3 - #4	TON	13.333
#5 - #6	TON	11.429
#7 - #8	TON	10.000
#9 - #10	TON	8.889
#11 - #12	TON	8.000
Epoxy Coated		

Reinforcement

03210.45 — Foundation Reinforcing

	UNIT	MAN/HOURS
#3 - #4	TON	14.545
#5 - #6	TON	12.308
#7 - #8	TON	10.667
#9 - #10	TON	9.412
#11 - #12	TON	8.421

03210.50 — Grade Beam Reinforcing

	UNIT	MAN/HOURS
Grade beams		
#3 - #4	TON	12.308
#5 - #6	TON	10.667
#7 - #8	TON	9.412
#9 - #10	TON	8.421
#11 - #12	TON	7.619
Galvanized		
#3 - #4	TON	12.308
#5 - #6	TON	10.667
#7 - #8	TON	9.412
#9 - #10	TON	8.421
#11 - #12	TON	7.619
Epoxy coated		
#3 - #4	TON	13.333
#5 - #6	TON	11.429
#7 - #8	TON	10.000
#9 - #10	TON	8.889
#11 - #12	TON	8.000

03210.53 — Pile Cap Reinforcing

	UNIT	MAN/HOURS
Pile caps		
#3 - #4	TON	20.000
#5 - #6	TON	17.778
#7 - #8	TON	16.000
#9 - #10	TON	14.545
#11 - #12	TON	13.333
Galvanized		
#3 - #4	TON	20.000
#5 - #6	TON	17.778
#7 - #8	TON	16.000
#9 - #10	TON	14.545
#11 - #12	TON	13.333
Epoxy coated		
#3 - #4	TON	22.857
#5 - #6	TON	20.000
#7 - #8	TON	17.778
#9 - #10	TON	16.000
#11 - #12	TON	14.545

03210.55 — Slab/mat Reinforcing

	UNIT	MAN/HOURS
Bars, slabs		
#3 - #4	TON	13.333
#5 - #6	TON	11.429
#7 - #8	TON	10.000
#9 - #10	TON	8.889
#11 - #12	TON	8.000
Galvanized		

Reinforcement	UNIT	MAN/HOURS
03210.55 Slab/mat Reinforcing		
#3 - #4	TON	13.333
#5 - #6	TON	11.429
#7 - #8	TON	10.000
#9 - #10	TON	8.889
#11 - #12	TON	8.000
Epoxy coated		
#3 - #4	TON	14.545
#5 - #6	TON	12.308
#7 - #8	TON	10.667
#9 - #10	TON	9.412
#11 - #12	TON	8.421
Wire mesh, slabs		
Galvanized		
4x4		
W1.4xW1.4	S.F.	0.005
W2.0xW2.0	S.F.	0.006
W2.9xW2.9	S.F.	0.006
W4.0xW4.0	S.F.	0.007
6x6		
W1.4xW1.4	S.F.	0.004
W2.0xW2.0	S.F.	0.004
W2.9xW2.9	S.F.	0.005
W4.0xW4.0	S.F.	0.005
Standard		
2x2		
W.9xW.9	S.F.	0.005
4x4		
W1.4xW1.4	S.F.	0.005
W2.0xW2.0	S.F.	0.006
W2.9xW2.9	S.F.	0.006
W4.0xW4.0	S.F.	0.007
6x6		
W1.4xW1.4	S.F.	0.004
W2.0xW2.0	S.F.	0.004
W2.9xW2.9	S.F.	0.005
W4.0xW4.0	S.F.	0.005
03210.60 Stair Reinforcing		
Stairs		
#3 - #4	TON	16.000
#5 - #6	TON	13.333
#7 - #8	TON	11.429
#9 - #10	TON	10.000
Galvanized		
#3 - #4	TON	16.000
#5 - #6	TON	13.333
#7 - #8	TON	11.429
#9 - #10	TON	10.000
Epoxy coated		
#3 - #4	TON	17.778
#5 - #6	TON	14.545
#7 - #8	TON	12.308
#9 - #10	TON	10.667

Reinforcement	UNIT	MAN/HOURS
03210.65 Wall Reinforcing		
Walls		
#3 - #4	TON	11.429
#5 - #6	TON	10.000
#7 - #8	TON	8.889
#9 - #10	TON	8.000
Galvanized		
#3 - #4	TON	11.429
#5 - #6	TON	10.000
#7 - #8	TON	8.889
#9 - #10	TON	8.000
Epoxy coated		
#3 - #4	TON	12.308
#5 - #6	TON	10.667
#7 - #8	TON	9.412
#9 - #10	TON	8.421
Masonry wall (horizontal)		
#3 - #4	TON	32.000
#5 - #6	TON	26.667
Galvanized		
#3 - #4	TON	32.000
#5 - #6	TON	26.667
Masonry wall (vertical)		
#3 - #4	TON	40.000
#5 - #6	TON	32.000
Galvanized		
#3 - #4	TON	40.000
#5 - #6	TON	32.000

Accessories	UNIT	MAN/HOURS
03250.40 Concrete Accessories		
Expansion joint, poured		
Asphalt		
1/2" x 1"	L.F.	0.016
1" x 2"	L.F.	0.017
Liquid neoprene, cold applied		
1/2" x 1"	L.F.	0.016
1" x 2"	L.F.	0.018
Polyurethane, 2 parts		
1/2" x 1"	L.F.	0.027
1" x 2"	L.F.	0.029
Rubberized asphalt, cold		
1/2" x 1"	L.F.	0.016
1" x 2"	L.F.	0.017
Hot, fuel resistant		
1/2" x 1"	L.F.	0.016
1" x 2"	L.F.	0.017

Accessories	UNIT	MAN/ HOURS
03250.40 Concrete Accessories		
Expansion joint, premolded, in slabs		
Asphalt		
1/2" x 6"	L.F.	0.020
1" x 12"	L.F.	0.027
Cork		
1/2" x 6"	L.F.	0.020
1" x 12"	L.F.	0.027
Neoprene sponge		
1/2" x 6"	L.F.	0.020
1" x 12"	L.F.	0.027
Polyethylene foam		
1/2" x 6"	L.F.	0.020
1" x 12"	L.F.	0.027
Polyurethane foam		
1/2" x 6"	L.F.	0.020
1" x 12"	L.F.	0.027
Polyvinyl chloride foam		
1/2" x 6"	L.F.	0.020
1" x 12"	L.F.	0.027
Rubber, gray sponge		
1/2" x 6"	L.F.	0.020
1" x 12"	L.F.	0.027
Asphalt felt control joints or bond breaker, screed joints		
4" slab	L.F.	0.016
6" slab	L.F.	0.018
8" slab	L.F.	0.020
10" slab	L.F.	0.023
Keyed cold expansion and control joints, 24 ga.		
4" slab	L.F.	0.050
5" slab	L.F.	0.050
6" slab	L.F.	0.053
8" slab	L.F.	0.057
10" slab	L.F.	0.062
Waterstops		
Polyvinyl chloride		
Ribbed		
3/16" thick x		
4" wide	L.F.	0.040
6" wide	L.F.	0.044
1/2" thick x		
9" wide	L.F.	0.050
Ribbed with center bulb		
3/16" thick x 9" wide	L.F.	0.050
3/8" thick x 9" wide	L.F.	0.050
Dumbbell type, 3/8" thick x 6" wide	L.F.	0.044
Plain, 3/8" thick x 9" wide	L.F.	0.050
Center bulb, 3/8" thick x 9" wide	L.F.	0.050
Rubber		
Flat dumbbell		
3/8" thick x		
6" wide	L.F.	0.044
9" wide	L.F.	0.050
Center bulb		
3/8" thick x		

Accessories	UNIT	MAN/ HOURS
03250.40 Concrete Accessories		
6" wide	L.F.	0.044
9" wide	L.F.	0.050
Vapor barrier		
4 mil polyethylene	S.F.	0.003
6 mil polyethylene	S.F.	0.003
Gravel porous fill, under floor slabs, 3/4" stone	C.Y.	1.333
Reinforcing accessories		
Beam bolsters		
1-1/2" high, plain	L.F.	0.008
Galvanized	L.F.	0.008
3" high		
Plain	L.F.	0.010
Galvanized	L.F.	0.010
Slab bolsters		
1" high		
Plain	L.F.	0.004
Galvanized	L.F.	0.004
2" high		
Plain	L.F.	0.004
Galvanized	L.F.	0.004
Chairs, high chairs		
3" high		
Plain	EA.	0.020
Galvanized	EA.	0.020
5" high		
Plain	EA.	0.021
Galvanized	EA.	0.021
8" high		
Plain	EA.	0.023
Galvanized	EA.	0.023
12" high		
Plain	EA.	0.027
Galvanized	EA.	0.027
Continuous, high chair		
3" high		
Plain	L.F.	0.005
Galvanized	L.F.	0.005
5" high		
Plain	L.F.	0.006
Galvanized	L.F.	0.006
8" high		
Plain	L.F.	0.006
Galvanized	L.F.	0.006
12" high		
Plain	L.F.	0.007
Galvanized	L.F.	0.007

03 CONCRETE

Cast-in-place Concrete	UNIT	MAN/HOURS
03350.10 Concrete Finishes		
Floor finishes		
Broom	S.F.	0.011
Screed	S.F.	0.010
Darby	S.F.	0.010
Steel float	S.F.	0.013
Granolithic topping		
1/2" thick	S.F.	0.036
1" thick	S.F.	0.040
2" thick	S.F.	0.044
Wall finishes		
Burlap rub, with cement paste	S.F.	0.013
Float finish	S.F.	0.020
Etch with acid	S.F.	0.013
Sandblast		
Minimum	S.F.	0.016
Maximum	S.F.	0.016
Bush hammer		
Green concrete	S.F.	0.040
Cured concrete	S.F.	0.062
Break ties and patch holes	S.F.	0.016
Carborundum		
Dry rub	S.F.	0.027
Wet rub	S.F.	0.040
Floor hardeners		
Metallic		
Light service	S.F.	0.010
Heavy service	S.F.	0.013
Non-metallic		
Light service	S.F.	0.010
Heavy service	S.F.	0.013
Rusticated concrete finish		
Beveled edge	L.F.	0.044
Square edge	L.F.	0.057
Solid board concrete finish		
Standard	S.F.	0.067
Rustic	S.F.	0.080
03360.10 Pneumatic Concrete		
Pneumatic applied concrete (gunite)		
2" thick	S.F.	0.030
3" thick	S.F.	0.040
4" thick	S.F.	0.048
Finish surface		
Minimum	S.F.	0.040
Maximum	S.F.	0.080
03370.10 Curing Concrete		
Sprayed membrane		
Slabs	S.F.	0.002
Walls	S.F.	0.002
Curing paper		
Slabs	S.F.	0.002
Walls	S.F.	0.002
Burlap		

Cast-in-place Concrete	UNIT	MAN/HOURS
03370.10 Curing Concrete		
7.5 oz.	S.F.	0.003
12 oz.	S.F.	0.003

Placing Concrete	UNIT	MAN/HOURS
03380.05 Beam Concrete		
Beams and girders		
2500# or 3000# concrete		
By crane	C.Y.	0.960
By pump	C.Y.	0.873
By hand buggy	C.Y.	0.800
3500# or 4000# concrete		
By crane	C.Y.	0.960
By pump	C.Y.	0.873
By hand buggy	C.Y.	0.800
5000# concrete		
By crane	C.Y.	0.960
By pump	C.Y.	0.873
By hand buggy	C.Y.	0.800
Bond beam, 3000# concrete		
By pump		
8" high		
4" wide	L.F.	0.019
6" wide	L.F.	0.022
8" wide	L.F.	0.024
10" wide	L.F.	0.027
12" wide	L.F.	0.030
16" high		
8" wide	L.F.	0.030
10" wide	L.F.	0.034
12" wide	L.F.	0.040
By crane		
8" high		
4" wide	L.F.	0.021
6" wide	L.F.	0.023
8" wide	L.F.	0.024
10" wide	L.F.	0.027
12" wide	L.F.	0.030
16" high		
8" wide	L.F.	0.030
10" wide	L.F.	0.032
12" wide	L.F.	0.037
03380.15 Column Concrete		
Columns		
2500# or 3000# concrete		
By crane	C.Y.	0.873

Placing Concrete	UNIT	MAN/HOURS
03380.15 Column Concrete		
By pump	C.Y.	0.800
3500# or 4000# concrete		
By crane	C.Y.	0.873
By pump	C.Y.	0.800
5000# concrete		
By crane	C.Y.	0.873
By pump	C.Y.	0.800
03380.20 Elevated Slab Concrete		
Elevated slab		
2500# or 3000# concrete		
By crane	C.Y.	0.480
By pump	C.Y.	0.369
By hand buggy	C.Y.	0.800
3500# or 4000# concrete		
By crane	C.Y.	0.480
By pump	C.Y.	0.369
By hand buggy	C.Y.	0.800
5000# concrete		
By crane	C.Y.	0.480
By pump	C.Y.	0.369
By hand buggy	C.Y.	0.800
Topping		
2500# or 3000# concrete		
By crane	C.Y.	0.480
By pump	C.Y.	0.369
By hand buggy	C.Y.	0.800
3500# or 4000# concrete		
By crane	C.Y.	0.480
By pump	C.Y.	0.369
By hand buggy	C.Y.	0.800
5000# concrete		
By crane	C.Y.	0.480
By pump	C.Y.	0.369
By hand buggy	C.Y.	0.800
03380.25 Equipment Pad Concrete		
Equipment pad		
2500# or 3000# concrete		
By chute	C.Y.	0.267
By pump	C.Y.	0.686
By crane	C.Y.	0.800
3500# or 4000# concrete		
By chute	C.Y.	0.267
By pump	C.Y.	0.686
By crane	C.Y.	0.800
5000# concrete		
By chute	C.Y.	0.267
By pump	C.Y.	0.686
By crane	C.Y.	0.800

Placing Concrete	UNIT	MAN/HOURS
03380.35 Footing Concrete		
Continuous footing		
2500# or 3000# concrete		
By chute	C.Y.	0.267
By pump	C.Y.	0.600
By crane	C.Y.	0.686
3500# or 4000# concrete		
By chute	C.Y.	0.267
By pump	C.Y.	0.600
By crane	C.Y.	0.686
5000# concrete		
By chute	C.Y.	0.267
By pump	C.Y.	0.600
By crane	C.Y.	0.686
Spread footing		
2500# or 3000# concrete		
Under 5 cy		
By chute	C.Y.	0.267
By pump	C.Y.	0.640
By crane	C.Y.	0.738
Over 5 cy		
By chute	C.Y.	0.200
By pump	C.Y.	0.565
By crane	C.Y.	0.640
3500# or 4000# concrete		
Under 5 c.y.		
By chute	C.Y.	0.267
By pump	C.Y.	0.640
By crane	C.Y.	0.738
Over 5 c.y.		
By chute	C.Y.	0.200
By pump	C.Y.	0.565
By crane	C.Y.	0.640
5000# concrete		
Under 5 c.y.		
By chute	C.Y.	0.267
By pump	C.Y.	0.640
By crane	C.Y.	0.738
Over 5 c.y.		
By chute	C.Y.	0.200
By pump	C.Y.	0.565
By crane	C.Y.	0.640
03380.50 Grade Beam Concrete		
Grade beam		
2500# or 3000# concrete		
By chute	C.Y.	0.267
By crane	C.Y.	0.686
By pump	C.Y.	0.600
By hand buggy	C.Y.	0.800
3500# or 4000# concrete		
By chute	C.Y.	0.267
By crane	C.Y.	0.686
By pump	C.Y.	0.600
By hand buggy	C.Y.	0.800

Placing Concrete	UNIT	MAN/HOURS

03380.50 — Grade Beam Concrete

	UNIT	MAN/HOURS
5000# concrete		
By chute	C.Y.	0.267
By crane	C.Y.	0.686
By pump	C.Y.	0.600
By hand buggy	C.Y.	0.800

03380.53 — Pile Cap Concrete

	UNIT	MAN/HOURS
Pile cap		
2500# or 3000 concrete		
By chute	C.Y.	0.267
By crane	C.Y.	0.800
By pump	C.Y.	0.686
By hand buggy	C.Y.	0.800
3500# or 4000# concrete		
By chute	C.Y.	0.267
By crane	C.Y.	0.800
By pump	C.Y.	0.686
By hand buggy	C.Y.	0.800
5000# concrete		
By chute	C.Y.	0.267
By crane	C.Y.	0.800
By pump	C.Y.	0.686
By hand buggy	C.Y.	0.800

03380.55 — Slab/mat Concrete

	UNIT	MAN/HOURS
Slab on grade		
2500# or 3000# concrete		
By chute	C.Y.	0.200
By crane	C.Y.	0.400
By pump	C.Y.	0.343
By hand buggy	C.Y.	0.533
3500# or 4000# concrete		
By chute	C.Y.	0.200
By crane	C.Y.	0.400
By pump	C.Y.	0.343
By hand buggy	C.Y.	0.533
5000# concrete		
By chute	C.Y.	0.200
By crane	C.Y.	0.400
By pump	C.Y.	0.343
By hand buggy	C.Y.	0.533
Foundation mat		
2500# or 3000# concrete, over 20 cy		
By chute	C.Y.	0.160
By crane	C.Y.	0.343
By pump	C.Y.	0.300
By hand buggy	C.Y.	0.400

03380.58 — Sidewalks

	UNIT	MAN/HOURS
Walks, cast in place with wire mesh, base not incl.		
4" thick	S.F.	0.027
5" thick	S.F.	0.032
6" thick	S.F.	0.040

Placing Concrete	UNIT	MAN/HOURS

03380.60 — Stair Concrete

	UNIT	MAN/HOURS
Stairs		
2500# or 3000# concrete		
By chute	C.Y.	0.267
By crane	C.Y.	0.800
By pump	C.Y.	0.686
By hand buggy	C.Y.	0.800
3500# or 4000# concrete		
By chute	C.Y.	0.267
By crane	C.Y.	0.800
By pump	C.Y.	0.686
By hand buggy	C.Y.	0.800
5000# concrete		
By chute	C.Y.	0.267
By crane	C.Y.	0.800
By pump	C.Y.	0.686
By hand buggy	C.Y.	0.800

03380.65 — Wall Concrete

	UNIT	MAN/HOURS
Walls		
2500# or 3000# concrete		
To 4'		
By chute	C.Y.	0.229
By crane	C.Y.	0.800
By pump	C.Y.	0.738
To 8'		
By crane	C.Y.	0.873
By pump	C.Y.	0.800
To 16'		
By crane	C.Y.	0.960
By pump	C.Y.	0.873
Over 16'		
By crane	C.Y.	1.067
By pump	C.Y.	0.960
3500# or 4000# concrete		
To 4'		
By chute	C.Y.	0.229
By crane	C.Y.	0.800
By pump	C.Y.	0.738
To 8'		
By crane	C.Y.	0.873
By pump	C.Y.	0.800
To 16'		
By crane	C.Y.	0.960
By pump	C.Y.	0.873
Over 16'		
By crane	C.Y.	1.067
By pump	C.Y.	0.960
5000# concrete		
To 4'		
By chute	C.Y.	0.229
By crane	C.Y.	0.800
By pump	C.Y.	0.738
To 8'		
By crane	C.Y.	0.873

03 CONCRETE

Placing Concrete		UNIT	MAN/HOURS
03380.65	Wall Concrete		
By pump		C.Y.	0.800
To 16'			
By crane		C.Y.	0.960
By pump		C.Y.	0.873
Filled block (CMU)			
3000# concrete, by pump			
4" wide		S.F.	0.034
6" wide		S.F.	0.040
8" wide		S.F.	0.048
10" wide		S.F.	0.056
12" wide		S.F.	0.069
Pilasters, 3000# concrete		C.F.	0.960
Wall cavity, 2" thick, 3000# concrete		S.F.	0.032

Precast Concrete		UNIT	MAN/HOURS
03400.10	Precast Beams		
Prestressed, double tee, 24" deep, 8' wide			
35' span			
115 psf		S.F.	0.008
140 psf		S.F.	0.008
40' span			
80 psf		S.F.	0.009
143 psf		S.F.	0.009
45' span			
50 psf		S.F.	0.007
70 psf		S.F.	0.007
100 psf		S.F.	0.007
130 psf		S.F.	0.007
50' span			
75 psf		S.F.	0.007
100 psf		S.F.	0.007
Precast beams, girders and joists			
1000 lb/lf live load			
10' span		L.F.	0.160
20' span		L.F.	0.096
30' span		L.F.	0.080
3000 lb/lf live load			
10' span		L.F.	0.160
20' span		L.F.	0.096
30' span		L.F.	0.080
5000 lb/lf live load			
10' span		L.F.	0.160
20' span		L.F.	0.096
30' span		L.F.	0.080

Precast Concrete		UNIT	MAN/HOURS
03400.20	Precast Columns		
Prestressed concrete columns			
10" x 10"			
10' long		EA.	0.960
15' long		EA.	1.000
20' long		EA.	1.067
25' long		EA.	1.143
30' long		EA.	1.200
12" x 12"			
20' long		EA.	1.200
25' long		EA.	1.297
30' long		EA.	1.371
16" x 16"			
20' long		EA.	1.200
25' long		EA.	1.297
30' long		EA.	1.371
20" x 20"			
20' long		EA.	1.263
25' long		EA.	1.333
30' long		EA.	1.412
24" x 24"			
20' long		EA.	1.333
25' long		EA.	1.412
30' long		EA.	1.500
28" x 28"			
20' long		EA.	1.500
25' long		EA.	1.600
30' long		EA.	1.714
32" x 32"			
20' long		EA.	1.600
25' long		EA.	1.714
30' long		EA.	1.846
36" x 36"			
20' long		EA.	1.714
25' long		EA.	1.846
30' long		EA.	2.000
03400.30	Precast Slabs		
Prestressed flat slab			
6" thick, 4' wide			
20' span			
80 psf		S.F.	0.020
110 psf		S.F.	0.020
25' span			
80 psf		S.F.	0.019
Cored slab			
6" thick, 4' wide			
20' span			
80 psf		S.F.	0.020
100 psf		S.F.	0.020
130 psf		S.F.	0.020
8" thick, 4' wide			
25' span			
70 psf		S.F.	0.019
125 psf		S.F.	0.019

Precast Concrete

Precast Concrete	UNIT	MAN/HOURS
03400.30 — Precast Slabs		
170 psf	S.F.	0.019
30' span		
70 psf	S.F.	0.016
90 psf	S.F.	0.016
35' span		
70 psf	S.F.	0.015
10" thick, 4' wide		
30' span		
75 psf	S.F.	0.016
100 psf	S.F.	0.016
130 psf	S.F.	0.016
35' span		
60 psf	S.F.	0.015
80 psf	S.F.	0.015
120 psf	S.F.	0.015
40' span		
65 psf	S.F.	0.012
Slabs, roof and floor members, 4' wide		
6" thick, 25' span	S.F.	0.019
8" thick, 30' span	S.F.	0.015
10" thick, 40' span	S.F.	0.013
Tee members		
Multiple tee, roof and floor		
Minimum	S.F.	0.012
Maximum	S.F.	0.024
Double tee wall member		
Minimum	S.F.	0.014
Maximum	S.F.	0.027
Single tee		
Short span, roof members		
Minimum	S.F.	0.015
Maximum	S.F.	0.030
Long span, roof members		
Minimum	S.F.	0.012
Maximum	S.F.	0.024
03400.40 — Precast Walls		
Wall panel, 8' x 20'		
Gray cement		
Liner finish		
4" wall	S.F.	0.014
5" wall	S.F.	0.014
6" wall	S.F.	0.015
8" wall	S.F.	0.015
Sandblast finish		
4" wall	S.F.	0.014
5" wall	S.F.	0.014
6" wall	S.F.	0.015
8" wall	S.F.	0.015
White cement		
Liner finish		
4" wall	S.F.	0.014
5" wall	S.F.	0.014
6" wall	S.F.	0.015

Precast Concrete	UNIT	MAN/HOURS
03400.40 — Precast Walls		
8" wall	S.F.	0.015
Sandblast finish		
4" wall	S.F.	0.014
5" wall	S.F.	0.014
6" wall	S.F.	0.015
8" wall	S.F.	0.015
Double tee wall panel, 24" deep		
Gray cement		
Liner finish	S.F.	0.016
Sandblast finish	S.F.	0.016
White cement		
Form liner finish	S.F.	0.016
Sandblast finish	S.F.	0.016
Partition panels		
4" wall	S.F.	0.016
5" wall	S.F.	0.016
6" wall	S.F.	0.016
8" wall	S.F.	0.016
Cladding panels		
4" wall	S.F.	0.017
5" wall	S.F.	0.017
6" wall	S.F.	0.017
8" wall	S.F.	0.017
Sandwich panel, 2.5" cladding panel, 2" insulation		
5" wall	S.F.	0.017
6" wall	S.F.	0.017
8" wall	S.F.	0.017
Adjustable tilt-up brace	EA.	0.200
03400.90 — Precast Specialties		
Precast concrete, coping, 4' to 8' long		
12" wide	L.F.	0.060
10" wide	L.F.	0.069
Splash block, 30"x12"x4"	EA.	0.400
Stair unit, per riser	EA.	0.400
Sun screen and trellis, 8' long, 12" high		
4" thick blades	EA.	0.300
5" thick blades	EA.	0.300
6" thick blades	EA.	0.320
8" thick blades	EA.	0.320
Bearing pads for precast members, 2" wide strips		
1/8" thick	L.F.	0.003
1/4" thick	L.F.	0.003
1/2" thick	L.F.	0.003
3/4" thick	L.F.	0.004
1" thick	L.F.	0.004
1-1/2" thick	L.F.	0.004

Cementitous Toppings

	UNIT	MAN/HOURS

03550.10   Concrete Toppings

	UNIT	MAN/HOURS
Gypsum fill		
2" thick	S.F.	0.005
2-1/2" thick	S.F.	0.005
3" thick	S.F.	0.005
3-1/2" thick	S.F.	0.005
4" thick	S.F.	0.006
Formboard		
Mineral fiber board		
1" thick	S.F.	0.020
1-1/2" thick	S.F.	0.023
Cement fiber board		
1" thick	S.F.	0.027
1-1/2" thick	S.F.	0.031
Glass fiber board		
1" thick	S.F.	0.020
1-1/2" thick	S.F.	0.023
Poured deck		
Vermiculite or perlite		
1 to 4 mix	C.Y.	0.800
1 to 6 mix	C.Y.	0.738
Vermiculite or perlite		
2" thick		
1 to 4 mix	S.F.	0.005
1 to 6 mix	S.F.	0.005
3" thick		
1 to 4 mix	S.F.	0.007
1 to 6 mix	S.F.	0.007
Concrete plank, lightweight		
2" thick	S.F.	0.024
2-1/2" thick	S.F.	0.024
3-1/2" thick	S.F.	0.027
4" thick	S.F.	0.027
Channel slab, lightweight, straight		
2-3/4" thick	S.F.	0.024
3-1/2" thick	S.F.	0.024
3-3/4" thick	S.F.	0.024
4-3/4" thick	S.F.	0.027
Gypsum plank		
2" thick	S.F.	0.024
3" thick	S.F.	0.024
Cement fiber, T and G planks		
1" thick	S.F.	0.022
1-1/2" thick	S.F.	0.022
2" thick	S.F.	0.024
2-1/2" thick	S.F.	0.024
3" thick	S.F.	0.024
3-1/2" thick	S.F.	0.027
4" thick	S.F.	0.027

Grout

	UNIT	MAN/HOURS

03600.10   Grouting

	UNIT	MAN/HOURS
Grouting for bases		
Nonshrink		
Metallic grout		
1" deep	S.F.	0.160
2" deep	S.F.	0.178
Non-metallic grout		
1" deep	S.F.	0.160
2" deep	S.F.	0.178
Fluid type		
Non-metallic		
1" deep	S.F.	0.160
2" deep	S.F.	0.178
Grouting for joints		
Portland cement grout (1 cement to 3 sand, by volume)		
1/2" joint thickness		
6" wide joints	L.F.	0.027
8" wide joints	L.F.	0.032
1" joint thickness		
4" wide joints	L.F.	0.025
6" wide joints	L.F.	0.028
8" wide joints	L.F.	0.033
Nonshrink, nonmetallic grout		
1/2" joint thickness		
4" wide joint	L.F.	0.023
6" wide joint	L.F.	0.027
8" wide joint	L.F.	0.032
1" joint thickness		
4" wide joint	L.F.	0.025
6" wide joint	L.F.	0.028
8" wide joint	L.F.	0.033

Concrete Restoration

	UNIT	MAN/HOURS

03730.10   Concrete Repair

	UNIT	MAN/HOURS
Epoxy grout floor patch, 1/4" thick	S.F.	0.080
Epoxy gel grout	S.F.	0.800
Injection valve, 1 way, threaded plastic	EA.	0.160
Grout crack seal, 2 component	C.F.	0.800
Grout, non shrink	C.F.	0.800
Concrete, epoxy modified		
Sand mix	C.F.	0.320
Gravel mix	C.F.	0.296
Concrete repair		
Soffit repair		
16" wide	L.F.	0.160
18" wide	L.F.	0.167
24" wide	L.F.	0.178

Concrete Restoration	UNIT	MAN/ HOURS
03730.10 Concrete Repair		
30" wide	L.F.	0.190
32" wide	L.F.	0.200
Edge repair		
2" spall	L.F.	0.200
3" spall	L.F.	0.211
4" spall	L.F.	0.216
6" spall	L.F.	0.222
8" spall	L.F.	0.235
9" spall	L.F.	0.267
Crack repair, 1/8" crack	L.F.	0.080
Reinforcing steel repair		
1 bar, 4 ft		
#4 bar	L.F.	0.100
#5 bar	L.F.	0.100
#6 bar	L.F.	0.107
#8 bar	L.F.	0.107
#9 bar	L.F.	0.114
#11 bar	L.F.	0.114
Pile repairs		
Polyethylene wrap		
30 mil thick		
60" wide	S.F.	0.267
72" wide	S.F.	0.320
60 mil thick		
60" wide	S.F.	0.267
80" wide	S.F.	0.364
Pile spall, average repair 3'		
18" x 18"	EA.	0.667
20" x 20"	EA.	0.800

Mortar And Grout

04100.10 — Masonry Grout

	UNIT	MAN/HOURS
Grout, non shrink, non-metallic, trowelable	C.F.	0.016
Grout door frame, hollow metal		
Single	EA.	0.600
Double	EA.	0.632
Grout-filled concrete block (CMU)		
4" wide	S.F.	0.020
6" wide	S.F.	0.022
8" wide	S.F.	0.024
12" wide	S.F.	0.025
Grout-filled individual CMU cells		
4" wide	L.F.	0.012
6" wide	L.F.	0.012
8" wide	L.F.	0.012
10" wide	L.F.	0.014
12" wide	L.F.	0.014
Bond beams or lintels, 8" deep		
6" thick	L.F.	0.022
8" thick	L.F.	0.024
10" thick	L.F.	0.027
12" thick	L.F.	0.030
Cavity walls		
2" thick	S.F.	0.032
3" thick	S.F.	0.032
4" thick	S.F.	0.034
6" thick	S.F.	0.040

04150.10 — Masonry Accessories

	UNIT	MAN/HOURS
Foundation vents	EA.	0.320
Bar reinforcing		
Horizontal		
#3 - #4	Lb.	0.032
#5 - #6	Lb.	0.027
Vertical		
#3 - #4	Lb.	0.040
#5 - #6	Lb.	0.032
Horizontal joint reinforcing		
Truss type		
4" wide, 6" wall	L.F.	0.003
6" wide, 8" wall	L.F.	0.003
8" wide, 10" wall	L.F.	0.003
10" wide, 12" wall	L.F.	0.004
12" wide, 14" wall	L.F.	0.004
Ladder type		
4" wide, 6" wall	L.F.	0.003
6" wide, 8" wall	L.F.	0.003
8" wide, 10" wall	L.F.	0.003
10" wide, 12" wall	L.F.	0.003
Rectangular wall ties		
3/16" dia., galvanized		
2" x 6"	EA.	0.013
2" x 8"	EA.	0.013
2" x 10"	EA.	0.013
2" x 12"	EA.	0.013
4" x 6"	EA.	0.016

Mortar And Grout

04150.10 — Masonry Accessories

	UNIT	MAN/HOURS
4" x 8"	EA.	0.016
4" x 10"	EA.	0.016
4" x 12"	EA.	0.016
1/4" dia., galvanized		
2" x 6"	EA.	0.013
2" x 8"	EA.	0.013
2" x 10"	EA.	0.013
2" x 12"	EA.	0.013
4" x 6"	EA.	0.016
4" x 8"	EA.	0.016
4" x 10"	EA.	0.016
4" x 12"	EA.	0.016
"Z" type wall ties, galvanized		
6" long		
1/8" dia.	EA.	0.013
3/16" dia.	EA.	0.013
1/4" dia.	EA.	0.013
8" long		
1/8" dia.	EA.	0.013
3/16" dia.	EA.	0.013
1/4" dia.	EA.	0.013
10" long		
1/8" dia.	EA.	0.013
3/16" dia.	EA.	0.013
1/4" dia.	EA.	0.013
Dovetail anchor slots		
Galvanized steel, filled		
24 ga.	L.F.	0.020
20 ga.	L.F.	0.020
16 oz. copper, foam filled	L.F.	0.020
Dovetail anchors		
16 ga.		
3-1/2" long	EA.	0.013
5-1/2" long	EA.	0.013
12 ga.		
3-1/2" long	EA.	0.013
5-1/2" long	EA.	0.013
Dovetail, triangular galvanized ties, 12 ga.		
3" x 3"	EA.	0.013
5" x 5"	EA.	0.013
7" x 7"	EA.	0.013
7" x 9"	EA.	0.013
Brick anchors		
Corrugated, 3-1/2" long		
16 ga.	EA.	0.013
12 ga.	EA.	0.013
Non-corrugated, 3-1/2" long		
16 ga.	EA.	0.013
12 ga.	EA.	0.013

04150.20 — Masonry Control Joints

	UNIT	MAN/HOURS
Control joint, cross shaped PVC	L.F.	0.020
Closed cell joint filler		
1/2"	L.F.	0.020

Mortar And Grout

	UNIT	MAN/HOURS
04150.20 Masonry Control Joints		
3/4"	L.F.	0.020
Rubber, for		
4" wall	L.F.	0.020
6" wall	L.F.	0.021
8" wall	L.F.	0.022
PVC, for		
4" wall	L.F.	0.020
6" wall	L.F.	0.021
8" wall	L.F.	0.022
04150.50 Masonry Flashing		
Through-wall flashing		
5 oz. coated copper	S.F.	0.067
0.030" elastomeric	S.F.	0.053

Unit Masonry

	UNIT	MAN/HOURS
04210.10 Brick Masonry		
Standard size brick, running bond		
Face brick, red (6.4/sf)		
Veneer	S.F.	0.133
Cavity wall	S.F.	0.114
9" solid wall	S.F.	0.229
Back-up		
4" thick	S.F.	0.100
8" thick	S.F.	0.160
Firewall		
12" thick	S.F.	0.267
16" thick	S.F.	0.364
Glazed brick (7.4/sf)		
Veneer	S.F.	0.145
Buff or gray face brick (6.4/sf)		
Veneer	S.F.	0.133
Cavity wall	S.F.	0.114
Jumbo or oversize brick (3/sf)		
4" veneer	S.F.	0.080
4" back-up	S.F.	0.067
8" back-up	S.F.	0.114
12" firewall	S.F.	0.200
16" firewall	S.F.	0.267
Norman brick, red face, (4.5/sf)		
4" veneer	S.F.	0.100
Cavity wall	S.F.	0.089
Chimney, standard brick, including flue		
16" x 16"	L.F.	0.800
16" x 20"	L.F.	0.800
16" x 24"	L.F.	0.800

Unit Masonry

	UNIT	MAN/HOURS
04210.10 Brick Masonry		
20" x 20"	L.F.	1.000
20" x 24"	L.F.	1.000
20" x 32"	L.F.	1.143
Window sill, face brick on edge	L.F.	0.200
04210.20 Structural Tile		
Structural glazed tile		
6T series, 5-1/2" x 12"		
Glazed on one side		
2" thick	S.F.	0.080
4" thick	S.F.	0.080
6" thick	S.F.	0.089
8" thick	S.F.	0.100
Glazed on two sides		
4" thick	S.F.	0.100
6" thick	S.F.	0.114
04210.60 Pavers, Masonry		
Brick walk laid on sand, sand joints		
Laid flat, (4.5 per sf)	S.F.	0.089
Laid on edge, (7.2 per sf)	S.F.	0.133
Precast concrete patio blocks		
2" thick		
Natural	S.F.	0.027
Colors	S.F.	0.027
Exposed aggregates, local aggregate		
Natural	S.F.	0.027
Colors	S.F.	0.027
Granite or limestone aggregate	S.F.	0.027
White tumblestone aggregate	S.F.	0.027
Stone pavers, set in mortar		
Bluestone		
1" thick		
Irregular	S.F.	0.200
Snapped rectangular	S.F.	0.160
1-1/2" thick, random rectangular	S.F.	0.200
2" thick, random rectangular	S.F.	0.229
Slate		
Natural cleft		
Irregular, 3/4" thick	S.F.	0.229
Random rectangular		
1-1/4" thick	S.F.	0.200
1-1/2" thick	S.F.	0.222
Granite blocks		
3" thick, 3" to 6" wide		
4" to 12" long	S.F.	0.267
6" to 15" long	S.F.	0.229
Crushed stone, white marble, 3" thick	S.F.	0.016
04220.10 Concrete Masonry Units		
Hollow, load bearing		
4"	S.F.	0.059
6"	S.F.	0.062
8"	S.F.	0.067

Unit Masonry	UNIT	MAN/HOURS
04220.10 Concrete Masonry Units		
10"	S.F.	0.073
12"	S.F.	0.080
Solid, load bearing		
4"	S.F.	0.059
6"	S.F.	0.062
8"	S.F.	0.067
10"	S.F.	0.073
12"	S.F.	0.080
Back-up block, 8" x 16"		
2"	S.F.	0.046
4"	S.F.	0.047
6"	S.F.	0.050
8"	S.F.	0.053
10"	S.F.	0.057
12"	S.F.	0.062
Foundation wall, 8" x 16"		
6"	S.F.	0.057
8"	S.F.	0.062
10"	S.F.	0.067
12"	S.F.	0.073
Solid		
6"	S.F.	0.062
8"	S.F.	0.067
10"	S.F.	0.073
12"	S.F.	0.080
Exterior, styrofoam inserts, standard weight, 8" x 16"		
6"	S.F.	0.062
8"	S.F.	0.067
10"	S.F.	0.073
12"	S.F.	0.080
Acoustical slotted block		
4"	S.F.	0.073
6"	S.F.	0.073
8"	S.F.	0.080
Filled cavities		
4"	S.F.	0.089
6"	S.F.	0.094
8"	S.F.	0.100
Hollow, split face		
4"	S.F.	0.059
6"	S.F.	0.062
8"	S.F.	0.067
10"	S.F.	0.073
12"	S.F.	0.080
Split rib profile		
4"	S.F.	0.073
6"	S.F.	0.073
8"	S.F.	0.080
10"	S.F.	0.080
12"	S.F.	0.080
High strength block, 3500 psi		
2"	S.F.	0.059
4"	S.F.	0.062
6"	S.F.	0.062

Unit Masonry	UNIT	MAN/HOURS
04220.10 Concrete Masonry Units		
8"	S.F.	0.067
10"	S.F.	0.073
12"	S.F.	0.080
Solar screen concrete block		
4" thick		
6" x 6"	S.F.	0.178
8" x 8"	S.F.	0.160
12" x 12"	S.F.	0.123
8" thick		
8" x 16"	S.F.	0.114
Glazed block		
Cove base, glazed 1 side, 2"	L.F.	0.089
4"	L.F.	0.089
6"	L.F.	0.100
8"	L.F.	0.100
Single face		
2"	S.F.	0.067
4"	S.F.	0.067
6"	S.F.	0.073
8"	S.F.	0.080
10"	S.F.	0.089
12"	S.F.	0.094
Double face		
4"	S.F.	0.084
6"	S.F.	0.089
8"	S.F.	0.100
Corner or bullnose		
2"	EA.	0.100
4"	EA.	0.114
6"	EA.	0.114
8"	EA.	0.133
10"	EA.	0.145
12"	EA.	0.160
04220.90 Bond Beams & Lintels		
Bond beam, no grout or reinforcement		
8" x 16" x		
4" thick	L.F.	0.062
6" thick	L.F.	0.064
8" thick	L.F.	0.067
10" thick	L.F.	0.070
12" thick	L.F.	0.073
Beam lintel, no grout or reinforcement		
8" x 16" x		
10" thick	L.F.	0.080
12" thick	L.F.	0.089
Precast masonry lintel		
6 lf, 8" high x		
4" thick	L.F.	0.133
6" thick	L.F.	0.133
8" thick	L.F.	0.145
10" thick	L.F.	0.145
10 lf, 8" high x		
4" thick	L.F.	0.080

Unit Masonry

Unit Masonry	UNIT	MAN/HOURS
04220.90 **Bond Beams & Lintels**		
6" thick	L.F.	0.080
8" thick	L.F.	0.089
10" thick	L.F.	0.089
Steel angles and plates		
Minimum	Lb.	0.011
Maximum	Lb.	0.020
Various size angle lintels		
1/4" stock		
3" x 3"	L.F.	0.050
3" x 3-1/2"	L.F.	0.050
3/8" stock		
3" x 4"	L.F.	0.050
3-1/2" x 4"	L.F.	0.050
4" x 4"	L.F.	0.050
5" x 3-1/2"	L.F.	0.050
6" x 3-1/2"	L.F.	0.050
1/2" stock		
6" x 4"	L.F.	0.050
04270.10 **Glass Block**		
Glass block, 4" thick		
6" x 6"	S.F.	0.267
8" x 8"	S.F.	0.200
12" x 12"	S.F.	0.160
Replacement glass blocks, 4" x 8" x 8"		
Minimum	S.F.	0.800
Maximum	S.F.	1.600
04295.10 **Parging/masonry Plaster**		
Parging		
1/2" thick	S.F.	0.053
3/4" thick	S.F.	0.067
1" thick	S.F.	0.080

Stone

Stone	UNIT	MAN/HOURS
04400.10 **Stone**		
Rubble stone		
Walls set in mortar		
8" thick	S.F.	0.200
12" thick	S.F.	0.320
18" thick	S.F.	0.400
24" thick	S.F.	0.533
Dry set wall		
8" thick	S.F.	0.133
12" thick	S.F.	0.200
18" thick	S.F.	0.267

Stone

Stone	UNIT	MAN/HOURS
04400.10 **Stone**		
24" thick	S.F.	0.320
Cut stone		
Facing panels		
3/4" thick	S.F.	0.320
1-1/2" thick	S.F.	0.364

Masonry Restoration

Masonry Restoration	UNIT	MAN/HOURS
04520.10 **Restoration And Cleaning**		
Masonry cleaning		
Washing brick		
Smooth surface	S.F.	0.013
Rough surface	S.F.	0.018
Steam clean masonry		
Smooth face		
Minimum	S.F.	0.010
Maximum	S.F.	0.015
Rough face		
Minimum	S.F.	0.013
Maximum	S.F.	0.020
Sandblast masonry		
Minimum	S.F.	0.016
Maximum	S.F.	0.027
Pointing masonry		
Brick	S.F.	0.032
Concrete block	S.F.	0.023
Cut and repoint		
Brick		
Minimum	S.F.	0.040
Maximum	S.F.	0.080
Stone work	L.F.	0.062
Cut and recaulk		
Oil base caulks	L.F.	0.053
Butyl caulks	L.F.	0.053
Polysulfides and acrylics	L.F.	0.053
Silicones	L.F.	0.053
Cement and sand grout on walls, to 1/8" thick		
Minimum	S.F.	0.032
Maximum	S.F.	0.040
Brick removal and replacement		
Minimum	EA.	0.100
Average	EA.	0.133
Maximum	EA.	0.400

Metal Fastening	UNIT	MAN/HOURS
05050.10 — Structural Welding		
Welding		
Single pass		
1/8"	L.F.	0.040
3/16"	L.F.	0.053
1/4"	L.F.	0.067
Miscellaneous steel shapes		
Plain	Lb.	0.002
Galvanized	Lb.	0.003
Plates		
Plain	Lb.	0.002
Galvanized	Lb.	0.003
05050.95 — Metal Lintels		
Lintels, steel		
Plain	Lb.	0.020
Galvanized	Lb.	0.020
05120.10 — Structural Steel		
Beams and girders, A-36		
Welded	TON	4.800
Bolted	TON	4.364
Columns		
Pipe		
6" dia.	Lb.	0.005
12" dia.	Lb.	0.004
Purlins and girts		
Welded	TON	8.000
Bolted	TON	6.857
Column base plates		
Up to 150 lb each	Lb.	0.005
Over 150 lb each	Lb.	0.007
Structural pipe		
3" to 5" o.d.	TON	9.600
6" to 12" o.d.	TON	6.857
Structural tube		
6" square		
Light sections	TON	9.600
Heavy sections	TON	6.857
6" wide rectangular		
Light sections	TON	8.000
Heavy sections	TON	6.000
Greater than 6" wide rectangular		
Light sections	TON	8.000
Heavy sections	TON	6.000
Miscellaneous structural shapes		
Steel angle	TON	12.000
Steel plate	TON	8.000
Trusses, field welded		
60 lb/lf	TON	6.000
100 lb/lf	TON	4.800
150 lb/lf	TON	4.000
Bolted		
60 lb/lf	TON	5.333
100 lb/lf	TON	4.364

Metal Fastening	UNIT	MAN/HOURS
05120.10 — Structural Steel		
150 lb/lf	TON	3.692

Cold Formed Framing	UNIT	MAN/HOURS
05410.10 — Metal Framing		
Furring channel, galvanized		
Beams and columns, 3/4"		
12" o.c.	S.F.	0.080
16" o.c.	S.F.	0.073
Walls, 3/4"		
12" o.c.	S.F.	0.040
16" o.c.	S.F.	0.033
24" o.c.	S.F.	0.027
1-1/2"		
12" o.c.	S.F.	0.040
16" o.c.	S.F.	0.033
24" o.c.	S.F.	0.027
Stud, load bearing		
16" o.c.		
16 ga.		
2-1/2"	S.F.	0.036
3-5/8"	S.F.	0.036
4"	S.F.	0.036
6"	S.F.	0.040
24" o.c.		
16 ga.		
2-1/2"	S.F.	0.031
3-5/8"	S.F.	0.031
4"	S.F.	0.031
6"	S.F.	0.033
8"	S.F.	0.033

Metal Fabrications	UNIT	MAN/HOURS
05510.10 — Stairs		
Stock unit, steel, complete, per riser		
Tread		
3'-6" wide	EA.	1.000
4' wide	EA.	1.143
5' wide	EA.	1.333
Metal pan stair, cement filled, per riser		

05 METALS

Metal Fabrications	UNIT	MAN/HOURS
05510.10 Stairs		
3'-6" wide	EA.	0.800
4' wide	EA.	0.889
5' wide	EA.	1.000
Landing, steel pan	S.F.	0.200
Cast iron tread, steel stringers, stock units, per riser		
Tread		
3'-6" wide	EA.	1.000
4' wide	EA.	1.143
5' wide	EA.	1.333
Stair treads, abrasive, 12" x 3'-6"		
Cast iron		
3/8"	EA.	0.400
1/2"	EA.	0.400
Cast aluminum		
5/16"	EA.	0.400
3/8"	EA.	0.400
1/2"	EA.	0.400
05515.10 Ladders		
Ladder, 18" wide		
With cage	L.F.	0.533
Without cage	L.F.	0.400
05520.10 Railings		
Railing, pipe		
1-1/4" diameter, welded steel		
2-rail		
Primed	L.F.	0.160
Galvanized	L.F.	0.160
3-rail		
Primed	L.F.	0.200
Galvanized	L.F.	0.200
Wall mounted, single rail, welded steel		
Primed	L.F.	0.123
Galvanized	L.F.	0.123
1-1/2" diameter, welded steel		
2-rail		
Primed	L.F.	0.160
Galvanized	L.F.	0.160
3-rail		
Primed	L.F.	0.200
Galvanized	L.F.	0.200
Wall mounted, single rail, welded steel		
Primed	L.F.	0.123
Galvanized	L.F.	0.123
2" diameter, welded steel		
2-rail		
Primed	L.F.	0.178
Galvanized	L.F.	0.178
3-rail		
Primed	L.F.	0.229
Galvanized	L.F.	0.229
Wall mounted, single rail, welded steel		
Primed	L.F.	0.133

Metal Fabrications	UNIT	MAN/HOURS
05520.10 Railings		
Galvanized	L.F.	0.133
05530.10 Metal Grating		
Floor plate, checkered, steel		
1/4"		
Primed	S.F.	0.011
Galvanized	S.F.	0.011
3/8"		
Primed	S.F.	0.012
Galvanized	S.F.	0.012
Aluminum grating, pressure-locked bearing bars		
3/4" x 1/8"	S.F.	0.020
1" x 1/8"	S.F.	0.020
1-1/4" x 1/8"	S.F.	0.020
1-1/4" x 3/16"	S.F.	0.020
1-1/2" x 1/8"	S.F.	0.020
1-3/4" x 3/16"	S.F.	0.020
Miscellaneous expenses		
Cutting		
Minimum	L.F.	0.053
Maximum	L.F.	0.080
Banding		
Minimum	L.F.	0.133
Maximum	L.F.	0.160
Toe plates		
Minimum	L.F.	0.160
Maximum	L.F.	0.200
Steel grating, primed		
3/4" x 1/8"	S.F.	0.027
1" x 1/8"	S.F.	0.027
1-1/4" x 1/8"	S.F.	0.027
1-1/4" x 3/16"	S.F.	0.027
1-1/2" x 1/8"	S.F.	0.027
1-3/4" x 3/16"	S.F.	0.027
Galvanized		
3/4" x 1/8"	S.F.	0.027
1" x 1/8"	S.F.	0.027
1-1/4" x 1/8"	S.F.	0.027
1-1/4" x 3/16"	S.F.	0.027
1-1/2" x 1/8"	S.F.	0.027
1-3/4" x 3/16"	S.F.	0.027
Miscellaneous expenses		
Cutting		
Minimum	L.F.	0.057
Maximum	L.F.	0.089
Banding		
Minimum	L.F.	0.145
Maximum	L.F.	0.178
Toe plates		
Minimum	L.F.	0.178
Maximum	L.F.	0.229

Metal Fabrications

Metal Fabrications	UNIT	MAN/ HOURS
05540.10 — Castings		
Miscellaneous castings		
Light sections	Lb.	0.016
Heavy sections	Lb.	0.011
Manhole covers and frames		
Regular, city type		
18" dia.		
100 lb	EA.	1.600
24" dia.		
200 lb	EA.	1.600
300 lb	EA.	1.778
400 lb	EA.	1.778
26" dia., 475 lb	EA.	2.000
30" dia., 600 lb	EA.	2.286
8" square, 75 lb	EA.	0.320
24" square		
126 lb	EA.	1.600
500 lb	EA.	2.000
Watertight type		
20" dia., 200 lb	EA.	2.000
24" dia., 350 lb	EA.	2.667
Steps, cast iron		
7" x 9"	EA.	0.160
8" x 9"	EA.	0.178
Manhole covers and frames, aluminum		
12" x 12"	EA.	0.320
18" x 18"	EA.	0.320
24" x 24"	EA.	0.400
Corner protection		
Steel angle guard with anchors		
2" x 2" x 3/16"	L.F.	0.114
2" x 3" x 1/4"	L.F.	0.114
3" x 3" x 5/16"	L.F.	0.114
3" x 4" x 5/16"	L.F.	0.123
4" x 4" x 5/16"	L.F.	0.123

Misc. Fabrications

Misc. Fabrications	UNIT	MAN/ HOURS
05580.10 — Metal Specialties		
Kick plate		
4" high x 1/4" thick		
Primed	L.F.	0.160
Galvanized	L.F.	0.160
6" high x 1/4" thick		
Primed	L.F.	0.178
Galvanized	L.F.	0.178

Misc. Fabrications

Misc. Fabrications	UNIT	MAN/ HOURS
05700.10 — Ornamental Metal		
Railings, vertical square bars, 6" o.c., with shaped top rails		
Steel	L.F.	0.400
Aluminum	L.F.	0.400
Bronze	L.F.	0.533
Stainless steel	L.F.	0.533
Laminated metal or wood handrails with metal supports		
2-1/2" round or oval shape	L.F.	0.400
05800.10 — Expansion Control		
Expansion joints with covers, floor assembly type		
With 1" space		
Aluminum	L.F.	0.133
Bronze	L.F.	0.133
Stainless steel	L.F.	0.133
With 2" space		
Aluminum	L.F.	0.133
Bronze	L.F.	0.133
Stainless steel	L.F.	0.133
Ceiling and wall assembly type		
With 1" space		
Aluminum	L.F.	0.160
Bronze	L.F.	0.160
Stainless steel	L.F.	0.160
With 2" space		
Aluminum	L.F.	0.160
Bronze	L.F.	0.160
Stainless steel	L.F.	0.160
Exterior roof and wall, aluminum		
Roof to roof		
With 1" space	L.F.	0.133
With 2" space	L.F.	0.133
Roof to wall		
With 1" space	L.F.	0.145
With 2" space	L.F.	0.145

06 WOOD AND PLASTICS

Fasteners And Adhesives	UNIT	MAN/HOURS
06050.10 Accessories		
Column/post base, cast aluminum		
4" x 4"	EA.	0.200
6" x 6"	EA.	0.200
Bridging, metal, per pair		
12" o.c.	EA.	0.080
16" o.c.	EA.	0.073
Anchors		
Bolts, threaded two ends, with nuts and washers		
1/2" dia.		
4" long	EA.	0.050
7-1/2" long	EA.	0.050
15" long	EA.	0.050
Bolts, carriage		
1/4 x 4	EA.	0.080
5/16 x 6	EA.	0.084
Joist and beam hangers		
18 ga.		
2 x 4	EA.	0.080
2 x 6	EA.	0.080
2 x 8	EA.	0.080
2 x 10	EA.	0.089
2 x 12	EA.	0.100
16 ga.		
3 x 6	EA.	0.089
3 x 8	EA.	0.089
3 x 10	EA.	0.094
3 x 12	EA.	0.107
3 x 14	EA.	0.114
4 x 6	EA.	0.089
4 x 8	EA.	0.089
4 x 10	EA.	0.094
4 x 12	EA.	0.107
4 x 14	EA.	0.114
Rafter anchors, 18 ga., 1-1/2" wide		
5-1/4" long	EA.	0.067
10-3/4" long	EA.	0.067
Sill anchors		
Embedded in concrete	EA.	0.080
Strap ties, 14 ga., 1-3/8" wide		
12" long	EA.	0.067

Rough Carpentry	UNIT	MAN/HOURS
06110.10 Blocking		
Steel construction		
Walls		
2x4	L.F.	0.053

Rough Carpentry	UNIT	MAN/HOURS
06110.10 Blocking		
2x6	L.F.	0.062
2x8	L.F.	0.067
2x10	L.F.	0.073
2x12	L.F.	0.080
Ceilings		
2x4	L.F.	0.062
2x6	L.F.	0.073
2x8	L.F.	0.080
2x10	L.F.	0.089
2x12	L.F.	0.100
Wood construction		
Walls		
2x4	L.F.	0.044
2x6	L.F.	0.050
2x8	L.F.	0.053
2x10	L.F.	0.057
2x12	L.F.	0.062
Ceilings		
2x4	L.F.	0.050
2x6	L.F.	0.057
2x8	L.F.	0.062
2x10	L.F.	0.067
2x12	L.F.	0.073
06110.20 Ceiling Framing		
Ceiling joists		
16" o.c.		
2x4	S.F.	0.015
2x6	S.F.	0.016
2x8	S.F.	0.017
2x10	S.F.	0.017
2x12	S.F.	0.018
Headers and nailers		
2x4	L.F.	0.026
2x6	L.F.	0.027
2x8	L.F.	0.029
2x10	L.F.	0.031
2x12	L.F.	0.033
Sister joists for ceilings		
2x4	L.F.	0.057
2x6	L.F.	0.067
2x8	L.F.	0.080
2x10	L.F.	0.100
2x12	L.F.	0.133
06110.30 Floor Framing		
Floor joists		
16" o.c.		
2x6	S.F.	0.013
2x8	S.F.	0.014
2x10	S.F.	0.014
2x12	S.F.	0.014
2x14	S.F.	0.015
3x6	S.F.	0.014

Rough Carpentry	UNIT	MAN/HOURS
06110.30 Floor Framing		
3x8	S.F.	0.014
3x10	S.F.	0.015
3x12	S.F.	0.015
3x14	S.F.	0.016
4x6	S.F.	0.014
4x8	S.F.	0.014
4x10	S.F.	0.015
4x12	S.F.	0.015
4x14	S.F.	0.016
Sister joists for floors		
2x4	L.F.	0.050
2x6	L.F.	0.057
2x8	L.F.	0.067
2x10	L.F.	0.080
2x12	L.F.	0.100
06110.40 Furring		
Furring, wood strips		
Walls		
On masonry or concrete walls		
1x2 furring		
12" o.c.	S.F.	0.025
16" o.c.	S.F.	0.023
24" o.c.	S.F.	0.021
1x3 furring		
12" o.c.	S.F.	0.025
16" o.c.	S.F.	0.023
24" o.c.	S.F.	0.021
On wood walls		
1x2 furring		
12" o.c.	S.F.	0.018
16" o.c.	S.F.	0.016
24" o.c.	S.F.	0.015
1x3 furring		
12" o.c.	S.F.	0.018
16" o.c.	S.F.	0.016
24" o.c.	S.F.	0.015
Ceilings		
On masonry or concrete ceilings		
1x2 furring		
12" o.c.	S.F.	0.044
16" o.c.	S.F.	0.040
24" o.c.	S.F.	0.036
1x3 furring		
12" o.c.	S.F.	0.044
16" o.c.	S.F.	0.040
24" o.c.	S.F.	0.036
On wood ceilings		
1x2 furring		
12" o.c.	S.F.	0.030
16" o.c.	S.F.	0.027
24" o.c.	S.F.	0.024
1x3		
12" o.c.	S.F.	0.030

Rough Carpentry	UNIT	MAN/HOURS
06110.40 Furring		
16" o.c.	S.F.	0.027
24" o.c.	S.F.	0.024
06110.50 Roof Framing		
Roof framing		
Rafters, gable end		
4-6 pitch (4-in-12 to 6-in-12)		
16" o.c.		
2x6	S.F.	0.015
2x8	S.F.	0.015
2x10	S.F.	0.016
2x12	S.F.	0.017
24" o.c.		
2x6	S.F.	0.013
2x8	S.F.	0.013
2x10	S.F.	0.014
2x12	S.F.	0.015
Ridge boards		
2x6	L.F.	0.040
2x8	L.F.	0.044
2x10	L.F.	0.050
2x12	L.F.	0.057
Hip rafters		
2x6	L.F.	0.029
2x8	L.F.	0.030
2x10	L.F.	0.031
2x12	L.F.	0.032
Jack rafters		
4-6 pitch (4-in-12 to 6-in-12)		
16" o.c.		
2x6	S.F.	0.024
2x8	S.F.	0.024
2x10	S.F.	0.026
2x12	S.F.	0.027
24" o.c.		
2x6	S.F.	0.018
2x8	S.F.	0.019
2x10	S.F.	0.020
2x12	S.F.	0.020
Sister rafters		
2x4	L.F.	0.057
2x6	L.F.	0.067
2x8	L.F.	0.080
2x10	L.F.	0.100
2x12	L.F.	0.133
Fascia boards		
2x4	L.F.	0.040
2x6	L.F.	0.040
2x8	L.F.	0.044
2x10	L.F.	0.044
2x12	L.F.	0.050
Cant strips		
Fiber		
3x3	L.F.	0.023

Rough Carpentry		UNIT	MAN/HOURS
06110.50	Roof Framing		
4x4		L.F.	0.024
Wood			
3x3		L.F.	0.024
06110.60	Sleepers		
Sleepers, over concrete			
12" o.c.			
1x2		S.F.	0.018
1x3		S.F.	0.019
2x4		S.F.	0.022
2x6		S.F.	0.024
16" o.c.			
1x2		S.F.	0.016
1x3		S.F.	0.016
2x4		S.F.	0.019
2x6		S.F.	0.020
06110.65	Soffits		
Soffit framing			
2x3		L.F.	0.057
2x4		L.F.	0.062
2x6		L.F.	0.067
2x8		L.F.	0.073
06110.70	Wall Framing		
Framing wall, studs			
12" o.c.			
2x3		S.F.	0.015
2x4		S.F.	0.015
2x6		S.F.	0.016
2x8		S.F.	0.017
16" o.c.			
2x3		S.F.	0.013
2x4		S.F.	0.013
2x6		S.F.	0.013
2x8		S.F.	0.014
24" o.c.			
2x3		S.F.	0.011
2x4		S.F.	0.011
2x6		S.F.	0.011
2x8		S.F.	0.012
Plates, top or bottom			
2x3		L.F.	0.024
2x4		L.F.	0.025
2x6		L.F.	0.027
2x8		L.F.	0.029
Headers, door or window			
2x8			
Single			
4' long		EA.	0.500
8' long		EA.	0.615
Double			
4' long		EA.	0.571
8' long		EA.	0.727

Rough Carpentry		UNIT	MAN/HOURS
06110.70	Wall Framing		
2x12			
Single			
6' long		EA.	0.615
12' long		EA.	0.800
Double			
6' long		EA.	0.727
12' long		EA.	0.889
06115.10	Floor Sheathing		
Sub-flooring, plywood, CDX			
1/2" thick		S.F.	0.010
5/8" thick		S.F.	0.011
3/4" thick		S.F.	0.013
Structural plywood			
1/2" thick		S.F.	0.010
5/8" thick		S.F.	0.011
3/4" thick		S.F.	0.012
Underlayment			
Hardboard, 1/4" tempered		S.F.	0.010
Plywood, CDX			
3/8" thick		S.F.	0.010
1/2" thick		S.F.	0.011
5/8" thick		S.F.	0.011
3/4" thick		S.F.	0.012
06115.20	Roof Sheathing		
Sheathing			
Plywood, CDX			
3/8" thick		S.F.	0.010
1/2" thick		S.F.	0.011
5/8" thick		S.F.	0.011
3/4" thick		S.F.	0.012
06115.30	Wall Sheathing		
Sheathing			
Plywood, CDX			
3/8" thick		S.F.	0.012
1/2" thick		S.F.	0.012
5/8" thick		S.F.	0.013
3/4" thick		S.F.	0.015
06125.10	Wood Decking		
Decking, T&G solid			
Fir			
3" thick		S.F.	0.020
4" thick		S.F.	0.021
Southern yellow pine			
3" thick		S.F.	0.023
4" thick		S.F.	0.025
White pine			
3" thick		S.F.	0.020
4" thick		S.F.	0.021

Rough Carpentry	UNIT	MAN/HOURS
06130.10 Heavy Timber		
Mill framed structures		
Beams to 20' long		
Douglas fir		
6x8	L.F.	0.080
6x10	L.F.	0.083
Southern yellow pine		
6x8	L.F.	0.080
6x10	L.F.	0.083
Columns to 12' high		
6x6	L.F.	0.120
10x10	L.F.	0.133
06190.20 Wood Trusses		
Truss, fink, 2x4 members		
3-in-12 slope		
24' span	EA.	0.686
30' span	EA.	0.727

Finish Carpentry	UNIT	MAN/HOURS
06200.10 Finish Carpentry		
Casing		
11/16 x 2-1/2	L.F.	0.036
11/16 x 3-1/2	L.F.	0.038
Half round		
1/2	L.F.	0.032
5/8	L.F.	0.032
Railings, balusters		
1-1/8 x 1-1/8	L.F.	0.080
1-1/2 x 1-1/2	L.F.	0.073
Stop		
5/8 x 1-5/8		
Colonial	L.F.	0.050
Ranch	L.F.	0.050
Exterior trim, casing, select pine, 1x3	L.F.	0.040
Douglas fir		
1x3	L.F.	0.040
1x4	L.F.	0.040
1x6	L.F.	0.044
Cornices, white pine, #2 or better		
1x2	L.F.	0.040
1x4	L.F.	0.040
1x8	L.F.	0.047
Shelving, pine		
1x8	L.F.	0.062
1x10	L.F.	0.064
1x12	L.F.	0.067

Finish Carpentry	UNIT	MAN/HOURS
06220.10 Millwork		
Countertop, laminated plastic		
25" x 7/8" thick		
Minimum	L.F.	0.200
Average	L.F.	0.267
Maximum	L.F.	0.320
Base cabinets, 34-1/2" high, 24" deep, hardwood, no tops		
Minimum	L.F.	0.320
Average	L.F.	0.400
Maximum	L.F.	0.533
Wall cabinets		
Minimum	L.F.	0.267
Average	L.F.	0.320
Maximum	L.F.	0.400
Oil borne		
Water borne		

Architectural Woodwork	UNIT	MAN/HOURS
06420.10 Panel Work		
Plywood unfinished, 1/4" thick		
Birch		
Natural	S.F.	0.027
Select	S.F.	0.027
Knotty pine	S.F.	0.027
Plywood, prefinished, 1/4" thick, premium grade		
Birch veneer	S.F.	0.032
Cherry veneer	S.F.	0.032
06430.10 Stairwork		
Risers, 1x8, 42" wide		
White oak	EA.	0.400
Pine	EA.	0.400
Treads, 1-1/16" x 9-1/2" x 42"		
White oak	EA.	0.500
06440.10 Columns		
Column, hollow, round wood		
12" diameter		
10' high	EA.	0.800
12' high	EA.	0.857
24" diameter		
16' high	EA.	1.200
18' high	EA.	1.263

Moisture Protection	UNIT	MAN/HOURS
07100.10 Waterproofing		
Membrane waterproofing, elastomeric		
Butyl		
1/32" thick	S.F.	0.032
1/16" thick	S.F.	0.033
Butyl with nylon		
1/32" thick	S.F.	0.032
1/16" thick	S.F.	0.033
Neoprene		
1/32" thick	S.F.	0.032
1/16" thick	S.F.	0.033
Neoprene with nylon		
1/32" thick	S.F.	0.032
1/16" thick	S.F.	0.033
Plastic vapor barrier (polyethylene)		
4 mil	S.F.	0.003
6 mil	S.F.	0.003
10 mil	S.F.	0.004
Bituminous membrane waterproofing, asphalt felt, 15 lb.		
One ply	S.F.	0.020
Two ply	S.F.	0.024
Three ply	S.F.	0.029
Four ply	S.F.	0.033
Five ply	S.F.	0.042
Modified asphalt membrane waterproofing, fibrous asphalt		
One ply	S.F.	0.033
Two ply	S.F.	0.040
Three ply	S.F.	0.044
Four ply	S.F.	0.053
Five ply	S.F.	0.064
Asphalt coated protective board		
1/8" thick	S.F.	0.020
1/4" thick	S.F.	0.020
3/8" thick	S.F.	0.020
1/2" thick	S.F.	0.021
Cement protective board		
3/8" thick	S.F.	0.027
1/2" thick	S.F.	0.027
Fluid applied, neoprene		
50 mil	S.F.	0.027
90 mil	S.F.	0.027
Tab extended polyurethane		
.050" thick	S.F.	0.020
Fluid applied rubber based polyurethane		
6 mil	S.F.	0.025
15 mil	S.F.	0.020
Bentonite waterproofing, panels		
3/16" thick	S.F.	0.020
1/4" thick	S.F.	0.020
5/8" thick	S.F.	0.021
Granular admixtures, trowel on, 3/8" thick	S.F.	0.020
Metallic oxide waterproofing, iron compound, troweled		
5/8" thick	S.F.	0.020
3/4" thick	S.F.	0.023

Moisture Protection	UNIT	MAN/HOURS
07150.10 Dampproofing		
Silicone dampproofing, sprayed on		
Concrete surface		
1 coat	S.F.	0.004
2 coats	S.F.	0.006
Concrete block		
1 coat	S.F.	0.005
2 coats	S.F.	0.007
Brick		
1 coat	S.F.	0.006
2 coats	S.F.	0.008
07160.10 Bituminous Dampproofing		
Building paper, asphalt felt		
15 lb	S.F.	0.032
30 lb	S.F.	0.033
Asphalt dampproofing, troweled, cold, primer plus		
1 coat	S.F.	0.027
2 coats	S.F.	0.040
3 coats	S.F.	0.050
Fibrous asphalt dampproofing, hot troweled, primer plus		
1 coat	S.F.	0.032
2 coats	S.F.	0.044
3 coats	S.F.	0.057
Asphaltic paint dampproofing, per coat		
Brush on	S.F.	0.011
Spray on	S.F.	0.009
07190.10 Vapor Barriers		
Vapor barrier, polyethylene		
2 mil	S.F.	0.004
6 mil	S.F.	0.004
8 mil	S.F.	0.004
10 mil	S.F.	0.004

Insulation	UNIT	MAN/HOURS
07210.10 Batt Insulation		
Ceiling, fiberglass, unfaced		
3-1/2" thick, R11	S.F.	0.009
6" thick, R19	S.F.	0.011
9" thick, R30	S.F.	0.012
Suspended ceiling, unfaced		
3-1/2" thick, R11	S.F.	0.009
6" thick, R19	S.F.	0.010
9" thick, R30	S.F.	0.011
Wall, fiberglass		
Paper backed		

Insulation	UNIT	MAN/ HOURS
07210.10 Batt Insulation		
2" thick, R7	S.F.	0.008
3" thick, R8	S.F.	0.009
4" thick, R11	S.F.	0.009
6" thick, R19	S.F.	0.010
Foil backed, 1 side		
2" thick, R7	S.F.	0.008
3" thick, R11	S.F.	0.009
4" thick, R14	S.F.	0.009
Foil backed, 2 sides		
Unfaced		
2" thick, R7	S.F.	0.008
3" thick, R9	S.F.	0.009
4" thick, R11	S.F.	0.009
6" thick, R19	S.F.	0.010
07210.20 Board Insulation		
Insulation, rigid		
0.75" thick, R2.78	S.F.	0.007
1.06" thick, R4.17	S.F.	0.008
1.31" thick, R5.26	S.F.	0.008
1.63" thick, R6.67	S.F.	0.008
2.25" thick, R8.33	S.F.	0.009
Perlite board, roof		
1.00" thick, R2.78	S.F.	0.007
1.50" thick, R4.17	S.F.	0.007
2.00" thick, R5.92	S.F.	0.007
2.50" thick, R6.67	S.F.	0.008
Rigid urethane		
Roof		
1" thick, R6.67	S.F.	0.007
1.20" thick, R8.33	S.F.	0.007
1.50" thick, R11.11	S.F.	0.007
2" thick, R14.29	S.F.	0.007
2.25" thick, R16.67	S.F.	0.008
Polystyrene		
Roof		
1.0" thick, R4.17	S.F.	0.007
1.5" thick, R6.26	S.F.	0.007
2.0" thick, R8.33	S.F.	0.007
Wall		
1.0" thick, R4.17	S.F.	0.008
1.5" thick, R6.26	S.F.	0.009
2.0" thick, R8.33	S.F.	0.009
07210.60 Loose Fill Insulation		
Blown-in type		
Fiberglass		
5" thick, R11	S.F.	0.007
6" thick, R13	S.F.	0.008
9" thick, R19	S.F.	0.011
Poured type		
Fiberglass		
1" thick, R4	S.F.	0.005
2" thick, R8	S.F.	0.006

Insulation	UNIT	MAN/ HOURS
07210.60 Loose Fill Insulation		
3" thick, R12	S.F.	0.007
4" thick, R16	S.F.	0.008
Vermiculite or perlite		
2" thick, R4.8	S.F.	0.006
3" thick, R7.2	S.F.	0.007
4" thick, R9.6	S.F.	0.008
Masonry, poured vermiculite or perlite		
4" block	S.F.	0.004
6" block	S.F.	0.005
8" block	S.F.	0.006
10" block	S.F.	0.006
12" block	S.F.	0.007
07210.70 Sprayed Insulation		
Foam, sprayed on		
Polystyrene		
1" thick, R4	S.F.	0.008
2" thick, R8	S.F.	0.011
Urethane		
1" thick, R4	S.F.	0.008
2" thick, R8	S.F.	0.011
07250.10 Fireproofing		
Sprayed on		
1" thick		
On beams	S.F.	0.018
On columns	S.F.	0.016
On decks		
Flat surface	S.F.	0.008
Fluted surface	S.F.	0.010
1-1/2" thick		
On beams	S.F.	0.023
On columns	S.F.	0.020
On decks		
Flat surface	S.F.	0.010
Fluted surface	S.F.	0.013

Shingles And Tiles	UNIT	MAN/ HOURS
07310.10 Asphalt Shingles		
Standard asphalt shingles, strip shingles		
210 lb/square	SQ.	0.800
240 lb/square	SQ.	1.000
Roll roofing, mineral surface		
90 lb	SQ.	0.571
140 lb	SQ.	0.800

Shingles And Tiles	UNIT	MAN/HOURS
07310.30 Metal Shingles		
Aluminum, .020" thick		
Plain	SQ.	1.600
Steel, galvanized		
Plain	SQ.	1.600
07310.60 Slate Shingles		
Slate shingles		
Ribbon	SQ.	4.000
Clear	SQ.	4.000
Replacement shingles		
Small jobs	EA.	0.267
Large jobs	S.F.	0.133
07310.70 Wood Shingles		
Wood shingles, on roofs		
White cedar, #1 shingles		
4" exposure	SQ.	2.667
5" exposure	SQ.	2.000
#2 shingles		
4" exposure	SQ.	2.667
5" exposure	SQ.	2.000
Resquared and rebutted		
4" exposure	SQ.	2.667
5" exposure	SQ.	2.000
07310.80 Wood Shakes		
Shakes, hand split, 24" red cedar, on roofs		
5" exposure	SQ.	4.000
7" exposure	SQ.	3.200
9" exposure	SQ.	2.667

Roofing And Siding	UNIT	MAN/HOURS
07410.10 Manufactured Roofs		
Aluminum roof panels, for structural steel framing		
Corrugated		
Unpainted finish		
.024"	S.F.	0.020
.030"	S.F.	0.020
Painted finish		
.024"	S.F.	0.020
.030"	S.F.	0.020
Steel roof panels, for structural steel framing		
Corrugated, painted		
18 ga.	S.F.	0.020
20 ga.	S.F.	0.020

Roofing And Siding	UNIT	MAN/HOURS
07460.10 Metal Siding Panels		
Aluminum siding panels		
Corrugated		
Plain finish		
.024"	S.F.	0.032
.032"	S.F.	0.032
Painted finish		
.024"	S.F.	0.032
.032"	S.F.	0.032
Steel siding panels		
Corrugated		
22 ga.	S.F.	0.053
24 ga.	S.F.	0.053
07460.70 Steel Siding		
Ribbed, sheets, galvanized		
22 ga.	S.F.	0.032
24 ga.	S.F.	0.032
Primed		
24 ga.	S.F.	0.032
26 ga.	S.F.	0.032

Membrane Roofing	UNIT	MAN/HOURS
07510.10 Built-up Asphalt Roofing		
Built-up roofing, asphalt felt, including gravel		
2 ply	SQ.	2.000
3 ply	SQ.	2.667
4 ply	SQ.	3.200
Walkway, for built-up roofs		
3' x 3' x		
1/2" thick	S.F.	0.027
3/4" thick	S.F.	0.027
1" thick	S.F.	0.027
Cant strip, 4" x 4"		
Treated wood	L.F.	0.023
Foamglass	L.F.	0.020
Mineral fiber	L.F.	0.020
New gravel for built-up roofing, 400 lb/sq	SQ.	1.600
Roof gravel (ballast)	C.Y.	4.000
Aluminum coating, top surfacing, for built-up roofing	SQ.	1.333
Remove 4-ply built-up roof (includes gravel)	SQ.	4.000
Remove & replace gravel, includes flood coat	SQ.	2.667
07530.10 Single-ply Roofing		
Elastic sheet roofing		
Neoprene, 1/16" thick	S.F.	0.010
EPDM rubber		

Membrane Roofing

	UNIT	MAN/HOURS
07530.10 Single-ply Roofing		
45 mil	S.F.	0.010
PVC		
45 mil	S.F.	0.010
Flashing		
Pipe flashing, 90 mil thick		
1" pipe	EA.	0.200
Neoprene flashing, 60 mil thick strip		
6" wide	L.F.	0.067
12" wide	L.F.	0.100
18" wide	L.F.	0.133
24" wide	L.F.	0.200
Adhesives		
Mastic sealer, applied at joints only		
1/4" bead	L.F.	0.004
Fluid applied roofing		
Urethane, 2 components, elastomeric top membrane		
1" thick	S.F.	0.013
Vinyl liquid roofing, 2 coats, 2 mils per coat	S.F.	0.011
Silicone roofing, 2 coats sprayed, 16 mil per coat	S.F.	0.013
Inverted roof system		
Insulated membrane with coarse gravel ballast		
3 ply with 2" polystyrene	S.F.	0.013
Ballast, 3/4" through 1-1/2" dia. river gravel, 100lb/sf	S.F.	0.800
Walkway for membrane roofs, 1/2" thick	S.F.	0.027

Flashing And Sheet Metal

	UNIT	MAN/HOURS
07610.10 Metal Roofing		
Sheet metal roofing, copper, 16 oz, batten seam	SQ.	5.333
Standing seam	SQ.	5.000
Aluminum roofing, natural finish		
Corrugated, on steel frame		
.0175" thick	SQ.	2.286
.0215" thick	SQ.	2.286
.024" thick	SQ.	2.286
.032" thick	SQ.	2.286
Ridge cap		
.019" thick	L.F.	0.027
Corrugated galvanized steel roofing, on steel frame		
28 ga.	SQ.	2.286
26 ga.	SQ.	2.286
24 ga.	SQ.	2.286
22 ga.	SQ.	2.286

Flashing And Sheet Metal

	UNIT	MAN/HOURS
07620.10 Flashing And Trim		
Counter flashing		
Aluminum, .032"	S.F.	0.080
Stainless steel, .015"	S.F.	0.080
Copper		
16 oz.	S.F.	0.080
20 oz.	S.F.	0.080
24 oz.	S.F.	0.080
32 oz.	S.F.	0.080
Valley flashing		
Aluminum, .032"	S.F.	0.050
Stainless steel, .015	S.F.	0.050
Copper		
16 oz.	S.F.	0.050
20 oz.	S.F.	0.067
24 oz.	S.F.	0.050
32 oz.	S.F.	0.050
Base flashing		
Aluminum, .040"	S.F.	0.067
Stainless steel, .018"	S.F.	0.067
Copper		
16 oz.	S.F.	0.067
20 oz.	S.F.	0.050
24 oz.	S.F.	0.067
32 oz.	S.F.	0.067
Flashing and trim, aluminum		
.019" thick	S.F.	0.057
.032" thick	S.F.	0.057
.040" thick	S.F.	0.062
Reglets, copper 10 oz.	L.F.	0.053
Stainless steel, .020"	L.F.	0.053
Gravel stop		
Aluminum, .032"		
4"	L.F.	0.027
10"	L.F.	0.031
Copper, 16 oz.		
4"	L.F.	0.027
10"	L.F.	0.031
07700.10 Manufactured Specialties		
Smoke vent, 48" x 48"		
Aluminum	EA.	2.000
Galvanized steel	EA.	2.000
Heat/smoke vent, 48" x 96"		
Aluminum	EA.	2.667
Galvanized steel	EA.	2.667
Ridge vent strips		
Mill finish	L.F.	0.053
Soffit vents		
Mill finish		
2-1/2" wide	L.F.	0.032
Roof hatches		
Steel, plain, primed		
2'6" x 3'0"	EA.	2.000
Galvanized steel		

4

Flashing And Sheet Metal	UNIT	MAN/HOURS
07700.10 Manufactured Specialties		
2'6" x 3'0"	EA.	2.000
Aluminum		
2'6" x 3'0"	EA.	2.000
Gravity ventilators, with curb, base, damper and screen		
Wind driven spinner		
6" dia.	EA.	0.533
12" dia.	EA.	0.533

Skylights	UNIT	MAN/HOURS
07810.10 Plastic Skylights		
Single thickness, not including mounting curb		
2' x 4'	EA.	1.000
4' x 4'	EA.	1.333
Double thickness, not including mounting curb		
2' x 4'	EA.	1.000
4' x 4'	EA.	1.333

Metal	UNIT	MAN/HOURS
08110.10 Metal Doors		
Flush hollow metal, standard duty, 20 ga., 1-3/8" thick		
2-6 x 6-8	EA.	0.889
2-8 x 6-8	EA.	0.889
3-0 x 6-8	EA.	0.889
1-3/4" thick		
2-6 x 6-8	EA.	0.889
2-8 x 6-8	EA.	0.889
3-0 x 6-8	EA.	0.889
Heavy duty, 20 ga., unrated, 1-3/4"		
2-8 x 6-8	EA.	0.889
3-0 x 6-8	EA.	0.889
08110.40 Metal Door Frames		
Hollow metal, stock, 18 ga., 4-3/4" x 1-3/4"		
2-0 x 7-0	EA.	1.000
2-4 x 7-0	EA.	1.000
2-6 x 7-0	EA.	1.000
3-0 x 7-0	EA.	1.000
08120.10 Aluminum Doors		
Aluminum doors, commercial		
Narrow stile		
2-6 x 7-0	EA.	4.000
3-0 x 7-0	EA.	4.000
3-6 x 7-0	EA.	4.000
Wide stile		
2-6 x 7-0	EA.	4.000
3-0 x 7-0	EA.	4.000
3-6 x 7-0	EA.	4.000
08300.10 Special Doors		
Overhead door, coiling insulated		
Chain gear, no frame, 12' x 12'	EA.	10.000
Sliding metal fire doors, motorized, fusible link, 3 hr.		
3-0 x 6-8	EA.	16.000
3-8 x 6-8	EA.	16.000
4-0 x 8-0	EA.	16.000
5-0 x 8-0	EA.	16.000
Counter doors, (roll-up shutters), standard, manual		
Opening, 4' high		
4' wide	EA.	6.667
6' wide	EA.	6.667
8' wide	EA.	7.273
10' wide	EA.	10.000
14' wide	EA.	10.000
6' high		
4' wide	EA.	6.667
6' wide	EA.	7.273
8' wide	EA.	8.000
10' wide	EA.	10.000
14' wide	EA.	11.429
Service doors, (roll up shutters), standard, manual		
Opening		
8' high x 8' wide	EA.	4.444

Metal	UNIT	MAN/HOURS
08300.10 Special Doors		
10' high x 10' wide	EA.	6.667
12' high x 12' wide	EA.	10.000
14' high x 14' wide	EA.	13.333
16' high x 14' wide	EA.	13.333
20' high x 14' wide	EA.	20.000
24' high x 16' wide	EA.	17.778
Roll-up doors		
13-0 high x 14-0 wide	EA.	11.429
12-0 high x 14-0 wide	EA.	11.429
Top coiling grilles, manually operated, steel or aluminum		
Opening, 4' high x		
4' wide	EA.	3.200
6' wide	EA.	3.200
8' wide	EA.	4.444
12' wide	EA.	4.444
16' wide	EA.	6.667
6' high x		
4' wide	EA.	6.667
6' wide	EA.	7.273
8' wide	EA.	8.000
12' wide	EA.	8.889
16' wide	EA.	11.429
Side coiling grilles, manually operated, aluminum		
Opening, 8' high x		
18' wide	EA.	60.000
24' wide	EA.	68.571
12' high x		
12' wide	EA.	60.000
18' wide	EA.	68.571
24' wide	EA.	80.000

Storefronts	UNIT	MAN/HOURS
08410.10 Storefronts		
Storefront, aluminum and glass		
Minimum	S.F.	0.100
Average	S.F.	0.114
Maximum	S.F.	0.133

Metal Windows	UNIT	MAN/HOURS
08510.10 Steel Windows		
Steel windows, primed		
Casements		
Operable		
Minimum	S.F.	0.047
Maximum	S.F.	0.053
Fixed sash	S.F.	0.040
Double hung	S.F.	0.044
Industrial windows		
Horizontally pivoted sash	S.F.	0.053
Fixed sash	S.F.	0.044
Security sash		
Operable	S.F.	0.053
Fixed	S.F.	0.044
Picture window	S.F.	0.044
Projecting sash		
Minimum	S.F.	0.050
Maximum	S.F.	0.050
Mullions	L.F.	0.040
08520.10 Aluminum Windows		
Fixed window		
6 sf to 8 sf	S.F.	0.114
12 sf to 16 sf	S.F.	0.089
Projecting window		
6 sf to 8 sf	S.F.	0.200
12 sf to 16 sf	S.F.	0.133
Horizontal sliding		
6 sf to 8 sf	S.F.	0.100
12 sf to 16 sf	S.F.	0.080
Double hung		
6 sf to 8 sf	S.F.	0.160
10 sf to 12 sf	S.F.	0.133

Hardware	UNIT	MAN/HOURS
08710.20 Locksets		
Latchset, heavy duty		
Cylindrical	EA.	0.500
Mortise	EA.	0.800
Lockset, heavy duty		
Cylindrical	EA.	0.500
Mortise	EA.	0.800
08710.30 Closers		
Door closers		
Surface mounted, traditional type, parallel arm		
Standard	EA.	1.000

Hardware	UNIT	MAN/HOURS
08710.30 Closers		
Heavy duty	EA.	1.000
08710.40 Door Trim		
Panic device		
Mortise	EA.	2.000
Vertical rod	EA.	2.000
Labelled, rim type	EA.	2.000
Mortise	EA.	2.000
Vertical rod	EA.	2.000
Door plates		
Kick plate, aluminum, 3 beveled edges		
10" x 28"	EA.	0.400
10" x 38"	EA.	0.400
Push plate, 4" x 16"		
Aluminum	EA.	0.160
Bronze	EA.	0.160
Stainless steel	EA.	0.160
08710.60 Weatherstripping		
Weatherstrip, head and jamb, metal strip, neoprene bulb		
Standard duty	L.F.	0.044
Heavy duty	L.F.	0.050
Thresholds		
Bronze	L.F.	0.200
Aluminum		
Plain	L.F.	0.200
Vinyl insert	L.F.	0.200
Aluminum with grit	L.F.	0.200
Steel		
Plain	L.F.	0.200
Interlocking	L.F.	0.667

Glazing	UNIT	MAN/HOURS
08810.10 Glazing		
Sheet glass, 1/8" thick	S.F.	0.044
Plate glass, bronze or grey, 1/4" thick	S.F.	0.073
Clear	S.F.	0.073
Polished	S.F.	0.073
Plexiglass		
1/8" thick	S.F.	0.073
1/4" thick	S.F.	0.044
Float glass, clear		
1/4" thick	S.F.	0.073
1/2" thick	S.F.	0.133
3/4" thick	S.F.	0.200
1" thick	S.F.	0.267

Glazing	UNIT	MAN/HOURS
08810.10 Glazing		
Tinted glass, polished plate, twin ground		
1/4" thick	S.F.	0.073
1/2" thick	S.F.	0.133
Total, full vision, all glass window system		
To 10' high		
Minimum	S.F.	0.200
Average	S.F.	0.200
Maximum	S.F.	0.200
10' to 20' high		
Minimum	S.F.	0.200
Average	S.F.	0.200
Maximum	S.F.	0.200
Insulated glass, bronze or gray		
1/2" thick	S.F.	0.133
1" thick	S.F.	0.200
Spandrel glass, polished bronze/grey, 1 side, 1/4" thick	S.F.	0.073
Tempered glass (safety)		
Clear sheet glass		
1/8" thick	S.F.	0.044
3/16" thick	S.F.	0.062
Clear float glass		
1/4" thick	S.F.	0.067
1/2" thick	S.F.	0.133
3/4" thick	S.F.	0.267
Tinted float glass		
3/16" thick	S.F.	0.062
1/4" thick	S.F.	0.067
3/8" thick	S.F.	0.100
1/2" thick	S.F.	0.133
Laminated glass		
Float safety glass with polyvinyl plastic interlayer		
1/4", sheet or float		
Two lites, 1/8" thick, clear glass	S.F.	0.067
1/2" thick, float glass		
Two lites, 1/4" thick, clear glass	S.F.	0.133
Tinted glass	S.F.	0.133
Insulating glass, two lites, clear float glass		
1/2" thick	S.F.	0.133
3/4" thick	S.F.	0.200
1" thick	S.F.	0.267
Glass seal edge		
3/8" thick	S.F.	0.133
Tinted glass		
1/2" thick	S.F.	0.133
1" thick	S.F.	0.267
Tempered, clear		
1" thick	S.F.	0.267
Wire reinforced	S.F.	0.267
Plate mirror glass		
1/4" thick		
15 sf	S.F.	0.080
Over 15 sf	S.F.	0.073
Door type, 1/4" thick	S.F.	0.080
Transparent, one way vision, 1/4" thick	S.F.	0.080

Glazing	UNIT	MAN/HOURS
08810.10 Glazing		
Sheet mirror glass		
3/16" thick	S.F.	0.080
1/4" thick	S.F.	0.067
Wall tiles, 12" x 12"		
Clear glass	S.F.	0.044
Veined glass	S.F.	0.044
Wire glass, 1/4" thick		
Clear	S.F.	0.267
Hammered	S.F.	0.267
Obscure	S.F.	0.267
Glazing accessories		
Neoprene glazing gaskets		
1/4" glass	L.F.	0.032
1/2" glass	L.F.	0.035
3/4" glass	L.F.	0.036
1" glass	L.F.	0.040
Mullion section		
1/4" glass	L.F.	0.016
3/8" glass	L.F.	0.020
1/2" glass	L.F.	0.023
3/4" glass	L.F.	0.027
1" glass	L.F.	0.032
Molded corners	EA.	0.533

Glazed Curtain Walls	UNIT	MAN/HOURS
08910.10 Glazed Curtain Walls		
Curtain wall, aluminum system, framing sections		
2" x 3"		
Jamb	L.F.	0.067
Horizontal	L.F.	0.067
Mullion	L.F.	0.067
2" x 4"		
Jamb	L.F.	0.100
Horizontal	L.F.	0.100
Mullion	L.F.	0.100
3" x 5-1/2"		
Jamb	L.F.	0.100
Horizontal	L.F.	0.100
Mullion	L.F.	0.100
4" corner mullion	L.F.	0.133
Coping sections		
1/8" x 8"	L.F.	0.133
1/8" x 9"	L.F.	0.133
1/8" x 12-1/2"	L.F.	0.160
Sill section		
1/8" x 6"	L.F.	0.080

Glazed Curtain Walls	UNIT	MAN/HOURS
08910.10 Glazed Curtain Walls		
1/8" x 7"	L.F.	0.080
1/8" x 8-1/2"	L.F.	0.080
Column covers, aluminum		
1/8" x 26"	L.F.	0.200
1/8" x 34"	L.F.	0.211
1/8" x 38"	L.F.	0.211
Doors		
Aluminum framed, standard hardware		
Narrow stile		
2-6 x 7-0	EA.	4.000
3-0 x 7-0	EA.	4.000
3-6 x 7-0	EA.	4.000
Wide stile		
2-6 x 7-0	EA.	4.000
3-0 x 7-0	EA.	4.000
3-6 x 7-0	EA.	4.000
Window wall system, complete		
Minimum	S.F.	0.080
Average	S.F.	0.089
Maximum	S.F.	0.114

Support Systems	UNIT	MAN/HOURS
09110.10 Metal Studs		
Studs, non load bearing, galvanized		
2-1/2", 20 ga.		
12" o.c.	S.F.	0.017
16" o.c.	S.F.	0.013
25 ga.		
12" o.c.	S.F.	0.017
16" o.c.	S.F.	0.013
24" o.c.	S.F.	0.011
3-5/8", 20 ga.		
12" o.c.	S.F.	0.020
16" o.c.	S.F.	0.016
24" o.c.	S.F.	0.013
25 ga.		
12" o.c.	S.F.	0.020
16" o.c.	S.F.	0.016
24" o.c.	S.F.	0.013
4", 20 ga.		
12" o.c.	S.F.	0.020
16" o.c.	S.F.	0.016
24" o.c.	S.F.	0.013
25 ga.		
12" o.c.	S.F.	0.020
16" o.c.	S.F.	0.016
24" o.c.	S.F.	0.013
6", 20 ga.		
12" o.c.	S.F.	0.025
16" o.c.	S.F.	0.020
24" o.c.	S.F.	0.017
25 ga.		
12" o.c.	S.F.	0.025
16" o.c.	S.F.	0.020
24" o.c.	S.F.	0.017
Load bearing studs, galvanized		
3-5/8", 16 ga.		
12" o.c.	S.F.	0.020
16" o.c.	S.F.	0.016
18 ga.		
12" o.c.	S.F.	0.013
16" o.c.	S.F.	0.016
4", 16 ga.		
12" o.c.	S.F.	0.020
16" o.c.	S.F.	0.016
6", 16 ga.		
12" o.c.	S.F.	0.025
16" o.c.	S.F.	0.020
Furring		
On beams and columns		
7/8" channel	L.F.	0.053
1-1/2" channel	L.F.	0.062
On ceilings		
3/4" furring channels		
12" o.c.	S.F.	0.033
16" o.c.	S.F.	0.032
24" o.c.	S.F.	0.029

Support Systems	UNIT	MAN/HOURS
09110.10 Metal Studs		
1-1/2" furring channels		
12" o.c.	S.F.	0.036
16" o.c.	S.F.	0.033
24" o.c.	S.F.	0.031
On walls		
3/4" furring channels		
12" o.c.	S.F.	0.027
16" o.c.	S.F.	0.025
24" o.c.	S.F.	0.024
1-1/2" furring channels		
12" o.c.	S.F.	0.029
16" o.c.	S.F.	0.027

Lath And Plaster	UNIT	MAN/HOURS
09205.10 Gypsum Lath		
Gypsum lath, 1/2" thick		
Clipped	S.Y.	0.044
Nailed	S.Y.	0.050
09205.20 Metal Lath		
Stucco lath		
1.8 lb.	S.Y.	0.100
3.6 lb.	S.Y.	0.100
Paper backed		
Minimum	S.Y.	0.080
Maximum	S.Y.	0.114
09210.10 Plaster		
Gypsum plaster, trowel finish, 2 coats		
Ceilings	S.Y.	0.250
Walls	S.Y.	0.235
3 coats		
Ceilings	S.Y.	0.348
Walls	S.Y.	0.308
Patch holes, average size holes		
1 sf to 5 sf		
Minimum	S.F.	0.133
Average	S.F.	0.160
Maximum	S.F.	0.200
Over 5 sf		
Minimum	S.F.	0.080
Average	S.F.	0.114
Maximum	S.F.	0.133
Patch cracks		
Minimum	S.F.	0.027
average	S.F.	0.040

Lath And Plaster

	UNIT	MAN/HOURS
09210.10 Plaster		
Maximum	S.F.	0.080
09220.10 Portland Cement Plaster		
Stucco, portland, gray, 3 coat, 1" thick		
Sand finish	S.Y.	0.348
Trowel finish	S.Y.	0.364
White cement		
Sand finish	S.Y.	0.364
Trowel finish	S.Y.	0.400
Scratch coat		
For ceramic tile	S.Y.	0.080
For quarry tile	S.Y.	0.080
Portland cement plaster		
2 coats, 1/2"	S.Y.	0.160
3 coats, 7/8"	S.Y.	0.200
09250.10 Gypsum Board		
Drywall, plasterboard, 3/8" clipped to		
Metal furred ceiling	S.F.	0.009
Columns and beams	S.F.	0.020
Walls	S.F.	0.008
Nailed or screwed to		
Wood framed ceiling	S.F.	0.008
Columns and beams	S.F.	0.018
Walls	S.F.	0.007
1/2", clipped to		
Metal furred ceiling	S.F.	0.009
Columns and beams	S.F.	0.020
Walls	S.F.	0.008
Nailed or screwed to		
Wood framed ceiling	S.F.	0.008
Columns and beams	S.F.	0.018
Walls	S.F.	0.007
5/8", clipped to		
Metal furred ceiling	S.F.	0.010
Columns and beams	S.F.	0.022
Walls	S.F.	0.009
Nailed or screwed to		
Wood framed ceiling	S.F.	0.010
Columns and beams	S.F.	0.022
Walls	S.F.	0.009
Taping and finishing joints		
Minimum	S.F.	0.005
Average	S.F.	0.007
Maximum	S.F.	0.008
Casing bead		
Minimum	L.F.	0.023
Average	L.F.	0.027
Maximum	L.F.	0.040
Corner bead		
Minimum	L.F.	0.023
Average	L.F.	0.027
Maximum	L.F.	0.040

Tile

	UNIT	MAN/HOURS
09310.10 Ceramic Tile		
Glazed wall tile, 4-1/4" x 4-1/4"		
Minimum	S.F.	0.057
Average	S.F.	0.067
Maximum	S.F.	0.080
Unglazed floor tile		
Portland cement bed, cushion edge, face mounted		
1" x 1"	S.F.	0.073
1" x 2"	S.F.	0.070
2" x 2"	S.F.	0.067
Adhesive bed, with white grout		
1" x 1"	S.F.	0.073
1" x 2"	S.F.	0.070
2" x 2"	S.F.	0.067
09330.10 Quarry Tile		
Floor		
4 x 4 x 1/2"	S.F.	0.107
6 x 6 x 1/2"	S.F.	0.100
6 x 6 x 3/4"	S.F.	0.100
Wall, applied to 3/4" portland cement bed		
4 x 4 x 1/2"	S.F.	0.160
6 x 6 x 3/4"	S.F.	0.133
Cove base		
5 x 6 x 1/2" straight top	L.F.	0.133
6 x 6 x 3/4" round top	L.F.	0.133
Stair treads 6 x 6 x 3/4"	L.F.	0.200
Window sill 6 x 8 x 3/4"	L.F.	0.160
For abrasive surface, add to material, 25%		
09410.10 Terrazzo		
Floors on concrete, 1-3/4" thick, 5/8" topping		
Gray cement	S.F.	0.114
White cement	S.F.	0.114
Sand cushion, 3" thick, 5/8" top, 1/4"		
Gray cement	S.F.	0.133
White cement	S.F.	0.133
Monolithic terrazzo, 3-1/2" base slab, 5/8" topping	S.F.	0.100
Terrazzo wainscot, cast-in-place, 1/2" thick	S.F.	0.200
Base, cast in place, terrazzo cove type, 6" high	L.F.	0.114
Curb, cast in place, 6" wide x 6" high, polished top	L.F.	0.400
Stairs, cast-in-place, topping on concrete or metal		
1-1/2" thick treads, 12" wide	L.F.	0.400
Combined tread and riser	L.F.	1.000
Precast terrazzo, thin set		
Terrazzo tiles, non-slip surface		
9" x 9" x 1" thick	S.F.	0.114
12" x 12"		
1" thick	S.F.	0.107
1-1/2" thick	S.F.	0.114
18" x 18" x 1-1/2" thick	S.F.	0.114
24" x 24" x 1-1/2" thick	S.F.	0.094
Terrazzo wainscot		
12" x 12" x 1" thick	S.F.	0.200
18" x 18" x 1-1/2" thick	S.F.	0.229

Tile

	UNIT	MAN/HOURS

09410.10   Terrazzo

	UNIT	MAN/HOURS
Base		
6" high		
Straight	L.F.	0.062
Coved	L.F.	0.062
8" high		
Straight	L.F.	0.067
Coved	L.F.	0.067
Terrazzo curbs		
8" wide x 8" high	L.F.	0.320
6" wide x 6" high	L.F.	0.267
Precast terrazzo stair treads, 12" wide		
1-1/2" thick		
Diamond pattern	L.F.	0.145
Non-slip surface	L.F.	0.145
2" thick		
Diamond pattern	L.F.	0.145
Non-slip surface	L.F.	0.160
Stair risers, 1" thick to 6" high		
Straight sections	L.F.	0.080
Cove sections	L.F.	0.080
Combined tread and riser		
Straight sections		
1-1/2" tread, 3/4" riser	L.F.	0.229
3" tread, 1" riser	L.F.	0.229
Curved sections		
2" tread, 1" riser	L.F.	0.267
3" tread, 1" riser	L.F.	0.267
Stair stringers, notched for treads and risers		
1" thick	L.F.	0.200
2" thick	L.F.	0.267
Landings, structural, nonslip		
1-1/2" thick	S.F.	0.133
3" thick	S.F.	0.160
Conductive terrazzo, spark proof industrial floor		
Epoxy terrazzo		
Floor	S.F.	0.050
Base	S.F.	0.067
Polyacrylate		
Floor	S.F.	0.050
Base	S.F.	0.067
Polyester		
Floor	S.F.	0.032
Base	S.F.	0.040
Synthetic latex mastic		
Floor	S.F.	0.050
Base	S.F.	0.067

Acoustical Treatment

	UNIT	MAN/HOURS

09510.10   Ceilings And Walls

	UNIT	MAN/HOURS
Acoustical panels, suspension system not included		
Fiberglass panels		
5/8" thick		
2' x 2'	S.F.	0.011
2' x 4'	S.F.	0.009
3/4" thick		
2' x 2'	S.F.	0.011
2' x 4'	S.F.	0.009
Mineral fiber panels		
5/8" thick		
2' x 2'	S.F.	0.011
2' x 4'	S.F.	0.009
3/4" thick		
2' x 2'	S.F.	0.011
2' x 4'	S.F.	0.009
Ceiling suspension systems		
T bar system		
2' x 4'	S.F.	0.008
2' x 2'	S.F.	0.009

Flooring

	UNIT	MAN/HOURS

09550.10   Wood Flooring

	UNIT	MAN/HOURS
Wood block industrial flooring		
Creosoted		
2" thick	S.F.	0.021
2-1/2" thick	S.F.	0.025
3" thick	S.F.	0.027
Gym floor, 2 ply felt, 25/32" maple, finished, in mastic	S.F.	0.044
Over wood sleepers	S.F.	0.050
Finishing, sand, fill, finish, and wax	S.F.	0.020
Refinish sand, seal, and 2 coats of polyurethane	S.F.	0.027
Clean and wax floors	S.F.	0.004

09630.10   Unit Masonry Flooring

	UNIT	MAN/HOURS
Clay brick		
9 x 4-1/2 x 3" thick		
Glazed	S.F.	0.067
Unglazed	S.F.	0.067
8 x 4 x 3/4" thick		
Glazed	S.F.	0.070
Unglazed	S.F.	0.070

09660.10   Resilient Tile Flooring

	UNIT	MAN/HOURS
Solid vinyl tile, 1/8" thick, 12" x 12"		
Marble patterns	S.F.	0.020
Solid colors	S.F.	0.020

Flooring

Flooring	UNIT	MAN/HOURS
09660.10 Resilient Tile Flooring		
Travertine patterns	S.F.	0.020
09665.10 Resilient Sheet Flooring		
Vinyl sheet flooring		
Minimum	S.F.	0.008
Average	S.F.	0.010
Maximum	S.F.	0.013
Cove, to 6"	L.F.	0.016
Fluid applied resilient flooring		
Polyurethane, poured in place, 3/8" thick	S.F.	0.067
Wall base, vinyl		
4" high	L.F.	0.027
6" high	L.F.	0.027
Stair accessories		
Treads, 1/4" x 12", rubber diamond surface		
Marbled	L.F.	0.067
Plain	L.F.	0.067
Grit strip safety tread, 12" wide, colors		
3/16" thick	L.F.	0.067
5/16" thick	L.F.	0.067
Risers, 7" high, 1/8" thick, colors		
Flat	L.F.	0.040
Coved	L.F.	0.040

Carpet

Carpet	UNIT	MAN/HOURS
09680.10 Floor Leveling		
Repair and level floors to receive new flooring		
Minimum	S.Y.	0.027
Average	S.Y.	0.067
Maximum	S.Y.	0.080
09682.10 Carpet Padding		
Carpet padding		
Jute padding		
Minimum	S.Y.	0.036
Average	S.Y.	0.040
Maximum	S.Y.	0.044
Sponge rubber cushion		
Minimum	S.Y.	0.036
Average	S.Y.	0.040
Maximum	S.Y.	0.044
Urethane cushion, 3/8" thick		
Minimum	S.Y.	0.036
Average	S.Y.	0.040
Maximum	S.Y.	0.044

Carpet

Carpet	UNIT	MAN/HOURS
09685.10 Carpet		
Carpet, acrylic		
24 oz., light traffic	S.Y.	0.089
28 oz., medium traffic	S.Y.	0.089
Commercial		
Nylon		
28 oz., medium traffic	S.Y.	0.089
35 oz., heavy traffic	S.Y.	0.089
Wool		
30 oz., medium traffic	S.Y.	0.089
36 oz., medium traffic	S.Y.	0.089
42 oz., heavy traffic	S.Y.	0.089
Carpet tile		
Foam backed		
Clean and vacuum carpet		
Minimum	S.Y.	0.004
Average	S.Y.	0.005
Maximum	S.Y.	0.008
09700.10 Special Flooring		
Epoxy flooring, marble chips		
Epoxy with colored quartz chips in 1/4" base	S.F.	0.044
Heavy duty epoxy topping, 3/16" thick	S.F.	0.044
Epoxy terrazzo		
1/4" thick chemical resistant	S.F.	0.050

Painting

Painting	UNIT	MAN/HOURS
09905.10 Painting Preparation		
Dropcloths		
Minimum	S.F.	0.001
Average	S.F.	0.001
Maximum	S.F.	0.001
Masking		
Paper and tape		
Minimum	L.F.	0.008
Average	L.F.	0.010
Maximum	L.F.	0.013
Doors		
Minimum	EA.	0.100
Average	EA.	0.133
Maximum	EA.	0.178
Windows		
Minimum	EA.	0.100
Average	EA.	0.133
Maximum	EA.	0.178
Sanding		
Walls and flat surfaces		

Painting

09905.10	Painting Preparation	UNIT	MAN/HOURS
Minimum		S.F.	0.005
Average		S.F.	0.007
Maximum		S.F.	0.008
Doors and windows			
Minimum		EA.	0.133
Average		EA.	0.200
Maximum		EA.	0.267
Trim			
Minimum		L.F.	0.010
Average		L.F.	0.013
Maximum		L.F.	0.018
Puttying			
Minimum		S.F.	0.012
Average		S.F.	0.016
Maximum		S.F.	0.020

09910.05	Ext. Painting, Sitework	UNIT	MAN/HOURS
Benches			
Brush			
First Coat			
Minimum		S.F.	0.008
Average		S.F.	0.010
Maximum		S.F.	0.013
Second Coat			
Minimum		S.F.	0.005
Average		S.F.	0.006
Maximum		S.F.	0.007
Roller			
First Coat			
Minimum		S.F.	0.004
Average		S.F.	0.004
Maximum		S.F.	0.005
Second Coat			
Minimum		S.F.	0.003
Average		S.F.	0.003
Maximum		S.F.	0.004
Brickwork			
Brush			
First Coat			
Minimum		S.F.	0.005
Average		S.F.	0.007
Maximum		S.F.	0.010
Second Coat			
Minimum		S.F.	0.004
Average		S.F.	0.005
Maximum		S.F.	0.007
Roller			
First Coat			
Minimum		S.F.	0.004
Average		S.F.	0.005
Maximum		S.F.	0.007
Second Coat			
Minimum		S.F.	0.003
Average		S.F.	0.004

Painting

09910.05	Ext. Painting, Sitework	UNIT	MAN/HOURS
Maximum		S.F.	0.005
Spray			
First Coat			
Minimum		S.F.	0.002
Average		S.F.	0.003
Maximum		S.F.	0.004
Second Coat			
Minimum		S.F.	0.002
Average		S.F.	0.003
Maximum		S.F.	0.003
Concrete Block			
Roller			
First Coat			
Minimum		S.F.	0.004
Average		S.F.	0.005
Maximum		S.F.	0.008
Second Coat			
Minimum		S.F.	0.003
Average		S.F.	0.004
Maximum		S.F.	0.007
Spray			
First Coat			
Minimum		S.F.	0.002
Average		S.F.	0.003
Maximum		S.F.	0.003
Second Coat			
Minimum		S.F.	0.001
Average		S.F.	0.002
Maximum		S.F.	0.003
Fences, Chain Link			
Brush			
First Coat			
Minimum		S.F.	0.008
Average		S.F.	0.009
Maximum		S.F.	0.010
Second Coat			
Minimum		S.F.	0.005
Average		S.F.	0.006
Maximum		S.F.	0.007
Roller			
First Coat			
Minimum		S.F.	0.006
Average		S.F.	0.007
Maximum		S.F.	0.008
Second Coat			
Minimum		S.F.	0.003
Average		S.F.	0.004
Maximum		S.F.	0.005
Spray			
First Coat			
Minimum		S.F.	0.003
Average		S.F.	0.003
Maximum		S.F.	0.003
Second Coat			

Painting	UNIT	MAN/HOURS
09910.05 Ext. Painting, Sitework		
Minimum	S.F.	0.002
Average	S.F.	0.002
Maximum	S.F.	0.003
Fences, Wood or Masonry		
Brush		
First Coat		
Minimum	S.F.	0.008
Average	S.F.	0.010
Maximum	S.F.	0.013
Second Coat		
Minimum	S.F.	0.005
Average	S.F.	0.006
Maximum	S.F.	0.008
Roller		
First Coat		
Minimum	S.F.	0.004
Average	S.F.	0.005
Maximum	S.F.	0.006
Second Coat		
Minimum	S.F.	0.003
Average	S.F.	0.004
Maximum	S.F.	0.005
Spray		
First Coat		
Minimum	S.F.	0.003
Average	S.F.	0.004
Maximum	S.F.	0.005
Second Coat		
Minimum	S.F.	0.002
Average	S.F.	0.003
Maximum	S.F.	0.003
Storage Tanks		
Roller		
First Coat		
Minimum	S.F.	0.003
Average	S.F.	0.004
Maximum	S.F.	0.005
Second Coat		
Minimum	S.F.	0.003
Average	S.F.	0.003
Maximum	S.F.	0.004
Spray		
First Coat		
Minimum	S.F.	0.002
Average	S.F.	0.002
Maximum	S.F.	0.003
Second Coat		
Minimum	S.F.	0.002
Average	S.F.	0.002
Maximum	S.F.	0.002

Painting	UNIT	MAN/HOURS
09910.15 Ext. Painting, Buildings		
Decks, Wood, Stained		
Brush		
First Coat		
Minimum	S.F.	0.004
Average	S.F.	0.004
Maximum	S.F.	0.005
Second Coat		
Minimum	S.F.	0.003
Average	S.F.	0.003
Maximum	S.F.	0.003
Roller		
First Coat		
Minimum	S.F.	0.003
Average	S.F.	0.003
Maximum	S.F.	0.003
Second Coat		
Minimum	S.F.	0.003
Average	S.F.	0.003
Maximum	S.F.	0.003
Spray		
First Coat		
Minimum	S.F.	0.003
Average	S.F.	0.003
Maximum	S.F.	0.003
Second Coat		
Minimum	S.F.	0.002
Average	S.F.	0.002
Maximum	S.F.	0.003
Doors, Metal		
Roller		
First Coat		
Minimum	S.F.	0.006
Average	S.F.	0.007
Maximum	S.F.	0.008
Second Coat		
Minimum	S.F.	0.004
Average	S.F.	0.004
Maximum	S.F.	0.005
Spray		
First Coat		
Minimum	S.F.	0.005
Average	S.F.	0.006
Maximum	S.F.	0.007
Second Coat		
Minimum	S.F.	0.004
Average	S.F.	0.004
Maximum	S.F.	0.004
Door Frames, Metal		
Brush		
First Coat		
Minimum	L.F.	0.010
Average	L.F.	0.013
Maximum	L.F.	0.015
Second Coat		

09910.15 Ext. Painting, Buildings

Painting	UNIT	MAN/HOURS
Minimum	L.F.	0.006
Average	L.F.	0.007
Maximum	L.F.	0.008
Spray		
First Coat		
Minimum	L.F.	0.004
Average	L.F.	0.006
Maximum	L.F.	0.008
Second Coat		
Minimum	L.F.	0.004
Average	L.F.	0.004
Maximum	L.F.	0.004
Siding, Metal		
Roller		
First Coat		
Minimum	S.F.	0.003
Average	S.F.	0.004
Maximum	S.F.	0.004
Second Coat		
Minimum	S.F.	0.003
Average	S.F.	0.003
Maximum	S.F.	0.004
Spray		
First Coat		
Minimum	S.F.	0.003
Average	S.F.	0.003
Maximum	S.F.	0.003
Minimum	S.F.	0.002
Average	S.F.	0.002
Maximum	S.F.	0.003
Stucco		
Roller		
First Coat		
Minimum	S.F.	0.004
Average	S.F.	0.004
Maximum	S.F.	0.005
Second Coat		
Minimum	S.F.	0.003
Average	S.F.	0.003
Maximum	S.F.	0.004
Spray		
First Coat		
Minimum	S.F.	0.003
Average	S.F.	0.003
Maximum	S.F.	0.003
Second Coat		
Minimum	S.F.	0.002
Average	S.F.	0.002
Maximum	S.F.	0.003
Trim		
Brush		
First Coat		
Minimum	L.F.	0.003
Average	L.F.	0.004

09910.15 Ext. Painting, Buildings

Painting	UNIT	MAN/HOURS
Maximum	L.F.	0.005
Second Coat		
Minimum	L.F.	0.003
Average	L.F.	0.003
Maximum	L.F.	0.005
Walls		
Roller		
First Coat		
Minimum	S.F.	0.003
Average	S.F.	0.003
Maximum	S.F.	0.003
Second Coat		
Minimum	S.F.	0.003
Average	S.F.	0.003
Maximum	S.F.	0.003
Spray		
First Coat		
Minimum	S.F.	0.001
Average	S.F.	0.002
Maximum	S.F.	0.002
Second Coat		
Minimum	S.F.	0.001
Average	S.F.	0.001
Maximum	S.F.	0.002
Windows		
Brush		
First Coat		
Minimum	S.F.	0.013
Average	S.F.	0.016
Maximum	S.F.	0.020
Second Coat		
Minimum	S.F.	0.011
Average	S.F.	0.013
Maximum	S.F.	0.016

09910.25 Ext. Painting, Misc.

Painting	UNIT	MAN/HOURS
Gratings, Metal		
Roller		
First Coat		
Minimum	S.F.	0.023
Average	S.F.	0.027
Maximum	S.F.	0.032
Second Coat		
Minimum	S.F.	0.016
Average	S.F.	0.020
Maximum	S.F.	0.027
Spray		
First Coat		
Minimum	S.F.	0.011
Average	S.F.	0.013
Maximum	S.F.	0.016
Second Coat		
Minimum	S.F.	0.009
Average	S.F.	0.010

Painting	UNIT	MAN/HOURS
09910.25 Ext. Painting, Misc.		
Maximum	S.F.	0.011
Ladders		
Brush		
First Coat		
Minimum	L.F.	0.020
Average	L.F.	0.023
Maximum	L.F.	0.027
Second Coat		
Minimum	L.F.	0.016
Average	L.F.	0.018
Maximum	L.F.	0.020
Spray		
First Coat		
Minimum	L.F.	0.013
Average	L.F.	0.015
Maximum	L.F.	0.016
Second Coat		
Minimum	L.F.	0.011
Average	L.F.	0.012
Maximum	L.F.	0.013
Shutters and Louvres		
Brush		
First Coat		
Minimum	EA.	0.160
Average	EA.	0.200
Maximum	EA.	0.267
Second Coat		
Minimum	EA.	0.100
Average	EA.	0.123
Maximum	EA.	0.160
Spray		
First Coat		
Minimum	EA.	0.053
Average	EA.	0.064
Maximum	EA.	0.080
Second Coat		
Minimum	EA.	0.040
Average	EA.	0.053
Maximum	EA.	0.064
Stairs, metal		
Brush		
First Coat		
Minimum	S.F.	0.009
Average	S.F.	0.010
Maximum	S.F.	0.011
Second Coat		
Minimum	S.F.	0.005
Average	S.F.	0.006
Maximum	S.F.	0.007
Spray		
First Coat		
Minimum	S.F.	0.004
Average	S.F.	0.006
Maximum	S.F.	0.006

Painting	UNIT	MAN/HOURS
09910.25 Ext. Painting, Misc.		
Second Coat		
Minimum	S.F.	0.003
Average	S.F.	0.004
Maximum	S.F.	0.005
09910.35 Int. Painting, Buildings		
Ceilings		
Roller		
First Coat		
Minimum	S.F.	0.003
Average	S.F.	0.004
Maximum	S.F.	0.004
Second Coat		
Minimum	S.F.	0.003
Average	S.F.	0.003
Maximum	S.F.	0.003
Spray		
First Coat		
Minimum	S.F.	0.002
Average	S.F.	0.002
Maximum	S.F.	0.003
Second Coat		
Minimum	S.F.	0.002
Average	S.F.	0.002
Maximum	S.F.	0.002
Doors, Metal		
Roller		
First Coat		
Minimum	L.F.	0.005
Average	L.F.	0.006
Maximum	L.F.	0.007
Second Coat		
Minimum	L.F.	0.004
Average	L.F.	0.004
Maximum	L.F.	0.005
Spray		
First Coat		
Minimum	L.F.	0.004
Average	L.F.	0.005
Maximum	L.F.	0.006
Second Coat		
Minimum	L.F.	0.003
Average	L.F.	0.004
Maximum	L.F.	0.004
Floors		
Roller		
First Coat		
Minimum	S.F.	0.003
Average	S.F.	0.003
Maximum	S.F.	0.003
Second Coat		
Minimum	S.F.	0.002
Average	S.F.	0.002
Maximum	S.F.	0.002

Painting	UNIT	MAN/HOURS
09910.35 Int. Painting, Buildings		
Spray		
First Coat		
Minimum	S.F.	0.002
Average	S.F.	0.002
Maximum	S.F.	0.002
Second Coat		
Minimum	S.F.	0.002
Average	S.F.	0.002
Maximum	S.F.	0.002
Pipes to 6" diameter		
Brush		
Minimum	L.F.	0.010
Average	L.F.	0.011
Maximum	L.F.	0.013
Spray		
Minimum	L.F.	0.003
Average	L.F.	0.004
Maximum	L.F.	0.005
Pipes to 12" diameter		
Brush		
Minimum	L.F.	0.020
Average	L.F.	0.023
Maximum	L.F.	0.027
Spray		
Minimum	L.F.	0.007
Average	L.F.	0.008
Maximum	L.F.	0.010
Trim		
Brush		
First Coat		
Minimum	L.F.	0.003
Average	L.F.	0.004
Maximum	L.F.	0.004
Second Coat		
Minimum	L.F.	0.002
Average	L.F.	0.003
Maximum	L.F.	0.004
Walls		
Roller		
First Coat		
Minimum	S.F.	0.003
Average	S.F.	0.003
Maximum	S.F.	0.003
Second Coat		
Minimum	S.F.	0.003
Average	S.F.	0.003
Maximum	S.F.	0.003
Spray		
First Coat		
Minimum	S.F.	0.001
Average	S.F.	0.002
Maximum	S.F.	0.002
Second Coat		
Minimum	S.F.	0.001

Painting	UNIT	MAN/HOURS
09910.35 Int. Painting, Buildings		
Average	S.F.	0.001
Maximum	S.F.	0.002
09955.10 Wall Covering		
Vinyl wall covering		
Medium duty	S.F.	0.011
Heavy duty	S.F.	0.013
Over pipes and irregular shapes		
Flexible gypsum coated wall fabric, fire resistant	S.F.	0.008
Vinyl corner guards		
3/4" x 3/4" x 8'	EA.	0.100
2-3/4" x 2-3/4" x 4'	EA.	0.100

Specialties	UNIT	MAN/HOURS
10110.10 Chalkboards		
Chalkboard, metal frame, 1/4" thick		
48"x60"	EA.	0.800
48"x96"	EA.	0.889
48"x144"	EA.	1.000
48"x192"	EA.	1.143
Liquid chalkboard		
48"x60"	EA.	0.800
48"x96"	EA.	0.889
48"x144"	EA.	1.000
48"x192"	EA.	1.143
Map rail, deluxe	L.F.	0.040
Average	PCT.	
10165.10 Toilet Partitions		
Toilet partition, plastic laminate		
Ceiling mounted	EA.	2.667
Floor mounted	EA.	2.000
Metal		
Ceiling mounted	EA.	2.667
Floor mounted	EA.	2.000
Wheel chair partition, plastic laminate		
Ceiling mounted	EA.	2.667
Floor mounted	EA.	2.000
Painted metal		
Ceiling mounted	EA.	2.667
Floor mounted	EA.	2.000
Urinal screen, plastic laminate		
Wall hung	EA.	1.000
Floor mounted	EA.	1.000
Porcelain enameled steel, floor mounted	EA.	1.000
Painted metal, floor mounted	EA.	1.000
Stainless steel, floor mounted	EA.	1.000
Metal toilet partitions		
Front door and side divider, floor mounted		
Porcelain enameled steel	EA.	2.000
Painted steel	EA.	2.000
Stainless steel	EA.	2.000
10185.10 Shower Stalls		
Shower receptors		
Precast, terrazzo		
32" x 32"	EA.	0.667
32" x 48"	EA.	0.800
Concrete		
32" x 32"	EA.	0.667
48" x 48"	EA.	0.889
Shower door, trim and hardware		
Porcelain enameled steel, flush	EA.	0.800
Baked enameled steel, flush	EA.	0.800
Aluminum frame, tempered glass, 48" wide, sliding	EA.	1.000
Folding	EA.	1.000
Shower compartment, precast concrete receptor		
Single entry type		
Porcelain enameled steel	EA.	8.000

Specialties	UNIT	MAN/HOURS
10185.10 Shower Stalls		
Baked enameled steel	EA.	8.000
Stainless steel	EA.	8.000
Double entry type		
Porcelain enameled steel	EA.	10.000
Baked enameled steel	EA.	10.000
Stainless steel	EA.	10.000
10210.10 Vents And Wall Louvres		
Vents w/screen, 4" deep, 8" wide, 5" high		
Modular	EA.	0.250
Aluminum gable louvers	S.F.	0.133
Vent screen aluminum, 4" wide, continuous	L.F.	0.027
Wall louvre, aluminum mill finish		
Under, 2 sf	S.F.	0.100
2 to 4 sf	S.F.	0.089
5 to 10 sf	S.F.	0.089
Galvanized steel		
Under 2 sf	S.F.	0.100
2 to 4 sf	S.F.	0.089
5 to 10 sf	S.F.	0.089
10225.10 Door Louvres		
Fixed, 1" thick, enameled steel		
8"x8"	EA.	0.100
12"x12"	EA.	0.114
20"x20"	EA.	0.320
24"x24"	EA.	0.364
10290.10 Pest Control		
Termite control		
Under slab spraying		
Minimum	S.F.	0.002
Average	S.F.	0.004
Maximum	S.F.	0.008
10350.10 Flagpoles		
Installed in concrete base		
Fiberglass		
25' high	EA.	5.333
50' high	EA.	13.333
Aluminum		
25' high	EA.	5.333
50' high	EA.	13.333
Bonderized steel		
25' high	EA.	6.154
50' high	EA.	16.000
Freestanding tapered, fiberglass		
30' high	EA.	5.714
40' high	EA.	7.273
50' high	EA.	8.000
60' high	EA.	9.412
Wall mounted, with collar, brushed aluminum finish		
15' long	EA.	4.000
18' long	EA.	4.000

Specialties	UNIT	MAN/HOURS
10350.10 Flagpoles		
20' long	EA.	4.211
24' long	EA.	4.706
Outrigger, wall, including base		
10' long	EA.	5.333
20' long	EA.	6.667
10400.10 Identifying Devices		
Directory and bulletin boards		
Open face boards		
Chrome plated steel frame	S.F.	0.400
Aluminum framed	S.F.	0.400
Bronze framed	S.F.	0.400
Stainless steel framed	S.F.	0.400
Tack board, aluminum framed	S.F.	0.400
Visual aid board, aluminum framed	S.F.	0.400
Glass encased boards, hinged and keyed		
Aluminum framed	S.F.	1.000
Bronze framed	S.F.	1.000
Stainless steel framed	S.F.	1.000
Chrome plated steel framed	S.F.	1.000
Metal plaque		
Cast bronze	S.F.	0.667
Aluminum	S.F.	0.667
Metal engraved plaque		
Porcelain steel	S.F.	0.667
Stainless steel	S.F.	0.667
Brass	S.F.	0.667
Aluminum	S.F.	0.667
Metal built-up plaque		
Bronze	S.F.	0.800
Copper and bronze	S.F.	0.800
Copper and aluminum	S.F.	0.800
Metal nameplate plaques		
Cast bronze	S.F.	0.500
Cast aluminum	S.F.	0.500
Engraved, 1-1/2" x 6"		
Bronze	EA.	0.500
Aluminum	EA.	0.500
Letters, on masonry or concrete, aluminum, satin finish		
1/2" thick		
2" high	EA.	0.320
4" high	EA.	0.400
6" high	EA.	0.444
3/4" thick		
8" high	EA.	0.500
10" high	EA.	0.571
1" thick		
12" high	EA.	0.667
14" high	EA.	0.800
16" high	EA.	1.000
3/8" thick		
2" high	EA.	0.320
4" high	EA.	0.400
1/2" thick, 6" high	EA.	0.444

Specialties	UNIT	MAN/HOURS
10400.10 Identifying Devices		
5/8" thick, 8" high	EA.	0.500
1" thick		
10" high	EA.	0.571
12" high	EA.	0.667
14" high	EA.	0.800
16" high	EA.	1.000
Interior door signs, adhesive, flexible		
2" x 8"	EA.	0.200
4" x 4"	EA.	0.200
6" x 7"	EA.	0.200
6" x 9"	EA.	0.200
10" x 9"	EA.	0.200
10" x 12"	EA.	0.200
Hard plastic type, no frame		
3" x 8"	EA.	0.200
4" x 4"	EA.	0.200
4" x 12"	EA.	0.200
Hard plastic type, with frame		
3" x 8"	EA.	0.200
4" x 4"	EA.	0.200
4" x 12"	EA.	0.200
10450.10 Control		
Access control, 7' high, indoor or outdoor impenetrability		
Remote or card control, type B	EA.	10.667
Free passage, type B	EA.	10.667
Remote or card control, type AA	EA.	10.667
Free passage, type AA	EA.	10.667
10500.10 Lockers		
Locker bench, floor mounted, laminated maple		
4'	EA.	0.667
6'	EA.	0.667
Wardrobe locker, 12" x 60" x 15", baked on enamel		
1-tier	EA.	0.400
2-tier	EA.	0.400
3-tier	EA.	0.421
4-tier	EA.	0.421
12" x 72" x 15", baked on enamel		
1-tier	EA.	0.400
2-tier	EA.	0.400
4-tier	EA.	0.421
5-tier	EA.	0.421
15" x 60" x 15", baked on enamel		
1-tier	EA.	0.400
4-tier	EA.	0.421
Wardrobe locker, single tier type		
12" x 15" x 72"	EA.	0.800
18" x 15" x 72"	EA.	0.842
12" x 18" x 72"	EA.	0.889
18" x 18" x 72"	EA.	0.941
Double tier type		
12" x 15" x 36"	EA.	0.400
18" x 15" x 36"	EA.	0.400

Specialties

Specialties	UNIT	MAN/HOURS

10500.10 — Lockers

	UNIT	MAN/HOURS
12" x 18" x 36"	EA.	0.400
18" x 18" x 36"	EA.	0.400
Two person unit		
18" x 15" x 72"	EA.	1.333
18" x 18" x 72"	EA.	1.600
Duplex unit		
15" x 15" x 72"	EA.	0.800
15" x 21" x 72"	EA.	0.800
Basket lockers, basket sets with baskets		
24 basket set	SET	4.000
30 basket set	SET	5.000
36 basket set	SET	6.667
42 basket set	SET	8.000

10520.10 — Fire Protection

	UNIT	MAN/HOURS
Portable fire extinguishers		
Water pump tank type		
2.5 gal.		
Red enameled galvanized	EA.	0.533
Red enameled copper	EA.	0.533
Polished copper	EA.	0.533
Carbon dioxide type, red enamel steel		
Squeeze grip with hose and horn		
2.5 lb	EA.	0.533
5 lb	EA.	0.615
10 lb	EA.	0.800
15 lb	EA.	1.000
20 lb	EA.	1.000
Wheeled type		
125 lb	EA.	1.600
250 lb	EA.	1.600
500 lb	EA.	1.600
Dry chemical, pressurized type		
Red enameled steel		
2.5 lb	EA.	0.533
5 lb	EA.	0.615
10 lb	EA.	0.800
20 lb	EA.	1.000
30 lb	EA.	1.000
Chrome plated steel, 2.5 lb	EA.	0.533
Other type extinguishers		
2.5 gal, stainless steel, pressurized water tanks	EA.	0.533
Soda and acid type	EA.	0.533
Cartridge operated, water type	EA.	0.533
Loaded stream, water type	EA.	0.533
Foam type	EA.	0.533
40 gal, wheeled foam type	EA.	1.600
Fire extinguisher cabinets		
Enameled steel		
8" x 12" x 27"	EA.	1.600
8" x 16" x 38"	EA.	1.600
Aluminum		
8" x 12" x 27"	EA.	1.600
8" x 16" x 38"	EA.	1.600

Specialties

Specialties	UNIT	MAN/HOURS

10520.10 — Fire Protection

	UNIT	MAN/HOURS
8" x 12" x 27"	EA.	1.600
Stainless steel		
8" x 16" x 38"	EA.	1.600

10550.10 — Postal Specialties

	UNIT	MAN/HOURS
Mail chutes		
Single mail chute		
Finished aluminum	L.F.	2.000
Bronze	L.F.	2.000
Single mail chute receiving box		
Finished aluminum	EA.	4.000
Bronze	EA.	4.000
Twin mail chute, double parallel		
Finished aluminum	FLR	4.000
Bronze	FLR	4.000
Receiving box, 36" x 20" x 12"		
Finished aluminum	EA.	6.667
Bronze	EA.	6.667
Locked receiving mail box		
Finished aluminum	EA.	4.000
Bronze	EA.	4.000
Commercial postal accessories for mail chutes		
Letter slot, brass	EA.	1.333
Bulk mail slot, brass	EA.	1.333
Mail boxes		
Residential postal accessories		
Letter slot	EA.	0.400
Rural letter box	EA.	1.000

10670.10 — Shelving

	UNIT	MAN/HOURS
Shelving, enamel, closed side and back, 12" x 36"		
5 shelves	EA.	1.333
8 shelves	EA.	1.778
Open		
5 shelves	EA.	1.333
8 shelves	EA.	1.778
Metal storage shelving, baked enamel		
7 shelf unit, 72" or 84" high		
12" shelf	L.F.	0.842
24" shelf	L.F.	1.000
36" shelf	L.F.	1.143
4 shelf unit, 40" high		
12" shelf	L.F.	0.727
24" shelf	L.F.	0.889
3 shelf unit, 32" high		
12" shelf	L.F.	0.421
24" shelf	L.F.	0.500
Single shelf unit, attached to masonry		
12" shelf	L.F.	0.145
24" shelf	L.F.	0.174

Specialties	UNIT	MAN/HOURS
10800.10 **Bath Accessories**		
Ash receiver, wall mounted, aluminum	EA.	0.400
Grab bar, 1-1/2" dia., stainless steel, wall mounted		
24" long	EA.	0.400
36" long	EA.	0.421
48" long	EA.	0.471
1" dia., stainless steel		
12" long	EA.	0.348
24" long	EA.	0.400
36" long	EA.	0.444
48" long	EA.	0.471
Hand dryer, surface mounted, 110 volt	EA.	1.000
Medicine cabinet, 16 x 22, baked enamel, steel, lighted	EA.	0.320
With mirror, lighted	EA.	0.533
Mirror, 1/4" plate glass, up to 10 sf	S.F.	0.080
Mirror, stainless steel frame		
18"x24"	EA.	0.267
24"x30"	EA.	0.400
24"x48"	EA.	0.667
30"x30"	EA.	0.800
48"x72"	EA.	1.333
With shelf, 18"x24"	EA.	0.320
Sanitary napkin dispenser, stainless steel, wall mounted	EA.	0.533
Shower rod, 1" diameter		
Chrome finish over brass	EA.	0.400
Stainless steel	EA.	0.400
Soap dish, stainless steel, wall mounted	EA.	0.533
Toilet tissue dispenser, stainless, wall mounted		
Single roll	EA.	0.200
Double roll	EA.	0.229
Towel dispenser, stainless steel		
Flush mounted	EA.	0.444
Surface mounted	EA.	0.400
Combination towel dispenser and waste receptacle	EA.	0.533
Towel bar, stainless steel		
18" long	EA.	0.320
24" long	EA.	0.364
30" long	EA.	0.400
36" long	EA.	0.444
Waste receptacle, stainless steel, wall mounted	EA.	0.667

11 EQUIPMENT

Architectural Equipment	UNIT	MAN/HOURS
11020.10 Security Equipment		
Office safes, 30" x 20" x 20", 1 hr rating	EA.	2.000
30" x 16" x 15", 2 hr rating	EA.	1.600
30" x 28" x 20", H&G rating	EA.	1.000
Surveillance system		
Minimum	EA.	16.000
Maximum	EA.	80.000
Insulated file room door		
1 hr rating		
32" wide	EA.	8.000
40" wide	EA.	8.889
11161.10 Loading Dock Equipment		
Dock leveler, 10 ton capacity		
6' x 8'	EA.	8.000
7' x 8'	EA.	8.000
Bumpers, laminated rubber		
4-1/2" thick		
6" x 14"	EA.	0.160
10" x 14"	EA.	0.200
10" x 36"	EA.	0.267
12" x 14"	EA.	0.211
12" x 36"	EA.	0.296
6" thick		
10" x 14"	EA.	0.229
10" x 24"	EA.	0.276
10" x 36"	EA.	0.400
Extruded rubber bumpers		
T-section, 22" x 22" x 3"	EA.	0.160
Molded rubber bumpers		
24" x 12" x 3" thick	EA.	0.400
Door seal, 12" x 12", vinyl covered	L.F.	0.200
Dock boards, heavy duty, 5' x 5'		
5000 lb		
Minimum	EA.	6.667
Maximum	EA.	6.667
9000 lb		
Minimum	EA.	6.667
Maximum	EA.	7.273
15,000 lb	EA.	7.273
Truck shelters		
Minimum	EA.	6.154
Maximum	EA.	11.429
11170.10 Waste Handling		
Incinerator, electric		
100 lb/hr		
Minimum	EA.	8.000
Maximum	EA.	8.000
400 lb/hr		
Minimum	EA.	16.000
Maximum	EA.	16.000
1000 lb/hr		
Minimum	EA.	24.242
Maximum	EA.	24.242

Architectural Equipment	UNIT	MAN/HOURS
11480.10 Athletic Equipment		
Basketball backboard		
Fixed	EA.	10.000
Swing-up	EA.	16.000
Portable, hydraulic	EA.	4.000
Suspended type, standard	EA.	16.000
Bleacher, telescoping, manual		
15 tier, minimum	SEAT	0.160
Maximum	SEAT	0.160
20 tier, minimum	SEAT	0.178
Maximum	SEAT	0.178
30 tier, minimum	SEAT	0.267
Maximum	SEAT	0.267
Boxing ring elevated, complete, 22' x 22'	EA.	114.286
Gym divider curtain		
Minimum	S.F.	0.011
Maximum	S.F.	0.011
Scoreboards, single face		
Minimum	EA.	8.000
Maximum	EA.	40.000
Parallel bars		
Minimum	EA.	8.000
Maximum	EA.	13.333
11500.10 Industrial Equipment		
Vehicular paint spray booth, solid back, 14'4" x 9'6"		
24' deep	EA.	8.000
26'6" deep	EA.	8.000
28'6" deep	EA.	8.000
Drive through, 14'9" x 9'6"		
24' deep	EA.	8.000
26'6" deep	EA.	8.000
28'6" deep	EA.	8.000
Water wash, paint spray booth		
5' x 11'2" x 10'8"	EA.	8.000
6' x 11'2" x 10'8"	EA.	8.000
8' x 11'2" x 10'8"	EA.	8.000
10' x 11'2" x 11'2"	EA.	8.000
12' x 12'2" x 11'2"	EA.	8.000
14' x 12'2" x 11'2"	EA.	8.000
16' x 12'2" x 11'2"	EA.	8.000
20' x 12'2" x 11'2"	EA.	8.000
Dry type spray booth, with paint arrestors		
5'4" x 7'2" x 6'8"	EA.	8.000
6'4" x 7'2" x 6'8"	EA.	8.000
8'4" x 7'2" x 9'2"	EA.	8.000
10'4" x 7'2" x 9'2"	EA.	8.000
12'4" x 7'6" x 9'2"	EA.	8.000
14'4" x 7'6" x 9'8"	EA.	8.000
16'4" x 7'7" x 9'8"	EA.	8.000
20'4" x 7'7" x 10'8"	EA.	8.000
Air compressor, electric		
1 hp		
115 volt	EA.	5.333
7.5 hp		

Architectural Equipment	UNIT	MAN/HOURS
11500.10 Industrial Equipment		
115 volt	EA.	8.000
230 volt	EA.	8.000
Hydraulic lifts		
8,000 lb capacity	EA.	20.000
11,000 lb capacity	EA.	32.000
24,000 lb capacity	EA.	53.333
Power tools		
Band saws		
10"	EA.	0.667
14"	EA.	0.800
Motorized shaper	EA.	0.615
Motorized lathe	EA.	0.667
Bench saws		
9" saw	EA.	0.533
10" saw	EA.	0.571
12" saw	EA.	0.667
Electric grinders		
1/3 hp	EA.	0.320
1/2 hp	EA.	0.348
3/4 hp	EA.	0.348

Interior	UNIT	MAN/ HOURS
12690.40	**Floor Mats**	
Recessed entrance mat, 3/8" thick, aluminum link	S.F.	0.400
Steel, flexible	S.F.	0.400

Construction	UNIT	MAN/HOURS
13121.10 Pre-engineered Buildings		
Pre-engineered metal building, 40'x100'		
14' eave height	S.F.	0.032
16' eave height	S.F.	0.037
20' eave height	S.F.	0.048
60'x100'		
14' eave height	S.F.	0.032
16' eave height	S.F.	0.037
20' eave height	S.F.	0.048
80'x100'		
14' eave height	S.F.	0.032
16' eave height	S.F.	0.037
20' eave height	S.F.	0.048
100'x100'		
14' eave height	S.F.	0.032
16' eave height	S.F.	0.037
20' eave height	S.F.	0.048
100'x150'		
14' eave height	S.F.	0.032
16' eave height	S.F.	0.037
20' eave height	S.F.	0.048
120'x150'		
14' eave height	S.F.	0.032
16' eave height	S.F.	0.037
20' eave height	S.F.	0.048
140'x150'		
14' eave height	S.F.	0.032
16' eave height	S.F.	0.037
20' eave height	S.F.	0.048
160'x200'		
14' eave height	S.F.	0.032
16' eave height	S.F.	0.037
20' eave height	S.F.	0.048
200'x200'		
14' eave height	S.F.	0.032
16' eave height	S.F.	0.037
20' eave height	S.F.	0.048
Liner panel, 26 ga, painted steel	S.F.	0.020
Wall panel insulated, 26 ga. steel, foam core	S.F.	0.020
Roof panel, 26 ga. painted steel	S.F.	0.011
Plastic (sky light)	S.F.	0.011
Insulation, 3-1/2" thick blanket, R11	S.F.	0.005

14 CONVEYING

Elevators	UNIT	MAN/HOURS

14210.10	Elevators		
Passenger elevators, electric, geared			
Based on a shaft of 6 stops and 6 openings			
50 fpm, 2000 lb	EA.	24.000
100 fpm, 2000 lb	EA.	26.667
150 fpm		
2000 lb	EA.	30.000
3000 lb	EA.	34.286
4000 lb	EA.	40.000

Lifts	UNIT	MAN/HOURS

14410.10	Personnel Lifts		
Residential stair climber, per story	EA.	6.667

14450.10	Vehicle Lifts		
Automotive hoist, one post, semi-hydraulic, 8,000 lb	EA.	24.000
Full hydraulic, 8,000 lb	EA.	24.000
2 post, semi-hydraulic, 10,000 lb	EA.	34.286
Full hydraulic		
10,000 lb	EA.	34.286
13,000 lb	EA.	60.000
18,500 lb	EA.	60.000
24,000 lb	EA.	60.000
26,000 lb	EA.	60.000
Pneumatic hoist, fully hydraulic		
11,000 lb	EA.	80.000
24,000 lb	EA.	80.000

Hoists And Cranes	UNIT	MAN/HOURS

14600.10	Industrial Hoists		
Industrial hoists, electric, light to medium duty			
500 lb	EA.	4.000
1000 lb	EA.	4.211
2000 lb	EA.	4.444
5000 lb	EA.	5.333
10,000 lb	EA.	5.926
20,000 lb	EA.	6.667
30,000 lb	EA.	8.000
Heavy duty		
500 lb	EA.	4.000

Hoists And Cranes	UNIT	MAN/HOURS

14600.10	Industrial Hoists		
1000 lb	EA.	4.211
2000 lb	EA.	4.444
5000 lb	EA.	5.333
10,000 lb	EA.	5.926
20,000 lb	EA.	6.667
30,000 lb	EA.	8.000
Air powered hoists		
500 lb	EA.	4.000
1000 lb	EA.	4.000
2000 lb	EA.	4.211
4000 lb	EA.	4.706
6000 lb	EA.	6.154
Overhead traveling bridge crane		
Single girder, 20' span		
3 ton	EA.	12.000
5 ton	EA.	12.000
7.5 ton	EA.	12.000
10 ton	EA.	15.000
15 ton	EA.	15.000
30' span		
3 ton	EA.	12.000
5 ton	EA.	12.000
10 ton	EA.	15.000
15 ton	EA.	15.000
Double girder, 40' span		
3 ton	EA.	26.667
5 ton	EA.	26.667
7.5 ton	EA.	26.667
10 ton	EA.	34.286
15 ton	EA.	34.286
25 ton	EA.	34.286
50' span		
3 ton	EA.	26.667
5 ton	EA.	26.667
7.5 ton	EA.	26.667
10 ton	EA.	34.286
15 ton	EA.	34.286
25 ton	EA.	34.286

14650.10	Jib Cranes		
Self supporting, swinging 8' boom, 200 deg rotation			
2000 lb	EA.	6.667
4000 lb	EA.	13.333
10,000 lb	EA.	13.333
Wall mounted, 180 deg rotation		
2000 lb	EA.	6.667
4000 lb	EA.	13.333
10,000 lb	EA.	13.333

Basic Materials	UNIT	MAN/HOURS
15100.10 Specialties		
Wall penetration		
Concrete wall, 6" thick		
2" dia.	EA.	0.267
4" dia.	EA.	0.400
12" thick		
2" dia.	EA.	0.364
4" dia.	EA.	0.571
15120.10 Backflow Preventers		
Backflow preventer, flanged, cast iron, with valves		
3" pipe	EA.	4.000
4" pipe	EA.	4.444
Threaded		
3/4" pipe	EA.	0.500
2" pipe	EA.	0.800
15140.11 Pipe Hangers, Light		
A band, black iron		
1/2"	EA.	0.057
1"	EA.	0.059
1-1/4"	EA.	0.062
1-1/2"	EA.	0.067
2"	EA.	0.073
2-1/2"	EA.	0.080
3"	EA.	0.089
4"	EA.	0.100
Copper		
1/2"	EA.	0.057
3/4"	EA.	0.059
1"	EA.	0.059
1-1/4"	EA.	0.062
1-1/2"	EA.	0.067
2"	EA.	0.073
2-1/2"	EA.	0.080
3"	EA.	0.089
4"	EA.	0.100
2 hole clips, galvanized		
3/4"	EA.	0.053
1"	EA.	0.055
1-1/4"	EA.	0.057
1-1/2"	EA.	0.059
2"	EA.	0.062
2-1/2"	EA.	0.064
3"	EA.	0.067
4"	EA.	0.073
Perforated strap		
3/4"		
Galvanized, 20 ga.	L.F.	0.040
Copper, 22 ga.	L.F.	0.040
J-Hooks		
1/2"	EA.	0.036
3/4"	EA.	0.036
1"	EA.	0.038
1-1/4"	EA.	0.039

Basic Materials	UNIT	MAN/HOURS
15140.11 Pipe Hangers, Light		
1-1/2"	EA.	0.040
2"	EA.	0.040
3"	EA.	0.042
4"	EA.	0.042
PVC coated hangers, galvanized, 28 ga.		
1-1/2" x 12"	EA.	0.053
2" x 12"	EA.	0.057
3" x 12"	EA.	0.062
4" x 12"	EA.	0.067
Copper, 30 ga.		
1-1/2" x 12"	EA.	0.053
2" x 12"	EA.	0.057
3" x 12"	EA.	0.062
4" x 12"	EA.	0.067
Wire hook hangers		
Black wire, 1/2" x		
4"	EA.	0.040
6"	EA.	0.042
Copper wire hooks		
1/2" x		
4"	EA.	0.040
6"	EA.	0.042
8"	EA.	0.044
10"	EA.	0.047
12"	EA.	0.050
15240.10 Vibration Control		
Vibration isolator, in-line, stainless connector, screwed		
3/4"	EA.	0.471
1"	EA.	0.500
2"	EA.	0.615
3"	EA.	0.727
4"	EA.	0.800

Insulation	UNIT	MAN/HOURS
15260.10 Fiberglass Pipe Insulation		
Fiberglass insulation on 1/2" pipe		
1" thick	L.F.	0.027
1-1/2" thick	L.F.	0.033
3/4" pipe		
1" thick	L.F.	0.027
1-1/2" thick	L.F.	0.033
1" pipe		
1" thick	L.F.	0.027
1-1/2" thick	L.F.	0.033
2" thick	L.F.	0.040

Insulation		UNIT	MAN/ HOURS
15260.10	**Fiberglass Pipe Insulation**		
1-1/4" pipe			
1" thick		L.F.	0.033
1-1/2" thick		L.F.	0.036
1-1/2" pipe			
1" thick		L.F.	0.033
1-1/2" thick		L.F.	0.036
2" pipe			
1" thick		L.F.	0.033
1-1/2" thick		L.F.	0.036
2-1/2" pipe			
1" thick		L.F.	0.033
1-1/2" thick		L.F.	0.036
3" pipe			
1" thick		L.F.	0.038
1-1/2" thick		L.F.	0.040
4" pipe			
1" thick		L.F.	0.038
1-1/2" thick		L.F.	0.040
6" pipe			
1" thick		L.F.	0.042
2" thick		L.F.	0.044
10" pipe			
2" thick		L.F.	0.042
3" thick		L.F.	0.044
15260.20	**Calcium Silicate**		
Calcium silicate insulation, 6" pipe			
2" thick		L.F.	0.057
3" thick		L.F.	0.067
6" thick		L.F.	0.080
12" pipe			
2" thick		L.F.	0.062
3" thick		L.F.	0.073
6" thick		L.F.	0.089
15260.60	**Exterior Pipe Insulation**		
Fiberglass insulation, aluminum jacket			
1/2" pipe			
1" thick		L.F.	0.062
1-1/2" thick		L.F.	0.067
1" pipe			
1" thick		L.F.	0.062
1-1/2" thick		L.F.	0.067
2" pipe			
1" thick		L.F.	0.073
1-1/2" thick		L.F.	0.076
3" pipe			
1" thick		L.F.	0.080
1-1/2" thick		L.F.	0.084
4" pipe			
1" thick		L.F.	0.080
1-1/2" thick		L.F.	0.084
6" pipe			
1" thick		L.F.	0.089

Insulation		UNIT	MAN/ HOURS
15260.60	**Exterior Pipe Insulation**		
2" thick		L.F.	0.094
10" pipe			
2" thick		L.F.	0.089
3" thick		L.F.	0.094
15260.90	**Pipe Insulation Fittings**		
Insulation protection saddle			
1" thick covering			
1/2" pipe		EA.	0.320
3/4" pipe		EA.	0.320
1" pipe		EA.	0.320
2" pipe		EA.	0.320
3" pipe		EA.	0.364
6" pipe		EA.	0.500
1-1/2" thick covering			
3/4" pipe		EA.	0.320
1" pipe		EA.	0.320
2" pipe		EA.	0.320
3" pipe		EA.	0.320
6" pipe		EA.	0.500
10" pipe		EA.	0.667
15280.10	**Equipment Insulation**		
Equipment insulation, 2" thick, cellular glass		S.F.	0.050
Urethane, rigid, field applied jacket, plastered finish		S.F.	0.100
Fiberglass, rigid, with vapor barrier		S.F.	0.044
15290.10	**Ductwork Insulation**		
Fiberglass duct insulation, plain blanket			
1-1/2" thick		S.F.	0.010
2" thick		S.F.	0.013
With vapor barrier			
1-1/2" thick		S.F.	0.010
2" thick		S.F.	0.013
Rigid with vapor barrier			
2" thick		S.F.	0.027

Fire Protection		UNIT	MAN/ HOURS
15330.10	**Wet Sprinkler System**		
Sprinkler head, 212 deg, brass, exposed piping		EA.	0.320
Chrome, concealed piping		EA.	0.444
Water motor alarm		EA.	1.333
Fire department inlet connection		EA.	1.600
Wall plate for fire dept connection		EA.	0.667
Swing check valve flanged iron body, 4"		EA.	2.667
Check valve, 6"		EA.	4.000

Fire Protection	UNIT	MAN/HOURS
15330.10 Wet Sprinkler System		
Wet pipe valve, flange to groove, 4"	EA.	0.889
Flange to flange		
6"	EA.	1.333
8"	EA.	2.667
Alarm valve, flange to flange, (wet valve)		
4"	EA.	0.889
8"	EA.	6.667
Inspector's test connection	EA.	0.667
Wall hydrant, polished brass, 2-1/2" x 2-1/2", single	EA.	0.571
2-way	EA.	0.571
3-way	EA.	0.571
Wet valve trim, includes retard chamber & gauges, 4"-6"	EA.	0.667
Retard pressure switch for wet systems	EA.	1.600
Air maintenance device	EA.	0.667
Wall hydrant non-freeze, 8" thick wall, vacuum breaker	EA.	0.400
12" thick wall	EA.	0.400

Plumbing	UNIT	MAN/HOURS
15410.05 C.i. Pipe, Above Ground		
No hub pipe		
1-1/2" pipe	L.F.	0.057
2" pipe	L.F.	0.067
3" pipe	L.F.	0.080
4" pipe	L.F.	0.133
No hub fittings, 1-1/2" pipe		
1/4 bend	EA.	0.267
1/8 bend	EA.	0.267
Sanitary tee	EA.	0.400
Sanitary cross	EA.	0.400
Wye	EA.	0.400
2" pipe		
1/4 bend	EA.	0.320
1/8 bend	EA.	0.320
Sanitary tee	EA.	0.533
Wye	EA.	0.667
3" pipe		
1/4 bend	EA.	0.400
1/8 bend	EA.	0.400
Sanitary tee	EA.	0.500
Wye	EA.	0.667
4" pipe		
1/4 bend	EA.	0.400
1/8 bend	EA.	0.400
Sanitary tee	EA.	0.667
Wye	EA.	0.667

Plumbing	UNIT	MAN/HOURS
15410.06 C.i. Pipe, Below Ground		
No hub pipe		
1-1/2" pipe	L.F.	0.040
2" pipe	L.F.	0.044
3" pipe	L.F.	0.050
4" pipe	L.F.	0.067
Fittings, 1-1/2"		
1/4 bend	EA.	0.229
1/8 bend	EA.	0.229
Wye	EA.	0.320
Wye & 1/8 bend	EA.	0.229
P-trap	EA.	0.229
2"		
1/4 bend	EA.	0.267
1/8 bend	EA.	0.267
Double wye	EA.	0.500
Wye & 1/8 bend	EA.	0.400
Double wye & 1/8 bend	EA.	0.500
P-trap	EA.	0.267
3"		
1/4 bend	EA.	0.320
1/8 bend	EA.	0.320
Wye	EA.	0.500
3x2" wye	EA.	0.500
Wye & 1/8 bend	EA.	0.500
Double wye & 1/8 bend	EA.	0.500
3x2" double wye & 1/8 bend	EA.	0.500
3x2" reducer	EA.	0.320
P-trap	EA.	0.320
4"		
1/4 bend	EA.	0.320
1/8 bend	EA.	0.320
Wye	EA.	0.500
15410.09 Service Weight Pipe		
Service weight pipe, single hub		
3" x 5'	EA.	0.170
4" x 5'	EA.	0.178
6" x 5'	EA.	0.200
1/8 bend		
3"	EA.	0.320
4"	EA.	0.364
6"	EA.	0.400
1/4 bend		
3"	EA.	0.320
4"	EA.	0.364
6"	EA.	0.400
Sweep		
3"	EA.	0.320
4"	EA.	0.364
6"	EA.	0.400
Sanitary T		
3"	EA.	0.571
4"	EA.	0.667
6"	EA.	0.727

Plumbing	UNIT	MAN/HOURS
15410.09 Service Weight Pipe		
Wye		
3"	EA.	0.444
4"	EA.	0.471
6"	EA.	0.571
15410.10 Copper Pipe		
Type "K" copper		
1/2"	L.F.	0.025
3/4"	L.F.	0.027
1"	L.F.	0.029
DWV, copper		
1-1/4"	L.F.	0.033
1-1/2"	L.F.	0.036
2"	L.F.	0.040
3"	L.F.	0.044
4"	L.F.	0.050
6"	L.F.	0.057
Type "L" copper		
1/4"	L.F.	0.024
3/8"	L.F.	0.024
1/2"	L.F.	0.025
3/4"	L.F.	0.027
1"	L.F.	0.029
Type "M" copper		
1/2"	L.F.	0.025
3/4"	L.F.	0.027
1"	L.F.	0.029
15410.11 Copper Fittings		
DWV fittings, coupling with stop		
1-1/4"	EA.	0.471
1-1/2"	EA.	0.500
1-1/2" x 1-1/4"	EA.	0.500
2"	EA.	0.533
2" x 1-1/4"	EA.	0.533
2" x 1-1/2"	EA.	0.533
3"	EA.	0.667
3" x 1-1/2"	EA.	0.667
3" x 2"	EA.	0.667
4"	EA.	0.800
Slip coupling		
1-1/2"	EA.	0.500
2"	EA.	0.533
3"	EA.	0.667
90 ells		
1-1/2"	EA.	0.500
1-1/2" x 1-1/4"	EA.	0.500
2"	EA.	0.533
2" x 1-1/2"	EA.	0.533
3"	EA.	0.667
4"	EA.	0.800
Street, 90 elbows		
1-1/2"	EA.	0.500
2"	EA.	0.533

Plumbing	UNIT	MAN/HOURS
15410.11 Copper Fittings		
3"	EA.	0.667
4"	EA.	0.800
45 ells		
1-1/4"	EA.	0.471
1-1/2"	EA.	0.500
2"	EA.	0.533
3"	EA.	0.667
4"	EA.	0.800
Street, 45 ell		
1-1/2"	EA.	0.500
2"	EA.	0.533
3"	EA.	0.667
Wye		
1-1/4"	EA.	0.471
1-1/2"	EA.	0.500
2"	EA.	0.533
3"	EA.	0.667
4"	EA.	0.800
Sanitary tee		
1-1/4"	EA.	0.471
1-1/2"	EA.	0.500
2"	EA.	0.533
3"	EA.	0.667
4"	EA.	0.800
No-hub adapters		
1-1/2" x 2"	EA.	0.500
2"	EA.	0.533
2" x 3"	EA.	0.533
3"	EA.	0.667
3" x 4"	EA.	0.667
4"	EA.	0.800
Fitting reducers		
1-1/2" x 1-1/4"	EA.	0.500
2" x 1-1/2"	EA.	0.533
3" x 1-1/2"	EA.	0.667
3" x 2"	EA.	0.667
Copper caps		
1-1/2"	EA.	0.500
2"	EA.	0.533
Copper pipe fittings		
1/2"		
90 deg ell	EA.	0.178
45 deg ell	EA.	0.178
Tee	EA.	0.229
Cap	EA.	0.089
Coupling	EA.	0.178
Union	EA.	0.200
3/4"		
90 deg ell	EA.	0.200
45 deg ell	EA.	0.200
Tee	EA.	0.267
Cap	EA.	0.094
Coupling	EA.	0.200
Union	EA.	0.229

Plumbing	UNIT	MAN/HOURS
15410.11 Copper Fittings		
1"		
90 deg ell	EA.	0.267
45 deg ell	EA.	0.267
Tee	EA.	0.320
Cap	EA.	0.133
Coupling	EA.	0.267
Union	EA.	0.267
1-1/4"		
90 deg ell	EA.	0.229
45 deg ell	EA.	0.229
Tee	EA.	0.400
Cap	EA.	0.133
Union	EA.	0.286
1-1/2"		
90 deg ell	EA.	0.286
45 deg ell	EA.	0.286
Tee	EA.	0.444
Cap	EA.	0.133
Coupling	EA.	0.267
Union	EA.	0.364
2"		
90 deg ell	EA.	0.320
45 deg ell	EA.	0.500
Tee	EA.	0.500
Cap	EA.	0.160
Coupling	EA.	0.320
Union	EA.	0.400
2-1/2"		
90 deg ell	EA.	0.400
45 deg ell	EA.	0.400
Tee	EA.	0.571
Cap	EA.	0.200
Coupling	EA.	0.400
Union	EA.	0.444
15410.15 Brass Fittings		
Compression fittings, union		
3/8"	EA.	0.133
1/2"	EA.	0.133
5/8"	EA.	0.133
Union elbow		
3/8"	EA.	0.133
1/2"	EA.	0.133
5/8"	EA.	0.133
Union tee		
3/8"	EA.	0.133
1/2"	EA.	0.133
5/8"	EA.	0.133
Male connector		
3/8"	EA.	0.133
1/2"	EA.	0.133
5/8"	EA.	0.133
Female connector		
3/8"	EA.	0.133

Plumbing	UNIT	MAN/HOURS
15410.15 Brass Fittings		
1/2"	EA.	0.133
5/8"	EA.	0.133
15410.30 Pvc/cpvc Pipe		
PVC schedule 40		
1/2" pipe	L.F.	0.033
3/4" pipe	L.F.	0.036
1" pipe	L.F.	0.040
1-1/4" pipe	L.F.	0.044
1-1/2" pipe	L.F.	0.050
2" pipe	L.F.	0.057
2-1/2" pipe	L.F.	0.067
3" pipe	L.F.	0.080
4" pipe	L.F.	0.100
6" pipe	L.F.	0.200
8" pipe	L.F.	0.267
Fittings, 1/2"		
90 deg ell	EA.	0.100
45 deg ell	EA.	0.100
Tee	EA.	0.114
Polypropylene, acid resistant, DWV pipe		
Schedule 40		
1-1/2" pipe	L.F.	0.057
2" pipe	L.F.	0.067
3" pipe	L.F.	0.080
4" pipe	L.F.	0.100
6" pipe	L.F.	0.200
Polyethylene pipe and fittings		
SDR-21		
3" pipe	L.F.	0.100
4" pipe	L.F.	0.133
6" pipe	L.F.	0.200
8" pipe	L.F.	0.229
10" pipe	L.F.	0.267
12" pipe	L.F.	0.320
14" pipe	L.F.	0.400
16" pipe	L.F.	0.500
18" pipe	L.F.	0.615
20" pipe	L.F.	0.800
22" pipe	L.F.	0.889
24" pipe	L.F.	1.000
Fittings, 3"		
90 deg elbow	EA.	0.400
45 deg elbow	EA.	0.400
Tee	EA.	0.667
45 deg wye	EA.	0.667
Reducer	EA.	0.500
Flange assembly	EA.	0.400
4"		
90 deg elbow	EA.	0.500
45 deg elbow	EA.	0.500
Tee	EA.	0.800
45 deg wye	EA.	0.800
Reducer	EA.	0.667

Plumbing	UNIT	MAN/HOURS
15410.30 Pvc/cpvc Pipe		
Flange assembly	EA.	0.500
8"		
90 deg elbow	EA.	1.000
45 deg elbow	EA.	1.000
Tee	EA.	1.600
45 deg wye	EA.	1.600
Reducer	EA.	1.333
Flange assembly	EA.	1.000
10"		
90 deg elbow	EA.	1.333
45 deg elbow	EA.	1.333
Tee	EA.	2.000
45 deg wye	EA.	2.000
Reducer	EA.	1.600
Flange assembly	EA.	1.333
12"		
90 deg elbow	EA.	1.600
45 deg elbow	EA.	1.600
Tee	EA.	2.667
45 deg wye	EA.	2.667
Reducer	EA.	2.000
Flange assembly	EA.	1.600
14"		
90 deg elbow	EA.	2.000
45 deg elbow	EA.	2.000
Tee	EA.	3.200
45 deg wye	EA.	3.200
Reducer	EA.	2.667
Flange assembly	EA.	2.000
16"		
90 deg elbow	EA.	2.000
45 deg elbow	EA.	2.000
Tee	EA.	3.200
45 deg wye	EA.	3.200
Reducer	EA.	2.667
Flange assembly	EA.	2.000
18"		
90 deg elbow	EA.	2.667
45 deg elbow	EA.	2.667
Tee	EA.	4.000
45 deg wye	EA.	4.000
Reducer	EA.	2.667
Flange assembly	EA.	2.667
20"		
90 deg elbow	EA.	2.667
45 deg elbow	EA.	2.667
15410.33 Abs Dwv Pipe		
Schedule 40 ABS		
1-1/2" pipe	L.F.	0.040
2" pipe	L.F.	0.044
3" pipe	L.F.	0.057
4" pipe	L.F.	0.080
6" pipe	L.F.	0.100

Plumbing	UNIT	MAN/HOURS
15410.35 Plastic Pipe		
Fiberglass reinforced pipe		
2" pipe	L.F.	0.062
3" pipe	L.F.	0.067
4" pipe	L.F.	0.073
6" pipe	L.F.	0.080
8" pipe	L.F.	0.133
10" pipe	L.F.	0.160
12" pipe	L.F.	0.200
Fittings		
90 deg elbow, flanged		
2"	EA.	0.800
3"	EA.	0.889
4"	EA.	1.000
6"	EA.	1.333
8"	EA.	1.600
10"	EA.	2.000
12"	EA.	2.667
45 deg elbow, flanged		
2"	EA.	0.667
3"	EA.	0.800
4"	EA.	1.000
6"	EA.	1.333
8"	EA.	1.600
10"	EA.	2.000
12"	EA.	2.667
Tee, flanged		
2"	EA.	1.000
3"	EA.	1.143
4"	EA.	1.333
6"	EA.	1.600
8"	EA.	2.000
10"	EA.	2.667
12"	EA.	4.000
Wye, flanged		
2"	EA.	1.000
3"	EA.	1.143
4"	EA.	1.333
6"	EA.	1.600
8"	EA.	2.000
10"	EA.	2.667
12"	EA.	4.000
Concentric reducer, flanged		
2"	EA.	0.667
4"	EA.	0.800
6"	EA.	1.143
8"	EA.	1.600
10"	EA.	2.000
12"	EA.	2.667
Adapter, bell x male or female		
2"	EA.	0.667
3"	EA.	0.727
4"	EA.	0.800
6"	EA.	1.143
8"	EA.	1.600

Plumbing		UNIT	MAN/HOURS
15410.35	Plastic Pipe		
10"		EA.	2.000
12"		EA.	2.667
Nipples			
2" x 6"		EA.	0.080
2" x 12"		EA.	0.100
3" x 8"		EA.	0.123
3" x 12"		EA.	0.133
4" x 8"		EA.	0.133
4" x 12"		EA.	0.160
6" x 12"		EA.	0.200
8" x 18"		EA.	0.200
8" x 24"		EA.	0.229
10" x 18"		EA.	0.267
10" x 24"		EA.	0.320
12" x 18"		EA.	0.364
12" x 24"		EA.	0.400
Sleeve coupling			
2"		EA.	0.667
3"		EA.	0.800
4"		EA.	1.143
6"		EA.	1.600
8"		EA.	2.000
10"		EA.	2.667
Flanges			
2"		EA.	0.667
3"		EA.	0.800
4"		EA.	1.143
6"		EA.	1.600
8"		EA.	2.000
10"		EA.	2.667
12"		EA.	2.667
15410.70	Stainless Steel Pipe		
Stainless steel, schedule 40, threaded			
1/2" pipe		L.F.	0.114
1" pipe		L.F.	0.123
1-1/2" pipe		L.F.	0.133
2" pipe		L.F.	0.145
2-1/2" pipe		L.F.	0.160
3" pipe		L.F.	0.178
4" pipe		L.F.	0.200
15410.80	Steel Pipe		
Black steel, extra heavy pipe, threaded			
1/2" pipe		L.F.	0.032
3/4" pipe		L.F.	0.032
1" pipe		L.F.	0.040
1-1/2" pipe		L.F.	0.044
2-1/2" pipe		L.F.	0.100
3" pipe		L.F.	0.133
4" pipe		L.F.	0.160
5" pipe		L.F.	0.200
6" pipe		L.F.	0.200
8" pipe		L.F.	0.267

Plumbing		UNIT	MAN/HOURS
15410.80	Steel Pipe		
10" pipe		L.F.	0.320
12" pipe		L.F.	0.400
Fittings, malleable iron, threaded, 1/2" pipe			
90 deg ell		EA.	0.267
45 deg ell		EA.	0.267
Tee		EA.	0.400
3/4" pipe			
90 deg ell		EA.	0.267
45 deg ell		EA.	0.400
Tee		EA.	0.400
1-1/2" pipe			
90 deg ell		EA.	0.400
45 deg ell		EA.	0.400
Tee		EA.	0.571
2-1/2" pipe			
90 deg ell		EA.	1.000
45 deg ell		EA.	1.000
Tee		EA.	1.333
3" pipe			
90 deg ell		EA.	1.333
45 deg ell		EA.	1.333
Tee		EA.	2.000
4" pipe			
90 deg ell		EA.	1.600
45 deg ell		EA.	1.600
Tee		EA.	2.667
6" pipe			
90 deg ell		EA.	1.600
45 deg ell		EA.	1.600
Tee		EA.	2.667
8" pipe			
90 deg ell		EA.	3.200
45 deg ell		EA.	3.200
Tee		EA.	5.000
10" pipe			
90 deg ell		EA.	4.000
45 deg ell		EA.	4.000
Tee		EA.	5.000
12" pipe			
90 deg ell		EA.	5.000
45 deg ell		EA.	5.000
Tee		EA.	6.667
Butt welded, 1/2" pipe			
90 deg ell		EA.	0.267
45 deg ell		EA.	0.267
Tee		EA.	0.400
3/4" pipe			
90 deg ell		EA.	0.267
45 deg. ell		EA.	0.267
Tee		EA.	0.400
1" pipe			
90 deg ell		EA.	0.320
45 deg ell		EA.	0.320
Tee		EA.	0.444

Plumbing	UNIT	MAN/HOURS
15410.80 Steel Pipe		
1-1/2" pipe		
90 deg ell	EA.	0.400
45 deg. ell	EA.	0.400
Tee	EA.	0.571
Reducing tee	EA.	0.571
Cap	EA.	0.320
2-1/2" pipe		
90 deg. ell	EA.	0.800
45 deg. ell	EA.	0.800
Tee	EA.	1.143
Reducing tee	EA.	1.143
Cap	EA.	0.400
3" pipe		
90 deg. ell	EA.	1.000
45 deg. ell	EA.	1.000
Tee	EA.	1.333
Reducing tee	EA.	1.333
Cap	EA.	0.667
4" pipe		
90 deg ell	EA.	1.333
45 deg. ell	EA.	1.333
Tee	EA.	2.000
Reducing tee	EA.	2.000
Cap	EA.	0.667
6" pipe		
90 deg. ell	EA.	1.600
45 deg. ell	EA.	1.600
Tee	EA.	2.667
Reducing tee	EA.	2.667
Cap	EA.	0.800
8" pipe		
90 deg. ell	EA.	2.667
45 deg. ell	EA.	2.667
Tee	EA.	4.000
Reducing tee	EA.	4.000
Cap	EA.	1.600
10" pipe		
90 deg ell	EA.	2.667
45 deg. ell	EA.	2.667
Tee	EA.	4.000
Reducing tee	EA.	4.000
Cap	EA.	2.000
12" pipe		
90 deg. ell	EA.	3.200
45 deg. ell	EA.	3.200
Tee	EA.	5.714
Reducing tee	EA.	5.714
Cap	EA.	2.000
Cast iron fittings		
1/2" pipe		
90 deg. ell	EA.	0.267
45 deg. ell	EA.	0.267
Tee	EA.	0.400
Reducing tee	EA.	0.400

Plumbing	UNIT	MAN/HOURS
15410.80 Steel Pipe		
3/4" pipe		
90 deg. ell	EA.	0.267
45 deg. ell	EA.	0.267
Tee	EA.	0.400
Reducing tee	EA.	0.400
1" pipe		
90 deg. ell	EA.	0.320
45 deg. ell	EA.	0.320
Tee	EA.	0.444
Reducing tee	EA.	0.444
1-1/2" pipe		
90 deg. ell	EA.	0.400
45 deg. ell	EA.	0.400
Tee	EA.	0.571
Reducing tee	EA.	0.571
2-1/2" pipe		
90 deg. ell	EA.	0.800
45 deg. ell	EA.	0.800
Tee	EA.	1.143
Reducing tee	EA.	1.143
3" pipe		
90 deg. ell	EA.	1.000
45 deg. ell	EA.	1.000
Tee	EA.	1.600
Reducing tee	EA.	1.600
4" pipe		
90 deg. ell	EA.	1.333
45 deg. ell	EA.	1.333
Tee	EA.	2.000
Reducing tee	EA.	2.000
6" pipe		
90 deg. ell	EA.	1.333
45 deg. ell	EA.	1.333
Tee	EA.	2.000
Reducing tee	EA.	2.000
8" pipe		
90 deg. ell	EA.	2.667
45 deg. ell	EA.	2.667
Tee	EA.	4.000
Reducing tee	EA.	4.000
15410.82 Galvanized Steel Pipe		
Galvanized pipe		
1/2" pipe	L.F.	0.080
3/4" pipe	L.F.	0.100
1" pipe	L.F.	0.114
1-1/4" pipe	L.F.	0.133
1-1/2" pipe	L.F.	0.160
2" pipe	L.F.	0.200
2-1/2" pipe	L.F.	0.267
3" pipe	L.F.	0.286
4" pipe	L.F.	0.333
6" pipe	L.F.	0.667

Plumbing	UNIT	MAN/HOURS
15430.23 Cleanouts		
Cleanout, wall		
2"	EA.	0.533
3"	EA.	0.533
4"	EA.	0.667
6"	EA.	0.800
8"	EA.	1.000
Floor		
2"	EA.	0.667
3"	EA.	0.667
4"	EA.	0.800
6"	EA.	1.000
8"	EA.	1.143
15430.24 Grease Traps		
Grease traps, cast iron, 3" pipe		
35 gpm, 70 lb capacity	EA.	8.000
50 gpm, 100 lb capacity	EA.	10.000
15430.25 Hose Bibbs		
Hose bibb		
1/2"	EA.	0.267
3/4"	EA.	0.267
15430.60 Valves		
Gate valve, 125 lb, bronze, soldered		
1/2"	EA.	0.200
3/4"	EA.	0.200
1"	EA.	0.267
1-1/2"	EA.	0.320
2"	EA.	0.400
2-1/2"	EA.	0.500
Threaded		
1/4", 125 lb	EA.	0.320
1/2"		
125 lb	EA.	0.320
150 lb	EA.	0.320
300 lb	EA.	0.320
3/4"		
125 lb	EA.	0.320
150 lb	EA.	0.320
300 lb	EA.	0.320
1"		
125 lb	EA.	0.320
150 lb	EA.	0.320
300 lb	EA.	0.400
1-1/2"		
125 lb	EA.	0.400
150 lb	EA.	0.400
300 lb	EA.	0.444
2"		
125 lb	EA.	0.571
150 lb	EA.	0.571
300 lb	EA.	0.667
Cast iron, flanged		

Plumbing	UNIT	MAN/HOURS
15430.60 Valves		
2", 150 lb	EA.	0.667
2-1/2"		
125 lb	EA.	0.667
150 lb	EA.	0.667
250 lb	EA.	0.667
3"		
125 lb	EA.	0.800
150 lb	EA.	0.800
250 lb	EA.	0.800
4"		
125 lb	EA.	1.143
150 lb	EA.	1.143
250 lb	EA.	1.143
6"		
125 lb	EA.	1.600
250 lb	EA.	1.600
8"		
125 lb	EA.	2.000
250 lb	EA.	2.000
OS&Y, flanged		
2"		
125 lb	EA.	0.667
250 lb	EA.	0.667
2-1/2"		
125 lb	EA.	0.667
250 lb	EA.	0.800
3"		
125 lb	EA.	0.800
250 lb	EA.	0.800
4"		
125 lb	EA.	1.333
250 lb	EA.	1.333
6"		
125 lb	EA.	1.600
250 lb	EA.	1.600
Check valve, bronze, soldered, 125 lb		
1/2"	EA.	0.200
3/4"	EA.	0.200
1"	EA.	0.267
1-1/4"	EA.	0.320
1-1/2"	EA.	0.320
2"	EA.	0.400
Threaded		
1/2"		
125 lb	EA.	0.267
150 lb	EA.	0.267
200 lb	EA.	0.267
3/4"		
125 lb	EA.	0.320
150 lb	EA.	0.320
200 lb	EA.	0.320
1"		
125 lb	EA.	0.400
150 lb	EA.	0.400

Plumbing — 15430.60 Valves

Description	UNIT	MAN/HOURS
200 lb	EA.	0.400
Flow check valve, cast iron, threaded		
1"	EA.	0.320
1-1/4"	EA.	0.400
1-1/2"		
125 lb	EA.	0.400
150 lb	EA.	0.400
200 lb	EA.	0.444
2"		
125 lb	EA.	0.444
150 lb	EA.	0.444
200 lb	EA.	0.500
2-1/2"		
125 lb	EA.	0.667
250 lb	EA.	0.800
3"		
125 lb	EA.	0.800
250 lb	EA.	1.000
4"		
125 lb	EA.	1.143
250 lb	EA.	1.333
6"		
125 lb	EA.	1.600
250 lb	EA.	1.600
Vertical check valve, bronze, 125 lb, threaded		
1/2"	EA.	0.320
3/4"	EA.	0.364
1"	EA.	0.400
1-1/4"	EA.	0.444
1-1/2"	EA.	0.500
2"	EA.	0.571
Cast iron, flanged		
2-1/2"	EA.	0.800
3"	EA.	1.000
4"	EA.	1.333
6	EA.	1.600
8"	EA.	2.000
10"	EA.	2.667
12"	EA.	3.200
Globe valve, bronze, soldered, 125 lb		
1/2"	EA.	0.229
3/4"	EA.	0.250
1"	EA.	0.267
1-1/4"	EA.	0.286
1-1/2"	EA.	0.333
2"	EA.	0.400
Threaded		
1/2"		
125 lb	EA.	0.267
150 lb	EA.	0.267
300 lb	EA.	0.267
3/4"		
125 lb	EA.	0.320
150 lb	EA.	0.320

Plumbing — 15430.60 Valves

Description	UNIT	MAN/HOURS
300 lb	EA.	0.320
1"		
125 lb	EA.	0.400
150 lb	EA.	0.400
300 lb	EA.	0.400
1-1/4"		
125 lb	EA.	0.400
150 lb	EA.	0.400
300 lb	EA.	0.400
1-1/2"		
125 lb	EA.	0.444
150 lb	EA.	0.444
300 lb	EA.	0.444
2"		
125 lb	EA.	0.533
150 lb	EA.	0.533
300 lb	EA.	0.533
Cast iron flanged		
2-1/2"		
125 lb	EA.	0.800
250 lb	EA.	0.800
3"		
125 lb	EA.	1.000
250 lb	EA.	1.000
4"		
125 lb	EA.	1.333
250 lb	EA.	1.333
6"		
125 lb	EA.	1.600
250 lb	EA.	1.600
8"		
125 lb	EA.	2.000
250 lb	EA.	2.000
Butterfly valve, cast iron, wafer type		
2"		
150 lb	EA.	0.571
200 lb	EA.	0.667
2-1/2"		
150 lb	EA.	0.667
200 lb	EA.	0.727
3"		
150 lb	EA.	0.800
200 lb	EA.	0.889
4"		
150 lb	EA.	1.143
200 lb	EA.	1.333
6"		
150 lb	EA.	1.600
200 lb	EA.	1.600
8"		
150 lb	EA.	1.778
200 lb	EA.	2.000
10"		
150 lb	EA.	2.000

Plumbing

15430.60	Valves	UNIT	MAN/HOURS
200 lb		EA.	2.667
Ball valve, bronze, 250 lb, threaded			
1/2"		EA.	0.320
3/4"		EA.	0.320
1"		EA.	0.400
1-1/4"		EA.	0.444
1-1/2"		EA.	0.500
2"		EA.	0.571
Angle valve, bronze, 150 lb, threaded			
1/2"		EA.	0.286
3/4"		EA.	0.320
1"		EA.	0.320
1-1/4"		EA.	0.400
1-1/2"		EA.	0.444
Balancing valve, with meter connections, circuit setter			
1/2"		EA.	0.320
3/4"		EA.	0.364
1"		EA.	0.400
1-1/4"		EA.	0.444
1-1/2"		EA.	0.533
2"		EA.	0.667
2-1/2"		EA.	0.800
3"		EA.	1.000
4"		EA.	1.333
Balancing valve, straight type			
1/2"		EA.	0.320
3/4"		EA.	0.320
Angle type			
1/2"		EA.	0.320
3/4"		EA.	0.320
Square head cock, 125 lb, bronze body			
1/2"		EA.	0.267
3/4"		EA.	0.320
1"		EA.	0.364
1-1/4"		EA.	0.400
Pressure regulating valve, bronze, class 300			
1"		EA.	0.500
1-1/2"		EA.	0.615
2"		EA.	0.800
3"		EA.	1.143
4"		EA.	1.600
5"		EA.	2.000
6"		EA.	2.667

15430.68	Strainers	UNIT	MAN/HOURS
Strainer, Y pattern, 125 psi, cast iron body, threaded			
3/4"		EA.	0.286
1"		EA.	0.320
1-1/4"		EA.	0.400
1-1/2"		EA.	0.400
2"		EA.	0.500
250 psi, brass body, threaded			
3/4"		EA.	0.320
1"		EA.	0.320

Plumbing

15430.68	Strainers	UNIT	MAN/HOURS
1-1/4"		EA.	0.400
1-1/2"		EA.	0.400
2"		EA.	0.500
Cast iron body, threaded			
3/4"		EA.	0.320
1"		EA.	0.320
1-1/4"		EA.	0.400
1-1/2"		EA.	0.400
2"		EA.	0.500

15430.70	Drains, Roof & Floor	UNIT	MAN/HOURS
Floor drain, cast iron, with cast iron top			
2"		EA.	0.667
3"		EA.	0.667
4"		EA.	0.667
6"		EA.	0.800
Roof drain, cast iron			
2"		EA.	0.667
3"		EA.	0.667
4"		EA.	0.667
5"		EA.	0.800
6"		EA.	0.800

Plumbing Fixtures

15440.15	Faucets	UNIT	MAN/HOURS
Washroom			
Minimum		EA.	1.333
Average		EA.	1.600
Maximum		EA.	2.000
Handicapped			
Minimum		EA.	1.600
Average		EA.	2.000
Maximum		EA.	2.667
For trim and rough-in			
Minimum		EA.	1.600
Average		EA.	2.000
Maximum		EA.	4.000

15440.18	Hydrants	UNIT	MAN/HOURS
Wall hydrant			
8" thick		EA.	1.333
12" thick		EA.	1.600
18" thick		EA.	1.778
24" thick		EA.	2.000
Ground hydrant			
2' deep		EA.	1.000

Plumbing Fixtures	UNIT	MAN/HOURS
15440.18 Hydrants		
4' deep	EA.	1.143
6' deep	EA.	1.333
8' deep	EA.	2.000
15440.20 Lavatories		
Lavatory, counter top, porcelain enamel on cast iron		
Minimum	EA.	1.600
Average	EA.	2.000
Maximum	EA.	2.667
Wall hung, china		
Minimum	EA.	1.600
Average	EA.	2.000
Maximum	EA.	2.667
Handicapped		
Minimum	EA.	2.000
Average	EA.	2.667
Maximum	EA.	4.000
For trim and rough-in		
Minimum	EA.	2.000
Average	EA.	2.667
Maximum	EA.	4.000
15440.30 Showers		
Shower, fiberglass, 36"x34"x84"		
Minimum	EA.	5.714
Average	EA.	8.000
Maximum	EA.	8.000
Steel, 1 piece, 36"x36"		
Minimum	EA.	5.714
Average	EA.	8.000
Maximum	EA.	8.000
Receptor, molded stone, 36"x36"		
Minimum	EA.	2.667
Average	EA.	4.000
Maximum	EA.	6.667
For trim and rough-in		
Minimum	EA.	3.636
Average	EA.	4.444
Maximum	EA.	8.000
15440.40 Sinks		
Service sink, 24"x29"		
Minimum	EA.	2.000
Average	EA.	2.667
Maximum	EA.	4.000
Mop sink, 24"x36"x10"		
Minimum	EA.	1.600
Average	EA.	2.000
Maximum	EA.	2.667
For trim and rough-in		
Minimum	EA.	2.667
Average	EA.	4.000
Maximum	EA.	5.333

Plumbing Fixtures	UNIT	MAN/HOURS
15440.50 Urinals		
Urinal, flush valve, floor mounted		
Minimum	EA.	2.000
Average	EA.	2.667
Maximum	EA.	4.000
Wall mounted		
Minimum	EA.	2.000
Average	EA.	2.667
Maximum	EA.	4.000
For trim and rough-in		
Minimum	EA.	2.000
Average	EA.	4.000
Maximum	EA.	5.333
15440.60 Water Closets		
Water closet flush tank, floor mounted		
Minimum	EA.	2.000
Average	EA.	2.667
Maximum	EA.	4.000
Handicapped		
Minimum	EA.	2.667
Average	EA.	4.000
Maximum	EA.	8.000
Bowl, with flush valve, floor mounted		
Minimum	EA.	2.000
Average	EA.	2.667
Maximum	EA.	4.000
Wall mounted		
Minimum	EA.	2.000
Average	EA.	2.667
Maximum	EA.	4.000
For trim and rough-in		
Minimum	EA.	2.000
Average	EA.	2.667
Maximum	EA.	4.000
15440.70 Water Heaters		
Water heater, electric		
6 gal	EA.	1.333
10 gal	EA.	1.333
20 gal	EA.	1.600
40 gal	EA.	1.600
80 gal	EA.	2.000
100 gal	EA.	2.667
120 gal	EA.	2.667
15440.90 Miscellaneous Fixtures		
Electric water cooler		
Floor mounted	EA.	2.667
Wall mounted	EA.	2.667
Wash fountain		
Wall mounted	EA.	4.000
Circular, floor supported	EA.	8.000
Deluge shower and eye wash	EA.	4.000

Plumbing Fixtures

	UNIT	MAN/HOURS
15440.95 Fixture Carriers		
Water fountain, wall carrier		
Minimum	EA.	0.800
Average	EA.	1.000
Maximum	EA.	1.333
Lavatory, wall carrier		
Minimum	EA.	0.800
Average	EA.	1.000
Maximum	EA.	1.333
Sink, industrial, wall carrier		
Minimum	EA.	0.800
Average	EA.	1.000
Maximum	EA.	1.333
Toilets, water closets, wall carrier		
Minimum	EA.	0.800
Average	EA.	1.000
Maximum	EA.	1.333
Floor support		
Minimum	EA.	0.667
Average	EA.	0.800
Maximum	EA.	1.000
Urinals, wall carrier		
Minimum	EA.	0.800
Average	EA.	1.000
Maximum	EA.	1.333
Floor support		
Minimum	EA.	0.667
Average	EA.	0.800
Maximum	EA.	1.000
15450.30 Pumps		
In-line pump, bronze, centrifugal		
5 gpm, 20' head	EA.	0.500
20 gpm, 40' head	EA.	0.500
50 gpm		
50' head	EA.	1.000
100' head	EA.	1.000
70 gpm, 100' head	EA.	1.333
100 gpm, 80' head	EA.	1.333
250 gpm, 150' head	EA.	2.000
Cast iron, centrifugal		
50 gpm, 200' head	EA.	1.000
100 gpm		
100' head	EA.	1.333
200' head	EA.	1.333
200 gpm		
100' head	EA.	2.000
200' head	EA.	2.000
Centrifugal, close coupled, c.i., single stage		
50 gpm, 100' head	EA.	1.000
100 gpm, 100' head	EA.	1.333
Base mounted		
50 gpm, 100' head	EA.	1.000
100 gpm, 50' head	EA.	1.333
200 gpm, 100' head	EA.	2.000

Plumbing Fixtures

	UNIT	MAN/HOURS
15450.30 Pumps		
300 gpm, 175' head	EA.	2.000
Suction diffuser, flanged, strainer		
3" inlet, 2-1/2" outlet	EA.	1.000
3" outlet	EA.	1.000
4" inlet		
3" outlet	EA.	1.333
4" outlet	EA.	1.333
6" inlet		
4" outlet	EA.	1.600
5" outlet	EA.	1.600
6" Outlet	EA.	1.600
8" inlet		
6" outlet	EA.	2.000
8" outlet	EA.	2.000
10" inlet		
8" outlet	EA.	2.667
Vertical turbine		
Single stage, C.I., 3550 rpm, 200 gpm, 50'head	EA.	2.667
Multi stage, 3550 rpm		
50 gpm, 100' head	EA.	2.000
100 gpm		
100' head	EA.	2.000
200 gpm		
50' head	EA.	2.667
100' head	EA.	2.667
Bronze		
Single stage, 3550 rpm, 100 gpm, 50' head	EA.	2.000
Multi stage, 3550 rpm, 50 gpm, 100' head	EA.	2.000
100 gpm		
100' head	EA.	2.000
200 gpm		
50' head	EA.	2.667
100' head	EA.	2.667
Sump pump, bronze, 1750 rpm, 25 gpm		
20' head	EA.	10.000
150' head	EA.	13.333
50 gpm		
100' head	EA.	10.000
100 gpm		
50' head	EA.	10.000
15480.10 Special Systems		
Air compressor, air cooled, two stage		
5.0 cfm, 175 psi	EA.	16.000
10 cfm, 175 psi	EA.	17.778
20 cfm, 175 psi	EA.	19.048
50 cfm, 125 psi	EA.	21.053
80 cfm, 125 psi	EA.	22.857
Single stage, 125 psi		
1.0 cfm	EA.	11.429
1.5 cfm	EA.	11.429
2.0 cfm	EA.	11.429
Automotive, hose reel, air and water, 50' hose	EA.	6.667
Lube equipment, 3 reel, with pumps	EA.	32.000

4

Plumbing Fixtures	UNIT	MAN/HOURS
15480.10 Special Systems		
Tire changer		
Truck	EA.	11.429
Passenger car	EA.	6.154
Air hose reel, includes, 50' hose	EA.	6.154
Hose reel, 5 reel, motor oil, gear oil, lube, air & water	EA.	32.000
Water hose reel, 50' hose	EA.	6.154
Pump, air operated, for motor or gear oil, fits 55 gal drum	EA.	0.800
For chassis lube	EA.	0.800
Fuel dispensing pump, lighted dial, one product		
One hose	EA.	6.667
Two hose	EA.	6.667
Two products, two hose	EA.	6.667

Heating & Ventilating	UNIT	MAN/HOURS
15610.10 Furnaces		
Electric, hot air		
40 mbh	EA.	4.000
80 mbh	EA.	4.444
100 mbh	EA.	4.706
160 mbh	EA.	5.000
200 mbh	EA.	5.161
400 mbh	EA.	5.333
Gas fired hot air		
40 mbh	EA.	4.000
80 mbh	EA.	4.444
100 mbh	EA.	4.706
160 mbh	EA.	5.000
200 mbh	EA.	5.161
400 mbh	EA.	5.333
Oil fired hot air		
40 mbh	EA.	4.000
80 mbh	EA.	4.444
100 mbh	EA.	4.706
160 mbh	EA.	5.000
200 mbh	EA.	5.161
400 mbh	EA.	5.333

15780.20 Rooftop Units	UNIT	MAN/HOURS
Packaged, single zone rooftop unit, with roof curb		
2 ton	EA.	8.000
3 ton	EA.	8.000
4 ton	EA.	10.000
5 ton	EA.	13.333
7.5 ton	EA.	16.000

Heating & Ventilating	UNIT	MAN/HOURS
15830.70 Unit Heaters		
Steam unit heater, horizontal		
12,500 btuh, 200 cfm	EA.	1.333
17,000 btuh, 300 cfm	EA.	1.333
40,000 btuh, 500 cfm	EA.	1.333
60,000 btuh, 700 cfm	EA.	1.333
70,000 btuh, 1000 cfm	EA.	2.000
Vertical		
12,500 btuh, 200 cfm	EA.	1.333
17,000 btuh, 300 cfm	EA.	1.333
40,000 btuh, 500 cfm	EA.	1.333
60,000 btuh, 700 cfm	EA.	1.333
70,000 btuh, 1000 cfm	EA.	1.333
Gas unit heater, horizontal		
27,400 btuh	EA.	3.200
38,000 btuh	EA.	3.200
56,000 btuh	EA.	3.200
82,200 btuh	EA.	3.200
103,900 btuh	EA.	5.000
125,700 btuh	EA.	5.000
133,200 btuh	EA.	5.000
149,000 btuh	EA.	5.000
172,000 btuh	EA.	5.000
190,000 btuh	EA.	5.000
225,000 btuh	EA.	5.000
Hot water unit heater, horizontal		
12,500 btuh, 200 cfm	EA.	1.333
17,000 btuh, 300 cfm	EA.	1.333
25,000 btuh, 500 cfm	EA.	1.333
30,000 btuh, 700 cfm	EA.	1.333
50,000 btuh, 1000 cfm	EA.	2.000
60,000 btuh, 1300 cfm	EA.	2.000
Vertical		
12,500 btuh, 200 cfm	EA.	1.333
17,000 btuh, 300 cfm	EA.	1.333
25,000 btuh, 500 cfm	EA.	1.333
30,000 btuh, 700 cfm	EA.	1.333
50,000 btuh, 1000 cfm	EA.	1.333
60,000 btuh, 1300 cfm	EA.	1.333
Cabinet unit heaters, ceiling, exposed, hot water		
200 cfrn	EA.	2.667
300 cfm	EA.	3.200
400 cfm	EA.	3.810
600 cfm	EA.	4.211
800 cfm	EA.	5.000
1000 cfm	EA.	5.714
1200 cfm	EA.	6.667
2000 cfm	EA.	8.889

Air Handling

Air Handling	UNIT	MAN/HOURS

15855.10   Air Handling Units

	UNIT	MAN/HOURS
Air handling unit, medium pressure, single zone		
1500 cfm	EA.	5.000
3000 cfm	EA.	8.889
4000 cfm	EA.	10.000
5000 cfm	EA.	10.667
6000 cfm	EA.	11.429
7000 cfm	EA.	12.308
8500 cfm	EA.	13.333
Rooftop air handling units		
4950 cfm	EA.	8.889
7370 cfm	EA.	11.429

15870.20   Exhaust Fans

	UNIT	MAN/HOURS
Belt drive roof exhaust fans		
640 cfm, 2618 fpm	EA.	1.000
940 cfm, 2604 fpm	EA.	1.000
1050 cfm, 3325 fpm	EA.	1.000
1170 cfm, 2373 fpm	EA.	1.000
2440 cfm, 4501 fpm	EA.	1.000

Air Distribution

Air Distribution	UNIT	MAN/HOURS

15890.10   Metal Ductwork

	UNIT	MAN/HOURS
Rectangular duct		
Galvanized steel		
Minimum	Lb.	0.073
Average	Lb.	0.089
Maximum	Lb.	0.133
Aluminum		
Minimum	Lb.	0.160
Average	Lb.	0.200
Maximum	Lb.	0.267
Fittings		
Minimum	EA.	0.267
Average	EA.	0.400
Maximum	EA.	0.800

15890.30   Flexible Ductwork

	UNIT	MAN/HOURS
Flexible duct, 1.25" fiberglass		
6" dia.	L.F.	0.044
8" dia.	L.F.	0.050
12" dia.	L.F.	0.062
16" dia.	L.F.	0.073
Flexible duct connector, 3" wide fabric	L.F.	0.133

Air Distribution

Air Distribution	UNIT	MAN/HOURS

15910.10   Dampers

	UNIT	MAN/HOURS
Horizontal parallel aluminum backdraft damper		
12" x 12"	EA.	0.200
24" x 24"	EA.	0.400
36" x 36"	EA.	0.571

15940.10   Diffusers

	UNIT	MAN/HOURS
Ceiling diffusers, round, baked enamel finish		
6" dia.	EA.	0.267
8" dia.	EA.	0.333
12" dia.	EA.	0.333
16" dia.	EA.	0.364
20" dia.	EA.	0.400
Rectangular		
6x6"	EA.	0.267
12x12"	EA.	0.400
18x18"	EA.	0.400
24x24"	EA.	0.500

15940.40   Registers And Grilles

	UNIT	MAN/HOURS
Lay in flush mounted, perforated face, return		
6x6/24x24	EA.	0.320
8x8/24x24	EA.	0.320
9x9/24x24	EA.	0.320
10x10/24x24	EA.	0.320
12x12/24x24	EA.	0.320
Rectangular, ceiling return, single deflection		
10x10	EA.	0.400
12x12	EA.	0.400
16x16	EA.	0.400
20x20	EA.	0.400
24x18	EA.	0.400
36x24	EA.	0.444
36x30	EA.	0.444
Wall, return air register		
12x12	EA.	0.200
16x16	EA.	0.200
18x18	EA.	0.200
20x20	EA.	0.200
24x24	EA.	0.200

Basic Materials	UNIT	MAN/HOURS
16050.30 Bus Duct		
Bus duct, 100a, plug-in		
10', 600v	EA.	2.759
With ground	EA.	4.211
Circuit breakers, with enclosure		
1 pole		
15a-60a	EA.	1.000
70a-100a	EA.	1.250
2 pole		
15a-60a	EA.	1.100
70a-100a	EA.	1.301
Circuit breaker, adapter cubicle		
225a	EA.	1.509
400a	EA.	1.600
Fusible switches, 240v, 3 phase		
30a	EA.	1.000
60a	EA.	1.250
100a	EA.	1.509
200a	EA.	2.105
16110.12 Cable Tray		
Cable tray, 6"	L.F.	0.059
Ventilated cover	L.F.	0.030
Solid cover	L.F.	0.030
16110.20 Conduit Specialties		
Rod beam clamp, 1/2"	EA.	0.050
Hanger rod		
3/8"	L.F.	0.040
1/2"	L.F.	0.050
Hanger channel, 1-1/2"		
No holes	EA.	0.030
Holes	EA.	0.030
Channel strap		
1/2"	EA.	0.050
1"	EA.	0.050
2"	EA.	0.080
3"	EA.	0.123
4"	EA.	0.145
5"	EA.	0.145
6"	EA.	0.145
Conduit penetrations, roof and wall, 8" thick		
1/2"	EA.	0.615
1"	EA.	0.800
2"	EA.	1.600
3"	EA.	1.600
4"	EA.	2.000
Fireproofing, for conduit penetrations		
1/2"	EA.	0.500
1"	EA.	0.500
2"	EA.	0.727
3"	EA.	0.899
4"	EA.	1.509

Basic Materials	UNIT	MAN/HOURS
16110.21 Aluminum Conduit		
Aluminum conduit		
1/2"	L.F.	0.030
3/4"	L.F.	0.040
1"	L.F.	0.050
1-1/4"	L.F.	0.059
1-1/2"	L.F.	0.080
2"	L.F.	0.089
2-1/2"	L.F.	0.100
3"	L.F.	0.107
3-1/2"	L.F.	0.123
4"	L.F.	0.145
5"	L.F.	0.182
6"	L.F.	0.200
16110.22 Emt Conduit		
EMT conduit		
1/2"	L.F.	0.030
3/4"	L.F.	0.040
1"	L.F.	0.050
1-1/4"	L.F.	0.059
1-1/2"	L.F.	0.080
2"	L.F.	0.089
2-1/2"	L.F.	0.100
3"	L.F.	0.123
3-1/2"	L.F.	0.145
4"	L.F.	0.182
16110.23 Flexible Conduit		
Flexible conduit, steel		
3/8"	L.F.	0.030
1/2	L.F.	0.030
3/4"	L.F.	0.040
1"	L.F.	0.040
1-1/4"	L.F.	0.050
1-1/2"	L.F.	0.059
2"	L.F.	0.080
2-1/2"	L.F.	0.089
3"	L.F.	0.107
16110.24 Galvanized Conduit		
Galvanized rigid steel conduit		
1/2"	L.F.	0.040
3/4"	L.F.	0.050
1"	L.F.	0.059
1-1/4"	L.F.	0.080
1-1/2"	L.F.	0.089
2"	L.F.	0.100
2-1/2"	L.F.	0.145
3"	L.F.	0.182
3-1/2"	L.F.	0.190
4"	L.F.	0.211
5"	L.F.	0.286
6"	L.F.	0.381

Basic Materials

	UNIT	MAN/HOURS

16110.25   Plastic Conduit

PVC conduit, schedule 40	UNIT	MAN/HOURS
1/2"	L.F.	0.030
3/4"	L.F.	0.030
1"	L.F.	0.040
1-1/4"	L.F.	0.040
1-1/2"	L.F.	0.050
2"	L.F.	0.050
2-1/2"	L.F.	0.059
3"	L.F.	0.059
3-1/2"	L.F.	0.080
4"	L.F.	0.080
5"	L.F.	0.089
6"	L.F.	0.100

16110.27   Plastic Coated Conduit

Rigid steel conduit, plastic coated	UNIT	MAN/HOURS
1/2"	L.F.	0.050
3/4"	L.F.	0.059
1"	L.F.	0.080
1-1/4"	L.F.	0.100
1-1/2"	L.F.	0.123
2"	L.F.	0.145
2-1/2"	L.F.	0.190
3"	L.F.	0.222
3-1/2"	L.F.	0.250
4"	L.F.	0.308
5"	L.F.	0.381
90 degree elbows		
1/2"	EA.	0.308
3/4"	EA.	0.381
1"	EA.	0.444
1-1/4"	EA.	0.500
1-1/2"	EA.	0.615
2"	EA.	0.800
2-1/2"	EA.	1.143
3"	EA.	1.333
3-1/2"	EA.	1.633
4"	EA.	2.000
5"	EA.	2.500
Couplings		
1/2"	EA.	0.059
3/4"	EA.	0.080
1"	EA.	0.089
1-1/4"	EA.	0.107
1-1/2"	EA.	0.123
2"	EA.	0.145
2-1/2"	EA.	0.182
3"	EA.	0.190
3-1/2"	EA.	0.200
4"	EA.	0.222
5"	EA.	0.250
1 hole conduit straps		
3/4"	EA.	0.050
1"	EA.	0.050

Basic Materials

	UNIT	MAN/HOURS

16110.27   Plastic Coated Conduit

	UNIT	MAN/HOURS
1-1/4"	EA.	0.059
1-1/2"	EA.	0.059
2"	EA.	0.059
3"	EA.	0.080
3-1/2"	EA.	0.080
4"	EA.	0.100

16110.28   Steel Conduit

Intermediate metal conduit (IMC)	UNIT	MAN/HOURS
1/2"	L.F.	0.030
3/4"	L.F.	0.040
1"	L.F.	0.050
1-1/4"	L.F.	0.059
1-1/2"	L.F.	0.080
2"	L.F.	0.089
2-1/2"	L.F.	0.119
3"	L.F.	0.145
3-1/2"	L.F.	0.182
4"	L.F.	0.190
90 degree ell		
1/2"	EA.	0.250
3/4"	EA.	0.308
1"	EA.	0.381
1-1/4"	EA.	0.444
1-1/2"	EA.	0.500
2"	EA.	0.571
2-1/2"	EA.	0.667
3"	EA.	0.889
3-1/2"	EA.	1.143
4"	EA.	1.333
Couplings		
1/2"	EA.	0.050
3/4"	EA.	0.059
1"	EA.	0.080
1-1/4"	EA.	0.089
1-1/2"	EA.	0.100
2"	EA.	0.107
2-1/2"	EA.	0.123
3"	EA.	0.145
3-1/2"	EA.	0.145
4"	EA.	0.160

16110.35   Surface Mounted Raceway

Single Raceway	UNIT	MAN/HOURS
3/4" x 17/32" Conduit	L.F.	0.040
Mounting Strap	EA.	0.053
Connector	EA.	0.053
Elbow		
45 degree	EA.	0.050
90 degree	EA.	0.050
internal	EA.	0.050
external	EA.	0.050
Switch	EA.	0.400
Utility Box	EA.	0.400

Basic Materials

	UNIT	MAN/HOURS
16110.35 Surface Mounted Raceway		
Receptacle	EA.	0.400
3/4" x 21/32" Conduit	L.F.	0.040
Mounting Strap	EA.	0.053
Connector	EA.	0.053
Elbow		
45 degree	EA.	0.050
90 degree	EA.	0.050
internal	EA.	0.050
external	EA.	0.050
Switch	EA.	0.400
Utility Box	EA.	0.400
Receptacle	EA.	0.400
16110.60 Trench Duct		
Trench duct, with cover		
9"	L.F.	0.170
12"	L.F.	0.200
18"	L.F.	0.267
Tees		
9"	EA.	1.739
12"	EA.	2.000
18"	EA.	2.222
Vertical elbows		
9"	EA.	0.800
12"	EA.	1.096
18"	EA.	1.356
Cabinet connectors		
9"	EA.	2.000
12"	EA.	2.105
18"	EA.	2.424
End closers		
9"	EA.	0.615
12"	EA.	0.667
18"	EA.	0.800
Horizontal elbows		
9"	EA.	1.509
12"	EA.	1.739
18"	EA.	2.105
Crosses		
9"	EA.	2.000
12"	EA.	2.222
18"	EA.	2.500
16110.80 Wireways		
Wireway, hinge cover type		
2-1/2" x 2-1/2"		
1' section	EA.	0.154
2'	EA.	0.190
3'	EA.	0.250
16120.41 Aluminum Conductors		
Type XHHW, stranded aluminum, 600v		
#8	L.F.	0.005
#6	L.F.	0.006

Basic Materials

	UNIT	MAN/HOURS
16120.41 Aluminum Conductors		
#4	L.F.	0.008
#2	L.F.	0.009
1/0	L.F.	0.011
2/0	L.F.	0.012
3/0	L.F.	0.014
4/0	L.F.	0.015
THW, stranded		
#8	L.F.	0.005
#6	L.F.	0.006
#4	L.F.	0.008
#3	L.F.	0.009
#1	L.F.	0.010
1/0	L.F.	0.011
2/0	L.F.	0.012
3/0	L.F.	0.012
4/0	L.F.	0.015
16120.43 Copper Conductors		
Copper conductors, type THW, solid		
#14	L.F.	0.004
#12	L.F.	0.005
#10	L.F.	0.006
Stranded		
#14	L.F.	0.004
#12	L.F.	0.005
#10	L.F.	0.006
#8	L.F.	0.008
#6	L.F.	0.009
#4	L.F.	0.010
#3	L.F.	0.010
#2	L.F.	0.012
#1	L.F.	0.014
1/0	L.F.	0.016
2/0	L.F.	0.020
3/0	L.F.	0.025
4/0	L.F.	0.028
THHN-THWN, solid		
#14	L.F.	0.004
#12	L.F.	0.005
#10	L.F.	0.006
Stranded		
#14	L.F.	0.004
#12	L.F.	0.005
#10	L.F.	0.006
#8	L.F.	0.008
#6	L.F.	0.009
#4	L.F.	0.010
#2	L.F.	0.012
#1	L.F.	0.014
1/0	L.F.	0.016
2/0	L.F.	0.020
3/0	L.F.	0.025
4/0	L.F.	0.028
XLP, 600v		

Basic Materials

	UNIT	MAN/HOURS
16120.43 Copper Conductors		
#12	L.F.	0.005
#10	L.F.	0.006
#8	L.F.	0.008
#6	L.F.	0.009
#4	L.F.	0.010
#3	L.F.	0.011
#2	L.F.	0.012
#1	L.F.	0.014
1/0	L.F.	0.016
2/0	L.F.	0.020
3/0	L.F.	0.026
4/0	L.F.	0.028
Bare solid wire		
#14	L.F.	0.004
#12	L.F.	0.005
#10	L.F.	0.006
#8	L.F.	0.008
#6	L.F.	0.009
#4	L.F.	0.010
#2	L.F.	0.012
Bare stranded wire		
#8	L.F.	0.008
#6	L.F.	0.010
#4	L.F.	0.010
#2	L.F.	0.011
#1	L.F.	0.014
1/0	L.F.	0.018
2/0	L.F.	0.020
3/0	L.F.	0.025
4/0	L.F.	0.028
Type "BX" solid armored cable		
#14/2	L.F.	0.025
#14/3	L.F.	0.028
#14/4	L.F.	0.031
#12/2	L.F.	0.028
#12/3	L.F.	0.031
#12/4	L.F.	0.035
#10/2	L.F.	0.031
#10/3	L.F.	0.035
#10/4	L.F.	0.040
#8/2	L.F.	0.035
#8/3	L.F.	0.040
Steel type, metal clad cable, solid, with ground		
#14/2	L.F.	0.018
#14/3	L.F.	0.020
#14/4	L.F.	0.023
#12/2	L.F.	0.020
#12/3	L.F.	0.025
#12/4	L.F.	0.030
#10/2	L.F.	0.023
#10/3	L.F.	0.028
#10/4	L.F.	0.033
Metal clad cable, stranded, with ground		
#8/2	L.F.	0.028

Basic Materials

	UNIT	MAN/HOURS
16120.43 Copper Conductors		
#8/3	L.F.	0.035
#8/4	L.F.	0.042
#6/2	L.F.	0.030
#6/3	L.F.	0.038
#6/4	L.F.	0.044
#4/2	L.F.	0.040
#4/3	L.F.	0.044
#4/4	L.F.	0.055
#3/3	L.F.	0.050
#3/4	L.F.	0.059
#2/3	L.F.	0.057
#2/4	L.F.	0.067
#1/3	L.F.	0.076
#1/4	L.F.	0.084
16120.47 Sheathed Cable		
Non-metallic sheathed cable		
Type NM cable with ground		
#14/2	L.F.	0.015
#12/2	L.F.	0.016
#10/2	L.F.	0.018
#8/2	L.F.	0.020
#6/2	L.F.	0.025
#14/3	L.F.	0.026
#12/3	L.F.	0.027
#10/3	L.F.	0.027
#8/3	L.F.	0.028
#6/3	L.F.	0.028
#4/3	L.F.	0.032
#2/3	L.F.	0.035
Type U.F. cable with ground		
#14/2	L.F.	0.016
#12/2	L.F.	0.019
#10/2	L.F.	0.020
#8/2	L.F.	0.023
#6/2	L.F.	0.027
#14/3	L.F.	0.020
#12/3	L.F.	0.022
#10/3	L.F.	0.025
#8/3	L.F.	0.028
#6/3	L.F.	0.032
Type S.F.U. cable, 3 conductor		
#8	L.F.	0.028
#6	L.F.	0.031
Type SER cable, 4 conductor		
#6	L.F.	0.036
#4	L.F.	0.039
Flexible cord, type STO cord		
#18/2	L.F.	0.004
#18/3	L.F.	0.005
#18/4	L.F.	0.006
#16/2	L.F.	0.004
#16/3	L.F.	0.004
#16/4	L.F.	0.005

Basic Materials

16120.47	Sheathed Cable	UNIT	MAN/HOURS
#14/2		L.F.	0.005
#14/3		L.F.	0.006
#14/4		L.F.	0.007
#12/2		L.F.	0.006
#12/3		L.F.	0.007
#12/4		L.F.	0.008
#10/2		L.F.	0.007
#10/3		L.F.	0.008
#10/4		L.F.	0.009
#8/2		L.F.	0.008
#8/3		L.F.	0.009
#8/4		L.F.	0.010

16130.40	Boxes	UNIT	MAN/HOURS
Round cast box, type SEH			
1/2"		EA.	0.348
3/4"		EA.	0.421
SEHC			
1/2"		EA.	0.348
3/4"		EA.	0.421
SEHL			
1/2"		EA.	0.348
3/4"		EA.	0.444
SEHT			
1/2"		EA.	0.421
3/4"		EA.	0.500
SEHX			
1/2"		EA.	0.500
3/4"		EA.	0.615
Blank cover		EA.	0.145
1/2", hub cover		EA.	0.145
Cover with gasket		EA.	0.178
Rectangle, type FS boxes			
1/2"		EA.	0.348
3/4"		EA.	0.400
1"		EA.	0.500
FSA			
1/2"		EA.	0.348
3/4"		EA.	0.400
FSC			
1/2"		EA.	0.348
3/4"		EA.	0.421
1"		EA.	0.500
FSL			
1/2"		EA.	0.348
3/4"		EA.	0.400
FSR			
1/2"		EA.	0.348
3/4"		EA.	0.400
FSS			
1/2"		EA.	0.348
3/4"		EA.	0.400
FSLA			
1/2"		EA.	0.348

Basic Materials

16130.40	Boxes	UNIT	MAN/HOURS
3/4"		EA.	0.400
FSCA			
1/2"		EA.	0.348
3/4"		EA.	0.400
FSCC			
1/2"		EA.	0.400
3/4"		EA.	0.500
FSCT			
1/2"		EA.	0.400
3/4"		EA.	0.500
1"		EA.	0.571
FST			
1/2"		EA.	0.500
3/4"		EA.	0.571
FSX			
1/2"		EA.	0.615
3/4"		EA.	0.727
FSCD boxes			
1/2"		EA.	0.615
3/4"		EA.	0.727
Rectangle, type FS, 2 gang boxes			
1/2"		EA.	0.348
3/4"		EA.	0.400
1"		EA.	0.500
Weatherproof cast aluminum boxes, 1 gang, 3 outlets			
1/2"		EA.	0.400
3/4"		EA.	0.500
2 gang, 3 outlets			
1/2"		EA.	0.500
3/4"		EA.	0.533
1 gang, 4 outlets			
1/2"		EA.	0.615
3/4"		EA.	0.727
2 gang, 4 outlets			
1/2"		EA.	0.615
3/4"		EA.	0.727
Weatherproof and type FS box covers, blank, 1 gang		EA.	0.145
Tumbler switch, 1 gang		EA.	0.145
1 gang, single recept		EA.	0.145
Duplex recept		EA.	0.145
Despard		EA.	0.145
Red pilot light		EA.	0.145
SW and			
Single recept		EA.	0.200
Duplex recept		EA.	0.200
2 gang			
Blank		EA.	0.182
Tumbler switch		EA.	0.182
Single recept		EA.	0.182
Duplex recept		EA.	0.182
Box covers			
Surface		EA.	0.200
Sealing		EA.	0.200
Dome		EA.	0.200

Basic Materials	UNIT	MAN/HOURS
16130.40 Boxes		
1/2" nipple	EA.	0.200
3/4" nipple	EA.	0.200
16130.60 Pull And Junction Boxes		
4"		
Octagon box	EA.	0.114
Box extension	EA.	0.059
Plaster ring	EA.	0.059
Cover blank	EA.	0.059
Square box	EA.	0.114
Box extension	EA.	0.059
Plaster ring	EA.	0.059
Cover blank	EA.	0.059
4-11/16"		
Square box	EA.	0.114
Box extension	EA.	0.059
Plaster ring	EA.	0.059
Cover blank	EA.	0.059
Switch and device boxes		
2 gang	EA.	0.114
3 gang	EA.	0.114
4 gang	EA.	0.160
Device covers		
2 gang	EA.	0.059
3 gang	EA.	0.059
4 gang	EA.	0.059
Handy box	EA.	0.114
Extension	EA.	0.059
Switch cover	EA.	0.059
Switch box with knockout	EA.	0.145
Weatherproof cover, spring type	EA.	0.080
Cover plate, dryer receptacle 1 gang plastic	EA.	0.100
For 4" receptacle, 2 gang	EA.	0.100
Duplex receptacle cover plate, plastic	EA.	0.059
4", vertical bracket box, 1-1/2" with		
RMX clamps	EA.	0.145
BX clamps	EA.	0.145
4", octagon device cover		
1 switch	EA.	0.059
1 duplex recept	EA.	0.059
4" octagon adjustable bar hangers		
18-1/2"	EA.	0.050
26-1/2"	EA.	0.050
With clip		
18-1/2"	EA.	0.050
26-1/2"	EA.	0.050
4" square to round plaster rings	EA.	0.059
2 gang device plaster rings	EA.	0.059
Surface covers		
1 gang switch	EA.	0.059
2 gang switch	EA.	0.059
1 single recept	EA.	0.059
1 20a twist lock recept	EA.	0.059
1 30a twist lock recept	EA.	0.059

Basic Materials	UNIT	MAN/HOURS
16130.60 Pull And Junction Boxes		
1 duplex recept	EA.	0.059
2 duplex recept	EA.	0.059
Switch and duplex recept	EA.	0.059
4" plastic round boxes, ground straps		
Box only	EA.	0.145
Box w/clamps	EA.	0.200
Box w/16" bar	EA.	0.229
Box w/24" bar	EA.	0.250
4" plastic round box covers		
Blank cover	EA.	0.059
Plaster ring	EA.	0.059
4" plastic square boxes		
Box only	EA.	0.145
Box w/clamps	EA.	0.200
Box w/hanger	EA.	0.250
Box w/nails and clamp	EA.	0.250
4" plastic square box covers		
Blank cover	EA.	0.059
1 gang ring	EA.	0.059
2 gang ring	EA.	0.059
Round ring	EA.	0.059
16130.65 Pull Boxes And Cabinets		
Galvanized pull boxes, screw cover		
4x4x4	EA.	0.190
4x6x4	EA.	0.190
16130.80 Receptacles		
Contractor grade duplex receptacles, 15a 120v		
Duplex	EA.	0.200
125 volt, 20a, duplex, grounding type, standard grade	EA.	0.200
Ground fault interrupter type	EA.	0.296
250 volt, 20a, 2 pole, single receptacle, ground type	EA.	0.200
120/208v, 4 pole, single receptacle, twist lock		
20a	EA.	0.348
50a	EA.	0.348
125/250v, 3 pole, flush receptacle		
30a	EA.	0.296
50a	EA.	0.296
60a	EA.	0.348
Clock receptacle, 2 pole, grounding type	EA.	0.200
125/250v, 3 pole, 3 wire surface recepts		
30a	EA.	0.296
50a	EA.	0.296
60a	EA.	0.348
Cord set, 3 wire, 6' cord		
30a	EA.	0.296
50a	EA.	0.296
125/250v, 3 pole, 3 wire cap		
30a	EA.	0.400
50a	EA.	0.400
60a	EA.	0.444

Basic Materials	UNIT	MAN/HOURS
16198.10 Electric Manholes		
Precast, handhole, 4' deep		
2'x2'	EA.	3.478
3'x3'	EA.	5.556
4'x4'	EA.	10.256
Power manhole, complete, precast, 8' deep		
4'x4'	EA.	14.035
6'x6'	EA.	20.000
8'x8'	EA.	21.053
6' deep, 9' x 12'	EA.	25.000
Cast in place, power manhole, 8' deep		
4'x4'	EA.	14.035
6'x6'	EA.	20.000
8'x8'	EA.	21.053
16199.10 Utility Poles & Fittings		
Wood pole, creosoted		
25'	EA.	2.353
30'	EA.	2.963
35'	EA.	3.478
40'	EA.	3.791
45'	EA.	6.957
50'	EA.	7.207
55'	EA.	7.547
Treated, wood preservative, 6"x6"		
8'	EA.	0.500
10'	EA.	0.800
12'	EA.	0.889
14'	EA.	1.333
16'	EA.	1.600
18'	EA.	2.000
20'	EA.	2.000
Aluminum, brushed, no base		
8'	EA.	2.000
10'	EA.	2.667
15'	EA.	2.759
20'	EA.	3.200
25'	EA.	3.810
30'	EA.	4.396
35'	EA.	5.000
40'	EA.	6.250
Steel, no base		
10'	EA.	2.500
15'	EA.	2.963
20'	EA.	3.810
25'	EA.	4.520
30'	EA.	5.096
35'	EA.	6.250
Concrete, no base		
13'	EA.	5.517
16'	EA.	7.273
18'	EA.	8.791
25'	EA.	10.000
30'	EA.	12.121
35'	EA.	14.035

Basic Materials	UNIT	MAN/HOURS
16199.10 Utility Poles & Fittings		
40'	EA.	16.000
45'	EA.	17.021
50'	EA.	18.182
55'	EA.	19.048
60'	EA.	20.000
Pole line hardware		
Wood crossarm		
4'	EA.	1.333
8'	EA.	1.667
10'	EA.	2.051
Angle steel brace		
1 piece	EA.	0.250
2 piece	EA.	0.348
Eye nut, 5/8"	EA.	0.050
Bolt (14-16"), 5/8"	EA.	0.200
Transformer, ground connection	EA.	0.250
Stirrup	EA.	0.308
Secondary lead support	EA.	0.400
Spool insulator	EA.	0.200
Guy grip, preformed		
7/16"	EA.	0.145
1/2"	EA.	0.145
Hook	EA.	0.250
Strain insulator	EA.	0.364
Wire		
5/16"	L.F.	0.005
7/16"	L.F.	0.006
1/2"	L.F.	0.008
Soft drawn ground, copper, #8	L.F.	0.008
Ground clamp	EA.	0.308
Perforated strapping for conduit, 1-1/2"	L.F.	0.145
Hot line clamp	EA.	0.800
Lightning arrester		
3kv	EA.	1.000
10kv	EA.	1.600
30kv	EA.	2.000
36kv	EA.	2.500
Fittings		
Plastic molding	L.F.	0.145
Molding staples	EA.	0.050
Ground wires staples	EA.	0.030
Copper butt plate	EA.	0.296
Anchor bond clamp	EA.	0.145
Guy wire		
1/4"	L.F.	0.030
3/8"	L.F.	0.050
Guy grip		
1/4"	EA.	0.050
3/8"	EA.	0.050

Power Generation	UNIT	MAN/ HOURS
16210.10 Generators		
Diesel generator, with auto transfer switch		
50kw	EA.	30.769
125kw	EA.	50.000
300kw	EA.	100.000
750kw	EA.	200.000
16320.10 Transformers		
Floor mounted, single phase, int. dry, 480v-120/240v		
3 kva	EA.	1.818
5 kva	EA.	3.077
7.5 kva	EA.	3.478
10 kva	EA.	3.810
15 kva	EA.	4.301
100 kva	EA.	11.594
Three phase, 480v-120/208v		
15 kva	EA.	6.015
30 kva	EA.	9.412
45 kva	EA.	10.811
225 kva	EA.	15.385
16350.10 Circuit Breakers		
Molded case, 240v, 15-60a, bolt-on		
1 pole	EA.	0.250
2 pole	EA.	0.348
70-100a, 2 pole	EA.	0.533
15-60a, 3 pole	EA.	0.400
70-100a, 3 pole	EA.	0.615
480v, 2 pole		
15-60a	EA.	0.296
70-100a	EA.	0.400
3 pole		
15-60a	EA.	0.400
70-100a	EA.	0.444
70-225a	EA.	0.615
Load center circuit breakers, 240v		
1 pole, 10-60a	EA.	0.250
2 pole		
10-60a	EA.	0.400
70-100a	EA.	0.667
110-150a	EA.	0.727
3 pole		
10-60a	EA.	0.500
70-100a	EA.	0.727
Load center, G.F.I. breakers, 240v		
1 pole, 15-30a	EA.	0.296
2 pole, 15-30a	EA.	0.400
Key operated breakers, 240v, 1 pole, 10-30a	EA.	0.296
Tandem breakers, 240v		
1 pole, 15-30a	EA.	0.400
2 pole, 15-30a	EA.	0.533
Bolt-on, G.F.I. breakers, 240v, 1 pole, 15-30a	EA.	0.348

Power Generation	UNIT	MAN/ HOURS
16360.10 Safety Switches		
Fused, 3 phase, 30 amp, 600v, heavy duty		
NEMA 1	EA.	1.143
NEMA 3r	EA.	1.143
NEMA 4	EA.	1.600
NEMA 12	EA.	1.739
60a		
NEMA 1	EA.	1.143
NEMA 3r	EA.	1.143
NEMA 4	EA.	1.600
NEMA 12	EA.	1.739
100a		
NEMA 1	EA.	1.739
NEMA 3r	EA.	1.739
NEMA 4	EA.	2.000
NEMA 12	EA.	2.500
200a		
NEMA 1	EA.	2.500
NEMA 3r	EA.	2.500
NEMA 4	EA.	2.759
NEMA 12	EA.	3.478
Non-fused, 240-600v, heavy duty, 3 phase, 30 amp		
NEMA 1	EA.	1.143
NEMA 3r	EA.	1.143
NEMA 4	EA.	1.739
NEMA 12	EA.	1.739
60a		
NEMA1	EA.	1.143
NEMA 3r	EA.	1.143
NEMA 4	EA.	1.739
NEMA 12	EA.	1.739
100a		
NEMA 1	EA.	1.739
NEMA 3r	EA.	1.739
NEMA 4	EA.	2.500
NEMA 12	EA.	2.500
200a, NEMA 1	EA.	2.500
600a, NEMA 12	EA.	12.308
16365.10 Fuses		
Fuse, one-time, 250v		
30a	EA.	0.050
60a	EA.	0.050
100a	EA.	0.050
200a	EA.	0.050
400a	EA.	0.050
600a	EA.	0.050
600v		
30a	EA.	0.050
60a	EA.	0.050
100a	EA.	0.050
200a	EA.	0.050
400a	EA.	0.050

4

Power Generation

16395.10   Grounding

	UNIT	MAN/ HOURS
Ground rods, copper clad, 1/2" x		
6'	EA.	0.667
8'	EA.	0.727
10'	EA.	1.000
5/8" x		
5'	EA.	0.615
6'	EA.	0.727
8'	EA.	1.000
10'	EA.	1.250
3/4" x		
8'	EA.	0.727
10'	EA.	0.800
Ground rod clamp		
5/8"	EA.	0.123
3/4"	EA.	0.123
Ground rod couplings		
1/2"	EA.	0.100
5/8"	EA.	0.100
Ground rod, driving stud		
1/2"	EA.	0.100
5/8"	EA.	0.100
3/4"	EA.	0.100
Ground rod clamps, #8-2 to		
1" pipe	EA.	0.200
2" pipe	EA.	0.250
3" pipe	EA.	0.296
5" pipe	EA.	0.348
6" pipe	EA.	0.444

Service And Distribution

16425.10   Switchboards

	UNIT	MAN/ HOURS
Switchboard, 90" high, no main disconnect, 208/120v		
400a	EA.	7.921
600a	EA.	8.000
1000a	EA.	8.000
1200a	EA.	10.000
1600a	EA.	11.940
2000a	EA.	14.035
2500a	EA.	16.000
277/480v		
600a	EA.	8.163
800a	EA.	8.163
1600a	EA.	11.940
2000a	EA.	14.035
2500a	EA.	16.000
3000a	EA.	27.586

Service And Distribution

16425.10   Switchboards

	UNIT	MAN/ HOURS
4000a	EA.	29.630

16430.20   Metering

	UNIT	MAN/ HOURS
Outdoor wp meter sockets, 1 gang, 240v, 1 phase		
Includes sealing ring, 100a	EA.	1.509
150a	EA.	1.778
200a	EA.	2.000
Die cast hubs, 1-1/4"	EA.	0.320
1-1/2"	EA.	0.320
2"	EA.	0.320

16470.10   Panelboards

	UNIT	MAN/ HOURS
Indoor load center, 1 phase 240v main lug only		
30a - 2 spaces	EA.	2.000
100a - 8 spaces	EA.	2.424
150a - 16 spaces	EA.	2.963
200a - 24 spaces	EA.	3.478
200a - 42 spaces	EA.	4.000
Main circuit breaker		
100a - 8 spaces	EA.	2.424
100a - 16 spaces	EA.	2.759
150a - 16 spaces	EA.	2.963
150a - 24 spaces	EA.	3.200
200a - 24 spaces	EA.	3.478
200a - 42 spaces	EA.	3.636
3 phase, 480/277v, main lugs only, 120a, 30 circuits	EA.	3.478
277/480v, 4 wire, flush surface		
225a, 30 circuits	EA.	4.000
400a, 30 circuits	EA.	5.000
600a, 42 circuits	EA.	6.015
208/120v, main circuit breaker, 3 phase, 4 wire		
100a		
12 circuits	EA.	5.096
20 circuits	EA.	6.299
30 circuits	EA.	7.018
400a		
30 circuits	EA.	14.815
42 circuits	EA.	16.000
600a, 42 circuits	EA.	18.182
120/208v, flush, 3 ph., 4 wire, main only		
100a		
12 circuits	EA.	5.096
20 circuits	EA.	6.299
30 circuits	EA.	7.018
225a		
30 circuits	EA.	7.767
42 circuits	EA.	9.524
400a		
30 circuits	EA.	14.815
42 circuits	EA.	16.000
600a, 42 circuits	EA.	18.182

Service And Distribution	UNIT	MAN/HOURS
16480.10 Motor Controls		
Motor generator set, 3 phase, 480/277v, w/controls		
10kw	EA.	27.586
15kw	EA.	30.769
20kw	EA.	32.000
40kw	EA.	38.095
100kw	EA.	61.538
200kw	EA.	72.727
300kw	EA.	80.000
2 pole, 230 volt starter, w/NEMA-1		
1 hp, 9 amp, size 00	EA.	1.000
2 hp, 18amp, size 0	EA.	1.000
3 hp, 27amp, size 1	EA.	1.000
5 hp, 45amp, size 1p	EA.	1.000
7-1/2 hp, 45a, size 2	EA.	1.000
15 hp, 90a, size 3	EA.	1.000
16490.10 Switches		
Fused interrupter load, 35kv		
20A		
1 pole	EA.	16.000
2 pole	EA.	17.021
3 way	EA.	17.021
4 way	EA.	18.182
30a, 1 pole	EA.	16.000
3 way	EA.	17.021
4 way	EA.	18.182
Weatherproof switch, including box & cover, 20a		
1 pole	EA.	16.000
2 pole	EA.	17.021
3 way	EA.	18.182
4 way	EA.	18.182
Photo electric switches		
1000 watt		
105-135v	EA.	0.727
Dimmer switch and switch plate		
600w	EA.	0.308
Contractor grade wall switch 15a, 120v		
Single pole	EA.	0.160
Three way	EA.	0.200
Four way	EA.	0.267
Specification grade toggle switches, 20a, 120-277v		
Single pole	EA.	0.200
Double pole	EA.	0.296
3 way	EA.	0.250
4 way	EA.	0.296
Switch plates, plastic ivory		
1 gang	EA.	0.080
2 gang	EA.	0.100
3 gang	EA.	0.119
4 gang	EA.	0.145
5 gang	EA.	0.160
6 gang	EA.	0.182
Stainless steel		
1 gang	EA.	0.080

Service And Distribution	UNIT	MAN/HOURS
16490.10 Switches		
2 gang	EA.	0.100
3 gang	EA.	0.123
4 gang	EA.	0.145
5 gang	EA.	0.160
6 gang	EA.	0.182
Brass		
1 gang	EA.	0.080
2 gang	EA.	0.100
3 gang	EA.	0.123
4 gang	EA.	0.145
5 gang	EA.	0.160
6 gang	EA.	0.182
16490.20 Transfer Switches		
Automatic transfer switch 600v, 3 pole		
30a	EA.	3.478
100a	EA.	4.762
400a	EA.	10.000
800a	EA.	18.182
1200a	EA.	22.857
2600a	EA.	42.105
16490.80 Safety Switches		
Safety switch, 600v, 3 pole, heavy duty, NEMA-1		
30a	EA.	1.000
60a	EA.	1.143
100a	EA.	1.600
200a	EA.	2.500
400a	EA.	5.517
600a	EA.	8.000
800a	EA.	10.526
1200a	EA.	14.286

Lighting	UNIT	MAN/HOURS
16510.05 Interior Lighting		
Recessed fluorescent fixtures, 2'x2'		
2 lamp	EA.	0.727
4 lamp	EA.	0.727
2 lamp w/flange	EA.	1.000
4 lamp w/flange	EA.	1.000
1'x4'		
2 lamp	EA.	0.667
3 lamp	EA.	0.667
2 lamp w/flange	EA.	0.727
3 lamp w/flange	EA.	0.727
2'x4'		

Lighting	UNIT	MAN/HOURS
16510.05 Interior Lighting		
2 lamp	EA.	0.727
3 lamp	EA.	0.727
4 lamp	EA.	0.727
2 lamp w/flange	EA.	1.000
3 lamp w/flange	EA.	1.000
4 lamp w/flange	EA.	1.000
4'x4'		
4 lamp	EA.	1.000
6 lamp	EA.	1.000
8 lamp	EA.	1.000
4 lamp w/flange	EA.	1.509
6 lamp w/flange	EA.	1.509
8 lamp, w/flange	EA.	1.509
Surface mounted incandescent fixtures		
40w	EA.	0.667
75w	EA.	0.667
100w	EA.	0.667
150w	EA.	0.667
Pendant		
40w	EA.	0.800
75w	EA.	0.800
100w	EA.	0.800
150w	EA.	0.800
Recessed incandescent fixtures		
40w	EA.	1.509
75w	EA.	1.509
100w	EA.	1.509
150w	EA.	1.509
Exit lights, 120v		
Recessed	EA.	1.250
Back mount	EA.	0.727
Universal mount	EA.	0.727
Emergency battery units, 6v-120v, 50 unit	EA.	1.509
With 1 head	EA.	1.509
With 2 heads	EA.	1.509
Mounting bucket	EA.	0.727
Light track single circuit		
2'	EA.	0.500
4'	EA.	0.500
8'	EA.	1.000
12'	EA.	1.509
Fixtures, square		
R-20	EA.	0.145
R-30	EA.	0.145
Mini spot	EA.	0.145
16510.10 Lighting Industrial		
Surface mounted fluorescent, wrap around lens		
1 lamp	EA.	0.800
2 lamps	EA.	0.889
4 lamps	EA.	1.000
Wall mounted fluorescent		
2-20w lamps	EA.	0.500
2-30w lamps	EA.	0.500

Lighting	UNIT	MAN/HOURS
16510.10 Lighting Industrial		
2-40w lamps	EA.	0.667
Indirect, with wood shielding, 2049w lamps		
4'	EA.	1.000
8'	EA.	1.600
Industrial fluorescent, 2 lamp		
4'	EA.	0.727
8'	EA.	1.333
Strip fluorescent		
4'		
1 lamp	EA.	0.667
2 lamps	EA.	0.667
8'		
1 lamp	EA.	0.727
2 lamps	EA.	0.889
Wire guard for strip fixture, 4' long	EA.	0.348
Strip fluorescent, 8' long, two 4' lamps	EA.	1.333
With four 4' lamps	EA.	1.600
Wet location fluorescent, plastic housing		
4' long		
1 lamp	EA.	1.000
2 lamps	EA.	1.333
8' long		
2 lamps	EA.	1.600
4 lamps	EA.	1.739
Parabolic troffer, 2'x2'		
With 2 "U" lamps	EA.	1.000
With 3 "U" lamps	EA.	1.143
2'x4'		
With 2 40w lamps	EA.	1.143
With 3 40w lamps	EA.	1.333
With 4 40w lamps	EA.	1.333
1'x4'		
With 1 T-12 lamp, 9 cell	EA.	0.727
With 2 T-12 lamps	EA.	0.889
With 1 T-12 lamp, 20 cell	EA.	0.727
With 2 T-12 lamps	EA.	0.889
Steel sided surface fluorescent, 2'x4'		
3 lamps	EA.	1.333
4 lamps	EA.	1.333
Outdoor sign fluor., 1 lamp, remote ballast		
4' long	EA.	6.015
6' long	EA.	8.000
Recess mounted, commercial, 2'x2', 13" high		
100w	EA.	4.000
250w	EA.	4.494
High pressure sodium, hi-bay open		
400w	EA.	1.739
1000w	EA.	2.424
Enclosed		
400w	EA.	2.424
1000w	EA.	2.963
Metal halide hi-bay, open		
400w	EA.	1.739
1000w	EA.	2.424

Lighting	UNIT	MAN/HOURS
16510.10 Lighting Industrial		
Enclosed		
400w	EA.	2.424
1000w	EA.	2.963
High pressure sodium, low bay, surface mounted		
100w	EA.	1.000
150w	EA.	1.143
250w	EA.	1.333
400w	EA.	1.600
Metal halide, low bay, pendant mounted		
175w	EA.	1.333
250w	EA.	1.600
400w	EA.	2.222
Indirect luminare, square, metal halide, freestanding		
175w	EA.	1.000
250w	EA.	1.000
400w	EA.	1.000
High pressure sodium		
150w	EA.	1.000
250w	EA.	1.000
400w	EA.	1.000
Round, metal halide		
175w	EA.	1.000
250w	EA.	1.000
400w	EA.	1.000
High pressure sodium		
150w	EA.	1.000
250w	EA.	1.000
400w	EA.	1.000
Wall mounted, metal halide		
175w	EA.	2.500
250w	EA.	2.500
400w	EA.	3.200
High pressure sodium		
150w	EA.	2.500
250w	EA.	2.500
400w	EA.	3.200
Wall pack lithonia, high pressure sodium		
35w	EA.	0.889
55w	EA.	1.000
150w	EA.	1.600
250w	EA.	1.739
Low pressure sodium		
35w	EA.	1.739
55w	EA.	2.000
Wall pack hubbell, high pressure sodium		
35w	EA.	0.889
150w	EA.	1.600
250w	EA.	1.739
Compact fluorescent		
2-7w	EA.	1.000
2-13w	EA.	1.333
1-18w	EA.	1.333
Handball & racquet ball court, 2'x2', metal halide		
250w	EA.	2.500

Lighting	UNIT	MAN/HOURS
16510.10 Lighting Industrial		
400w	EA.	2.759
High pressure sodium		
250w	EA.	2.500
400w	EA.	2.759
Bollard light, 42" w/found., high pressure sodium		
70w	EA.	2.581
100w	EA.	2.581
150w	EA.	2.581
Light fixture lamps		
Lamp		
20w med. bipin base, cool white, 24"	EA.	0.145
30w cool white, rapid start, 36"	EA.	0.145
40w cool white "U", 3"	EA.	0.145
40w cool white, rapid start, 48"	EA.	0.145
70w high pressure sodium, mogul base	EA.	0.200
75w slimline, 96"	EA.	0.200
100w		
Incandescent, 100a, inside frost	EA.	0.100
Mercury vapor, clear, mogul base	EA.	0.200
High pressure sodium, mogul base	EA.	0.200
150w		
Par 38 flood or spot, incandescent	EA.	0.100
High pressure sodium, 1/2 mogul base	EA.	0.200
175w		
Mercury vapor, clear, mogul base	EA.	0.200
Metal halide, clear, mogul base	EA.	0.200
High pressure sodium, mogul base	EA.	0.200
250w		
Mercury vapor, clear, mogul base	EA.	0.200
Metal halide, clear, mogul base	EA.	0.200
High pressure sodium, mogul base	EA.	0.200
400w		
Mercury vapor, clear, mogul base	EA.	0.200
Metal halide, clear, mogul base	EA.	0.200
High pressure sodium, mogul base	EA.	0.200
1000w		
Mercury vapor, clear, mogul base	EA.	0.250
High pressure sodium, mogul base	EA.	0.250
16510.30 Exterior Lighting		
Exterior light fixtures		
Rectangle, high pressure sodium		
70w	EA.	2.500
100w	EA.	2.581
150w	EA.	2.581
250w	EA.	2.759
400w	EA.	3.478
Flood, rectangular, high pressure sodium		
70w	EA.	2.500
100w	EA.	2.581
150w	EA.	2.581
400w	EA.	3.478
1000w	EA.	4.494
Round		

4

Lighting	UNIT	MAN/HOURS
16510.30 Exterior Lighting		
400w	EA.	3.478
1000w	EA.	4.494
Round, metal halide		
400w	EA.	3.478
1000w	EA.	4.494
Light fixture arms, cobra head, 6', high press. sodium		
100w	EA.	2.000
150w	EA.	2.500
250w	EA.	2.500
400w	EA.	2.963
Flood, metal halide		
400w	EA.	3.478
1000w	EA.	4.494
1500w	EA.	6.015
Mercury vapor		
250w	EA.	2.759
400w	EA.	3.478
Incandescent		
300w	EA.	1.739
500w	EA.	2.000
1000w	EA.	3.200
16510.90 Power Line Filters		
Heavy duty power line filter, 240v		
100a	EA.	10.000
300a	EA.	16.000
600a	EA.	24.242
16610.30 Uninterruptible Power		
Uninterruptible power systems, (U.P.S.), 3kva	EA.	8.000
5 kva	EA.	11.004
7.5 kva	EA.	16.000
10 kva	EA.	21.978
15 kva	EA.	22.857
20 kva	EA.	24.024
25 kva	EA.	25.000
30 kva	EA.	25.974
35 kva	EA.	27.027
40 kva	EA.	27.972
45 kva	EA.	28.986
50 kva	EA.	29.963
62.5 kva	EA.	32.000
75 kva	EA.	34.934
100 kva	EA.	36.036
150 kva	EA.	50.000
200 kva	EA.	55.172
300 kva	EA.	74.766
400 kva	EA.	89.888
500 kva	EA.	109.589
16670.10 Lightning Protection		
Lightning protection		
Copper point, nickel plated, 12'		
1/2" dia.	EA.	1.000

Lighting	UNIT	MAN/HOURS
16670.10 Lightning Protection		
5/8" dia.	EA.	1.000

Communications	UNIT	MAN/HOURS
16720.10 Fire Alarm Systems		
Master fire alarm box, pedestal mounted	EA.	16.000
Master fire alarm box	EA.	6.015
Box light	EA.	0.500
Ground assembly for box	EA.	0.667
Bracket for pole type box	EA.	0.727
Pull station		
Waterproof	EA.	0.500
Manual	EA.	0.400
Horn, waterproof	EA.	1.000
Interior alarm	EA.	0.727
Coded transmitter, automatic	EA.	2.000
Control panel, 8 zone	EA.	8.000
Battery charger and cabinet	EA.	2.000
Batteries, nickel cadmium or lead calcium	EA.	5.000
CO2 pressure switch connection	EA.	0.727
Annunciator panels		
Fire detection annunciator, remote type, 8 zone	EA.	1.818
12 zone	EA.	2.000
16 zone	EA.	2.500
Fire alarm systems		
Bell	EA.	0.615
Weatherproof bell	EA.	0.667
Horn	EA.	0.727
Siren	EA.	2.000
Chime	EA.	0.615
Audio/visual	EA.	0.727
Strobe light	EA.	0.727
Smoke detector	EA.	0.667
Heat detection	EA.	0.500
Thermal detector	EA.	0.500
Ionization detector	EA.	0.533
Duct detector	EA.	2.759
Test switch	EA.	0.500
Remote indicator	EA.	0.571
Door holder	EA.	0.727
Telephone jack	EA.	0.296
Fireman phone	EA.	1.000
Speaker	EA.	0.800
Remote fire alarm annunciator panel		
24 zone	EA.	6.667
48 zone	EA.	13.008
Control panel		

Communications	UNIT	MAN/HOURS
16720.10 Fire Alarm Systems		
12 zone	EA.	2.963
16 zone	EA.	4.444
24 zone	EA.	6.667
48 zone	EA.	16.000
Power supply	EA.	1.509
Status command	EA.	5.000
Printer	EA.	1.509
Transponder	EA.	0.899
Transformer	EA.	0.667
Transceiver	EA.	0.727
Relays	EA.	0.500
Flow switch	EA.	2.000
Tamper switch	EA.	2.963
End of line resistor	EA.	0.348
Printed ckt. card	EA.	0.500
Central processing unit	EA.	6.154
UPS backup to c.p.u.	EA.	8.999
Smoke detector, fixed temp. & rate of rise comb.	EA.	1.600
16720.50 Security Systems		
Sensors		
Balanced magnetic door switch, surface mounted	EA.	0.500
With remote test	EA.	1.000
Flush mounted	EA.	1.860
Mounted bracket	EA.	0.348
Mounted bracket spacer	EA.	0.348
Photoelectric sensor, for fence		
6 beam	EA.	2.759
9 beam	EA.	4.255
Photoelectric sensor, 12 volt dc		
500' range	EA.	1.600
800' range	EA.	2.000
Monitor cabinet, wall mounted		
1 zone	EA.	1.000
5 zone	EA.	1.600
10 zone	EA.	1.739
20 zone	EA.	2.000
16730.20 Clock Systems		
Clock systems		
Single face	EA.	0.800
Double face	EA.	0.800
Skeleton	EA.	2.759
Master	EA.	5.000
Signal generator	EA.	4.000
Elapsed time indicator	EA.	0.800
Controller	EA.	0.533
Clock and speaker	EA.	1.096
Bell		
Standard	EA.	0.533
Weatherproof	EA.	0.800
Horn		
Standard	EA.	0.727
Weatherproof	EA.	0.952

Communications	UNIT	MAN/HOURS
16730.20 Clock Systems		
Chime	EA.	0.533
Buzzer	EA.	0.533
Flasher	EA.	0.615
Control Board	EA.	3.478
Program unit	EA.	5.000
Block back box	EA.	0.500
Double clock back box	EA.	0.667
Wire guard	EA.	0.200
16740.10 Telephone Systems		
Communication cable		
25 pair	L.F.	0.026
100 pair	L.F.	0.029
150 pair	L.F.	0.033
200 pair	L.F.	0.040
300 pair	L.F.	0.042
400 pair	L.F.	0.044
Cable tap in manhole or junction box		
25 pair cable	EA.	3.810
50 pair cable	EA.	7.547
75 pair cable	EA.	11.268
100 pair cable	EA.	15.094
150 pair cable	EA.	22.222
200 pair cable	EA.	29.630
300 pair cable	EA.	44.444
400 pair cable	EA.	61.538
Cable terminations, manhole or junction box		
25 pair cable	EA.	3.756
50 pair cable	EA.	7.477
100 pair cable	EA.	15.094
150 pair cable	EA.	22.222
200 pair cable	EA.	29.630
300 pair cable	EA.	44.444
400 pair cable	EA.	61.538
Telephones, standard		
1 button	EA.	2.963
2 button	EA.	3.478
6 button	EA.	5.333
12 button	EA.	7.619
18 button	EA.	8.889
Hazardous area		
Desk	EA.	7.273
Wall	EA.	5.000
Accessories		
Standard ground	EA.	1.600
Push button	EA.	1.600
Buzzer	EA.	1.600
Interface device	EA.	0.800
Long cord	EA.	0.800
Interior jack	EA.	0.400
Exterior jack	EA.	0.615
Hazardous area		
Selector switch	EA.	3.200
Bell	EA.	3.200

4

16 ELECTRICAL

Communications	UNIT	MAN/HOURS
16740.10 Telephone Systems		
Horn	EA.	4.211
Horn relay	EA.	3.077
16770.30 Sound Systems		
Power amplifiers	EA.	3.478
Pre-amplifiers	EA.	2.759
Tuner	EA.	1.455
Horn		
Equalizer	EA.	1.600
Mixer	EA.	2.222
Tape recorder	EA.	1.860
Microphone	EA.	1.000
Cassette Player	EA.	2.162
Record player	EA.	1.905
Equipment rack	EA.	1.290
Speaker		
Wall	EA.	4.000
Paging	EA.	0.800
Column	EA.	0.533
Single	EA.	0.615
Double	EA.	4.444
Volume control	EA.	0.533
Plug-in	EA.	0.800
Desk	EA.	0.400
Outlet	EA.	0.400
Stand	EA.	0.296
Console	EA.	8.000
Power supply	EA.	1.290
16780.10 Antennas And Towers		
Guy cable, alumaweld		
1x3, 7/32"	L.F.	0.050
1x3, 1/4"	L.F.	0.050
1x3, 25/64"	L.F.	0.059
1x19, 1/2"	L.F.	0.070
1x7, 35/64"	L.F.	0.080
1x19, 13/16"	L.F.	0.100
Preformed alumaweld end grip		
1/4" cable	EA.	0.100
3/8" cable	EA.	0.100
1/2" cable	EA.	0.145
9/16" cable	EA.	0.200
5/8" cable	EA.	0.250
Fiberglass guy rod, white epoxy coated		
1/4" dia.	L.F.	0.145
3/8" dia	L.F.	0.145
1/2" dia	L.F.	0.200
5/8" dia	L.F.	0.250
Preformed glass grip end grip, guy rod		
1/4" dia.	EA.	0.145
3/8" dia.	EA.	0.200
1/2" dia.	EA.	0.250
5/8" dia.	EA.	0.250
Spelter socket end grip, 1/4" dia. guy rod		

Communications	UNIT	MAN/HOURS
16780.10 Antennas And Towers		
Standard strength	EA.	0.500
High performance	EA.	0.500
3/8" dia. guy rod		
Standard strength	EA.	0.348
High performance	EA.	0.500
Timber pole, Douglas Fir		
80-85 ft	EA.	19.512
90-95 ft	EA.	22.222
Southern yellow pine		
35-45 ft	EA.	10.959
50-55 ft	EA.	14.035
16780.50 Television Systems		
TV outlet, self terminating, w/cover plate	EA.	0.308
Thru splitter	EA.	1.600
End of line	EA.	1.333
In line splitter multitap		
4 way	EA.	1.818
2 way	EA.	1.702
Equipment cabinet	EA.	1.600
Antenna		
Broad band uhf	EA.	3.478
Lightning arrester	EA.	0.727
TV cable	L.F.	0.005
Coaxial cable rg	L.F.	0.005
Cable drill, with replacement tip	EA.	0.500
Cable blocks for in-line taps	EA.	0.727
In-line taps ptu-series 36 tv system	EA.	1.143
Control receptacles	EA.	0.449
Coupler	EA.	2.424
Head end equipment	EA.	6.667
TV camera	EA.	1.667
TV power bracket	EA.	0.800
TV monitor	EA.	1.455
Video recorder	EA.	2.105
Console	EA.	8.502
Selector switch	EA.	1.379
TV controller	EA.	1.404

Resistance Heating	UNIT	MAN/HOURS
16850.10 Electric Heating		
Baseboard heater		
2', 375w	EA.	1.000
3', 500w	EA.	1.000
4', 750w	EA.	1.143
5', 935w	EA.	1.333

Resistance Heating	UNIT	MAN/HOURS
16850.10 Electric Heating		
6', 1125w	EA.	1.600
7', 1310w	EA.	1.818
8', 1500w	EA.	2.000
9', 1680w	EA.	2.222
10', 1875w	EA.	2.286
Unit heater, wall mounted		
750w	EA.	1.600
1500w	EA.	1.667
2000w	EA.	1.739
2500w	EA.	1.818
3000w	EA.	2.000
4000w	EA.	2.286
Thermostat		
Integral	EA.	0.500
Line voltage	EA.	0.500
Electric heater connection	EA.	0.250
Fittings		
Inside corner	EA.	0.400
Outside corner	EA.	0.400
Receptacle section	EA.	0.400
Blank section	EA.	0.400
Infrared heaters		
600w	EA.	1.000
2000w	EA.	1.194
3000w	EA.	2.000
4000w	EA.	2.500
Controller	EA.	0.667
Wall bracket	EA.	0.727
Radiant ceiling heater panels		
500w	EA.	1.000
750w	EA.	1.000
Unit heaters, suspended, single phase		
3.0 kw	EA.	2.759
5.0 kw	EA.	2.759
7.5 kw	EA.	3.200
10.0 kw	EA.	3.810
Three phase		
5 kw	EA.	2.759
7.5 kw	EA.	3.200
10 kw	EA.	3.810
15 kw	EA.	4.211
20 kw	EA.	5.333
25 kw	EA.	6.400
30 kw	EA.	8.000
35 kw	EA.	8.000
Unit heater thermostat	EA.	0.533
Mounting bracket	EA.	0.727
Relay	EA.	0.615
Duct heaters, three phase		
10 kw	EA.	3.810
15 kw	EA.	3.810
17.5 kw	EA.	4.000
20 kw	EA.	6.154

Controls	UNIT	MAN/HOURS
16910.40 Control Cable		
Control cable, 600v, #14 THWN, PVC jacket		
2 wire	L.F.	0.008
4 wire	L.F.	0.010
6 wire	L.F.	0.131
8 wire	L.F.	0.145
10 wire	L.F.	0.160
12 wire	L.F.	0.182
14 wire	L.F.	0.211
16 wire	L.F.	0.222
18 wire	L.F.	0.242
20 wire	L.F.	0.250
22 wire	L.F.	0.286
Audio cables, shielded, #24 gauge		
3 conductor	L.F.	0.004
4 conductor	L.F.	0.006
5 conductor	L.F.	0.007
6 conductor	L.F.	0.009
7 conductor	L.F.	0.011
8 conductor	L.F.	0.012
9 conductor	L.F.	0.014
10 conductor	L.F.	0.015
15 conductor	L.F.	0.018
20 conductor	L.F.	0.023
25 conductor	L.F.	0.027
30 conductor	L.F.	0.030
40 conductor	L.F.	0.036
50 conductor	L.F.	0.042
#22 gauge		
3 conductor	L.F.	0.004
4 conductor	L.F.	0.006
#20 gauge		
3 conductor	L.F.	0.004
10 conductor	L.F.	0.015
15 conductor	L.F.	0.018
#18 gauge		
3 conductor	L.F.	0.004
4 conductor	L.F.	0.006
Microphone cables, #24 gauge		
2 conductor	L.F.	0.004
3 conductor	L.F.	0.005
#20 gauge		
1 conductor	L.F.	0.004
2 conductor	L.F.	0.004
2 conductor	L.F.	0.004
3 conductor	L.F.	0.006
4 conductor	L.F.	0.007
5 conductor	L.F.	0.009
7 conductor	L.F.	0.011
8 conductor	L.F.	0.012
Computer cables shielded, #24 gauge		
1 pair	L.F.	0.004
2 pair	L.F.	0.004
3 pair	L.F.	0.006
4 pair	L.F.	0.007

Controls	UNIT	MAN/HOURS
16910.40 Control Cable		
5 pair	L.F.	0.009
6 pair	L.F.	0.011
7 pair	L.F.	0.012
8 pair	L.F.	0.014
50 pair	L.F.	0.039
Fire alarm cables, #22 gauge		
6 conductor	L.F.	0.010
9 conductor	L.F.	0.015
12 conductor	L.F.	0.016
#18 gauge		
2 conductor	L.F.	0.005
4 conductor	L.F.	0.007
#16 gauge		
2 conductor	L.F.	0.007
4 conductor	L.F.	0.008
#14 gauge		
2 conductor	L.F.	0.008
#12 gauge		
2 conductor	L.F.	0.010
Plastic jacketed thermostat cable		
2 conductor	L.F.	0.004
3 conductor	L.F.	0.005
4 conductor	L.F.	0.006
5 conductor	L.F.	0.008
6 conductor	L.F.	0.009
7 conductor	L.F.	0.012
8 conductor	L.F.	0.013

Supporting Construction Reference Data

This section contains information, text, charts and tables on various aspects of construction. The intent is to provide the user with a better understanding of unfamiliar areas in order to be able to estimate better. This information includes actual takeoff data for some areas and also selected explanations of common construction materials, methods and common practices.

TYPICAL BUILDING COST BROKEN DOWN
BY CSI FORMAT
(Commercial Construction)

Division	New Construction	Remodeling Construction
1. General Requirements	6 to 8%	Up to 30%
2. Sitework	4 to 6%	
3. Concrete	15 to 20%	
4. Masonry	8 to 12%	
5. Metals	5 to 7%	
6. Wood and Plastics	1 to 5 %	
7. Thermal and Moisture Protection	4 to 6%	
8. Doors and Windows	5 to 7%	} Up to 30%
9. Finishes	8 to 12 %	
10. Specialties		
11. Architectural Equipment		
12. Furnishings	} 6 to 10%	
13. Special Construction		
14. Conveying Systems		
15. Mechanical	15 to 25%	} Up to 30%
16. Electrical	8 to 12%	
TOTAL COST	100%	

CONVERSION FACTORS

Change	To	Multiply By
ATMOSPHERES	POUNDS PER SQUARE INCH	14.696
ATMOSPHERES	INCHES OF MERCURY	29.92
ATMOSPHERES	FEET OF WATER	34
BARRELS, OIL	GALLONS, OF OIL	42
BARRELS, CEMENT	POUNDS OF CEMENT	376
BOGS OR SACKS, CEMENT	POUNDS OF CEMENT	94
BTU/MIN	FOOT-POUNDS/SEC	12.96
BTU/MIN	HORSE-POWER	0.02356
BTU/MIN	KILOWATTS	0.01757
BTU/MM	WATTS	17.57
CENTIMETERS	INCHES	0.3937
CENTIMETERS OF MERCURY	ATMOSPHERES	0.01316
CENTIMETERS OF MERCURY	FEET OF WATER	0.4461
CUBIC INCHES	CUBIC FEET	0.00058
CUBIC FEET	CUBIC INCHES	1728
CUBIC FEET	CUBIC YARDS	0.03703
CUBIC YARDS	CUBIC FEET	27
CUBIC INCHES	GALLONS	0.00433
CUBIC FEET	GALLONS	7.48
FEET	INCHES	12
FEET	YARDS	0.3333
YARDS	FEET	3
FEET OF WATER	ATMOSPHERES	0.02950
FEET OF WATER	INCHES OF MERCURY	0.8826
GALLONS	CUBIC INCHES	231
GALLONS	CUBIC FEET	0.1337
GALLONS	POUNDS OF WATER	8.33
GALLONS	QUARTS	4
GALLONS PER MIN	CUBIC FEET SEC	0.002228
GALLONS PER MIN	CUBIC FEET HOUR	8.0208
GALLONS WATER PER MIN	TONS WATER/24 HOURS	6.0086
HORSE-POWER	FOOT-LBS./SEC	550
INCHES	CENTIMETERS	2.540
INCHES	FEET	0.0833
INCHES	MILLIMETERS	25.4
INCHES OF WATER	POUNDS PER SQ. INCH	0.0361
INCHES OF WATER	INCHES OF MERCURY	0.0735
INCHES OF WATER	OUNCES PER SQUARE INCH	0.578
INCHES OF WATER	OUNCES PER SQUARE FOOT	5.2
INCHES OF MERCURY	INCHES OF WATER	13.6
INCHES OF MERCURY	FEET OF WATER	1.1333
INCHES OF MERCURY	POUNDS PER SQUARE INCH	0.4914
KILOMETERS	MILES	0.6214
METERS	INCHES	39.37
MILES	FEET	5280
MILLIMETERS	CENTIMETERS	0.1
MILLIMETERS	INCHES	0.03937
OUNCES (FLUID)	CUBIC INCHES	1.805
OUNCES	POUNDS	0.0625
POUNDS	OUNCES	16
POUNDS PER SQUARE INCH	INCHES OF WATER	27.72
POUNDS PER SQUARE INCH	FEET OF WATER	2.310
POUNDS PER SQUARE INCH	INCHES OF MERCURY	2.04
POUNDS PER SQUARE INCH	ATMOSPHERES	0.0681
QUARTS	CUBIC INCHES	67.20
SQUARE INCHES	SQUARE FEET	0.00694
SQUARE FEET	SQUARE INCHES	144
SQUARE FEET	SQUARE YARDS	0.11111
SQUARE YARDS	SQUARE FEET	9
SQUARE MILES	ACRES	640
SHORT TONS	POUNDS	2000
SHORT TONS	LONG TONS	0.89285
TONS OF WATER/24 HOURS	GALLONS PER MINUTE	0.16643
YARDS	FEET	3
YARDS	CENTIMETERS	91.44
YARDS	INCHES	36

CONVERSION CALCULATIONS

Commercial Measure

16 grams .... = 1 ounce
16 ounces .... = 1 pound
2,000 pounds .... = 1 ton

Long Measure

12 inches .... = 1 foot
3 feet .... = 1 yard
16 ½ feet .... = 1 rod
40 rods .... = 1 furlong
8 furlongs (5,280 ft.) .... = 1 mile
3 miles .... = 1 league

Square Measure

144 square inches .... = 1 square foot
9 square feet .... = 1 square yard
30 ¼ square yards .... = 1 square rod
160 square rods .... = 1 acre
4,840 square yards .... = 1 acre
640 acres .... = 1 square mile
36 square miles .... = 1 township

Surveyor's Measure

7.92 inches .... = 1 link
25 links .... = 1 rod
4 rods (66 ft.) .... = 1 chain
10 chains .... = 1 furlong
8 furlongs .... = 1 mile
1 square mile .... = 1 section

Cubic Measure

1728 cubic inches .... = 1 cubic foot
27 cubic feet .... = 1 cubic yard
128 cubic feet .... = 1 cord (wood/stone)
231 cubic inches .... = 1 U.S. gallon
7.48 U.S. Gallons .... = 1 cubic foot
2150.4 cubic inches .... = 1 U.S. bushel

Liquid Measure

4 fluid ounces .... = 1 gill
4 gills .... = 1 pint
2 pints .... = 1 quart
4 quarts .... = 1 gallon
9 gallons .... = 1 firkin
31 ½ gallons .... = 1 barrel
2 barrels .... = 1 hogshead

Dry Measure

2 pints .... = 1 quart
8 quarts .... = 1 peck
4 pecks .... = 1 bushel
2150.42 cubic inches .... = 1 bushel

SQUARE

$$A = a^2$$

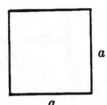

RECTANGLE

$$A = bh$$

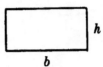

TRIANGLE

$$A = \frac{1}{2}bh$$

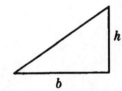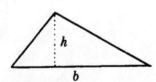

PARALLELOGRAM

$$A = bh = ab \; Sin\phi$$

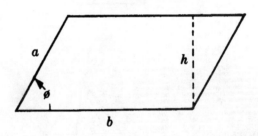

TRAPEZOID

$$A = \left(\frac{a+b}{2}\right)h$$

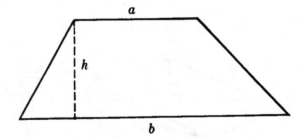

CIRCLE

$$A = \pi r^2 = \frac{\pi d^2}{4}$$

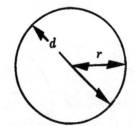

Circumference $= C = 2\pi r = \pi d$

ELLIPSE

$A = \pi ab$

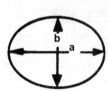

PARABOLA

$A = \frac{2}{3}bh$

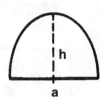

VOLUMES

CUBE

$V = a^3$

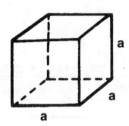

CYLINDER

$V = \pi r^3 h$

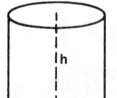

PYRAMID

$V = \frac{1}{3}(\text{Base})\, h$

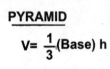

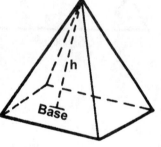

CONE

$V = \frac{1}{3}\pi r^2 h$

SPHERE

$V = \frac{4}{3}\pi r^3 = \frac{1}{6}\pi d^3$

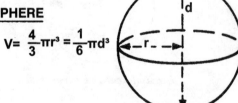

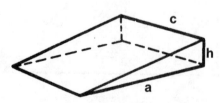

WEDGE

$V = \frac{1}{2}abc$

CONVERSION FACTORS
ENGLISH TO SI (SYSTEM INTERNATIONAL)

To Convert from	To	Multiply by
LENGTH		
Inches	Millimetres	25.4[a]
Feet	Metres	0.3048[a]
Yards	Metres	0.9144[a]
Miles (statute)	Kilometres	1.609
AREA		
Square inches	Square millimetres	645.2
Square feet	Square metres	0.0929
Square yards	Square metres	0.8361
VOLUME		
Cubic inches	Cubic millimetres	16.387
Cubic feet	Cubic metres	0.02832
Cubic yards	Cubic metres	0.7646
Gallons (U.S. liquid) [b]	Cubic metres[c]	0.003785
Gallons (Canadian liquid) [b]	Cubic metres[c]	0.004546
Ounces (U.S. liquid) [b]	Millilitres [c,d]	29.57
Quarts (U.S. liquid) [b]	Litres [c,d]	0.9464
Gallons (U.S. liquid) [b]	Litres [c]	3.785
FORCE		
Kilograms force	Newtons	9.807
Pounds force	Newtons	4.448
Pounds force	Kilograms force [d]	0.4536
Kips	Newtons	4448
Kips	Kilograms force [d]	453.6
PRESSURE, STRESS, STRENGTH (FORCE PER UNIT AREA)		
Kilograms force per sq. centimetre	Megapascals	0.09807
Pounds force per square inch (psi)	Megapascals	6895
Kips per square inch	Megapascals	6.895
Pounds force per square inch (psi)	Kilograms force per square centimetre [d]	0.07031
Pounds force per square foot	Pascals	47.88
Pounds force per square foot	Kilograms force per square metre [d]	4.882
SENDING MOMENT OR TORQUE		
Inch-pounds force	Metre-kilog. force [d]	0.01152
Inch-pounds force	Newton-metres	0.1130
Foot-pounds force	Metre-kilog. force [d]	0.1383
Foot-pounds force	Newton-metres	1.356
Metre-kilograms force	Newton-metres	9.807
MASS		
Ounce (avoirdupois)	Grams	28.35
Pounds (avoirdupois)	Kilograms	0.4536
Tons (metric)	Kilograms	1000[a]
Tons, short (2000 pounds)	Kilograms	907.2
Tons, short (2000 pounds)	Megagrams [e]	0.9072
MASS PER UNIT VOLUME		
Pounds mass per cubic foot	Kilog. per cubic metre	16.02
Pounds mass per cubic yard	Kilog. per cubic metre	0.5933
Pds. mass per gallon (U.S. liquid) [b]	Kilog. per cubic metre	119.8
Pds. mass p/gal. (Canadian liquid) [b]	Kilog. per cubic metre	99.78
TEMPERATURE		
Degrees Fahrenheit	Degrees Celsius	$tK = (1F - 32)/1.8$
Degrees Fahrenheit	Degrees Kelvin	$tK = (1F + 459.67)/1.8$
Degree Celsius	Degree Kelvin	$tK = 1C + 273.15$

[a] The factor given is exact.
[b] One U.S. gallon equals 0.8327 Canadian gallon.
[c] 1 litre = 1000 millilitres = 10,000 cubic centimetres = 1 cubic decimetre = 0.001 cubic metre.
[d] Metric but not SI unit.
[e] Called "tonne" in England. Called "metric ton" in other metric systems.

TRENCH BRACING

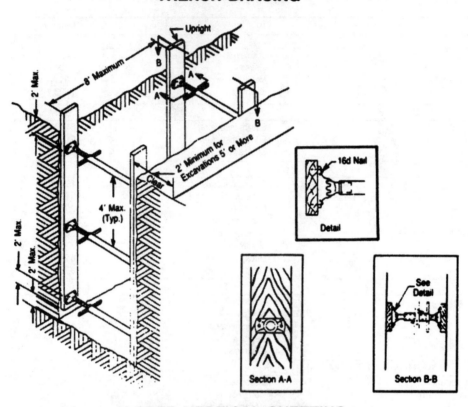

Upright

8' Maximum

2' Max.

2' Minimum for Excavations 5' or More

Clear

4' Max. (Typ.)

2' Max.

2' Max.

16d Nail

Detail

Section A-A

See Detail

Section B-B

CLOSED VERTICAL SHEETING

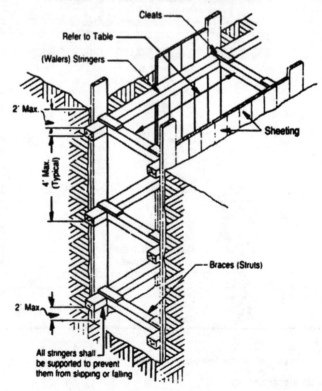

Cleats

Refer to Table

(Walers) Stringers

2' Max.

Sheeting

4' Max. (Typical)

Braces (Struts)

2' Max.

All stringers shall be supported to prevent them from slipping or falling

Soil Identification. For most purposes, soils can usually be identified visually and by texture, as described in the chart that follows. For design purposes, however, soils must be formally identified and their performance characteristics determined in a laboratory by skilled soil mechanics.

Classification	Identifying Characteristics
Gravel	Rounded or water-worn pebbles or bulk rock grains. No cohesion or plasticity. Gritty, granular and crunchy underfoot.
Sand	Granular, gritty, loose grains, passing a No. 4 sieve and between .002 and .079 inches in diameter. Individual grains readily seen and felt. No plasticity or cohesion. When dry, it cannot be molded but will crumble when touched. The coarse grains are rounded; the fine grains are visible and angular.
Silt	Fine, barely visible grains passing a No. 200 sieve and between .0002 and .002 inches in diameter. Little or no plasticity and no cohesion. A dried cast is easily crushed. Is permeable and movement of water through the voids occurs easily and is visible. Feels gritty when bitten and will not form a thread.
Clay	Invisible particles under .0002 inches in diameter. Cohesive and highly plastic when moist. Will form a long, thin, flexible thread when rolled between the hands. Does not feel gritty when bitten. Will form hard lumps or clods when dry which resist crushing. Impermeable, with no apparent movement of water through voids.
Muck and Organic Silt	Thoroughly decomposed organic material often mixed with other soils of mineral origin. Usually black with fibrous remains. Odorous when dried and burnt. Found as deposits in swamps, peat bogs and muskeg flats.
Peat	Partly decayed plant material. Mostly organic. Highly fibrous with visible plant remains. Spongy and easily identified.

Classification by Particle Size. Soils can be classified in general terms by the nature of their predominant particle size or the grading of the particle sizes. These particle sizes are usually grouped into gravel, coarse sand, medium sand, fine sand, silt, clay and colloids.

The major divisions of soils are:

Coarse-Grained(Granular)		Fine-Grained		Organic	
Gravel	Sand	Silt	Clay	Muck	Peat

Soils comprised primarily of sand particles are referred to as "granular soils," while fine-grained soils are commonly called "heavy soils." It is accepted practice in the field to refer to a particular soil as a coarse sand, or silt, or by any of the particle size groupings which describe the soil generally from a visual examination.

Classification of Soil Mixtures.

Class	% Sand	% Silt	% Clay
Sandy	80-100	0-20	0-20
Sandy clay loam	50-80	0-30	20-30
Sandy loam	50-80	0-50	0-20
Loam	30-50	30-50	0-20
Silty loam	0-50	50-80	0-20
Silt	0-20	80-100	0-20
Silty clay	0-30	50-80	20-30
Silty clay	0-20	50-70	30-50
Clay	20-50	20-50	20-30
Sandy clay	50-70	0-20	30-50
Clay	0-50	0-50	30-100

Material	Approx. In-Bank Weight (lbs. per cu. yd.)	Percent Swell
Clay, dry	2300	40
Clay, wet	3000	40
Granite, decomposed	4500	65
Gravel, dry	3250	10-15
Gravel, wet	3600	10-15
Loam, dry	2800	15-35
Loam, wet	3370	25
Rock, well blasted	4200	65
Sand, dry	3250	10-15
Sand, wet	3600	10-15
Shale and soft rock	3000	65
Slate	4700	65

PILES AND PILE DRIVING

General. A pile is a column driven or jetted into the ground which derives its supporting capabilities from end-bearing on the underlying strata, skin friction between the pile surface and the soil, or from a combination of end-bearing and skin friction.

Piles can be divided into two major classes: **Sheet piles** and **load-bearing piles.** Sheet piling is used primarily to restrain lateral forces as in trench sheeting and bulkheads, or to resist the flow of water as in cofferdams. It is prefabricated and is available in steel, wood or concrete. Load-bearing piles are used primarily to transmit loads through soil formations of low bearing values to formations that are capable of supporting the designed loads. If the load is supported predominantly by the action of soil friction on the surface of the pile, it is called a **friction pile.** If the load is transmitted to the soil primarily through the lower tip, it is called an **end-bearing pile.**

There are several load-bearing pile types, which can be classified according to the material from which they are fabricated:

* Timber (Treated and untreated)
* Concrete (Precast and cast in place)
* Steel (H-Section and steel pipe)
* Composite (A combination of two or more materials)

Some of the additional uses of piling are to: eliminate or control settlement of structures, support bridge piers and abutments and protect them from scour, anchor structures against uplift or overturning, and for numerous marine structures such as docks, wharves, fenders, anchorages, piers, trestles and jetties.

Timber Piles. Timber piles, treated or untreated, are the piles most commonly used throughout the world, primarily because they are readily available, economical, easily handled, can be easily cut off to any desired length after driving and can be easily removed if necessary. On the other hand, they have some serious disadvantages which include: difficulty in securing straight piles of long length, problems in driving them into hard formations and difficulty in splicing to increase their length. They are generally not suitable for use as end-bearing piles under heavy load and they are subject to decay and insect attack. Timber piles are resilient and particularly adaptable for use in waterfront structures such as wharves, docks and piers for anchorages since they will bend or give under load or impact where other materials may break. The ease with which they can be worked and their economy makes them popular for trestle construction and for temporary structures such as falsework or centering. Where timber piles can be driven and cut off below the permanent groundwater level, they will last indefinitely; but above this level in the soil, a timber pile will rot or will be attacked by insects and eventually destroyed. In sea water, marine borers and fungus will act to deteriorate timber piles. Treatment of timber piles increases their life but does not protect them indefinitely.

Concrete Piles. Concrete piles are of two general types, precast and cast-in-place. The advantages in the use of concrete piles are that they can be fabricated to meet the most exacting conditions of design, can be cast in any desired shape or length, possess high strength and have excellent resistance to chemical and biological attack. Certain disadvantages are encountered in the use of precast piles, such as:

(a) Their heavy weight and bulk (which introduces problems in handling and driving).
(b) Problems with hair cracks which often develop in the concrete as a result of shrinkage after curing (which may expose the steel reinforcement to deterioration).
(c) Difficulty encountered in cut-off or splicing.
(d) Susceptibility to damage or breakage in handling and driving.
(e) They are more expensive to fabricate, transport and drive.

Precast piles are fabricated in casting yards. Centrifugally spun piles (or piles with square or octagonal cross-sections) are cast in horizontal forms, while round piles are usually cast in vertical forms. With the exception of relatively short lengths, precast piles must be reinforced to provide the designed column strengths and to resist damage or breakage while being transported or driven.

Precast piles can be tapered or have parallel sides. The reinforcement can be of deformed bars or be prestressed or poststressed with high strength steel tendons. Prestressing or prestressing eliminates the problem of open shrinkage cracks in the concrete. Otherwise, the pile must be protected by coating it with a bituminous or plastic material to prevent ultimate deterioration of the reinforcement. Proper curing of the precast concrete in piles is essential.

Cast-in-place pile types are numerous and vary according to the manufacturer of the shell or inventor of the method. In general, they can be classified into two groups: shell-less types and the shell types. The shell-less type is constructed by driving a steel shell into the ground and filling it with concrete as the shell is pulled from the ground. The shell type is constructed by driving a steel shell into the ground and filling it in place with concrete. Some of the advantages of cast-in-place concrete piles are: lightweight shells are handled and driven easily, lengths of the shell may be increased or decreased easily, shells may be transported in short lengths and quickly assembled, the problem of breakage is eliminated and a driven shell may be inspected for shell damage or an uncased hole for "pinching off." Among the disadvantages are problems encountered in the proper centering of the reinforcement cages, in placing and consolidating the concrete without displacement of the reinforcement steel or segregation of the concrete, and shell damage or "pinching-off" of uncased holes.

Shell type piles are fabricated of heavy gage metal or are fluted, corrugated or spirally reinforced with heavy wire to make them strong enough to be driven without a mandrel.

Other thin-shell types are driven with a collapsible steel mandrel or core inside the casing. In addition to making the driving of a long thin shell possible, the mandrel prevents or minimizes damage to the shell from tearing, buckling, collapsing or from hard objects encountered in driving.

Some shell type piles are fabricated of heavy gauge metal with enlargement at the lower end to increase the end bearing.

These enlargements are formed by withdrawing the casing two to three feet after placing concrete in the lower end of the shell. This wet concrete is then struck by a blow of the pile hammer on a core in the casing and the enlargement is formed. As the shell is withdrawn, the core is used to consolidate the concrete after each batch is placed in the shell. The procedure results in completely filling the hole left by the withdrawal of the shell.

Steel Piles. A steel pile is any pile fabricated entirely of steel. They are usually formed of rolled steel H sections, but heavy steel pipe or box piles (fabricated from sections of steel sheet piles welded together) are also used. The advantages of steel piles are that they are readily available, have a thin uniform section and high strength, will take hard driving, will develop high load-bearing values, are easily cut off or extended, are easily adapted to the structure they are to support, and breakage is eliminated. Some disadvantages are: they will rust and deteriorate unless protected from the elements; acid, soils or water will result in corrosion of the pile; and greater lengths may be required than for other types of piles to achieve the same bearing value unless bearing on rock strata. Pipe pile can either be driven open-end or closed-end and can be unfilled, sand filled or concrete filled. After open-end pipe piles are driven, the material from inside can be removed by an earth auger, air or water jets, or other means, inspected, and then filled with concrete. Concrete filled pipe piles are subject to corrosion on the outside surface only.

Composite Piles. Any pile that is fabricated of two or more materials is called a composite pile. There are three general classes of composite piles: wood with concrete, steel with concrete, and wood with steel. Composite piles are usually used for a special purpose or for reasons of economy.

Where a permanent ground-water table exists and a composite pile is to be used, it will generally be of concrete and wood. The wood portion is driven to below the water table level and the concrete upper portion eliminates problems of decay and insect infestation above the water table. Composite piles of steel and concrete are used where high bearing loads are desired or where driving in hard or rocky soils is expected. Composite wood and steel piles are relatively uncommon.

It is important that the pile design provides for a permanent joint between the two materials used, so constructed that the parts do not separate or shift out of axial alignment during driving operations.

Sheet Piles. Sheet piles are made from the same basic materials as other piling: wood, steel and concrete. They are ordinarily designed so as to interlock along the edges of adjacent piles.

Sheet piles are used where support of a vertical wall of earth is required, such as trench walls, bulkheads, waterfront structures or cofferdams. Wood sheet piling is generally used in temporary installations, but is seldom used where water-tightness is required or hard driving expected. Concrete sheet piling has the capability of resisting much larger lateral loads than wood sheet piling, but considerable difficulty is experienced in securing water-tight joints. The type referred to as "fishmouth" type is designed to permit jetting out the joint and filling with grout, but a seal is not always effected unless the adjacent piles are wedged tightly together. Concrete sheet piling has the advantage that it is the most permanent of all types of sheet piling.

Steel sheet piling is manufactured with a tension-type interlock along its edges. Several different shapes are available to permit versatility in its use. It has the advantages that it can take hard driving, has reasonably water-tight joints and can be easily cut, patched, lengthened or reinforced. It can also be easily extracted and reused. Its principal disadvantage is its vulnerability to corrosion.

Types of Pile Driving Hammers. A pile-driving hammer is used to drive load-bearing or sheet piles. The commonly used types are: drop, single-acting, double-acting, differential acting and diesel hammers. The most recent development is a type of hammer that utilizes high-frequency sound and a dead load as the principal sources of driving energy.

Drop Hammers. These hammers employ the principle of lifting a heavy weight by a cable and releasing it to fall on top of the pile. This type of hammer is rapidly disappearing from use, primarily because other types of pile driving hammers are more efficient. Its disadvantages are that it has a slow rate of driving (four to eight blows per minute), that there is some risk of damaging the pile from excessive impact, that damage may occur in adjacent structures from heavy vibration and that it cannot be used directly for driving piles under water. Drop hammers have the advantages of simplicity of operation, ability to vary the energy by changing the height of fall and they represent a small investment in equipment.

Single-Acting Hammers. These hammers can be operated either on steam or compressed air. The driving energy is provided by a free-falling weight (called a ram) which is raised after each stroke by the action of steam or air on a piston. They are manufactured as either open or closed types. Single-acting hammers are best suited for jobs where dense or elastic soil materials must be penetrated or where long heavy timber or precast concrete piles must be driven. The closed type can be used for underwater pile driving. Its advantages include: faster driving (50 blows or more per minute), reduction in skin friction as a result of

SITEWORK / PILE DRIVING | 02355

more frequent blows, lower velocity of the ram which transmits a greater proportion of its energy to the pile and minimizes piles damage during driving, and it has underwater driving capability. Some of its disadvantages are: requires higher investment in equipment (i.e. steam boiler, air compressor, etc.), higher maintenance costs, greater set-up and moving time required, and a larger operating crew.

Double-Acting Hammers. These hammers are similar to the single-acting hammers except that steam or compressed air is used both to lift the ram and to impart energy to the falling ram. While the action is approximately twice as fast as the single-acting hammer (100 blows per minute or more), the ram is much lighter and operates at a greater velocity, thereby making it particularly useful in high production driving of light or medium-weight piles of moderate lengths in granular soils. The hammer is nearly always fully encased by a steel housing which also permits direct driving of piles under water.

Some of its advantages are: faster driving rate, less static skin friction develops between blows, has underwater driving capability and piles can be driven more easily without leads.

Among its disadvantages are: it is less suitable for driving heavy piles in high-friction soils and the more complicated mechanism results in higher maintenance costs.

Differential-Acting Hammers. This type of hammer is, in effect, a modified double-acting hammer with the actuating mechanism having two different diameters. A large-diameter piston operates in an upper cylinder to accelerate the ram on the downstroke and a small-diameter piston operates in a lower cylinder to raise the ram. The additional energy added to the falling ram is the difference in areas of the two pistons multiplied by the unit pressure of the steam or air used. This hammer is a short-stroke, fast-acting hammer with a cycle rate approximately that of the double-acting hammer.

Its advantages are that it has the speed and characteristics of the double-acting hammer with a ram weight comparable to the single-acting type, and it uses 25 to 35 percent less steam or air. It is also more suitable for driving heavy piles under more difficult driving conditions than the double-acting hammer. It is available in the open or closed-type cases, the latter permitting direct underwater pile driving. Its principal disadvantage is higher maintenance costs.

Diesel Hammers. This hammer is a self-contained driving unit which does not require an auxiliary steam boiler or air compressor. It consists essentially of a ram operating as a piston in a cylinder. When the ram is lifted and allowed to fall in the cylinder, diesel fuel is injected in the compression space between the ram and an anvil placed on top of the pile. The continued downstroke of the ram compresses the air and fuel to ignition heat and the resultant explosion drives the pile downward and the ram upward to start another cycle. This hammer is capable of driving at a rate of from 80 to 100 blows per minute. Its advantages are that it has a low equipment investment cost, is easily moved, requires a small crew, has a high driving rate, does not require a steam boiler or air compressor and can be used with or without leads for most work. Its disadvantages are that it is not self-starting (the ram must be mechanically lifted to start the action) and it does not deliver a uniform blow. The latter disadvantage arises from the fact that as the reaction of the pile to driving increases, the reaction to the ram increases correspondingly. That is, when the pile encounters considerable resistance, the rebound of the ram is higher and the energy is increased automatically. The operator is required to observe the driving operations closely to identify changing driving conditions and compensate for such changes with his controls to avoid damaging the pile.

Diesel hammers can be used on all types of piles and they are best suited to jobs where mobility or frequent relocation of the pile driving equipment is necessary.

383

PILE CHART

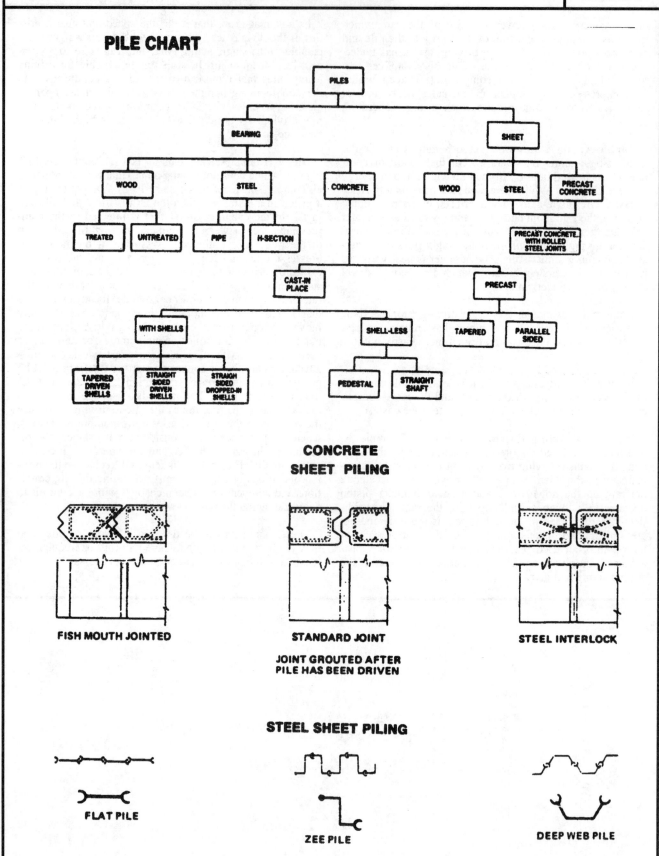

CONCRETE SHEET PILING

FISH MOUTH JOINTED

STANDARD JOINT

JOINT GROUTED AFTER
PILE HAS BEEN DRIVEN

STEEL INTERLOCK

STEEL SHEET PILING

FLAT PILE

ZEE PILE

DEEP WEB PILE

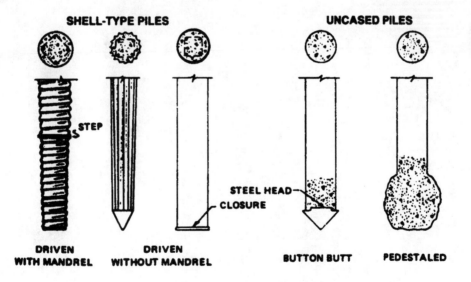

BEARING PILES

TIMBER PILE

PRECAST
CONCRETE PILES

STEEL PILES

STEEL
PIPE

CONCRETE
FILL

SPUN STANDARD "H" SECT. PIPE

DRIVEN PILES

COMPOSITE WOOD PILE

PIPE

PLATE

TURNED
HEAD OF
WOOD
PILE

WOOD
PILE

COMPOSITE STEEL PILE

REINF
STEEL

WELD LONG.
BARS TO
PIPE OR
H-PILE

SHELL-TYPE PILES

STEP

UNCASED PILES

STEEL HEAD
CLOSURE

DRIVEN
WITH MANDREL

DRIVEN
WITHOUT MANDREL

BUTTON BUTT

PEDESTALED

CAST-IN-PLACE PILES

STANDARD NOMENCLATURE
FOR STREET CONSTRUCTION

SLOPE EASEMENT

PROPERTY LINE

X ft.

RIGHT OF WAY

ROADBED

ROADWAY

SIDEWALK

CURB & GUTTER

FINISHED SURFACE

Structural section

PAVEMENT SUBGRADE (FINE GRADE)

PAVEMENT

BASE

PROPERTY LINE

SLOPE EASEMENT

Y ft.

ROUGH GRADE

FOUNDATION

When used, subbase is placed under a base course

COMPACTED FILL

ORIGINAL GROUND LINE

CONCRETE MASONRY PAVING UNITS

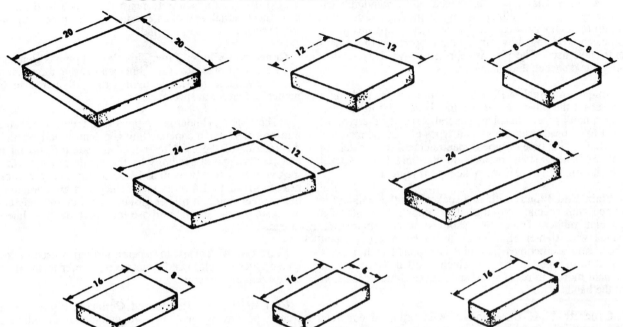

NOTE: Sizes are nominal and will vary by manufacturer.

HEXAGON PAVER UNITS
Various Sizes Available

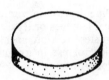

ROUND PAVING UNITS
Various Sizes Available

VEHICULAR PAVING UNITS

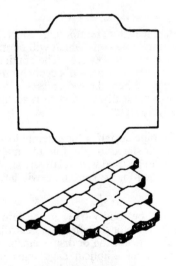

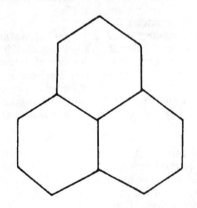

INTERLOCKING PAVER
7¼" x 3" x 8½"

INTERLOCKING PAVER
12" x 3⅝" x 12"

TURF PAVER
24" x 3⅝" x 24"

PIPE

Clay Pipe. Clay pipe is manufactured by blending various clays together, milling, mixing, extruding and firing in a kiln to obtain vitrification. The physical properties of the pipe can be changed by varying the proportions of the several clays used. The pipe is supplied in two basic styles: spigot and socket; and plain end.

Spigot and Socket Pipe has a spigot on one end and a socket on the other, and is commonly referred to as "bell and spigot" pipe. The plans generally specify the type of joint to be used from the several types of jointing methods available. This type of pipe is manufactured with matching polyurethane gaskets molded on the spigot and socket which form a tight seal when the pipe is jointed.

Plain End Pipe is without a socket on either end and is joined with special couplings. The coupling consists of a circular rubber sleeve, two stainless steel compression bands with tightening devices and a corrosion resistant shear ring. Sometimes this joint is supplied with a cardboard form, open at the top, which is filled with portland cement mortar to resist shear and prevent future corrosion of the bands.

Concrete Pipe. Unreinforced and reinforced concrete pipe is manufactured by casting in stationary or revolving metal molds. At the present time, the design practice is to specify reinforced concrete pipe far all purposes.

Unreinforced Concrete Pipe is cast in vertical steel molds, usually in pipe sizes of 21 inches or less, and is of the spigot and socket type. No steel reinforcement is used and the pipe is usually intended for use in irrigation systems and under light loading conditions.

Reinforced Concrete Pipe (RCP) is made in a number of different manufacturing processes and for a wide variety of pressure and non-pressure classes. It is available in standard sizes or it can be made to order to any diameter desired. Some of the larger diameters include diameters of 12 and 14 feet. A large variety of joint details are used with RCP. Tongue and groove joints are used for storm drain pipelines.

Reinforced concrete pipe for wastewater pipeline projects is supplied with gasketed joints and a polyvinyl chloride (PVC) plastic liner cast into the pipe.

(a) **Cast Pipe** is cast vertically in steel forms with the reinforcing cage securely held in place. The reinforcement is generally elliptical in shape to provide the maximum structural strength to resist the loads imposed on the pipe by the backfill and other stresses. Consolidation of the concrete is obtained by the use of external form vibrators.

(b) **Centrifugally Spun Pipe** is manufactured by introducing concrete into a spinning horizontal steel cylinder into which the reinforcement cage has been previously installed and which is equipped with end dams to provide the proper pipe wall thickness. The speed of rotation of the mold is increased and the centrifugal force produces a smooth, dense concrete pipe.

(c) **Pressure Pipe** may be cast or centrifugally spun pipe but it usually has a circular steel reinforcement cage (or cages) designed not only to resist the trench loading, but also the internal pressures exerted on the pipe from the fluid under pressure in the line.

Concrete Cylinder Pipe. This class of pipe is generally used for high pressure water lines and sewer force mains and is available in sizes ranging from 10 inches to 60 inches and larger in special cases.

A sheet steel cylinder is wrapped with the designed steel reinforcement and a concrete lining is centrifugally spun in the interior of the steel cylinder. An exterior coating of concrete is applied generally by the gunite process, while the cylinder is slowly rotated. These coatings vary in thickness from 1/2 to 3/4 of an inch. The joints are commonly of the steel ring and rubber gasket type, but are generally designed for the special purpose for which the pipe line is intended.

Definition of Terms. In general, the terms used to designate types of reinforced concrete pipe refer to the process used in manufacture.

Cast RCP (Cast Reinforced Concrete Pipe). A concrete pipe having one or more cylindrical or elliptical cages of reinforcement steel embedded in it, the concrete for which is cast with the forms in a vertical position.

CSRCP (Centrifugally Spun Reinforced Concrete Pipe). A concrete pipe having one or more cylindrical or elliptical cages of reinforcement steel embedded in it, and cast in a horizontal position while the forms are spinning rapidly. This type of pipe may be designated as Spun RCP or as CCP (Centrifugal Concrete Pipe).

RCP (Reinforced Concrete Pipe). A reinforced concrete pipe manufactured by either the casting or spinning method.

Steel Reinforcement. Steel for reinforcing concrete pipe is generally furnished in large coils which will permit the use of machines to fabricate the "cages." The continuous steel rod is wound spirally at a prescribed pitch on a drum of the proper diameter. Where the rod crosses a longitudinal spacer rod, it is electrically welded to it so that the complete cage is relatively rigid.

Reinforcement cages for pipe designed for external loading are generally elliptical in shape to take full advantage of the steel in tension. Pipe to be used with relatively small external loads or pipe designed for pressure lines will have circular cages.

Reinforcement cages must be rigidly fixed in the forms so that the placement of concrete or the effects of centrifugal spinning will not result in distortion or displacement of the steel The orientation of an elliptical cage must be marked on the forms to assure that the minor axis can be located after the concrete is placed.

CAPACITIES FOR SEPTIC TANKS SERVING
AN INDIVIDUAL DWELLING

No. of bedrooms	Capacity of tank (gals.)
2 or less	750
3	900
4	1,000

FORM NOMENCLAURE

FALSEWORK NOMENCLATURE

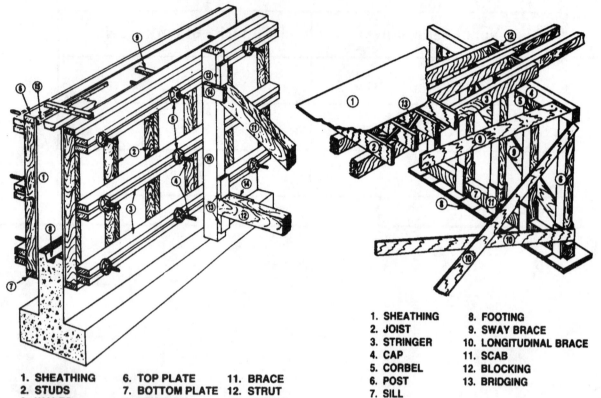

1. SHEATHING	6. TOP PLATE	11. BRACE
2. STUDS	7. BOTTOM PLATE	12. STRUT
3. WALES	8. KEY-WAY	13. CLEATS
4. FORM BOLTS	9. SPREADER	14. SCAB
5. NUT WASHER	10. STRONGBACK	14. POUR STRIP

1. SHEATHING	8. FOOTING
2. JOIST	9. SWAY BRACE
3. STRINGER	10. LONGITUDINAL BRACE
4. CAP	11. SCAB
5. CORBEL	12. BLOCKING
6. POST	13. BRIDGING
7. SILL	

TYPICAL PAN-JOIST FORM CONSTRUCTION

TYPICAL WAFFLE SLAB FORM CONSTRUCTION

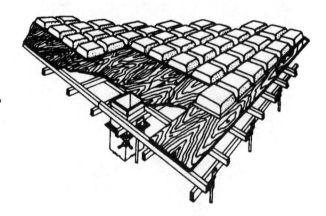

3 FOOT SINGLE TAPERED END FORMS
3 FOOT INTERMEDIATE STEEL FORMS
END CAPS
WOOD SOFFIT PLANK
END CAP
HEADER FOR TEE-HEADED BEAM
STRINGER
BEAM FORM

COMMON TYPES OF STEEL REINFORCEMENT BARS

ASTM specifications for billet steel reinforcing bars (A 615) require identification marks to be rolled into the surface of one side of the bar to denote the producer's mill designation, bar size and type of steel. For Grade 60 and Grade 75 bars, grade marks indicating yield strength must be show. Grade 40 bars show only three marks (no grade mark) in the following order:

1st — Producing Mill (usually an initial)
2nd — Bar Size Number (#3 through # 18)
3rd — Type (N for New Billet)

NUMBER SYSTEM — GRADE MARKS

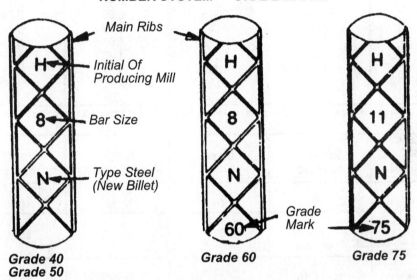

Main Ribs

Initial Of Producing Mill

Bar Size

Type Steel (New Billet)

Grade Mark

Grade 40
Grade 50

Grade 60

Grade 75

LINE SYSTEM — GRADE MARKS

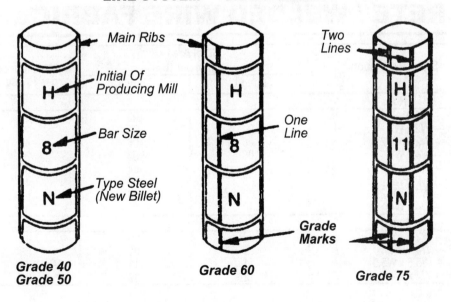

Main Ribs

Initial Of Producing Mill

Bar Size

Type Steel (New Billet)

Two Lines

One Line

Grade Marks

Grade 40
Grade 50

Grade 60

Grade 75

CONCRETE / REINFORCING STEEL 03210

STANDARD SIZES OF STEEL REINFORCEMENT BARS

STANDARD REINFORCEMENT BARS				
Bar Designation Number*	Nominal Weight lb. per ft.	Nominal Dimensions		
		Diameter, in.	Cross Sectional Area, sq. in.	Perimeter, in.
3	0.376	0.375	0.11	1.178
4	0.668	0.500	0.20	1.571
5	1.043	0.625	0.31	1.963
6	1.502	0.750	0.44	2.356
7	2.044	0.875	0.60	2.749
8	2.670	1.000	0.79	3.142
9	3.400	1.128	1.00	3.544
10	4.303	1.270	1.27	3.990
11	5.313	1.410	1.56	4.430
14	7.65	1.693	2.25	5.32
18	13.60	2.257	4.00	7.09

*The bar numbers are based on the number of 1/8 inches included in the nominal diameter of the bar.

Type of Steel & ASTM Specification No.	Size Nos. Inclusive	Grade	Tensile Strength Min., psi.	Yield (a) Min., psi
Billet Steel A 615	3-11	40	70,000	40,000
	3-11 14, 18	60	90,000	60,000
	11, 14, 18	75	100,000	75,000

CONCRETE / WELDED WIRE FABRIC 03220

Style Designation	Steel Area sq. in per ft.		Weight Approx. lbs. per 100 sq. ft.
	Longit.	Transv.	
Rolls			
6 x 6 — W1.4 x W1.4	.03	.03	21
6 x 8 — W2 x W2	.04	.04	29
6 x 6 — W2.9 x W2.9	.08	.06	42
6 x 6 — W4 x W4	.08	.08	58
4 x 4 — W1.4 x W1.4	.04	.04	31
4 x 4 — W2 x W2	.06	.06	43
4 x 4 — W2.9 x W2.9	.09	.09	62
4 x 4 — W4 x W4	.12	.12	
Sheets			
6 x 6 — W2.9 x W2.9	.06	.06	42
6 x 6 — W4 x W4	.08	.08	58
6 x 6 — W5.5 x W5.5	.11	.11	80
4 x 4 — W4 x W4	.12	.12	86

Insofar as is possible, the moisture content should be kept uniform to avoid problems in determining the proper amount of water to be added for mixing. Mixing water must be reduced to compensate for moisture in the aggregate in order to control the slump of the concrete and avoid exceeding the specified water-cement ratio.

Handling Concrete by Pumping Methods. Transportation and placement of concrete by pumping is another method gaining increased popularity. Pumps have several advantages, the primary one being that a pump will high-lift concrete without the need for an expensive crane and bucket. Since the concrete is delivered through pipe and hoses, concrete can be conveyed to remote locations in buildings, in tunnels, to locations otherwise inaccessible on steep hillside slopes for anchor walls, pipe bedding or encasement, or for placing concrete for chain link fence post bases. Concrete pumps have been found to be economical and expedient in the placement of concrete, and this has promoted the use and acceptance of this development. The essence of proper concrete pumping is the placement of the concrete in its final location without segregation.

Modern concrete pumps, depending on the mix design and size of line, can pump to a height of 200 feet or a horizontal distance of 1,000 feet. They can handle, economically, structural mixes, standard mixes, low slump mixes, mixes with two-inch maximum size aggregate and light weight concrete. When a special pump mix is required for structural concrete in a major structure, the mix design must be approved by the Engineer and checked and confirmed by the Supervisor of the Materials Control Group. The Inspector should obtain the pump manufacturer's printed information and evaluate its characteristics and ability to handle the concrete mixture specified for the project.

If concrete is being placed for a major reinforced structure, it is important that the placement continue without interruption. The Inspector should be sure that the contractor has ready access to a back-up pump to be used in the event of a breakdown. In order to further insure the success of the concrete placement by the pumping method, the user should be aware of the following points:

(a) A protective grating over the receiving hopper of the pump is necessary to exclude large pieces of aggregate or foreign material.

(b) The pump and lines require lubrication with a grout of cement and water. All of the excess grout is to be wasted prior to pumping the concrete.

(c) All changes in direction must be made by a large radius bend with a maximum bend of 90 degrees. Wye connections induce segregation and shall not be used.

(d) Pump lines should be made of a material capable of resisting abrasion and with a smooth interior surface having a low coefficient of friction. Steel is commonly used for pump lines, because a chemical reaction occurs between the concrete and the aluminum. Aluminum pipe should not be used for pumping concrete and some of the new plastic or rubber tubing is gaining acceptance. Hydrogen is generated which results in a swelling of the concrete, causing a significant reduction in compressive strength. This reaction is aggravated by any of the following: abrasive coarse aggregate, non-uniformly graded sand, low-slump concrete, low sand-aggregate ratio, high-alkali cement or when no air-entraining agent is used.

(e) During temporary interruptions in pumping, the hopper must remain nearly full, with an occasional turning and pumping to avoid developing a hard slug of concrete in the lines.

(f) Excessive line pressures must be avoided. When this occurs, check these points as the probable cause: segregation caused by too low a slump or too high a slump; large particle contamination caused by large pieces of aggregate or frozen lumps not eliminated by the grating; poor gradation of aggregates or particle shape; rich or lean spots caused by improper mixing.

(g) Corrections must be made to correct excessive slump loss as measured at the transit-mixed concrete truck and as measured at the hose outlet. This may be attributable to porous aggregate, high temperature or rapid setting mixes.

(h) Two transit-mix concrete trucks must be used simultaneously to deliver concrete into the pump hopper. These trucks must be discharged alternately to assure a continuous flow of concrete as trucks are replaced.

(i) Samples of concrete for test specimens prepared to determine the acceptance of the concrete quality are to be taken as required for conventional concrete.

Sampling is done before the concrete is deposited in the pump hopper. However, it is suggested that, where possible, the effect of pumping on the compressive strength be checked by taking companion samples, so identified, from the end of the pump line at the same time. The Record of Test must be properly noted as being a special mix used for pumping purposes. This will enable the Materials Control Group to compile a complete history of mix designs and their respective compressive strengths.

The prudent use of pumped concrete can result in economy and improved quality. However, only the control exercised by the operator will assure continued high standards of quality concrete.

Pump lines must be properly fastened to supports to eliminate excessive vibration. Couplings must be easily and securely fastened in a manner that will prevent mortar leakage. It is preferable to use the flexible hose only at the discharge point. This hose must be moved in such a manner as to avoid kinks or sharp bends. The pump line should be protected from excessive heat during hot weather by water sprinkling or shade.

COMPRESSIVE STRENGTH FOR VARIOUS WATER-CEMENT RATIOS
(The strengths listed are based on the use of normal portland cement)

WATER/CEMENT RATIO		PROBABLE 28-DAY STRENGTH	
WEIGHT	GALS./100#	PSI	MEGAPASCALS*
.40	4.8	5000	34
.45	5.4	4500	31
.50	6.0	4000	28
.55	6.6	3500	24
.60	7.2	3000	21
.65	7.8	2500	17
.70	8.4	2000	14

* International system equivalent.

APPROXIMATE CONTENT OF SAND, CEMENT AND WATER PER CUBIC YARD OF CONCRETE

Based on aggregates of average grading and physical characteristics in concrete mixes having a water-cement ratio (W/C) of about .65 by weight (or 7.8 gallons) per sack of cement; 3-in, slump; and a medium natural sand having a fineness modulus of about 2.75.

COURSE AGGREGATE MAX. SIZE	WATER		CEMENT	% SAND
	POUNDS	GALLONS		
3/8	385	46	590	57
½	365	44	560	50
¾	340	41	525	43
1	325	39	500	39
1 1/2	300	36	460	37

It can be noted from the above chart that, for a given slump, the amount of mixing water increases as the size of the course aggregate decreases. The size of the course aggregate controls the sand content in the same way; that is, the amount of sand required in the mix increases as the size of the course aggregate decreases.

Other typical examples are contained in the pamphlet published by the Portland Cement Association entitled "Design and Control of Concrete Mixtures."

Effects of Temperature on Concrete. Concrete mixtures gain strength rapidly in the first few days after placement. While the rate of gain in strength diminishes, concrete continues to become stronger with time over a period of many years, so long as drying of the concrete is prevented. Its strength at 28 days is considered to be the compressive strength upon which the Engineer bases his calculations. The temperature of the atmosphere has a significant effect upon the development of strength in concrete. Lower temperatures retard and higher temperatures accelerate the gain in strength.

Most destructive of the natural forces is freezing and thawing action. While the concrete is still wet or moist, expansion of the water as it is converted into ice results in severe damage to the fresh concrete. In situations where freezing may be encountered, high early strength cement may be used. Also, the mixing water or the aggregate (or both) may be preheated before mixing. Covering the concrete, and using steam or salamanders to heat the concrete under the covering, will help prevent freezing. Air-entraining agents help to diminish the effects of freezing of fresh concrete as well as in subsequent freezing and thawing cycles throughout the life of the concrete.

Hot weather will present problems of a different nature in placing concrete. Concrete will set up faster and tend to shrink and crack at the surface. To minimize this problem, the concrete should be placed without delay after mixing. Avoid the use of accelerators (perhaps even use a retarding agent), dampen all subgrade and forms, protect the freshly placed concrete from hot dry winds, and provide for adequate curing. Crushed ice or chilled water can be used as part of the mixing water to reduce the temperature of the mix in extremely hot areas.

Admixture	Purpose	Effects on Concrete	Advantages	Disadvantages
Accelerator	Hasten setting.	Improves cement dispersion and increases early strength.	Permits earlier finishing, form removal, and use of the structure.	Increases shrinkage, decreases sulfate resistance, tends to clog mixing and handling equipment.
Air-Entraining Agent	Increase workability and reduce mixing water.	Reduces segregation, bleeding and increases freeze-thaw resistance. Increases strength	Increases workability and reduces finishing time.	Excess will reduce strength and increase slump. Bulks concrete volume.
Bonding Agent	Increase bond to old concrete.	Produces a non-dusting, slip resistant finish,	Permits a thin topping without roughening old concrete, self-curing, ready in one day.	Quick setting and susceptible to damage from fats, oils and solvents.
Densifier	To obtain dense concrete.	Increased workability and strength.	Increases workability and increases water-proofing characteristics, more impermeable.	Care must be used to reduce mixing water in proportion to amount used.
Foaming Agent	Reduce weight.	Increases insulating properties.	Produces a more plastic mix, reduces dead weight loads.	Its use must be very carefully regulated — following instructions explicitly.
Retarder	Retard setting.	Increases control of setting.	Provides more time to work and finish concrete.	Performance varies with cement used — adds to slump. Requires stronger forms.
Water Reducer and Retarder	Increase compressive and flexural strength.	Reduces segregation, bleeding, absorption, shrinkage, and increases cement dispersion.	Easier to place work, provides better control.	Performance varies with cement. Of no use in cold weather.
Water Reducer, Retarder and Air-Entraining Agent	Increases workability.	Improves cohesiveness. Reduces bleeding and segregation.	Easier to place and work.	Care must be taken to avoid excessive air entrainment.

ARCHITECTURAL WALL PATTERNS (BONDS)

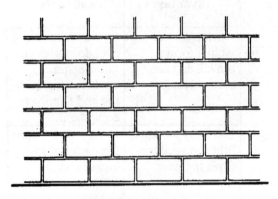

COMMON BOND
8" x 16" UNITS

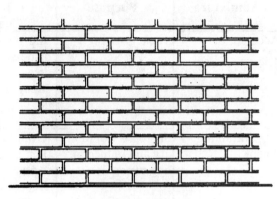

COMMON BOND
4" x 16" UNITS

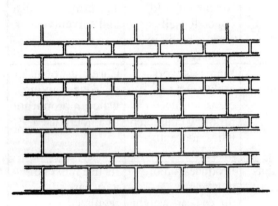

COURSED ASHLAR
8" x 16", 4"x 16" UNITS

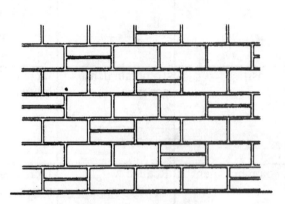

COURSED ASHLAR
8" x 16", 4"x 16" UNITS

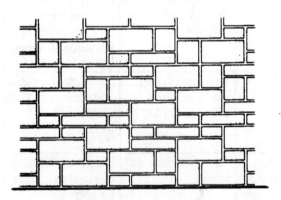

RANDOM ASHLAR
8" x 16", 8"x 8"
AND 4" x 8" UNITS

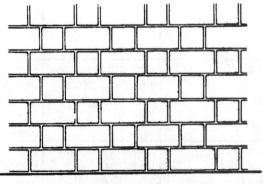

COURSED ASHLAR
8" x 16", 8"x 8" UNITS

ARCHITECTURAL WALL PATTERNS (BONDS) — (Continued)

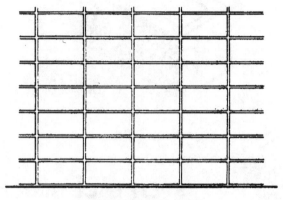

STACKED BOND
8" x 16" UNITS

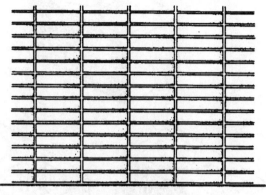

STACKED BOND
8" x 16" UNITS

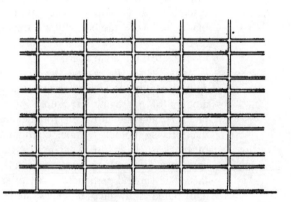

STACKED BOND
8" x 16", 4" x 16" UNITS

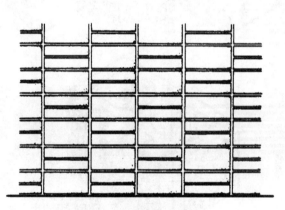

STACKED BOND
8" x 16", 4" x 16" UNITS

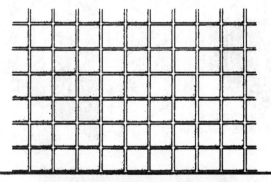

**STACKED BOND VERTICAL
SCORED UNITS**

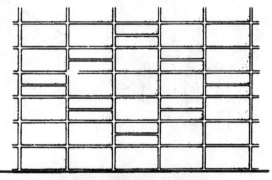

**USE OF BLOCK DESIGN
IN STACKED BOND**

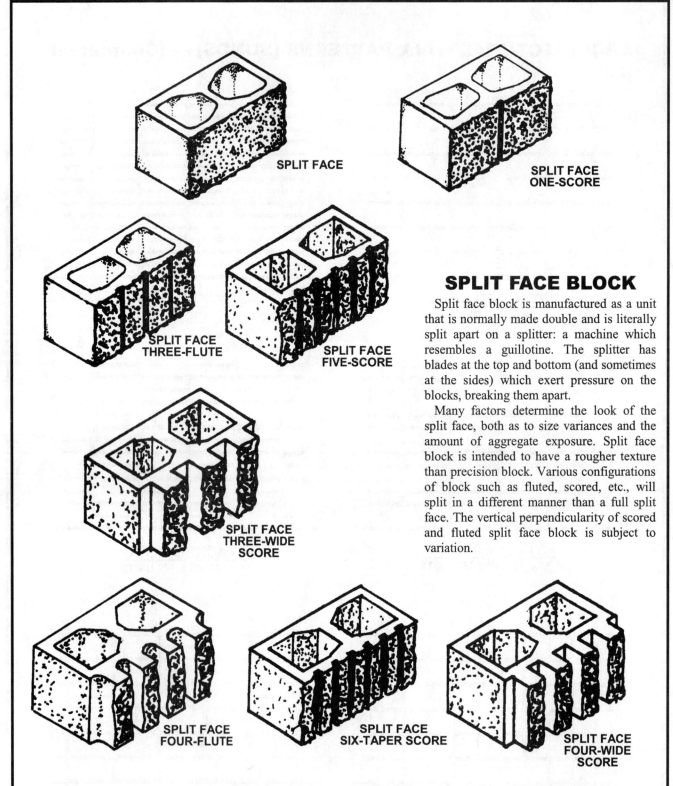

SPLIT FACE

SPLIT FACE
ONE-SCORE

SPLIT FACE
THREE-FLUTE

SPLIT FACE
FIVE-SCORE

SPLIT FACE
THREE-WIDE
SCORE

SPLIT FACE
FOUR-FLUTE

SPLIT FACE
SIX-TAPER SCORE

SPLIT FACE
FOUR-WIDE
SCORE

SPLIT FACE BLOCK

Split face block is manufactured as a unit that is normally made double and is literally split apart on a splitter: a machine which resembles a guillotine. The splitter has blades at the top and bottom (and sometimes at the sides) which exert pressure on the blocks, breaking them apart.

Many factors determine the look of the split face, both as to size variances and the amount of aggregate exposure. Split face block is intended to have a rougher texture than precision block. Various configurations of block such as fluted, scored, etc., will split in a different manner than a full split face. The vertical perpendicularity of scored and fluted split face block is subject to variation.

NOTE: Split face units shown in this manual are a small sampling of the broad range of concrete masonry architectural units available from the industry on special order. Depths and widths of scores vary. Consult a local manufacturer for specific information.

TYPICAL DETAILS — LINTELS AND BOND BEAMS

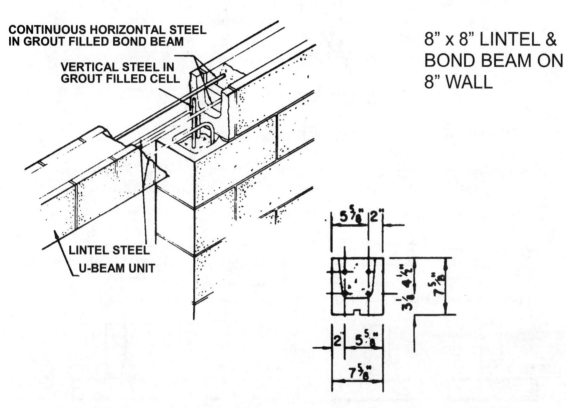

CONTINUOUS HORIZONTAL STEEL
IN GROUT FILLED BOND BEAM

VERTICAL STEEL IN
GROUT FILLED CELL

LINTEL STEEL
U-BEAM UNIT

8" x 8" LINTEL &
BOND BEAM ON
8" WALL

8" x 16"
BOND BEAM ON
8" WALL

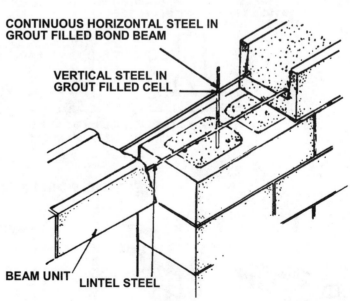

CONTINUOUS HORIZONTAL STEEL IN
GROUT FILLED BOND BEAM

VERTICAL STEEL IN
GROUT FILLED CELL

BEAM UNIT   LINTEL STEEL

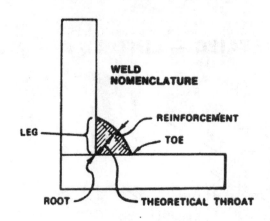

WELD NOMENCLATURE

WELDED JOINTS

SQUARE BUTT

SINGLE VEE BUTT

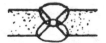

DOUBLE VEE BUTT

SINGLE U BUTT

DOUBLE U BUTT

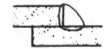

SINGLE FILLET LAP

DOUBLE FILLET LAP

STRAP JOINT

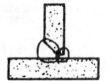

SINGLE BEVEL TEE

DOUBLE BEVEL TEE

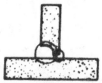

SINGLE J TEE

SQUARE TEE

DOUBLE J TEE

CLOSED CORNER (FLUSH) JOINT

HALF OPEN CORNER JOINT

WELDING POSITIONS

FLAT (F)

HORIZONTAL (H)

VERTICAL (V)

OVERHEAD (OH)

BOLTS IN COMMON USAGE

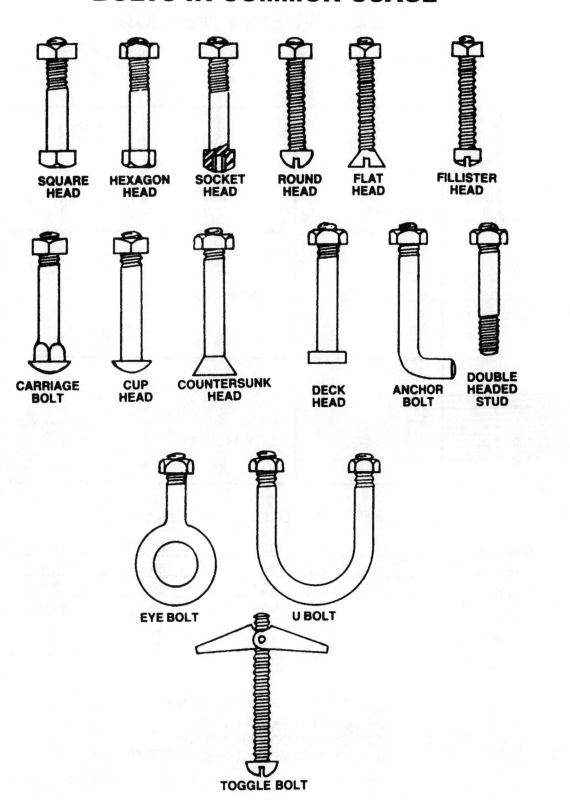

SQUARE HEAD   HEXAGON HEAD   SOCKET HEAD   ROUND HEAD   FLAT HEAD   FILLISTER HEAD

CARRIAGE BOLT   CUP HEAD   COUNTERSUNK HEAD   DECK HEAD   ANCHOR BOLT   DOUBLE HEADED STUD

EYE BOLT   U BOLT

TOGGLE BOLT

EXAMPLE OF SIMPLIFIED STRUCTURAL STEEL TAKEOFF METHOD

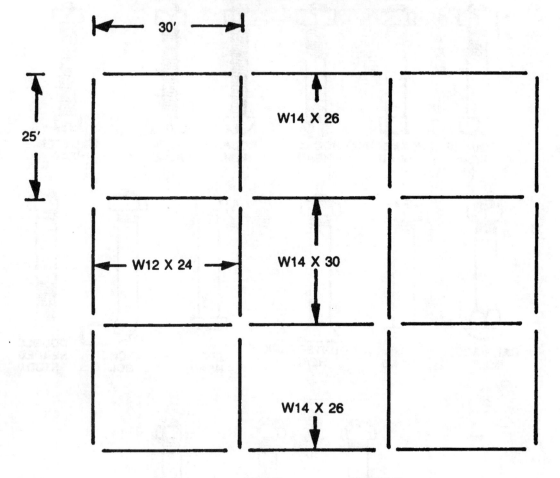

	#		LF. EA.		LBS./LF.			
W14 X 26	6	×	30	×	26	=	4,680	LBS.
W14 X 30	6	×	30	×	30	=	5,400	
W12 X 24	12	×	25	×	24	=	7,200	
							17,280	LBS.
							OR	
							9 ±	TONS

AFTER MAIN MEMBERS ARE ESTIMATED, ADD:

2 TO 3% FOR BASE PLATES
4 TO 5% FOR COLUMN SPLICES
4 TO 5% FOR MISCELLANEOUS COSTS

COMMON WIRE NAILS (ACTUAL SIZE)

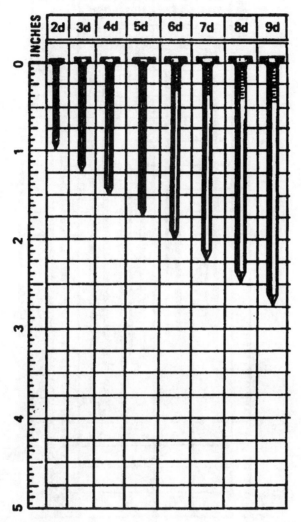

Cut Nails. Cut nails are angular-sided, wedge-shaped with a blunt point.

Wire Nails. Wire nails are round shafted, straight, pointed nails, and are used more generally than cut nails. They are stronger than cut nails and do not buckle as easily when driven into hard wood, but usually split wood more easily than cut nails. Wire nails are available in a variety of sizes varying from two penny to sixty penny.

Nail Finishes. Nails are available with special finishes. Some are galvanized or cadmium plated to resist rust. To increase the resistance to withdrawal, nails are coated with resins or asphalt cement (called cement coated). Nails which are small, sharp-pointed, and often placed in the craftsman's mouth (such as lath or plaster board nails) are generally blued and sterilized.

COMMON WIRE NAILS (ACTUAL SIZE) (Cont.)

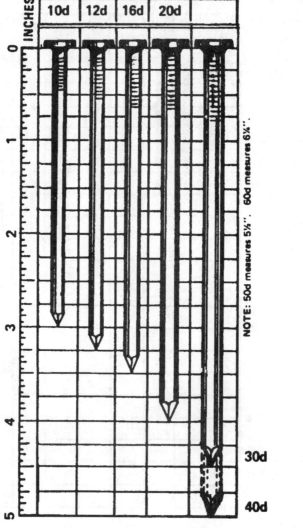

INCHES

| 10d | 12d | 16d | 20d | |

NOTE: 50d measures 5½".   60d measures 6¼".

30d

40d

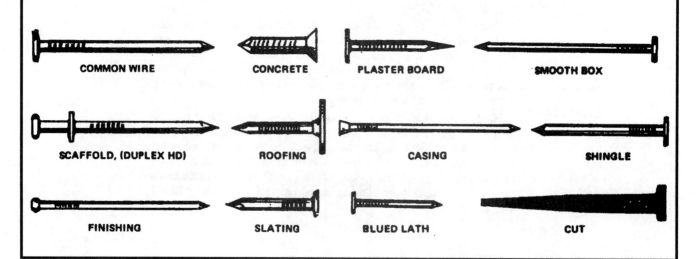

| COMMON WIRE | CONCRETE | PLASTER BOARD | SMOOTH BOX |

| SCAFFOLD, (DUPLEX HD) | ROOFING | CASING | SHINGLE |

| FINISHING | SLATING | BLUED LATH | CUT |

PLYWOOD — BASIC GRADE MARKS
AMERICAN PLYWOOD ASSOCIATION (APA)

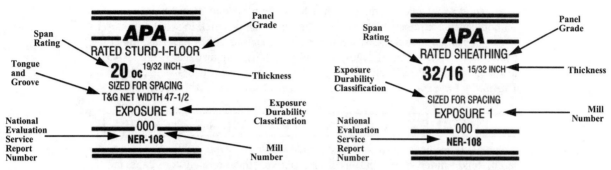

The American Plywood Association's trademarks appear only on products manufactured by APA member mills. The marks signify that the product is manufactured in conformance with APA performance standards and/or U.S. Product Standard PS 1-83 for Construction and Industrial Plywood.

APA A-C

For use where appearance of one side is important in exterior applications such as soffits, fences, structural uses, boxcar and truck linings, farm buildings, tanks, trays, commercial refrigerators, etc. **Exposure Durability Classification: Exterior. Common Thicknesses:** ¼, 11/32, ¾, 15/32, ½, 19/32, 5/8, 23/32, ¾.

APA A-D

For use where appearance of only one side is important in interior applications, such as paneling, built-ins, shelving, partitions, flow racks, etc. **Exposure Durability Classifications: Interior, Exposure 1. Common Thicknesses:** ¼, 11/32, 3/8, 15/32, ½, 19/32, 5/8, 23/32, ¾.

APA B-C

Utility panel for farm service and work buildings, boxcar and truck linings, containers, tanks, agricultural equipment, as a base for exterior coatings and other exterior uses. **Exposure Durability Classification: Exterior. Common Thicknesses:** ¼, 11/32, ¾, 15/32, ½, 19/32, 5/8, 23/32, ¾.

APA B-D

Utility panel for backing, sides or built-ins, industry shelving, slip sheets, separator boards, bins and other interior or protected applications. **Exposure Durability Classifications: Interior, Exposure 1. Common Thicknesses:** ¼, 11/32, 3/8, 15/32, ½, 19/32, 5/8, 23/32, ¾.

APA proprietary concrete form panels designed for high reuse. Sanded both sides and mill-oiled unless otherwise specified. Class I, the strongest, stiffest and more commonly available, is limited to Group 1 faces, Group 1 or 2 crossbands, and Group 1, 2, 3 or 4 inner plies. Class II is limited to Group 1 or 2 faces (Group 3 under certain conditions) and Group 1, 2, 3 or 4 inner plies. Also available in HDO for very smooth concrete finish, in Structural I, and with special overlays. **Exposure Durability Classification: Exterior. Common Thicknesses:** 19/32, ¾, 23/32, ¼.

Plywood panel manufactured with smooth, opaque, resin-treated fiber overlay providing ideal base for paint on one or both sides. Excellent material choice for shelving, factory work surfaces, paneling, built-ins, signs and numerous other construction and industrial applications. Also available as a 303 Siding with texture-embossed or smooth surface on one side only and Structural I. **Exposure Durability Classification: Exterior. Common Thicknesses:** 11/32, 3/8, 19/32, ½, 19/32, 5/8, 23/32, ¾.

SPECIALTY PANELS

```
HDO • A • A • G-1 • EXT APA • 000 • PS1  83
```

Plywood panel manufactured with a hard, semi-opaque resin-fiber overlay on both sides. Extremely abrasion resistant and ideally suited to scores of punishing construction and industrial applications, such as concrete forms, industrial tanks, work surfaces, signs, agricultural bins, exhaust ducts, etc. Also available with skid-resistant screen-grid surface and in Structural I. *Exposure Durability Classification:* **Exterior.** *Common Thicknesses:* **3/8, ½, 5/8, 3/4**

```
MARINE• A • A • EXT APA • 000 • PS1  83
```

Specialty designed plywood panel made only with Douglas fir or western larch, solid jointed cores, and highly restrictive limitations on core gaps and faces repairs. Ideal for both hulls and other marine applications. Also available with HDO or MDO faces. *Exposure Durability Classification:* **Exterior.** *Common Thicknesses:* **1/4, 3/8, ½, 5/8, 3/4.**

Unsanded and touch-sanded panels, and panels with "B" or better veneer on one side only, usually carry the APA trademark on the panel back. Panels with both sides of "B" or better veneer, or with special overlaid surfaces (such as Medium Density Overlay), carry the APA trademark on the panel edge, like this:

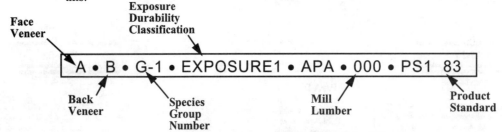

GLOSSARY OF TERMS
Some of the words and terms used in the grading of lumber follow:

Bow. A deviation flatwise from a straight line drawn from end to end of the piece. It is measured at the point of greatest distance from the straight line.

Checks. A separation of the wood which normally occurs across the annual rings and usually as a result of seasoning.

Crook. A deviation edgewise from a straight line drawn from end to end of the piece. It is measured at the point of greatest distance from the straight line.

Cup. A deviation from a straight line drawn across the piece from edge to edge. It is measured at the point of greatest distance from the straight line.

Flat Grain. The annual growth rings pass through the piece at an angle of less than 45 degrees with the flat surface of the piece.

Warp. Any deviation from a true or plane surface, including crook, cup, bow or any combination thereof.

Mixed Grain. The piece may have vertical grain, flat grain or a combination of both vertical and flat grain.

Pitch. An accumulation of resin which occurs in separations in the wood or in the wood cells themselves.

Shake. A separation of the wood which usually occurs between the rings of annual growth.

Splits. A separation of the wood due to tearing apart of the wood cells.

Vertical Grain. The annual growth rings pass through the piece at an angle of 45 degrees or more with the flat surface of the piece.

Wane. Bark or lack of wood from any cause, except eased edges (rounded) on the edge or corner of a piece of lumber.

LUMBER GRADING
GRADING-MARK ABBREVIATIONS

GRADES
(Listed alphabetically — not by quality)

COM	Common
CONST	Construction
ECON	Economy
No. 1	Number One
SEL-MER	Select Merchantable
SEL-STR	Select Structural
STAN	Standard
UTIL	Utility

ALSC TRADEMARKS

CLIS	California Lumber Inspection Service
NELMA	Northeastern Lumber Mfrs. Assoc., Inc.
NH&PMA	Northern Hardwood & Pine Mfrs. Assoc., Inc.
PLIB	Pacific Lumber Inspection Bureau
RIS	Redwood Inspection Service
SPIB	Southern Pine Inspection Bureau
TP	Timber Products Inspection
WCLB	West Coast Lumber Inspection Bureau
WWP	Western Wood Products Association

SPECIES GROUPINGS

AF	Alpine Fir
DF	Douglas Fir
HF	Hem Fir
SP	Sugar Pine
PP	Ponderosa Pipe
LP	Lodgepole Pine
IWP	Idaho White Pine
ES	Engelmann Spruce
WRC	Western Red Cedar
INC CDR	Incense Cedar
L	Larch
LP	Lodgepole Pine
MH	Mountain Hemlock
WW	White Wood

MOISTURE CONTENT

S-GRN	Surfaced at a moisture content of more than 19%.
S-DRY	Surfaced at a moisture content of 19% or less.
MC-15	Surfaced at a moisture content of 15% or less.

FRAMING ESTIMATING RULES OF THUMB

For 16" O.C. stud partitions figure 1 stud for every L.F. of wall; add for top and bottom plates.

For any type of framing, the quantity of basic framing members (in L.F.) can be determined based on spacing and surface area (S.F.):

12" O.C.	1.2 L.F./S.F.
16" O.C.	1.0 L.F./S.F.
24" O.C.	0.8 L.F./S.F.

(Doubled-up members, bands, plates, framed openings, etc., must be added.)

Framing accessories, nails, joist hangers, connectors, etc., should be estimated as separate material costs. Installation should be included with framing. Rule of thumb allowance is 0.5 to 1.5% of lumber cost for rough hardware. Another is 30 to 40 pounds of nails per M.B.F.

BOARD FEET/LINEAR FEET FOR LUMBER

Nominal Size	Actual Size	Board Feet Per Linear Foot	Linear Feet Per 1000 Board Feet
1 x 2	¾ x 1 ½	.167	6000
1 x 3	¾ x 2 ½	.250	4000
1 x 4	¾ x 3 ½	.333	3000
1 x 6	¾ x 5 ½	.500	2000
1 x 8	¾ x 7 ¼	.666	1500
1 x 10	¾ x 9 ¼	.833	1200
1 x 12	¾ x 11 ¼	1.0	1000
2 x 2	1 ½ x 1 ½	.333	3000
2 x 3	1 ½ x 2 ½	.500	2000
2 x 4	1 ½ x 3 ½	.666	1500
2 x 6	1 ½ x 5 ½	1.0	1000
2 x 8	1 ½ x 7 ¼	1.333	750
2 x 10	1 ½ x 9 ¼	1.666	600
2 x 12	1 ½ x 11 ¼	2.0	500

Redwood. Redwood is a fairly strong and moderately lightweight material. The heartwood is red but the sapwood is white. One of the principal advantages of redwood is that the heartwood is highly resistant (but not entirely immune) to decay, fungus and insects. Standard Specifications require that all redwood used in permanent installations shall be "select heart." Grade marking shall be in accordance with the standards established in the California Redwood Association. Grade marking shall be done by, or under the supervision of the Redwood Inspection Service.

Redwood is graded for specific uses as indicated in the following table:

REDWOOD GRADING

Type of Lumber	Grade	Typical Use
Grades for Dimension Only Listed Here	Clear All Heart	Exceptionally fine, knot free, straight-grained timbers. This grade is used primarily for stain finish work of high quality.
	Clear	Same as Clear All Heart except that this grade may contain sound sapwood and medium stain.
	Select Heart	**This grade only is to be used in Agency work, unless otherwise specified in the plans or specifications.** It is sound, live heartwood free from splits or streaks with sound knots. It is generally used where the timber is in contact with the ground, as in posts, mudsills, etc.
	Select Construction Heart	Slightly less quality than Select Heart. It may have some sapwood in the piece. Used for general construction purposes when redwood is needed.
	Construction Common	Same requirement as Construction Heart except that it will contain sapwood and medium stain. Its resistance to decay and insect attack is reduced.
	Merchantable	Used for fence posts, garden stakes, etc.
	Economy	Suitable for crating, bracing and temporary construction.

DOUGLAS FIR GRADING

Type of Lumber	Grade	Typical Use
Select Structural Joists and Planks	Select Structural	Used where strength is the primary consideration, with appearance desirable.
	No. 1	Used where strength is less critical and appearance not a major consideration.
	No. 2	Used for framing elements that will be covered by subsequent construction.
	No. 3	Used for structural framing where strength is required but appearance is not a factor.
Finish Lumber	Superior	For all types of uses as casings, cabinet, exposed members, etc., where a fine appearance is desired.
	Prime	
	E	
Boards (WCLIB)* * Grading is by West Coast Lumber Inspection Bureau rules, but sizes conform to Western Wood Products Assn. rules. These boards are still manufactured by some mills.	Select Merchantable	Intended for use in housing and light construction where a knotty type of lumber with finest appearance is required.
	Construction	Used for sub-flooring, roof and wall sheathing, concrete forms, etc. Has a high degree of serviceability.
	Standard	Used widely for general construction purposes, including subfloors, roof and wall sheathing, concrete forms, etc. Seldom used in exposed construction because appearance.
	Utility	Used in general construction where low cost is a factor and appearance is not important. (Storage shelving, crates, bracing, temporary scaffolding etc.)

BOARD FEET CONVERSION TABLE

Nominal Size (In.)	ACTUAL LENGTH IN FEET								
	8	10	12	14	16	18	20	22	24
1 x 2		1 2/3	2	2 1/3	2 2/3	3	3 ½	3 2/3	4
1 x 3		2 ½	3	3 ½	4	4 ½	5	5 ½	6
1 x 4	2 ¾	3 1/3	4	4 2/3	5 1/3	6	6 2/3	7 1/3	8
1 x 5		4 1/6	5	5 5/6	6 2/3	7 ½	8 1/3	9 1/6	10
1 x 6	4	5	6	7	8	9	10	11	12
1 x 7		5 5/8	7	8 1/6	9 1/3	10 ½	11 2/3	12 5/6	14
1 x 8	5 1/3	6 2/3	8	9 1/3	10 2/3	12	13 1/3	14 2/3	16
1 x 10	6 2/3	8 1/3	10	11 2/3	13 1/3	15	16 2/3	18 1/3	20
1 x 12	8	10	12	14	16	18	20	22	24
1¼ x 4		4 1/6	5	5 5/6	6 2/3	7 ½	8 1/3	9 1/6	10
1¼ x 6		6 ¼	7 ½	8 ¾	10	11 ¼	12 ½	13 ¾	15
1¼ x 8		8 1/3	10	11 2/3	13 1/3	15	16 2/3	18 1/3	20
1¼ x 10		10 5/12	12 ½	14 7/12	16 2/3	18 ¾	20 5/6	22 11/12	25
1¼ x 12		12 ½	15	17 ½	20	22 ½	25	27 ½	30
1½ x 4	4	5	6	7	8	9	10	11	12
1½ x 6	6	7 ½	9	10 ½	12	13 ½	15	16 ½	18
1½ x 8	8	10	12	14	16	18	20	22	24
1½ x 10	10	12 ½	15	17 ½	20	22 ½	25	27 ½	30
1½ x 12	12	15	18	21	24	27	30	33	36
2 x 4	5 1/3	6 2/3	8	9 1/3	10 1/3	12	13 1/3	14 2/3	16
2 x 6	8	10	12	14	16	18	20	22	24
2 x 8	10 2/3	13 1/3	16	18 2/3	21 1/3	24	26 2/3	29 1/3	32
2 x 10	13 1/3	16 2/3	20	23 1/3	26 2/3	30	33 1/3	36 2/3	40
2 x 12	16	20	24	28	32	36	40	44	48
3 x 6	12	15	18	21	24	27	30	33	36
3 x 8	16	20	24	28	32	36	40	44	48
3 x 10	20	25	30	35	40	45	50	55	60
3 x 12	24	30	36	42	48	54	60	66	72
4 x 4	10 2/3	13 1/3	16	18 2/3	21 1/3	24	26 2/3	29 1/3	32
4 x 6	16	20	24	28	32	36	40	44	48
4 x 8	21 1/3	26 2/3	32	37 1/3	42 2/3	48	53 1/3	58 2/3	64
4 x 10	26 2/3	33 1/3	40	46 2/3	53 1/3	60	66 2/3	73 1/3	80
4 x 12	32	40	48	56	64	72	80	88	96

MOISTURE PROTECTION / ROOFING | 07000

SLOPE AREA CALCULATIONS

Rise and Run	Multiply Flat Area by	LF of Hips or Valleys per LF of Common Run
2 in 12	1.014	1.424
3 in 12	1.031	1.436
4 in 12	1.054	1.453
5 in 12	1.083	1.474
6 in 12	1.118	1.500
7 in 12	1.158	1.530
8 in 12	1.202	1.564
9 in 12	1.250	1.600
10 in 12	1.302	1.641
11 in 12	1.357	1.685
12 in 12	1.413	1.732

MOISTURE PROTECTION / DOWNSPOUTS | 07600

DOWNSPOUT/VERTICAL LEADER CALCULATIONS

Roof Type	Slope	S.F. Roof/ Sq. In. Leader
Gravel	Less than ¼" per foot	300
Gravel	Greater than ¼" per foot	250
Metal or Shingle	Any	200

Alternate calculations:

$$\text{Diameter of downspout/leader} = 1.128 \sqrt{\frac{\text{Area of drainage}}{\text{SF Roof/Sq. Inch}}}$$

TYPICAL MINIMUM SIZE OF VERTICAL CONDUCTORS AND LEADERS

Size of leader or conductor (Inches)	Maximum projected roof area (Square feet)
2	544
2 ½	987
3	1,610
4	3,460
5	6,280
6	10,200
8	22,000

TYPICAL MINIMUM SIZE OF ROOF GUTTERS

Diameter gutter (Inches)	MAXIMUM PROJECTED ROOF AREA FOR GUTTERS OF VARIOUS SLOPES			
	1/16 in. Ft. slope (Sq. ft.)	1/8 in. per Ft. slope (Sq. ft.)	¼ in. per Ft. slope (Sq. ft.)	1/2 in. per Ft. /slope (Sq. ft.)
3	170	240	340	480
4	360	510	720	1,020
5	625	880	1,250	1,770
6	960	1,360	1,920	2,770
7	1,380	1,950	2,760	3,900
8	1,990	2,800	3,980	5,600
10	3,600	5,100	7,200	10,000

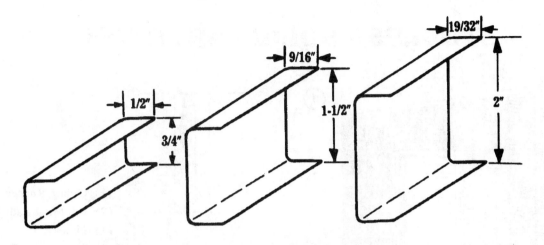

COLD ROLLED CHANNELS

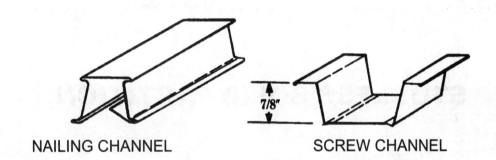

NAILING CHANNEL

SCREW CHANNEL

CHANNEL STUD

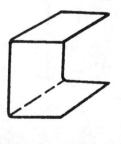

WIDE FLANGE CHANNEL

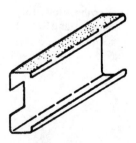

CEE STUD

STUDLESS SOLID PARTITION

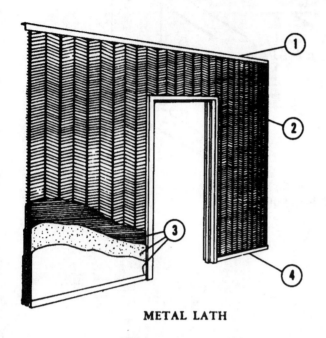
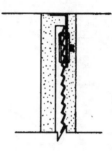

(1) Ceiling Runner
(2) Rib Metal Lath
(3) Plaster
(4) Combination Floor
    Runner and Screed

METAL LATH

STUDLESS SOLID PARTITION

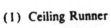
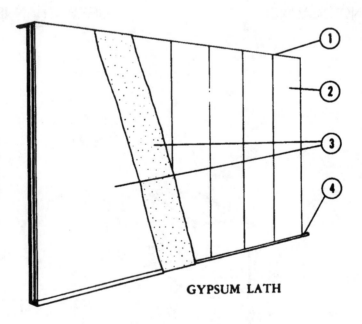
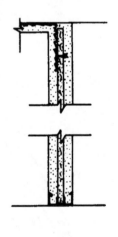

(1) Ceiling Runner
(2) Long Length
    Gypsum Lath
(3) Plaster
(4) Combination Floor
    Runner and Screed

GYPSUM LATH

SUSPENDED CEILINGS

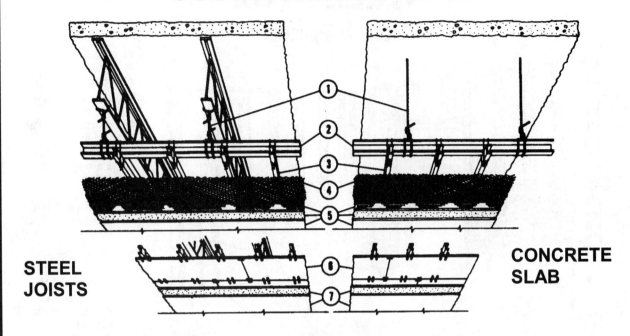

STEEL JOISTS

CONCRETE SLAB

(1) Hanger
(2) Main Runner Channel
(3) Furring Channel
(4) Metal or Wire Fabric Lath
(5) Plaster
(6) Gypsum Lath
(7) Plaster

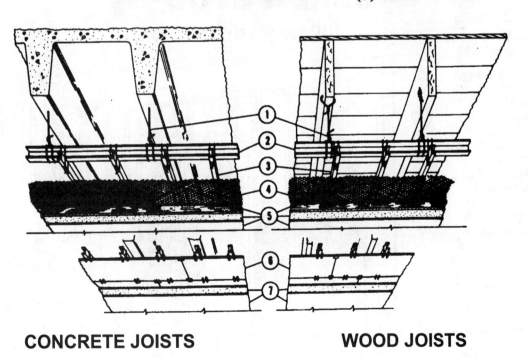

CONCRETE JOISTS

WOOD JOISTS

STEEL STUD
Hollow Partition

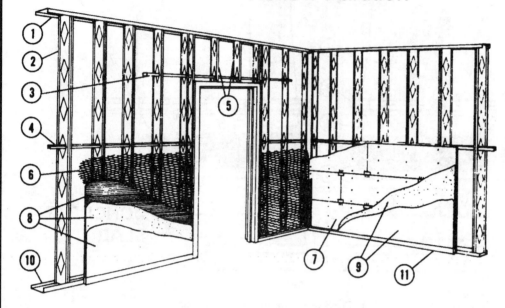

(1) Ceiling Runner Track
(2) Nailable Stud
(3) Door Opening Stiffener
(4) Partition Stiffener
(5) Jack Studs
(6) Metal or Wire Fabric Lath (screwed or wire tied)
(7) Gypsum Lath (nailed, clipped or screwed)
(8) Three Coats of Plaster (Scratch, Brown, Finish)
(9) Two Coats of Plaster (Brown, Finish)
(10) Floor Runner Track
(11) Flush Metal Base

SCREW STUD
Hollow Partition

(1) Ceiling Runner Track
(2) Screw Stud
(3) Door Opening Stiffener
(4) Partition Stiffener
(5) Jack Studs
(6) Metal or Wire Fabric Lath (screwed on)
(7) Gypsum Lath (screwed on)
(8) Three Coats of Plaster (Scratch, Brown, Finish)
(9) Two Coats of Plaster (Brown, Finish)
(10) Floor Runner Track
(11) Flush Metal Base

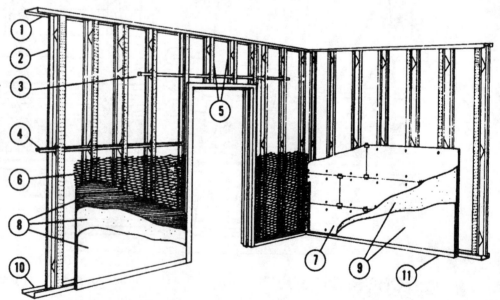

LOAD-BEARING HOLLOW PARTITION
Structural Stud

(1) Ceiling Runner Track
(2) Structural Stud (prefabricated)
(3) Structural Stud (nailable)
(4) Jack Studs
(5) Partition Stiffener (bridging)
(6) Metal or Wire Fabric Lath (wire-tied, nailed or stapled)
(7) Gypsum Lath (nailed or stapled)
(8) Three Coats of Plaster (Scratch, Brown, Finish)
(9) Two Coats of Plaster (Brown, Finish)

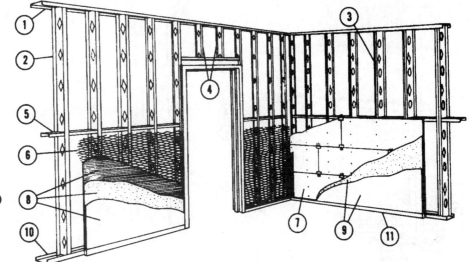

(10) Floor Runner Track   (11) Flush Metal Base

VERTICAL FURRING
With Studs

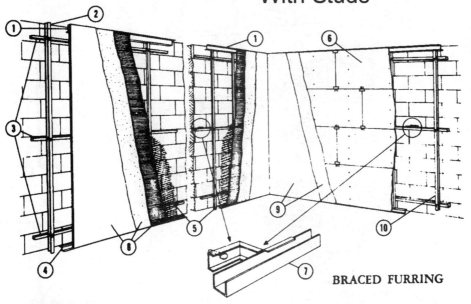

(1) Ceiling Runner
(2) Channel Stud
(3) Horizontal Stiffener
(4) Floor Runner
(5) Metal or Wire Fabric Lath
(6) Gypsum Lath
(7) Bracing
(8) Three Coats of Plaster (Scratch, Brown, Finish)
(9) Two Coats of Plaster (Brown, Finish)
(10) Screw Channel Studs

FREE STANDING FURRING

BRACED FURRING

417

DOUBLE CHANNEL STUD
Hollow Partition

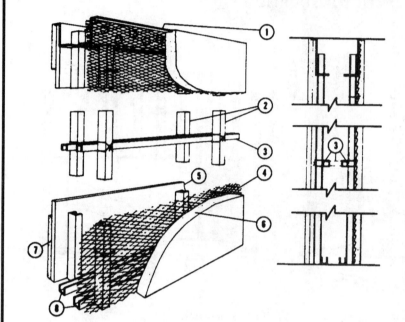

(1) Ceiling Runner
(2) Channel Studs
(3) Partition Stiffener and Channel Spacer
(4) Metal or Wire Fabric Lath (wire-tied)
(5) Gypsum Lath (clipped on)
(6) Three Coats of Plaster (Scratch, Brown, Finish)
(7) Two Coats of Plaster (Brown, Finish)
(8) Floor Runners (channel)

SINGLE CHANNEL STUD
Solid Partition

(1) Ceiling Runner
(2) Channel Stud
(3) Metal or Wire Fabric Lath (wire-tied)
(4) Plaster
(5) Combination Floor Runner and Screed

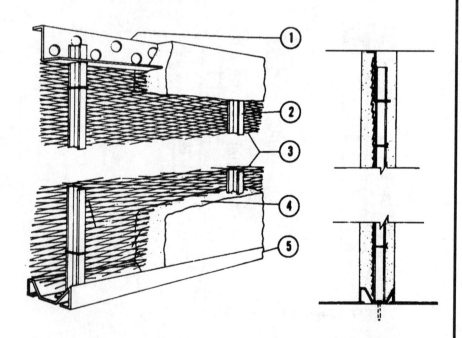

FURRED CEILINGS

STEEL JOISTS

CONCRETE JOISTS

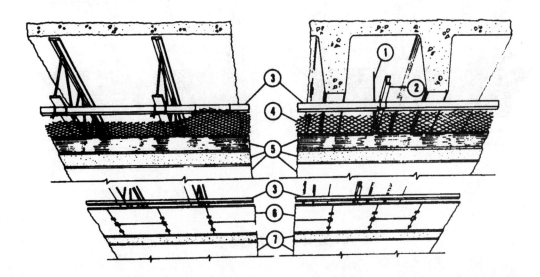

WOOD JOISTS

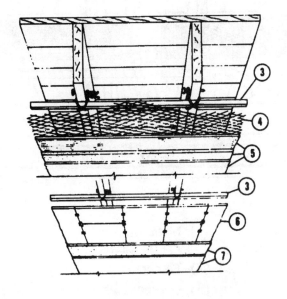

(1) Hanger

(2) ¾-inch Channel

(3) Cross Furring

(4) Metal or Wire Fabric Lath

(5) Plaster

(6) Gypsum Lath

(7) Plaster

CEILINGS

STEEL JOISTS   CONCRETE JOISTS

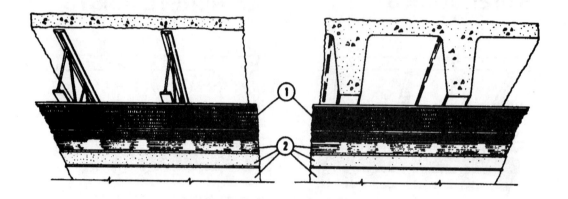

WOOD JOISTS

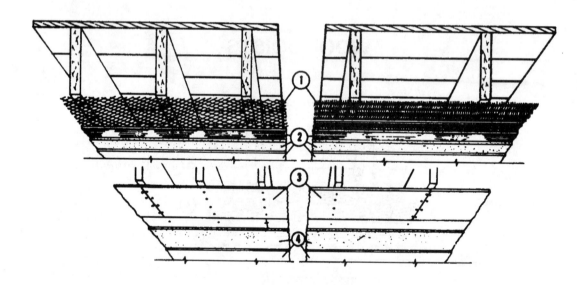

(1) Metal or Wire
    Fabric Lath
(2) Plaster
(3) Gypsum Lath
(4) Plaster

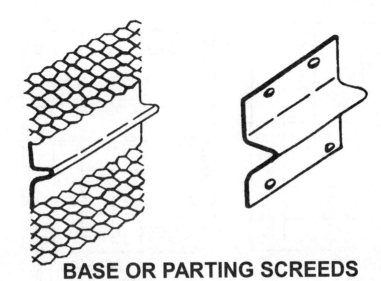

BASE OR PARTING SCREEDS

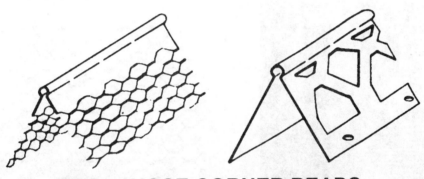

SMALL NOSE CORNER BEADS

WIRE BULL NOSE CORNER BEADS

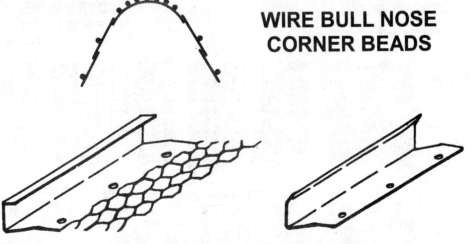

SQUARE CASING BEADS

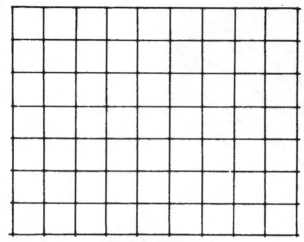

**PLAIN WIRE
FABRIC LATH**

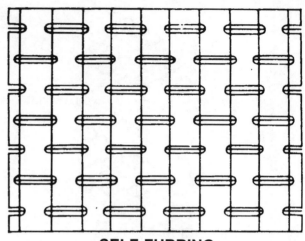

**SELF-FURRING
WIRE FABRIC LATH**

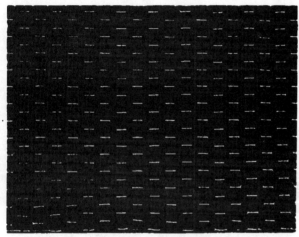

**PAPER BACKED
WOVEN WIRE
FABRIC LATH**

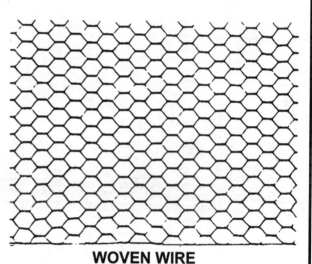

**WOVEN WIRE
FABRIC LATH**
(Also Available Self-Furred)

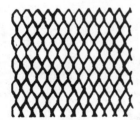

**FLAT
DIAMOND MESH
METAL LATH**

**SELF-
FURRING
METAL LATH**

**FLAT RIB
METAL LATH**

**RIB
METAL LATH**

**RIB
METAL LATH**

VERTICAL FURRING
Studless

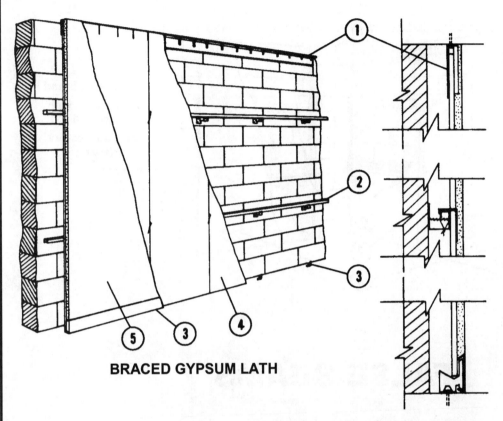

BRACED GYPSUM LATH

(1) Ceiling Runner
(2) Horizontal Stiffener (secured to bracing attachment)
(3) Metal Base and Clips
(4) Gypsum Lath
(5) Three Coats of Plaster (Scratch, Brown, Finish) (Minimum plaster thickness is ¾ inch.)

COLUMN FURRING

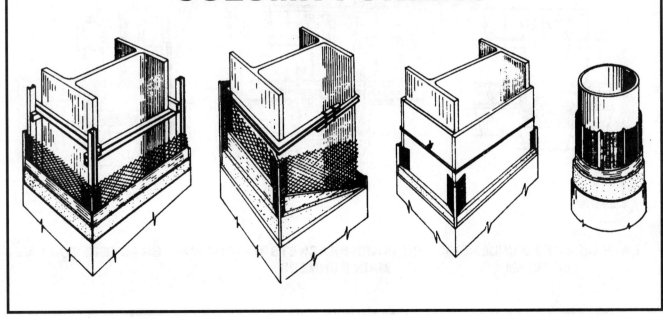

CONTACT FURRING

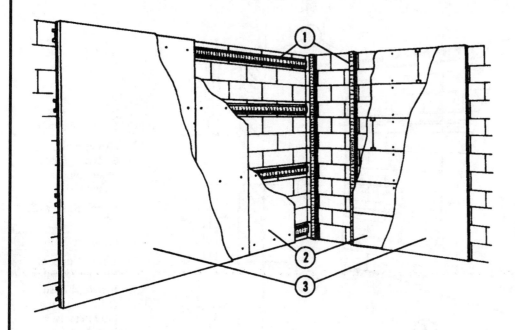

(1) Screw Channel
(2) Gypsum Lath (screwed on)
(3) Two Coats of Plaster (Brown, Finish)

FALSE BEAMS

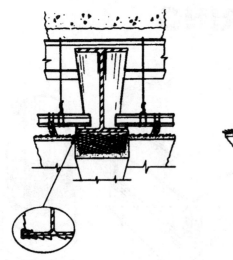 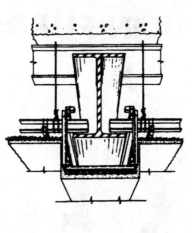 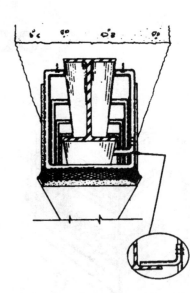

LATH DIRECT TO UNDERSIDE OF BEAM   **CHANNEL BRACKETS TO MAIN RUNNERS**   **CHANNEL BRACKETS TO SLAB**

MAXIMUM SPACING OF SUPPORTS FOR METAL LATH (Inches)

Type Of Lath	Weight of Lath Lb. Per Sq. Yd.	WALLS AND PARTITIONS			CEILINGS	
		Wood Studs	Solid Partitions	Steel Studs Wall Furring, Etc.	Wood or Concrete	Metal
Diamond Mesh (flat expanded)	2.5	16	16	13 1/2	12	12
	3.4	16	16	16	16	
Flat Rib	2.75	16	16	16	16	16
	3.4	19	24 (3)	19	19	19
3/8" Rib (1) (2)	3.4	24	(4)	24	24	24
	4.0	24	(4)	24	24	24
3/4" Rib	5.4	-	(4)	24 (5)	36 (6)	36 (6)
Sheet Lath	4.5	24	(4)	24	24	24

NOTE: Weights are exclusive of paper, fiber or other backing.
(1) 3.4 lb. 3/8" Rib Lath is permissible under Concrete Joists at 27" c.c.
(2) These spacings are based on a narrow bearing surface for the lath. When supports with a relatively wide bearing surface are used, these spacings may be increased accordingly, and still assure satisfactory work.
(3) This spacing permissible for Solid Partitions not exceeding 16' in height. For greater heights, permanent horizontal stiffener channels or rods must be provided on channel side of partitions, every 6' vertically, or else spacing shall be reduced 25%.
(4) For studless solid partitions, lath erected vertically.
(5) For interior wall furring or for application over solid surfaces for stucco.
(6) For contact or ceilings only.

TYPES OF LATH-ATTACHMENT TO WOOD AND METAL SUPPORTS

TYPE OF LATH	NAILS Type & Size	NAILS MAXIMUM SPACING (In Inches) Vertical	NAILS MAXIMUM SPACING (In Inches) Horizontal	SCREWS MAXIMUM SPACING (In Inches) Vertical	SCREWS MAXIMUM SPACING (In Inches) Horizontal	STAPLES Wire Gauge No.	STAPLES Crown	STAPLES Leg	STAPLES MAXIMUM SPACING (In Inches) Vertical	STAPLES MAXIMUM SPACING (In Inches) Horizontal
1. Diamond Mesh Expanded Metal Lath and Flat Rib Metal Lath	4d blued smooth box 1 ½ No. 14 gauge 7/32" head (clinched); 1" No.11 gauge 7/16" head, barbed; 1 ½" No.11 gauge 7/16" head, barbed	6 / 6 / 6	- / - / 6	6	6	16	¾	7/8	6	6
2. 3/8" Rib Metal Lath and Sheet Lath	1 ½" No. 11 ga. 7/16" head, barbed	6	6	6	6	16	¾	1 ½	At Ribs	At Ribs
3. ¾" Rib Metal Lath	4d common 1 ½" No.12 ½ gauge ¼" head; 2" No.11 gauge 7/16" head, barbed	At Ribs	- / At Ribs	At Ribs	At Ribs	16	¾	1 5/8	At Ribs	At Ribs
4. Wire Fabric Lath	4d blued smooth box (clinched); 1" No.11 gauge 7/16" head, barbed; 1 ½" No.11 gauge 7/16" head, barbed; 1 ¼" No.12 ga. 3/8" head, furring; 1" No.12 gauge 3/8" head	6 / 6 / 6 / 6 / 6	- / - / 6 / 6	6	6	16	7/16	7/8	6	6
5. 3/8" Gypsum Lath	1 1/8" No.13 gauge 12/61" head, blued	8	8	8	8	16	¾	7/8	8	8
6. ½" Gypsum Lath	1 ¼" No.13 gauge 12/61" head, blued	8	8 / 6	8	8 / 6	16	¾	1 1/8	8	8 / 6

STRESS RELIEF (CONTROL JOINTS)

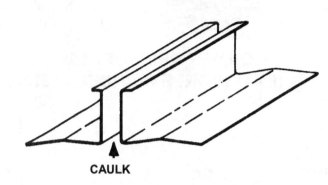

CAULK

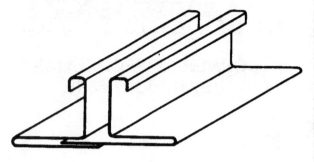

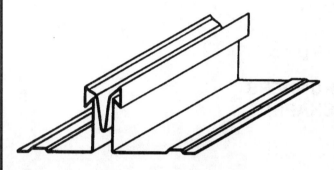

REVEALS

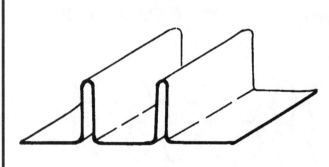

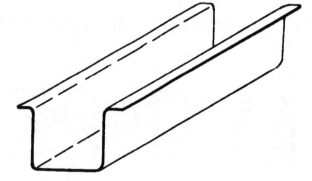

**CORNER REINFORCEMENT
(EXTERIOR) WIRE**

**CORNER REINFORCEMENT
(EXTERIOR) EXPANDED METAL**

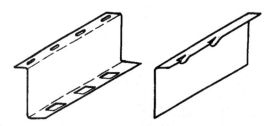

**PARTITION RUNNERS
(Z AND L SHAPE)**

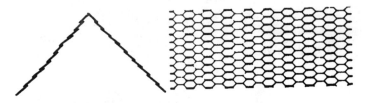

EXPANDED METAL CORNERITE

WIRE CORNERITE

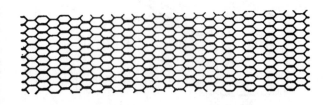

**STRIP REINFORCEMENT
(EXPANDED METAL)**

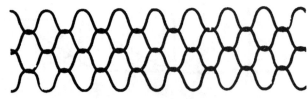

**STRIP REINFORCEMENT
(WIRE)**

 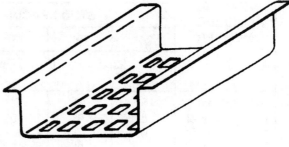

VENTILATING SCREEDS

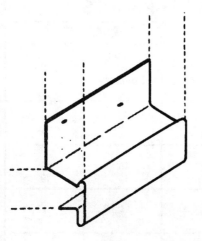 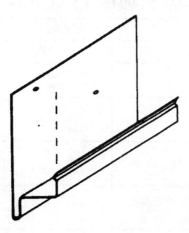 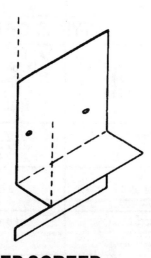

DRIP SCREEDS

WEEP SCREED
(Also Available with Perforations)

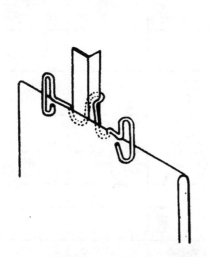 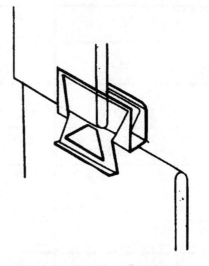

GYPSUM LATH ATTACHMENTS CLIPS

VERTICAL FURRING

VERTICAL FURRING MEMBER	UNBRACED				BRACED			
	STUD SPACING				STUD SPACING			
	24"	19"	16"	12"	24"	19"	16"	12"
	Maximum Furring Heights				Maximum Vertical Distance Between Braces			
3/4" Channel	6'	7'	8'	9'	5'	5'	6'	7'
1 1/2" Channel	8'	9'	10'	12'	6'	7'	8'	9'
2" Channel	9'	10'	11'	13'	7'	8'	9'	10'
2" Prefab. Stud	8'	9'	10'	11'	6'	7'	8'	9'
2 1/2" Prefab. Stud	10'	11'	12'	14'	8'	9'	10'	11'
	14'	16'	17'	20'	11'	13'	14'	16'

TYPES OF LATH—MAXIMUM SPACING OF SUPPORTS

TYPE OF LATH	Minimum Weight (psy), Gauge & Mesh Size	VERTICAL			HORIZONTAL	
		WOOD	METAL		Wood or Concrete	Metal
			Solid Plaster Partitions	Other		
Expanded Metal Lath (Diamond Mesh)	2.5	16"	16"	12"	12"	12"
	3.4	16"	16"	16"	16"	16"
Flat rib Expanded Metal Lath	2.75	16"	16"	16"	16"	16"
	3.4	19"	24"	19"	19"	19"
Stucco Mesh Expanded Metal Lath	1.8 and 3.6	16"	-	-	-	-
3/8" Rib Expanded Metal Lath	3.4	24"	-	24"	24"	24"
	4.0	24"		24"	24"	24"
Sheet Lath	4.5	24"	-	24"	24"	24"
3/4" Rib Expanded Metal Lath (Not manufactured in West)	5.4	-	-	-	36"	36"
Wire Fabric Lath — Welded	1.95 lbs.,11 ga.,2"x2"	24"	24"	24"	24"	24"
	1.4 lbs.,16 ga.,2"x2"	16"	16"	16"	16"	16"
	1.4 lbs.,18 ga.,1"x1"	16"	-	-	-	-
Wire Fabric Lath — Woven	1.4 lbs.,17 ga.,1 1/2" Hex.	24"	16"	16"	24"	16"
	1.4 lbs.,18 ga.,1" Hex.	24"	16"	16"	24"	16"
3/8" Gypsum Lath (plain)	-	16"	-	16"	16"	16"
(Large Size)	-	16"	-	16"	16"	16"
1/2" Gypsum Lath (plain)	-	24"	-	24"	24"	24"
(Large Size)		24"	No supports; Erected vertically		24"	24"	16"
5/8" Gypsum Lath (Large Size)	-	24"	No supports; Erected vertically		24"	24"	16"

PIPE WEIGHTS

CAST IRON PIPE

SERVICE WEIGHT			
Size, Inches	Weight of Pipe	Weight of Water	Total Weight— Lbs.
2"	3.8	1.45	5.3
3"	5.6	3.2	8.8
4"	7.5	5.5	13.0
5"	9.8	8.7	18.5
6"	12.4	12.5	24.9
8"	18.5	21.7	40.2

EXTRA HEAVY			
Size, Inches	Weight of Pipe	Weight of Water	Total Weight — Lbs.
2"	4.3	1.45	5.8
3"	8.3	3.2	11.5
4"	10.8	5.5	16.3
5"	13.3	8.7	22.0
6"	16.0	12.5	28.5
8"	26.5	21.7	48.2

STEEL PIPE

Pipe Size	W/40	H_2O/Lbs.	Total Lbs./L.F.
2"	3.65	1.45	5.1
2 1/2"	5.79	2.07	7.86
3"	7.57	3.2	10.77
3 1/2"	9.11	4.28	13.39
4"	10.8	5.51	16.31
5"	14.6	8.66	23.26
6"	18.0	12.5	30.5
8"	28.6	21.66	50.26
10"	40.5	34.15	74.65

SPRINKLER AREA CALCULATIONS

Typical maximum floor area allowed per system riser:

Light Hazard	**Ordinary Hazard**	**Extra Hazard**
52,000 S.F.	40,000-52,000 S.F.	25,000 S.F.

Typical maximum floor area coverage allowed per sprinkler head:

Light Hazard	**Ordinary Hazard**	**Extra Hazard**
130-200 S.F.	100-130 S.F.	90 S.F.

Typical maximum spacing between lines and sprinkler heads:

Light Hazard	**Ordinary Hazard**	**Extra Hazard**
12-15 feet	12-15 feet	12 feet

Note: This data is for estimating purposes only. Check all applicable codes and regulations for specific requirements.

SPRINKLER HEAD CALCULATIONS
Typical maximum quantity of sprinkler heads allowed by pipe size.

Light Hazard:

For sprinklers below ceiling:

Steel		Copper	
1 in. pipe	2 sprinklers	1 in. tube	2 sprinklers
1 ¼ in. pipe	3 sprinklers	1 ¼ in. tube	3 sprinklers
1 ½ in. pipe	5 sprinklers	1 ½ in. tube	5 sprinklers
2 in. pipe	10 sprinklers	2 in. tube	12 sprinklers
2 ½ in. pipe	30 sprinklers	2 ½ in. tube	40 sprinklers
3 in. pipe	60 sprinklers	3 in. tube	65 sprinklers
3 ½ in. pipe	100 sprinklers	3 ½ in. tube	115 sprinklers

For sprinklers above and below ceiling:

Steel		Copper	
1 in.	2 sprinklers	1 in.	2 sprinklers
1 ¼ in.	4 sprinklers	1 ¼ in.	4 sprinklers
1 ½ in.	7 sprinklers	1 ½ in.	7 sprinklers
2 in.	15 sprinklers	2 in.	18 sprinklers
2 ½ in.	50 sprinklers	2 ½ in.	65 sprinklers

Ordinary Hazard:

For sprinklers above ceiling:

Steel		Copper	
1 in. pipe	2 sprinklers	1 in. tube	2 sprinklers
1 ¼ in. pipe	3 sprinklers	1 ¼ in. tube	3 sprinklers
1 ½ in. pipe	5 sprinklers	1 ½ in. tube	5 sprinklers
2 in. pipe	10 sprinklers	2 in. tube	12 sprinklers
2 ½ in. pipe	20 sprinklers	2 ½ in. tube	25 sprinklers
3 in. pipe	40 sprinklers	3 in. tube	45 sprinklers
3 ½ in. pipe	65 sprinklers	3 ½ in. tube	75 sprinklers
4 in. pipe	100 sprinklers	4 in. tube	115 sprinklers
5 in. pipe	160 sprinklers	5 in. tube	180 sprinklers
6 in. pipe	275 sprinklers	6 in. tube	300 sprinklers

For sprinklers above and below ceiling:

Steel		Copper	
1 in.	2 sprinklers	1 in.	2 sprinklers
1 ¼ in.	4 sprinklers	1 ¼ in.	4 sprinklers
1 ½ in.	7 sprinklers	1 ½ in.	7 sprinklers
2 in.	15 sprinklers	2 in.	18 sprinklers
2 ½ in.	30 sprinklers	2 ½ in.	40 sprinklers
3 in.	60 sprinklers	3 in.	65 sprinklers

Extra Hazard:

For sprinklers below ceiling:

Steel		Copper	
1 in. pipe	1 sprinkler	1 in. tube	1 sprinkler
1 ¼ in. pipe	2 sprinklers	1 ¼ in. tube	2 sprinklers
1 ½ in. pipe	5 sprinklers	1 ½ in. tube	5 sprinklers
2 in. pipe	8 sprinklers	2 in. tube	8 sprinklers
2 ½ in. pipe	15 sprinklers	2 ½ in. tube	20 sprinklers
3 in. pipe	27 sprinklers	3 in. tube	30 sprinklers
3 ½ in. pipe	40 sprinklers	3 ½ in. tube	45 sprinklers
4 in. pipe	55 sprinklers	4 in. tube	65 sprinklers
5 in. pipe	90 sprinklers	5 in. tube	100 sprinklers
6 in. pipe	150 sprinklers	6 in. tube	170 sprinklers

Note: This data is for estimating purposes only. Check all applicable codes and regulations for specific requirements.

SPRINKLER HAZARD OCCUPANCIES

Typical Light Hazard Occupancies:

Churches
Clubs
Eaves and overhangs, if combustible construction with
    no combustible beneath
Educational
Hospitals
Institutional
Libraries, except large stack rooms
Museums

Nursing or convalescent homes
Office, including data processing
Residential
Restaurant seating areas
Theaters seating areas
Theaters and auditoriums excluding stages and pro-
    sceniums
Unused attics

Typical Ordinary Hazard Occupancies (Group 1):

Automobile parking garages
Bakeries
Beverage manufacturing
Canneries
Dairy products manufacturing and processing

Electronic plants
Glass and glass products manufacturing
Laundries
Restaurant service areas

Typical Ordinary Hazard Occupancies (Group 2):

Cereal mills
Chemical plants - ordinary
Cold Storage warehouses
Confectionery products
Distilleries
Leather goods mfg.
Libraries-large stack room areas

Mercantiles
Machine shops
Metal working
Printing and publishing
Textile mfg.
Tobacco Products mfg.
Wood product assembly

Typical Ordinary Hazard Occupancies (Group 3):

Feed mills
Paper and pulp mills
Paper process plants
Piers and wharves
Repair garages
Tire manufacturing

Warehouses (having moderate to higher combustibil-
    ity of content, such as paper, household furni-
    ture, paint, general storage, whiskey, etc.)[1]
Wood machining

Typical Extra Hazard Occupancies (Group 1):

Combustible hydraulic fluid use areas
Die casting
Metal extruding
Plywood and particle board manufacturing
Printing (using inks with below 100°F [37.8°C] flash
    points)
Rubber reclaiming, compounding, drying, milling, vul-
    canizing

Saw mills
Textile picking, opening, blending, garnetting, card-
    ing, combining of cotton, synthetics, wool
    shoddy or burlap
Upholstering with plastic foams

Typical Extra Hazard Occupancies (Group 2):

Asphalt saturating
Flammable liquids spraying
Flow coating
Mobile Home or Modular Building assemblies (where
    finished enclosure is present and has combustible
    interiors)

Open Oil quenching
Solvent cleaning
Varnish and paint dipping

MECHANICAL / PLUMBING 15400

TYPICAL MINIMUM SIZE OF HORIZONTAL BUILDING STORM DRAINS AND BUILDING STORM SEWERS

Diameter of drain	Maximum projected area in square feet for various slopes		
	1/8 inch per feet slope	1/4 inch per feet slope	1/2 inch per feet slope
3	822	1160	1644
4	1880	2650	3760
5	3340	4720	6680
6	5350	7550	10700
8	11500	16300	23000
10	20700	29200	41400
12	33300	47000	66600
15	59500	84000	119000

TYPICAL VENTILATION AIR REQUIREMENTS
FOR SPECIAL USES

Occupancy Classification	Required ventilation air in cfm per human occupant
Special areas	
Lockers	2 *
	(or 30 per locker)
Wardrobes	2 *
Public bathrooms	40 **
Private bathrooms	25 **
Swimming pools	15
	(per occupant)
Water closet (flush valve type)	1
Exitways and corridors	1 1/2 *

*Per square foot floor area.
**Per water closet or urinal.

TYPICAL VENTILATION AIR REQUIREMENTS
FOR RETAIL USES

Occupancy Classification	Required ventilation air in cfm per human occupant
Mercantile	
Sales floors and showrooms (basement & grade floors)	7
Sales and showrooms (upper floors)	7
Storage areas	5
Dressing rooms	7
Malls	7
Shipping areas	15
Elevators	7
Supermarkets	
Meat processing rooms	5
Drugs stores	
Pharmacists' work rooms	20
Specialty shops	
Pet shops	1.0*
Florists	5
Greenhouses	5

*cfm per sq. ft. floor area.

TYPICAL VENTILATION AIR REQUIREMENTS
FOR FACTORY AND INDUSTRIAL USES

Occupany Classification	Required ventilation air in cfm per human occupant
Factory and industrial	
Metalworking & finishing	35
Automotive engine test	
Paint spray booths	*Require*
Picking, etching & plating lines	*Special*
Degreasing booths	*Exhaust*
Sandblasting booths	*Systems*
Chemicals and pharmaceuticals	
Dusty operations	30
Rooms containing potential gas emitters	20
Drying oven rooms	15
Fermentation rooms	15
Pillmaking booths	10
Packaging areas	10
Utility rooms	7
Computer rooms	7
Textiles-clothes manufacturer	15
Electronics & aerospace circuit board & soldering rooms	20
Wood products, papermaking	20
Brewing, distilling, wineries, bottling	20*
Food processing	20
Tobacco processing	20
Power plants	
Control rooms	10
Boiler rooms	35
Generator rooms	20
Sewage treatment plants	
Control rooms	10
Compressor/blower motor rooms	20
Glass & ceramic manufacturer	20
Agricultural	20

TYPICAL VENTILATION AIR REQUIREMENTS
FOR BUSINESS USES

Occupany Classification	Required ventilation air in cfm per human occupant
Business	
Banks	
(see offices)	
Vaults	5
Barber, beauty and health services	
Beauty shops (hair dressers)	25
Reducing salons	25
Sauna baths, steam rooms	5
Barber shops	7
Photo studios	
Camera rooms, stages	5
Dark rooms	
Shoe repair shops	
Workrooms/trade areas	10
Offices	
General office space and showrooms	15
Conference rooms	25
Drafting/art rooms	7
Doctor's consultation rooms	10
Waiting rooms	10
Lithographing rooms	7
Diazo printing rooms	7
Computer rooms	5
Keypunch rooms	7
Communication	
TV/radio broadcasting booths, studios	30
Motion picture and TV stages	30
Pressrooms	15
Composing rooms	7
Engraving rooms	7
Telephone switchboard rooms (manual)	7
Telephone switchgear rooms (automatic)	7
Teletypewriter/facsimile rooms	5
Research institutes	
Laboratories:	
Light duty; non-chemical	15
Chemical	15
Heavy-duty	15
Radioisotope, chemical & biologically toxic	15
Machine shops	15
Dark rooms, spectroscopy rooms	10
Animal rooms	40
Veterinary hospitals	
Kennels, stalls	25
Operating rooms	25
Reception rooms	10

TYPICAL VENTILATION AIR REQUIREMENTS
FOR INSTITUTIONAL USES

Occupancy Classification	Required ventilation air in cfm per human occupant
Institutional	
Prisons	
Cell blocks	7
Eating halls..	15
Guard stations	7

APPLICATIONS FOR CONDUCTORS
USED FOR GENERAL WIRING

	AMBIENT TEMPERATURE								FEATURES
	60°C 140°F	75°C 167°F	85°C 185°F	90°C 194°F	110°C 230°F	200°C 392°F	Dry	Dry or Wet	
R	X						X		Code Rubber
RH		X					X		Heat Resistant
RHH				X			X		More Heat Resistant
RW	X							X	Moisture Resistant
RH-RW	X							X	Moisture and Heat Resistant
		X					X		Moisture and Heat Resistant
RHW		X						X	Moisture and Heat Resistant
RU	X						X		Latex Rubber
RUH		X					X		Heat Resistant
RUW	X							X	Moisture Resistant
T	X						X		Thermoplastic
TW	X							X	Moisture Resistant
THHN				X			X		Heat Resistant
THW		X						X	Moisture and Heat Resistant
THWN		X						X	Moisture and Heat Resistant
MI			X					X	Mineral Insulated Metal Sheathed
V			X				X		Varnished Cambric
AVA					X		X		With Asbestos
AVB				X			X		With Asbestos
AVL					X			X	With Asbestos

This table does not include special condition conductors, thickness of conductor insulation, or reference to all other protective coverings.

GENERAL CLASSIFICATION OF INSULATIONS:

A .... Asbestos
H .... Heat Resistant
MI........... Mineral Insulation
R .... Rubber

RU.......... Latex Rubber
V .... Varnished Cambric
T .... Thermoplastic
W .... (Water) Moisture Resistant

WIRE AND SHEET METAL GAGES
(In Decimals of an Inch)

Name of Gage	American Wire Gage (A.W.G.) (Corresponds to Brown & Sharpe Gage)	Birmingham Iron Wire Gage (B.W.G.)	United States Standard Gage (U.S.S.G.)	
Principal Use	Electrical Wire & Non-Ferrous Sheet Metal	Iron or Steel Wire	Ferrous Sheet Metal	
Gage No.				**Gage No.**
00 00000				00 00000
0 00000	.5800			0 00000
00000	.5165	.500		00000
0000	.4600	.454		0000
000	.4096	.425		000
00	.3648	.380		00
0	.3249	.340		0
1	.2893	.300		1
2	.2576	.284		2
3	.2294	.259	23.91	3
4	.2048	.238	.2242	4
5	.1819	.220	.2092	5
6	.1620	.203	.1943	6
7	.1443	.180	.1793	7
8	.1285	.165	.1644	8
9	.1144	.148	.1495	9
10	.1019	.134	.1345	10
11	.0907	.120	.1196	11
12	.0808	.109	.1046	12
13	.0720	.095	.0897	13
14	.0641	.083	.0747	14
15	.0571	.072	.0673	15
16	.0508	.065	.0598	16
17	.0453	.058	.0538	17
18	.0403	.049	.0478	18
19	.0359	.042	.0418	19
20	.0320	.035	.0359	20
21	.0285	.032	.0329	21
22	.0253	.028	.0299	22
23	.0226	.025	.0269	23
24	.0201	.022	.0239	24
25	.0179	.020	.0209	25
26	.0159	.018	.0179	26
27	.0142	.016	.0164	27
28	.0126	.014	.0149	28
29	.0113	.013	.0135	29
30	.0100	.012	.0120	30
31	.0089	.010	.0105	31
32	.0080	.009	.0097	32
33	.0071	.008	.0090	33
34	.0063	.007	.0082	34
35	.0056	.005	.0075	35
36	.0050	.004	.0067	36
37	.0045		.0064	37
38	.0040		.0060	38
39	.0035			39
40	.0031			40

Geographic Cost Modifiers

The costs as presented in this book attempt to represent national averages. Costs, however, vary among regions, states and even between adjacent localities.

In order to more closely approximate the probable costs for specific locations throughout the U.S., this table of Geographic Cost Modifiers is provided. These adjustment factors are used to modify costs obtained from this book to help account for regional variations of construction costs and to provide a more accurate estimate for specific areas. The factors are formulated by comparing costs in a specific area to the costs as presented in the Costbook pages. An example of how to use these factors is shown below. Whenever local current costs are known, whether material prices or labor rates, they should be used when more accuracy is required.

$$\text{Cost Obtained from Costbook Pages} \times \frac{\text{Location Cost Adjustment Factor}}{100} = \text{Adjusted Cost}$$

For example, a project estimated to cost $125,000 using the Costbook pages can be adjusted to more closely approximate the cost in Los Angeles:

$$\$125,000 \times \frac{105}{100} = \$131,250$$

GEOGRAPHIC COST MODIFERS		01025
State	**Metropolitan Areas**	**Multiplier**
AK	ANCHORAGE	122
AL	ANNISTON	80
	AUBURN-OPELIKA	80
	BIRMINGHAM	79
	DOTHAN	77
	GADSDEN	77
	HUNTSVILLE	79
	MOBILE	82
	MONTGOMERY	77
	TUSCALOOSA	79
AR	FAYETTEVILLE-SPRINGDALE-ROGERS	72
	FORT SMITH	77
	JONESBORO	76
	LITTLE ROCK-NORTH LITTLE ROCK	78
	PINE BLUFF	77
	TEXARKANA	77
AZ	FLAGSTAFF	88
	PHOENIX-MESA	88
	TUCSON	87
	YUMA	89
CA	BAKERSFIELD	100
	FRESNO	102
	LOS ANGELES-LONG BEACH	105
	MODESTO	99
	OAKLAND	108
	ORANGE COUNTY	102
	REDDING	99
	RIVERSIDE-SAN BERNARDINO	100
	SACRAMENTO	102
	SALINAS	104
	SAN DIEGO	101
	SAN FRANCISCO	111
	SAN JOSE	109
	SAN LUIS OBISPO	98
	SANTA CRUZ-WATSONVILLE	104
	SANTA ROSA	105
	STOCKTON-LODI	101
	VALLEJO-FAIRFIELD-NAPA	104
	VENTURA	100
	SANTA BARBARA	103

GEOGRAPHIC COST MODIFERS		01025
State	**Metropolitan Areas**	**Multiplier**
CO	BOULDER-LONGMONT	86
	COLORADO SPRINGS	91
	DENVER	91
	FORT COLLINS-LOVELAND	84
	GRAND JUNCTION	86
	GREELEY	84
	PUEBLO	88
CT	BRIDGEPORT	100
	DANBURY	100
	HARTFORD	99
	NEW HAVEN-MERIDEN	100
	NEW LONDON-NORWICH	98
	STAMFORD-NORWALK	103
	WATERBURY	99
DC	WASHINGTON	94
DE	DOVER	93
	WILMINGTON-NEWARK	94
FL	DAYTONA BEACH	83
	FORT LAUDERDALE	86
	FORT MYERS-CAPE CORAL	79
	FORT PIERCE-PORT ST. LUCIE	85
	FORT WALTON BEACH	87
	GAINESVILLE	81
	JACKSONVILLE	84
	LAKELAND-WINTER HAVEN	81
	MELBOURNE-TITUSVILLE-PALM BAY	88
	MIAMI	86
	NAPLES	88
	OCALA	85
	ORLANDO	85
	PANAMA CITY	75
	PENSACOLA	79
	SARASOTA-BRADENTON	80
	TALLAHASSEE	77
	TAMPA-ST. PETERSBURG-CLEARWATER	83
	WEST PALM BEACH-BOCA RATON	86
GA	ALBANY	76
	ATHENS	78
	ATLANTA	85
	AUGUSTA	74
	COLUMBUS	75
	MACON	78
	SAVANNAH	78

GEOGRAPHIC COST MODIFERS		01025
State	**Metropolitan Areas**	**Multiplier**
HI	HONOLULU	121
IA	CEDAR RAPIDS	87
	DAVENPORT	89
	DES MOINES	90
	DUBUQUE	85
	IOWA CITY	89
	SIOUX CITY	85
	WATERLOO-CEDAR FALLS	84
ID	BOISE CITY	88
	POCATELLO	87
IL	BLOOMINGTON-NORMAL	95
	CHAMPAIGN-URBANA	94
	CHICAGO	103
	DECATUR	93
	KANKAKEE	96
	PEORIA-PEKIN	95
	ROCKFORD	95
	SPRINGFIELD	93
IN	BLOOMINGTON	91
	EVANSVILLE	89
	FORT WAYNE	90
	GARY	97
	INDIANAPOLIS	93
	KOKOMO	89
	LAFAYETTE	90
	MUNCIE	90
	SOUTH BEND	90
	TERRE HAUTE	90
KS	KANSAS CITY	88
	LAWRENCE	84
	TOPEKA	83
	WICHITA	83
KY	LEXINGTON	84
	LOUISVILLE	86
	OWENSBORO	84
LA	ALEXANDRIA	79
	BATON ROUGE	82
	HOUMA	82
	LAFAYETTE	81
	LAKE CHARLES	82
	MONROE	79
	NEW ORLEANS	85
	SHREVEPORT-BOSSIER CITY	80

GEOGRAPHIC COST MODIFERS

State	Metropolitan Areas	Multiplier
MA	BARNSTABLE-YARMOUTH	103
	BOSTON	105
	BROCKTON	102
	FITCHBURG-LEOMINSTER	99
	LAWRENCE	99
	LOWELL	98
	NEW BEDFORD	102
	PITTSFIELD	98
	SPRINGFIELD	98
	WORCESTER	98
MD	BALTIMORE	90
	CUMBERLAND	86
	HAGERSTOWN	87
ME	BANGOR	85
	LEWISTON-AUBURN	86
	PORTLAND	88
MI	ANN ARBOR	95
	DETROIT	96
	FLINT	92
	GRAND RAPIDS-MUSKEGON-HOLLAND	89
	JACKSON	91
	KALAMAZOO-BATTLE CREEK	86
	LANSING-EAST LANSING	91
	SAGINAW-BAY CITY-MIDLAND	90
MN	DULUTH	95
	MINNEAPOLIS-ST. PAUL	100
	ROCHESTER	95
	ST. CLOUD	97
MO	COLUMBIA	89
	JOPLIN	85
	KANSAS CITY	91
	SPRINGFIELD	86
	ST. JOSEPH	89
	ST. LOUIS	89
MS	BILOXI-GULFPORT-PASCAGOULA	78
	JACKSON	77
MT	BILLINGS	88
	GREAT FALLS	88
	MISSOULA	86
NC	ASHEVILLE	73
	CHARLOTTE	75

GEOGRAPHIC COST MODIFERS

01025

State	Metropolitan Areas	Multiplier
NC	FAYETTEVILLE	75
	GREENSBORO-WINSTON-SALEM-HIGH POINT	74
	GREENVILLE	74
	HICKORY-MORGANTON-LENOIR	71
	RALEIGH-DURHAM-CHAPEL HILL	74
	ROCKY MOUNT	71
	WILMINGTON	75
ND	BISMARCK	86
	FARGO	89
	GRAND FORKS	87
NE	LINCOLN	82
	OMAHA	86
NH	MANCHESTER	90
	NASHUA	88
	PORTSMOUTH	86
NJ	ATLANTIC-CAPE MAY	99
	BERGEN-PASSAIC	101
	JERSEY CITY	100
	MIDDLESEX-SOMERSET-HUNTERDON	97
	MONMOUTH-OCEAN	99
	NEWARK	102
	TRENTON	99
	VINELAND-MILLVILLE-BRIDGETON	98
NM	ALBUQUERQUE	86
	LAS CRUCES	83
	SANTA FE	90
NV	LAS VEGAS	97
	RENO	96
NY	ALBANY-SCHENECTADY-TROY	91
	BINGHAMTON	90
	BUFFALO-NIAGARA FALLS	97
	ELMIRA	85
	GLENS FALLS	84
	JAMESTOWN	92
	NASSAU-SUFFOLK	103
	NEW YORK	118
	ROCHESTER	95
	SYRACUSE	92
	UTICA-ROME	92

GEOGRAPHIC COST MODIFERS		01025
State	**Metropolitan Areas**	**Multiplier**
OH	AKRON	92
	CANTON-MASSILLON	90
	CINCINNATI	90
	CLEVELAND-LORAIN-ELYRIA	93
	COLUMBUS	90
	DAYTON-SPRINGFIELD	88
	LIMA	90
	MANSFIELD	87
	STEUBENVILLE	93
	TOLEDO	92
	YOUNGSTOWN-WARREN	87
OK	ENID	79
	LAWTON	80
	OKLAHOMA CITY	81
	TULSA	80
OR	EUGENE-SPRINGFIELD	93
	MEDFORD-ASHLAND	91
	PORTLAND	95
	SALEM	94
PA	ALLENTOWN-BETHLEHEM-EASTON	94
	ALTOONA	92
	ERIE	93
	HARRISBURG-LEBANON-CARLISLE	90
	JOHNSTOWN	93
	LANCASTER	91
	PHILADELPHIA	102
	PITTSBURGH	93
	READING	93
	SCRANTON-WILKES-BARRE-HAZLETON	91
	STATE COLLEGE	88
	WILLIAMSPORT	89
	YORK	92
RI	PROVIDENCE	98
SC	AIKEN	81
	CHARLESTON-NORTH CHARLESTON	76
	COLUMBIA	76
	FLORENCE	73
	GREENVILLE-SPARTANBURG-ANDERSON	76
	MYRTLE BEACH	81
SD	RAPID CITY	80
	SIOUX FALLS	80

GEOGRAPHIC COST MODIFERS

01025

State	Metropolitan Areas	Multiplier
TN	CHATTANOOGA	79
	JACKSON	78
	JOHNSON CITY	75
	KNOXVILLE	79
	MEMPHIS	83
	NASHVILLE	82
TX	ABILENE	77
	AMARILLO	78
	AUSTIN-SAN MARCOS	78
	BEAUMONT-PORT ARTHUR	79
	BROWNSVILLE-HARLINGEN-SAN BENITO	80
	BRYAN-COLLEGE STATION	78
	CORPUS CHRISTI	76
	DALLAS	83
	EL PASO	76
	FORT WORTH-ARLINGTON	82
	GALVESTON-TEXAS CITY	81
	HOUSTON	84
	LAREDO	70
	LONGVIEW-MARSHALL	75
	LUBBOCK	78
	MCALLEN-EDINBURG-MISSION	75
	ODESSA-MIDLAND	76
	SAN ANGELO	75
	SAN ANTONIO	80
	TEXARKANA	77
	TYLER	77
	VICTORIA	77
	WACO	77
	WICHITA FALLS	77
UT	PROVO-OREM	84
	SALT LAKE CITY-OGDEN	83
VA	CHARLOTTESVILLE	79
	LYNCHBURG	79
	NORFOLK-VIRGINIA BEACH-NEWPORT NEWS	81
	RICHMOND-PETERSBURG	83
	ROANOKE	76
VT	BURLINGTON	91
WA	BELLINGHAM	100
	BREMERTON	98
	OLYMPIA	97

GEOGRAPHIC COST MODIFERS

State	Metropolitan Areas	Multiplier
WA	RICHLAND-KENNEWICK-PASCO	95
	SEATTLE-BELLEVUE-EVERETT	102
	SPOKANE	97
	TACOMA	99
	YAKIMA	95
WI	APPLETON-OSHKOSH-NEENAH	90
	EAU CLAIRE	90
	GREEN BAY	91
	JANESVILLE-BELOIT	90
	KENOSHA	92
	LA CROSSE	89
	MADISON	89
	MILWAUKEE-WAUKESHA	96
	RACINE	92
	WAUSAU	90
WV	CHARLESTON	89
	HUNTINGTON	90
	PARKERSBURG	87
	WHEELING	89
WY	CASPER	87
	CHEYENNE	89

BNi® Building News

Square Foot Tables

The following Square Foot Tables list hundreds of actual projects for dozens of building types, each with associated building size, total square foot building cost and percentage of project costs for total mechanical and electrical components. This data provides an overview of construction costs by building type. These costs are for actual projects. The variations within similar building types may be due, among other factors, to size, location, quality and specified components, materials and processes. Depending upon all such factors, specific building costs can vary significantly and may not necessarily fall within the range of costs as presented. The data has been updated to reflect current construction costs.

SQUARE FOOT TABLES

COMMERCIAL

AUTO DEALERSHIP

Project Size Gross S.F.	Project Cost $/S.F.	% Cost Mechanical	% Cost Electrical
7,700	138.70	16.7	9.4
16,100	78.70	10.2	15.9
20,000	82.70	12.9	23.4
26,300	84.30	12.5	22.0
43,600	66.80	19.4	13.2
53,600	111.30	12.5	11.5

BUSINESS CENTER

3,900	83.10	12.0	9.2
9,900	80.40	9.1	7.6
54,400	53.80	3.4	12.2
135,000	58.40	8.2	1.5

CINEMA

18,000	190.00	10.9	6.7
22,500 A	116.90	6.6	4.2

MALL/PLAZA

9,700	58.80	15.0	13.3
10,500	94.00	8.0	13.5
16,300	85.60	9.4	10.6
26,900	85.30	15.0	7.0
36,000	72.20	10.0	11.0
36,300	82.00	12.4	8.2
44,720	85.60	18.3	12.4
59,100	83.90	9.8	9.5
60,000 R	86.00	10.0	9.5
64,100	86.50	22.4	18.4
66,000	99.00	13.5	11.5
67,400	72.00	21.0	15.0
73,500	104.10	14.9	6.9

MALL/PLAZA (Cont.)

Project Size Gross S.F.	Project Cost $/S.F.	% Cost Mechanical	% Cost Electrical
142,000	65.40	7.1	8.0
220,000	172.80	11.0	6.4
223,700	50.80	9.0	9.3
321,200	60.40	7.3	7.4
379,900	78.80	11.2	6.2
405,100	81.30	13.9	6.0
482,000	135.30	10.5	9.4
630,000	90.50	12.2	12.4

RESTAURANT

4,300 R	149.40	6.9	8.7
4,400 R	219.90	14.6	8.5
5,800	178.70	28.0	10.6
6,800 A	208.90	7.0	11.1
7,360 R	225.00	16.0	6.5
9,600	223.40	24.7	13.1
10,000 R	232.40	21.0	10.0
10,100	200.50	28.6	18.4
10,600	369.30	20.4	6.4
22,900 R	240.00	15.8	16.9

RETAIL STORE

1,000	225.00	12.8	6.7
3,000 R	201.40	14.3	10.5
12,300	276.00	14.0	10.0
30,000	139.50	15.6	26.2
61,300	72.20	13.3	13.0
115,000	99.80	14.6	11.3
154,700	141.50	11.2	12.4
314,700 R	119.30	13.8	9.4

A = Addition   R = Remodel

For more information subscribe to **Design Cost & Data**

SQUARE FOOT TABLES

RESIDENTIAL

APARTMENTS

Project Size Gross S.F.	Project Cost $/S.F.	% Cost Mechanical	% Cost Electrical
3,700	83.60	14.9	4.4
13,900	114.50	7.9	7.2
19,200 R	181.80	45.3	7.5
19,700	106.50	7.4	10.4
23,700	117.00	10.6	4.3
26,500	110.80	25.2	12.8
35,100	90.60	16.4	5.6
54,000	156.80	23.3	13.1
62,700	114.00	17.0	9.0
67,300	104.10	13.8	8.4
70,600	58.60	18.1	7.8
75,300	129.30	13.2	8.1
75,600	125.80	14.5	8.9
72,200	109.00	18.4	10.9
77,600	141.10	26.9	14.3
88,100	131.00	15.3	9.3
89,500	122.80	10.7	11.1
94,100	74.00	8.5	6.8
96,000	92.40	17.0	13.3
102,000	160.30	17.8	12.5
103,200	72.90	12.1	8.9
103,600	117.40	19.1	9.0
105,200	149.40	14.9	8.9
106,200	107.60	12.8	9.3
110,900	103.40	15.6	8.4
111,800	146.80	17.3	7.4
115,900	110.10	12.5	8.6
117,200	68.80	12.9	8.0
119,000	94.50	15.6	8.4

APARTMENTS (Cont.)

Project Size Gross S.F.	Project Cost $/S.F.	% Cost Mechanical	% Cost Electrical
119,400	61.90	18.6	8.7
144,300	137.60	15.0	8.6
176,300	117.00	19.1	9.0
192,300	68.80	10.1	6.0
210,900	135.40	19.1	9.5
220,200	139.40	14.8	7.5
253,900	181.10	20.6	7.7
369,500	132.30	15.8	9.0

CONDOS/TOWNHOUSE

8,600	118.70	8.5	4.4
16,700	95.70	13.2	6.5
18,000	201.40	14.6	9.7
18,400	103.30	12.9	5.8
74,800	93.70	13.8	5.2
111,700	118.20	9.2	7.1
150,300	132.00	15.9	7.9
278,800	206.30	14.1	7.9
1,109,900	95.00	9.8	4.7

SINGLE-FAMILY HOMES

600 R	85.50	16.3	2.0
900	111.10	33.0	3.0
2,100	128.50	8.8	4.0
2,200	275.50	23.8	3.4
2,500	135.00	6.1	7.1
2,900	130.30	7.7	2.8
3,000	91.50	9.5	6.8
3,100	204.60	15.5	4.6
3,600	128.10	8.5	3.0
3,700	179.10	9.8	3.4

A = Addition   R = Remodel

SQUARE FOOT TABLES

RESIDENTIAL (Cont.)

SINGLE-FAMILY HOMES (Cont.)

Project Size Gross S.F.	Project Cost $/S.F.	% Cost Mechanical	% Cost Electrical
4,200	155.70	15.5	5.7
4,600	247.30	9.0	4.7
5,200	321.40	8.3	6.0
5,700	188.30	7.4	3.7
5,700	128.00	8.7	12.6
21,300*	91.30	26.0	4.0
22,700*	84.80	27.0	4.6
45,000*	129.00	7.8	2.5
51,458*	93.50	11.0	5.0

*TOWNHOUSES

EDUCATIONAL

ADMINISTRATION (OFFICES)

Project Size Gross S.F.	Project Cost $/S.F.	% Cost Mechanical	% Cost Electrical
53,700	219.90	15.4	9.0

ATHLETIC FACILITY

38,100	218.20	16.8	9.8
44,100	201.40	16.8	8.4
100,000	137.60	19.2	5.3
160,000	249.30	13.7	7.9
247,500	209.10	11.2	9.0
271,000	196.50	13.2	7.6
283,100	236.70	14.6	6.0

AUDITORIUM/PERFORMING ARTS

9,900	352.50	17.5	29.2
17,800	322.30	11.4	16.1
29,200	318.90	16.2	10.5
62,700	231.90	13.0	12.9

CLASSROOM

Project Size Gross S.F.	Project Cost $/S.F.	% Cost Mechanical	% Cost Electrical
35,400	319.80	10.2	6.8
70,000	144.40	24.3	13.1
78,900	268.60	13.3	14.3
80,100	218.20	16.9	10.5
100,000	217.40	21.1	9.8
166,000	150.20	16.1	11.2
298,400	140.90	11.3	11.9

COMPLETE COLLEGE FACILITIES

95,300	226.60	19.4	11.7
450,000	270.40	18.6	10.8

ELEMENTARY SCHOOL

18,000	165.80	19.1	13.8
30,800	152.50	16.0	10.0
31,600	127.60	12.1	11.3
35,700	186.40	17.3	8.7
40,000	162.00	18.5	13.4
40,500	142.00	22.1	11.3
57,000	122.70	22.1	7.5
69,700	191.40	20.6	9.3
91,400	154.30	18.2	7.6

HIGH SCHOOL

116,400	169.40	18.1	12.9
133,000	145.90	17.8	10.7
184,000	257.00	23.0	10.0
217,200 R	138.40	26.4	10.6
254,000 R	106.80	17.2	14.6
431,700	162.80	13.1	9.6

A = Addition   R = Remodel

For more information subscribe to **Design Cost & Data**

SQUARE FOOT TABLES

EDUCATIONAL (Cont.)

JUNIOR HIGH SCHOOL

Project Size Gross S.F.	Project Cost $/S.F.	% Cost Mechanical	% Cost Electrical
26,000	213.40	9.5	9.3
28,100	132.30	11.9	9.5
52,800	171.20	18.3	8.6
91,600	210.50	21.2	11.0
123,700	172.20	29.1	9.1

LABORATORY/RESEARCH

Project Size Gross S.F.	Project Cost $/S.F.	% Cost Mechanical	% Cost Electrical
9,200	369.30	25.4	4.5
80,300	290.40	20.2	15.5

LIBRARY

Project Size Gross S.F.	Project Cost $/S.F.	% Cost Mechanical	% Cost Electrical
6,900	193.60	17.9	10.3
8,200	177.70	18.8	10.6
12,000	230.40	19.4	15.9
15,000	201.40	15.7	18.7
16,300	170.60	11.3	7.4
28,600	152.80	15.7	9.0
30,100	207.30	13.0	11.0
37,700	162.80	14.6	8.0
43,500	137.60	16.6	6.7
47,900	241.20	29.7	9.0
51,400	246.40	13.1	12.4
63,400 A	185.30	13.5	8.3
64,000	173.50	10.9	11.4
74,000	196.50	17.2	8.0
75,600	260.80	12.5	16.7
176,000	144.50	11.2	9.8

SPECIAL NEEDS FUNCTION

Project Size Gross S.F.	Project Cost $/S.F.	% Cost Mechanical	% Cost Electrical
15,200	163.80	16.6	8.4
27,900	197.40	19.4	11.2

STUDENT CENTER/MULTIPURPOSE

Project Size Gross S.F.	Project Cost $/S.F.	% Cost Mechanical	% Cost Electrical
90,000	249.10	16.2	10.0
49,600	184.00	18.2	9.2
187,700	277.00	15.3	8.8
194,800	146.30	17.2	8.5

HOTEL/MOTEL

CONVENTION/CONFERENCE CENTER

Project Size Gross S.F.	Project Cost $/S.F.	% Cost Mechanical	% Cost Electrical
8,600 A	218.70	20.7	16.3
71,900	242.50	12.5	13.8
433,800	126.80	22.1	8.3

HOTEL

Project Size Gross S.F.	Project Cost $/S.F.	% Cost Mechanical	% Cost Electrical
19,900 A	125.00	16.8	5.8
25,875 R	112.10	11.8	10.5
48,400 A	224.20	23.6	8.2
64,300 R	302.10	20.3	10.1
104,200 A	140.40	15.0	8.8
108,040	119.90	13.0	7.0
110,100	155.20	18.4	10.5
132,000	290.10	16.4	5.4
135,900 A	179.30	15.2	7.7
144,100 A	201.40	19.3	11.5
231,000	217.80	15.2	8.4
449,800 A	125.80	13.1	7.0

HOTEL/INN

Project Size Gross S.F.	Project Cost $/S.F.	% Cost Mechanical	% Cost Electrical
57,400	145.50	13.0	10.0
73,000	95.30	24.4	18.1
75,900	126.80	16.5	7.6
162,000	152.50	17.5	8.0
197,000	146.00	15.7	7.7
277,900	107.20	18.8	9.4

A = Addition   R = Remodel

SQUARE FOOT TABLES

INDUSTRIAL

MANUFACTURING

Project Size Gross S.F.	Project Cost $/S.F.	% Cost Mechanical	% Cost Electrical
14,300	123.90	13.0	7.0
18,500	186.80	20.5	13.5
26,600	66.80	6.1	12.1
31,400	147.60	18.9	17.7
33,400	85.30	23.1	15.8
37,300	63.60	3.0	24.0
43,400	84.80	14.7	11.7
45,400	137.60	15.9	15.0
79,800	143.00	16.0	14.5
81,100	152.80	8.2	8.4
137,400	95.90	41.6	13.6
179,600	110.70	26.3	13.6
186,000	103.40	19.5	11.7

RESEARCH AND DEVELOPMENT

Project Size Gross S.F.	Project Cost $/S.F.	% Cost Mechanical	% Cost Electrical
89,140	197.60	20.8	9.0
100,400	261.70	36.1	25.1
114,200	256.30	21.4	9.8
125,000	174.30	20.8	8.4
140,000	243.60	20.1	11.2

WAREHOUSE W/OFFICE

Project Size Gross S.F.	Project Cost $/S.F.	% Cost Mechanical	% Cost Electrical
14,000	56.90	6.5	9.2
19,000	51.00	2.3	1.8
19,700	67.00	9.5	7.0
31,200	57.50	7.0	7.0
40,500	73.40	6.6	10.5
62,000	93.40	10.8	10.0
96,200	54.10	2.2	6.3
105,000	52.50	5.3	11.1
149,800	54.90	14.5	8.6

WAREHOUSE W/OFFICE (Cont.)

Project Size Gross S.F.	Project Cost $/S.F.	% Cost Mechanical	% Cost Electrical
168,600	60.40	11.4	6.3
209,600	55.70	4.9	10.3
402,400	75.70	14.9	8.3

MEDICAL

EDUCATION CENTER

Project Size Gross S.F.	Project Cost $/S.F.	% Cost Mechanical	% Cost Electrical
35,400	338.90	10.2	6.8

HOSPITALS

Project Size Gross S.F.	Project Cost $/S.F.	% Cost Mechanical	% Cost Electrical
9,300 R	334.90	29.5	12.0
15,900 A	247.10	27.4	15.3
16,600 R	89.00	14.7	9.6
22,000	562.30	31.6	17.5
39,100	280.20	23.3	7.9
63,800	225.70	23.4	7.8
98,000 A	324.80	20.5	17.0
100,200 A	518.10	22.2	9.6
103,900 A	287.10	31.1	11.7
109,300	284.50	20.7	15.7
148,700	223.50	25.2	11.8
154,700	363.00	19.3	10.5
165,484	315.50	21.5	14.8
165,700 A	307.90	26.2	17.7
179,400 A	187.60	28.9	20.3
182,800	279.20	19.1	14.0
265,000	333.10	31.2	14.1
281,100	319.10	24.1	14.6
435,000	330.60	21.5	13.7
694,300	183.10	28.9	9.7
772,300	337.40	31.5	13.4

A = Addition   R = Remodel

For more information subscribe to **Design Cost & Data**

SQUARE FOOT TABLES

| MEDICAL (Cont.) | PUBLIC FACILITIES |

MEDICAL OFFICES/CENTERS

Project Size Gross S.F.	Project Cost $/S.F.	% Cost Mechanical	% Cost Electrical
3,000	141.60	13.7	11.5
5,500	147.40	8.5	18.7
10,000	178.20	13.9	9.4
10,600	225.60	13.2	8.9
16,300	186.70	21.8	13.2
18,300	101.80	7.1	13.4
20,600	146.30	14.3	6.4
24,900	257.60	21.0	15.1
27,000	260.10	19.7	10.1
28,400	181.40	13.6	9.3
30,500	196.50	17.2	12.7
32.000	155.70	18.1	10.5
44,300	157.00	24.4	16.2
50,200	90.60	9.8	4.9
51,200	229.50	21.0	12.0
64,600	109.30	13.2	6.4
66,000	101.80	9.8	8.8
80,000	87.40	8.2	8.3
137,175	146.00	12.8	6.6

NURSING HOMES

Project Size Gross S.F.	Project Cost $/S.F.	% Cost Mechanical	% Cost Electrical
11,600 A	428.00	53.2	7.9
16,800	278.60	33.3	7.8
31,900 A	209.50	22.0	11.0
64,100	179.60	20.6	11.1
290,000	251.80	16.1	13.6

RESEARCH

Project Size Gross S.F.	Project Cost $/S.F.	% Cost Mechanical	% Cost Electrical
34,600	238.40	18.1	3.0

PUBLIC FACILITIES

ANIMAL CENTER

Project Size Gross S.F.	Project Cost $/S.F.	% Cost Mechanical	% Cost Electrical
20,000	302.10	20.7	4.6
39,100	225.70	22.9	6.8
44,300	215.10	8.1	5.8

AUTO DEALERSHIP

7,700	140.80	16.7	9.4

BROADCASTING

20,000	411.80	20.0	13.0
29,500	317.80	16.6	15.0
45,000 R	230.40	15.0	13.0

CIVIC CENTER

6,000	226.90	9.2	2.8
23,900	285.00	12.3	10.9
34,400	129.90	3.5	17.8
69,800 A	340.40	17.7	8.8
206,500	184.10	15.0	11.0

CORRECTION FACILITIES

44,600	275.20	20.9	13.1
66,000	168.00	15.0	23.0
257,800 A	290.60	20.9	10.7
360,000	195.70	32.7	13.2

FIRE STATION

6,900	245.60	12.4	9.7
7,600	188.70	16.0	9.5
8,430	259.50	12.8	9.6
9,600	226.30	13.5	11.8

A = Addition   R = Remodel

SQUARE FOOT TABLES

PUBLIC FACILITIES (Cont.)

GOVERMENT BUILDINGS

Project Size Gross S.F.	Project Cost $/S.F.	% Cost Mechanical	% Cost Electrical
12,300	176.10	13.5	10.7
23,500	288.50	11.1	15.6
27,300	227.80	19.5	9.3
31,600	256.50	27.1	11.3
46,600	241.40	17.4	13.8
72,100	262.80	24.4	10.7
78,200	218.10	19.7	15.2
332,900	211.60	16.2	14.2
364,100	277.10	14.6	12.9
771,000	306.20	17.6	11.3

MUSEUM

Project Size Gross S.F.	Project Cost $/S.F.	% Cost Mechanical	% Cost Electrical
27,600	211.40	17.8	14.1
30,100	242.80	18.6	7.9
43,264	226.30	11.1	8.3
63,000	244.90	8.8	18.1

PARKING GARAGE

Project Size Gross S.F.	Project Cost $/S.F.	% Cost Mechanical	% Cost Electrical
66,000	64.70	2.8	3.1
169,000	47.70	10.3	3.7
562,700	43.00	2.4	6.2

TRANSPORTATION

Project Size Gross S.F.	Project Cost $/S.F.	% Cost Mechanical	% Cost Electrical
7,300	388.50	15.1	3.2
14,300	312.20	13.3	16.6
23.000	215.70	9.6	13.7
35,500	179.60	1.0	19.0
49,100	267.90	35.5	11.6

TRANSPORTATION (Cont.)

Project Size Gross S.F.	Project Cost $/S.F.	% Cost Mechanical	% Cost Electrical
288,100	154.40	8.3	13.3
2,160,000	250.10	23.3	11.5

OFFICES

BANKS

Project Size Gross S.F.	Project Cost $/S.F.	% Cost Mechanical	% Cost Electrical
2,900	359.20	5.3	4.3
3,100	160.30	5.9	6.7
3,300	233.20	10.3	16.4
3,600	175.70	10.3	12.2
4,000	200.10	8.0	9.0
4,100	198.00	21.4	13.0
4,200	213.60	8.6	14.21
4,400	246.80	12.2	12.7
4,500	153.20	12.4	13.5
4,900	242.00	11.7	11.2
5,900	179.90	9.3	13.8
6,000	202.30	11.6	7.3
6,100	272.00	11.0	8.0
7,000	365.90	6.0	9.0
7,300	223.80	11.9	11.3
7,700	250.80	8.0	7.5
7,800	274.90	11.0	11.7
8,000	139.70	10.0	14.0
9,200	221.60	9.9	12.1
9,400	160.40	11.7	11.8
10,200	334.70	12.6	12.6
12,600	119.60	7.0	18.0

A = Addition   R = Remodel

For more information subscribe to **Design Cost & Data**

SQUARE FOOT TABLES

OFFICES (Cont.)

BANKS (Cont.)

Project Size Gross S.F.	Project Cost $/S.F.	% Cost Mechanical	% Cost Electrical
13,300	210.80	9.5	8.3
13,800	188.70	10.00	9.7
15,000	161.60	15.4	12.4
15,200	129.10	9.2	12.9
15,500	164.70	9.8	10.3
16,000	108.20	13.4	23.1
20,100	101.70	13.0	11.0
21,700	215.10	8.8	11.3
44,800	183.80	13.0	8.2
53,200	331.90	14.9	7.2
62,100	190.60	10.1	7.9
95,100	250.70	13.5	4.3

OFFICE BUILDINGS

Project Size Gross S.F.	Project Cost $/S.F.	% Cost Mechanical	% Cost Electrical
2,600	225.40	17.2	9.4
3,400	184.30	10.5	11.3
3,800	180.90	16.4	11.8
4,400	178.70	12.8	8.5
4,500	153.70	13.0	7.0
5,100	111.70	16.6	10.2
5,200	146.50	8.0	5.7
6,700	218.20	16.8	10.4
7,500	234.90	10.1	8.0
7,900	182.90	17.4	9.0
8,100	282.70	10.6	11.0
10,600	163.50	9.9	9.7
10,900	94.10	13.8	10.8

OFFICE BUILDINGS (Cont.)

Project Size Gross S.F.	Project Cost $/S.F.	% Cost Mechanical	% Cost Electrical
11,300	185.70	17.0	6.0
13,000	126.50	15.0	9.0
14,400	165.90	19.8	12.9
14,500	127.20	17.3	12.5
17,000	181.60	14.7	7.9
17,800 A	98.20	10.4	11.0
18,100	190.20	22.5	11.6
19,300	103.30	11.1	8.1
24,600	95.40	18.5	14.1
27,700	114.80	19.6	5.5
27,800	208.30	12.7	5.1
27,800	112.10	17.8	10.3
32,500 R	191.90	13.9	6.4
35,400	112.00	15.0	12.0
36.500	97.00	10.2	10.2
42,300	120.40	10.3	7.7
44,400	164.00	23.5	14.7
44,400	86.20	11.0	5.0
44,500	118.70	11.5	3.1
45,400	102.50	19.1	13.2
47,300	105.50	18.5	8.0
49,700	177.20	22.1	7.2
50,000	168.90	19.4	15.6
50,400	183.20	23.2	7.8
52,200	119.00	18.3	7.8
52,900	138.70	4.4	3.9
53,700	212.30	15.4	9.0

A = Addition   R = Remodel

SQUARE FOOT TABLES

OFFICES (Cont.)

OFFICE BUILDINGS (Cont.)

Project Size Gross S.F.	Project Cost $/S.F.	% Cost Mechanical	% Cost Electrical
54,000	85.90	14.4	2.6
56,000	97.40	10.6	6.2
56,500	134.10	19.1	11.0
72,000 R	47.10	12.9	20.2
74,000	93.40	13.5	6.8
80,800	94.40	12.0	6.0
81,800	129.90	21.1	9.5
81,900	109.30	19.9	9.0
82,000	151.90	14.0	4.2
83,100	179.10	16.0	8.6
85,400	157.00	18.7	8.6
86,200	123.00	14.7	11.0
99,900	142.30	16.6	6.6
100,000	159.00	10.6	12.1
100,000	93.80	16.3	10.4
116,400	150.20	12.6	10.0
134,500	306.40	14.1	12.4
140,000	237.50	20.1	11.2
155,700	295.80	11.1	6.1
171,000	138.60	24.0	7.7
174,300	170.70	12.3	9.1
203,300	230.80	19.0	13.2
265,800	319.40	11.0	10.0
287,300	88.40	10.7	4.1
319,800	138.60	13.4	5.6
350,000	204.90	20.0	13.0
360,900	124.00	14.2	11.1
394,000	98.50	22.5	8.7

OFFICE BUILDINGS (Cont.)

Project Size Gross S.F.	Project Cost $/S.F.	% Cost Mechanical	% Cost Electrical
430,000	147.60	21.8	9.3
490,000	156.90	11.2	7.5
588,400	322.60	15.0	9.0
606,000	129.00	9.4	8.8
620,000	355.80	12.6	12.8
733,500	98.50	10.8	4.2

RECREATIONAL

ARENA

Project Size Gross S.F.	Project Cost $/S.F.	% Cost Mechanical	% Cost Electrical
315,200	369.30	10.4	8.00
385,800	211.40	13.2	8.80
727,000	191.20	14.9	7.40

HEALTH CLUB

15,900	103.30	8.7	9.7
21,800	146.20	10.3	10.3
30,100	226.00	11.4	19.4
66,400	111.30	10.7	8.5

RECREATIONAL CENTER

9,900	200.80	6.6	9.8
14,000	131.00	11.2	5.0
14,000	157.00	11.3	16.7
15,700	119.60	17.8	14.3
20,000	271.20	19.1	8.9
21,200	152.60	16.0	9.6

A = Addition   R = Remodel

For more information subscribe to **Design Cost & Data**

SQUARE FOOT TABLES

RECREATIONAL (Cont.)

RECREATIONAL CENTER (Cont.)

Project Size Gross S.F.	Project Cost $/S.F.	% Cost Mechanical	% Cost Electrical
26,000	177.70	9.3	7.0
53,400 A	212.60	11.7	6.4
69,800	344.70	17.7	8.8

RELIGIOUS

CHURCH

Project Size Gross S.F.	Project Cost $/S.F.	% Cost Mechanical	% Cost Electrical
4,100	242.00	8.8	13.5
10,400 R	329.40	12.8	8.1
11,100	145.10	10.9	12.7
13,400	217.40	5.5	6.0
14,500	148.40	12.8	7.4
15,200	192.30	18.3	8.0
15,700	167.40	14.4	8.4

CHURCH (Cont.)

Project Size Gross S.F.	Project Cost $/S.F.	% Cost Mechanical	% Cost Electrical
16,000	272.40	14.1	9.6
20,900	169.90	16.0	14.0
21,500	186.50	7.3	8.0
22,900	168.40	12.1	9.5
30,600	127.30	15.5	8.0
42,700	143.80	18.6	7.7

MULTI-PURPOSE

Project Size Gross S.F.	Project Cost $/S.F.	% Cost Mechanical	% Cost Electrical
4,400	148.70	11.5	17.5
5,800 A	189.60	8.9	7.5
6,400	258.80	15.6	15.8
9,000	126.80	7.7	5.9
9,000	179.90	16.0	6.6
10,100	120.70	11.1	12.0
12,000	238.60	13.1	10.7
18,400	130.70	10.8	10.1
19,500	230.40	16.0	17.3

A = Addition   R = Remodel

For more information subscribe to **Design Cost & Data**

BNi. Building News

INDEX

INDEX

INDEX

INDEX

Notes

Notes

Notes

Notes

Notes